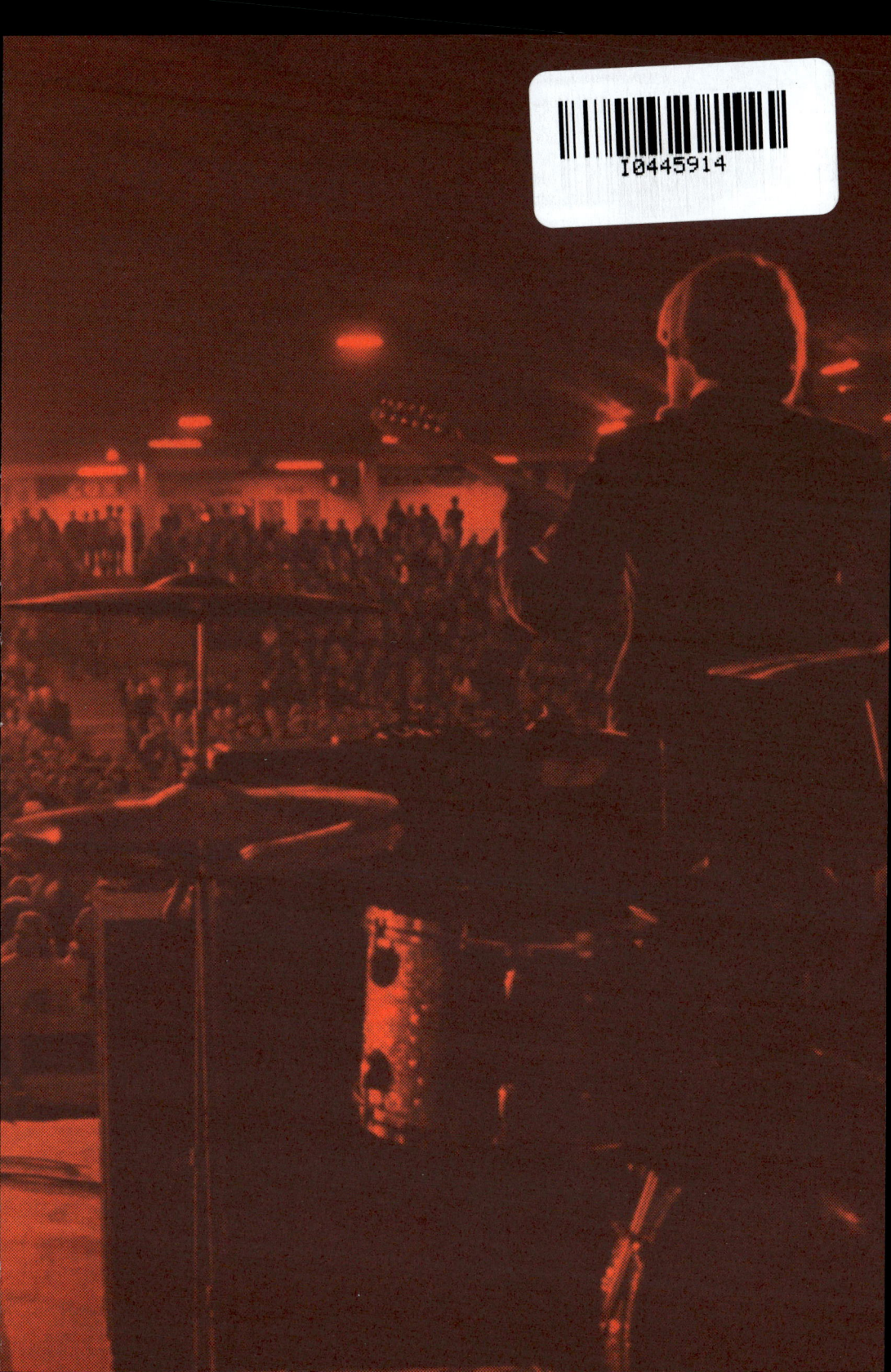

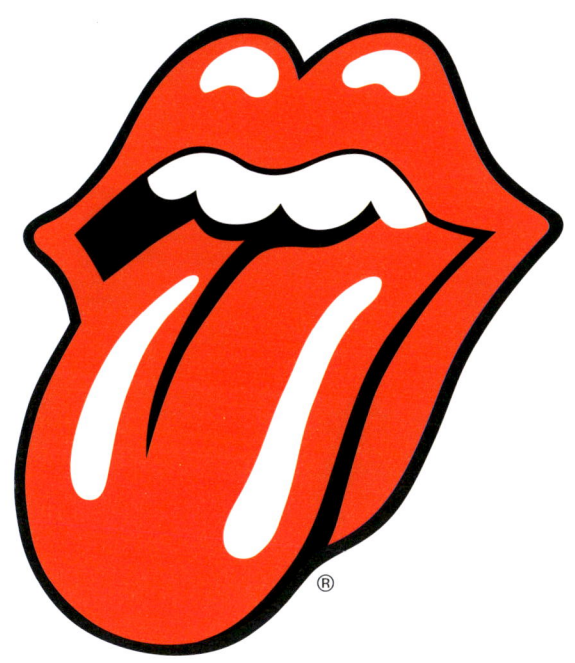

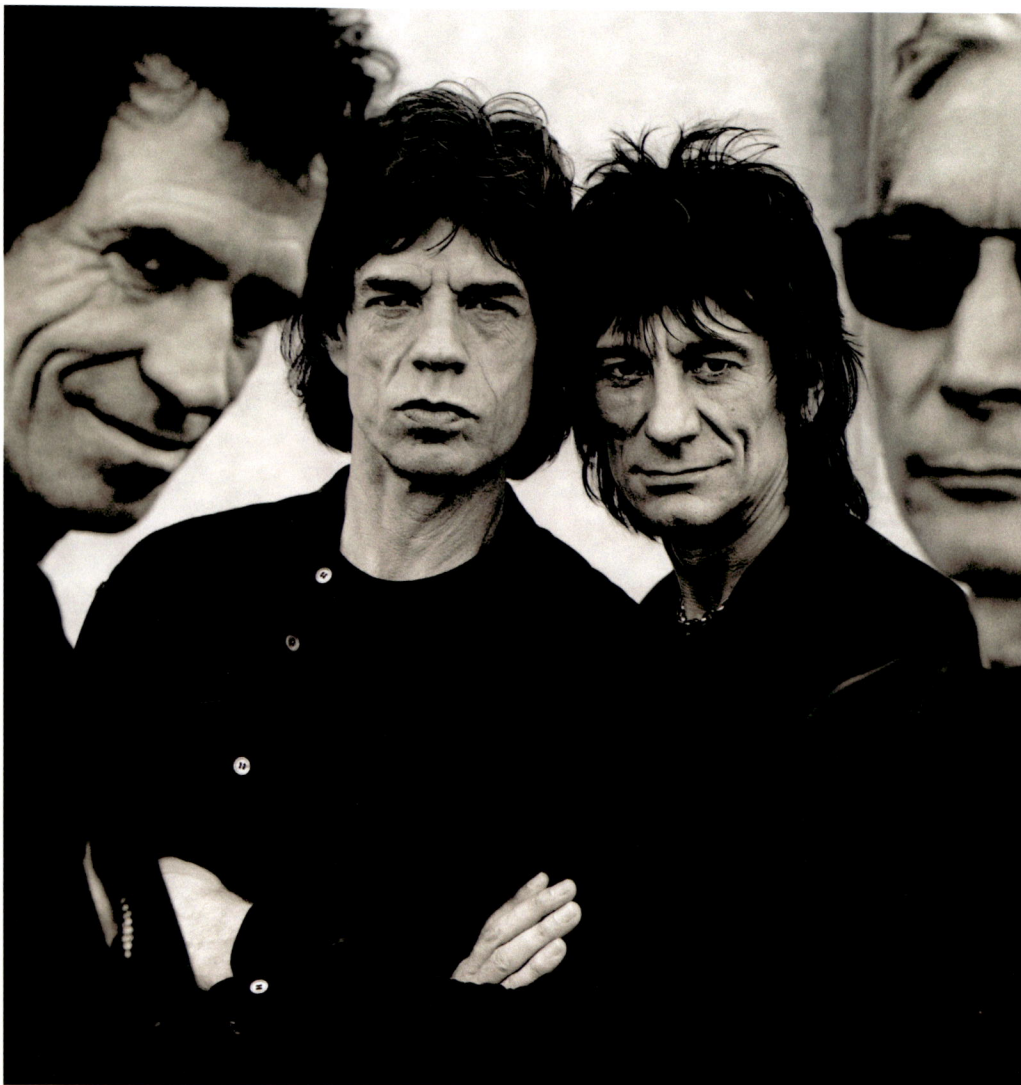

THE ROLLING STONES

Edited by **REUEL GOLDEN**
Essays by **LUCY SANTE, DAVID DALTON** and
WALDEMAR JANUSZCZAK
Captions by **SIMON WELLS**
Designed by **ANDY DISL**
Directed and produced by **BENEDIKT TASCHEN**

TASCHEN

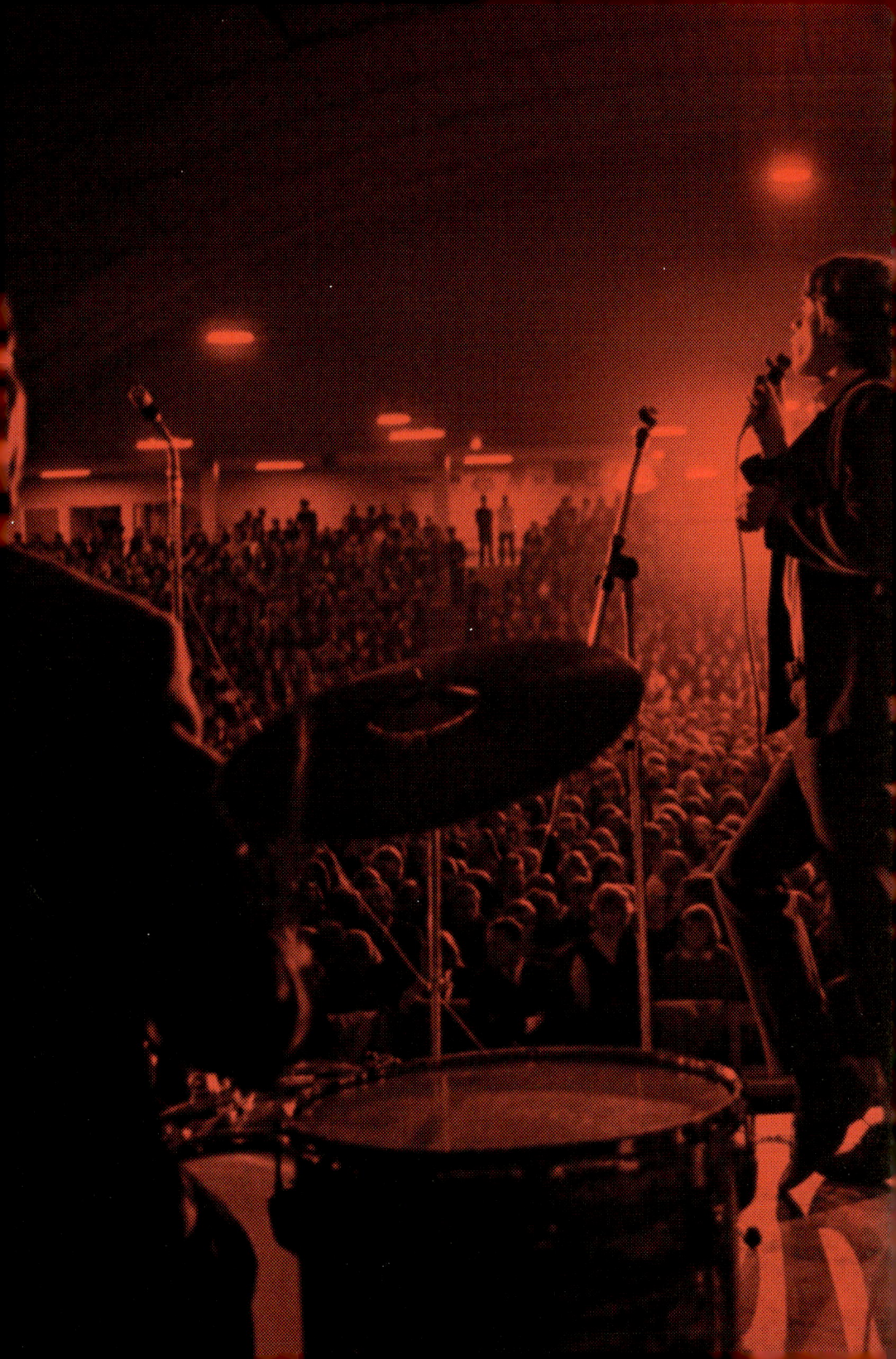

TABLE OF CONTENTS

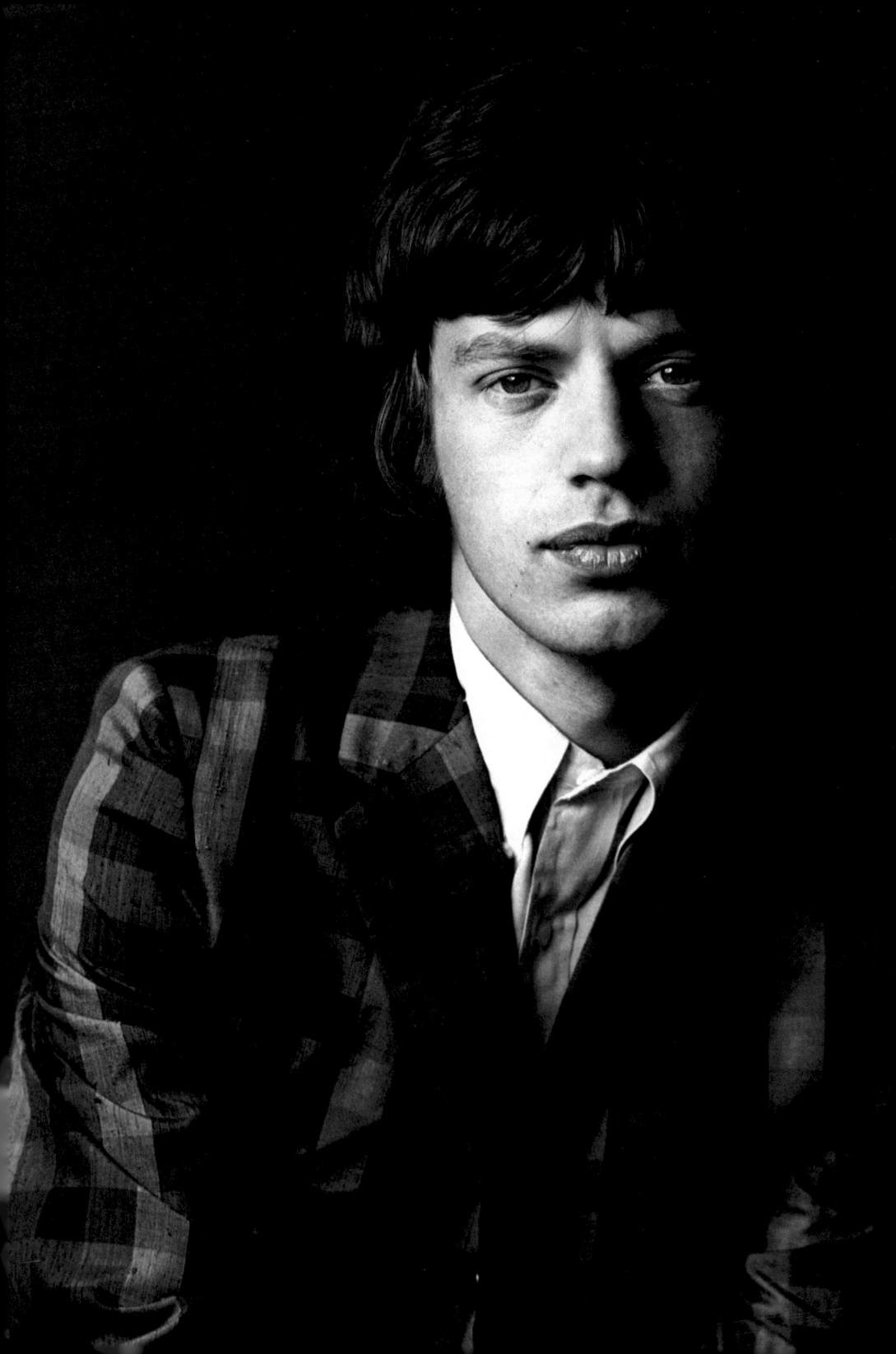

It's Just a Shot Away: The Rolling Stones in Photographs

By Lucy Sante

No one in 1962 could have imagined that The Rolling Stones would still be going strong close to 60 years later. Pop bands were as perishable as they were immediate. Their impact was time-stamped – they were the moment, and who knew if there would even still be a world past that moment? The Stones in particular seemed volatile, unstable; the very qualities that made them exciting surely doomed their long-term prospects. And who were they, anyway? They could not be understood according to the standard pop criteria that existed in the early 1960s. They weren't like film stars, who were issued new names and new teeth and perhaps even new biographies before they were allowed to stand under the hot lights of fame.

> *"I never really wanted to be the leader, but somehow I automatically got all the attention. I had the most recognisable features etc., though I didn't really know or care."*
>
> Mick Jagger in David Dalton,
> *Rolling Stones: In Their Own Words*, 1980

Quite to the contrary, the Stones had already begun projecting their personalities on to the crowd before anyone took them in hand and undertook to supervise their image, and of course, the teenage crowd responded most feverishly to exactly those qualities that responsible adults would expect to airbrush away.

The very first thing anybody noticed about The Rolling Stones was that they were emphatically not cuddly. And 1964 was the peak of cuddliness in pop music – you could say that The Beatles, seen from that angle, merely represented a further evolutionary step along the line from Fabian and Frankie Avalon and Tommy Steele; mothers were invited to imagine pinching their cheeks. The Stones, on the other hand, were gaunt, hard-faced, dour. In those early days, photographed by Philip Townsend and Terry O'Neill, in particular, they were most often pictured in black and white against the backdrop of a London that was still post-war, a backdrop they simultaneously harmonised and clashed with. They had long hair and sometimes dressed flash – although sometimes they didn't.

That might have helped them seem familiar in Britain, but in America, it made them exotic. The toughness they emanated was nothing like that of the corn-fed Hollywood ideal of the time. They were feral, but they instinctively knew how to wear clothes, and which clothes to wear. Initially, it was hard to tell them apart; they all seemed to share the same wide mouths and high cheekbones, and seldom smiled.

As the years drew on, the photographic record of the Stones became nearly as important as the phonographic. For a long time, there were no music videos, while television appearances were intermittent, so magazine coverage had a weight that may be difficult to appreciate today. In addition, the 45 RPM singles arrived in stores with the impact of breaking news, and their picture sleeves would give the first clue of what lay within. Might the boys be clad in leather and huddled in a high-contrast alley? Or were they perhaps wearing brocade and sheepskin, standing in a field, photographed in full colour, maybe with a fisheye lens? Very likely, the image would match the sound, at least to a degree, and gazing at the images would enhance the listening experience for their fans. The synesthesia was so strong that even today, those who first encountered the music by sliding the discs from those sleeves may be unable to hear, say, 'Jumpin' Jack Flash" without the subliminal presence in their mind's eye of the accompanying David Bailey photo: Keith in aviator's helmet and red nail polish; Mick with a dagger between his teeth, his hands joined above his head.

"What has proved to be the ruination of many people has been the making of me. I went against everything I had been brought up to believe in."

Brian Jones, *New Musical Express*, 29 May 1964

And then the march of images made for a compelling illusion of intimacy, even if the staged photos far outnumbered the spontaneous ones. The fans became acquainted with the Stones as individuals. Mick was immediately the prettiest, perhaps the most socially chameleonic, with a range of poses and outfits that let him one minute appear thuggish and the next remind you – wearing a crewneck sweater or an anorak – that he had recently attended classes at the London School of Economics. From the earliest days, he absorbed and reflected the most light, and anyone spotting the five of them in a railway buffet in 1963 would have picked him out as the frontman.

Keith, perhaps surprisingly in retrospect (but then again, perhaps not, given his seeming indestructibility), came off as the healthiest and most athletic, with a purposeful jaw and an air of grace under pressure. Brian came from Elsewhere, some hitherto unvisited planet of cool. His hair was unprecedented in this world – a golden helmet that hooded his eyes, it made him look androgynous and impenetrable. Bill was relentlessly vertical, from the way he held his bass to his air of being able to hide behind a lamp post. His face was a closed door, until a smile broke it open and revealed all.

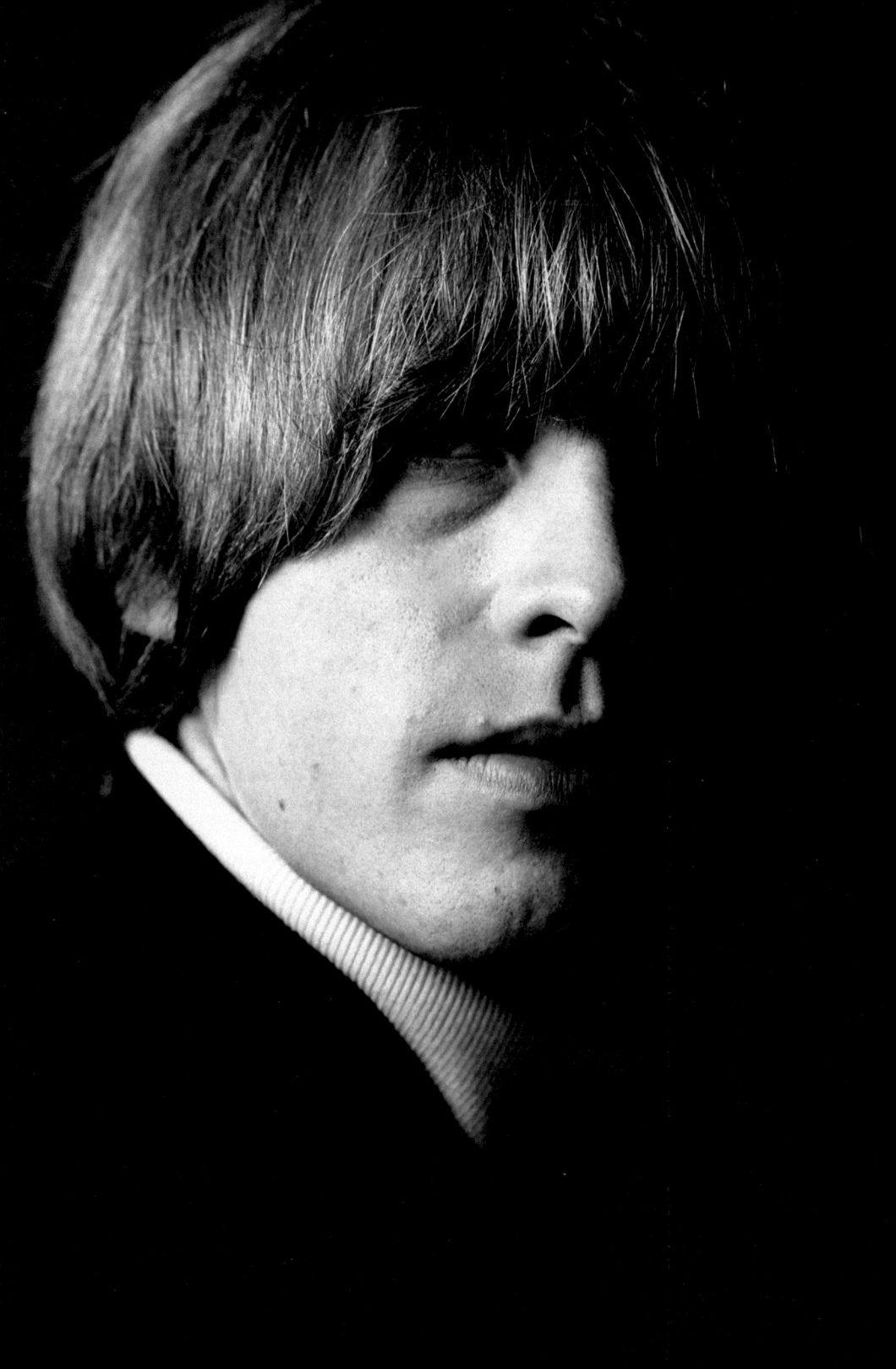

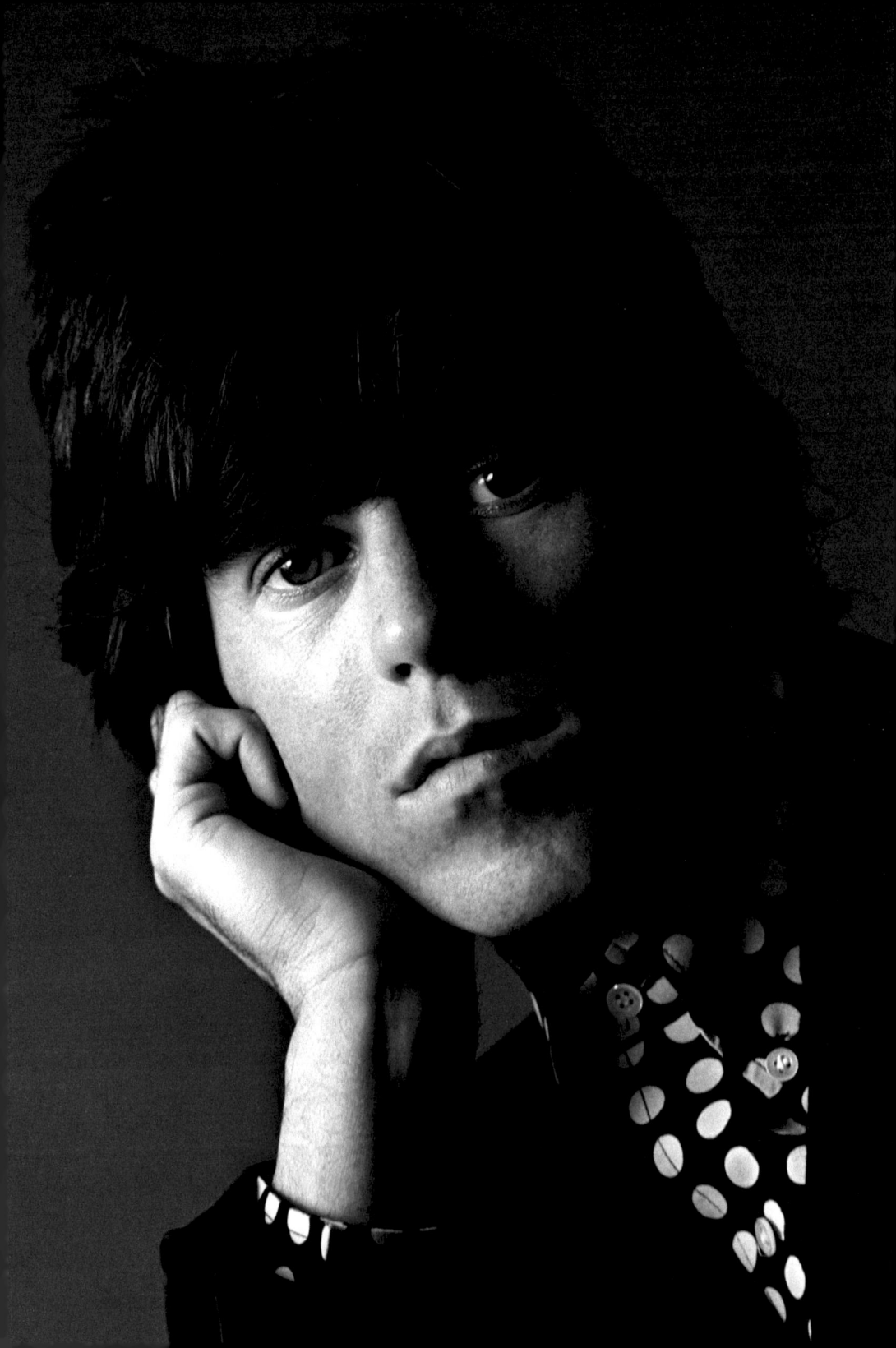

And Charlie, who always looked faintly amused, as if in possession of a secret known only to him – perhaps it was the knowledge of time signatures far beyond the capacity of the pop-rock of the era – had the physical proportions required to be known not just as well-dressed but as dapper. Even then, it was evident that he would age exceptionally well.

The most endearing of the early pictures are the ones by the Danish photographer Bent Rej, that purport to show them relaxing in their homes. But are those even their homes, those airy apartments, spotlessly clean, faintly anonymous, pleasantly and uncontroversially furnished, presumably by other hands, with a minimum of personal touches? Although Bill does have a child, and Charlie has a wife and quite a number of wall-mounted firearms, while Keith's spectacular and temporary hotel penthouse overlooking Hyde Park is either a prop or an invasion. But taken singly, minus all the bravado expressed in group shots, they are vulnerable, even touching.

It was surely the intended effect, for readers of glossies who needed such reassurance, but that does not diminish an essential modesty thus

"This is a job. It's a man's job, and it's a lifelong job. And if there's ever a sucker to prove it, I hope to be the sucker."

Keith Richards, *Rolling Stone* magazine, 6 October 1988

far untroubled by the scarring exigencies of international trade – rock 'n' roll was already a moneymaker, to be sure, but the waters were not yet as warm with sharks to the degree that would soon be the norm. Just a year or two later, when they are photographed by Gered Mankowitz, the settings have changed considerably. They now have manors and showy vehicles and lavish furnishings that may have just been uncrated.

Around that same time, the focus shifted from the urban realism of rhythm and blues to the multicoloured inner spaces of psychedelia. Initially, this shift affected the Stones less in their music than in their image-mongering. In the session photographed also by Mankowitz for what would be the cover of *Between The Buttons,* you, the viewer, are apparently tripping with the boys on a heath in north London in November.

Soon enough, their clothing lost any remaining Modness and everything was imported from India and Morocco and Middle Earth. The Beatles may have been cosily revisiting Victoria's reign, but the Stones were out there in the poppy fields off the Khyber Pass – although the conceit never quite adhered, since they were too physical, too urbane, by then, too wised-up to subscribe to any transcendental foolishness for very long.

At last, in Michael Joseph's photos for *Beggars Banquet,* the Stones find their true riposte to *Sgt. Pepper*: they are the elegant wastrels of history. Keith is in chainmail, Bill in a leather jerkin, Mick in sodden opera garb, Charlie has emerged from the Renaissance and Brian from the court of Harun al-Rashid. There are lutes, tankards, dripping candles, live or stuffed or roasted beasts. Outside, the fields may be rotting or the populace may be advancing on the chateau with torches and pitchforks. Inside, everyone is too dissipated to know or care. They managed to sustain the performance right through *Rock and Roll Circus*, when in addition, Mick can be seen for the first time sporting ostentatious make-up. But even then, a certain world was ending, that of the 1960s and its starry-eyed ideals, and Swinging London and its relative intimacy, which included the ability to socialise out in the world, more or less normally, despite international fame. Then Brian died, and all at once, the game had changed irrevocably.

"All I wanted was a nice home, good car, nice wife and family. That was what I'd wanted all my life."

Bill Wyman, *The Huffington Post*, 13 May 2013

The 1970s were tougher, less affected, more American. Their music had always flowed from an American source, one that was at first intuited, with somewhat spooky accuracy, from a world away. Now they set about assembling what would arguably be their finest and most sustained expression of the blues, the epochal *Exile On Main St* – in the parlours and verandas and mottled cellars of Keith's rented villa, Nellcôte, in the south of France. Dominique Tarlé's photographs of that interlude are a whole movie: the chandeliers and polished parquets, the exteriors looking like a set from *Les Vampires*, the suggested bacchanals in the off-hours, the apparent unspoilt youthfulness of Gram Parsons, the endless legs of Anita Pallenberg...

Further indelible images come from the tours of that period, gruelling affairs that might swallow half the globe. The protruding-tongue logo makes its maiden appearance; it is the dawn of branding. Keith famously demonstrates his concern for a drug-free America. Mick again and again demonstrates to millions of people his views on the dignity of labour, as he pushes his body to new extremes of exertion. By then, the Stones were dwelling in a newly minted social sphere, an instant aristocracy of glamour and public hijinks that brought together artists, models, couturiers, rogue heirs, professional partygoers. They hung with Andy, Liza, Halston, Truman Capote; Peter Beard photographed them in the Hamptons, still then a low-key ocean-side artists' retreat, and those images contributed to its dawning aura of exclusivity.

The photos from the mid-1970s define the term "rock star" as it has come to be applied to status indicators having nothing to do with music. The Rolling Stones owned the world; no arena anywhere could possibly be large enough to contain the number of people who wanted to witness them in action. They were mythical, deathless – for the audience, a portion of the thrill consisted in simply confirming their corporeal presence on earth.

And yet they were, after all, still a rock 'n' roll band that had come of age in the 1960s. The imagery of the 1980s and beyond seemed designed to remind everyone of

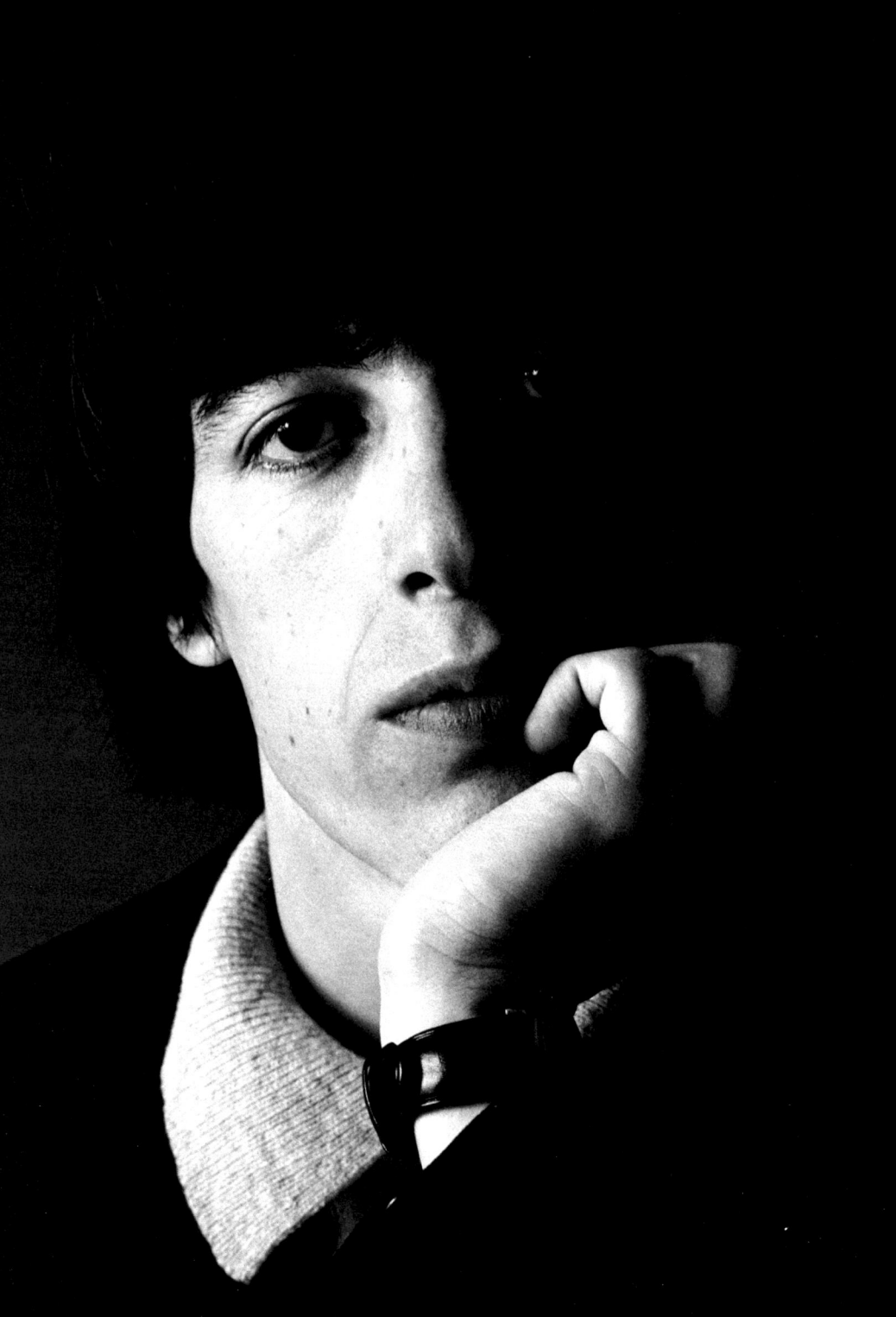

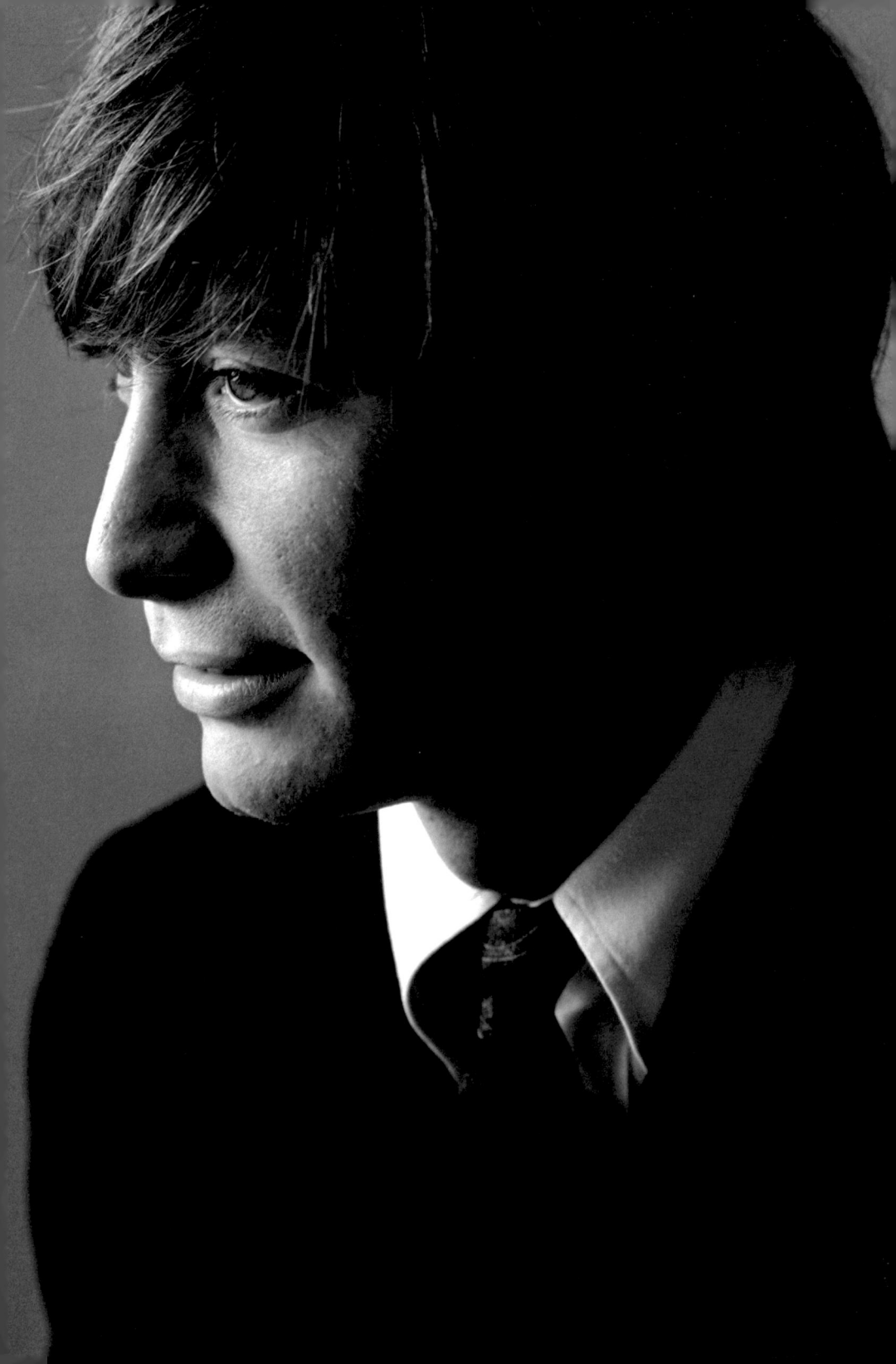

this fact. The settings and poses are chastened – barring the occasional outbreak of crazy clothing – and the band members are allowed to age visibly in just the way we might have hoped they would. The lines and wrinkles on their faces become indicators of a kind of authenticity that might otherwise seem unavailable to people who have spent so much of their lives so far from the common clutter.

By now, Bill Wyman has quit the band, and Ron Wood has been a member so long that he might always have been one. He looks like a dangerous businessman. Mick could be a somewhat flamboyant Oxford don. Charlie might be a Member of Parliament. And Keith – what can be said of Keith that has not already been said? He looks like the paramount chief of a lost Amazonian tribe; or a marooned sailor who has lived for decades on an undiscovered atoll.

The Rolling Stones have been a constant and inescapable presence in the world's image banks for half a century. They either originated or refined a large number of the visual tropes and commonplaces associated with rock 'n' roll: the sullen stare (which utterly annihilated the earlier generation's Pepsodent grin), the non-matching outfits, the aggressively foppish garb, the randomly deployed sunglasses, the Indian scarves, the private-plane scenario, the massive stage set, the stage show choreographed as modern dance rather than as Broadway musical, and photographed as if it were combat.

> *"Playing the drums was all I was ever interested in. The rest of it made me cringe. The girls only really loved Mick, Brian and Keith anyway."*
>
> Charlie Watts, *Observer*, 9 July 2000

Their pictorial record constitutes, among other things, a stylebook that has continued to define how a rock 'n' roll band should appear: how its members should lounge, wait, work, doze, stand, walk, play. You could also say that these are stills from an ongoing motion picture that is already one of the longest ever made. Anyone perusing this book has been watching that movie, at intervals, for decades – very likely since childhood – and has been influenced by it, subliminally or otherwise, in matters of behaviour, pose and dress.

The Stones didn't just write and perform great songs, they also sustained a continually evolving performance that included photo shoots, interviews, films, police-blotter items, nightclub paparazzi snaps, profiles in *Tiger Beat*, society columns, condemnations from the pulpit. The clothes and the hair are always impeccable. They were playing themselves, but with such consistent finesse you knew they were instinctively aware of the camera and how good they will look in the photos. They constructed a collective identity, a five-headed literary character that remains as singular an artistic achievement as their music.

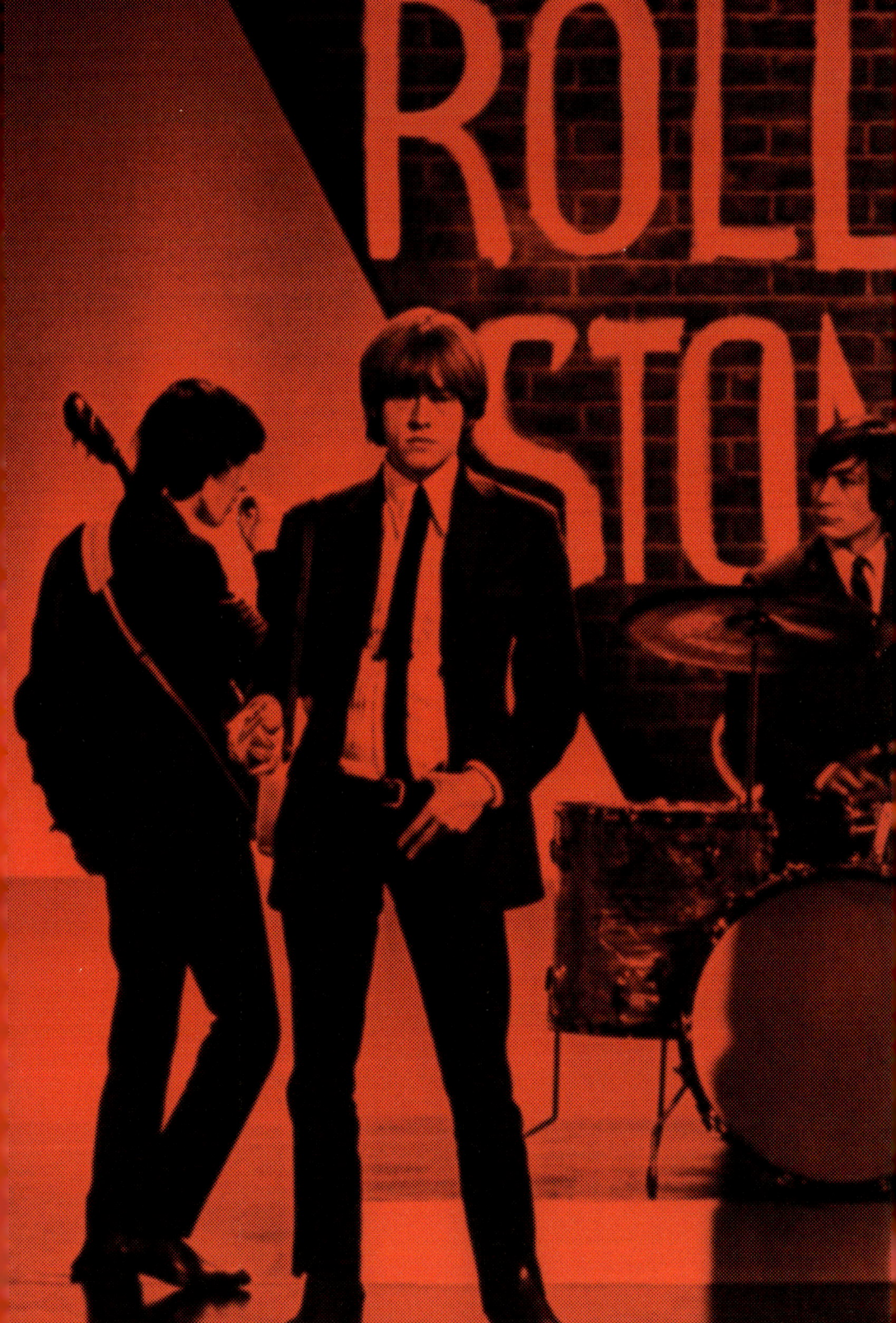

Act One

TIME IS ON MY SIDE
1962–1969

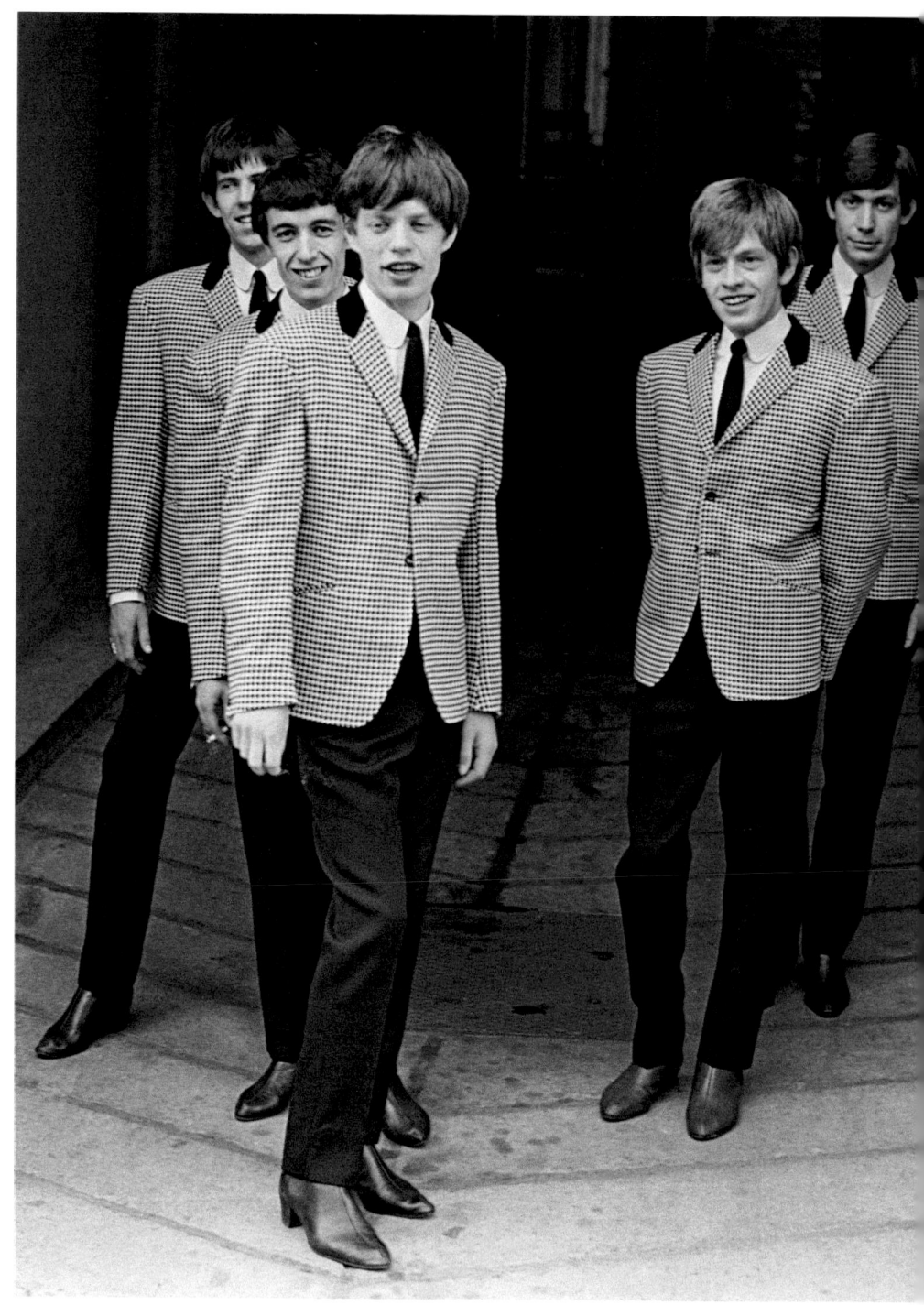

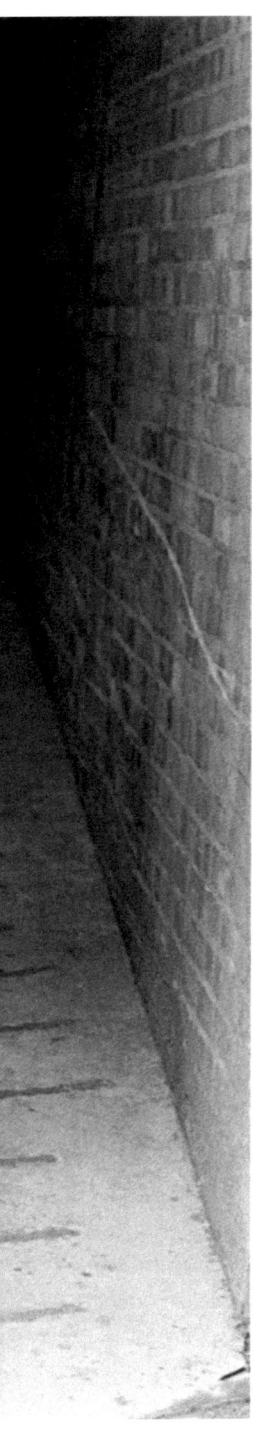

P. 2
Anton Corbijn
Budapest, Hungary, 10 August 1995.
Time out following a show at the city's Népstadion venue on 8 August 1995, as part of the *Voodoo Lounge* tour. *"The band's new album,* Voodoo Lounge, *is ragged and glorious, revelling in the quintessential rock & roll the Stones marked as their own some 30 years ago."* Barbara O'Dair, *Rolling Stone* magazine, 11 August 1994

PP. 4–5
Bent Rej
Fyens Forum, Odense, Denmark, 26 March 1965.
This iconic shot would be used for the back sleeve of the UK EP release *Got Live If You Want It!*

PP. 6–14
Guy Webster
Los Angeles, March 1966. Cover shoot for the *Aftermath* album.

PP. 16–17
Terry O'Neill
In rehearsal for *Thank Your Lucky Stars* at Alpha Television Studios in Birmingham, England, on 29 November 1964 – a show that would preview the single "Little Red Rooster". With viewing figures of over 20 million, an appearance on *Thank Your Lucky Stars* could guarantee enormous coverage for any new release. Despite the Stones' tabloid reputation as anarchic, wayward personalities, they dutifully fulfilled numerous media engagements. *"The suits, the ties and getting ready for* Thank Your Lucky Stars, *the innocence and naiveté of it all, and famous photographers wanting to take your picture and being in* Vogue *... Things happened so quickly. There were a lot of popular bands then, all from the North of England. Most people in England don't live in the North, and the English are snobby so they wanted a band from the South. We were it."* Mick Jagger, *Rolling Stone* magazine, 14 December 1995

Philip Townsend
London, May 1963.
"He [Oldham] put us in those dogtooth-checked suits with the black velvet collars ... For a month on the first tour we said, 'All right. We'll do it. You know the game. We'll try it out.' But then the Stones' thing started taking over. Charlie would leave his jacket in some dressing room and I'd pull mine out and there would be whisky stains all over it or chocolate pudding." Keith Richards, quoted in *According To The Rolling Stones*, 2003

19

Philip Townsend
Chelsea, hours before a show at London's
Battersea Park on 4 May 1963.
*"That 'just-out-of-bed-and-fuck-you' look was
the beginning of the image that would define and
divine them. Word got out that the results of the
session were 'disgusting'. I loved the photos, got
the picture, the penny dropped."* Andrew Loog
Oldham, *Stoned*, 2011

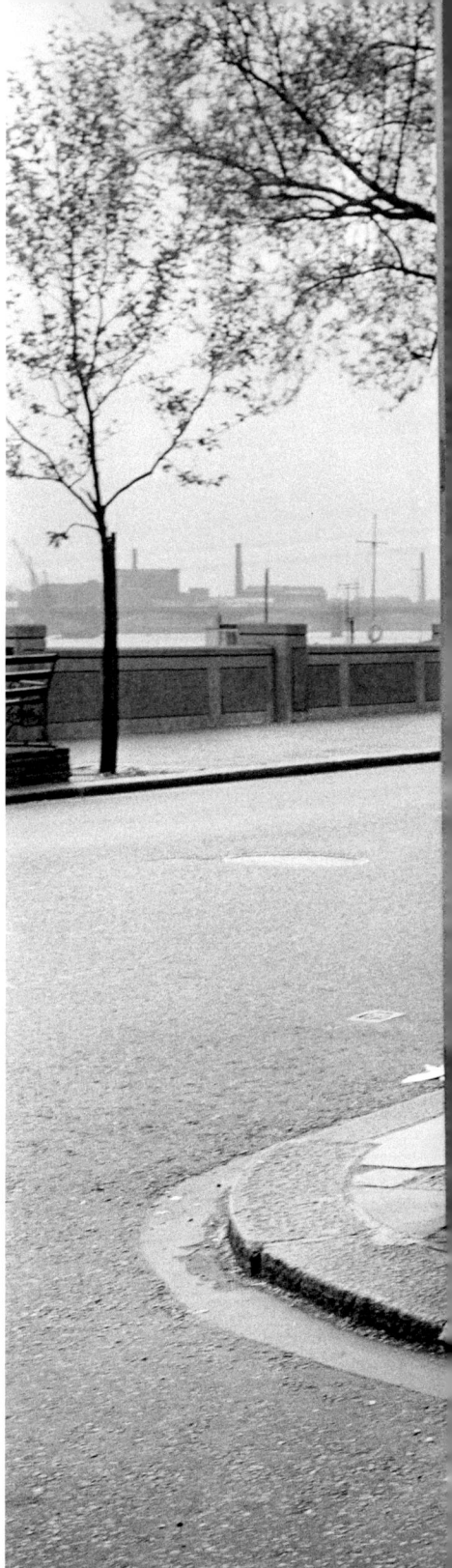

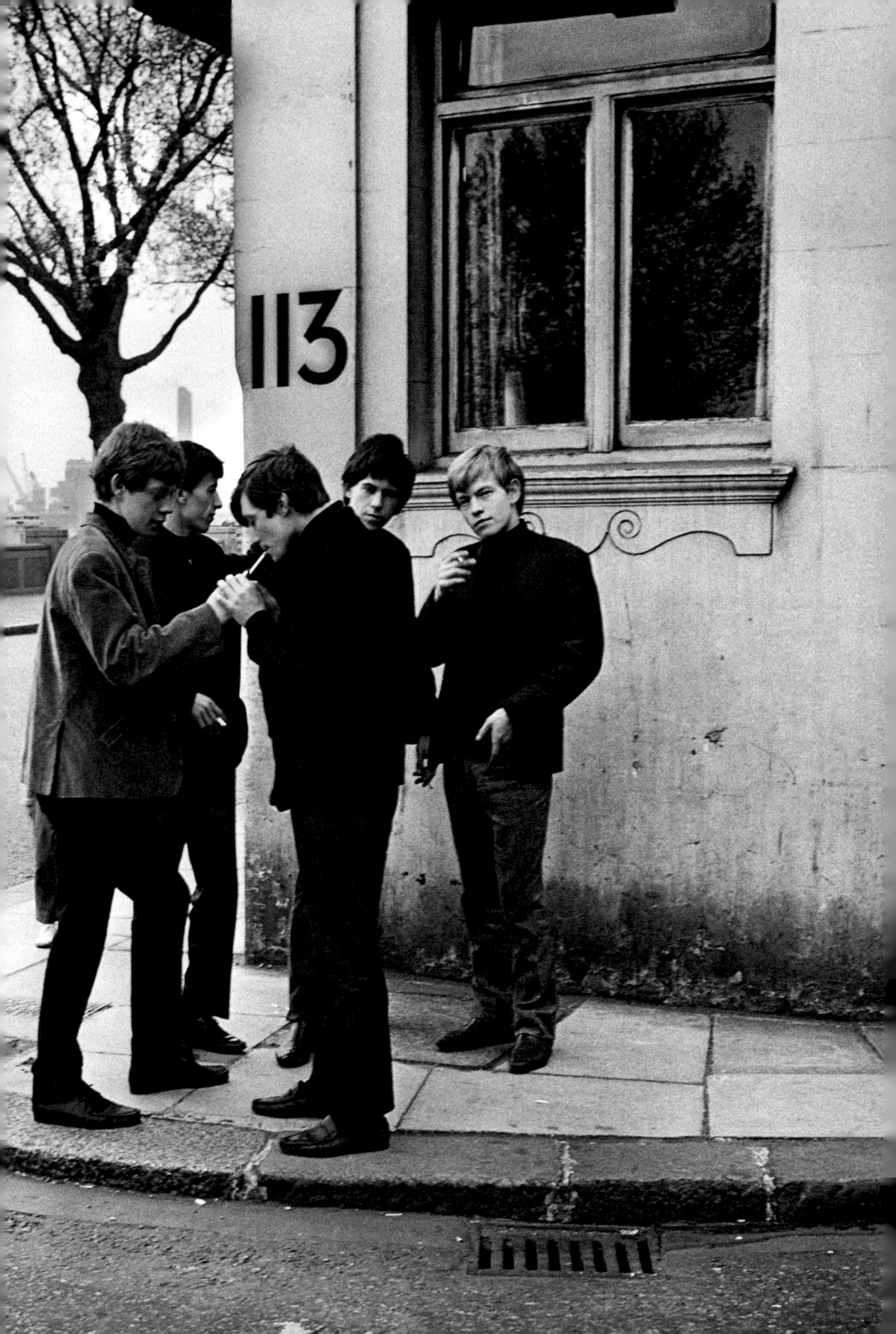

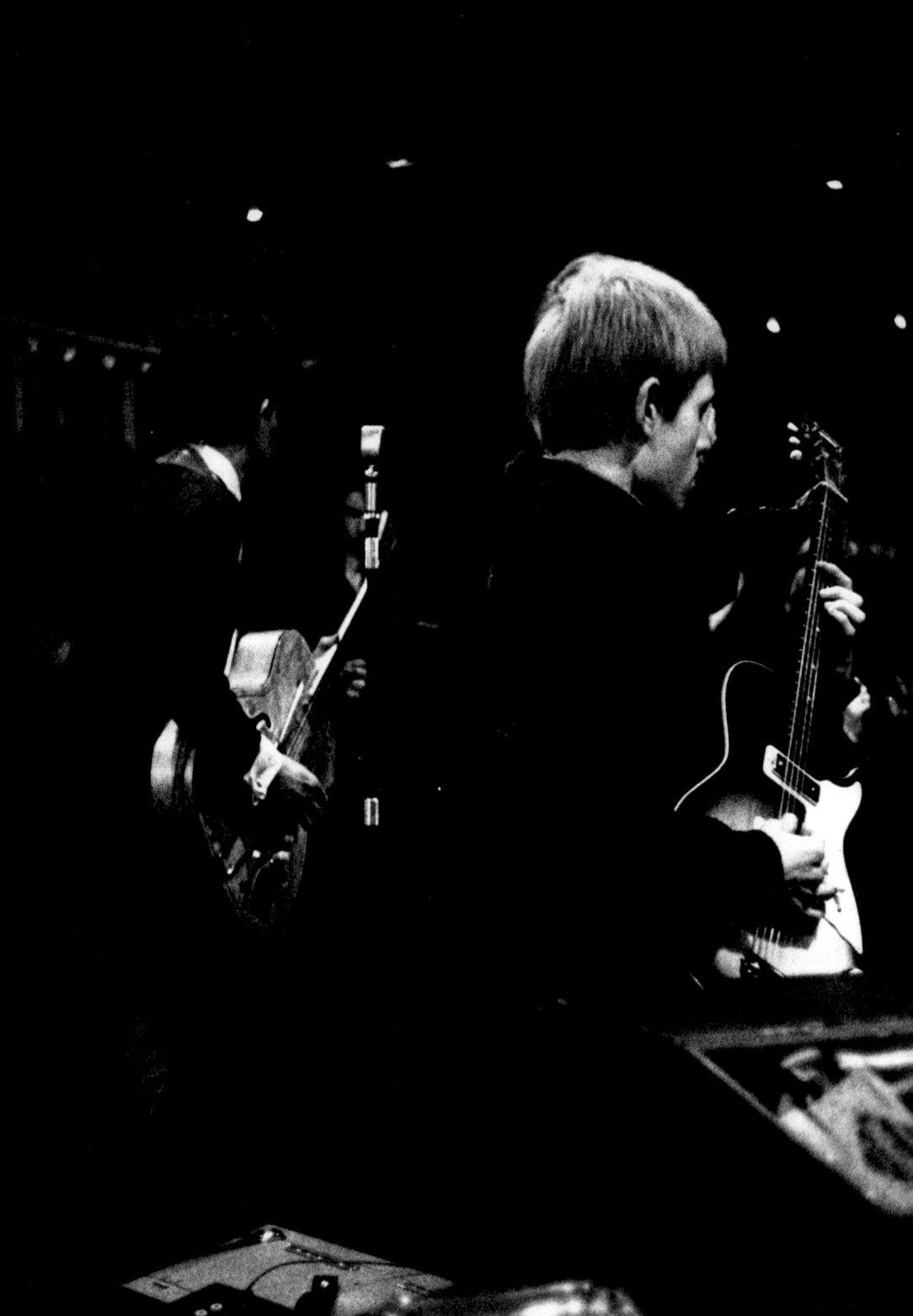

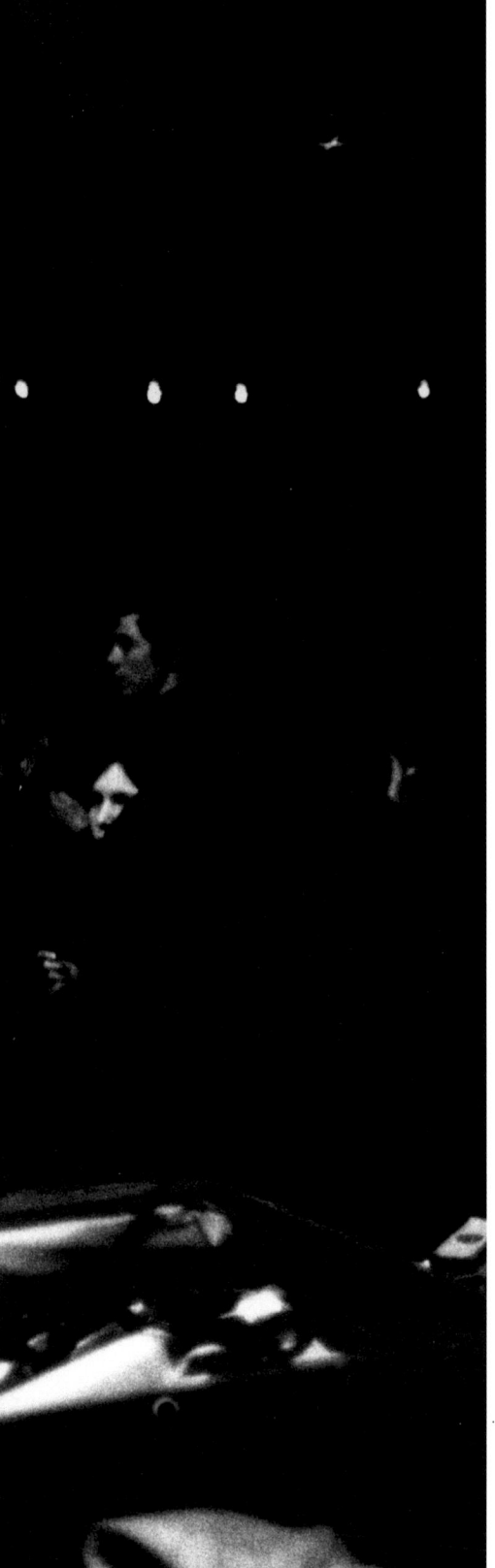

Anonymous
The Stones' first public appearance was at London's Marquee Club on 12 July 1962, a last-minute booking playing support to Long John Baldry. The group's blunt infusion of blues, rock 'n' roll and nervous energy served to affront some of the jazz purists present.
"Mick Jagger, R&B vocalist, is taking a rhythm and blues group into the Marquee tomorrow night while Blues Inc is doing its Jazz Club gig. Called 'The Rollin' Stones' ('I hope they don't think we're a rock and roll outfit,' says Mick), the line-up is Jagger (vocals), Keith Richards, Elmo Lewis (guitars), Dick Taylor (bass), 'Stew' (piano) and Mick Avery [sic] (drums)." Jazz News magazine, 11 July 1962

PP. 24–25
Gus Coral
Harmonising on the first national tour of the UK, which lasted from 29 September to 3 November 1963. They did 60 shows in 30 locations across the UK supporting the Everly Brothers, Bo Diddley and (in later shows) Little Richard.

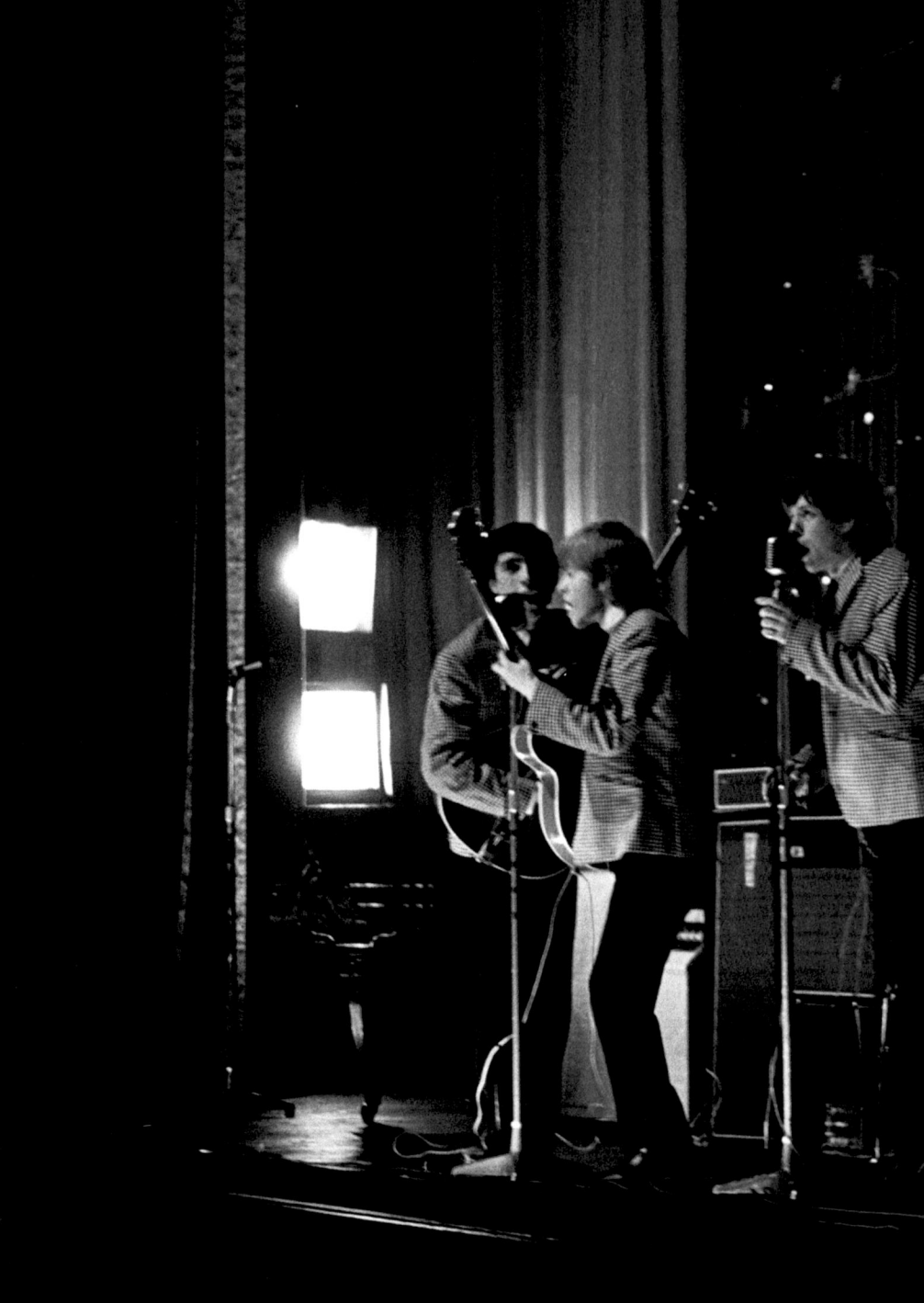

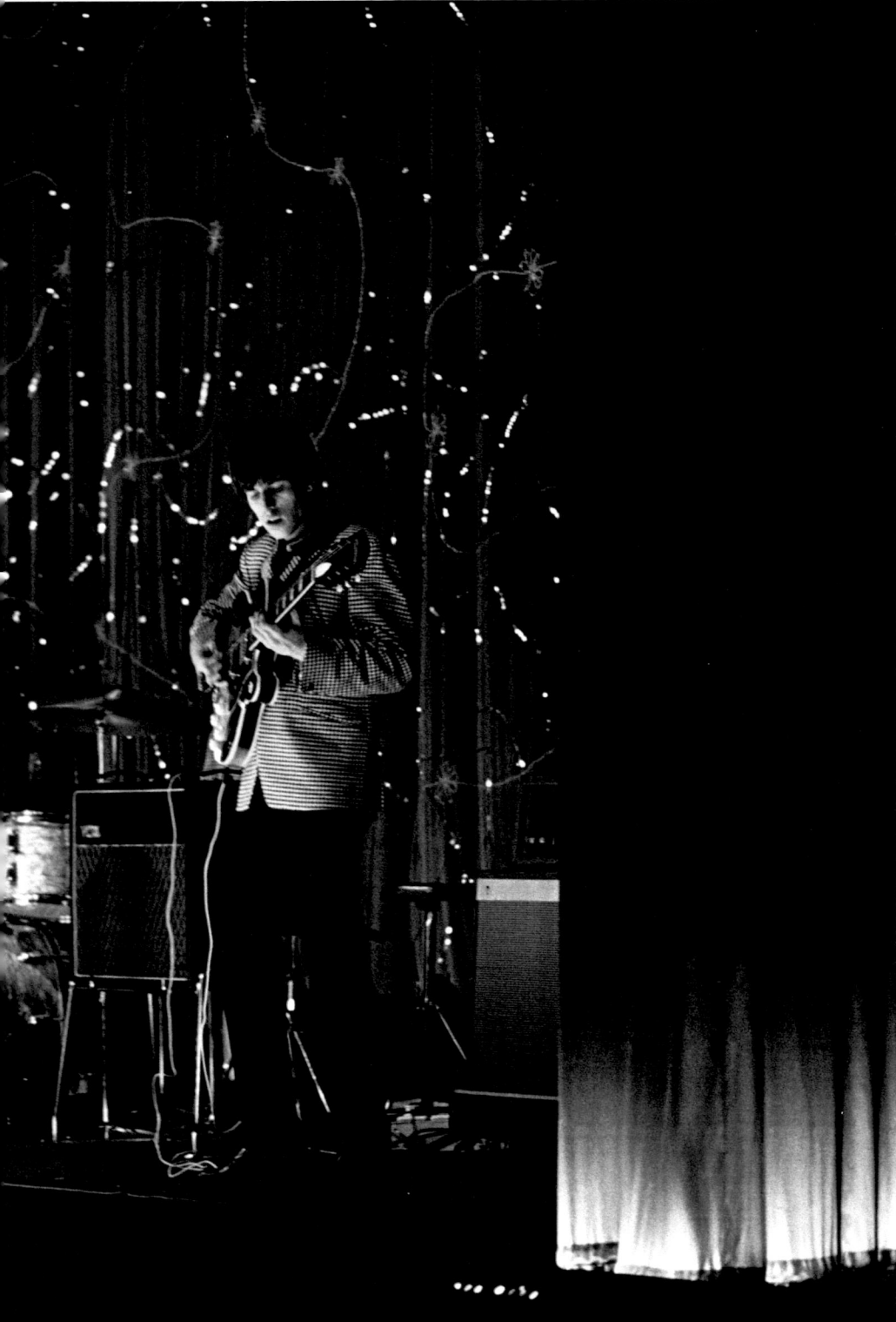

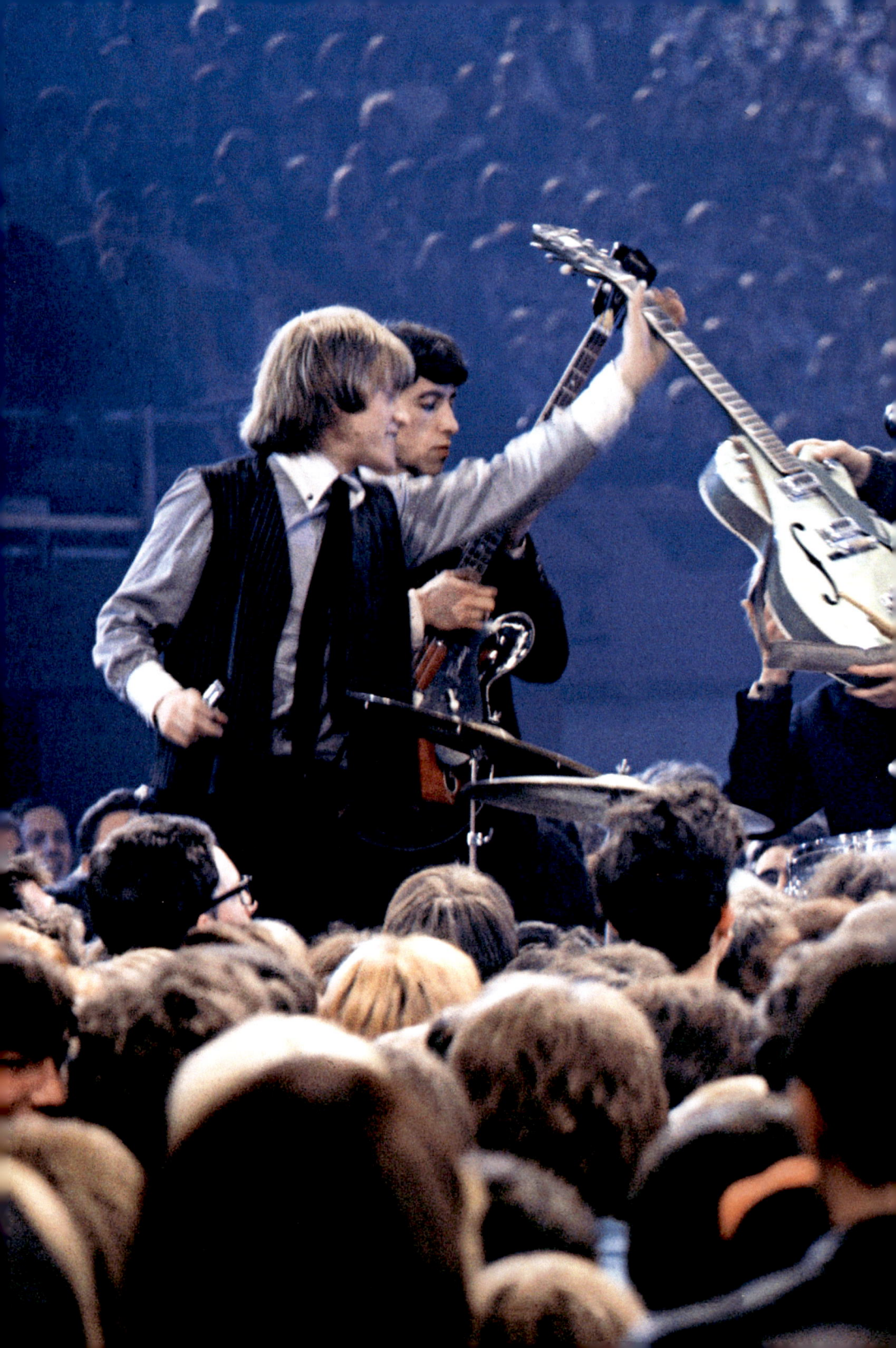

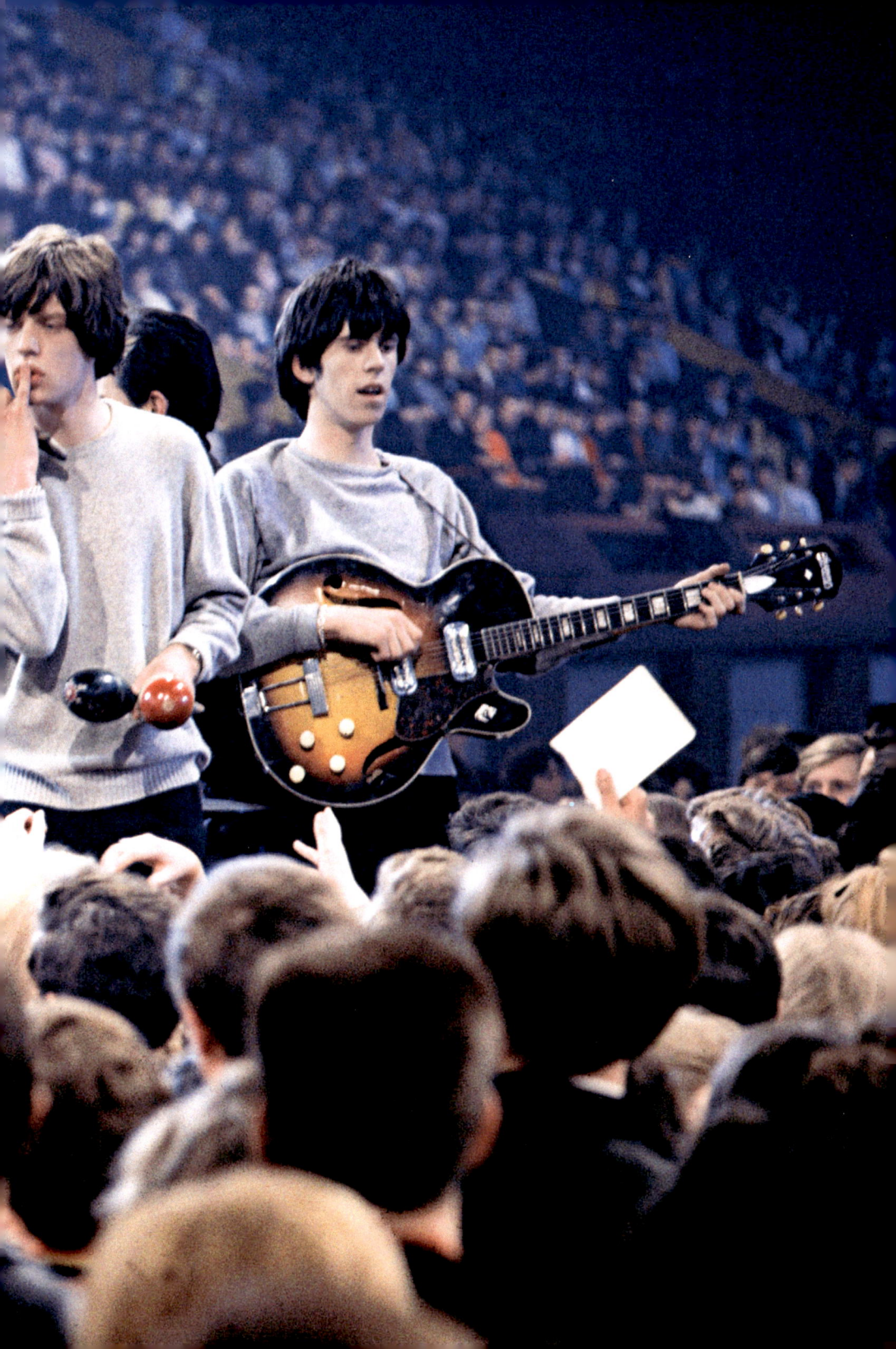

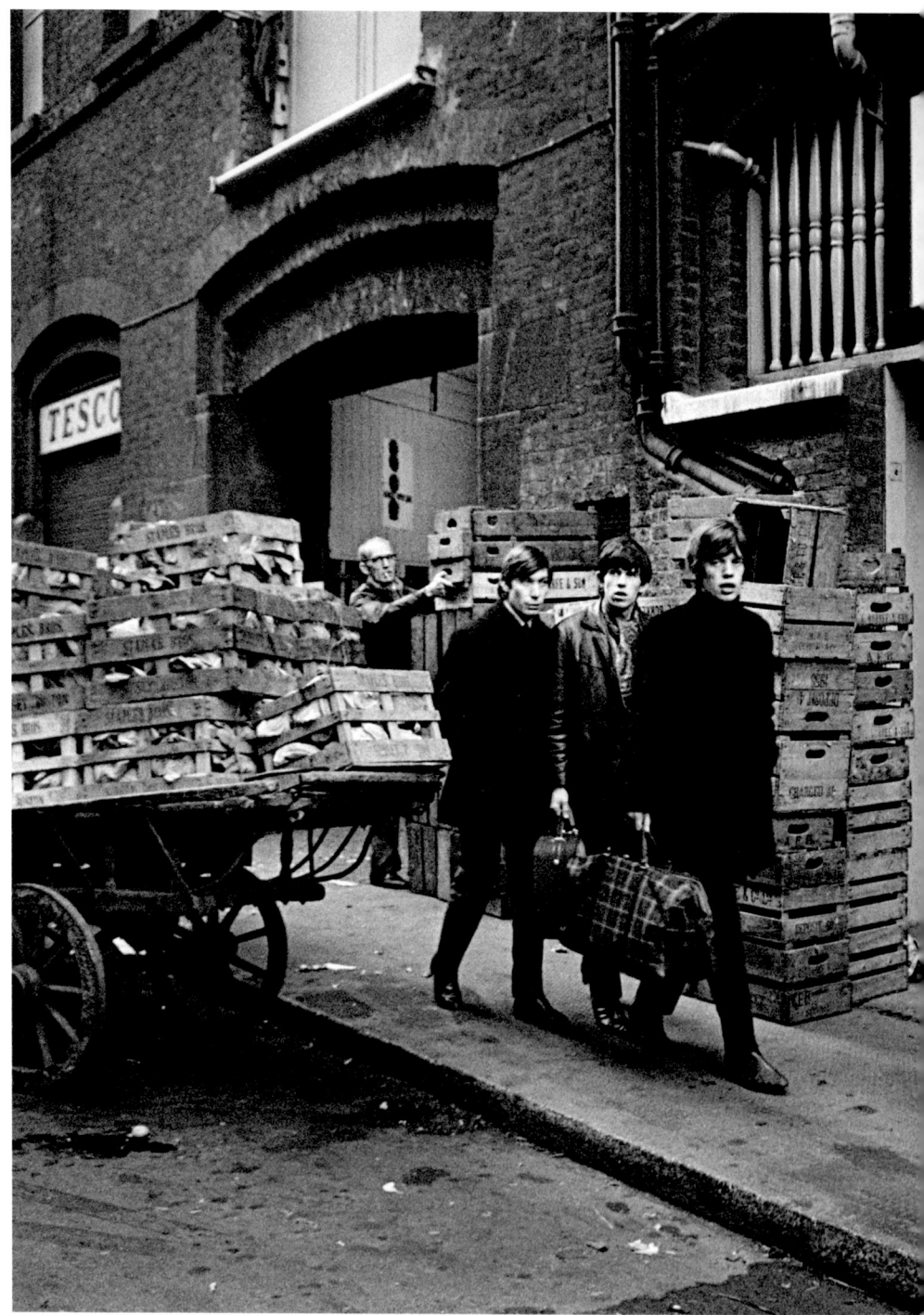

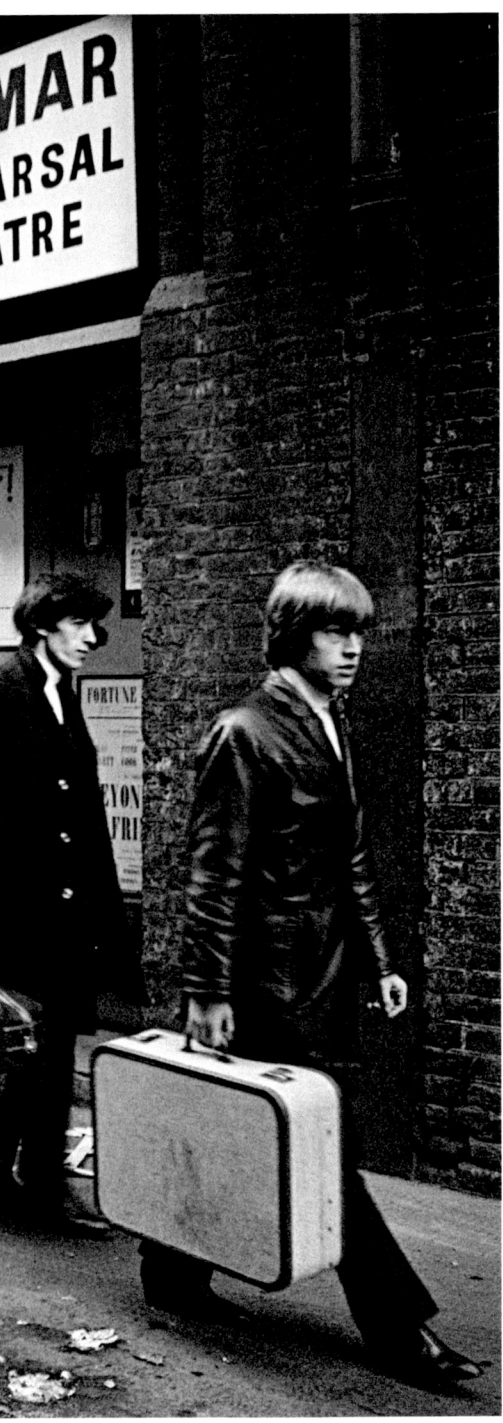

PP. 26–27

Anonymous

Playing "in the round" at London's Wembley Empire Pool on 8 April. The Stones were the most riotous act on a bill that included the more conventional artists Gerry and The Pacemakers, Cilla Black and Manfred Mann. They played four songs – "Not Fade Away", "Walking The Dog", "Hi-Heel Sneakers" and "I'm Alright" – with fans clambering on to the stage and mobbing them while television cameras beamed the action live.

"More than 30 teenagers were arrested last night outside the Empire Pool at Wembley where a Mod Ball was being held ... One group – The Rolling Stones – were mobbed as they left the stage. Commissionaires fought to protect them." Daily Mail, 9 April 1964

Terry O'Neill

Outside the Donmar Studios in Covent Garden, central London, late 1963: it was a popular rehearsal spot that was used by many musicians of the era.

29

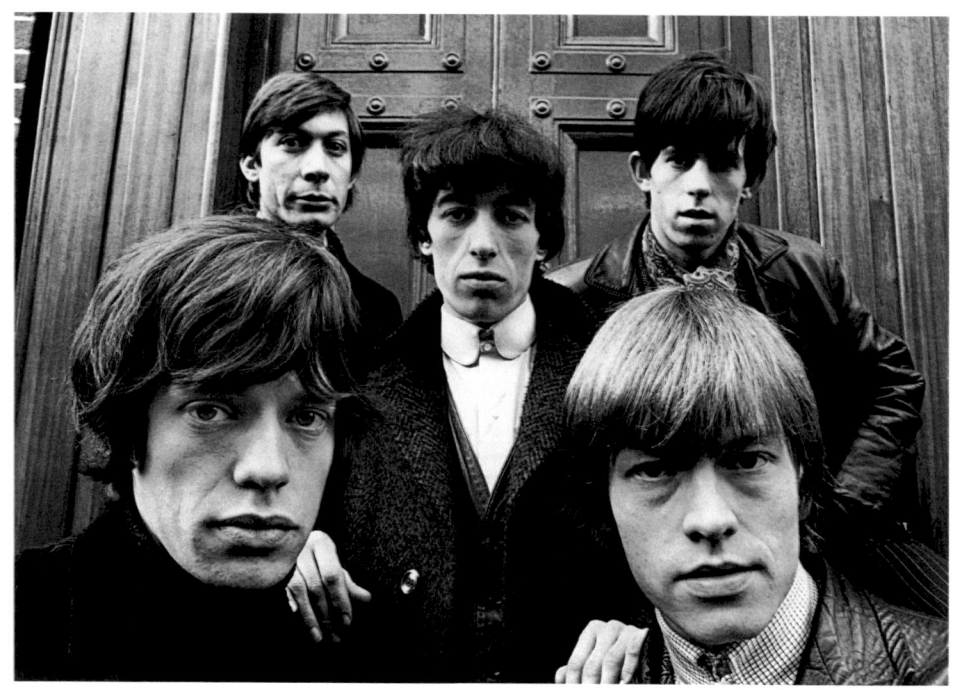

Terry O'Neill
Shot on the steps of St George's Church in London's Hanover Square, late 1963.
"They look like boys whom any self-respecting mum would lock in a bathroom! But The Rolling Stones – five tough, young, London-based music makers with doorstep mouths, pallid cheeks and unkempt hair – are not worried what mums think!" Daily Express, 28 February 1964

Terry O'Neill
Bill, Mick and Keith take a stroll near Ivor Court, off Baker Street, where Andrew Loog Oldham's management offices were located, in the summer of 1964.
"I only photographed musicians I liked … I got asked to do these Beatles. The paper published them and the paper sold out. So the picture editor said to me: Who else was out there? I had been watching a group called The Rolling Stones who were playing down in a little town called Richmond. I told them I wanted to photograph them. They were horrified how they looked. So they said 'God, aren't there any good-looking groups?'" Terry O'Neill, *Relix* magazine, March 2010

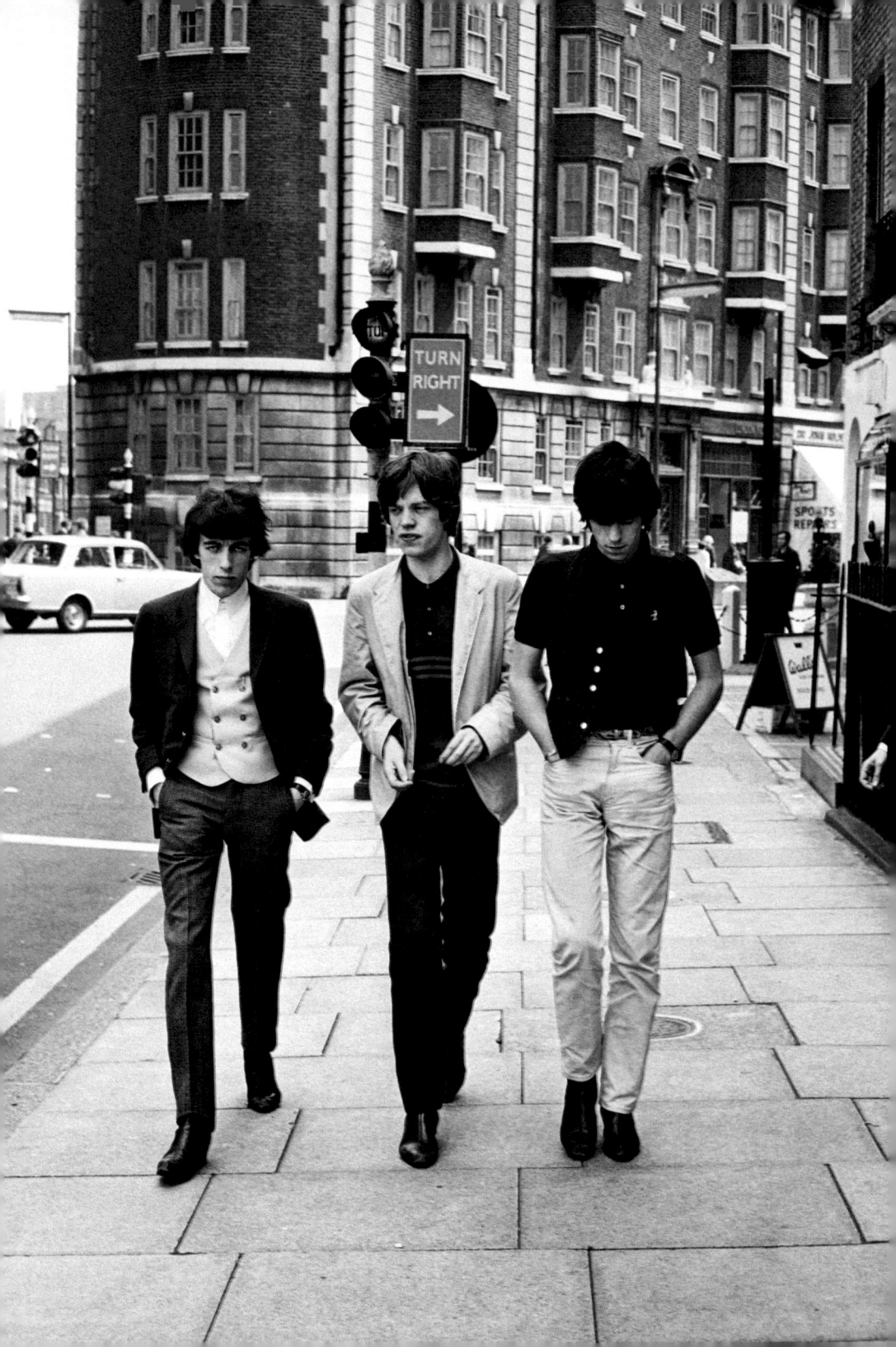

Terry O'Neill

London's "Tin Pan Alley" – more conventionally known as Denmark Street, the creative hub for songwriters and location (at number 4) of Regent Sound Studios – was an early recording base for the Stones. It was here that the group recorded their first album in early 1964.

PP. 34–35
Gus Coral

7 October 1963 was an auspicious date in the history of The Rolling Stones. They spent the best part of the day recording both sides of their next single, "I Wanna Be Your Man" and "Stoned", at Kingsway (later renamed De Lane Lea) Studios in London.

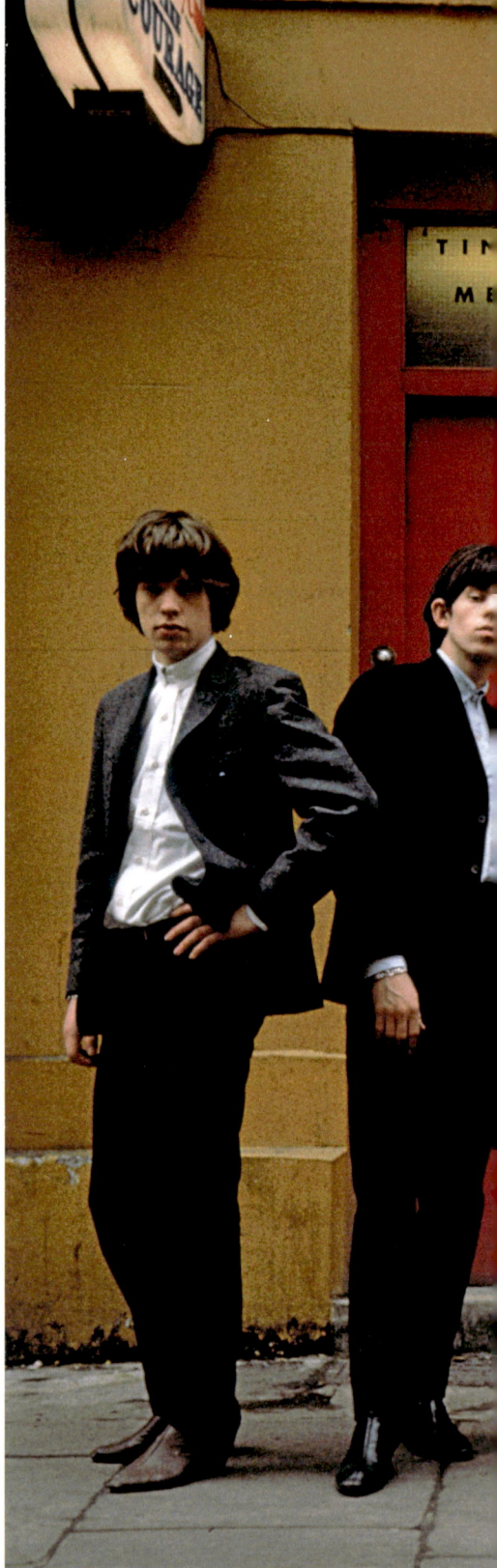

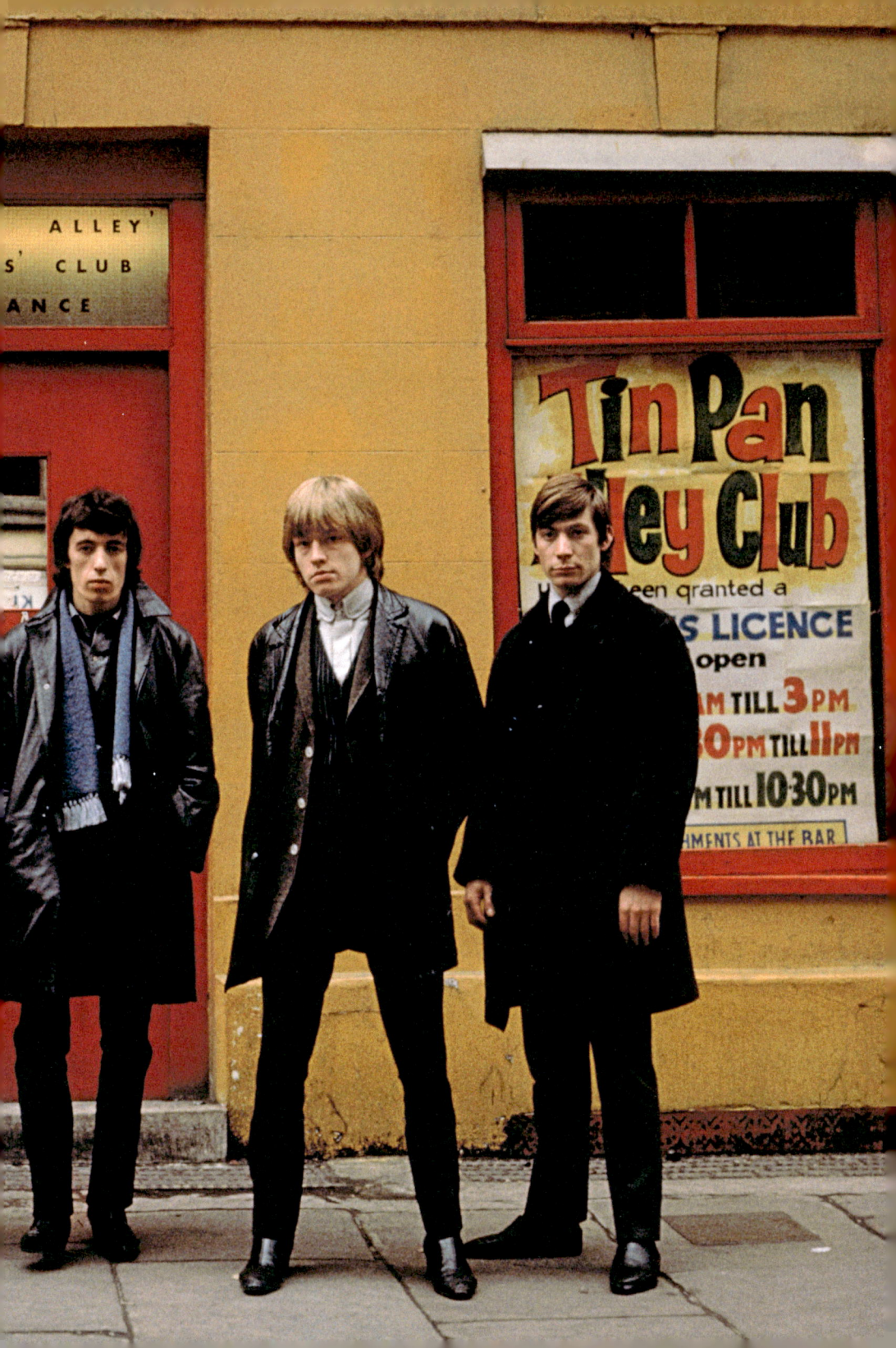

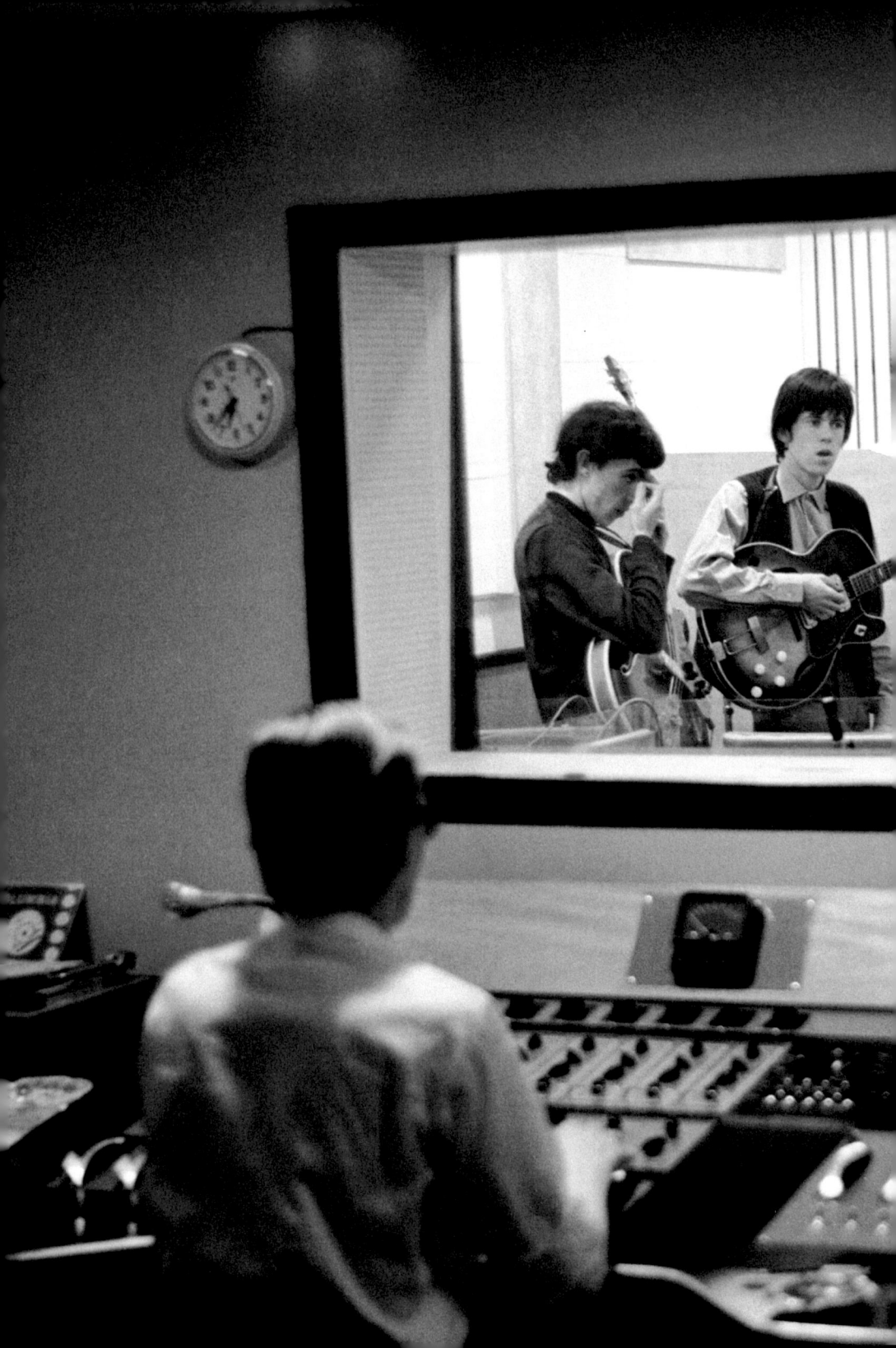

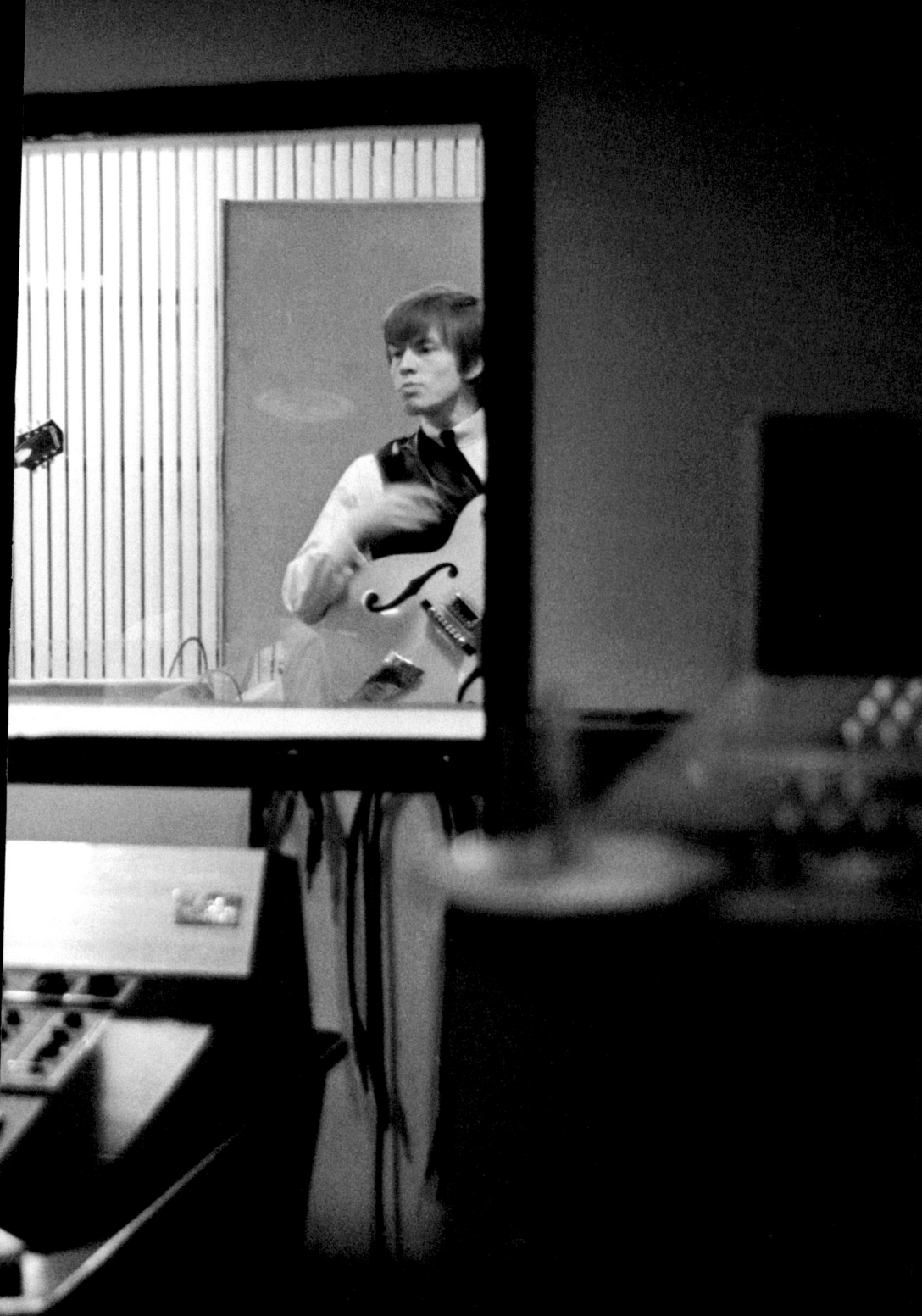

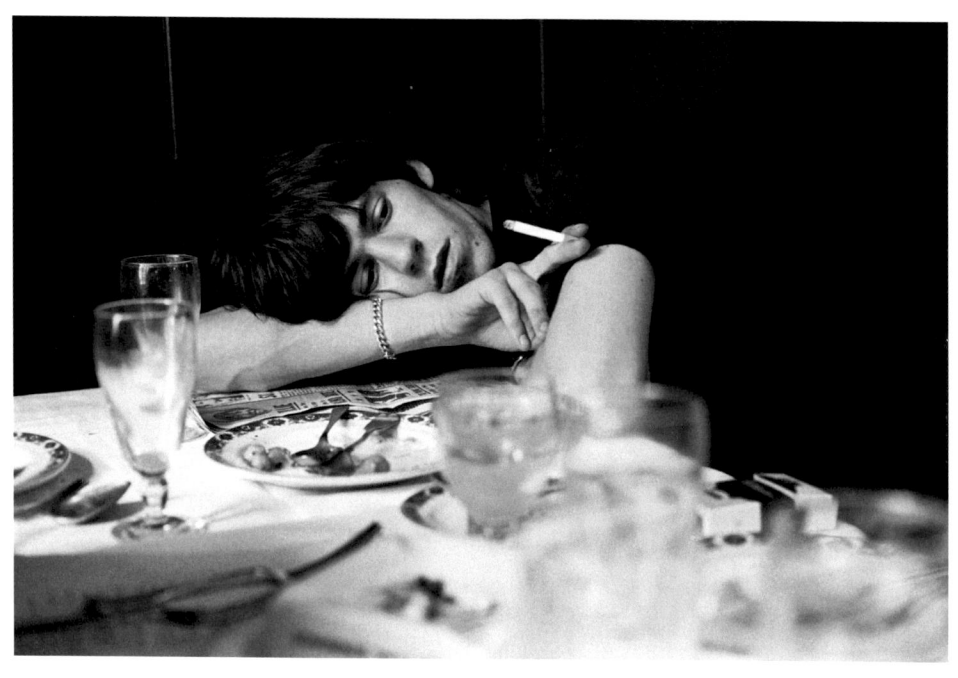

Terry O'Neill
Keith enjoys a cigarette
over lunch, summer 1964.

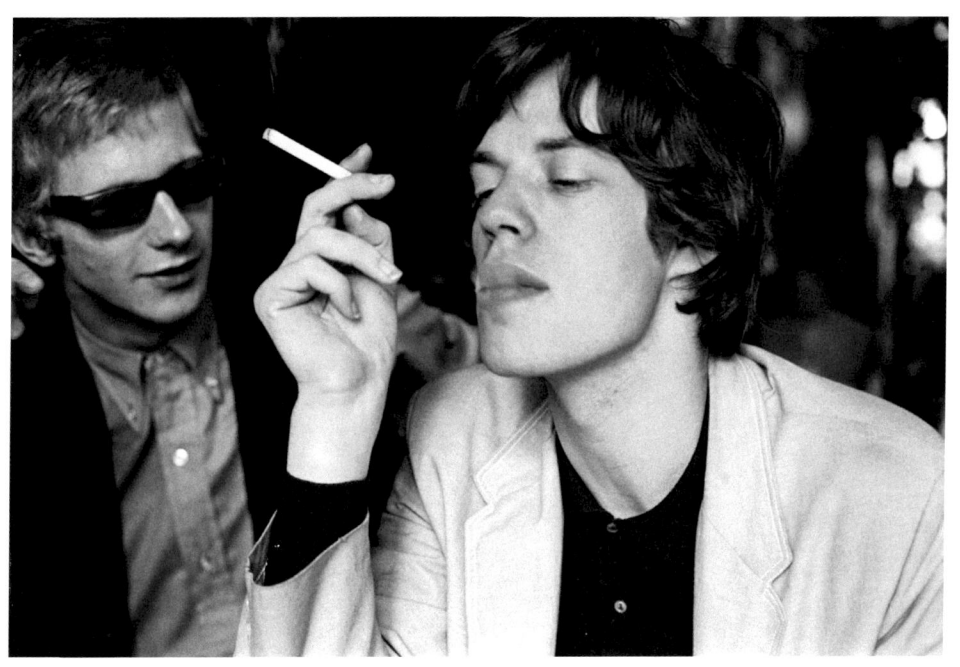

Terry O'Neill
Manager and principal star,
London, summer 1964.

David Bailey

1960s London had no finer photographer than David Bailey, a personality who shared many of the Stones' instinctive tastes and attitudes. This photograph entitled "Mick Jagger – Fur Hood" was included in Bailey's first collective work *Box Of Pin-Ups* in 1965. The collection benefitted from imaginative liner notes written by eminent critic and social commentator Francis Wyndham: "In the age of Mick Jagger, it is the boys who are the pin-ups: and Bailey's pictures give them all the inward, self-sufficient look of Narcissus."

P. 40
Eric Swayne
Focus of the lens. London, circa 1966.

P. 41
Eric Swayne
A baby seal-skin jacket was an unusual item of apparel in the mid 1960s.
"Put out of your mind the nonsense talked about this young man. He is not a long-haired idiot, but a highly intelligent university man. The Duke of Wellington had much longer hair and he won some famous battles." Dale Parkinson (Mick's barrister), Tettenhall Magistrates Court, Wolverhampton, 26 November 1964

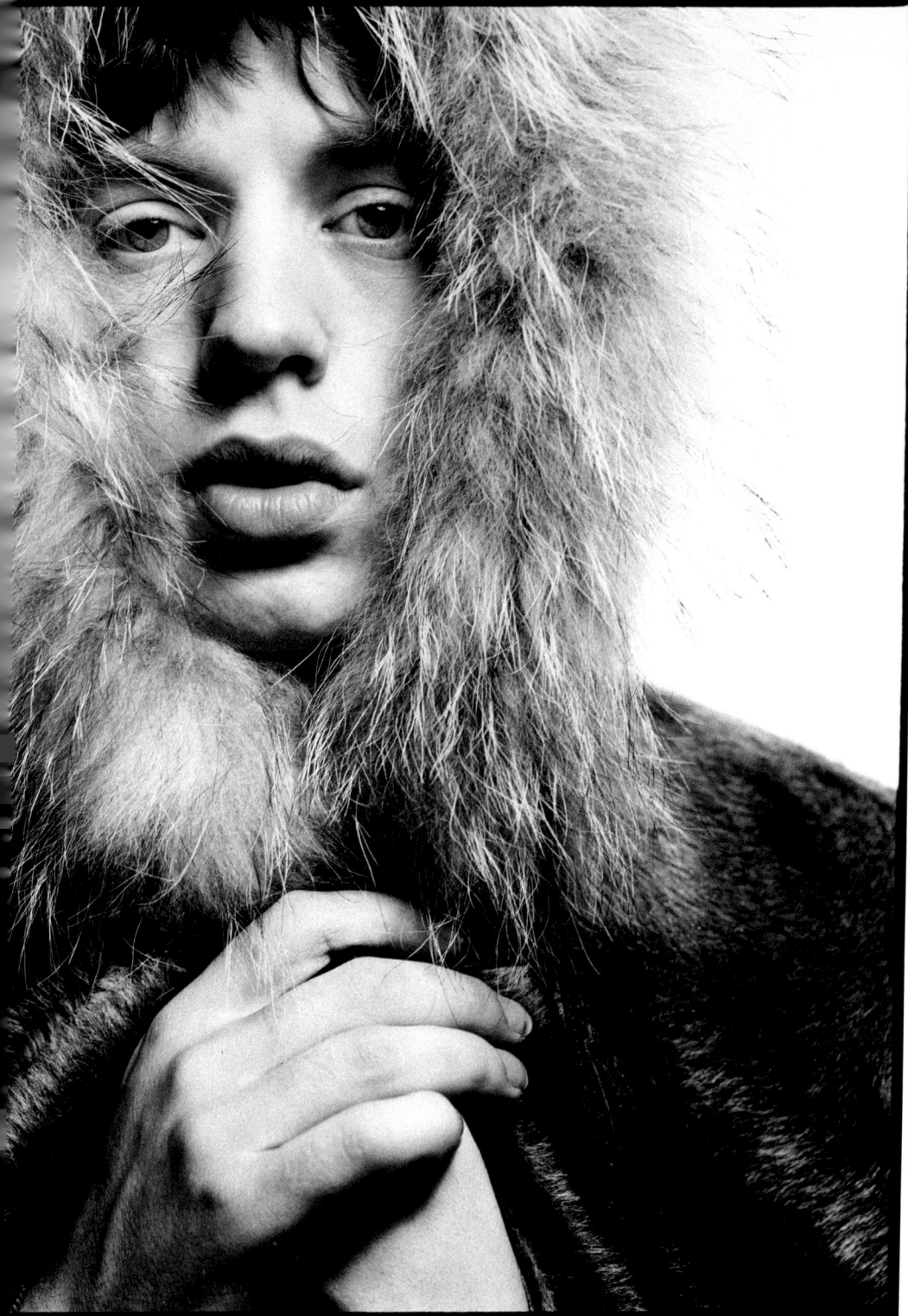

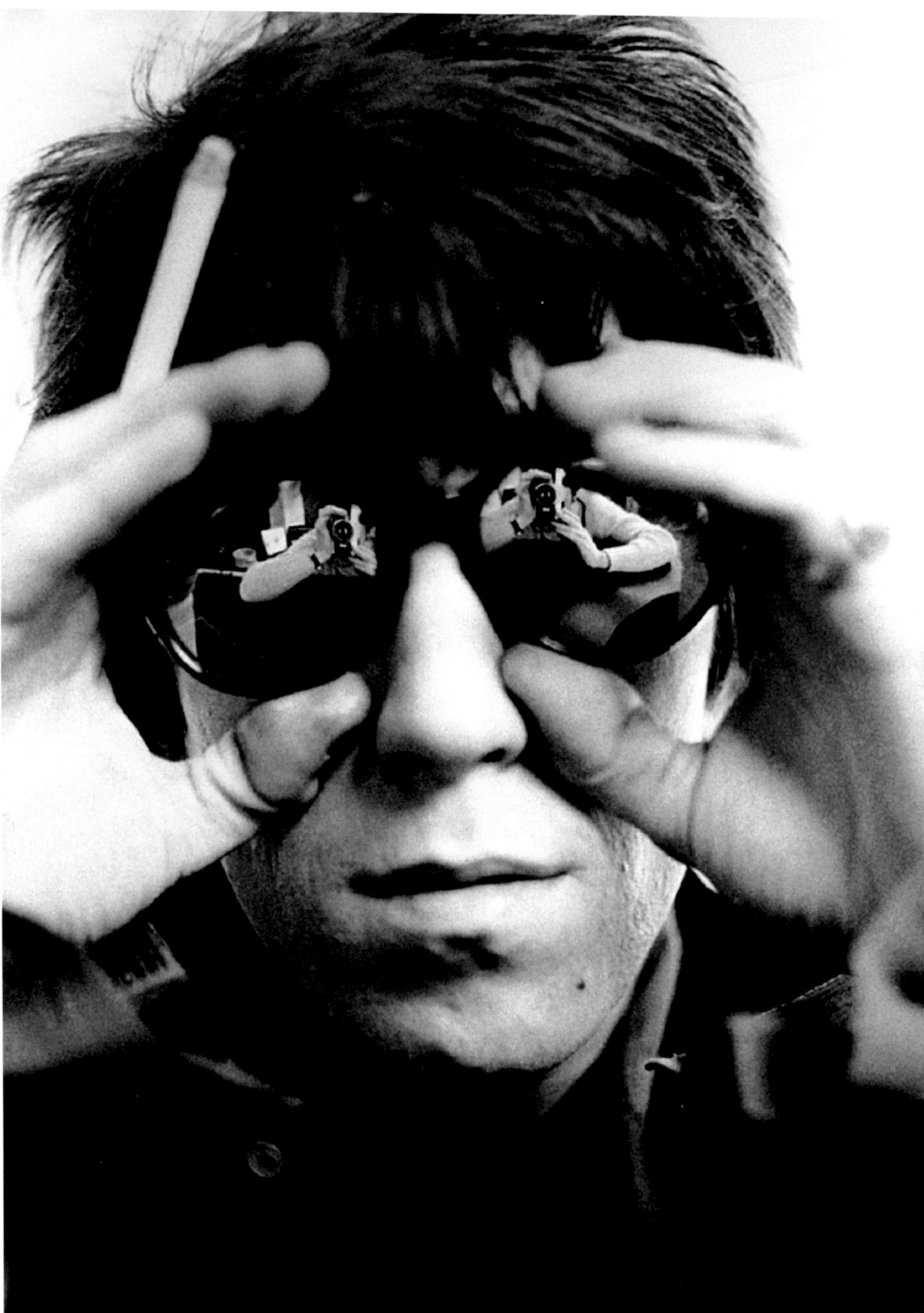

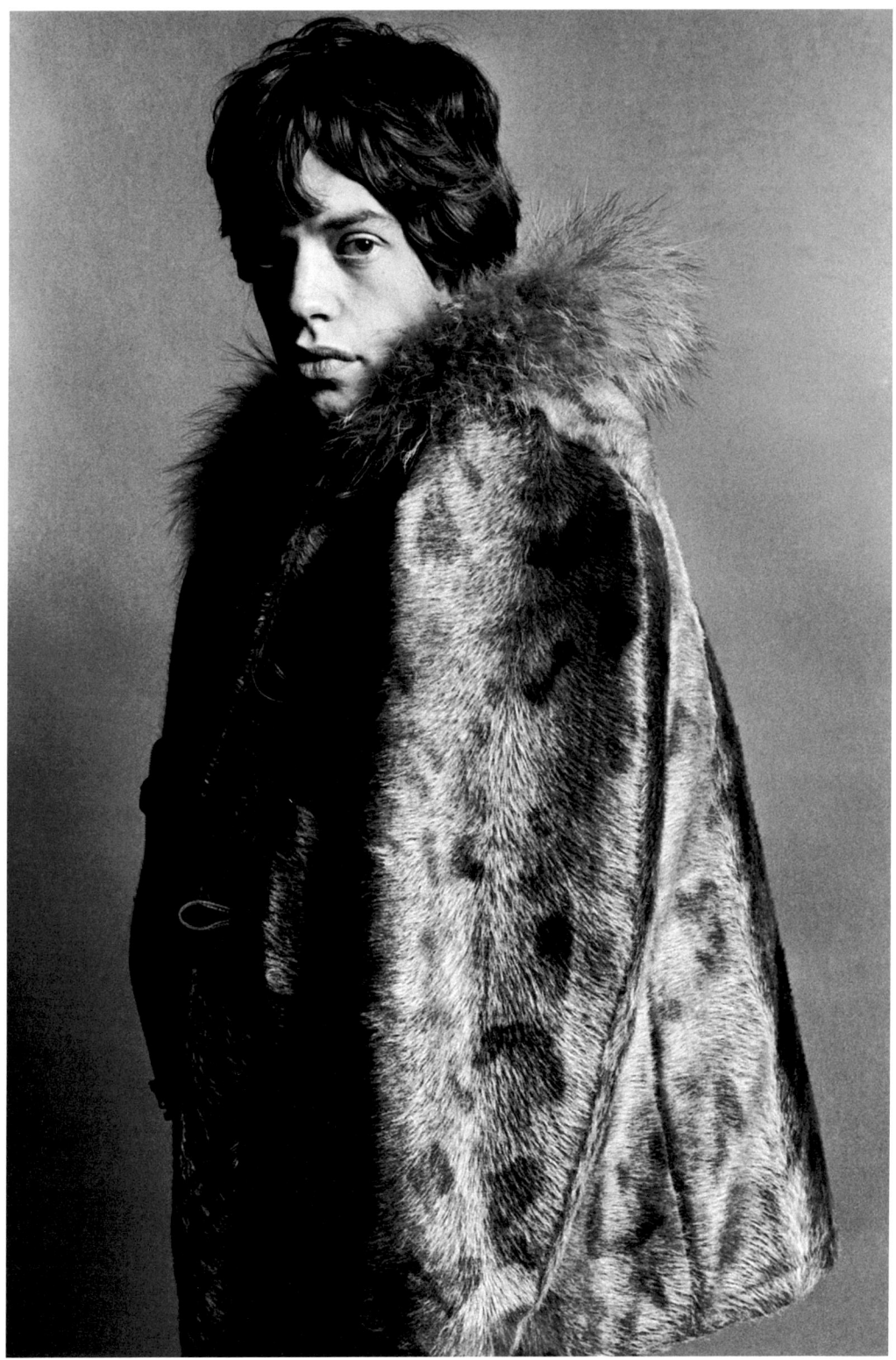

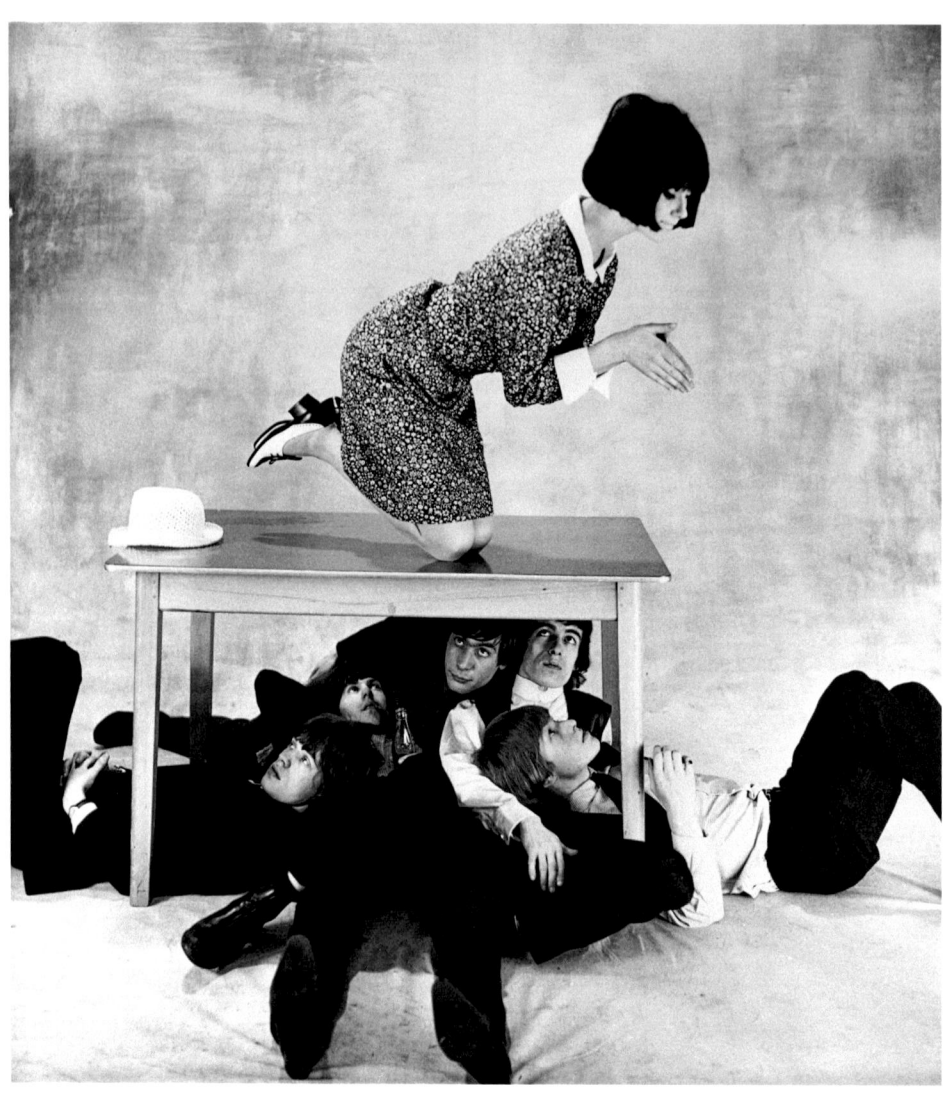

Norman Parkinson
With the help of French model Nicole de Lamargé, high-society fashion photographer Parkinson created a series of striking images that were unlike the standard type of "pop star" presentation. The fashion story for the April issue of *Queen* magazine featured the model in a Mary Quant outfit and was entitled "How To Kill 5 Stones With One Bird". London, 1964.

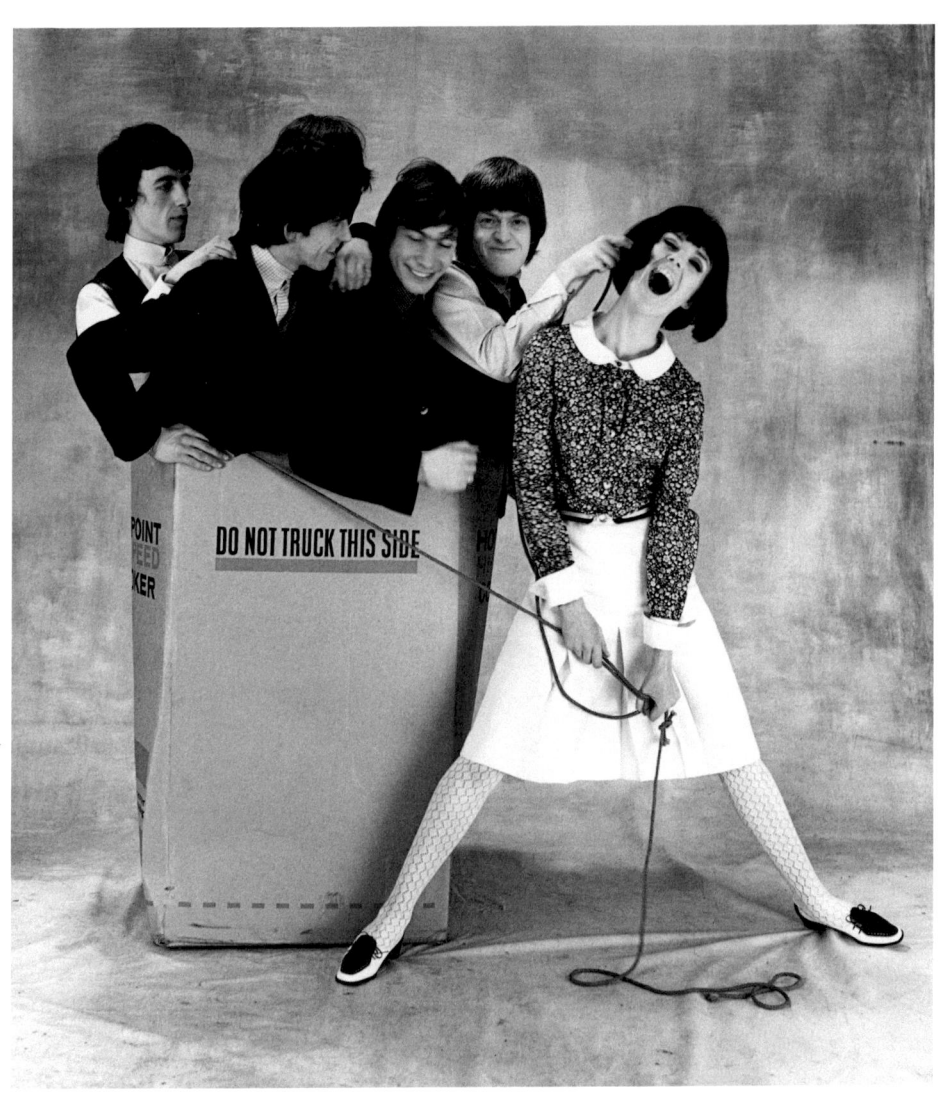

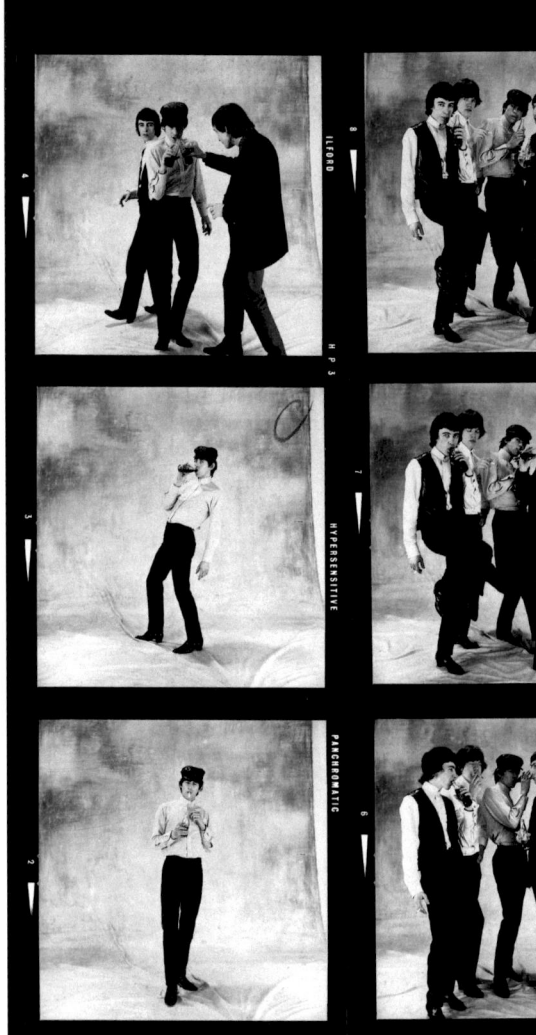
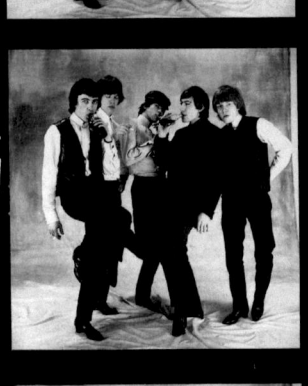
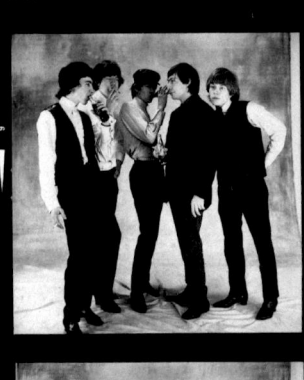
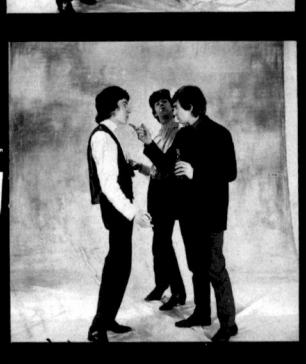
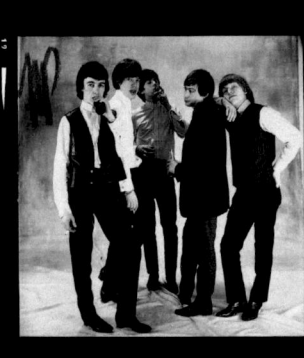
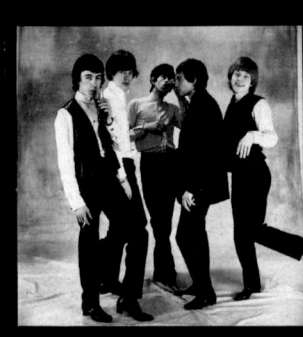
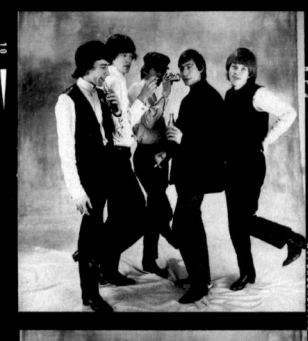
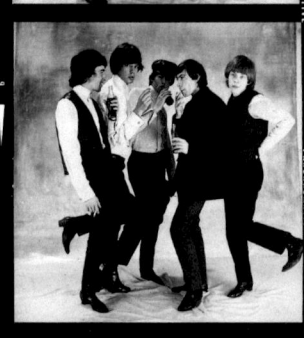

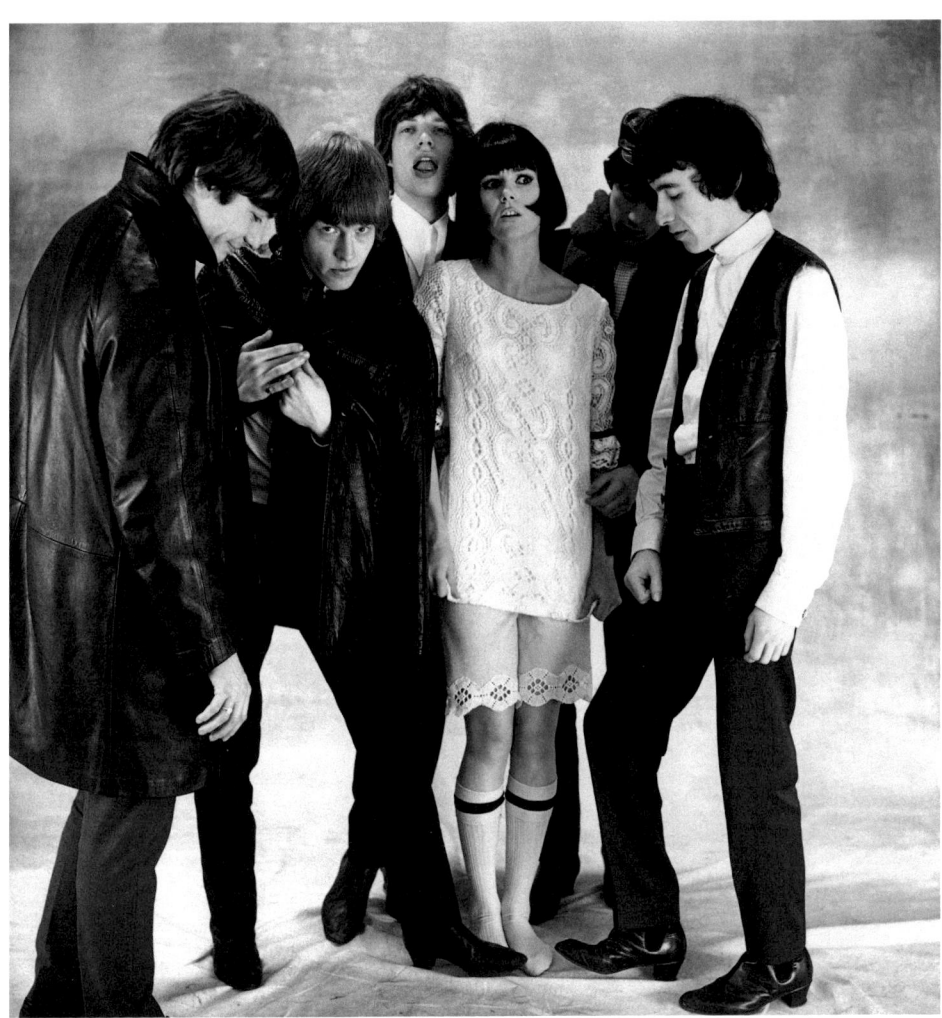

Norman Parkinson
London, 1964.
"Five meteoric boys (average age 21) are gathering mossy fans all over the country. They list among their likes and hobbies: women, science fiction, records, women, girls, poetry, cashew nuts, girls, sleeping, boats, records, girls, clothes, boats, having showers, and girls. Three out of five like black." Queen magazine, April 1964

Norman Parkinson
London, 1964.
"It takes a thief to catch a thief. So any girl who wants to get herself noticed by boys in the limelight like The Rolling Stones had better get herself the super aid of that phenomenal stealer of limelight, Mary Quant." Queen magazine, April 1964

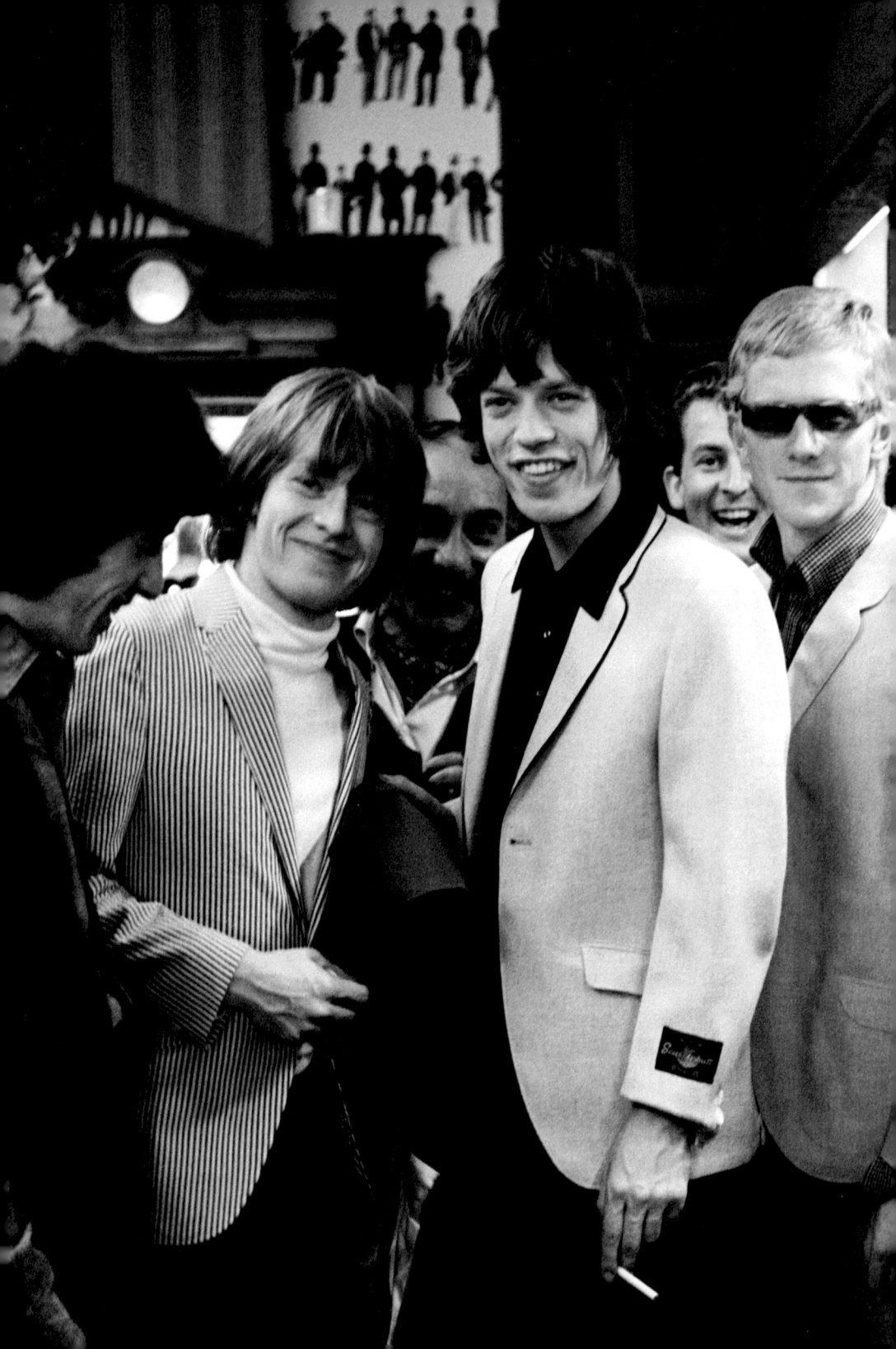

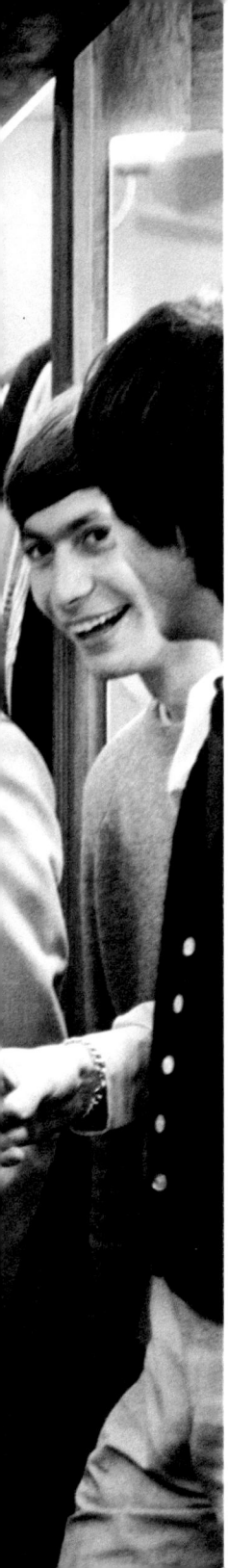

Anonymous

On 4 June 1964, prior to an appearance on *The Hollywood Palace*, hosted that week by Dean Martin, the band – with a sizable advance from the show's producers – were driven over to the fashionable store "Beau Gentry" on Hollywood's North Vine Street to be kitted out with some new threads.

"Dean Martin was a little bit out of it and made an awful lot of fun of the band. The producer gave them money to go out and buy themselves uniforms. We said, 'They don't wear uniforms.' Dean Martin and I got into an argument, and Keith was about to pop him one with his guitar." Bob Bonis (tour manager), quoted in Bill Wyman, *Rolling With The Stones*, 2002

Anonymous
Hollywood, 4 June 1964.
"The Beatles want to hold your hand, but the Stones want to burn down your town." Tom Wolfe, *Esquire* magazine, July 1965

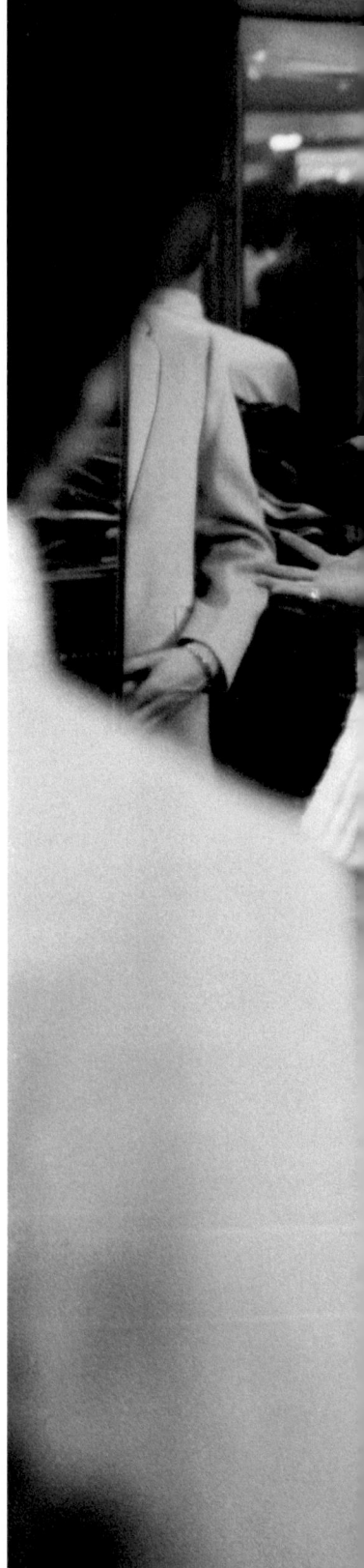

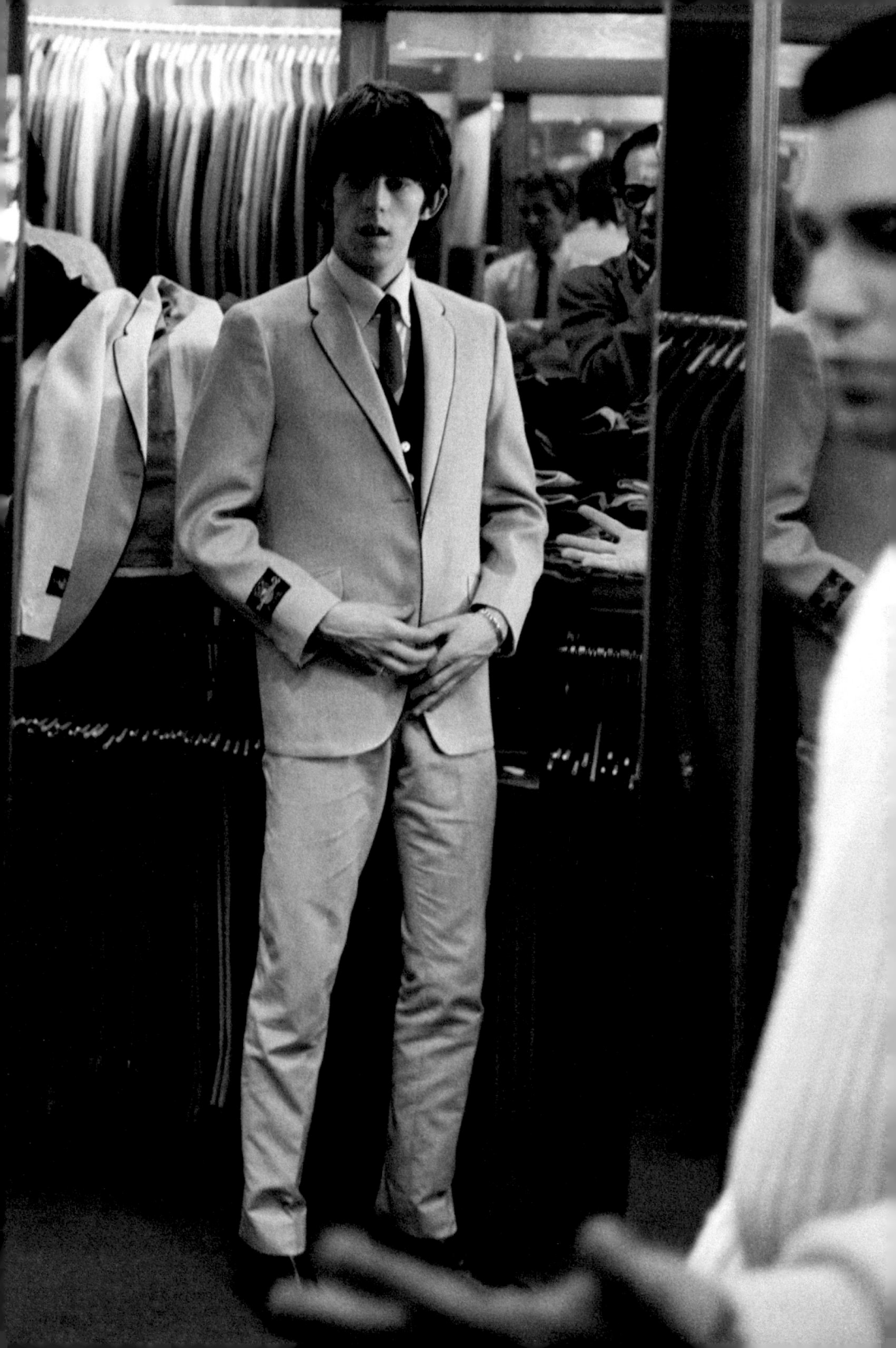

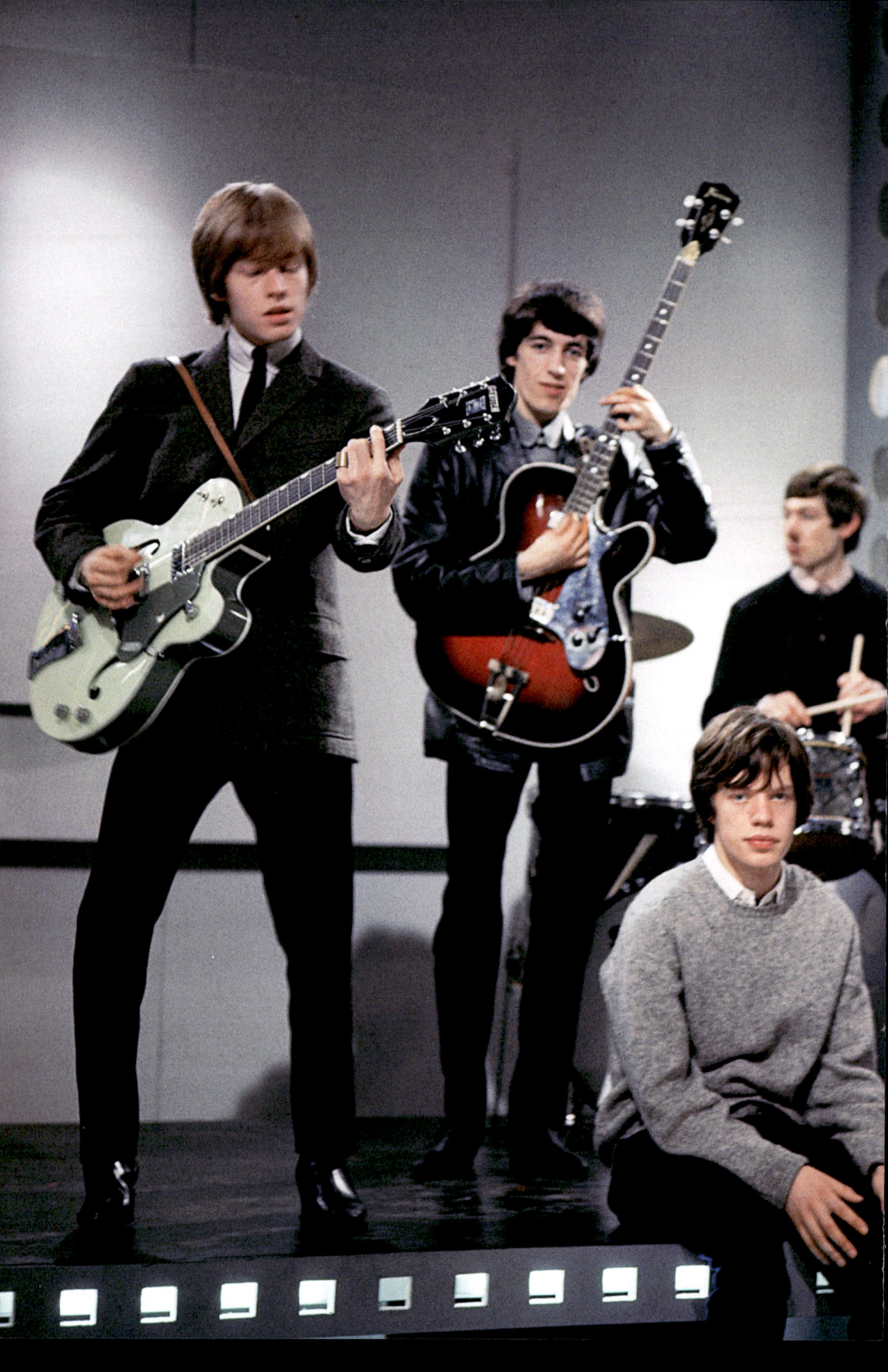

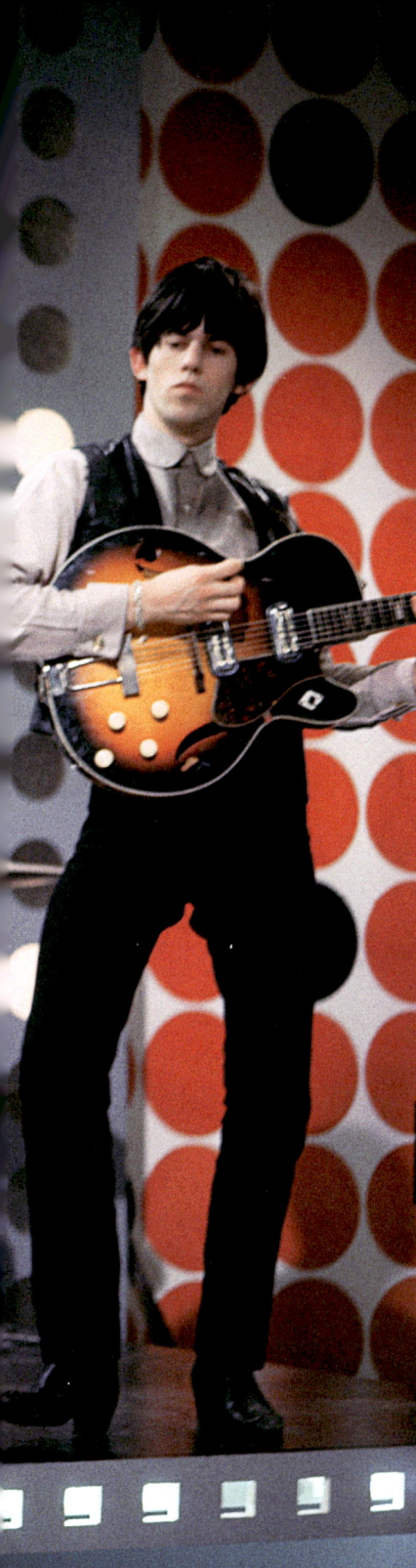

Paul Popper
The Stones featured on the BBC TV show *Top Of The Pops* numerous times during the 1960s, and are pictured here during their first-ever appearance on the first-ever show, New Year's Day, 1964. The group performed "I Wanna Be Your Man" then sped back from Manchester to London to prepare for recording sessions for their first album.

PP. 52–53
Bob Bonis
Backstage on the Stones' third US tour, April–May 1965. Keith is playing his new Gibson Firebird guitar while Brian plays his custom-made 12-string Vox Teardrop guitar, an instrument that was specially designed for him.

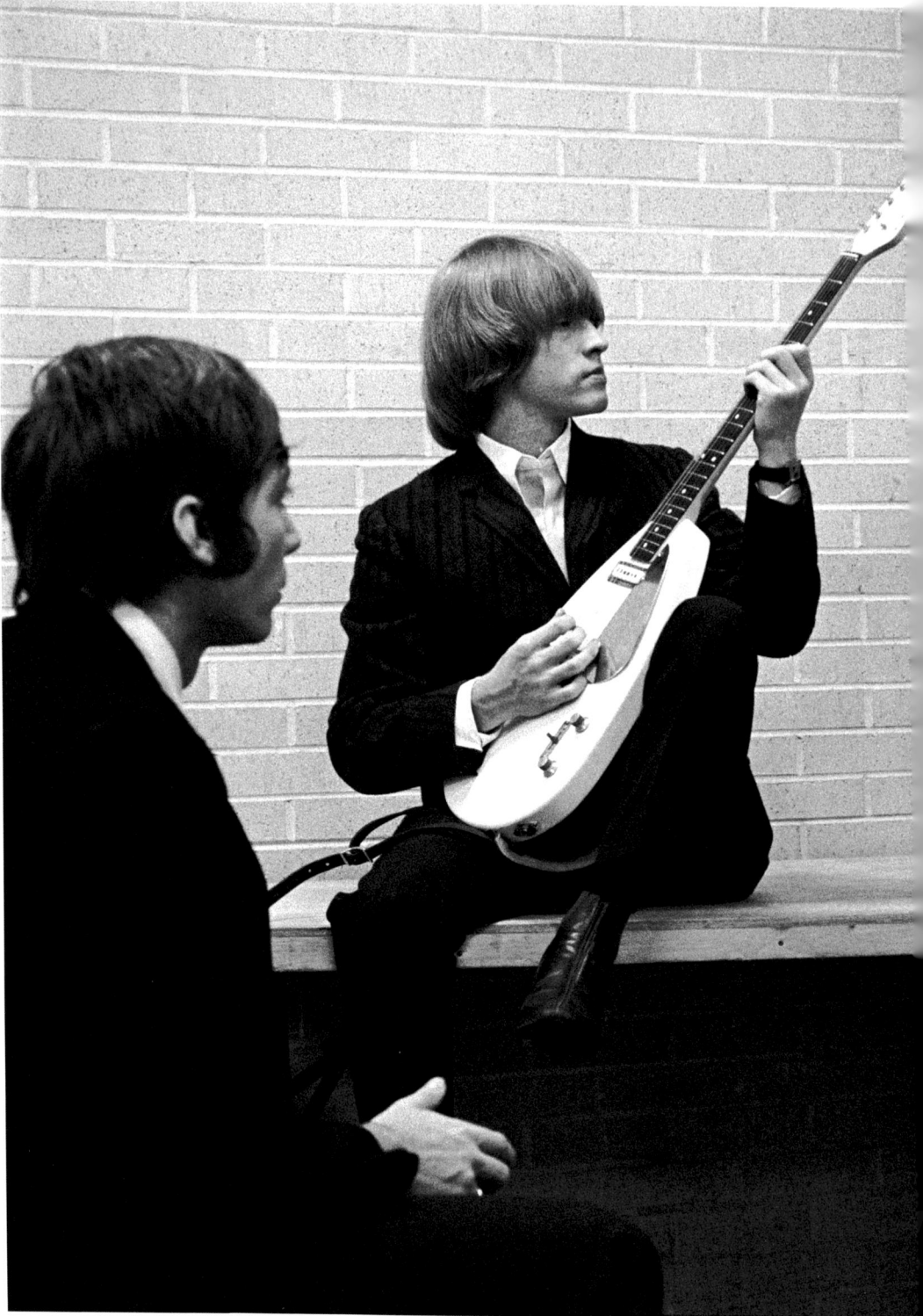

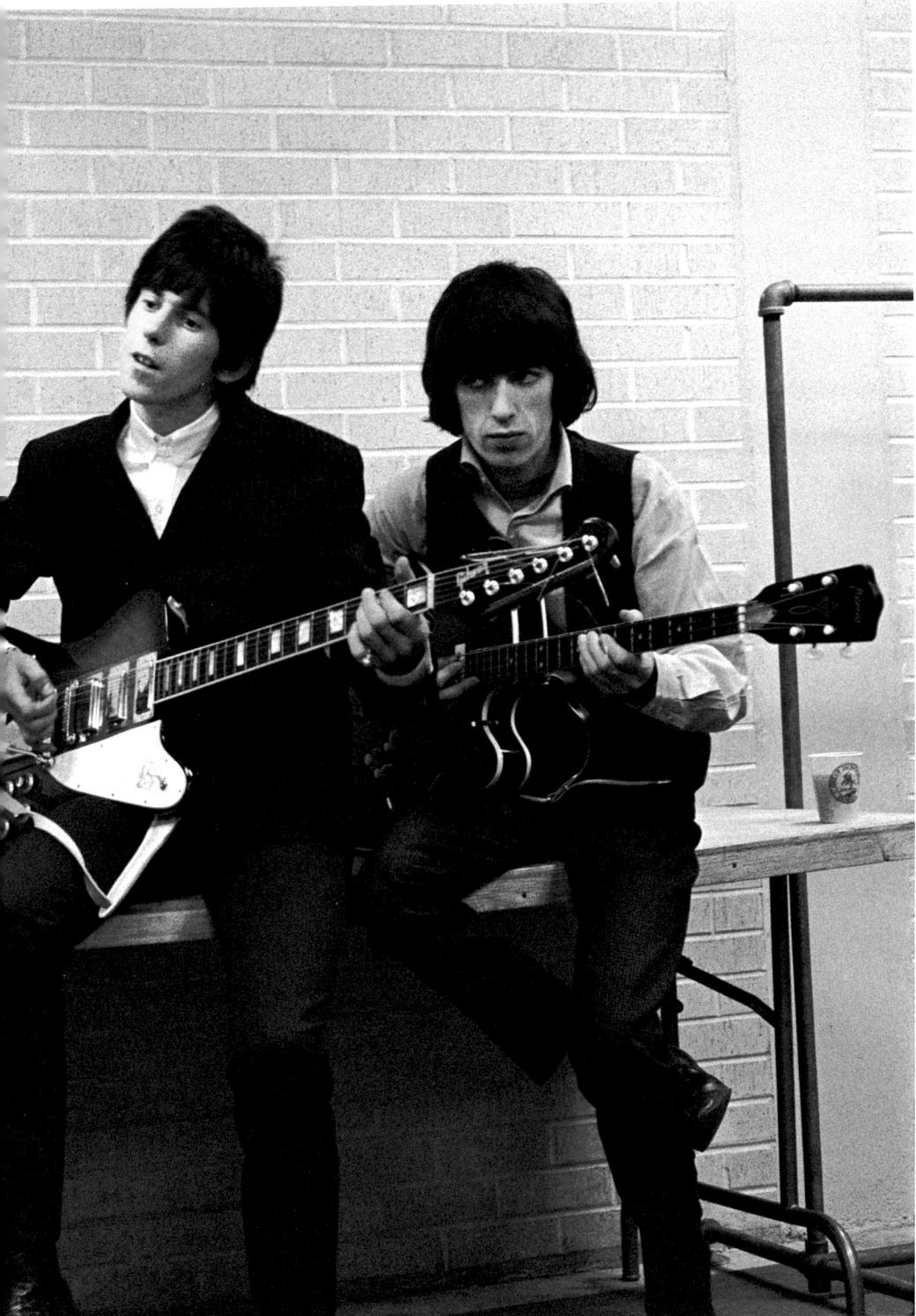

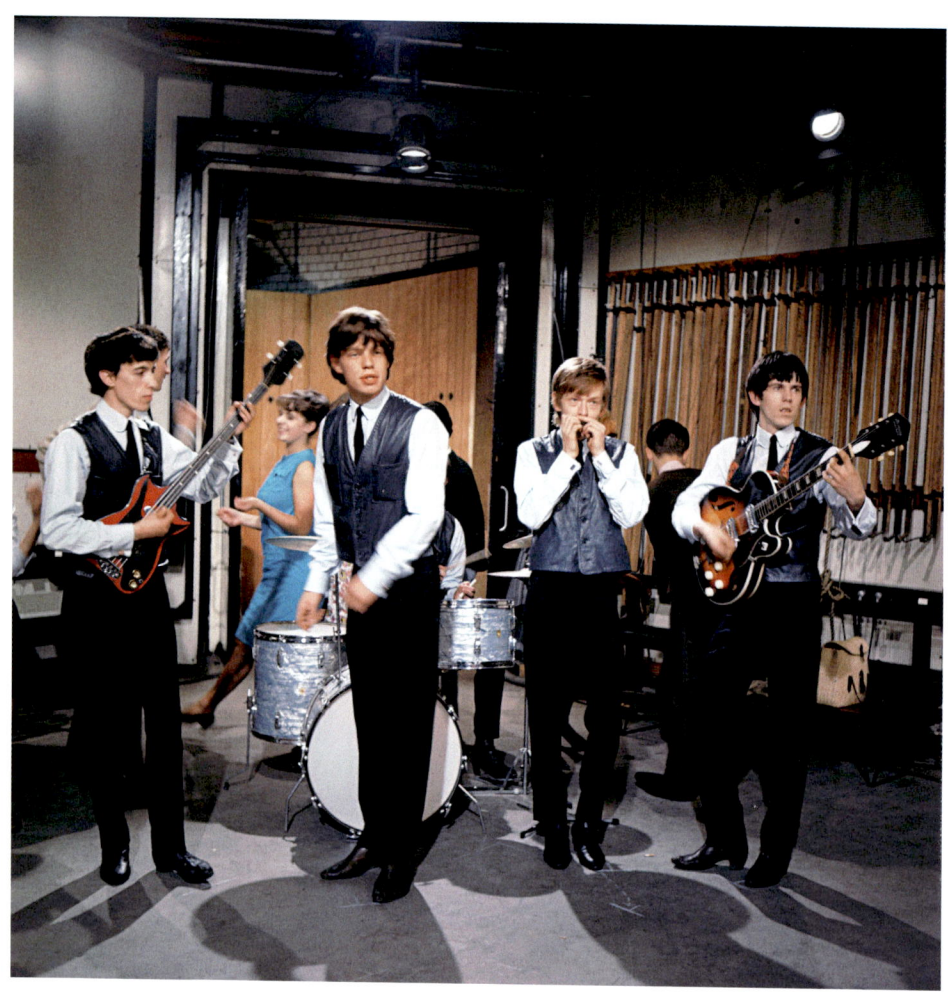

Anonymous
The Stones made their second national
television appearance on ITV's *Ready, Steady, Go!*,
23 August 1963. The engagement at Associated-
Rediffusion's London studios allowed them to
preview their debut single, "Come On".

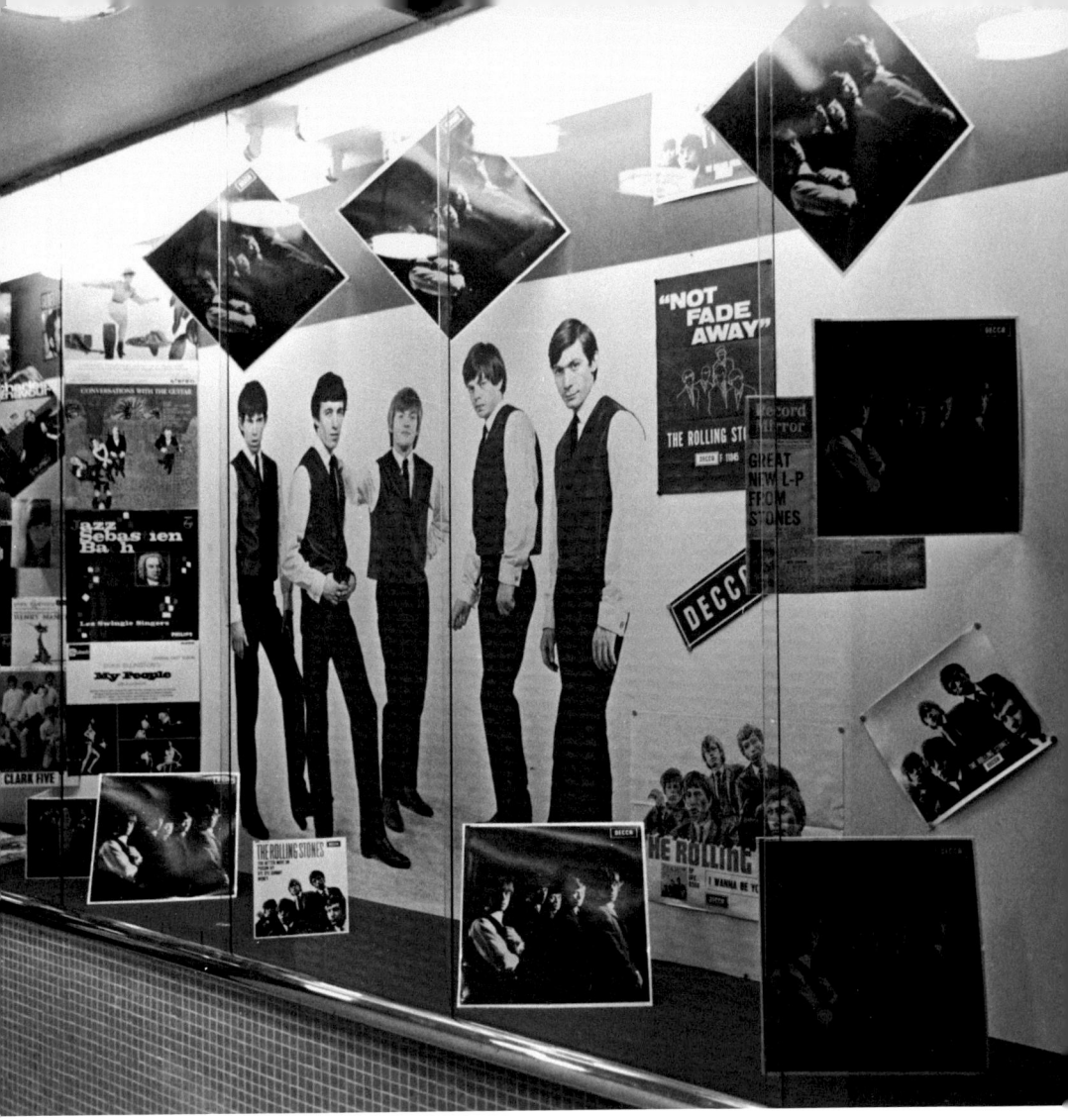

Dezo Hoffman

Following the modest success of the singles "Come On" and "I Wanna Be Your Man", in April 1964 the Stones made serious inroads into the singles charts with "Not Fade Away", the classic Buddy Holly song updated to the Stones' R&B formula, and the release of their first album. Soon record stores, such as The Soho Record Centre in London's Old Compton Street, were getting in on the act.

"At first it was an esoteric thing but gradually people began to realise that it was the thing to like it, so they listened to it. Then they found that they did enjoy it and it caught on in a big way." Brian Jones, *New Musical Express*, 31 January 1964

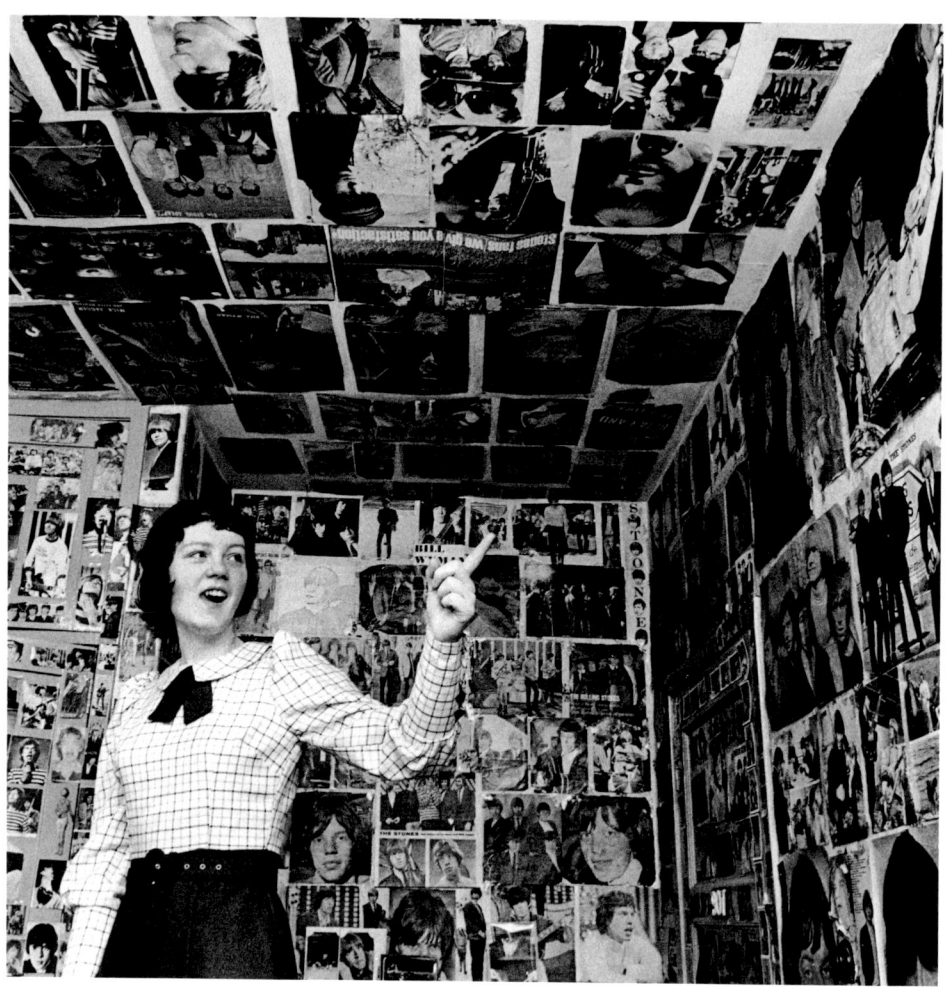

Anonymous
Superfan 18-year-old "Alice" showing off her
bedroom shrine to the band, October 1966.
Dear Mick and Boys,
Just a line to thank you for coming right down to
Colchester last Tuesday, 8th December!! I vowed
that I wouldn't scream – I wanted to hear you so
much! But when I saw you I helped "raise the roof"
because you gave such a wonderful performance.

Nothing quite so spectacular has happened round
this way for some time now, but this sure made
up for it. Hoping to see you again some time down
our way.
Lots of love, Julie Butcher xxx
Letter to *The Rolling Stones Book*, a monthly
magazine, October 1964

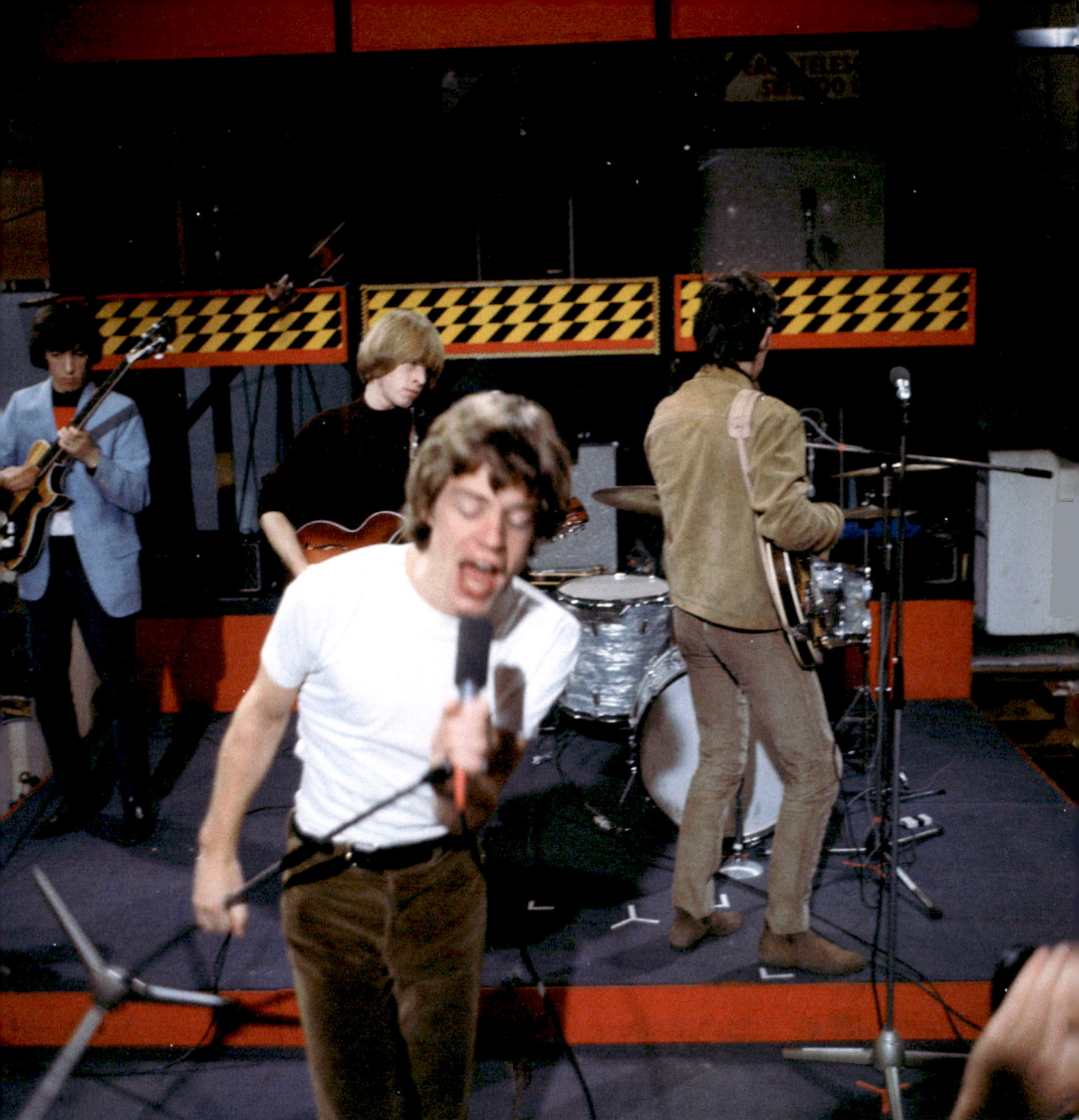

Tony Gale

Television rehearsals on 22 October 1965 for an appearance on *Ready, Steady, Go!* to promote the single "Get Off Of My Cloud". Tiring of cover versions and fired by the financial rewards to be made from homespun compositions, Mick and Keith focused on songwriting, drawing inspiration from what they saw around them.

"It's a stop-bugging-me, post-teenage-alienation song. The grown-up world was a very ordered society in the early 1960s, and I was coming out of it. America was even more ordered than any-where else. I found it a very restrictive society in thought and behaviour and dress." Mick Jagger, *Rolling Stone* magazine, 14 December 1994

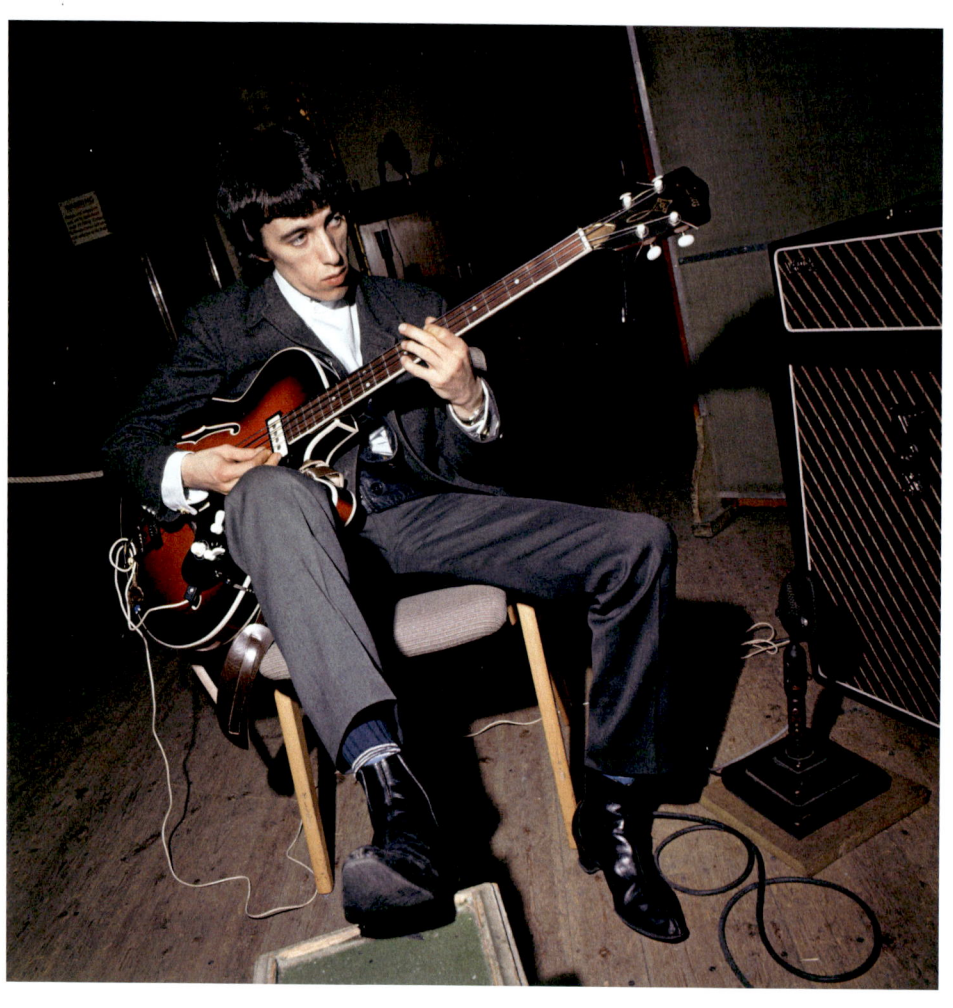

Tony Gale
Bill taking a moment to tune up backstage, 1964.

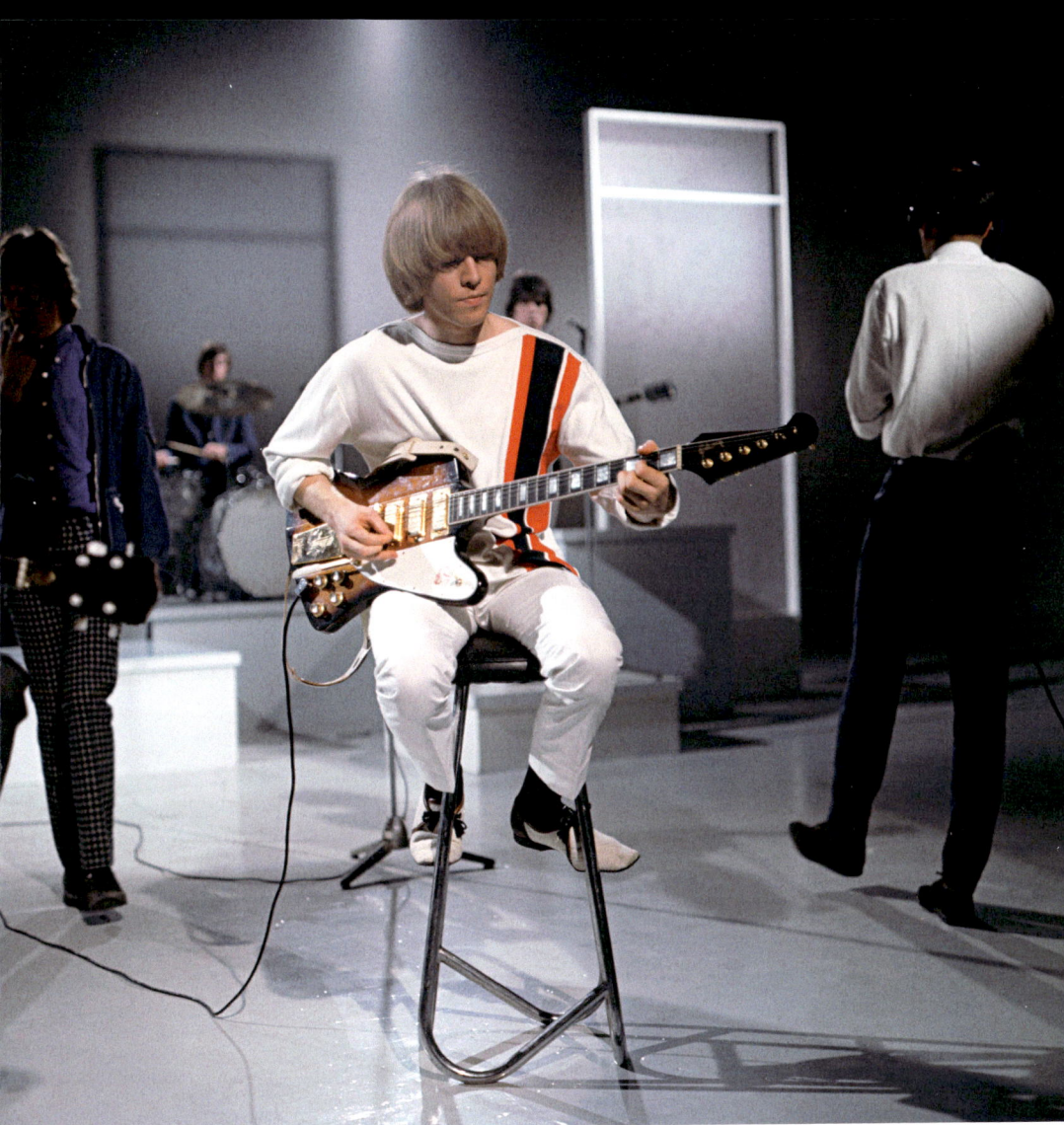

Tony Gale

American teenagers had an insatiable appetite for the British pop boom, so filmed musical segments were regularly sent over as inserts for programmes in the States. On 28 July 1965, the Stones took over a set at London's Twickenham Studios to record six songs for use in *Shindig!*, a lively entertainment show that often featured British acts and whose producer, Jack Good, was the father of British rock 'n' roll on the small screen. With sensitivities still somewhat delicate, ABC television censors cut the line "Trying to make some girl" from the broadcast of "Satisfaction".

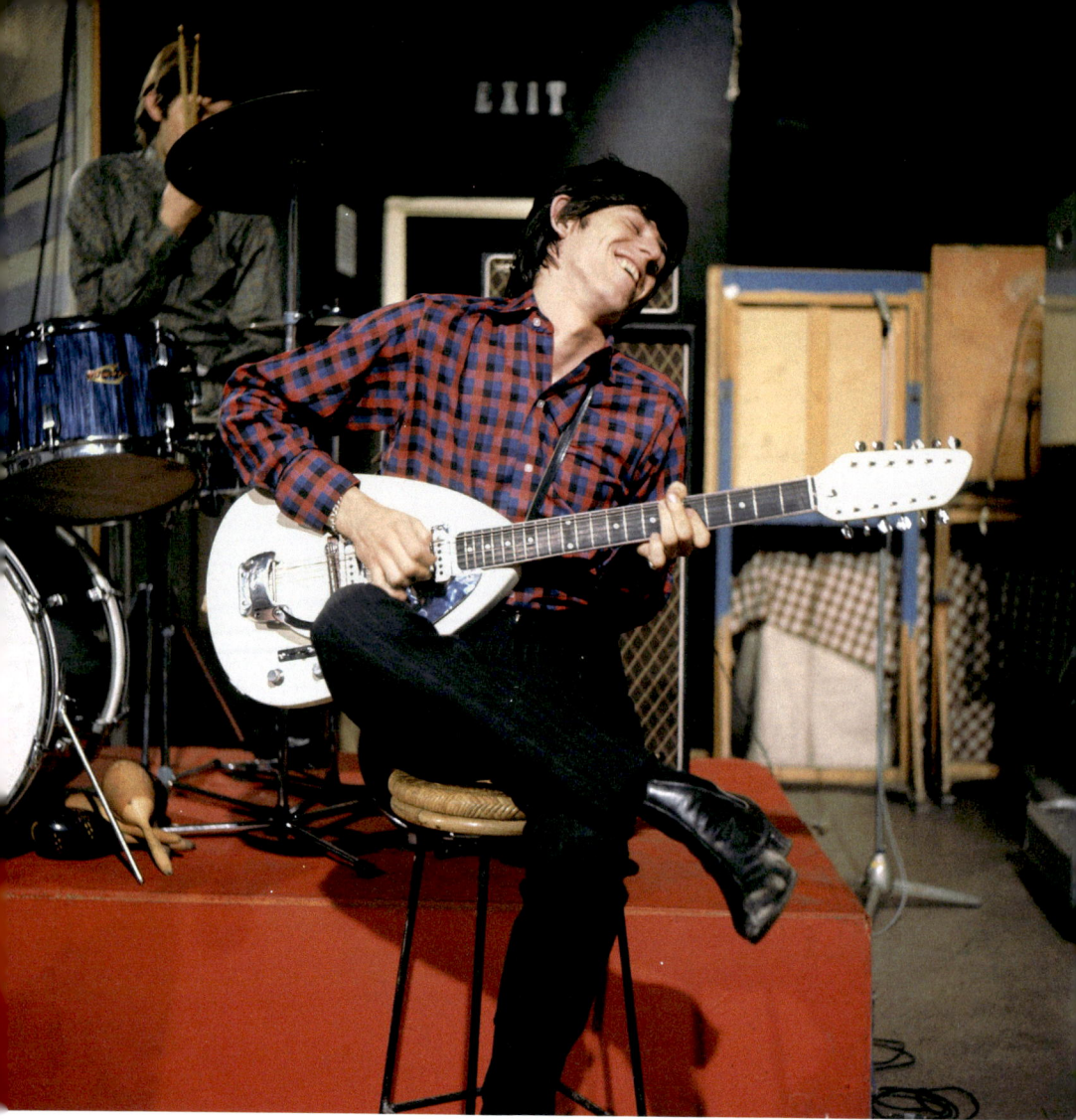

Peter Francis
During rehearsals for ITV's *Ready, Steady, Go!* on 26 June 1964, Keith took the opportunity to try out Brian's custom-made 12-string Vox Teardrop guitar.

"The girls were really going mad. Mick did all the jumping around that made the girls scream. We had literally thousands of letters in the office asking to see them again." Cathy McGowan (*RSG!* host), quoted in Bill Wyman, *Rolling With The Stones*, 2002

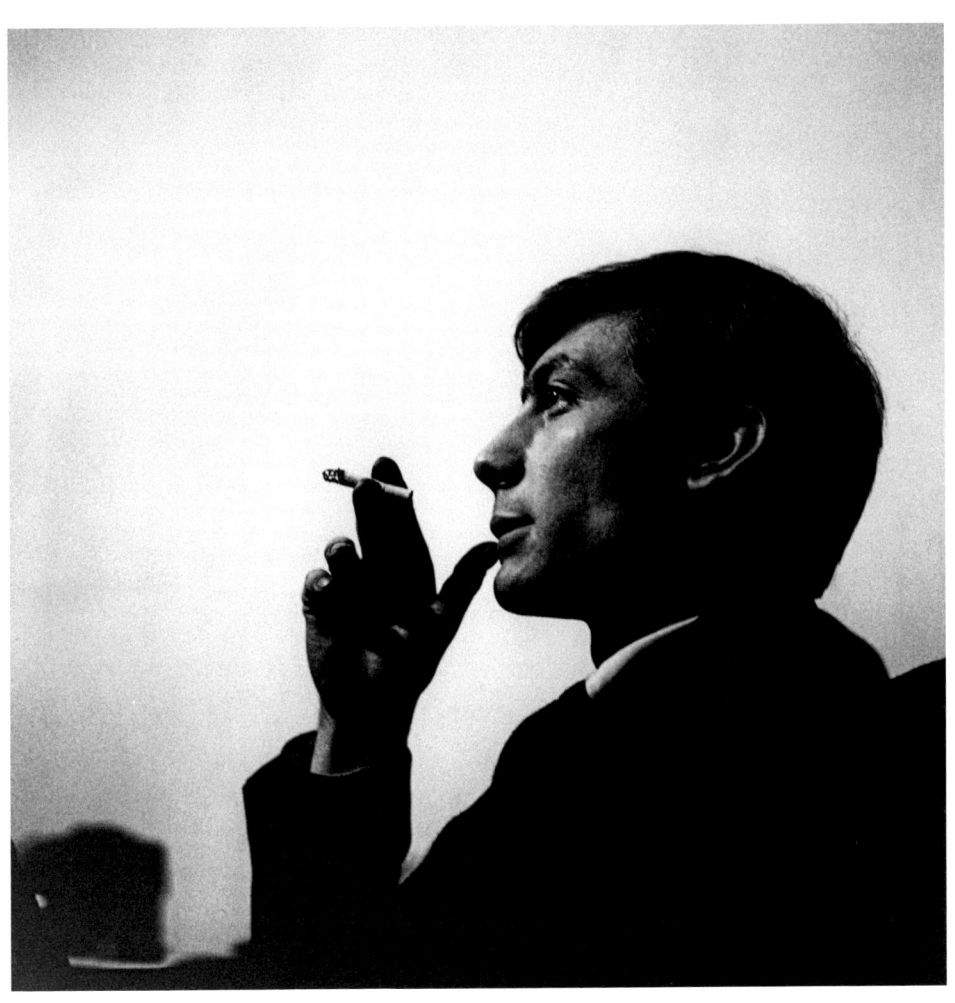

Jeremy Fletcher
A thoughtful Charlie pictured in 1963. Charlie's
prowess on the drums had marked him out
as one of the most skilled musicians in Britain.

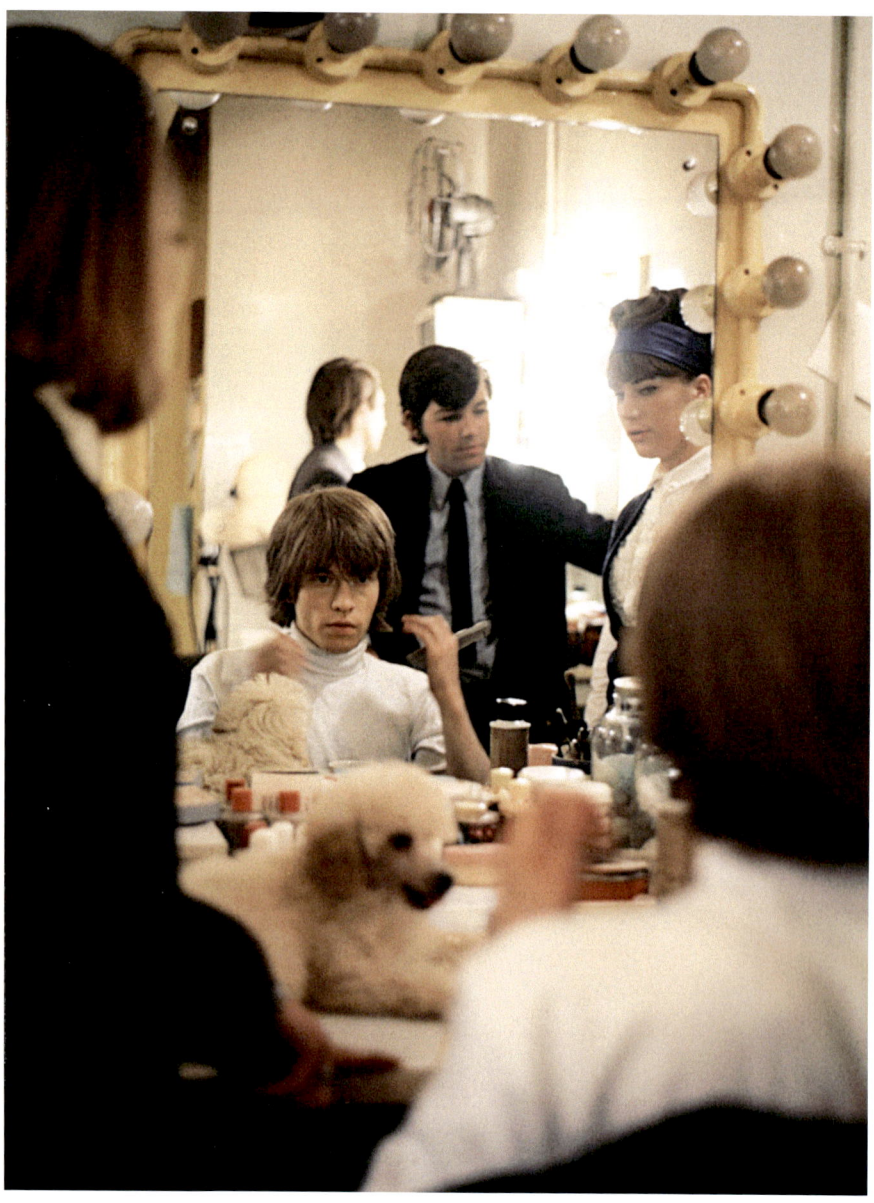

Michael Ward

His face in lights, Brian evidently enjoyed the company of a poodle in his dressing room, 1964. *"He was charming. He was articulate. He was – as he always was with me when I did interviews with him – urbane and intelligent. He was Prince Charming. He was also a complete bastard."* Keith Altham (former Rolling Stones press officer), quoted in *Who Killed The Rolling Stone – Brian Jones*, Channel 4, 2005

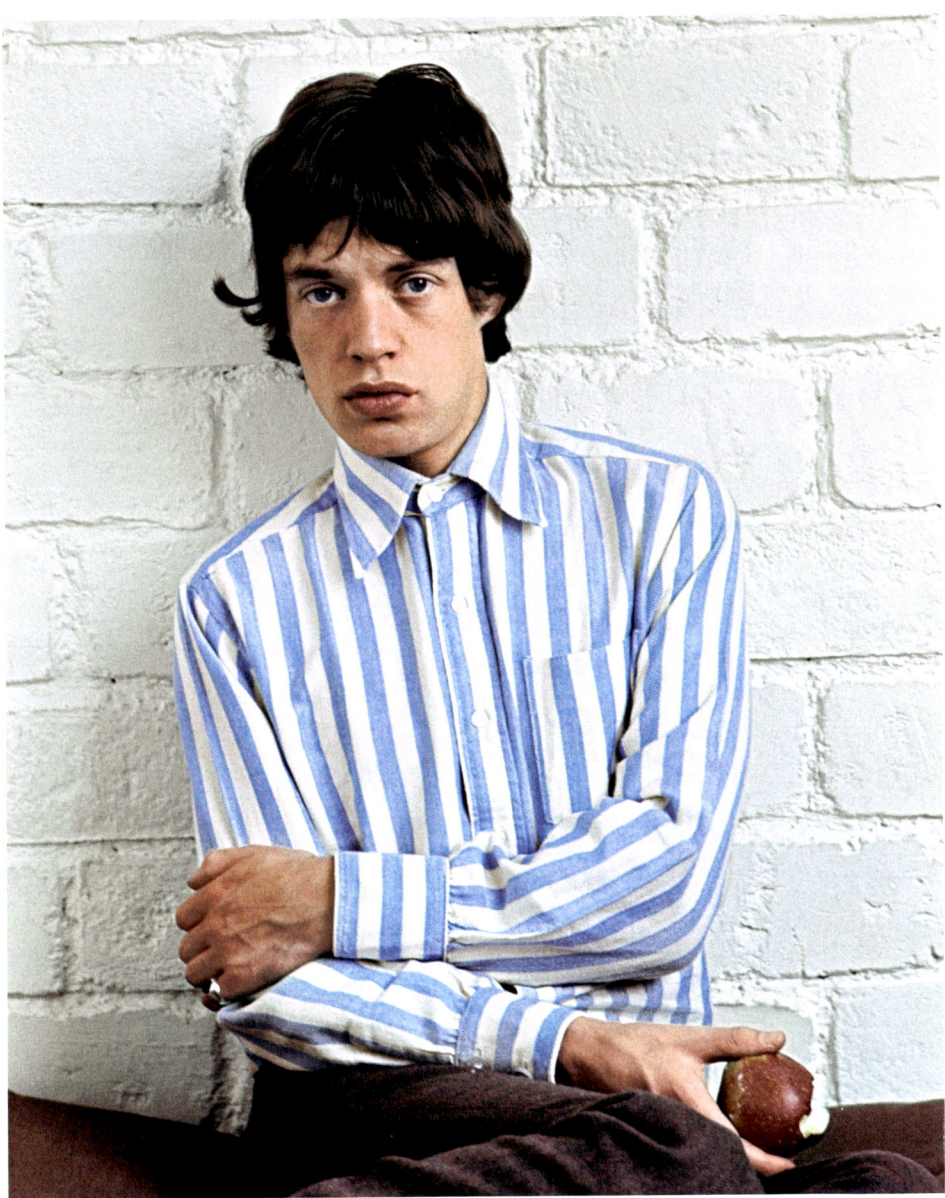

Jean-Marie Périer
Mick with an apple in a photographer's Paris studio during the Stones' French tour, March 1966. The somewhat weary look stems from an all-night drive from Marseilles to Paris in the photographer's car.

PP. 64–65
Jean-Marie Périer
By 1966, the Stones had upgraded from a basic tour bus to a private train carriage. France, March 1966.

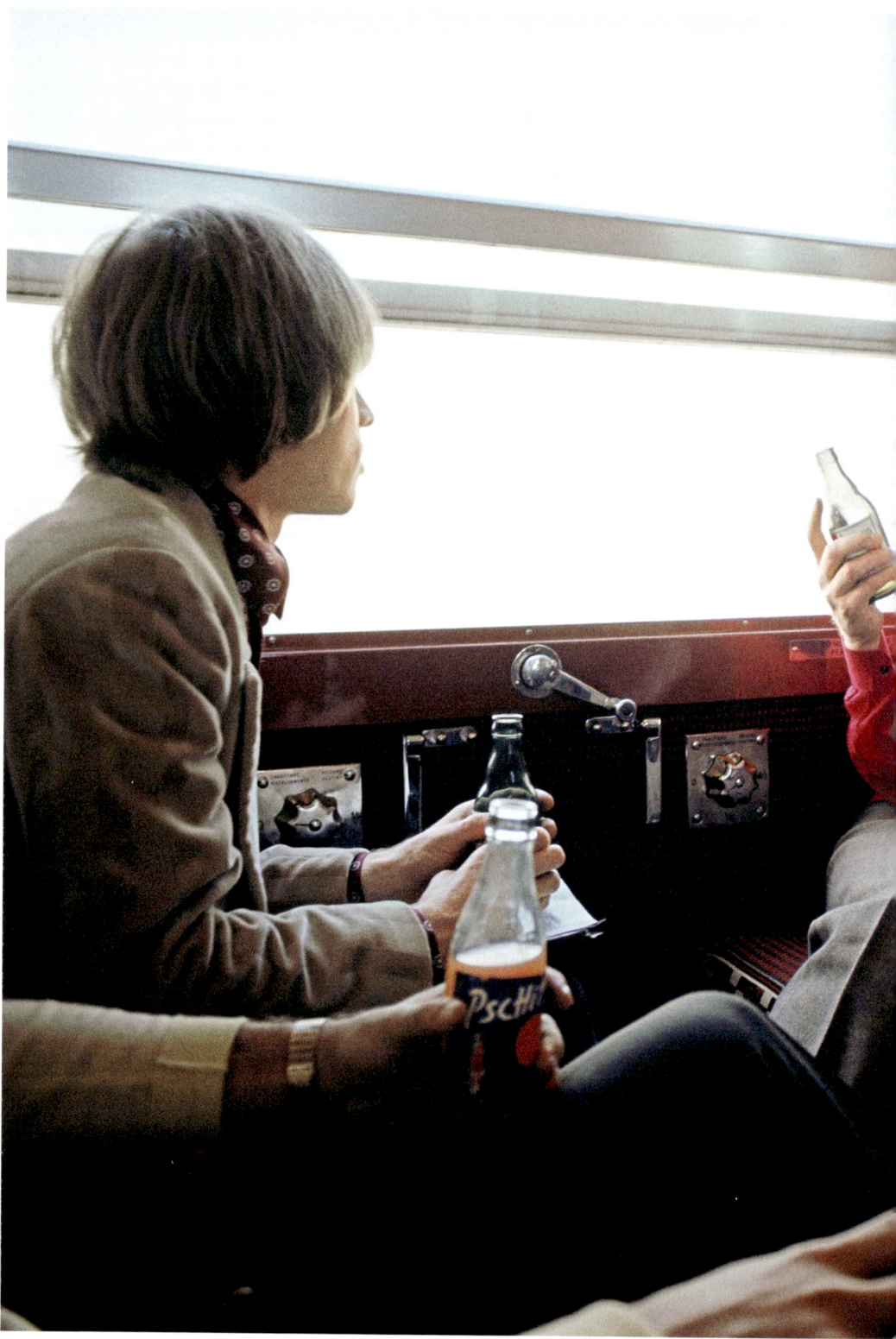

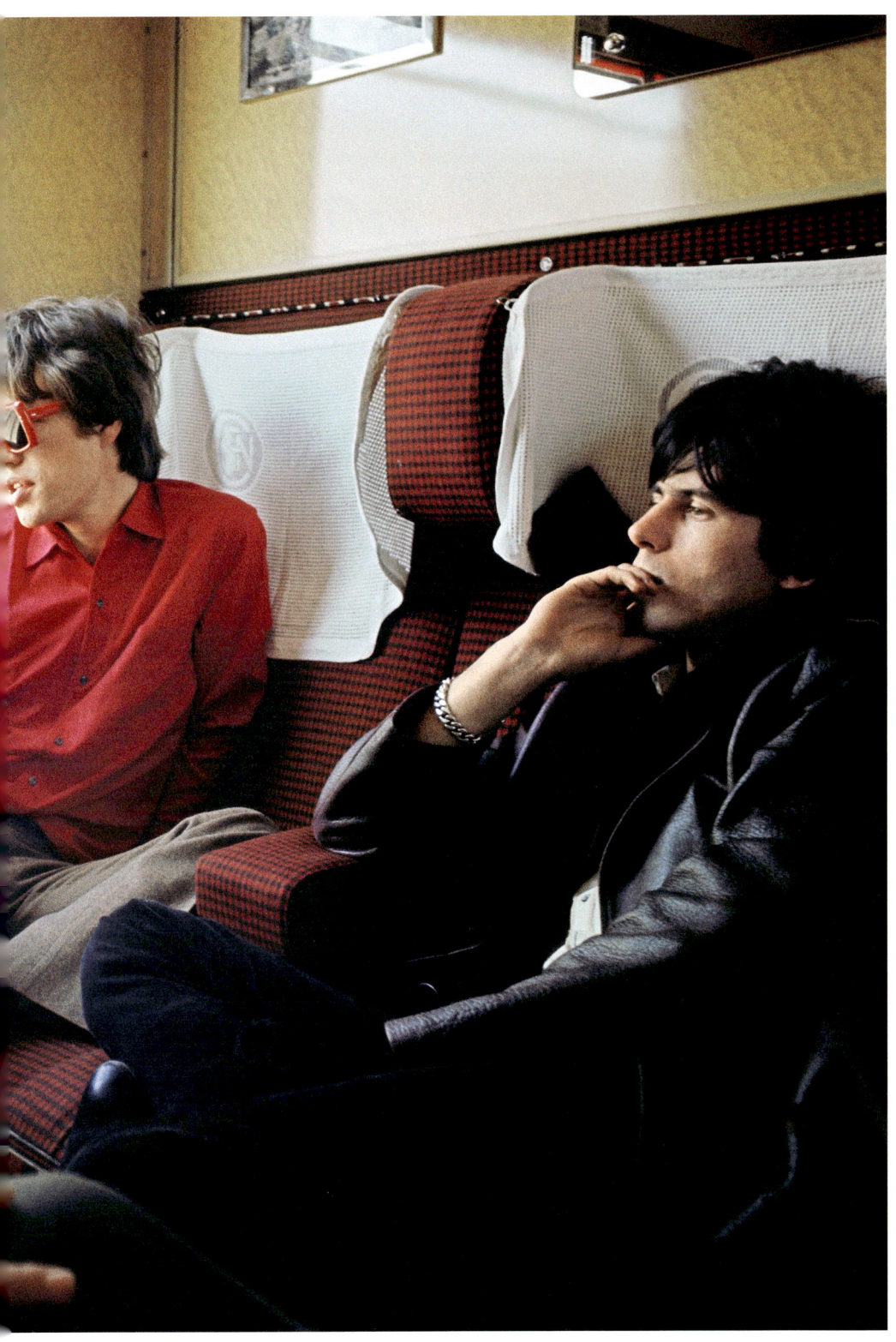

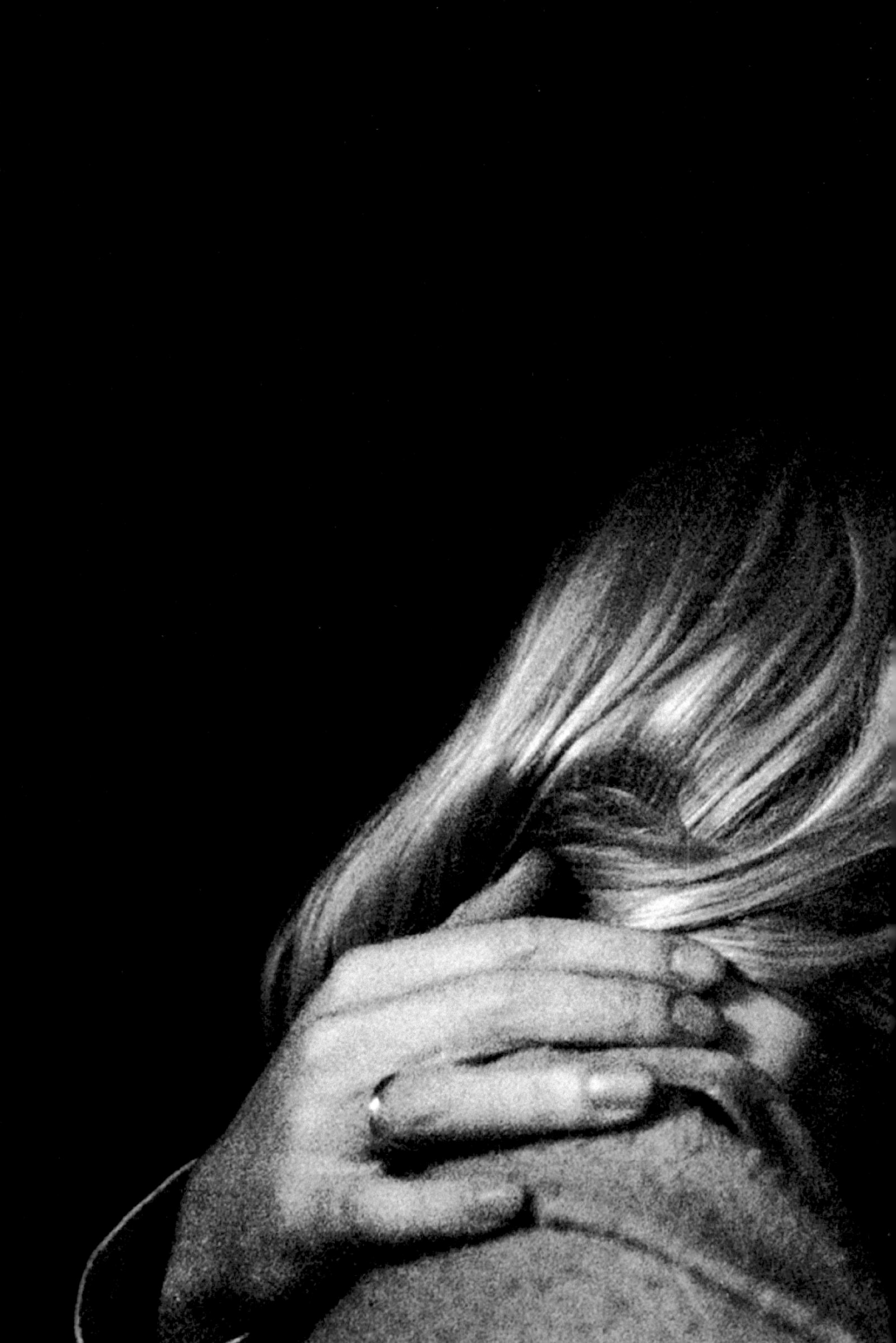

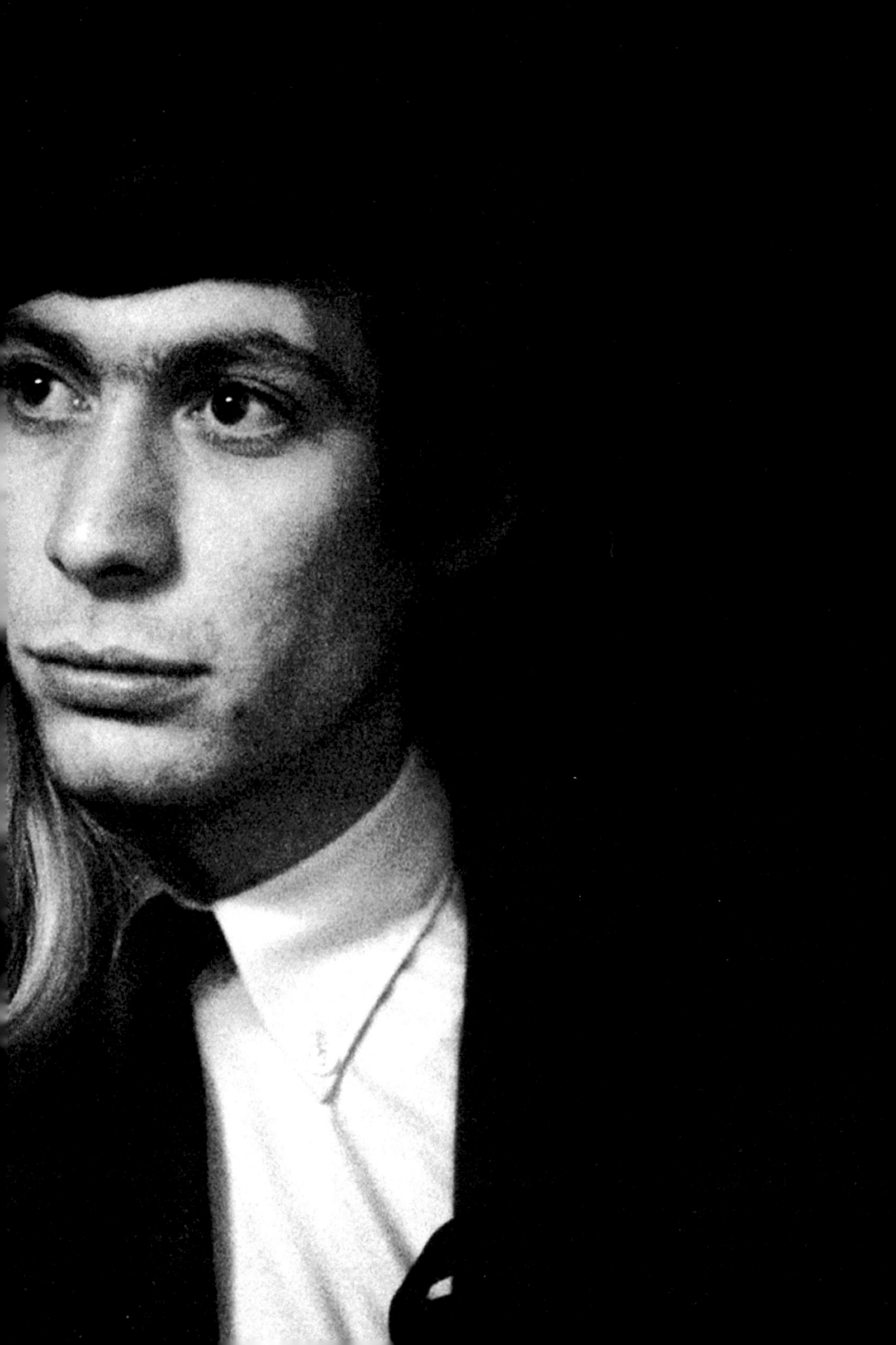

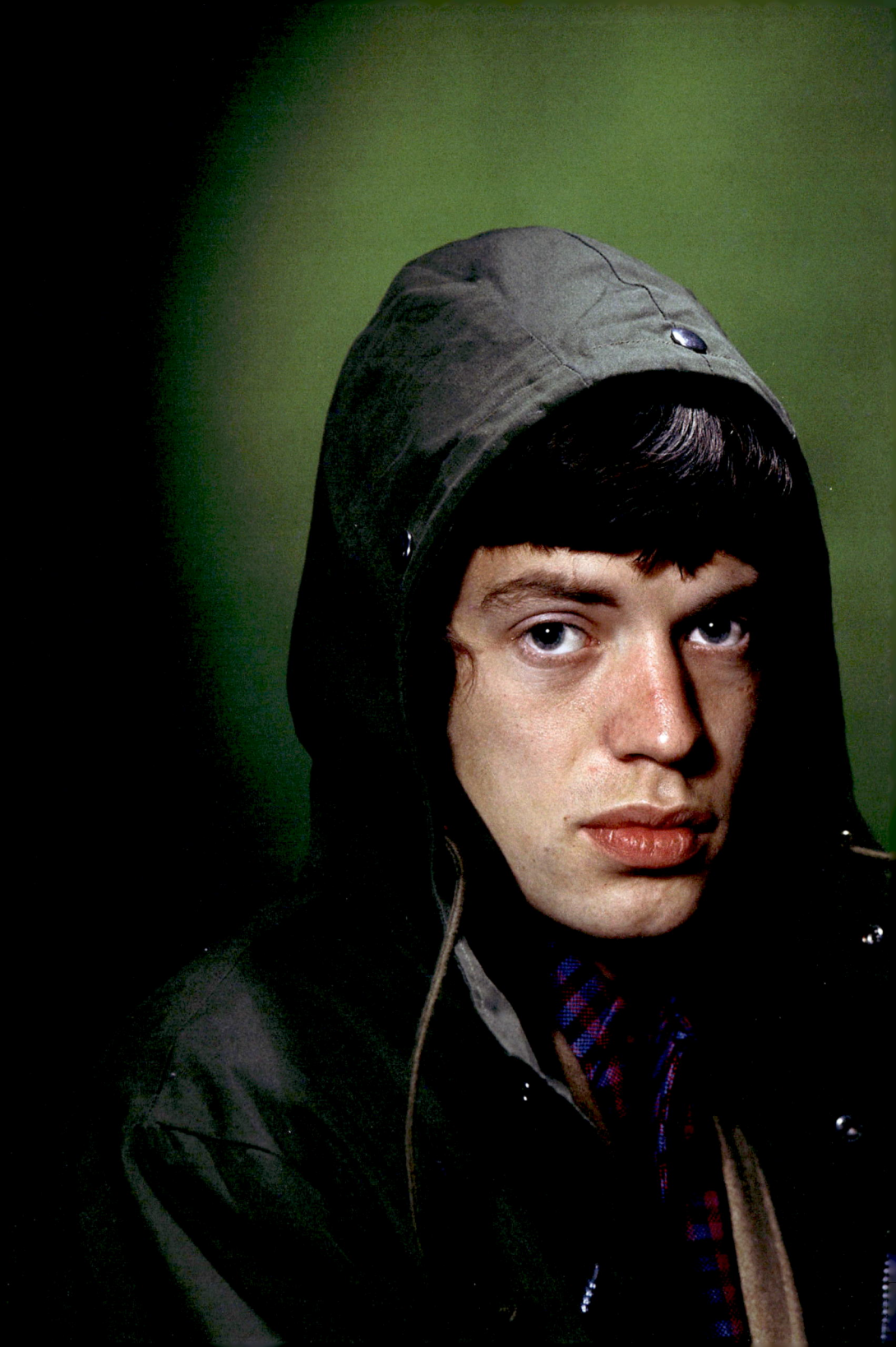

PP. 66–67

Eric Swayne

Charlie sheltering his partner Shirley Ann Shepherd from attention in late 1963. Shirley was on the scene before the Stones' tumultuous rise to fame, and she and Charlie stayed happily married for 57 years.

"I didn't meet my wife doing this. I was actually playing with Alexis Korner and she came to the very, very first rehearsal that I had with him and that's how I met her. So I don't know her from this world." Charlie Watts, *Daily Mirror*, 11 July 2012

Anonymous

Mick, mid 1960s.

"To the inner group in London, the new spectacular is a solemn young man, Mick Jagger, one of the five Rolling Stones, those singers who set out to cross America by bandwagon in June. For the British, the Stones have a perverse, unsettling sex appeal with Jagger out in front of his teammates … To women, Jagger looks fascinating, to men, a scare … They are quite different from The Beatles, and more terrifying." *Vogue*, May 1964

Bill Wyman

In addition to keeping a fastidiously detailed diary, Bill would not be averse to taking shots of his time on the road with the Stones. This candid portrait of Keith was taken backstage at San Francisco's Cow Palace on 26 July 1966. The 20,000-capacity arena doubled – as its name suggested – as a livestock exhibition hall, and by all accounts maintained a distinctly aromatic ambience. Of greater significance that night was the support roster for the Stones; many of the bands were drawn from the burgeoning San Francisco psychedelic scene, including one Jefferson Airplane.

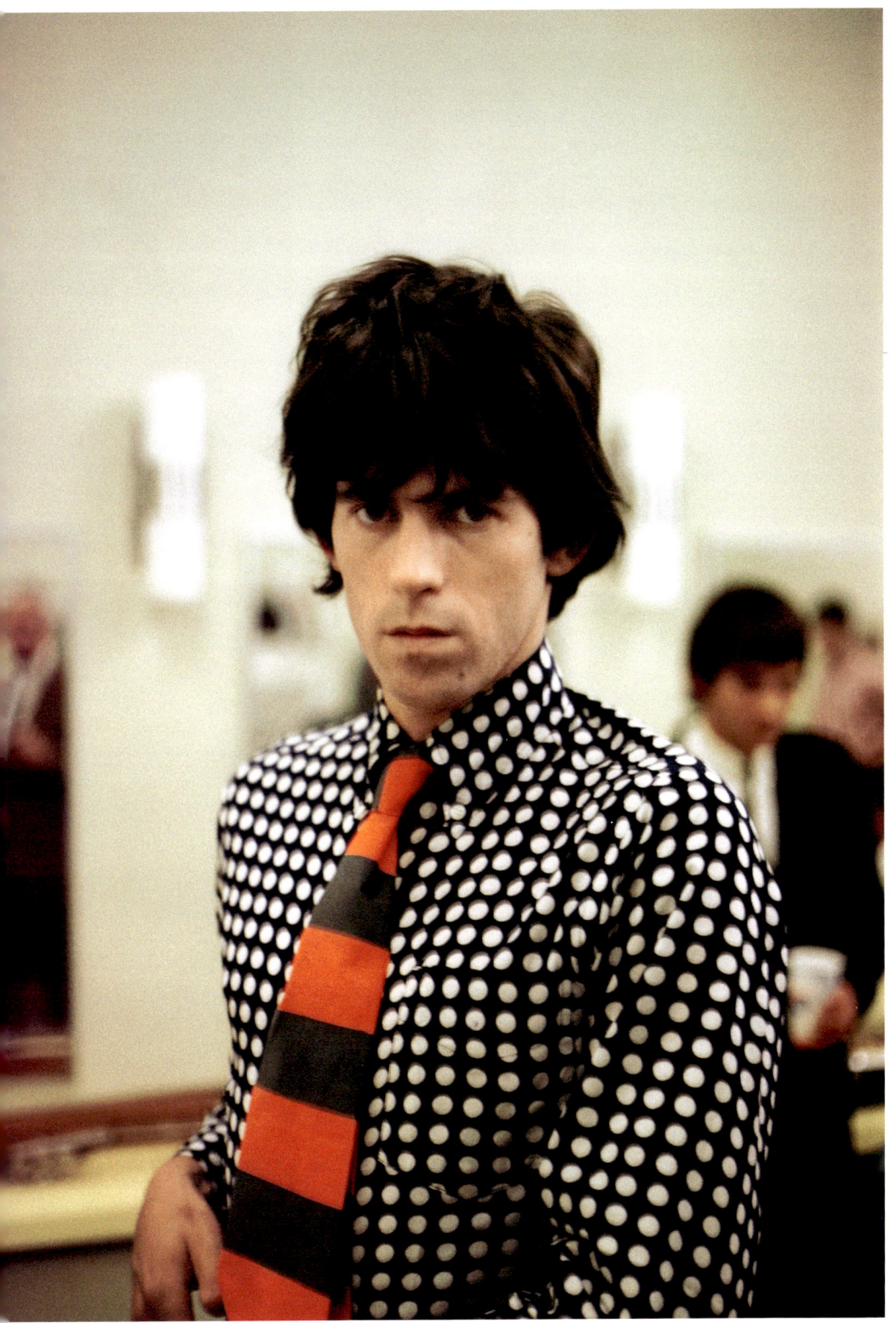

Michael Ward
East Sussex, spring 1964.

PP. 74–75
Anonymous
With his suit, sunglasses and cigarette, Keith
was evolving into a photogenic and charismatic
star. This was taken in Paris down by the Seine,
during the Stones' first visit to the City of Light
in October 1964.

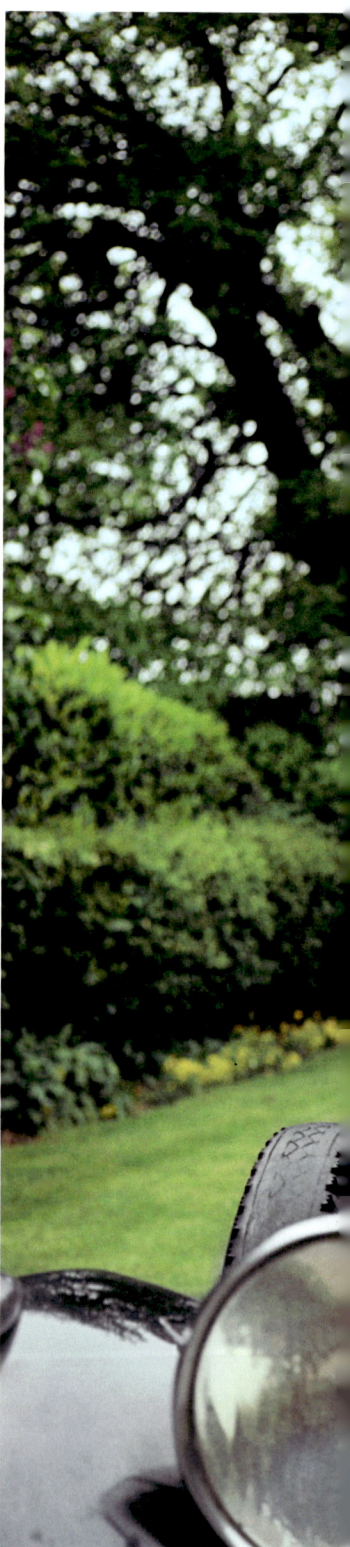

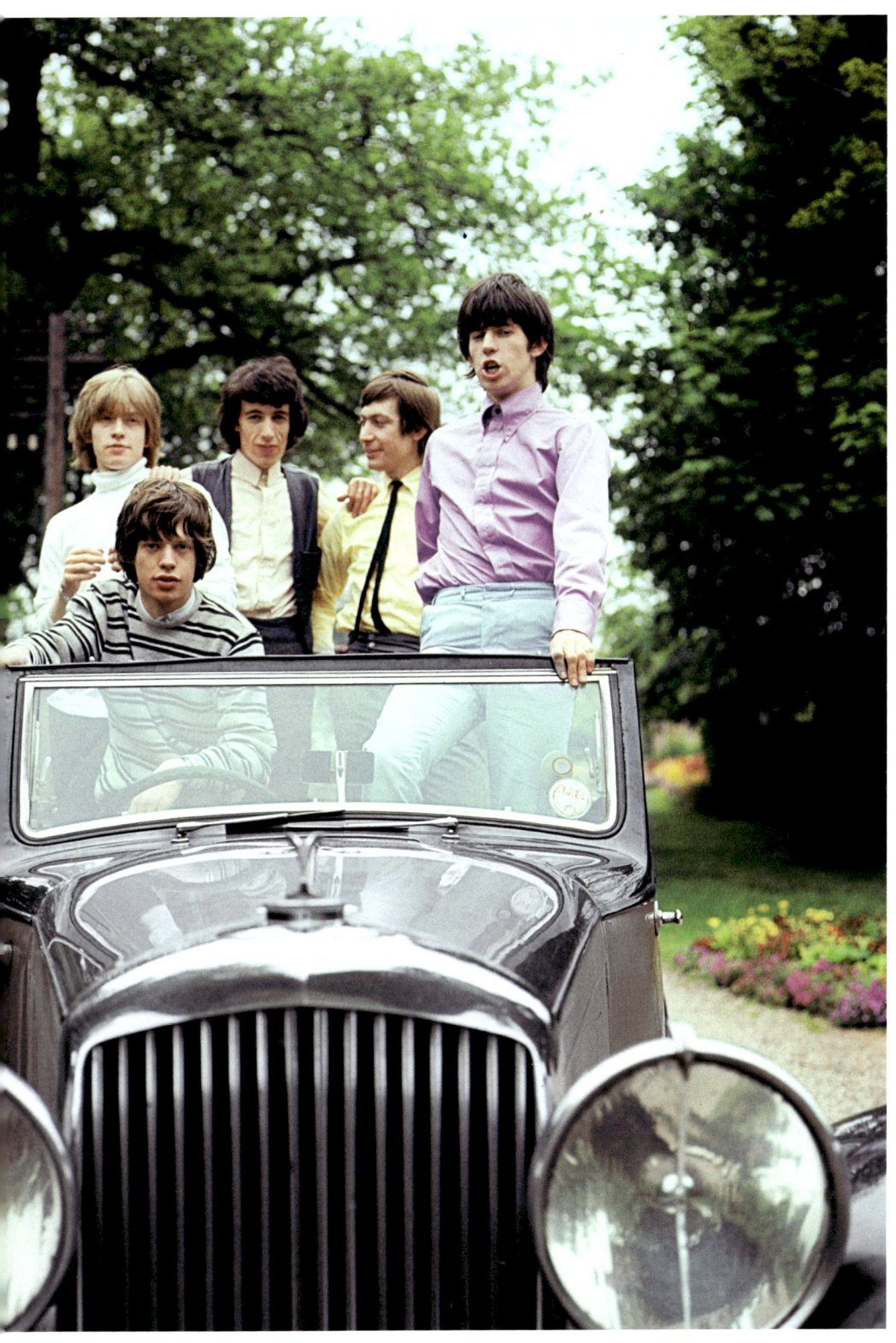

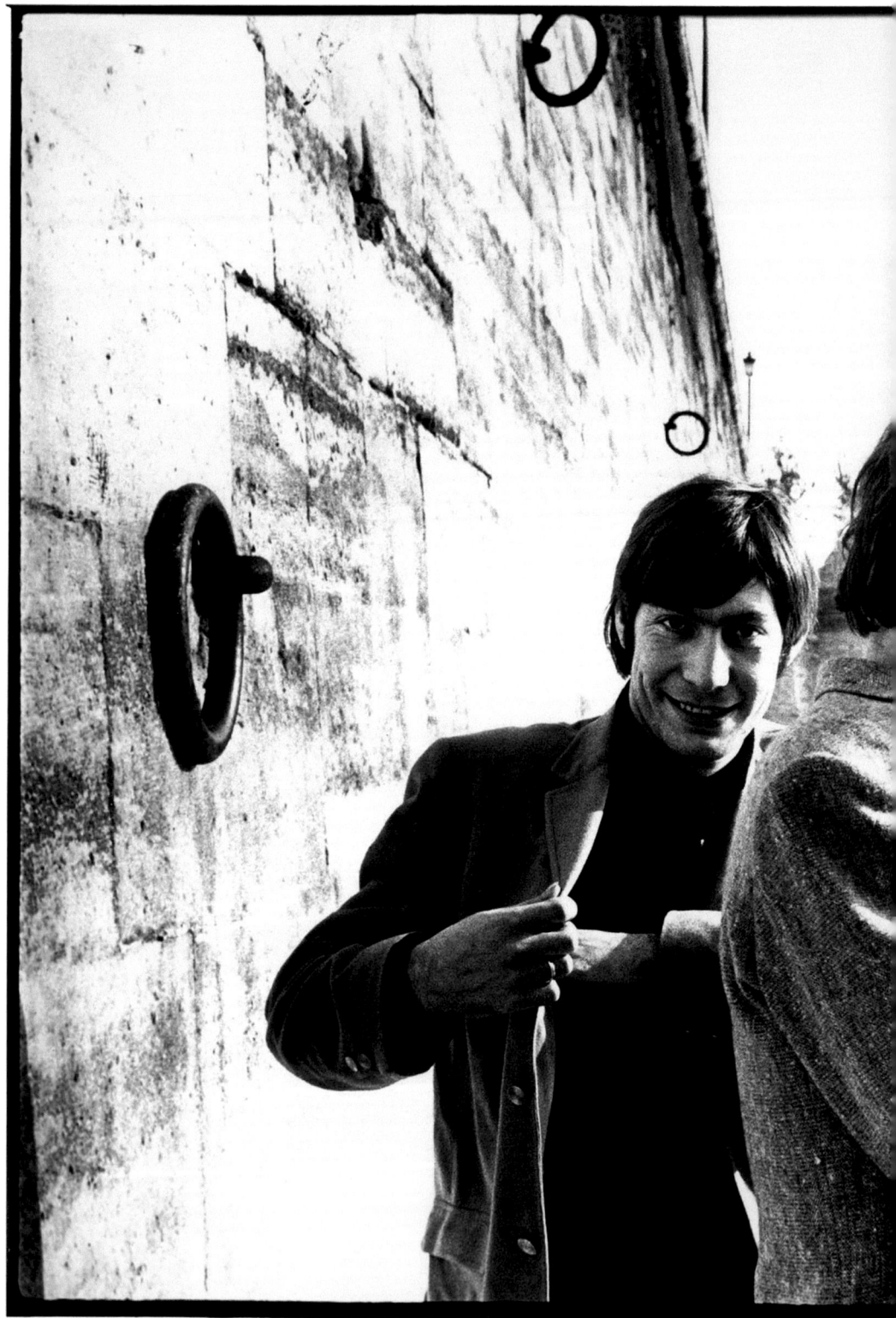

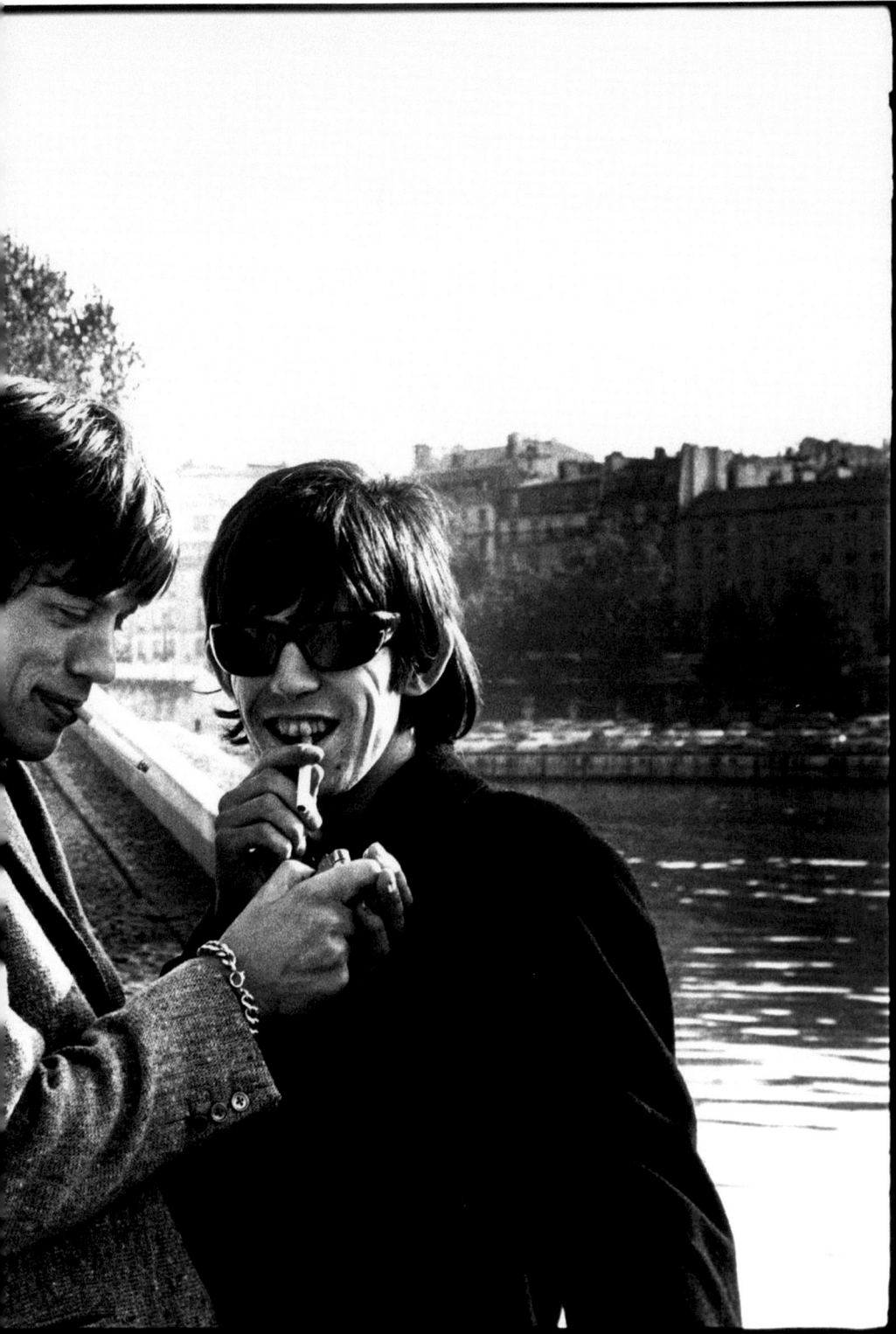

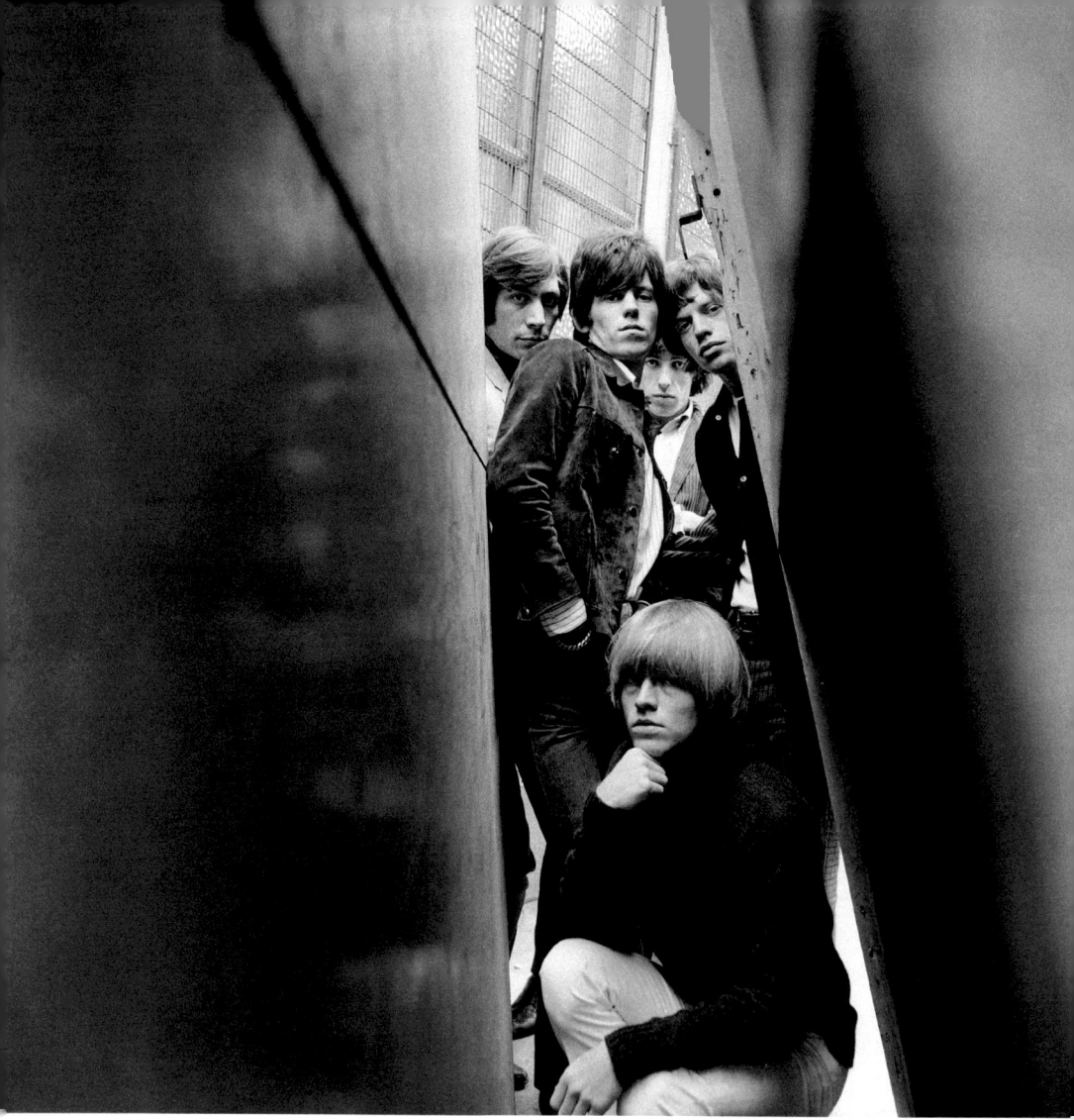

Gered Mankowitz

The photographer hosted this key session at his studio at 9, Mason's Yard, Westminster, London. He found plenty of props to augment his shoots when the action ventured outside – as seen here in September 1965. The use of sheets of hardboard made for an excellent shot that really captured the Stones' aura. This would become the cover for their third UK album, *Out Of Our Heads*.

"It was wonderful for me to have a photo like this used for a cover. It broke a lot of rules by not giving equal space to [each of] the band members. It was very unusual for the time. The people loved it." Gered Mankowitz, *Satisfaction: The Rolling Stones Photographs Of Gered Mankowitz*, 1984

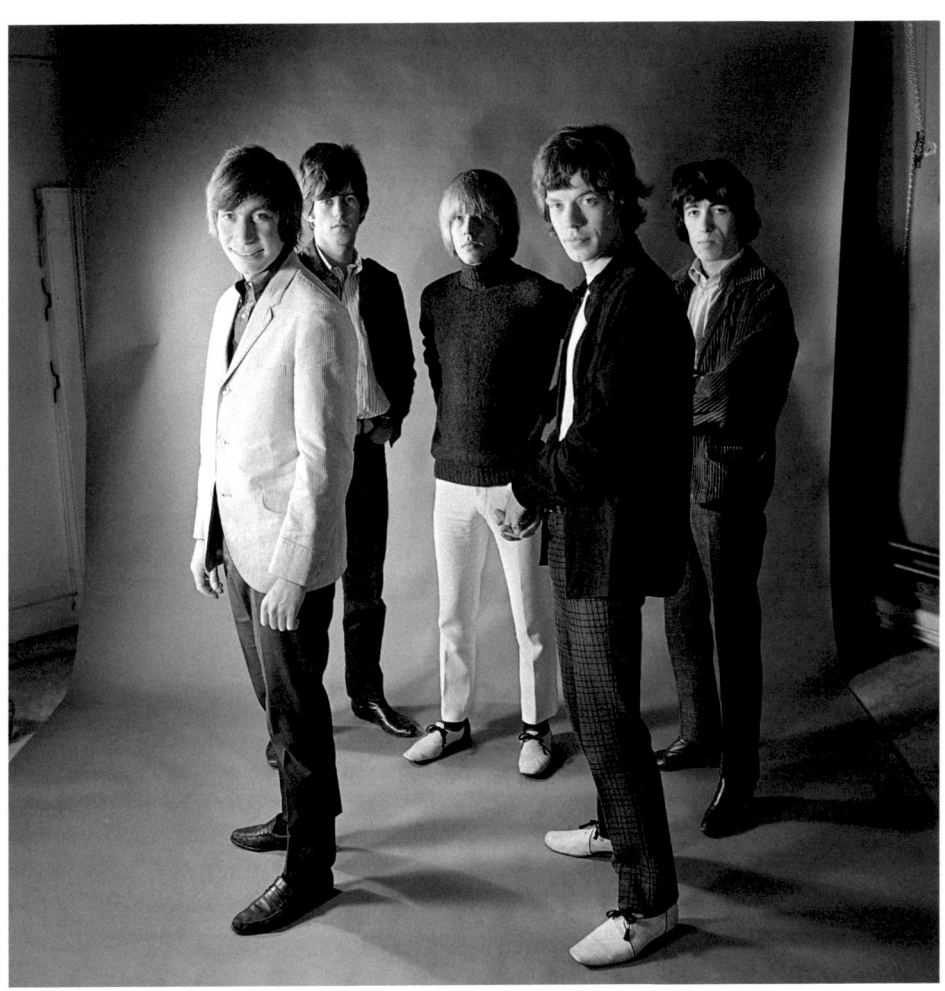

Gered Mankowitz
The area around Mankowitz's London studio was
popular in mid-1960s London, with the left-field
Indica Gallery and fashionable nightclub Scotch
Of St James both situated in Mason's Yard in 1965.

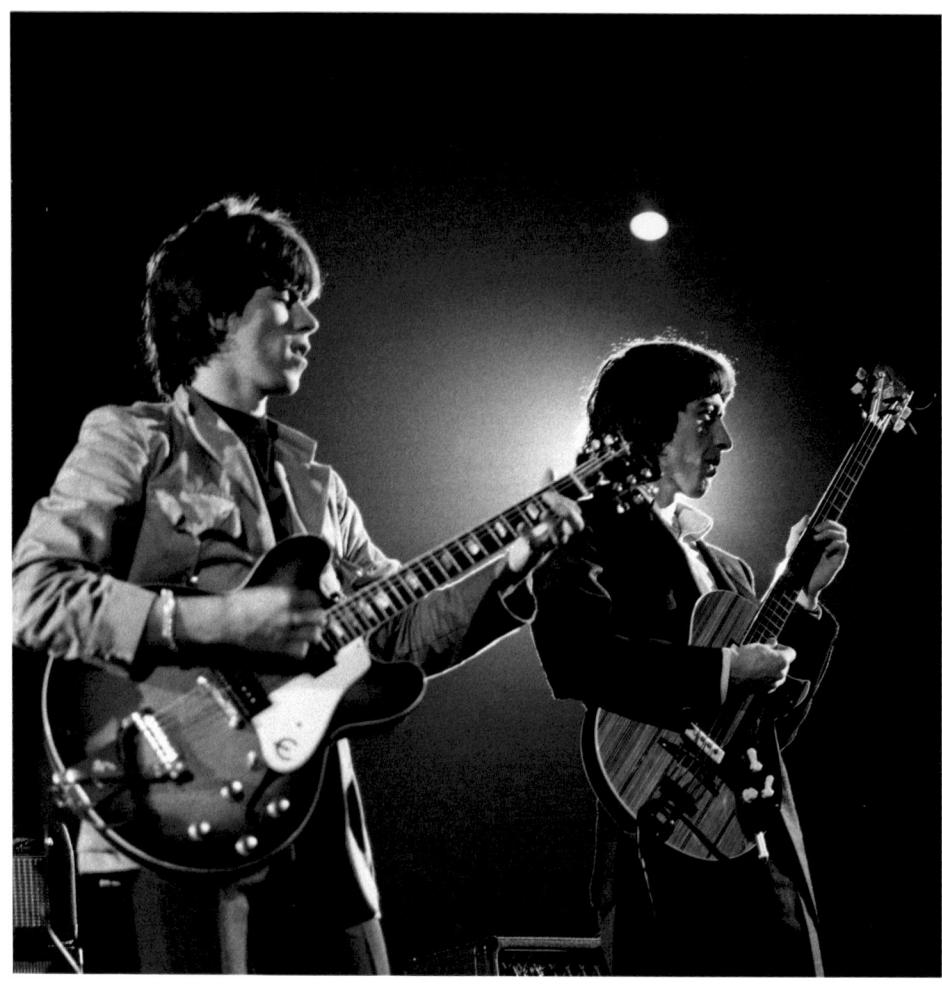

Gered Mankowitz
On tour in the States during late 1965.
"The British quintet knows what it is doing.
But so does Father Time. One fine day they'll
all be sitting around their solar-heated pad,
telling their grandchildren about those
'It's what's happening, baby' days." San Diego
Evening Tribune, 6 December 1965

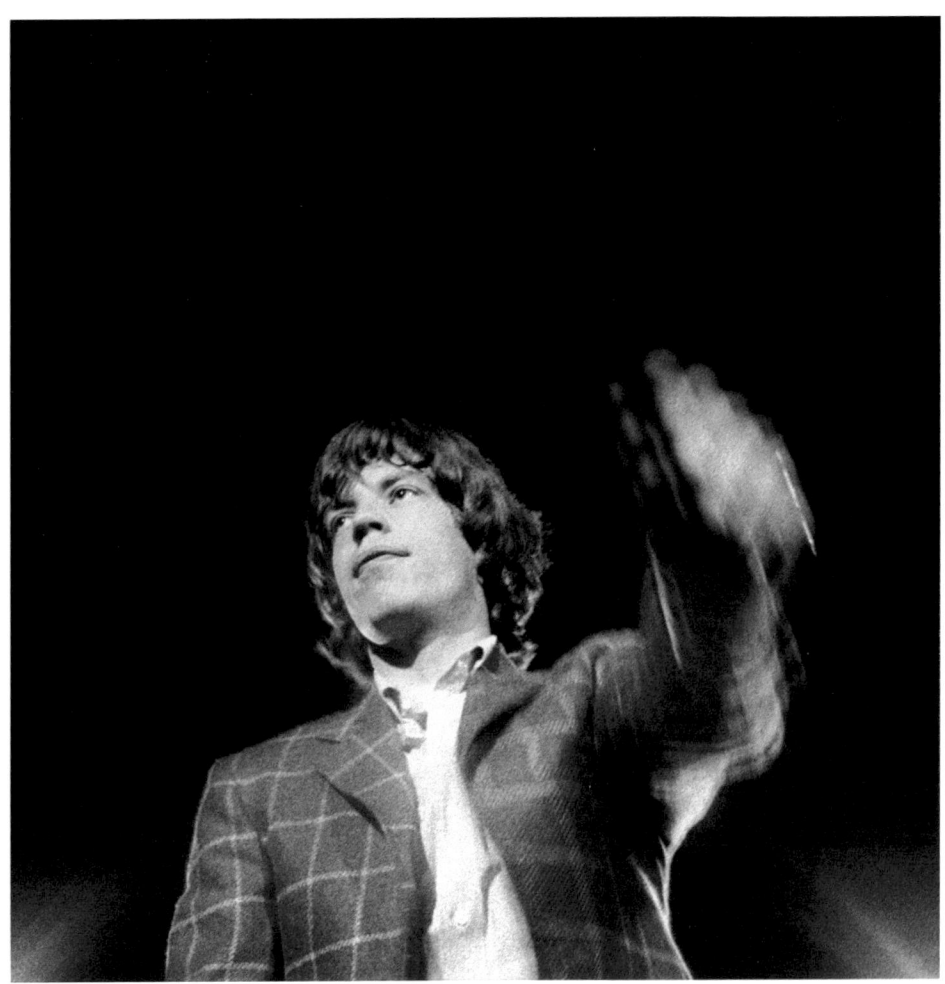

Gered Mankowitz
On stage during the US tour, late 1965.
*"I feel all this energy coming from an audience.
I often want to smash the microphone up or
something because I don't feel the same person
on stage as I am normally ... I entice the audience,
of course I do. I do it every way I can think."*
Mick Jagger, *Sunday People*, 9 October 1966

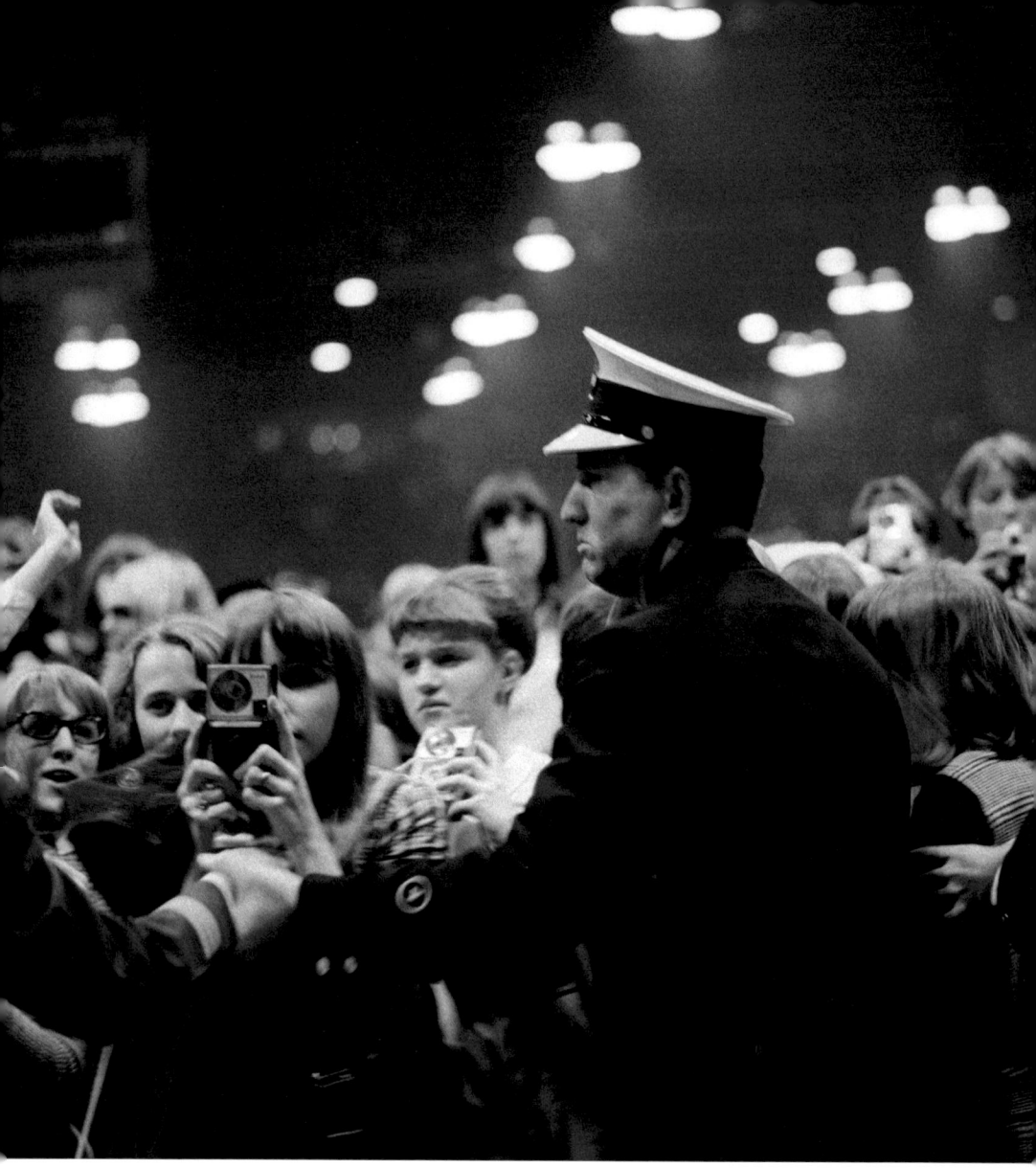

Gered Mankowitz
Pre-iPhones, an American fan photographs
a live performance, US tour, late 1965.
*"They relished the crowd reaction, although
on the occasions when the girls were able to
get close they were quite vicious, probably*
*without meaning to be, in their desperation to
touch the band, or to grab a tie or a shirt sleeve
or something."* Gered Mankowitz, interview
with the author, 18 February 2011

PP. 82–83
Jean-Marie Périer
Keith in the stalls, prior to an appearance on
ABC TV's *Shindig!*, Los Angeles, May 1965.
"Some of my friends have said I am in love with
guitars and they could well be right. I think it
is a wonderful instrument and it's especially

wonderful because you can never ever learn
all there is to know about it." Keith Richards,
The Rolling Stones Book, June 1964

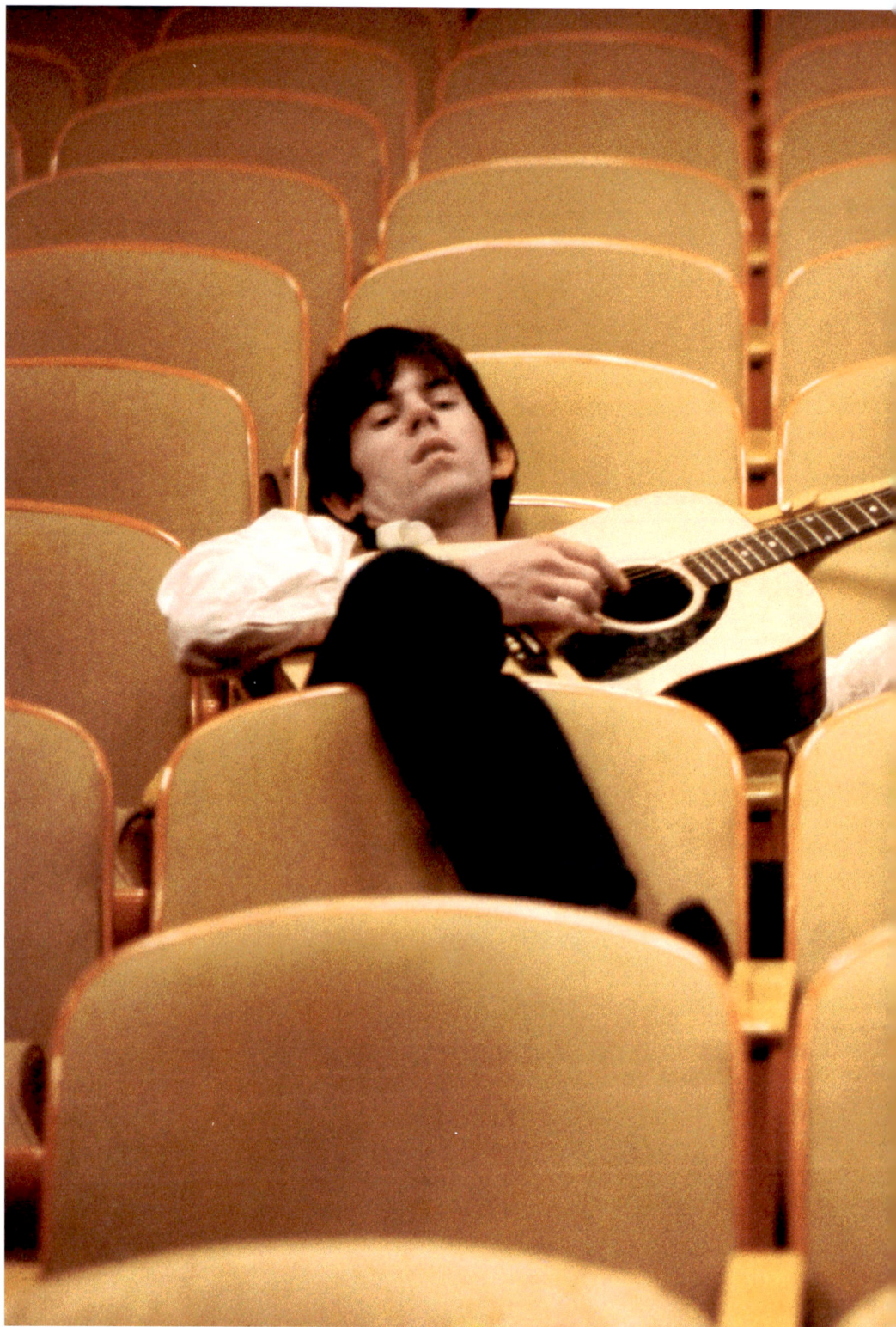

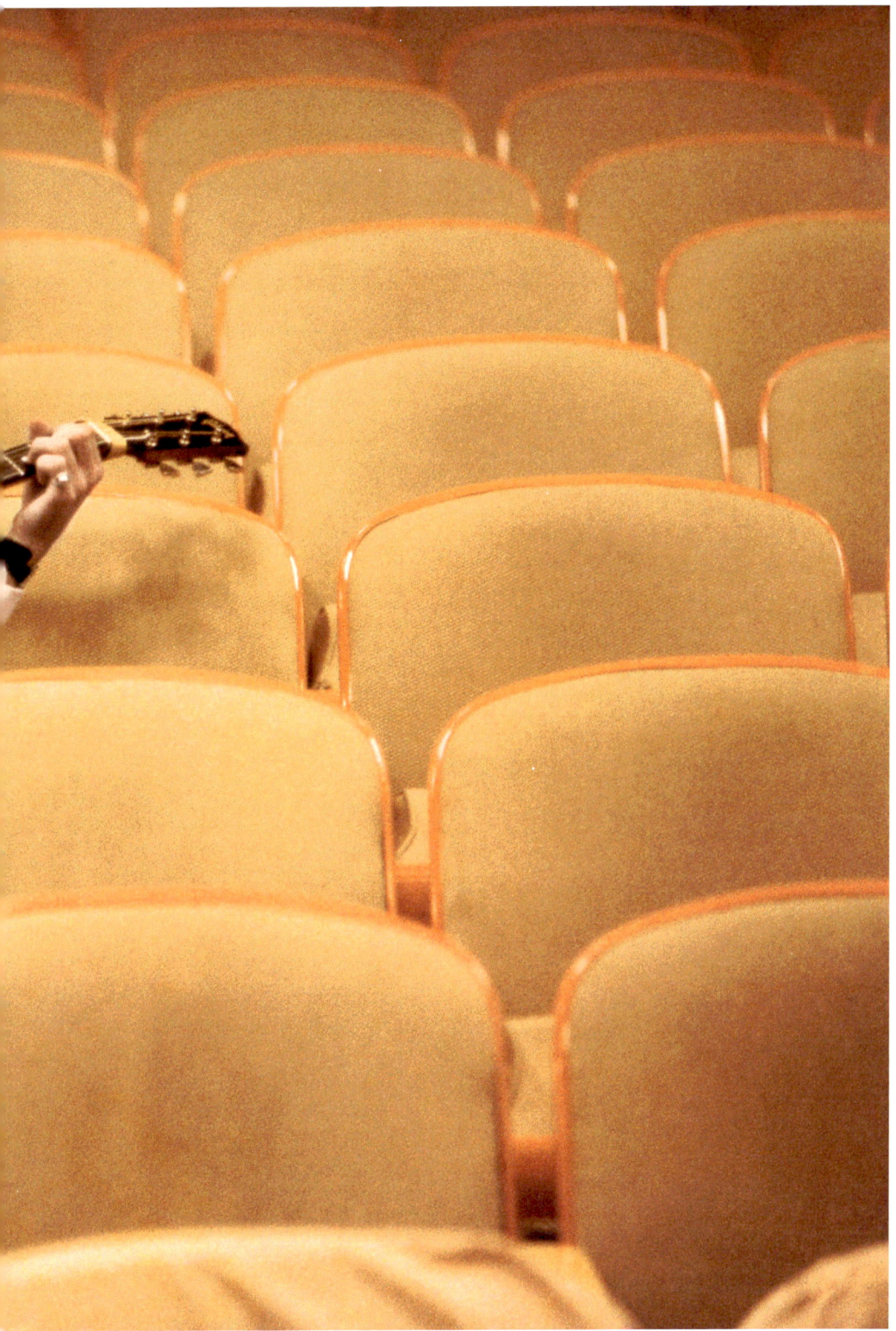

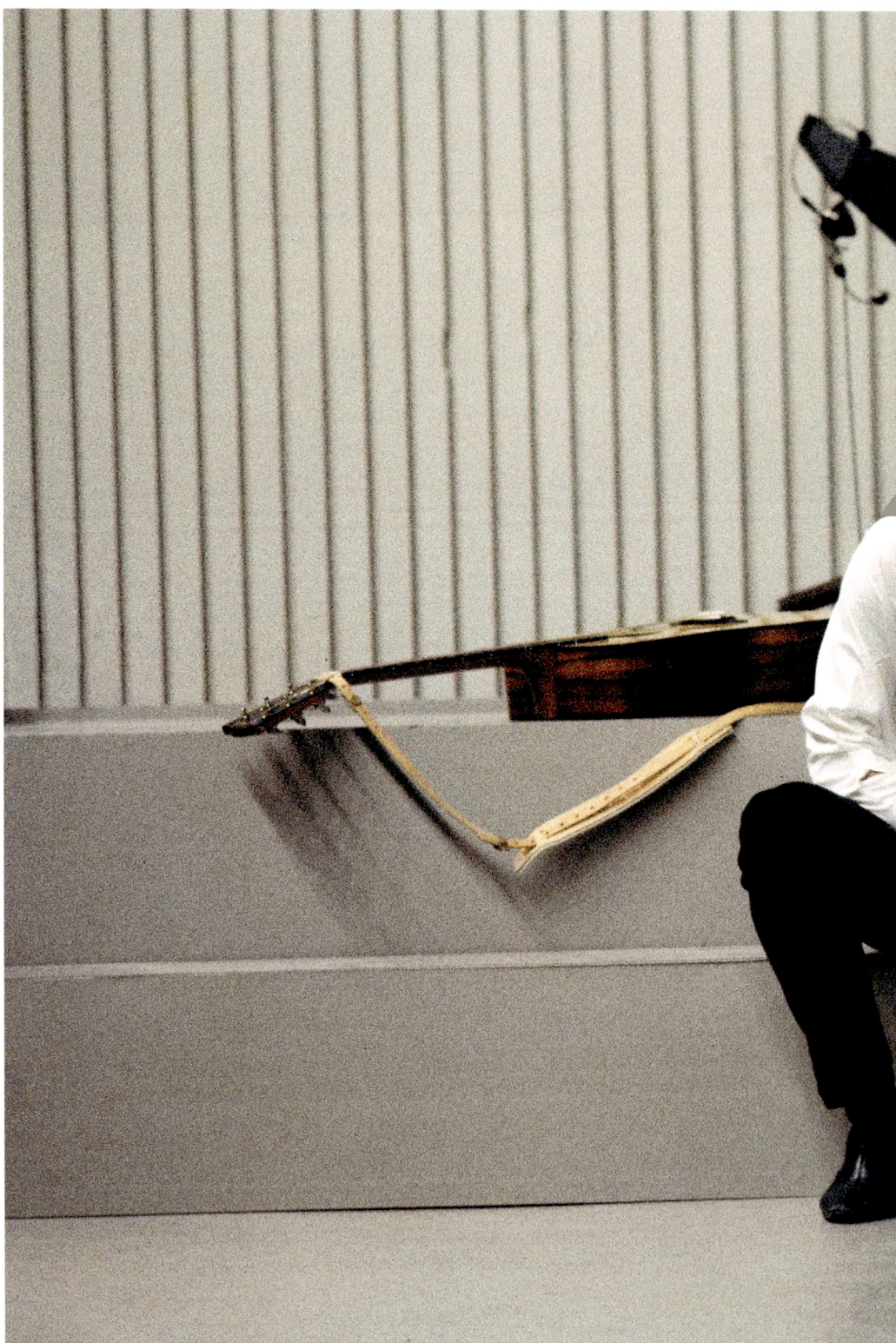

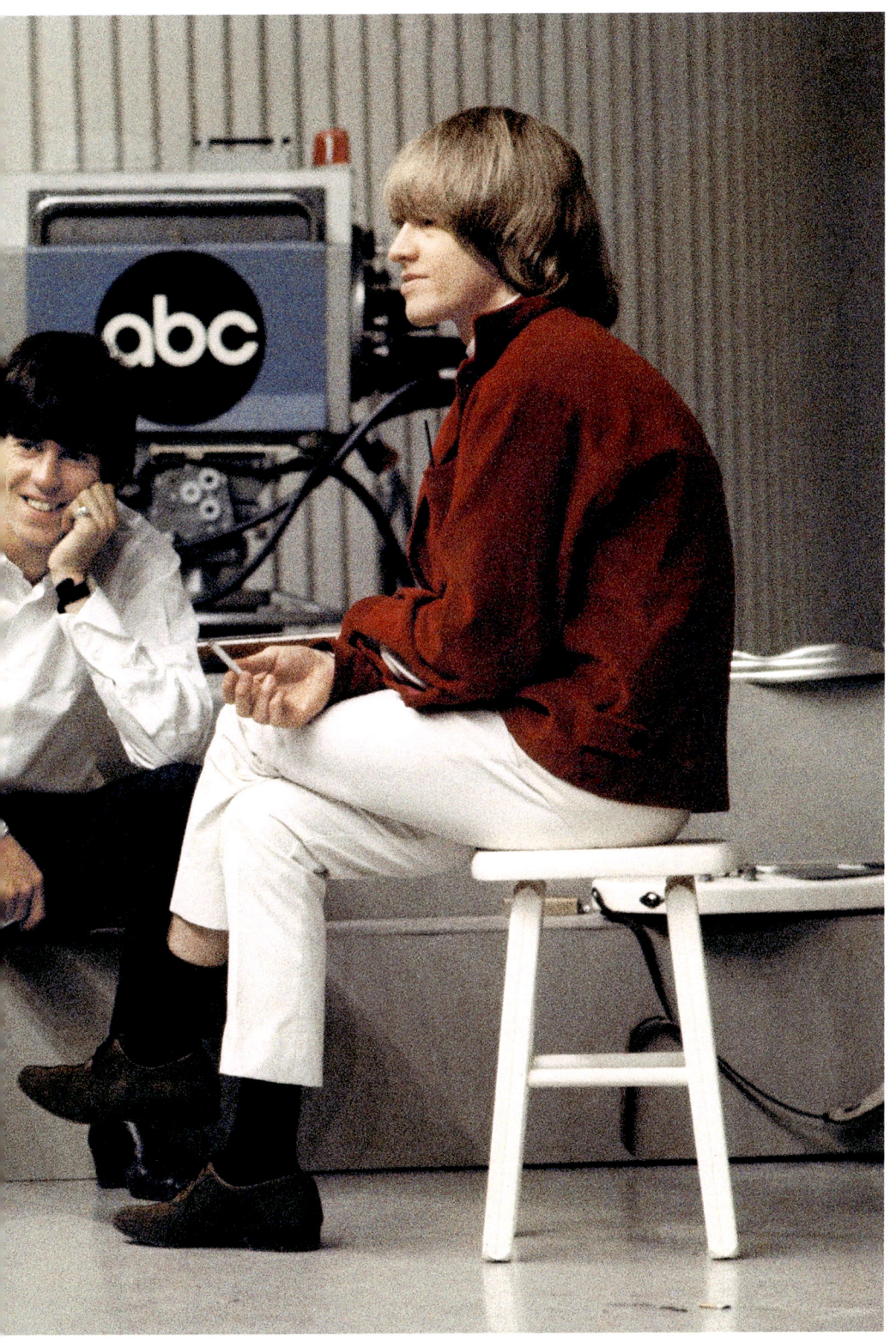

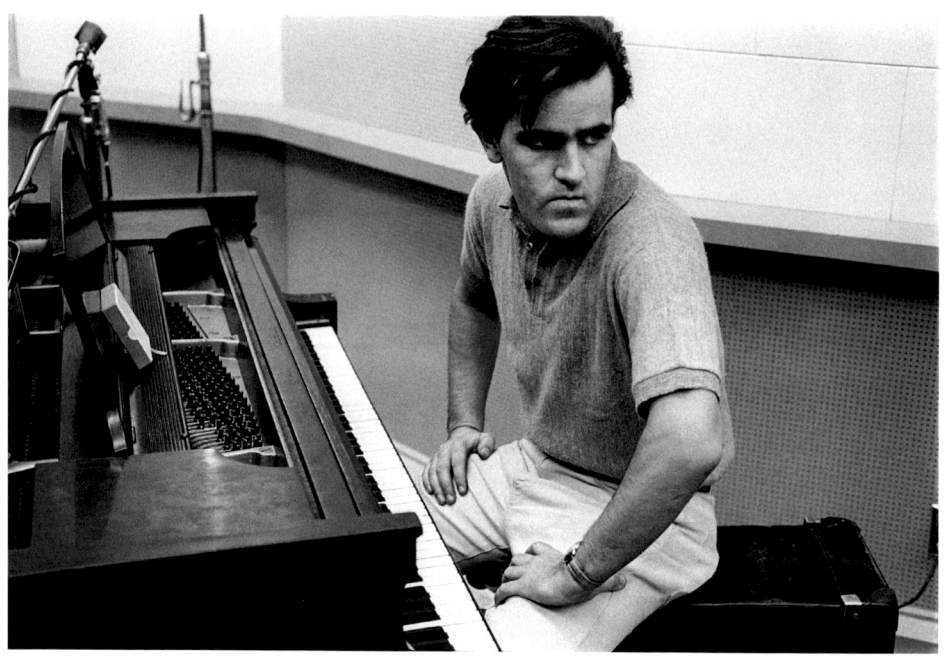

PP. 84–85
Jean-Marie Périer
Keith and Brian share a relaxed moment in
Los Angeles prior to a US television appearance
for ABC TV's *Shindig!*, May 1965.

Bob Bonis
In addition to tour manager duties, Ian Stewart
provided keyboard accompaniments throughout
his tenure with the group – both on stage and
in the studio. With his legendary unflappability
and prowess, Stewart garnered massive respect
from those around him, 1965.
*"I don't think the Stones would have coagulated
without Ian Stewart pulling it together. He was
the one that rented the first rehearsal room, told
people to get there at a certain time. Otherwise
it was so nebulous ... Without Stu we would have
been lost."* Keith Richards, *Life*, 2011

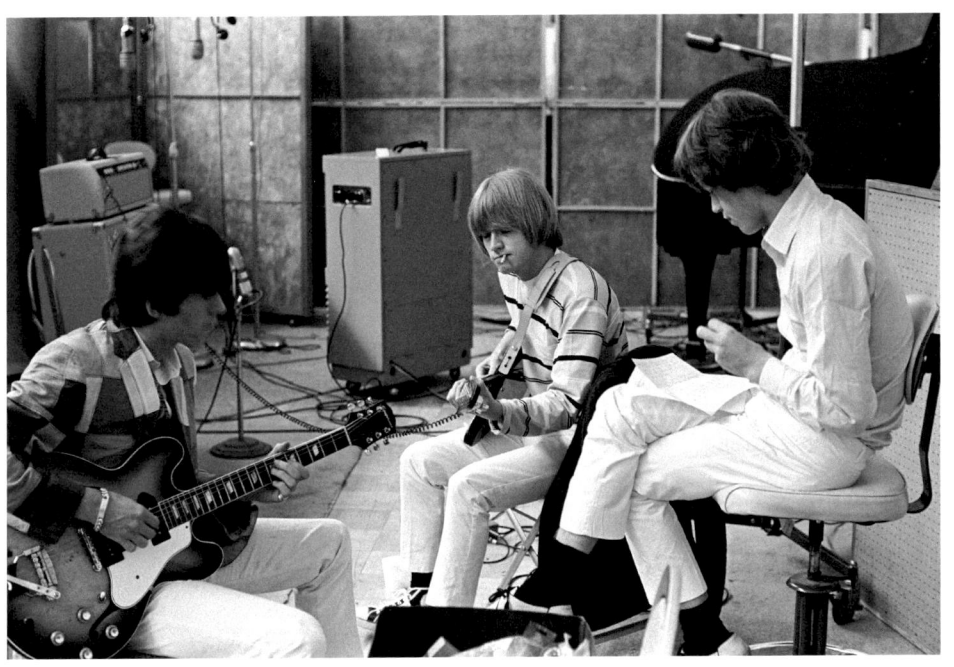

Bob Bonis

Sessions at RCA studios would provide material
for the group's up-and-coming album, *Out Of
Our Heads* (*December's Children* in the States).
*"Recording in England – it's just one slow painful
drag … For a start the whole attitude of record
engineers is slapdash. They just want to get the
record knocked out as quickly as possible so they
can all go home. They don't care about what they
are recording; they are not interested. In America,
the engineers are just as excited over new songs
as we are."* Mick Jagger, *KRLA – The Beat* (magazine), 11 September 1965

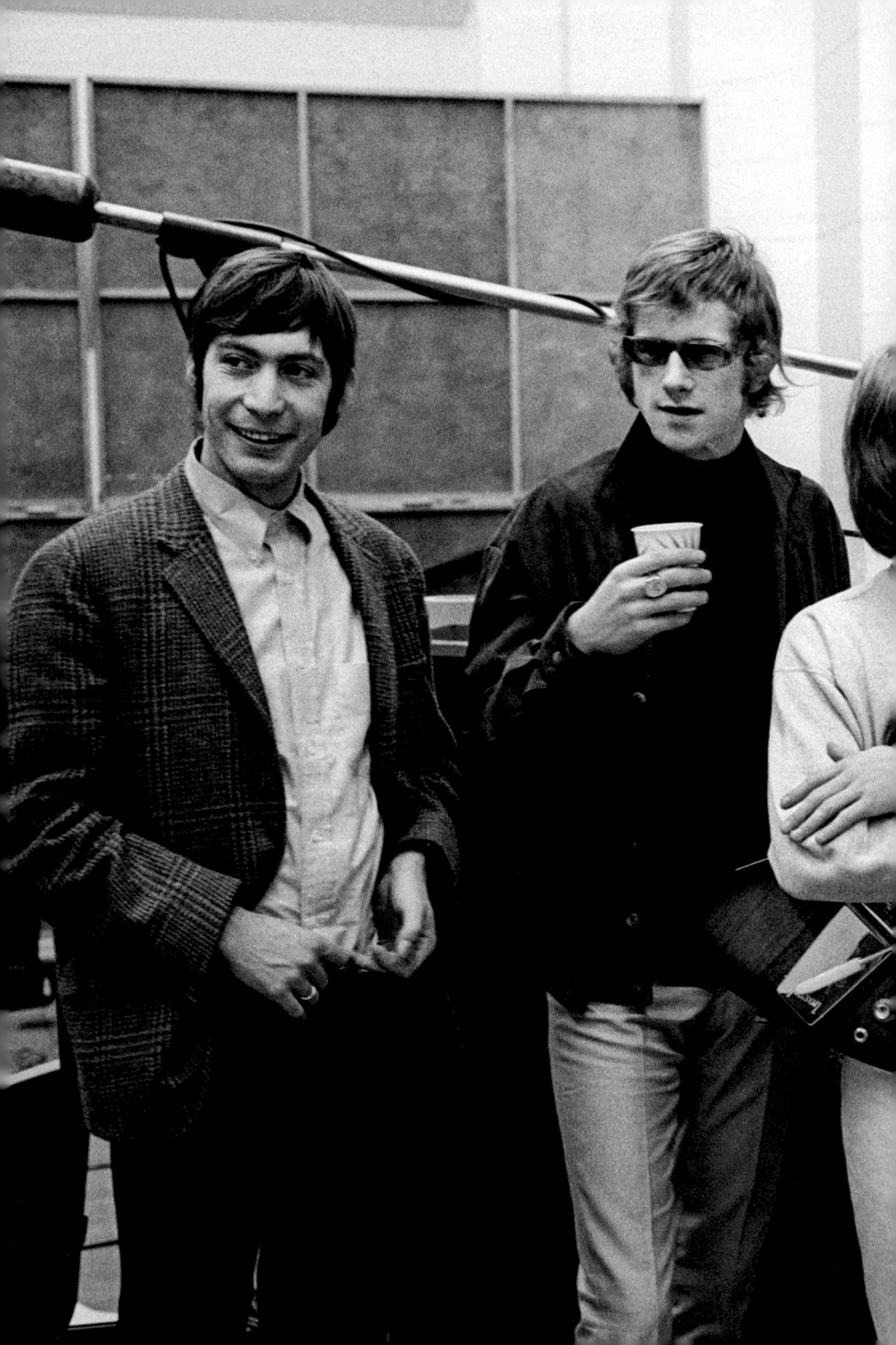

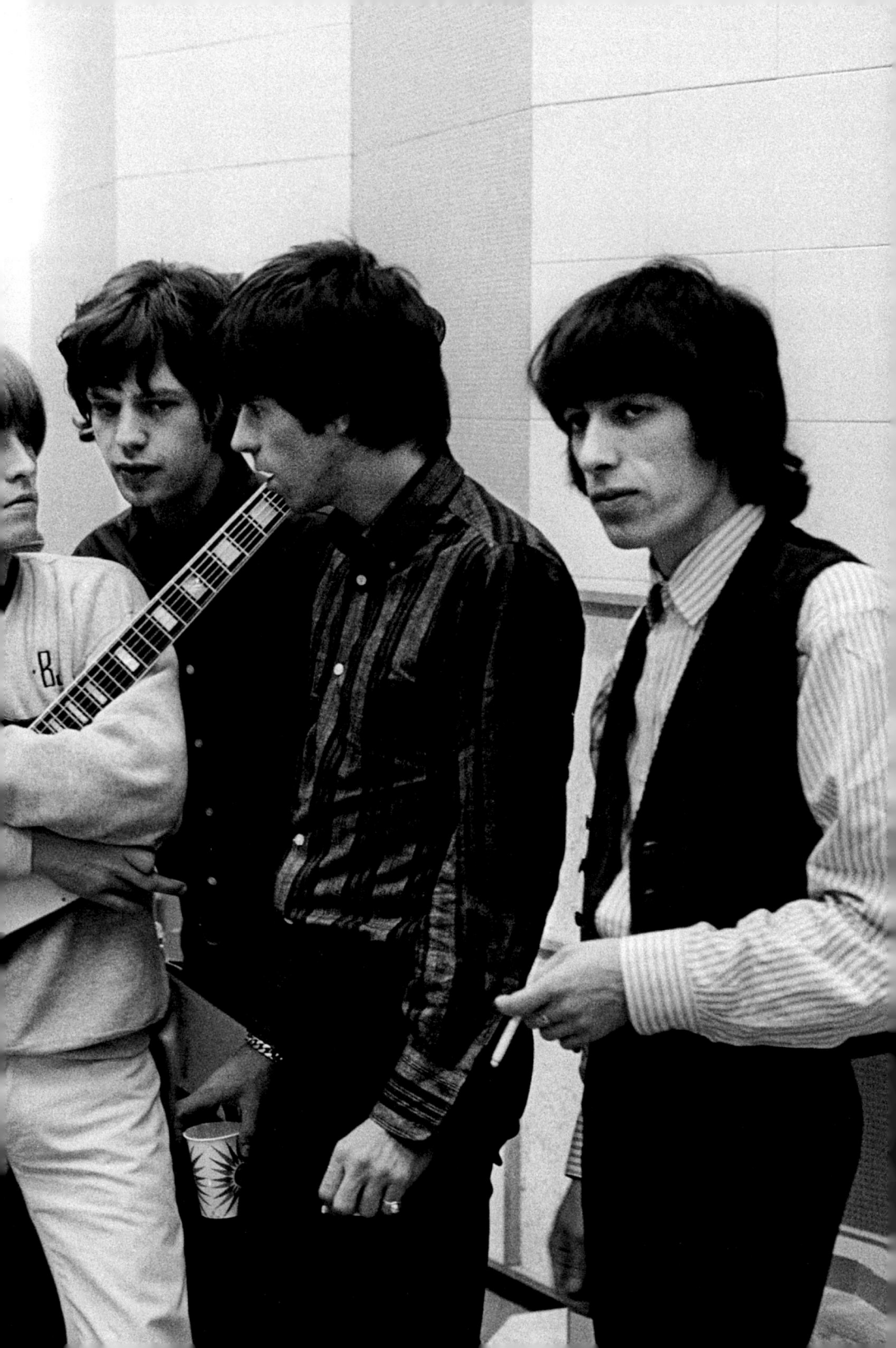

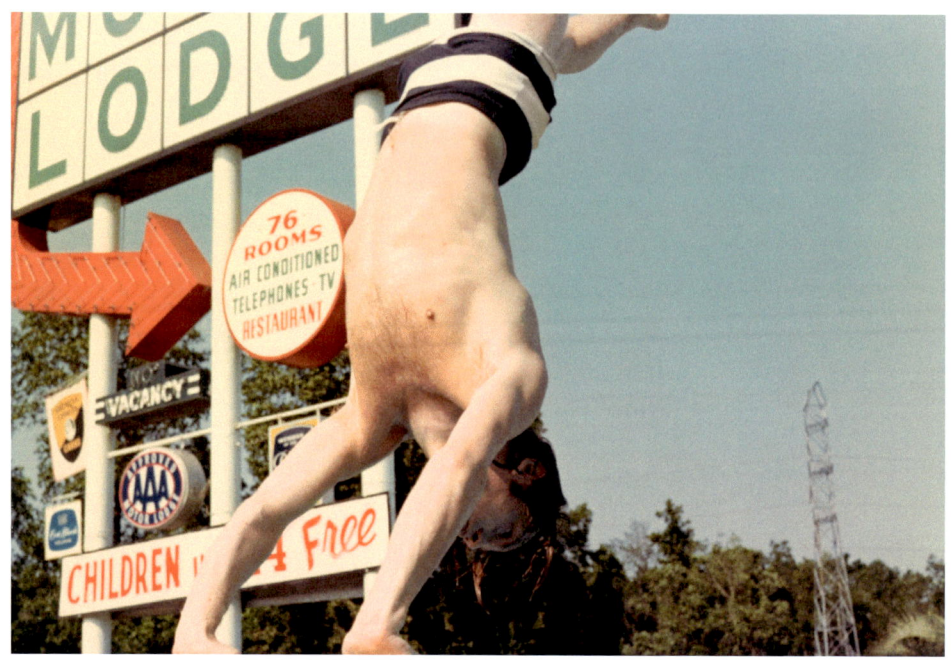

PP. 88–89

Bob Bonis

RCA Studios, Los Angeles, May 1965.
Manager Andrew Loog Oldham was omnipresent in the control room throughout 1965. His independent record label Immediate was launched that year, and Oldham was slowly being drawn to the more creative side of production, his proven ear for detecting hit material superseding the more predictable toils of business.
"We realised right from the beginning that we were making our appeal to young people and by *making a concerted effort towards freedom on their behalf we would upset those we neglected. We chose the young instead of the old, that's all. The old resented it. The Stones are still the social outcasts, the rebels. We worked on the principle that if you are going to kick conformity in the teeth, you may as well use both feet."* Andrew Loog Oldham, *New Musical Express*: Summer Special, June 1966

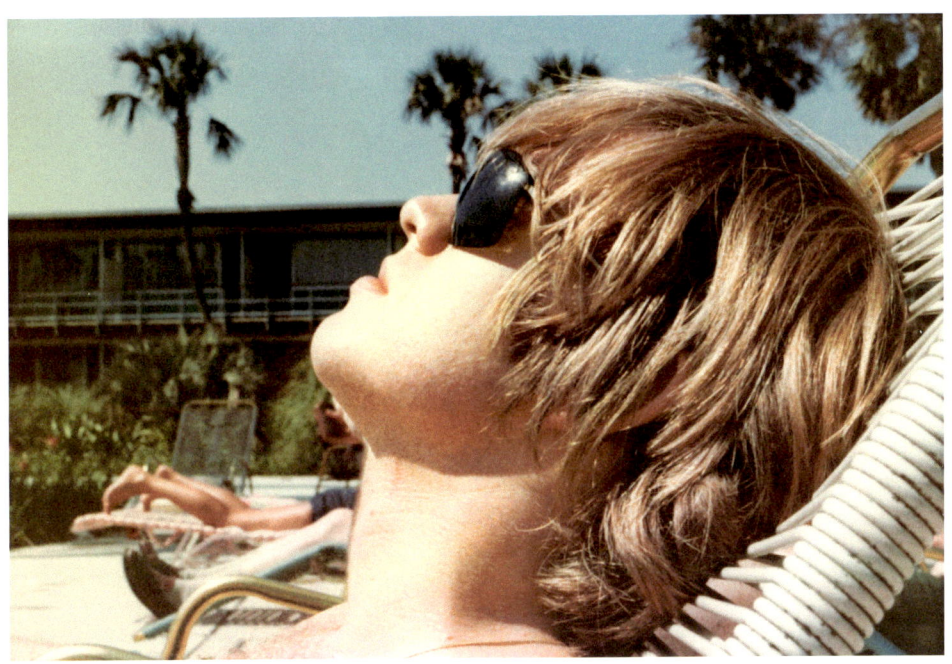

Bob Bonis

Brian had been something of an athlete prior to his immersion in The Rolling Stones and swimming was a particular passion. Some saw his prowess in the water as further evidence that he didn't accidentally drown in 1969. The Manger Towne and Country Motor Lodge in Savannah, Georgia, 5 May 1965.

Bob Bonis

Catching a few rays of Florida sun at the Fort Harrison Hotel in Clearwater, Florida, on 6 May 1965. Brian's demons got the better of him later that day. After assaulting a female fan, road manager Mike Dorsey got involved in a fight with Jones and the guitarist sustained two fractured ribs in the exchange. To support him through the evening's show at the Jack Russell Stadium, Jones had to resort to wearing a corset.

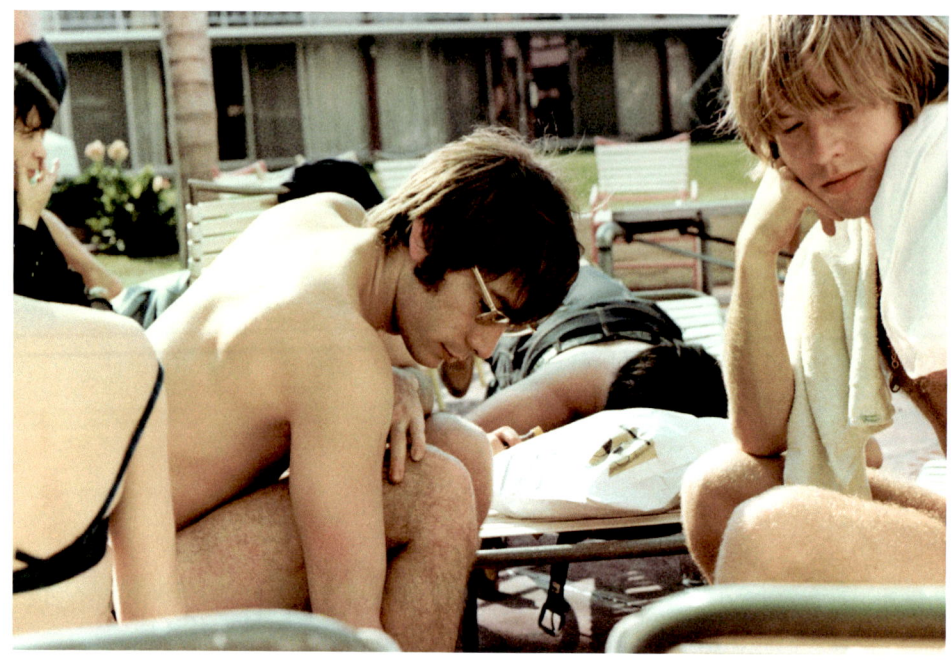

Bob Bonis
Charlie and Brian relaxing in Clearwater, Florida, 1965. Later that day the Stones played to 3,000 fans at Clearwater's Jack Russell Stadium. Four songs into their set the crowd turned rowdy, with some male members of the audience hurling toilet rolls at the band. Police feared a riot, so the group were swiftly hustled off stage to safety.

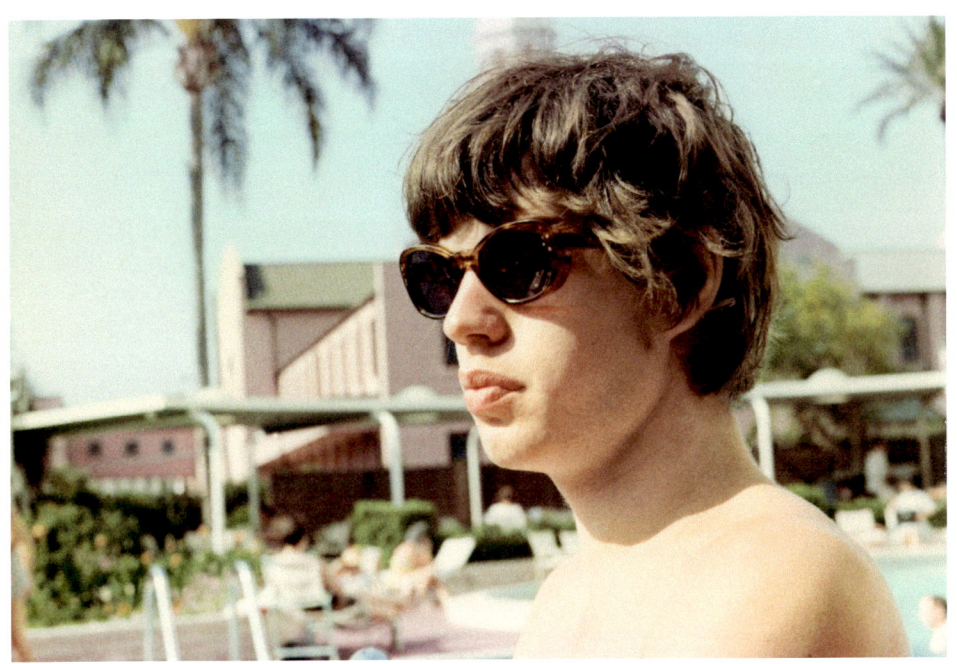

Bob Bonis

Mick poolside at the Fort Harrison Hotel, 1965. It was in Clearwater that the song "(I Can't Get No) Satisfaction" came into being. Keith allegedly came up with the famous riff during the night.

"It was Keith really. I mean it was his initial idea. It sounded like a folk song when we first started working on it and Keith didn't like it much. He didn't want it to be a single; he didn't think it would do very well. That's the only time we have had a disagreement." Mick Jagger, *Rolling Stone* magazine, 12 October 1968

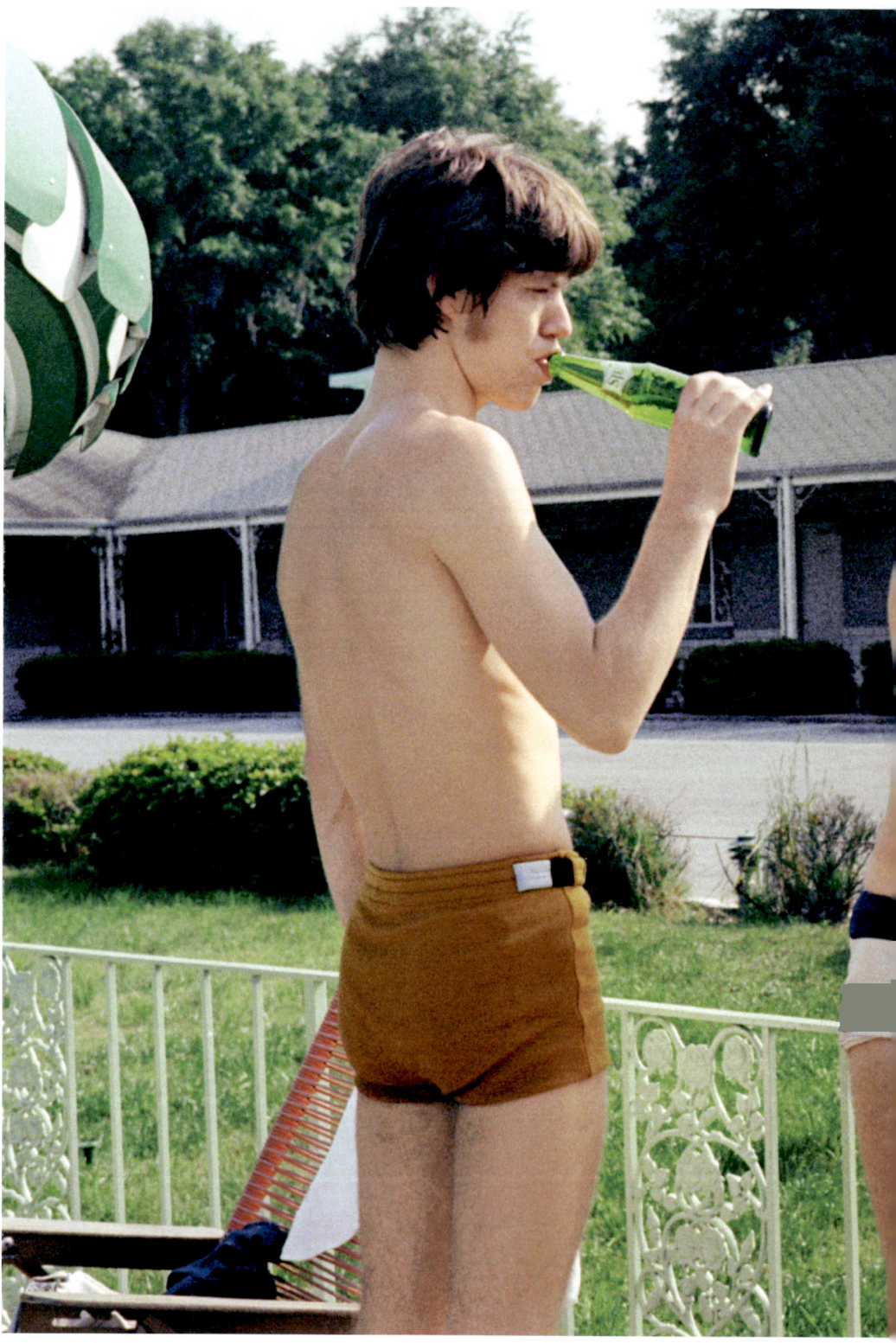

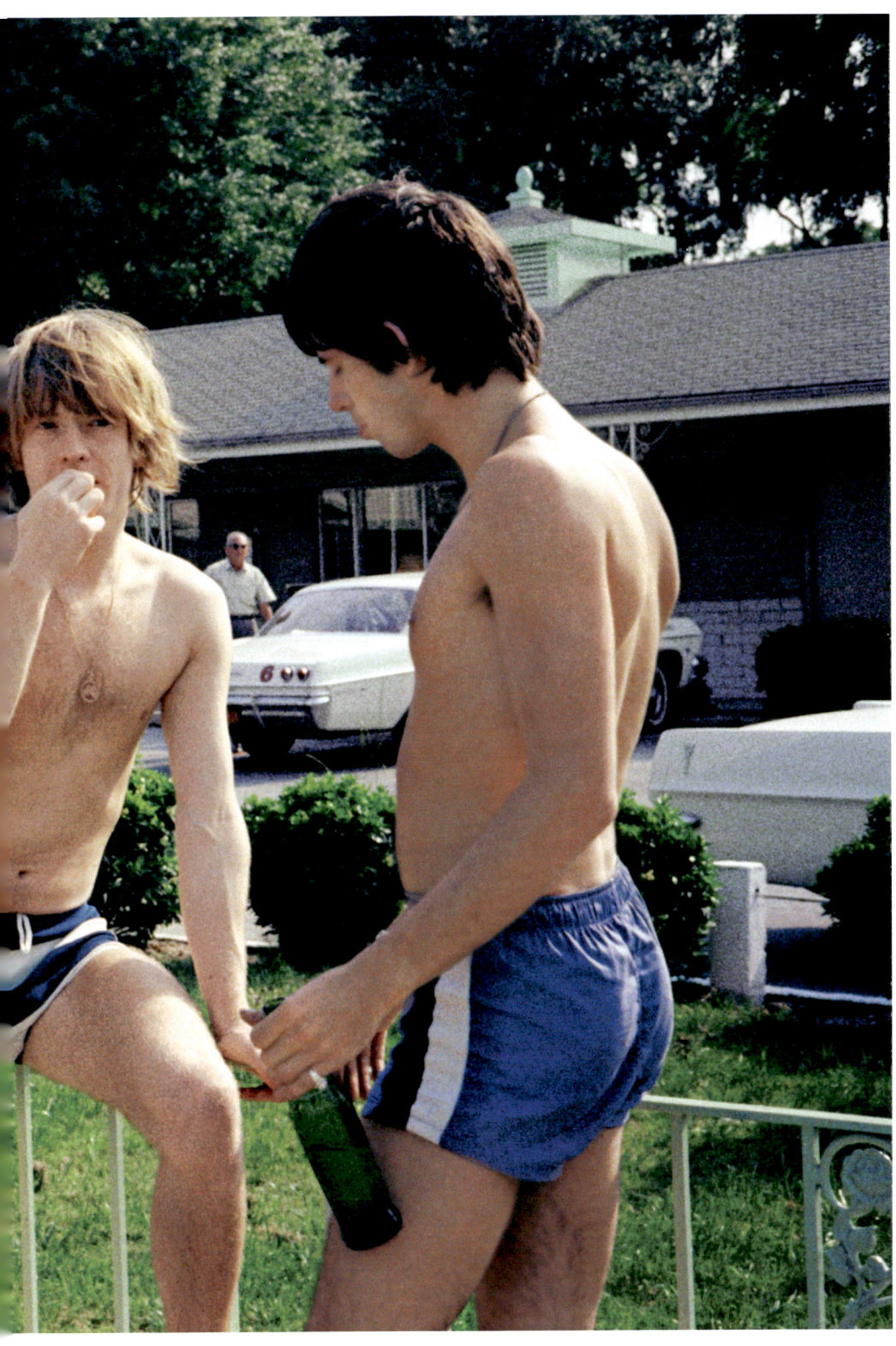

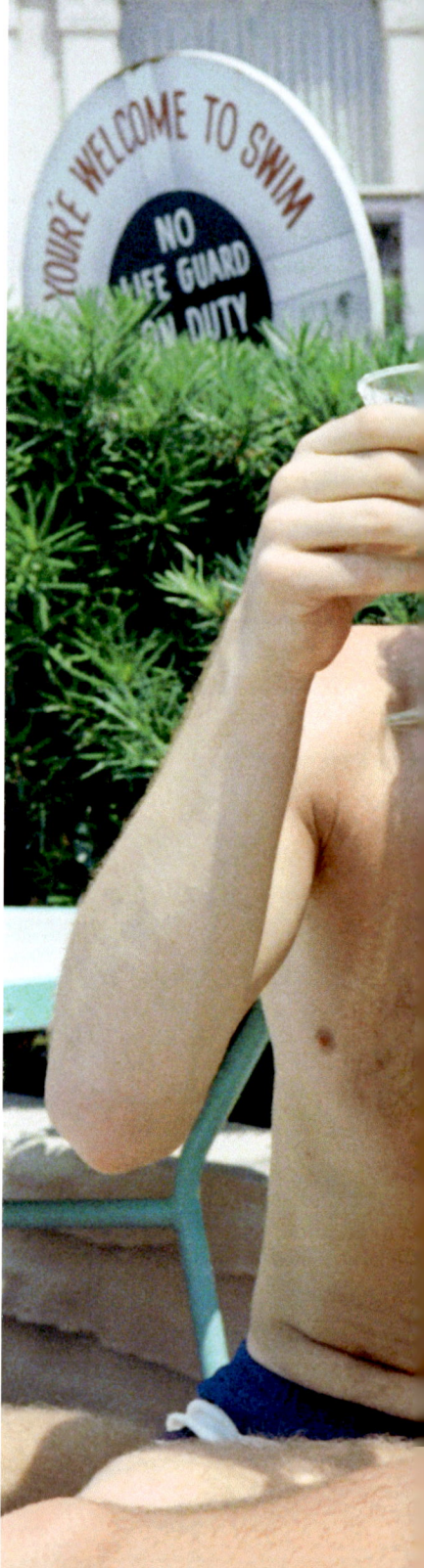

PP. 94–95
Bob Bonis
At the Manger Towne and Country Motor Lodge
in Savannah, Georgia, 5 May 1965.
*"Early Sixties America, you had an incredible
difference between what we called the outside,
the edge, which was New York, Chicago, Frisco,
LA, you know, Florida, maybe, but the difference between the big cities and Oklahoma was
immense at the time. I mean, we could make
contact with a lot of the city people, but quite
honestly for a year or so we were total freaks
out there, you know, you got used to being, 'I'm
a freak, you know, have a good laugh.'"* Keith
Richards in conversation with Anthony DeCurtis,
New York Public Library, 29 October 2010

Bob Bonis
Keith and Brian at Savannah's Manger Towne and
Country Motor Lodge, 5 May 1965. This cheeky
moment reveals considerable warmth between
the two musicians – testament to their early
camaraderie, despite their later falling out.
*"He was a gas. He was a cat who could play any
instrument. It was like, 'There it is, music comes
out of it, if I work at it for a bit, I can do it.'"* Keith
Richards, *Rolling Stone* magazine, 19 August 1971

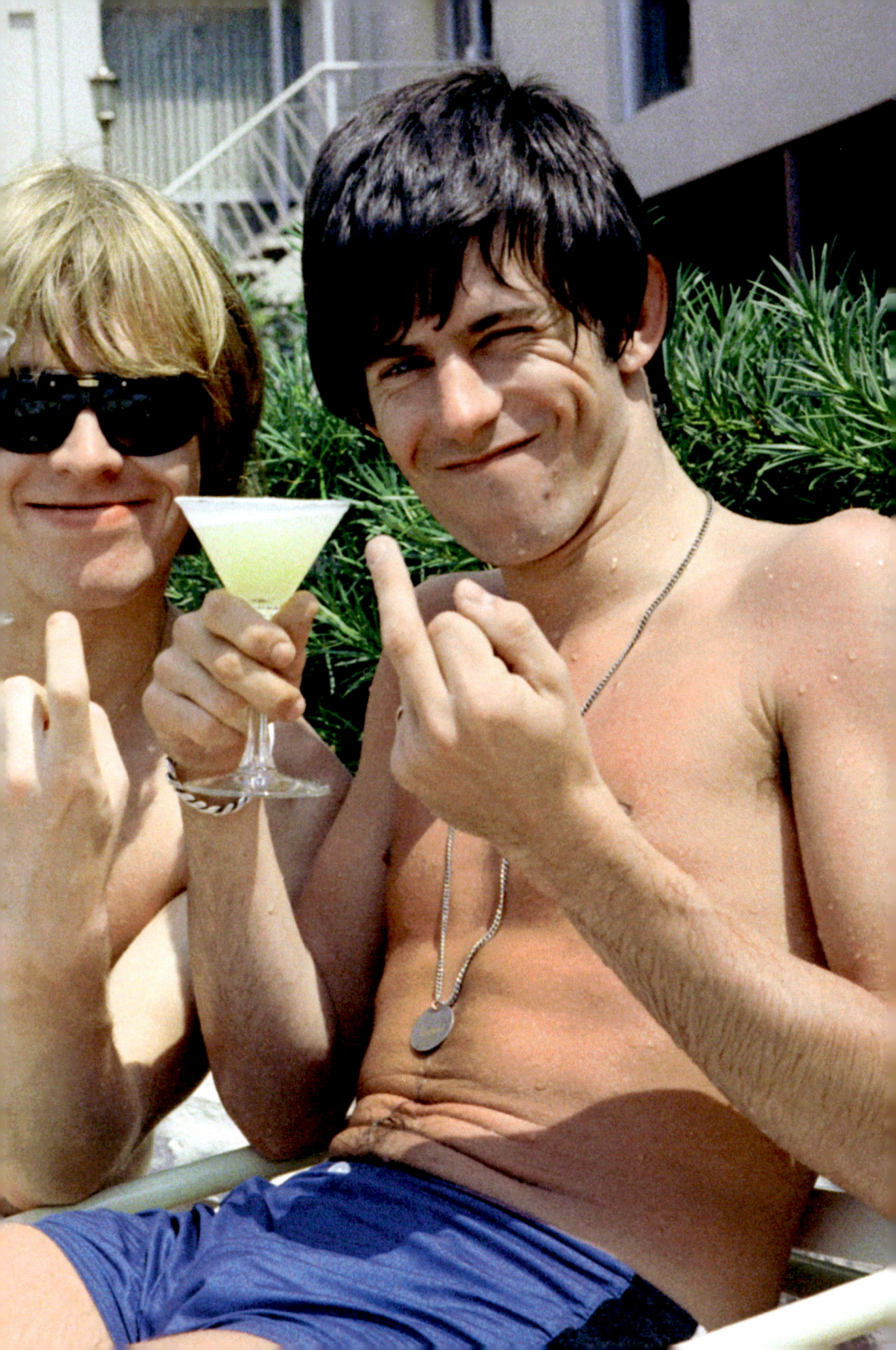

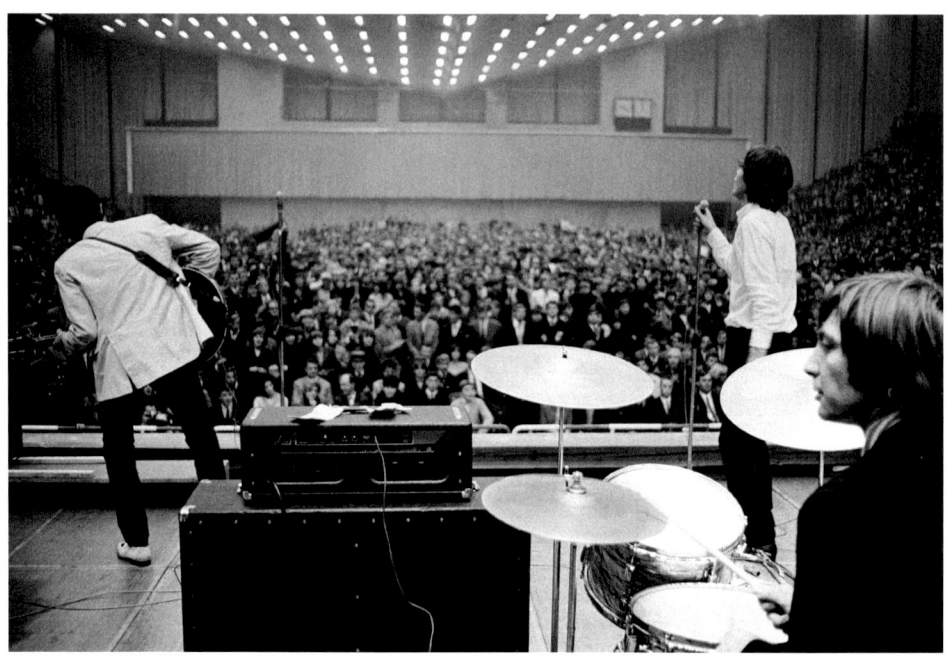

Bent Rej
A view from the rear at Grugahalle, Essen, West Germany, 12 September 1965. People compared the rowdy atmosphere at the Stones' show in Essen with the fevered mania of Nazi Germany just three decades earlier.
"I have seen nothing like this since the old days of a Nazi or Communist rally." Essen policeman, *Daily Mail*, 13 September 1965

Bob Bonis
Grugahalle, Essen, West Germany, 12 September 1965.
"It's a very strange feeling being on the stage and feeling all this energy coming from the audience directed straight into you. You can feel it, but you don't really understand it. I sometimes get perplexed by what they are trying to say to me, or what they want from me as a performer or as a person." Mick Jagger, *BBC TV Look Of The Week*, 21 May 1967

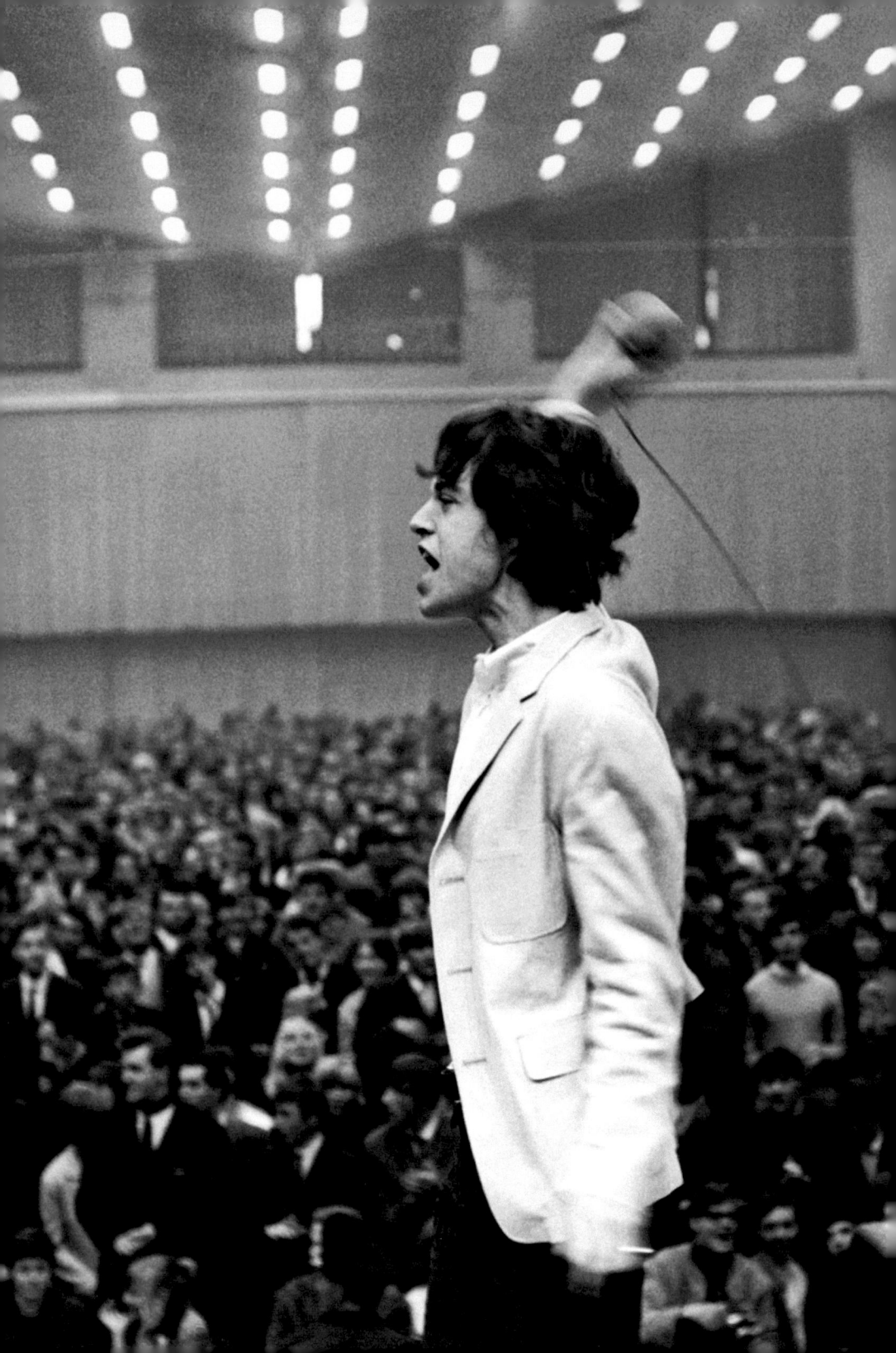

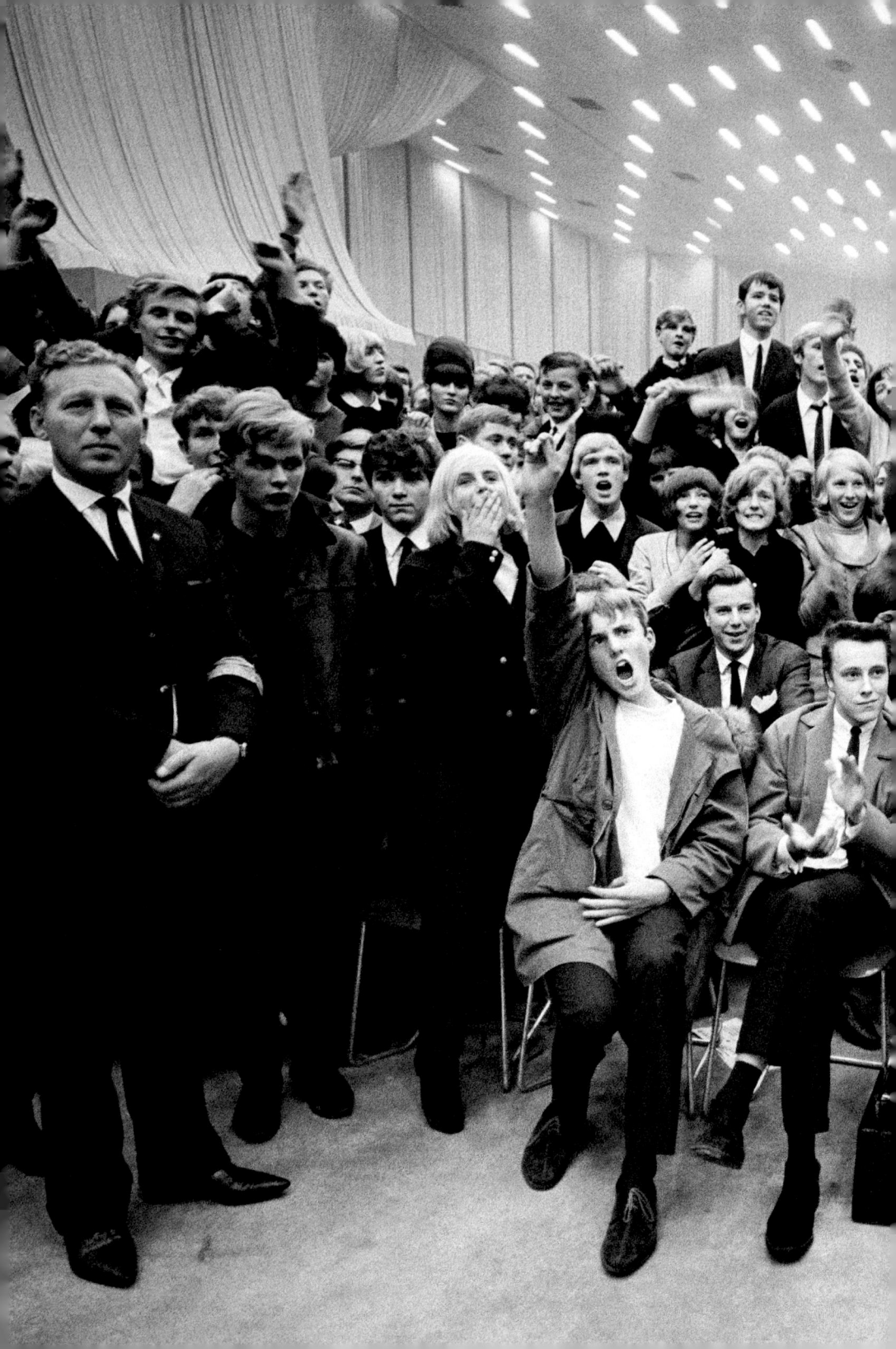

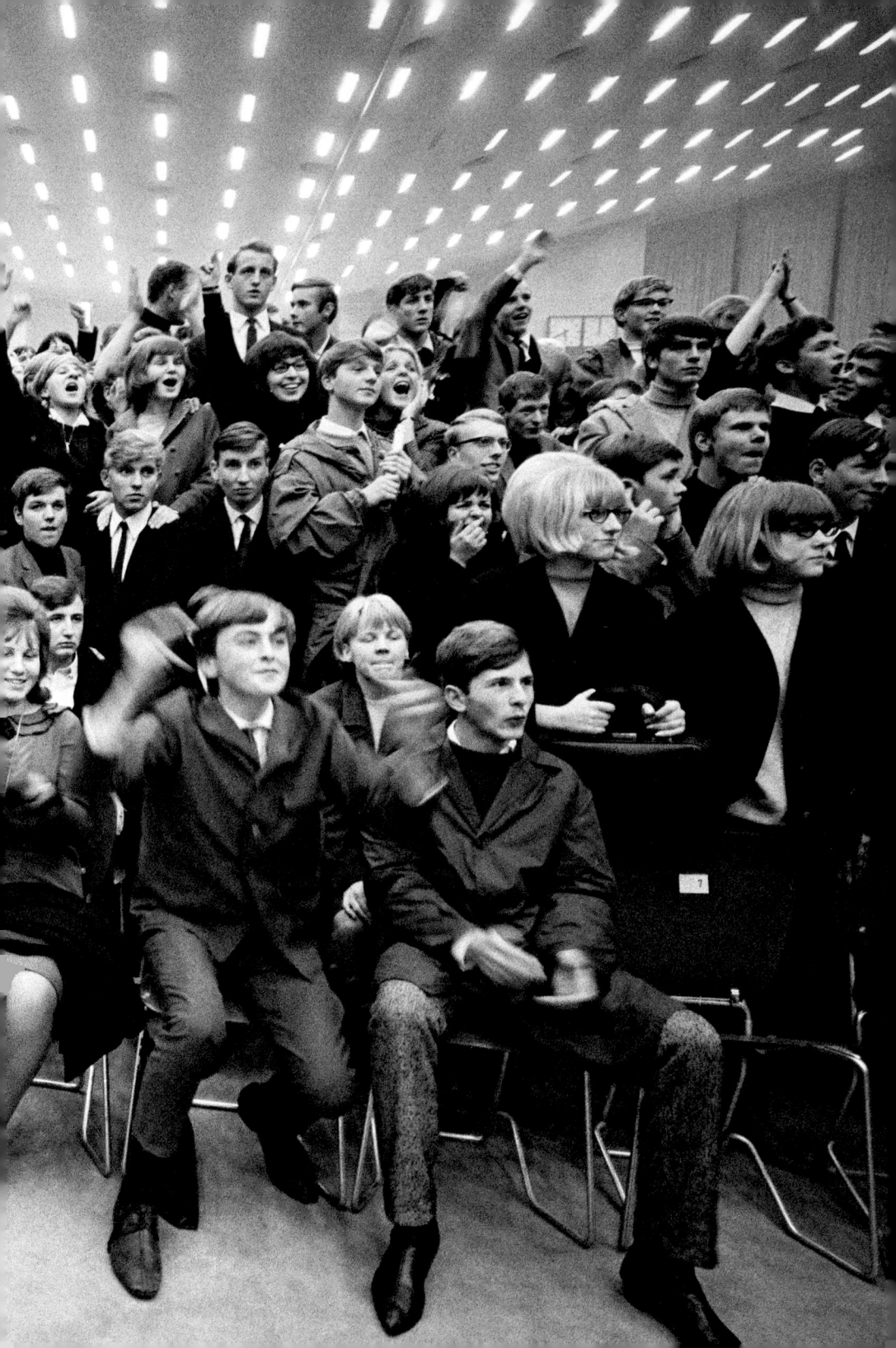

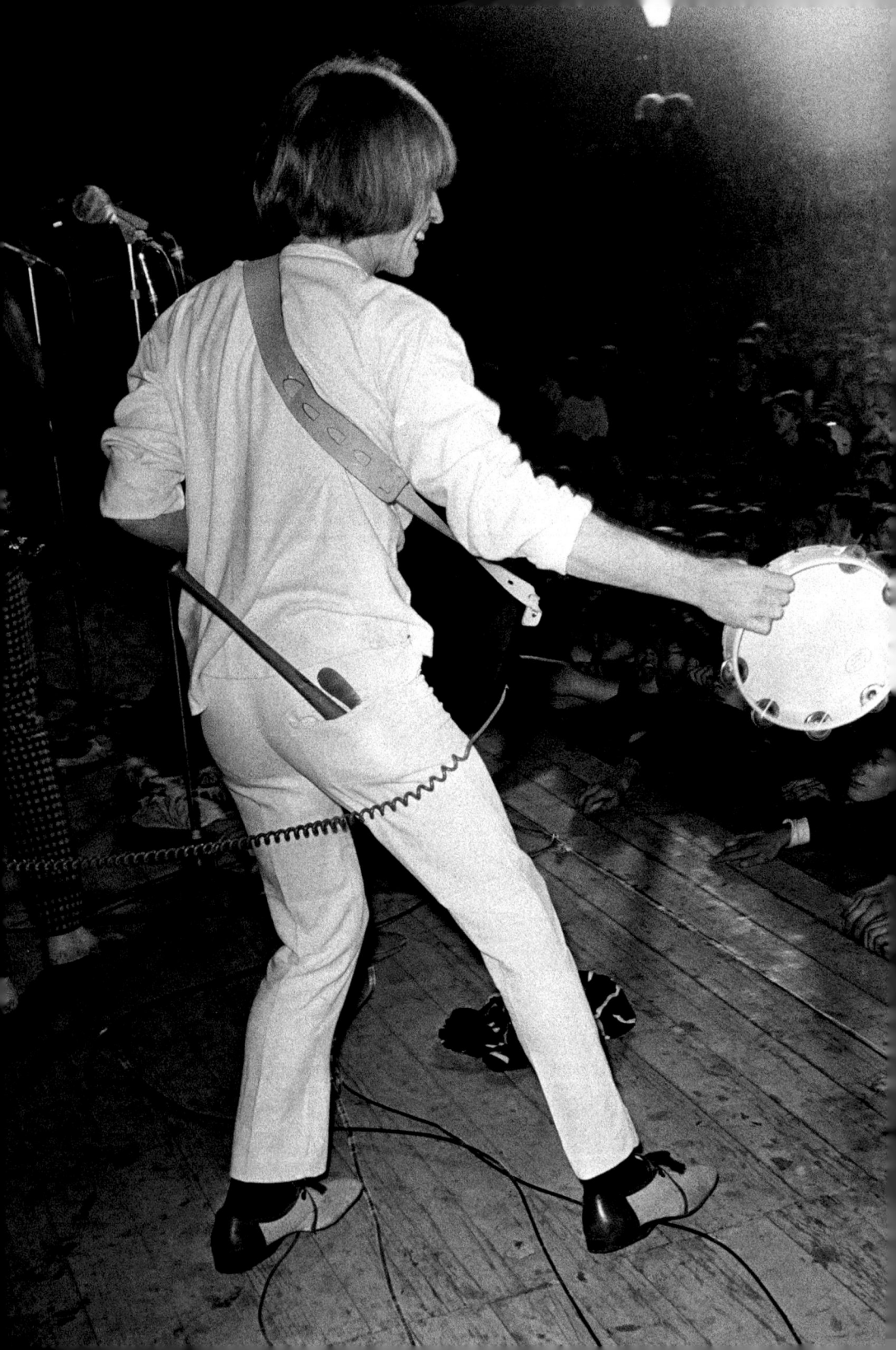

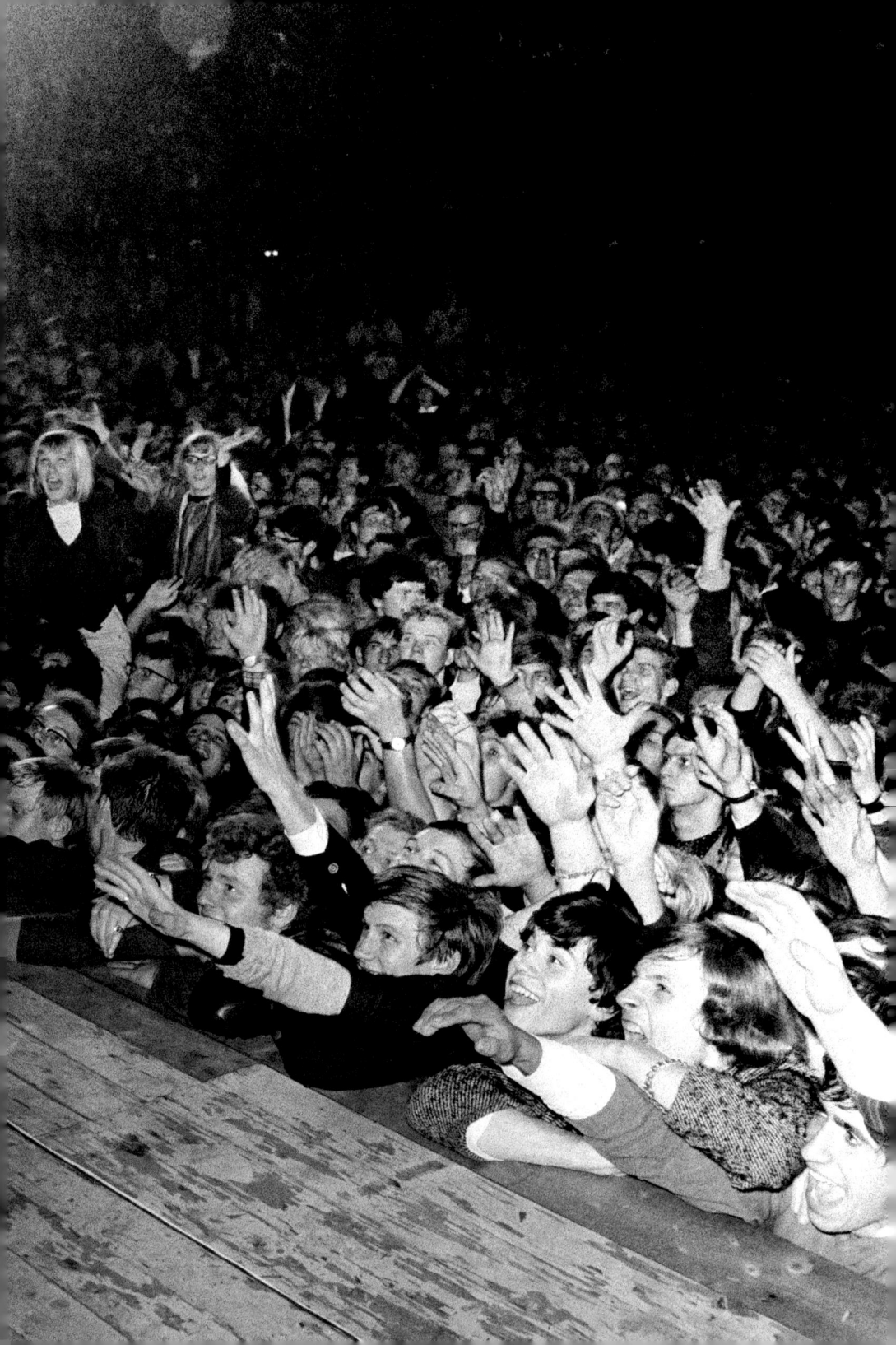

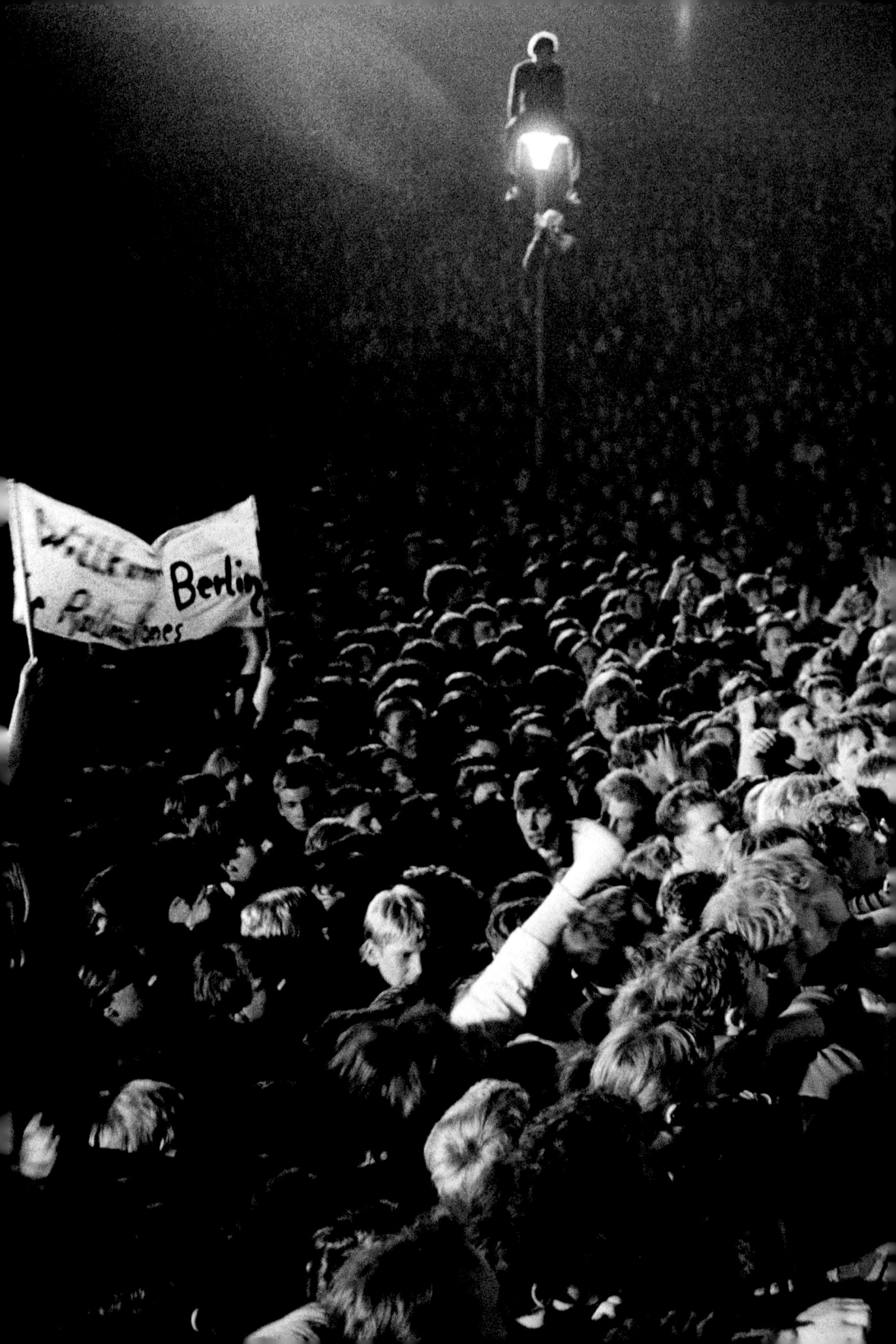

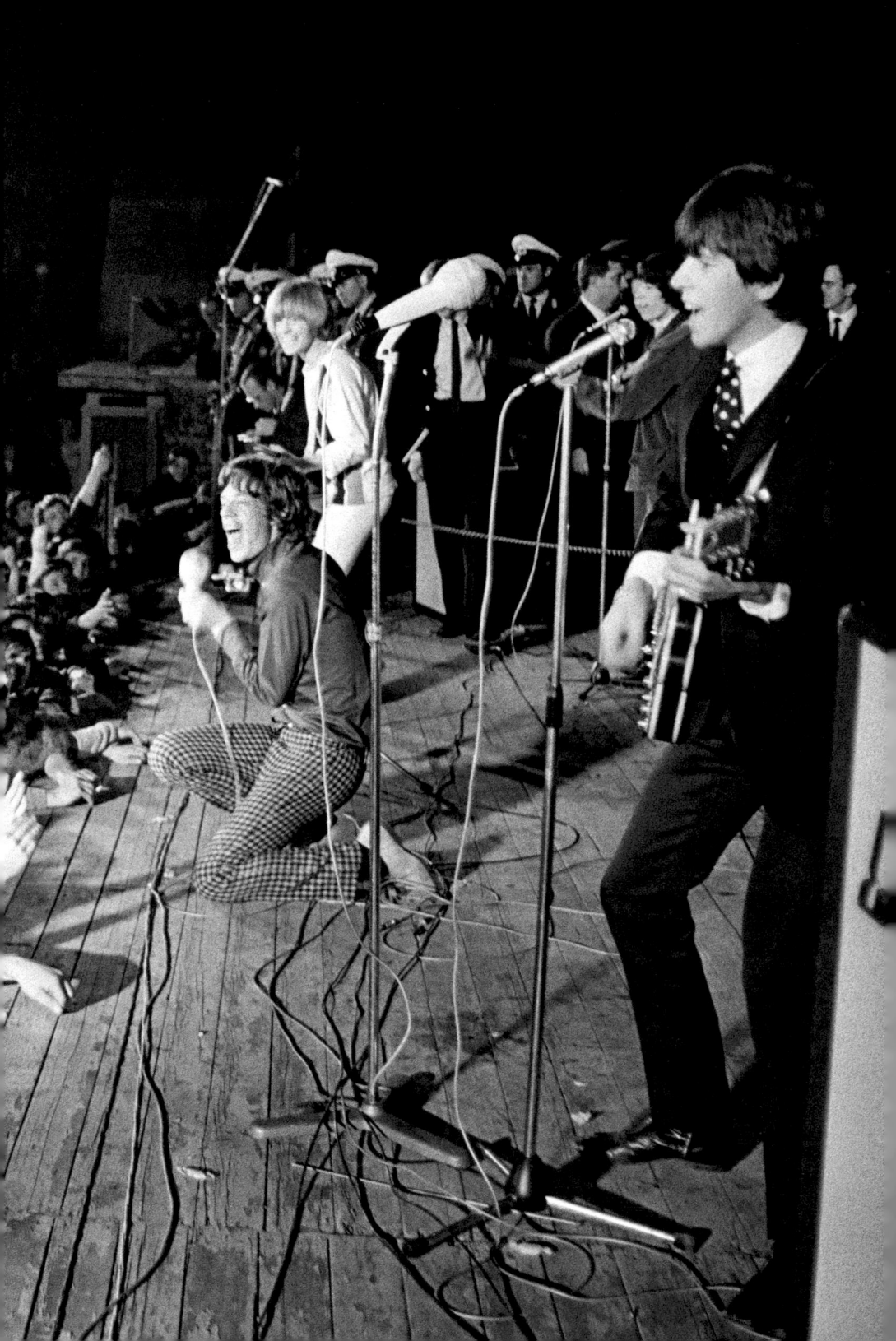

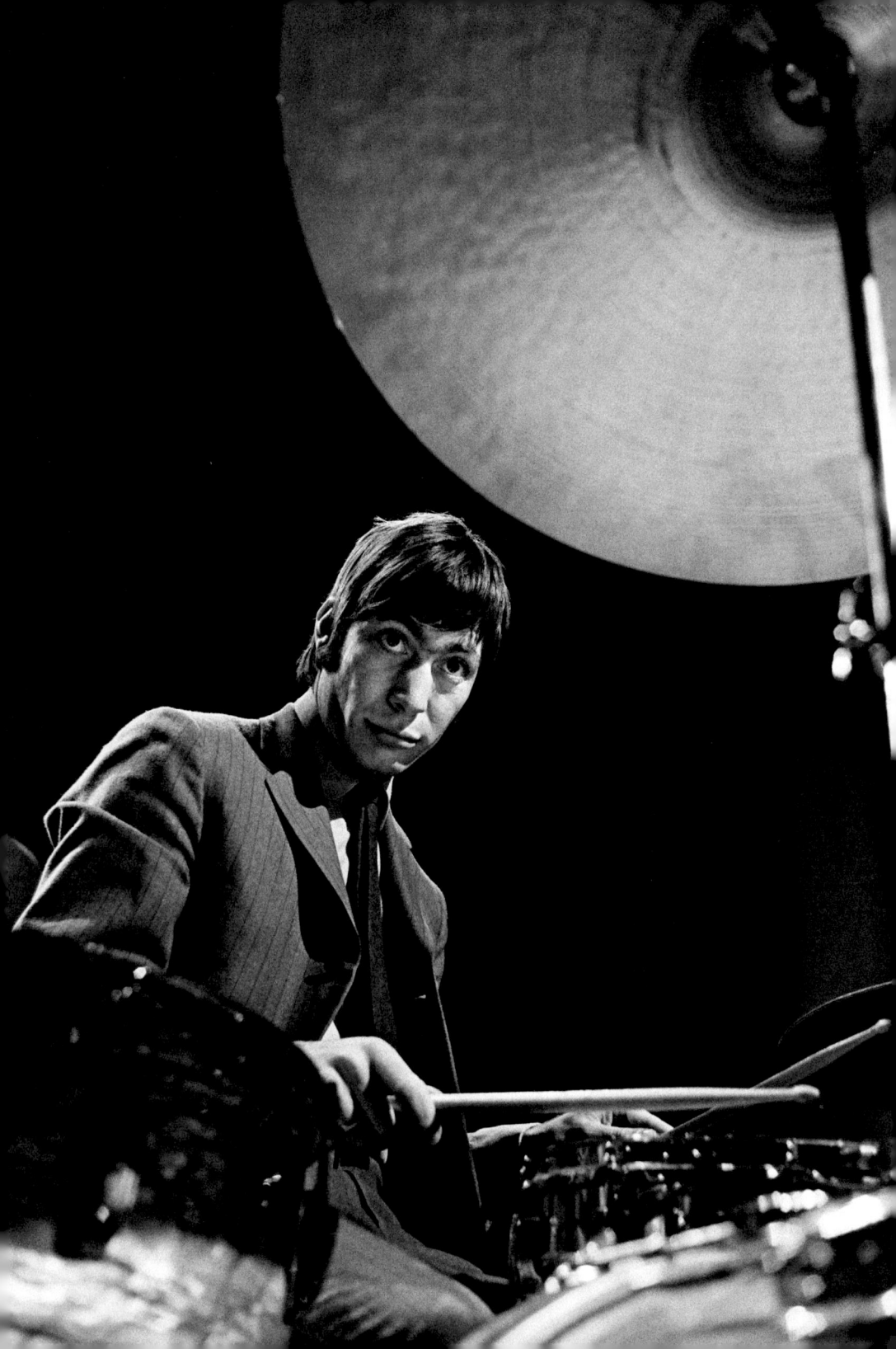

PP. 100–101
Bent Rej

Stylish young fans at the Grugahalle, Essen, West Germany, 12 September 1965.

"While the Stones whipped up a musical storm outside Essen's Grugahalle, fans without tickets continued battling outside with the police. They stormed the barricades in an attempt to gain entry using eggs, tin cans, tomatoes and even a dead rat as missiles against the police." Bent Rej, *The Rolling Stones: In The Beginning*, 2006

PP. 102–103
Bent Rej

The most extreme display of crazed adoration occurred at the Stones' gig at Berlin's Waldbühne on 15 September 1965. The band played for just 20 minutes before being ushered off stage under a hail of missiles. The gig became a low point in entertainment history, with the arena's seating entirely destroyed while scores of people had to be treated for injuries in a makeshift tent set up on the stage.

PP. 104–105
Bent Rej

On stage at the Waldbühne, Berlin, West Germany, 15 September 1965.

"Riots aren't the sign of a good show. It's enough if people just clap and cheer. When there's a lot of screaming, I know that most people can't hear us playing, but what can you do?" Mick Jagger, *New Musical Express*, 24 September 1965

Bent Rej

Malmö, Sweden, 29 June 1965.

"I don't actually like touring, you see. I don't like living out of suitcases. I hate being away from home. I always do tours thinking they're the last one, and at the end of them, I always leave the band. Because of what I do, I can't play the drums at home … And to play the drums I have to go on the road, and to go on the road I have to leave home. And so it's like a terribly vicious circle that has always been my life." Charlie Watts, *25x5: The Continuing Adventures Of The Rolling Stones*, 1989

PP. 108–109
Bent Rej

Mick's extraordinary stage presence was the dominant element of The Rolling Stones' live act – as demonstrated here at the K.B. Hallen, Copenhagen, 5 April 1966. Note how their style of dress is becoming more eclectic and 1960s dandy.

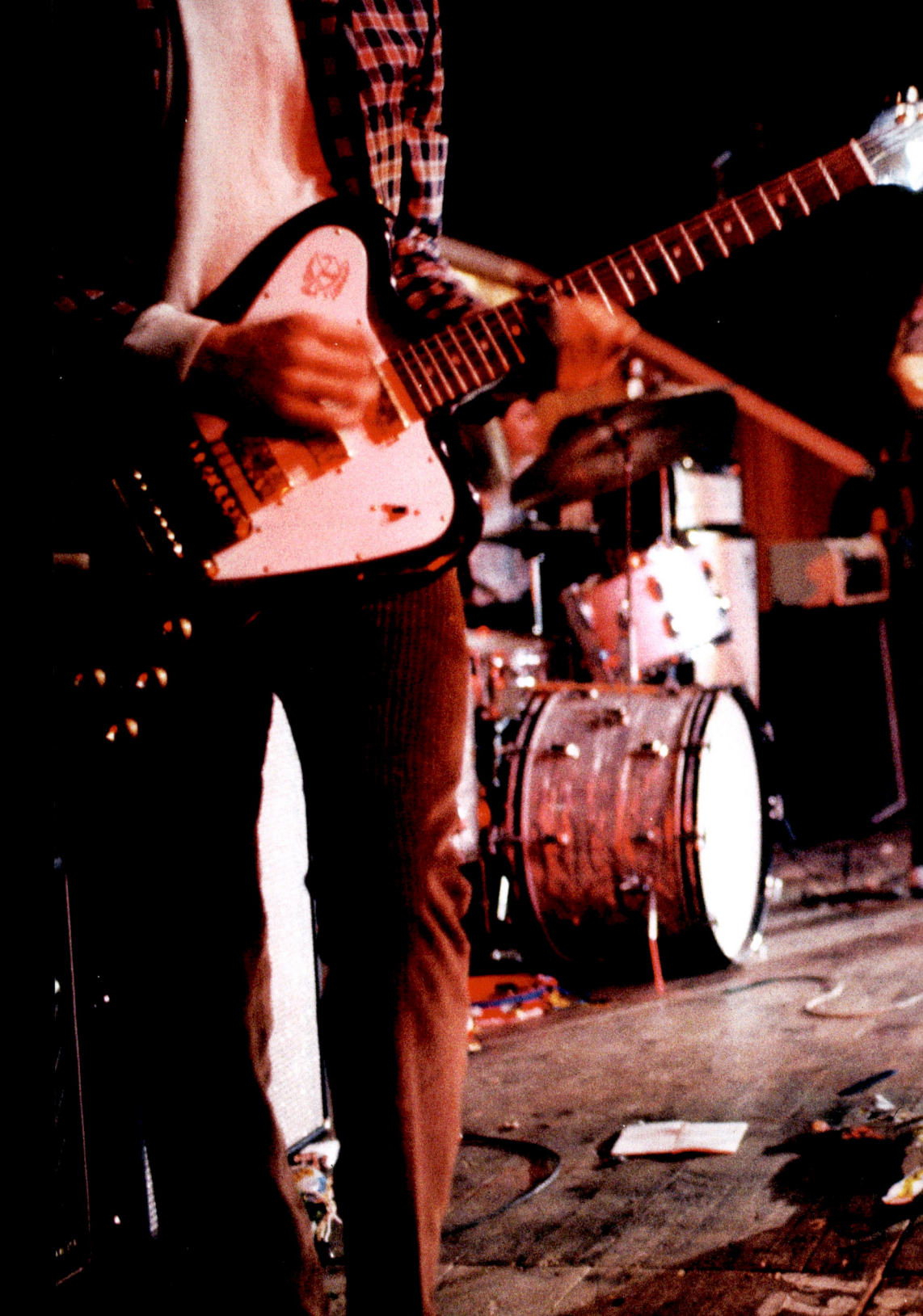

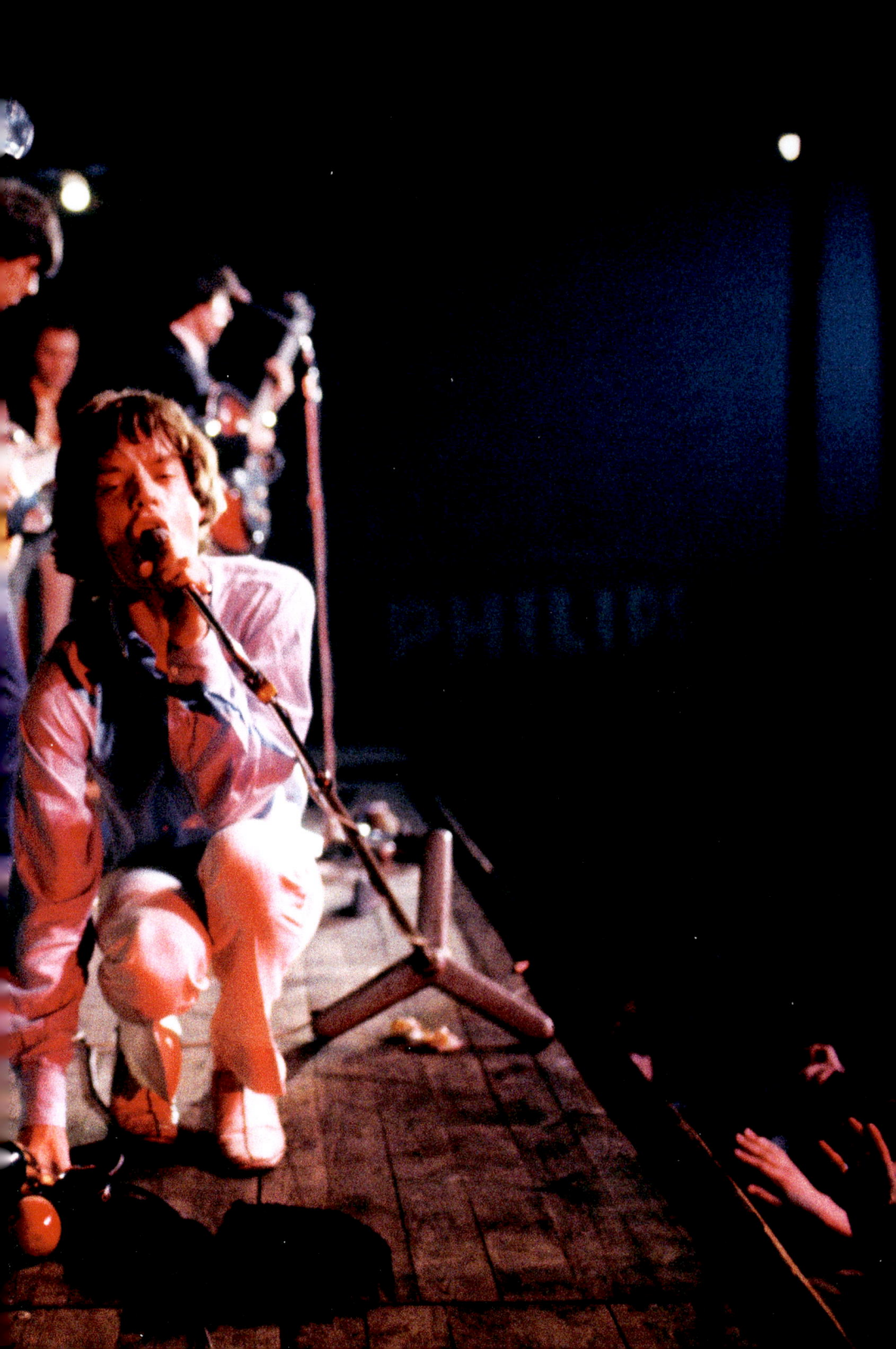

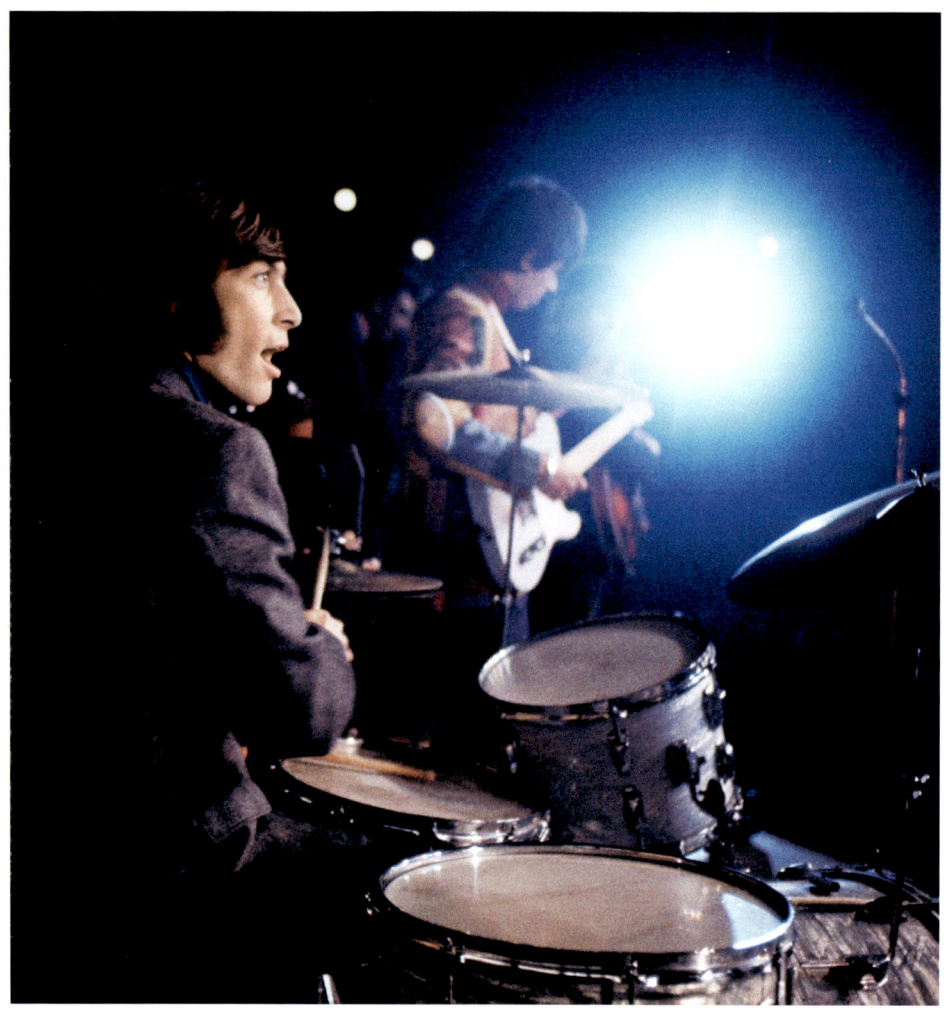

Bent Rej

Pounding the skins in Copenhagen on 5 April 1966: Charlie's solid percussive skills served to anchor the largely disparate energies of the performers in front of him.

"Charlie Watts is one of the greatest drummers the damn world is ever going to see. [He's] so beautifully spontaneous." Keith Richards' website video message, 2003

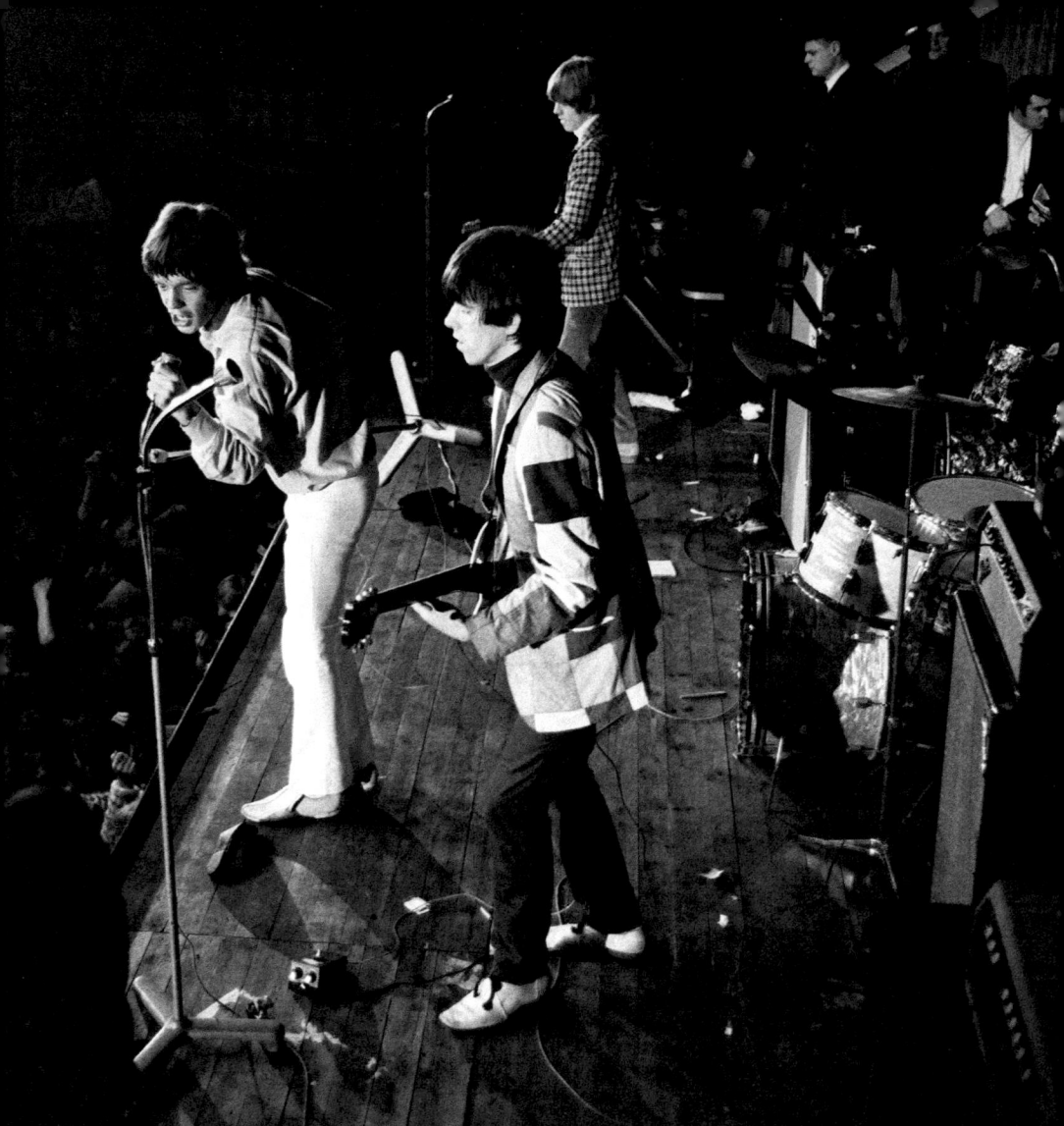

Bent Rej

On 3 April 1966, the Stones began a short Scandinavian tour. Five days earlier, in Marseilles, France, Mick received an eye injury courtesy of an over-enthusiastic fan who threw a broken chair at the stage. Although he was sporting a large facial gash and black eye, Jagger's appearance for the two shows at Copenhagen's K.B. Hallen on 5 April was restored courtesy of some stage make-up.

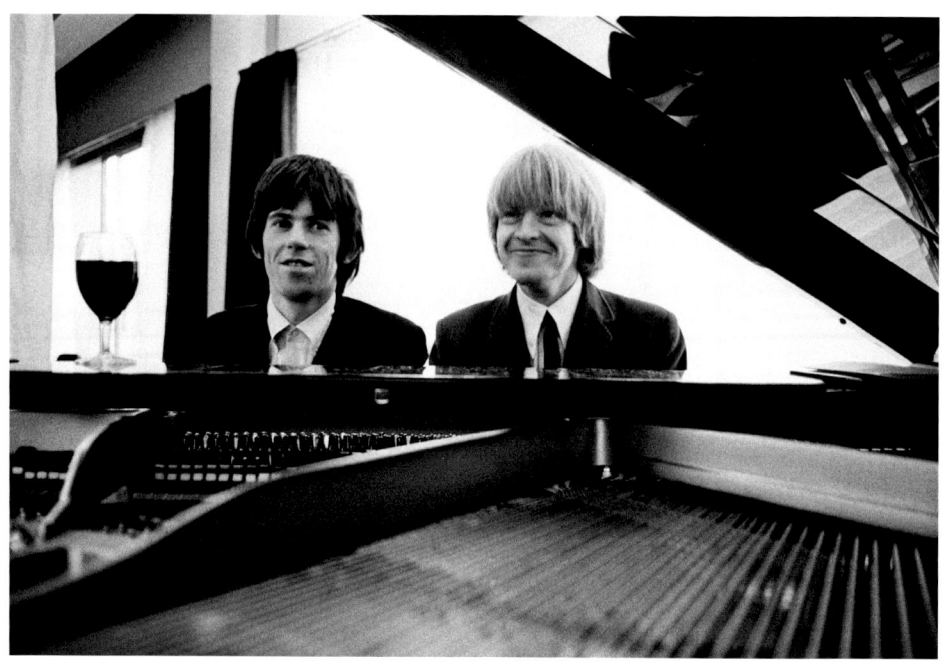

Bent Rej

Keith and Brian caught tinkling the ivories during a celebratory lunch held in their honour by the Danish branch of Decca during a visit to Copenhagen, 26 March 1965. Following a luncheon where Brian ordered 500 grams of high-end caviar, several bottles of expensive vintage wine were devoured by those present, presumably at the expense of the record company.

Bent Rej

A calm moment between Keith and Brian before going on stage at West Berlin's Waldbühne on 15 September 1965.

"I think the most important thing to us when we go on stage is that we succeed in communicating with the audience, and the only way we can do this is to produce an exciting atmosphere. Therefore if the kids scream, we love it. We react to their reaction." Brian Jones, press conference, Denmark, 26 June 1965

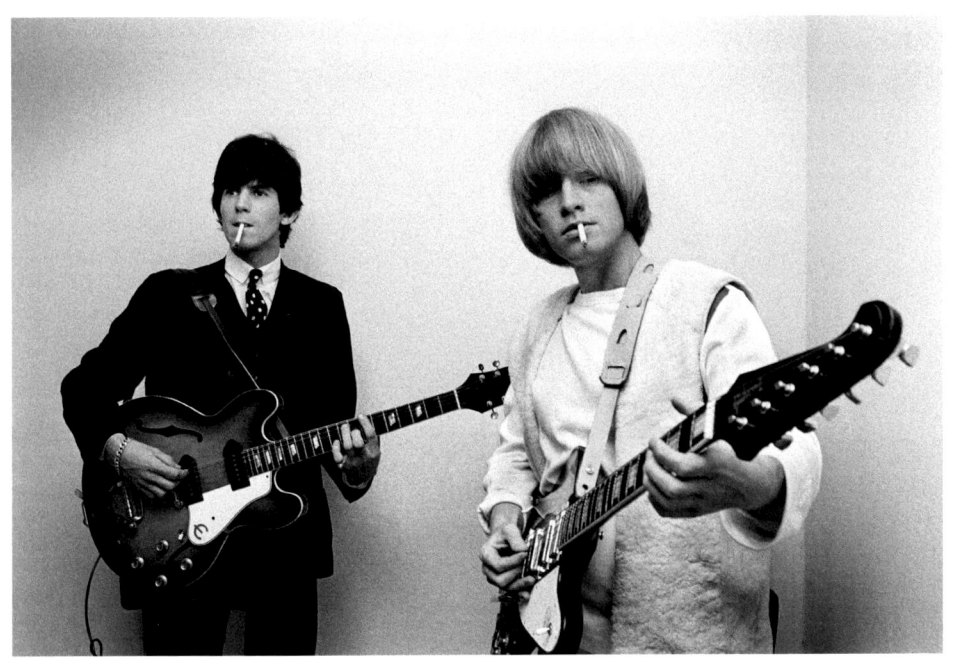

PP. 114–115

Bent Rej

A breath of fresh air following a reception held in the Stones' honour in Copenhagen, 26 March 1965. Despite their popular association with non-conformity, they paid great attention to their wardrobe, and, equally, to the feature that prompted considerable outrage – their hair. Bill is wearing dark glasses because of an eye infection.

"Simply because we chose to do something different and wear our hair long they had to make up these ridiculous stories about our hygiene. Any girl will tell you that once you grow your hair long, it's necessary to keep it washed far more regularly because it gets dirtier quicker!" Brian Jones, *New Musical Express: Summer Special*, June 1966

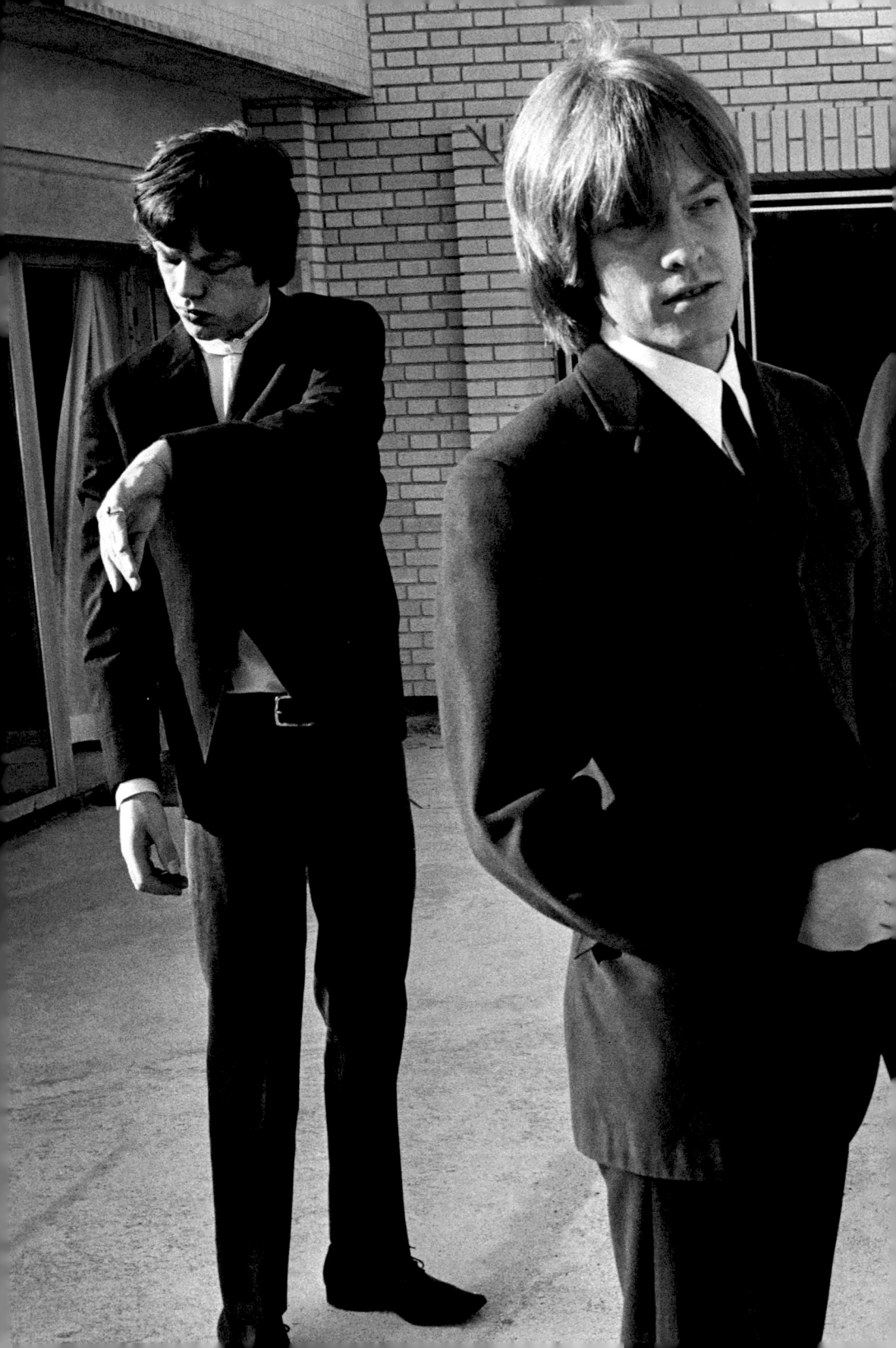

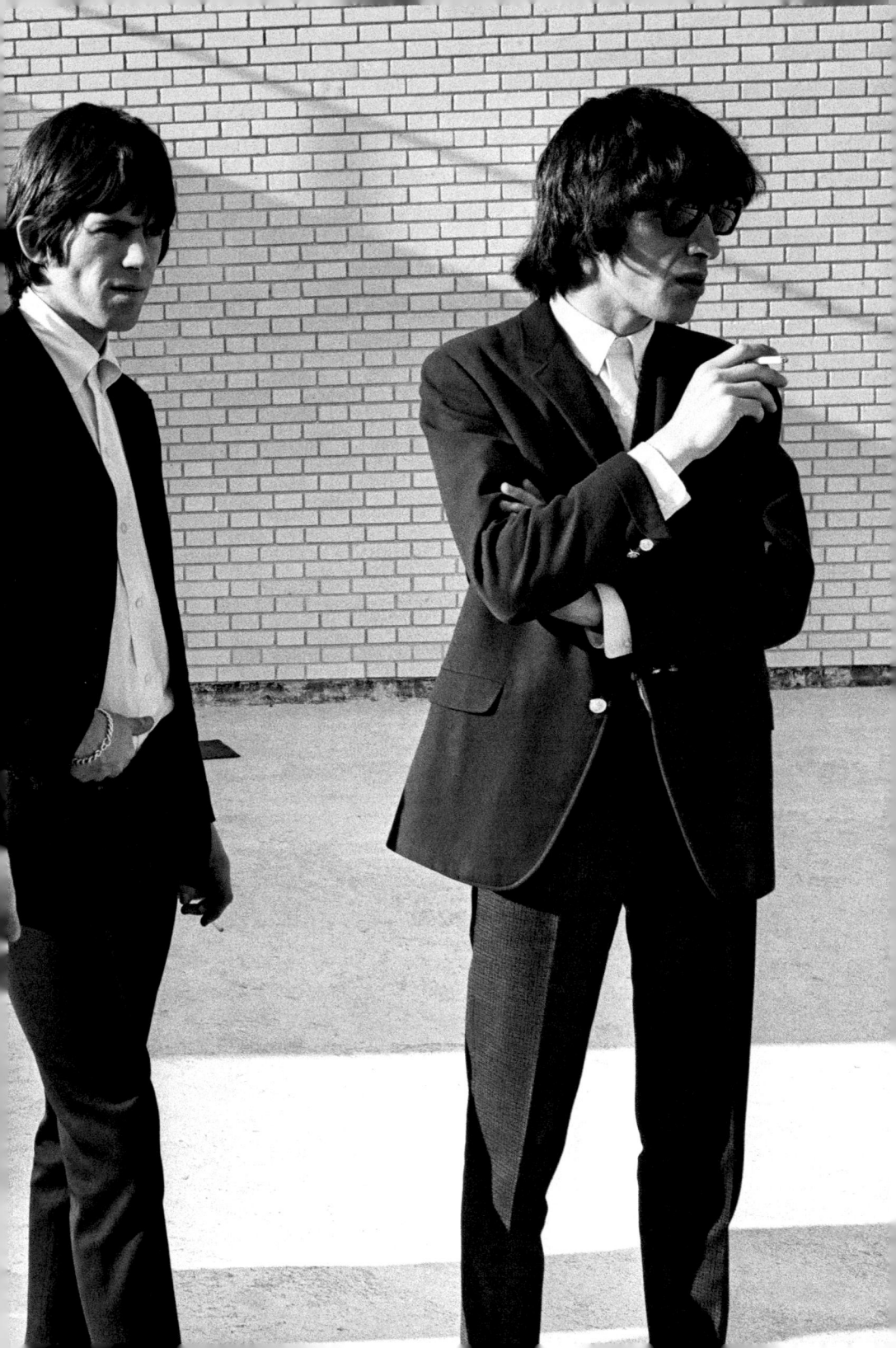

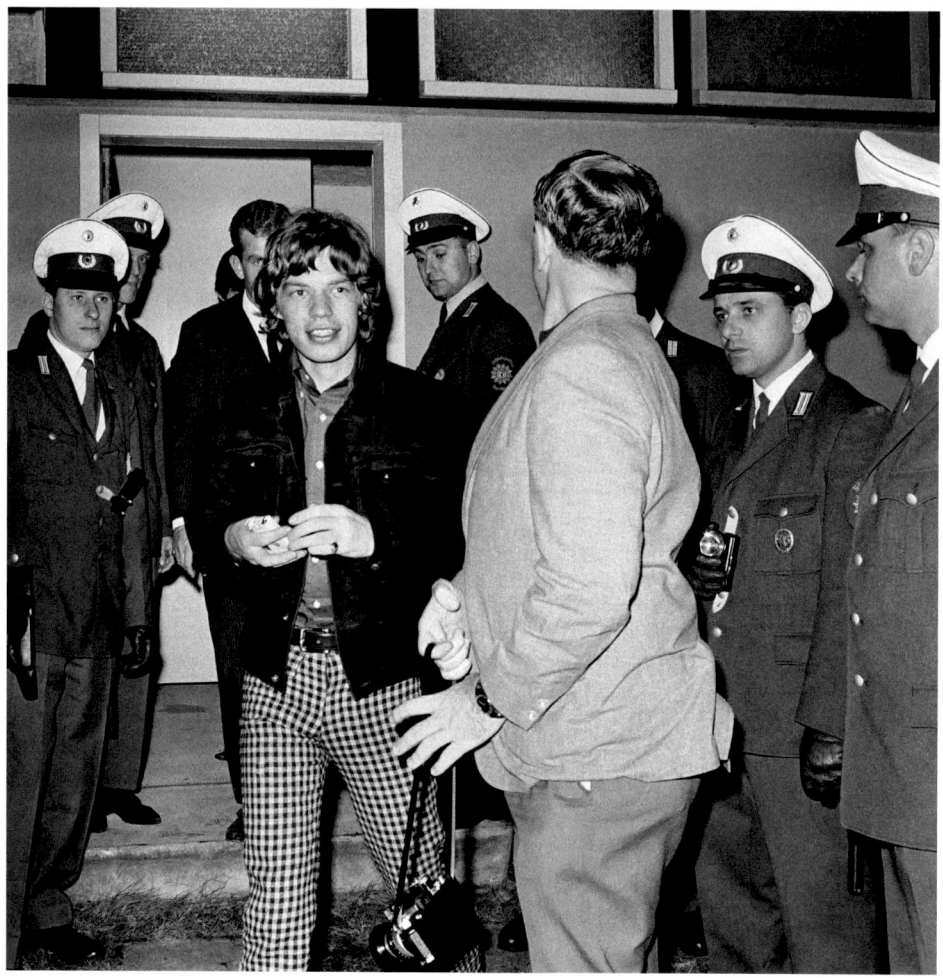

Bent Rej
Mick entering West Berlin's Waldbühne, before the famous riot, 15 September 1965.

Bent Rej
The Stones' gig at West Berlin's Waldbühne on 15 September 1965 came with a variety of issues, not least because the venue had hosted some of Adolf Hitler's Nazi rallies in the 1930s. Evidently aware of the connection, Brian arranged with the photographer to make a controversial "Sieg Heil" gesture moments before the band entered the arena.

"We had to walk for quite a way through the woods and underground bunkers to get to the stage. We agreed that on a given signal, Bent would take a photograph of Brian doing a Nazi signal with the police escort." Bill Wyman, quoted in Bent Rej, *The Rolling Stones: In The Beginning*, 2006

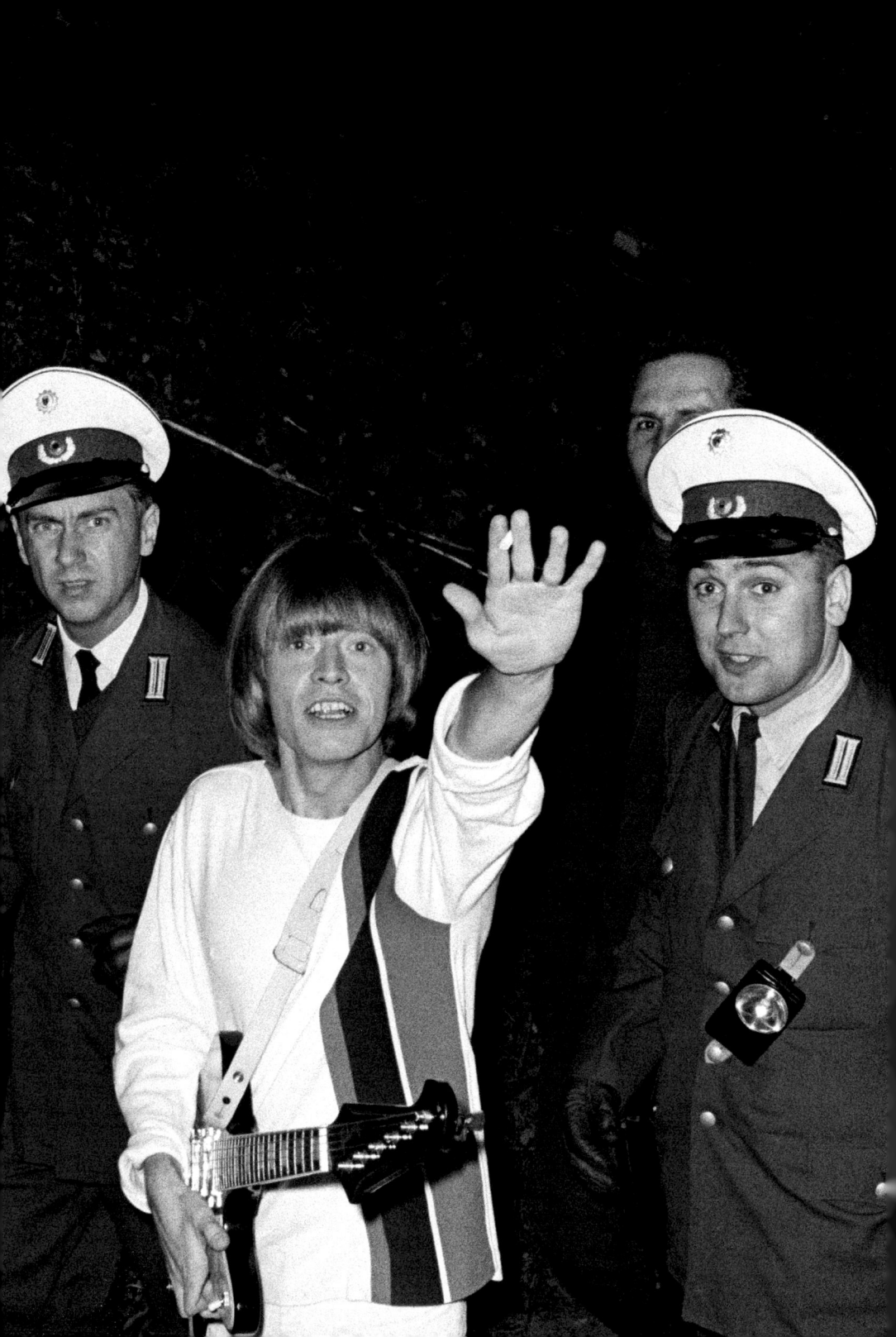

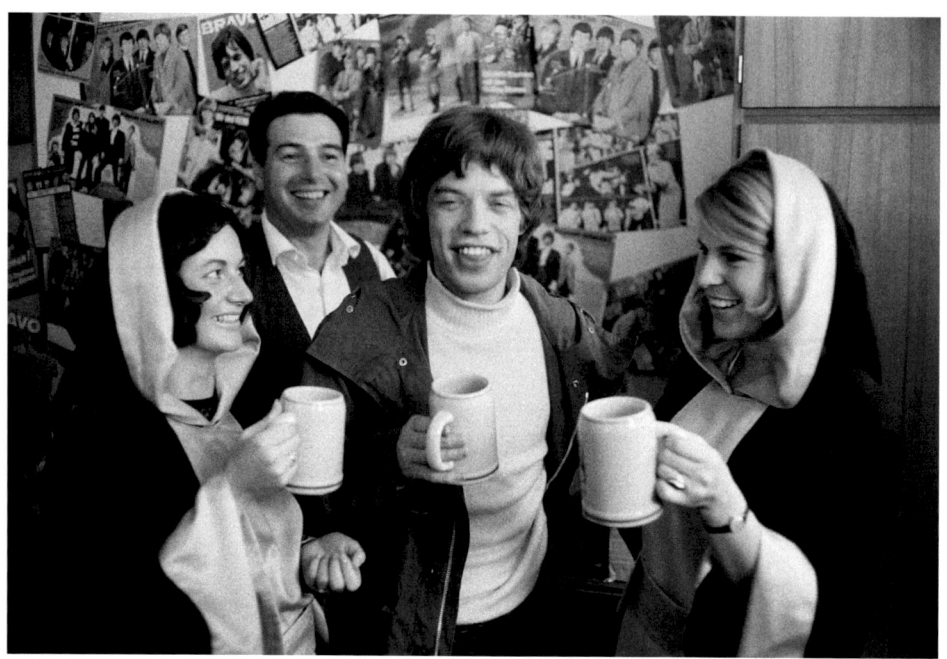

Bent Rej

All smiles in Munich on 14 September 1965 at a reception hosted by *Bravo* magazine. The visit to Munich was eventful in many ways, not least for the arrival of Anita Pallenberg backstage at Munich's Circus-Krone-Bau. Brian was instantly smitten with Pallenberg, who became a permanent fixture in the Stones community from then on.

"This photographer asked if I wanted to come backstage, it was in some bierhaus *in Munich. I didn't really know who was in the band, or their names – not even Brian Jones. But he could speak German, so I ended up talking with him all night."* Anita Pallenberg, *Mojo* magazine, Rolling Stones special issue, 2003

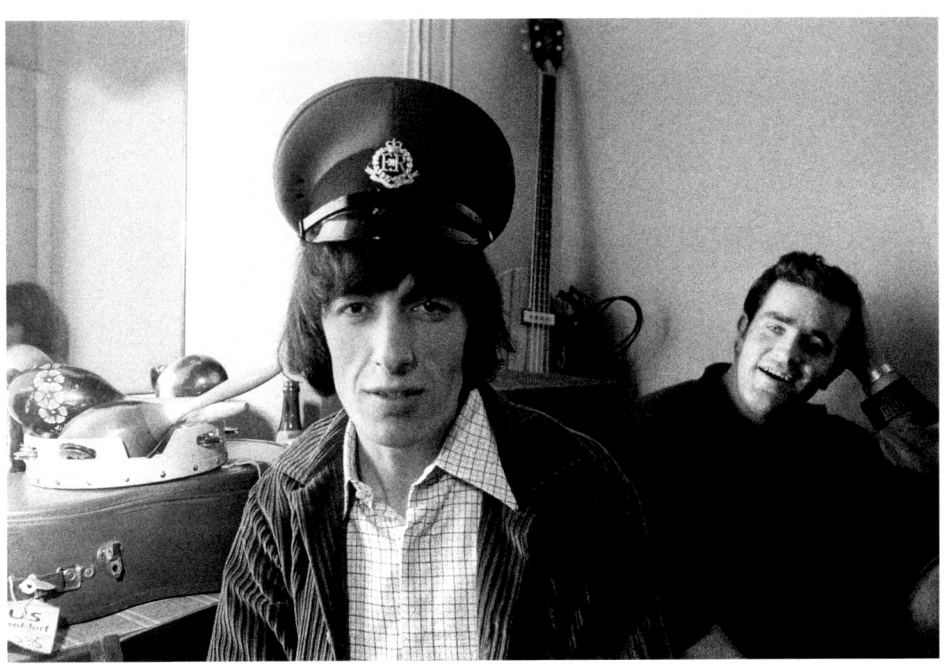

Bent Rej

Bill shares a joke with the Stones' sixth member, Ian "Stu" Stewart, backstage in Münster, Germany, 11 September 1965.
"He didn't get any rest. In those first two or three years we were working 300 days of the year, sometimes doing three or four things each day.

Morning, photo sessions with the girlie magazines or interviews for Melody Maker, Disc *and all that sort of stuff."* Bill Wyman on Ian Stewart, in Bill Wyman, *Stu*, 2013

Bent Rej

The readers of Germany's *Bravo* magazine wanted to give an award to the Stones for their achievements during 1965. The band was notoriously difficult to pin down, so *Bravo*'s editor Thomas Beyl flew to Copenhagen on 5 April 1966 to present the band with their trophies. Formalities over, Keith and Charlie's faces reveal little other than weariness.

Gered Mankowitz

Sessions for *Aftermath* mostly took place at night. The Stones committed a dozen songs to tape during their time at RCA's Hollywood studios, including "Mother's Little Helper", "Goin' Home" and future single "19th Nervous Breakdown".

"Keith and Mick acted as musical directors until the others got the gist of the numbers and then it was a free-for-all with everyone chipping in with their own particular ideas." Kevin Swift, *Beat Instrumental*, February 1966

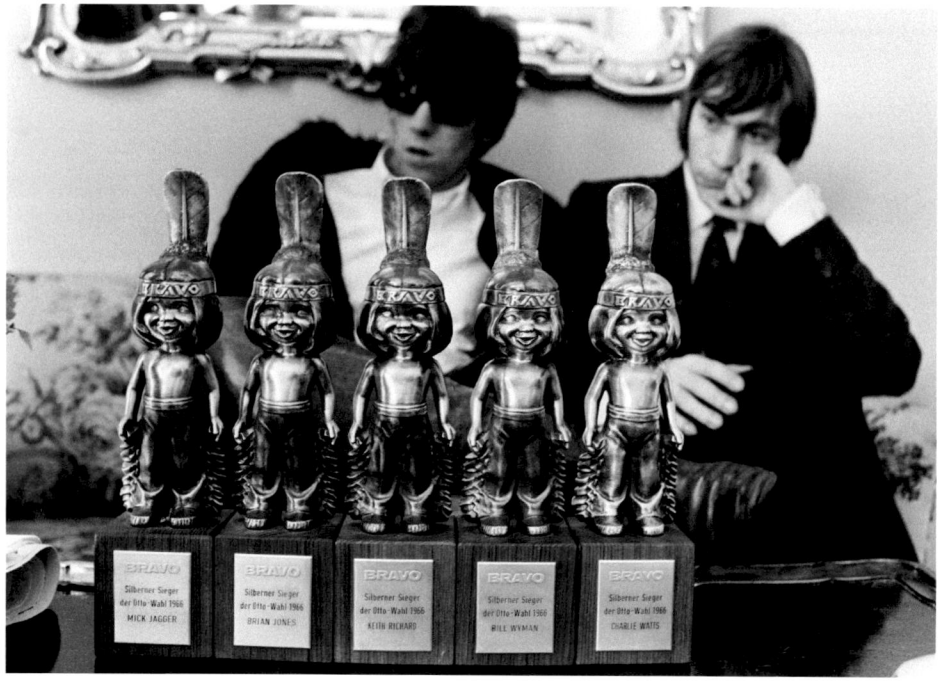

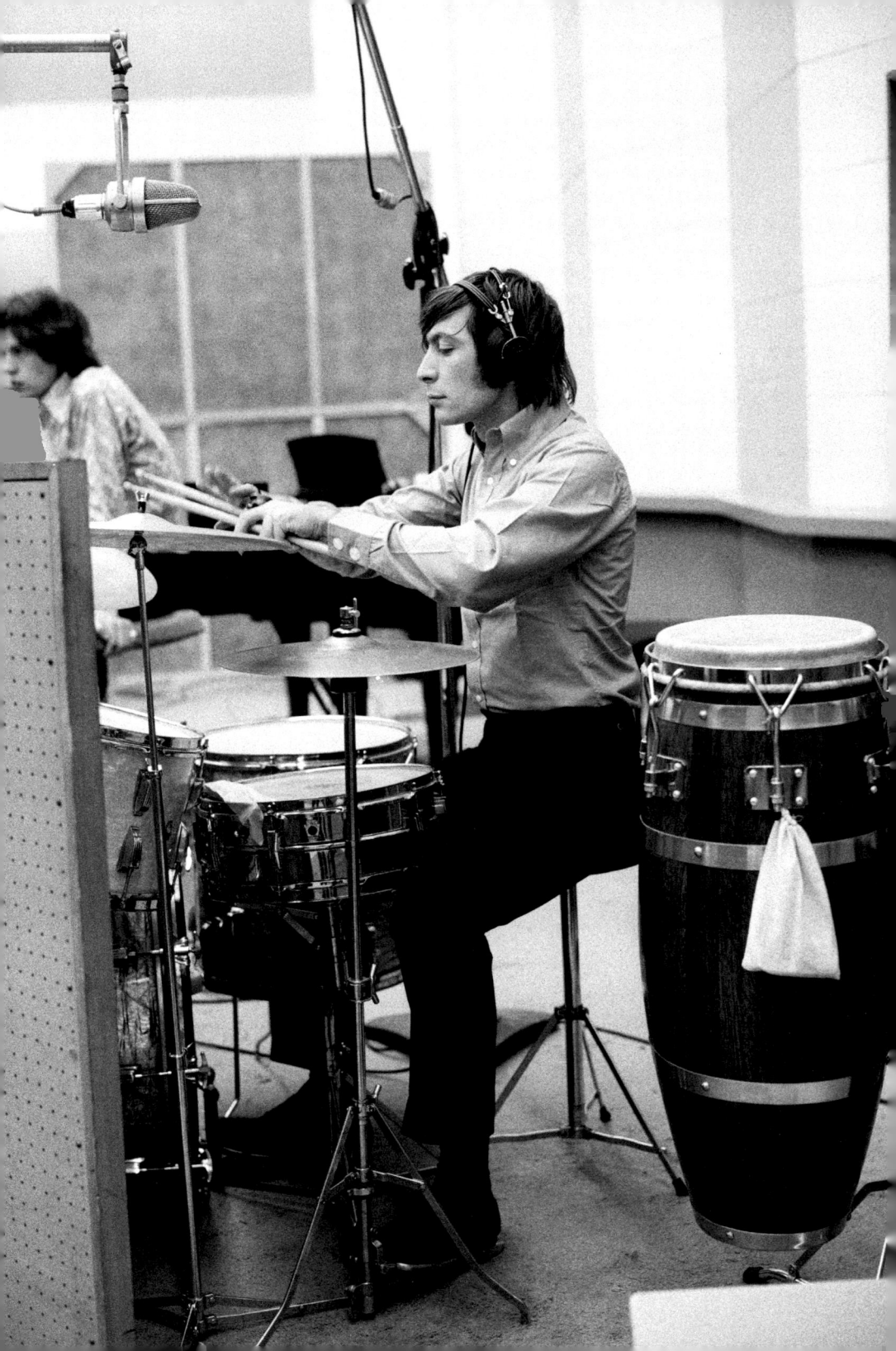

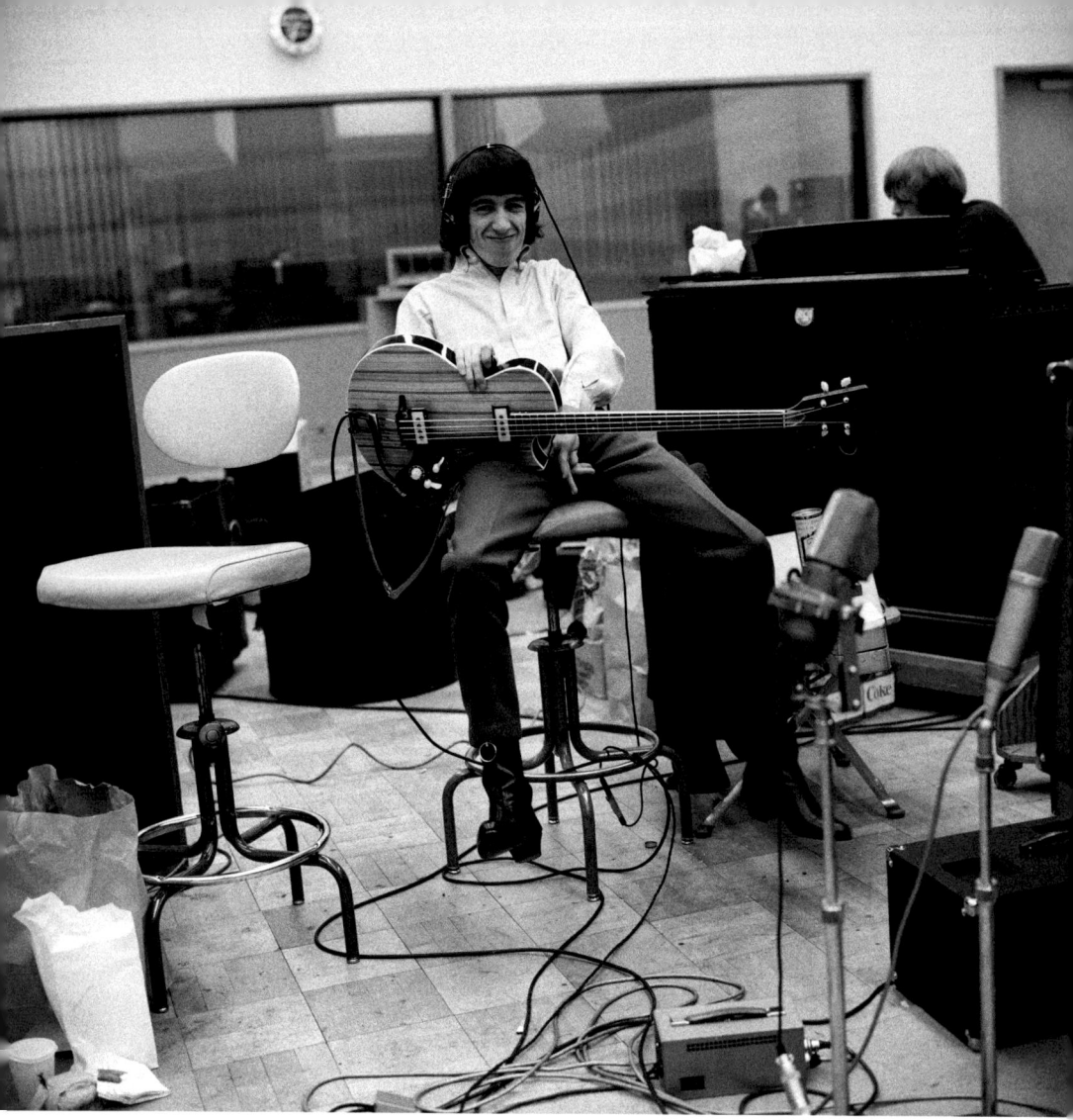

Gered Mankowitz
Bill at RCA's Hollywood studios in December
1965, giving the photographer what he liked
to call "the willy signal".

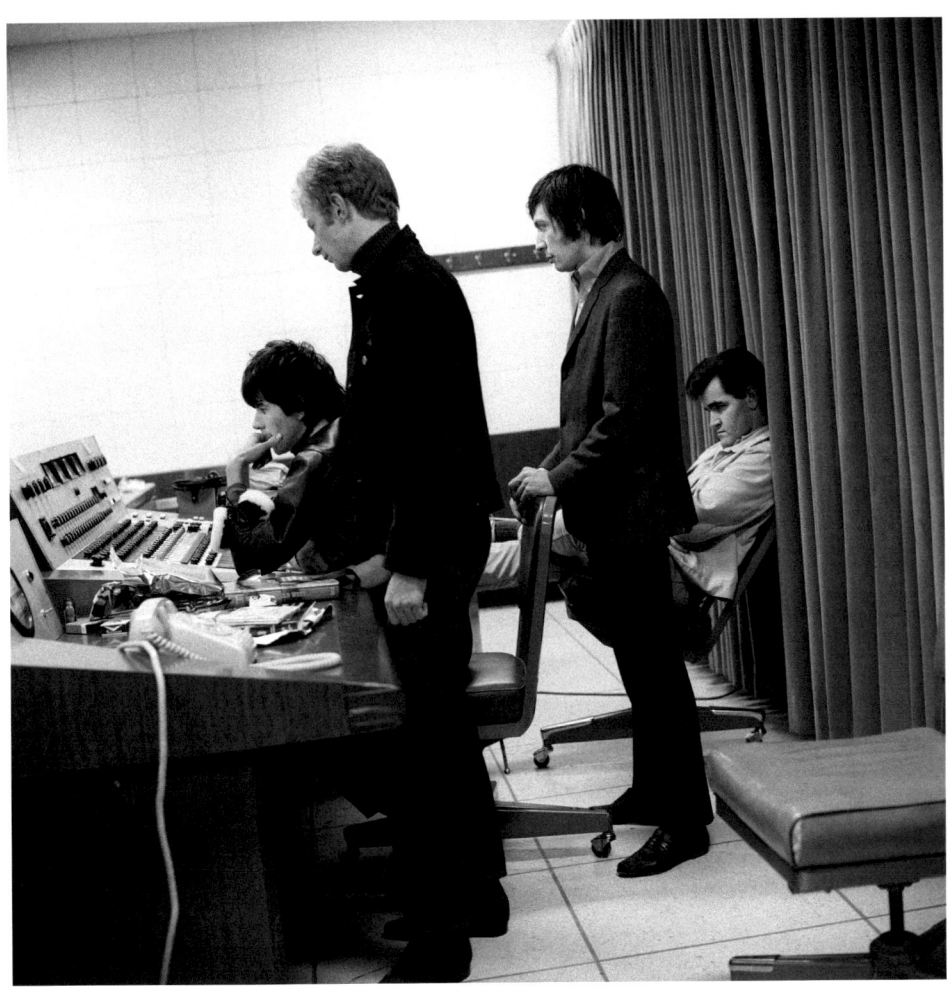

Gered Mankowitz
With Andrew Loog Oldham maintaining a heavy creative presence at RCA studios, sessions for *Aftermath* were often long, but nonetheless hugely productive.

"*Mick and Keith write about the things that are happening. Everyday things. Their songs reflect the world about them. I think it's better than anything they have done before.*" Andrew Loog Oldham, *Disc And Music Echo*, April 1966

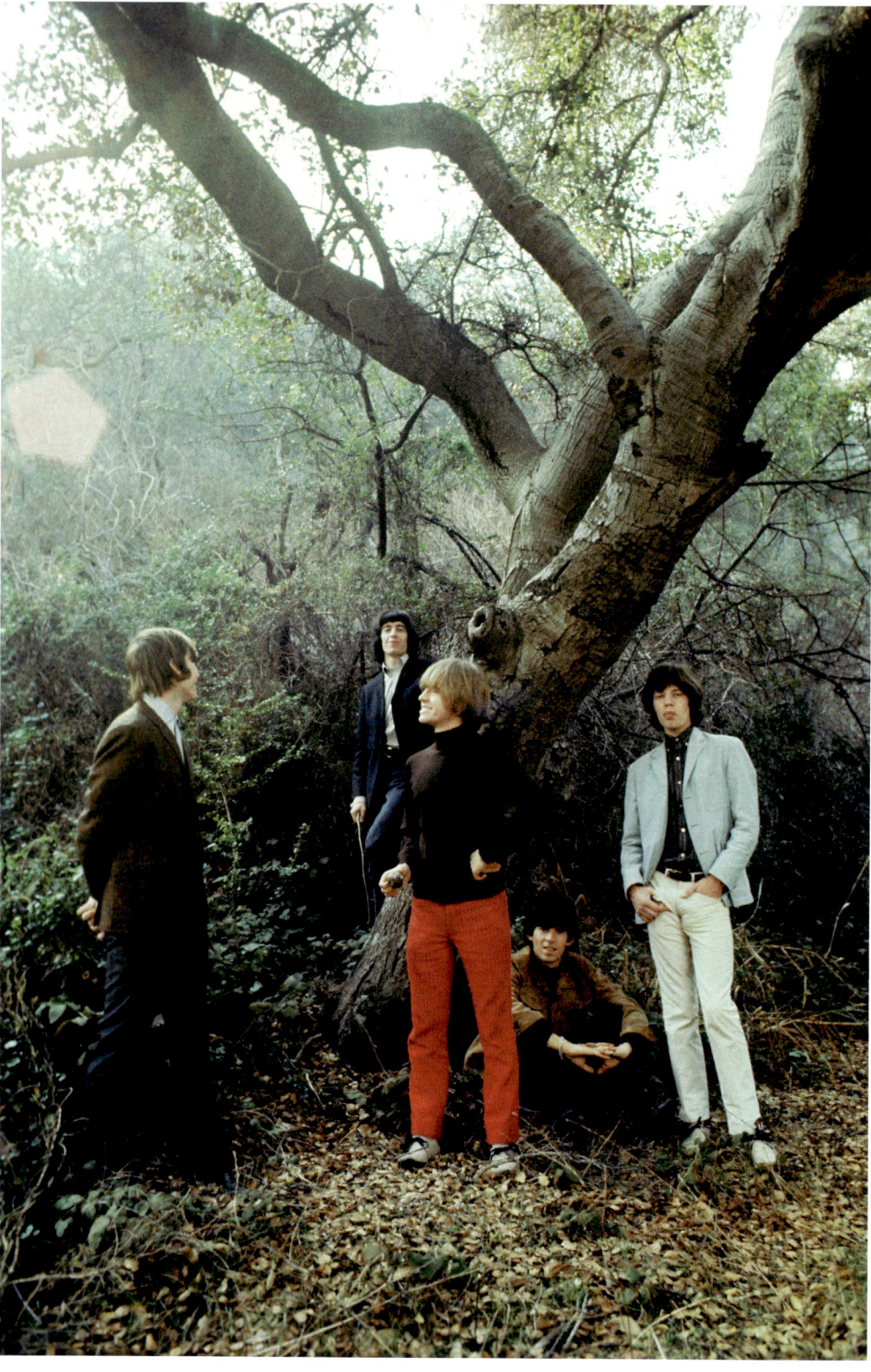

Guy Webster
On 7 December 1965, the group posed for photographs at Franklin Canyon Park in Beverly Hills, California. Some of the images taken that day would later adorn the front and back cover of the US version of the Stones' 1966 compilation album, *Big Hits* (*High Tide And Green Grass*).

Guy Webster
Just three days after the Stones' concert at
San Jose's Civic Auditorium on 4 December 1965,
the group enjoy the leafy Californian ambience.
Following the San Jose gig, Brian and Keith took
LSD during one of the Merry Pranksters' "Acid
Tests", held close to the San Jose concert venue.
The drug would have a profound effect on their
visual and aural senses.

PP. 128–129
Guy Webster
This unique 1965 shot of the Stones would
predate the band's flirtation with psychedelia –
a full year before assimilating with nature would
become a fashionable pursuit.

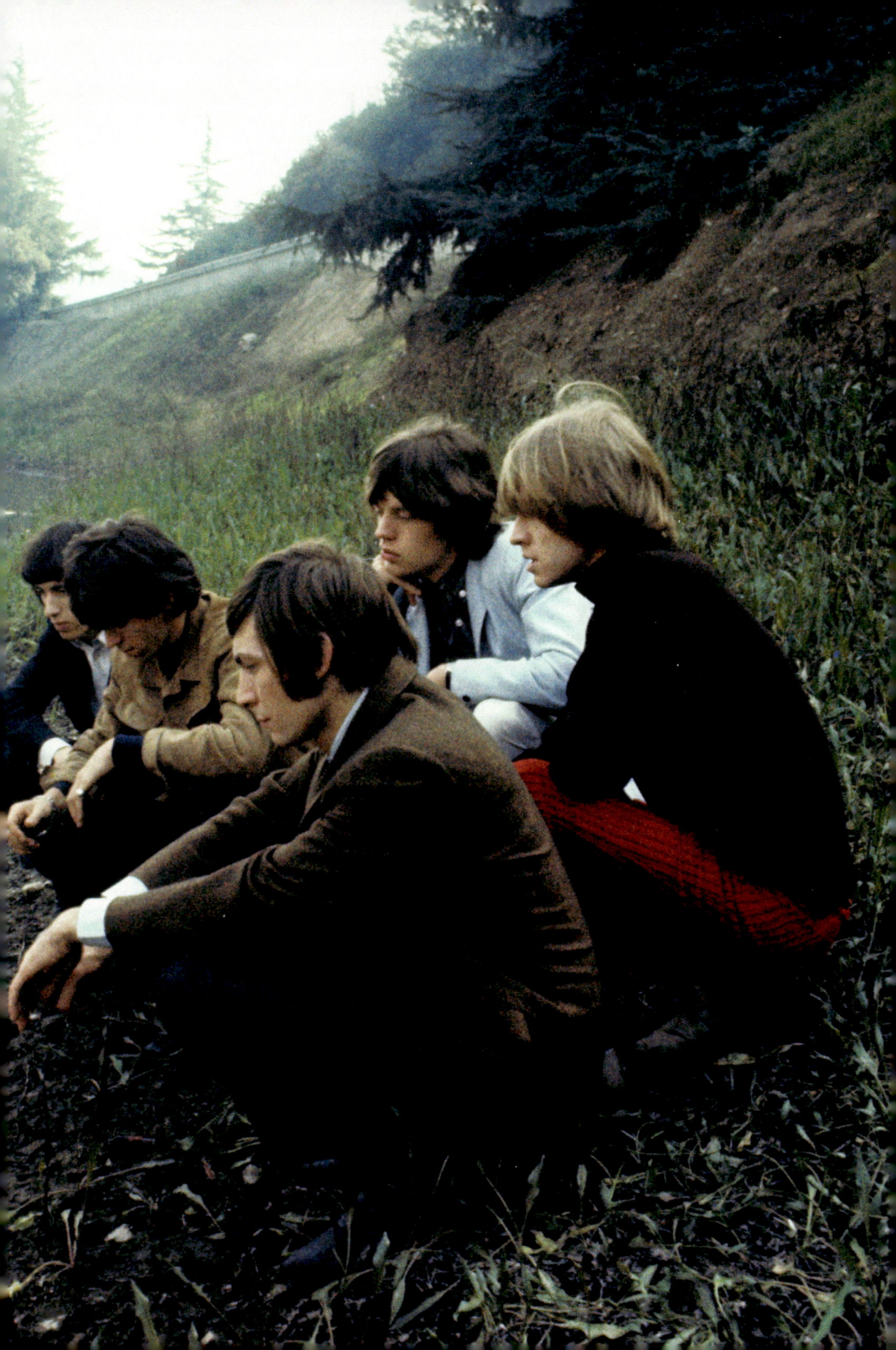

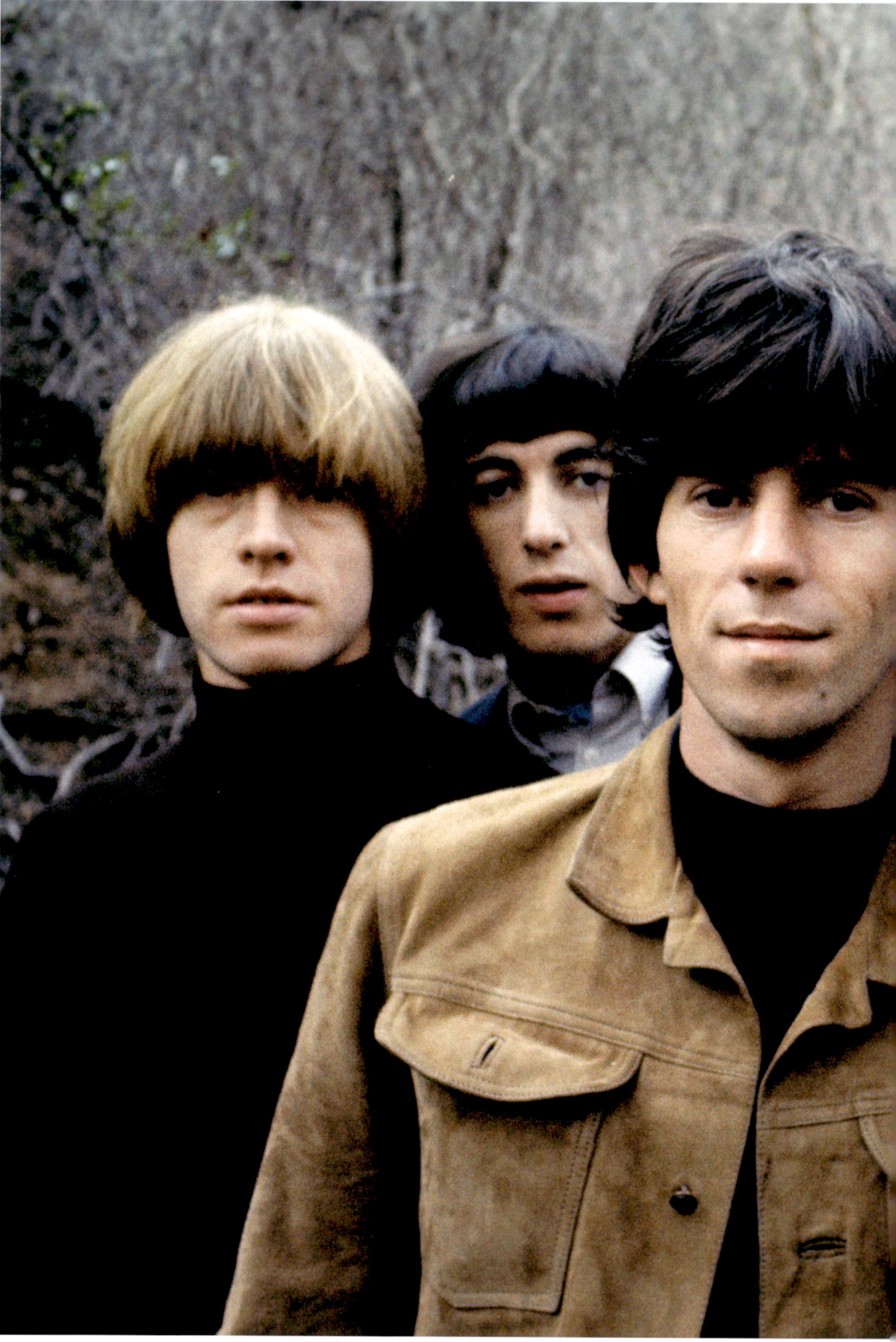

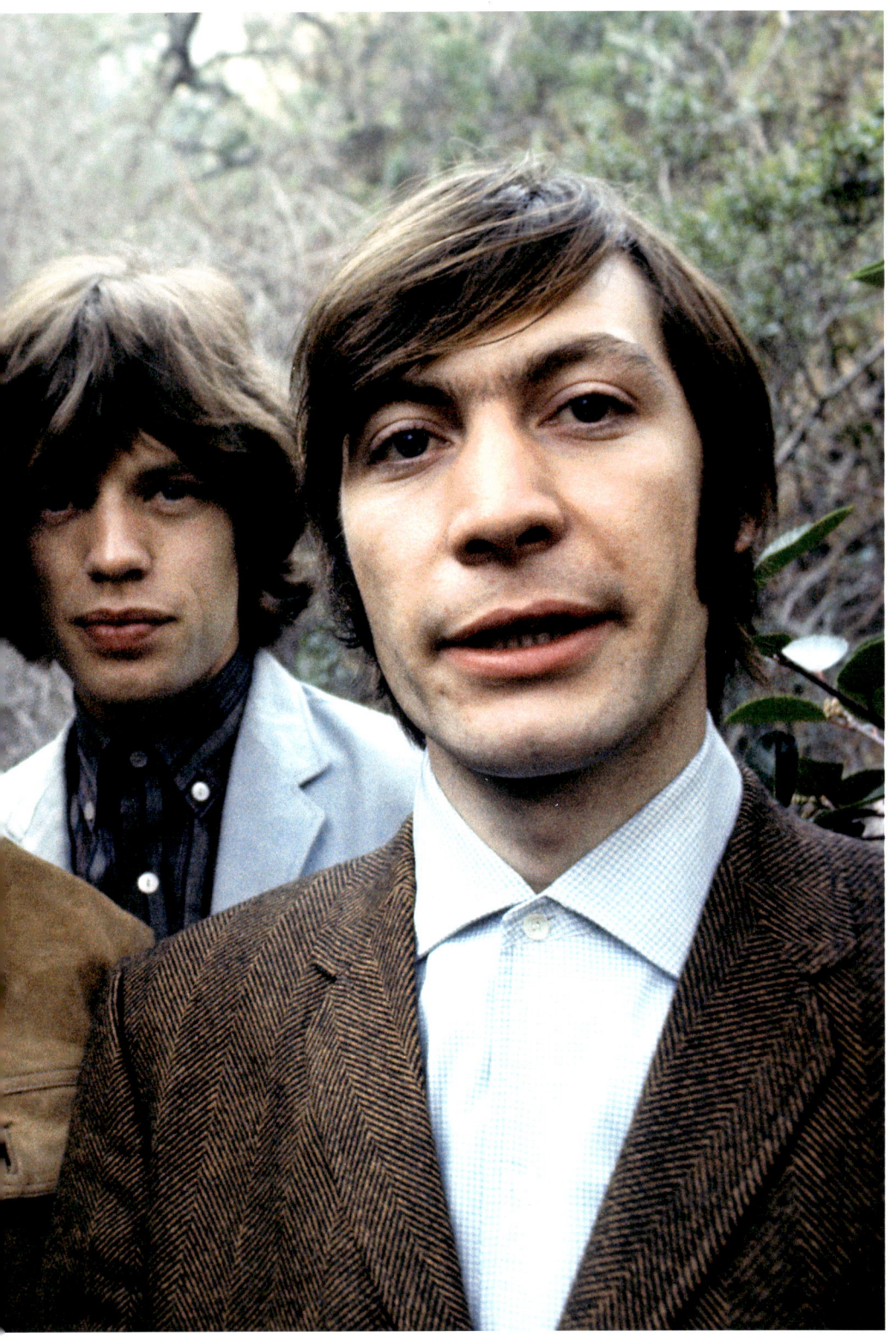

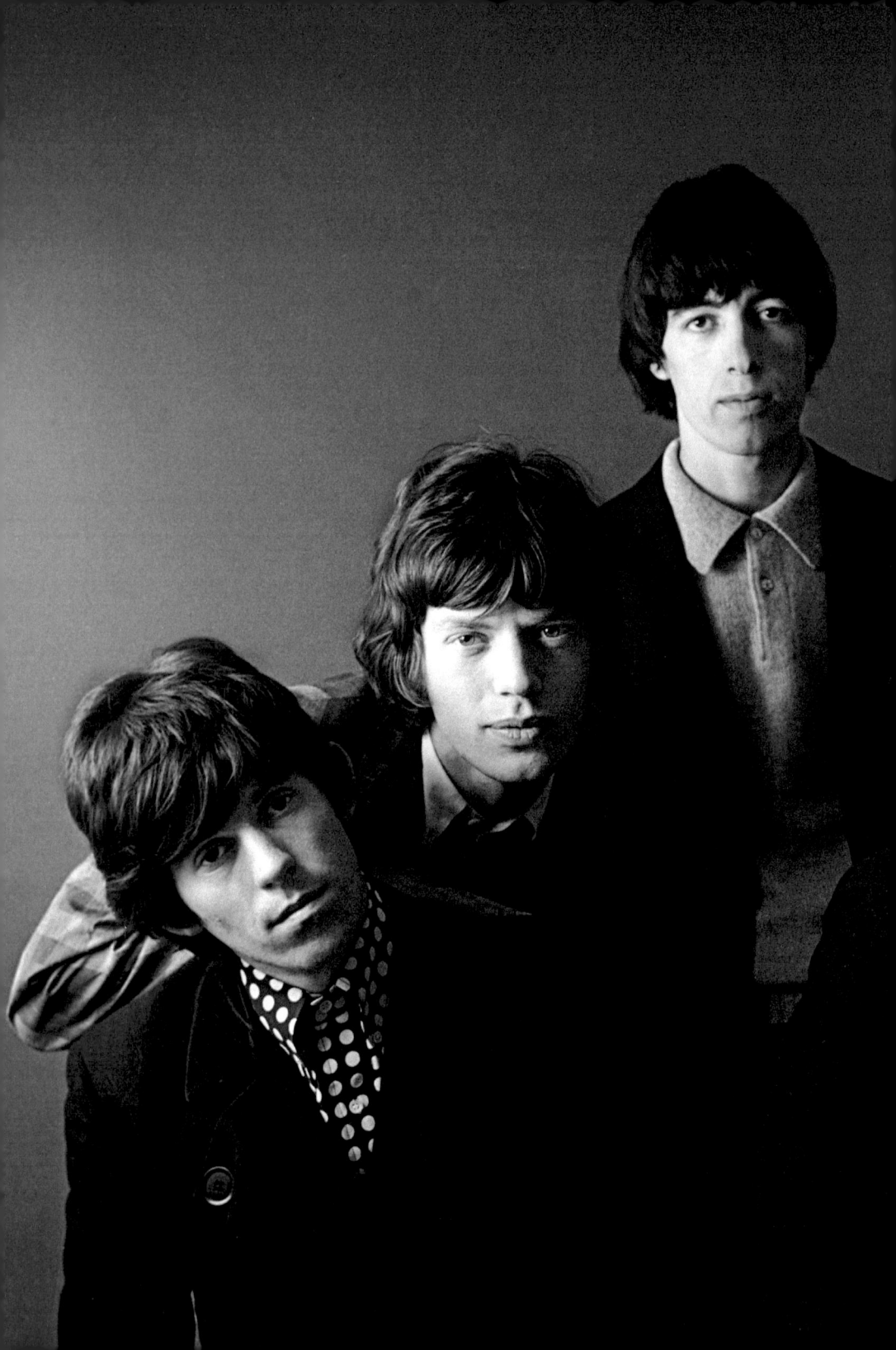

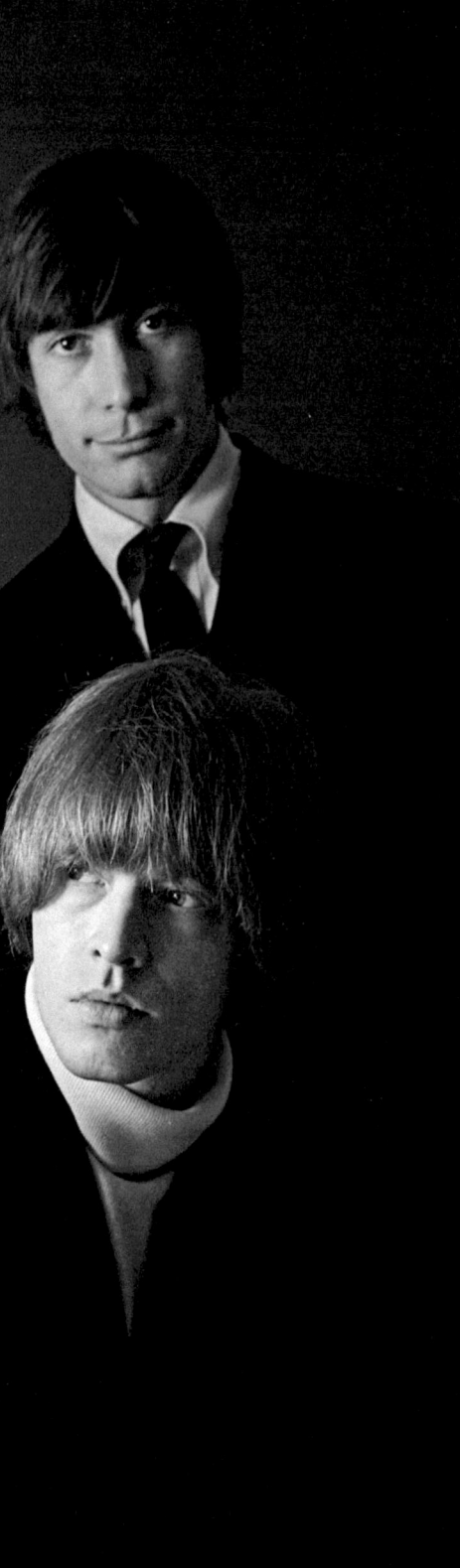

Guy Webster
The cover shot of the British version of *Aftermath*,
March 1965. Historic in that every track was
written by the Jagger/Richards partnership,
it included such classics as "Lady Jane" and
"Under My Thumb".
"We don't ask ourselves what is most commercial.
We simply say – 'we like this one best...' This is
probably the way Mozart wrote. He wrote for
himself, so do we. And it is a happy coincidence
that what we like should also be what our public
likes." Keith Richards, *New Musical Express*,
23 September 1966

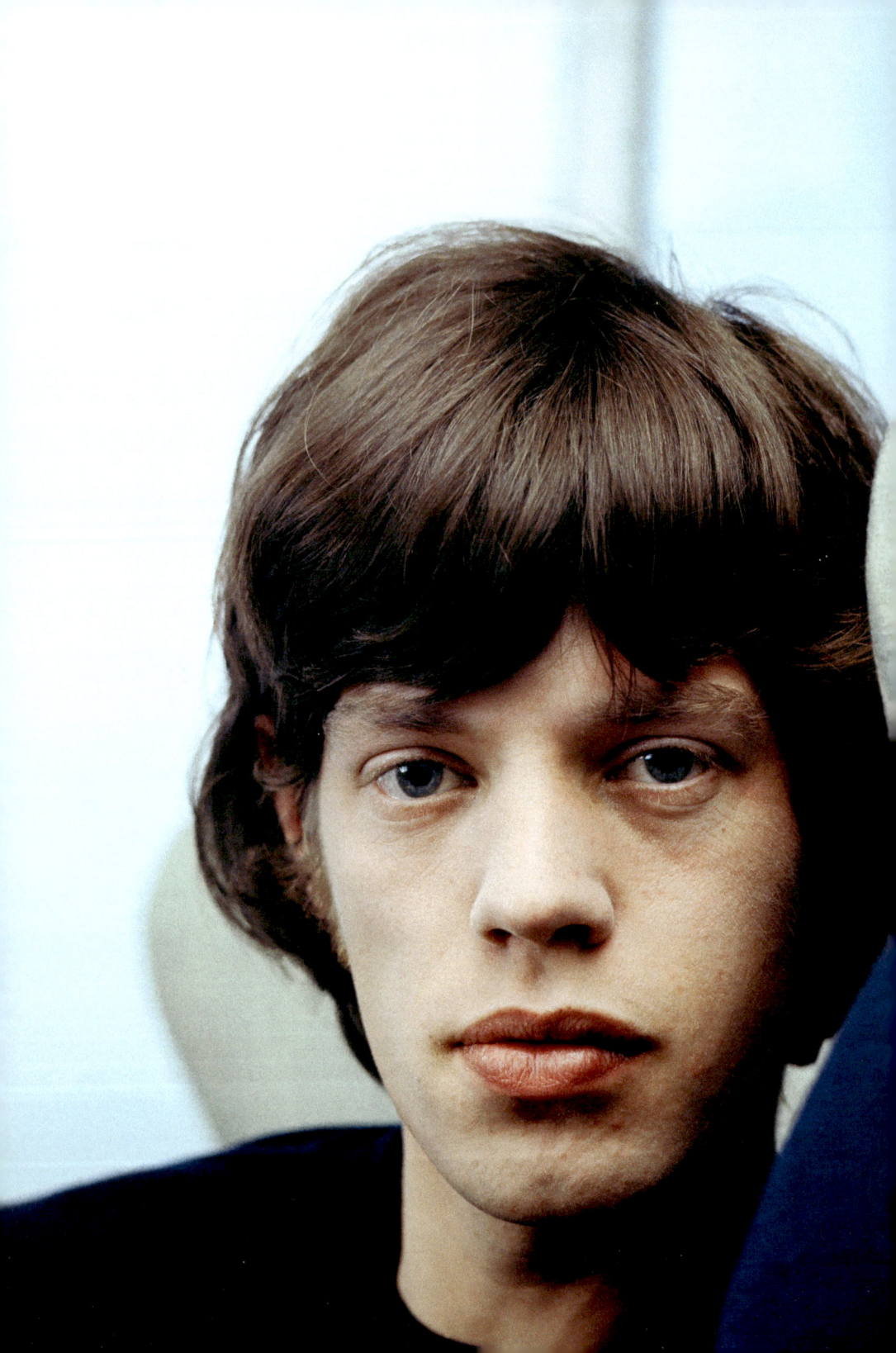

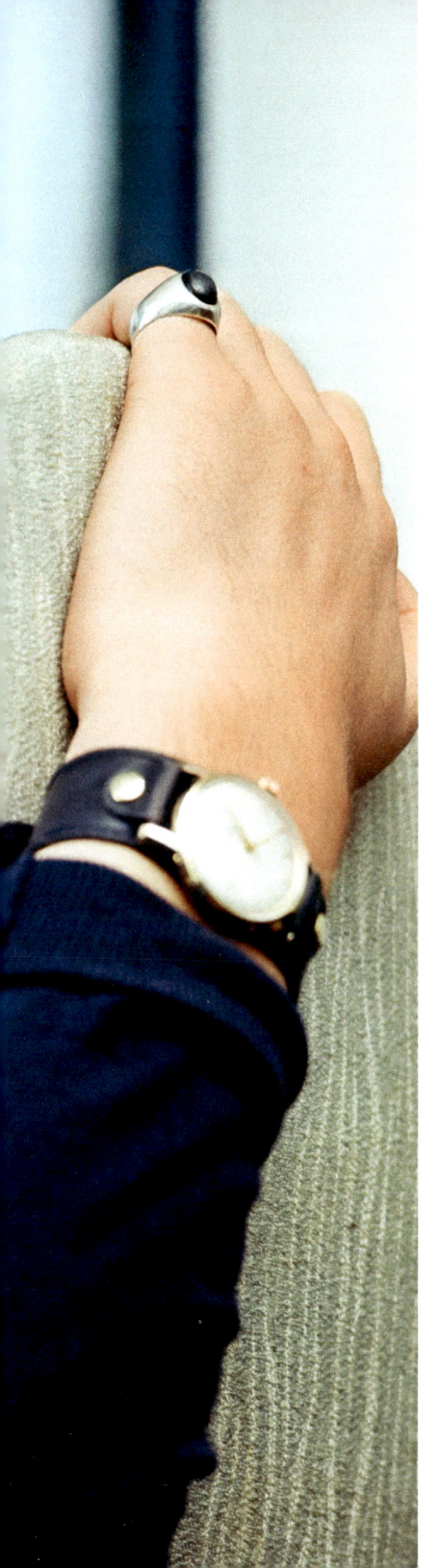

Bent Rej
At a press conference at Copenhagen's Royal Hotel, 29 March 1965.
"Everybody has their own moral code. I conduct myself as I think fit and what I do is my own affair ... Stars and celebrities should not try to set any level in morals. Who are we to say what is right and what is wrong?" Mick Jagger, *Melody Maker*, 30 January 1965

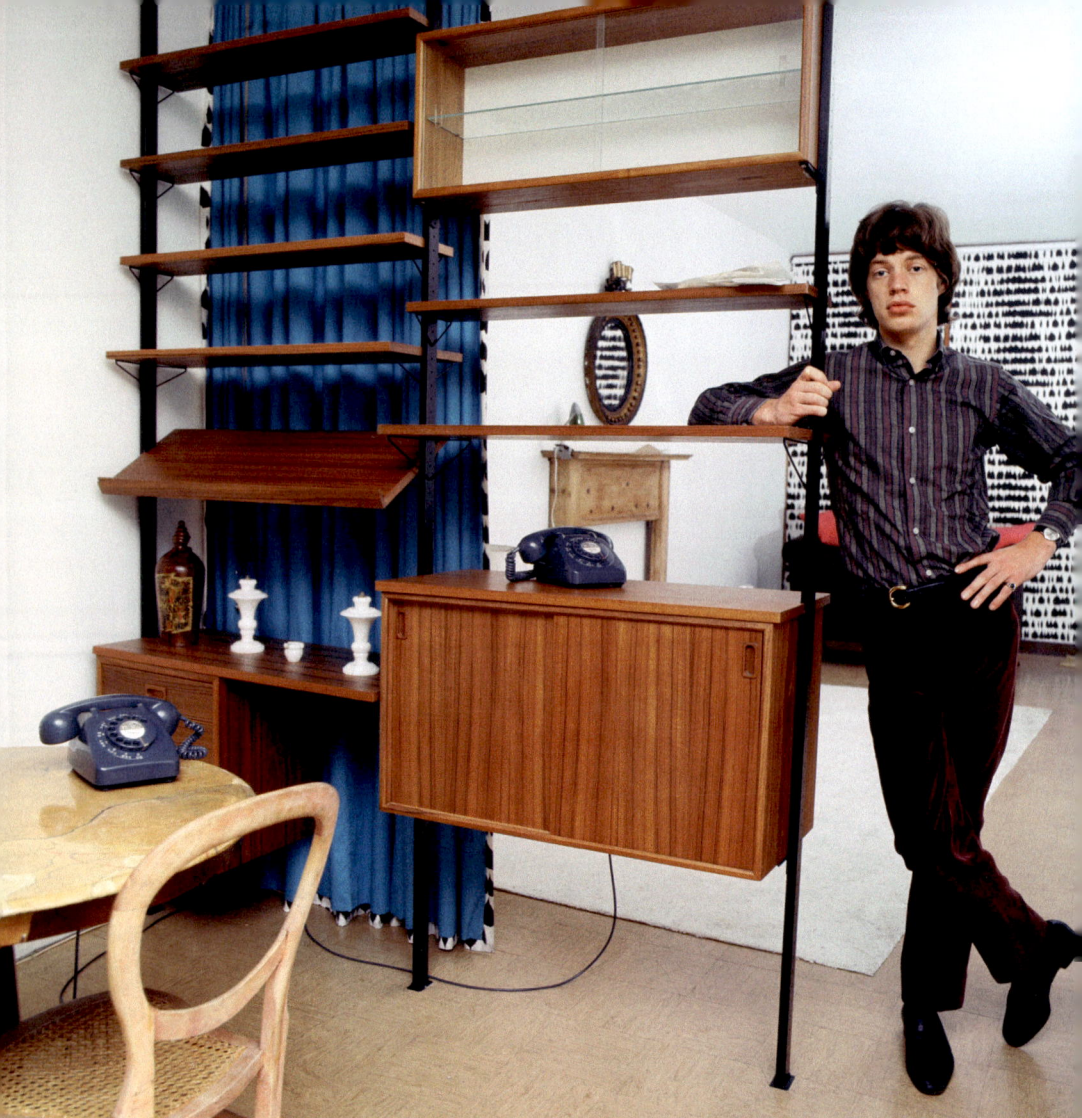

Bent Rej

Revelling in the freedom of his own space, Mick was occasionally happy to show trusted photographers around his distinctly bachelor pad in central London. The modest West End property at 13a Bryanstone Mews was a mere stone's throw from Oxford Street and convenient for his many activities, 1966.

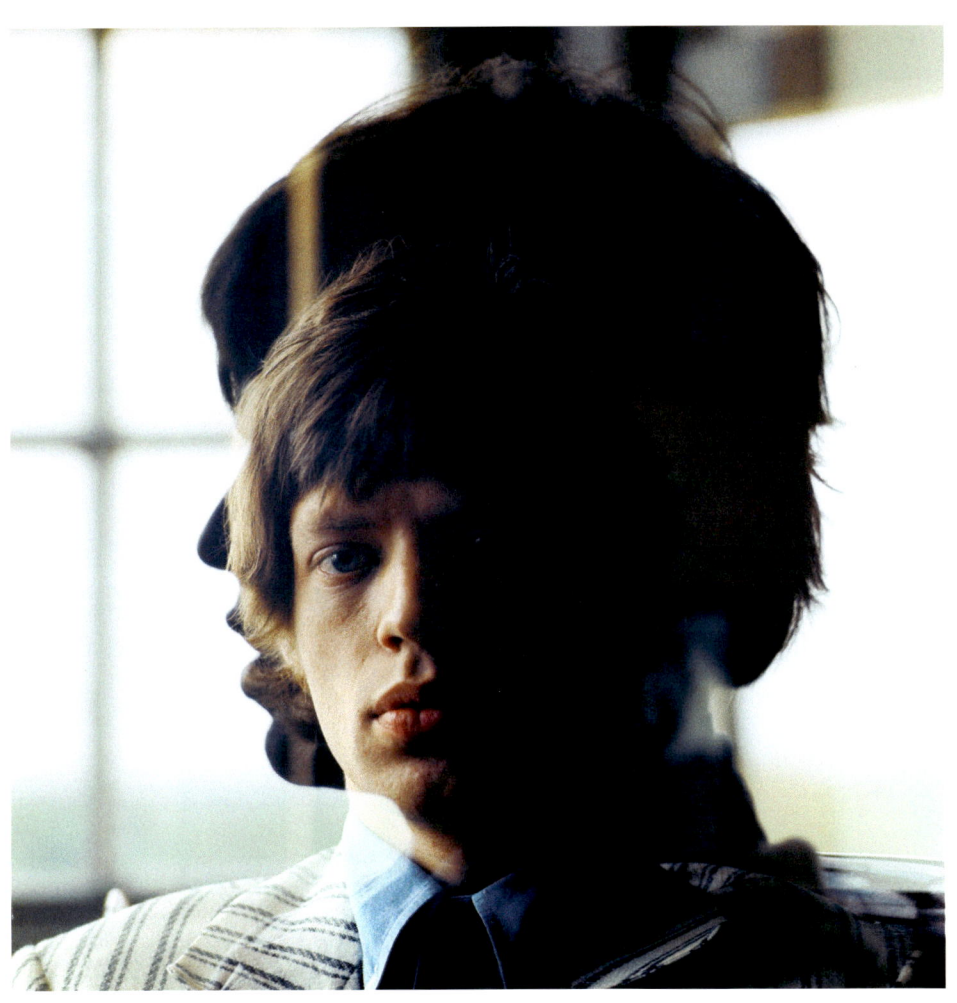

Bent Rej
London, September 1966.

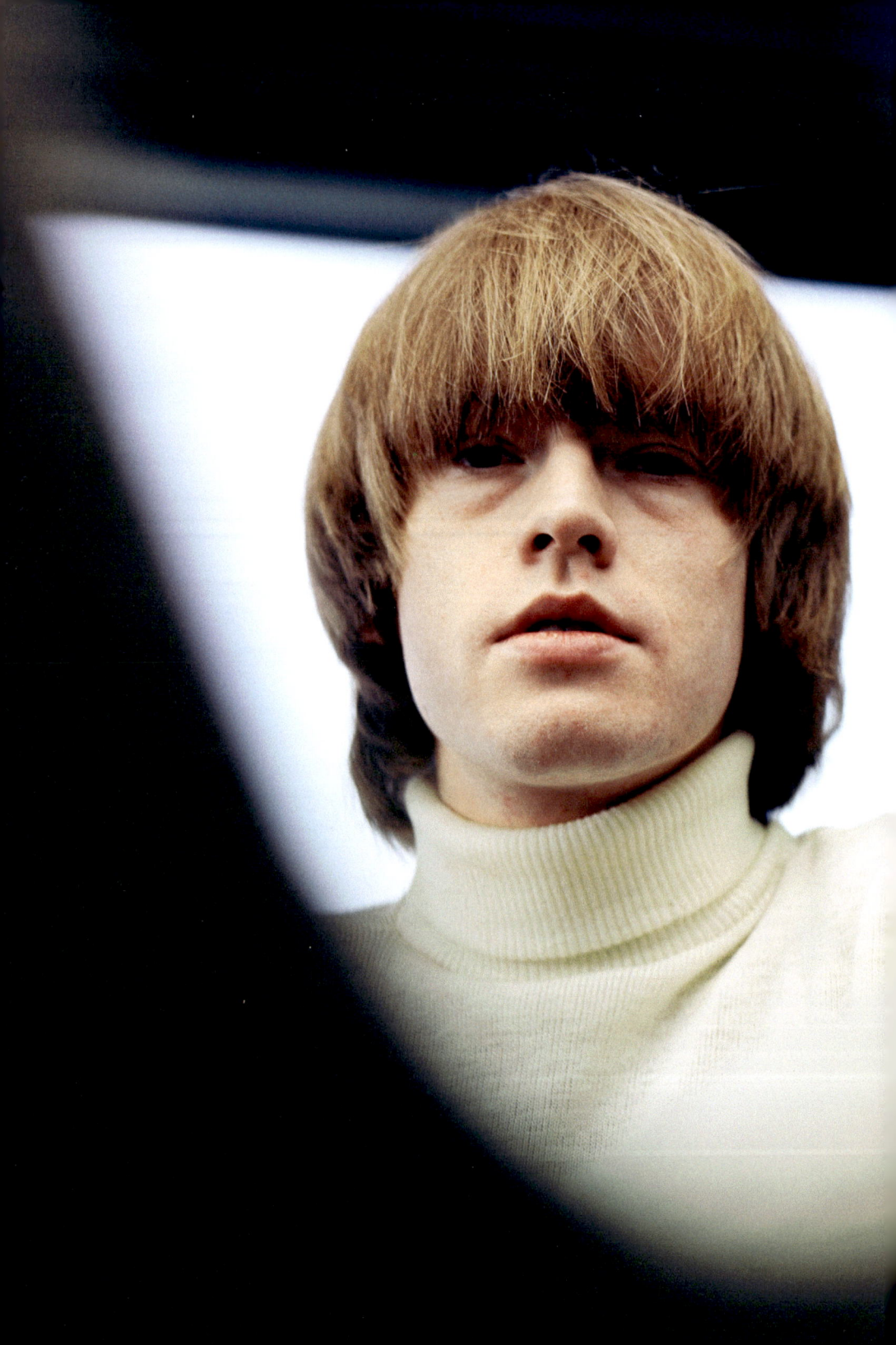

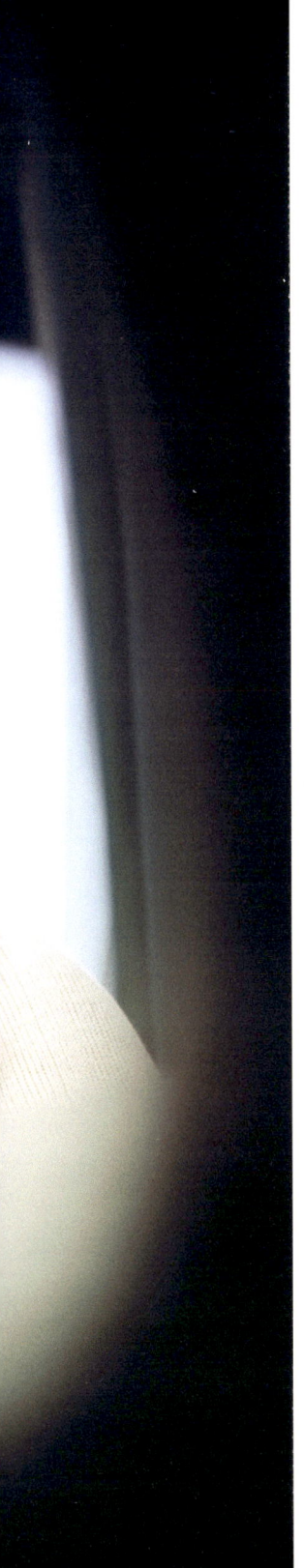

Bent Rej
The angelic-cum-demonesque Brian, at
Copenhagen's Royal Hotel, 29 March 1965.
*"We never deliberately went out to antagonise
parents – as many suspected – although I will
confess here and now we are not particularly
interested in pleasing parents. I don't think the
youngsters are any different now than in yester-
year."* Brian Jones, *Melody Maker*, 22 May 1965

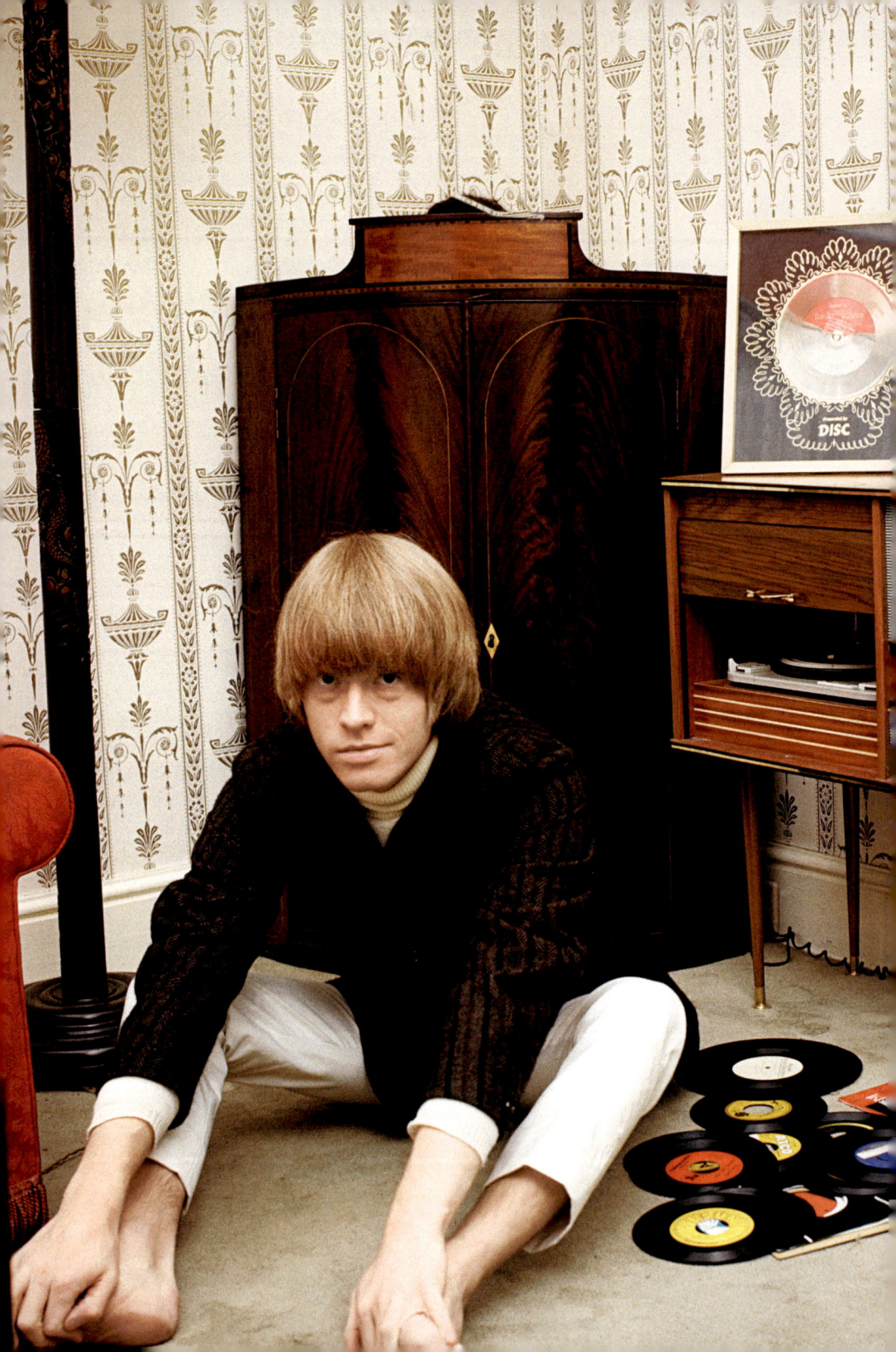

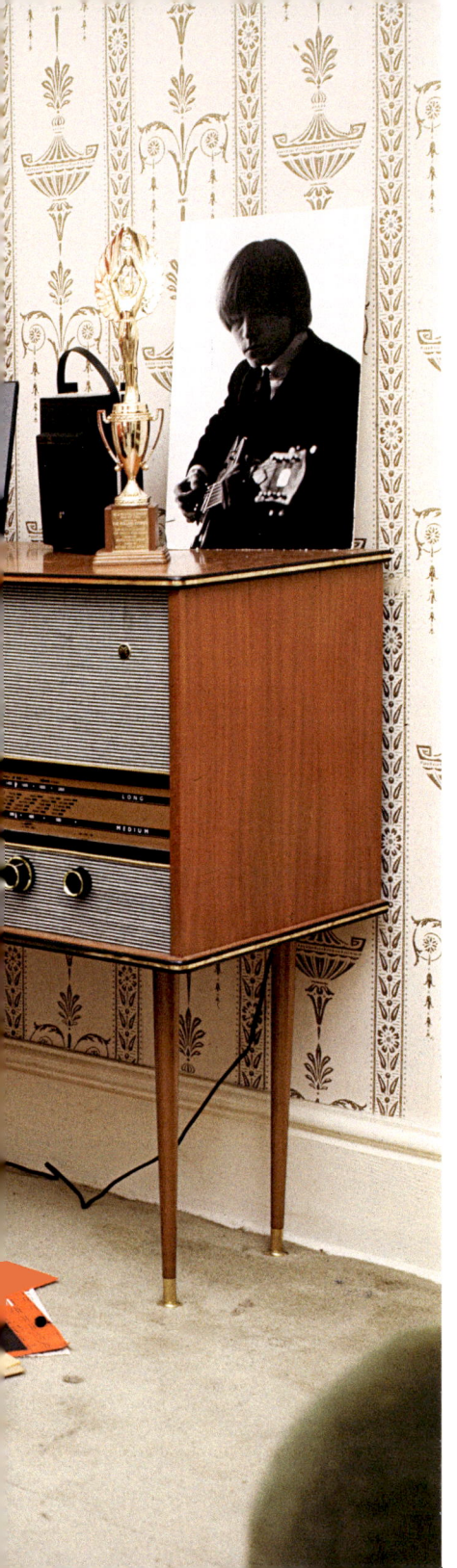

Bent Rej

During the Stones' rise to fame, Brian maintained a fairly peripatetic existence around central London but in 1965 he found time to establish a more permanent base in fashionable Chelsea, renting a property in Elm Park Mews for the best part of a year, April 1965.

"Brian's flat was like Aladdin's cave. Records, bottles, souvenirs, books and even a large amplifier were liberally scattered about the room. There seemed to be a struggle going on inside him. Something that wanted to break out in a creative form." Record Mirror, 12 February 1966

Bent Rej
At home in Chelsea with a 12-string guitar
in April 1965. Brian's Chelsea property was
beginning to assume the appearance of a music
emporium. In time, he'd outgrow the modest
dwelling and find a larger space just down the
road in Kensington to accommodate his library
of sound.

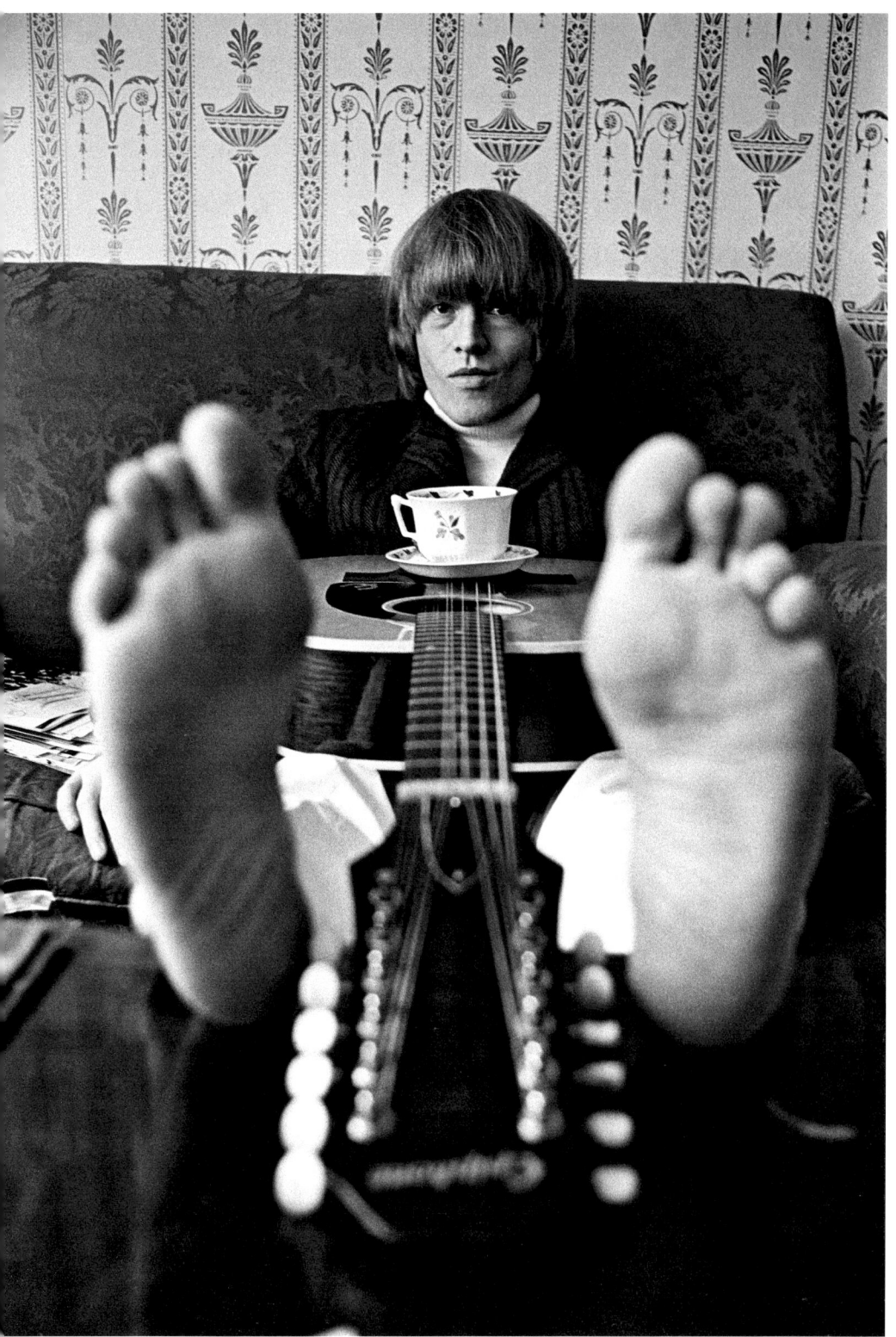

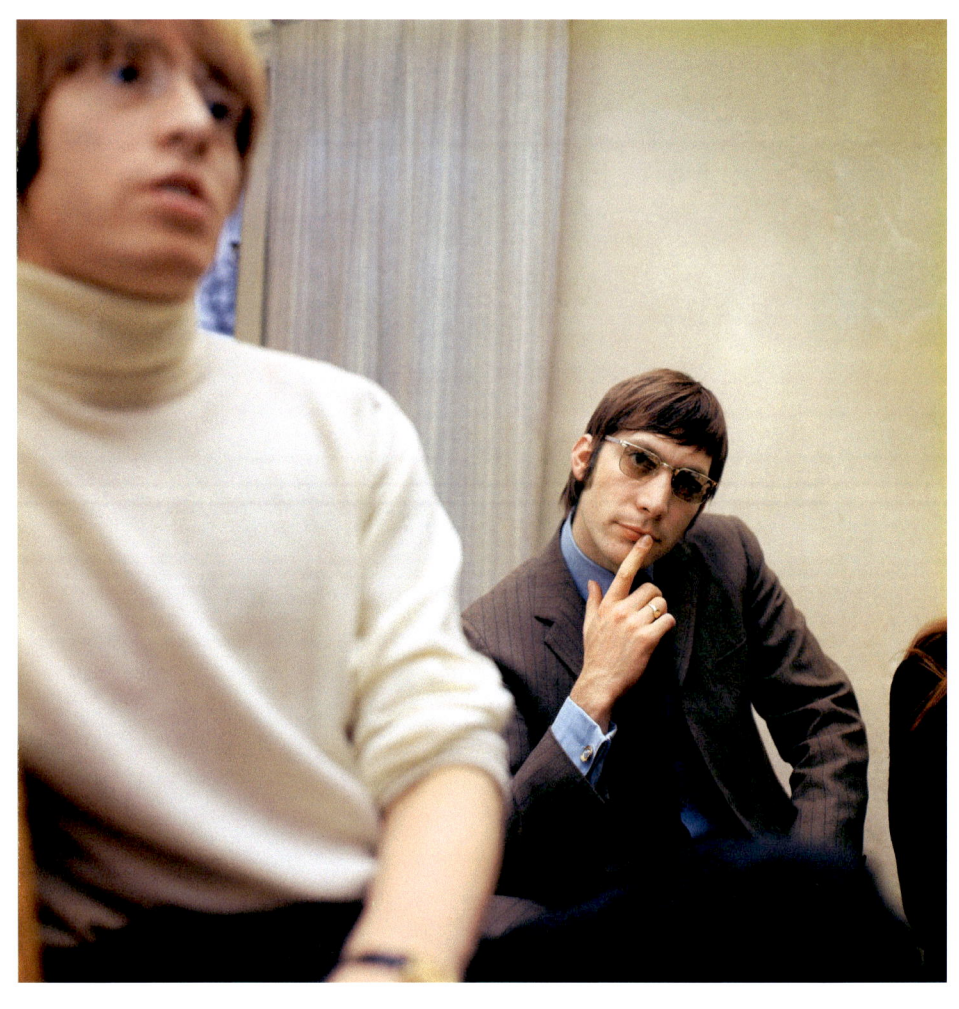

Bent Rej
Royal Hotel, Copenhagen, 29 March 1965.

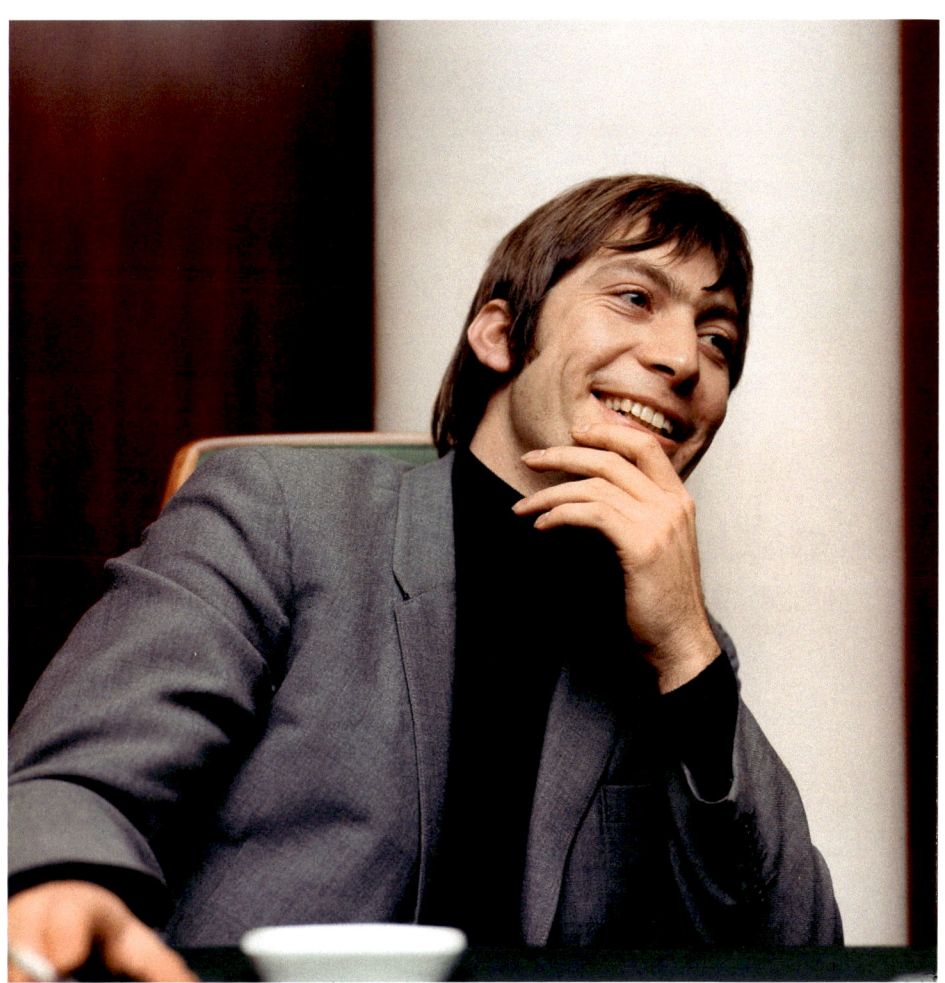

Bent Rej
Press conference in Copenhagen, 25 March 1965.
"We would not be human if we occasionally didn't   *together out of a suitcase most of the time*
have an odd word to say to one another. But there   *may make you feel a little edgy sometimes."*
has never been any major row between us. Living   Charlie Watts, *Melody Maker*, 30 January 1965

Bent Rej
Charlie captured at his modest flat in Ivor Court,
central London, in July 1965. The riches that were
being heaped on the Stones sat at odds with his
simple view of life.
"I suppose I find it difficult to justify to myself
everything I have, and because of this I'm at a
crossroads between grandeur and straight living.
Everything I have means a lot to me, of course,
but it's not really as good as a good laugh, is it?"
Charlie Watts, *Evening Standard*, 11 July 1969

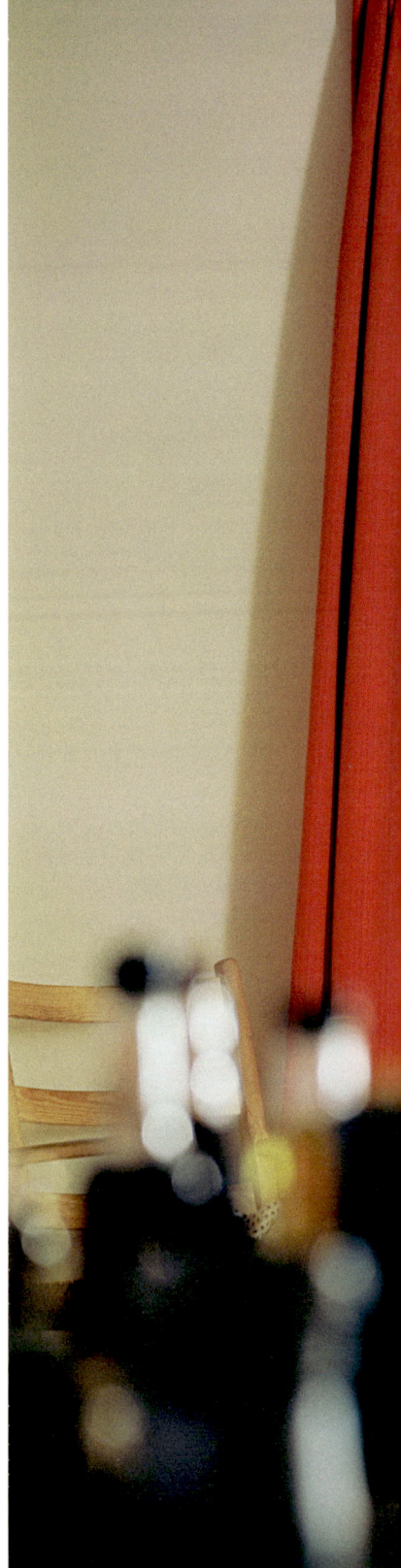

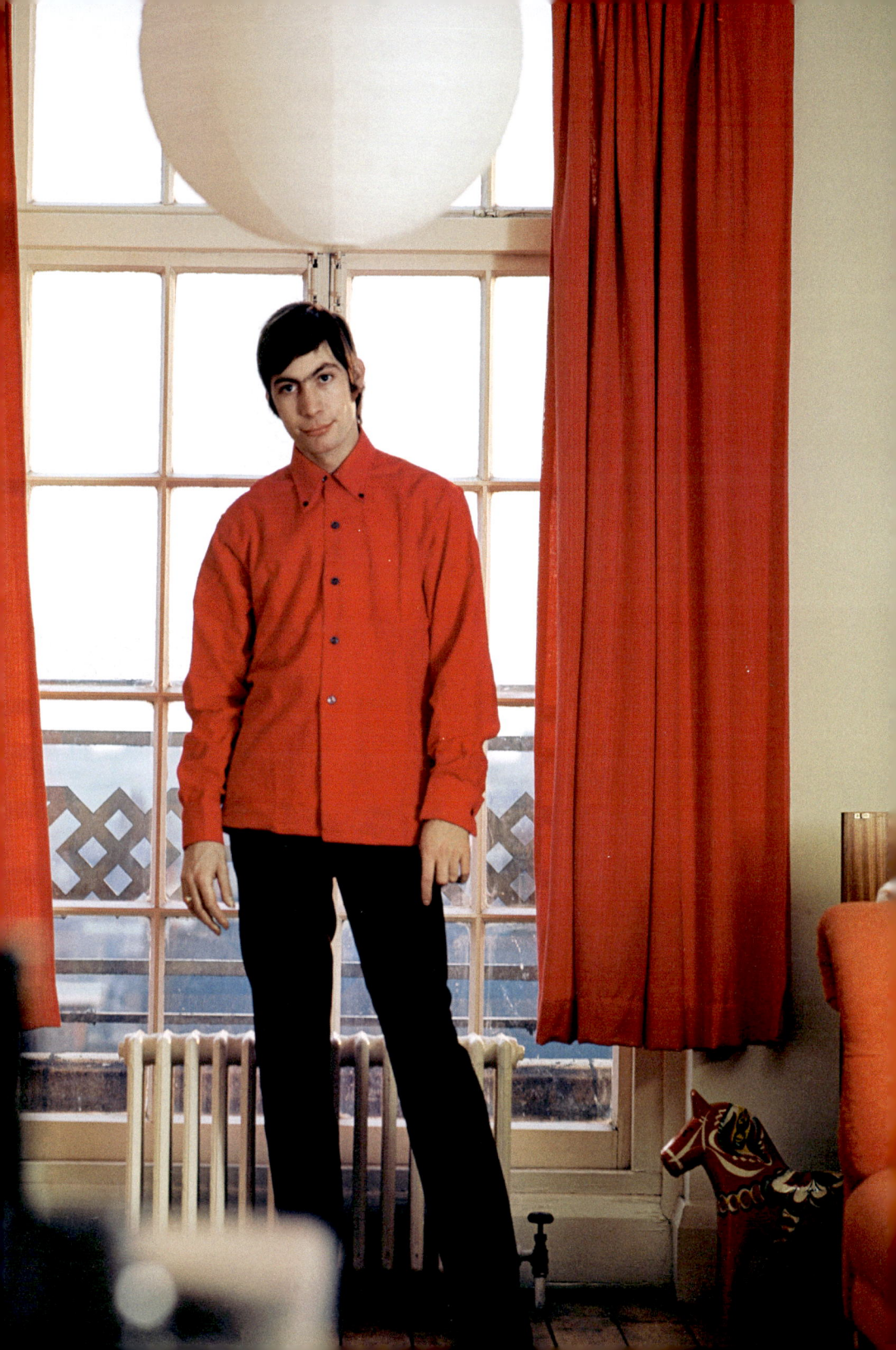

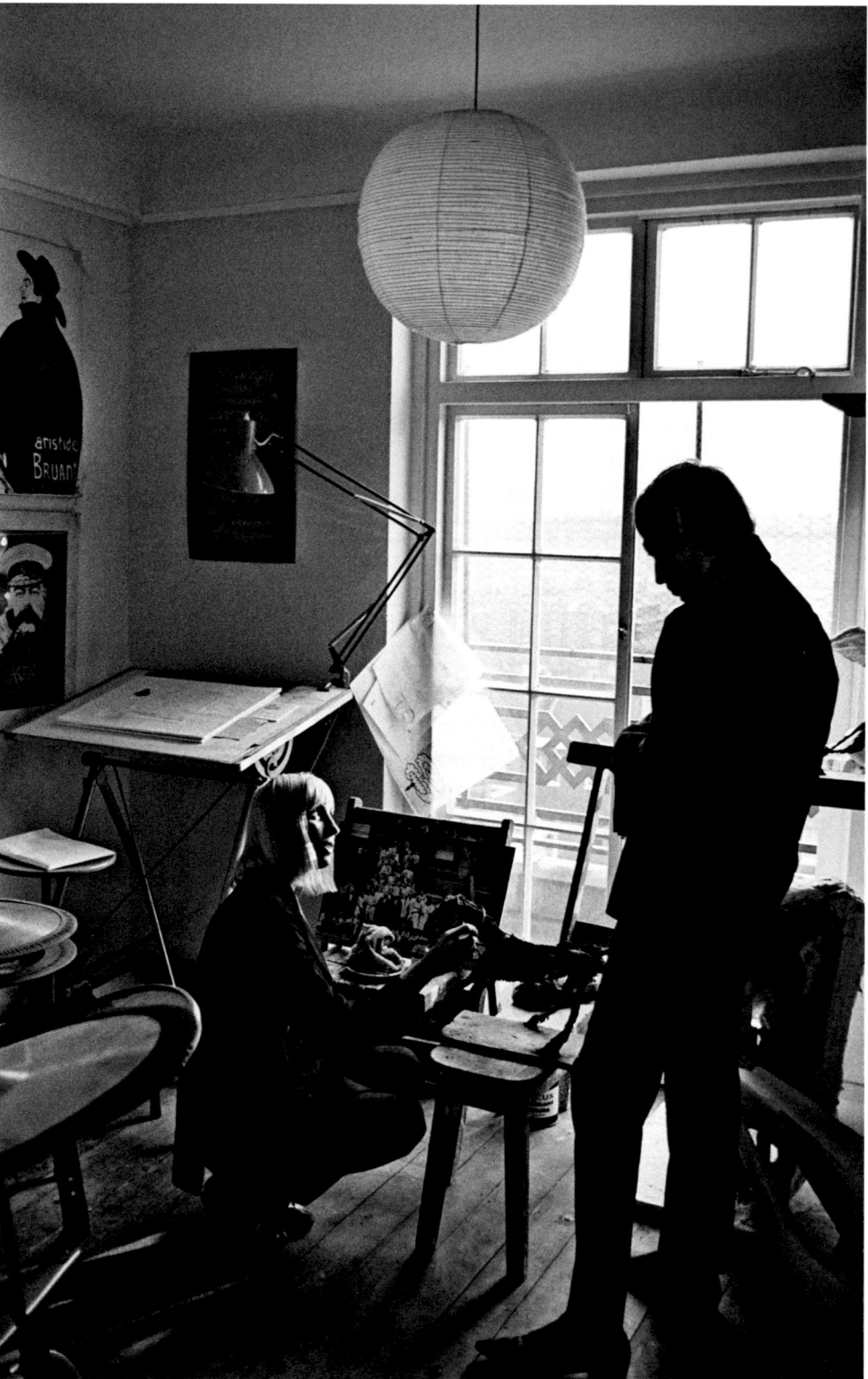

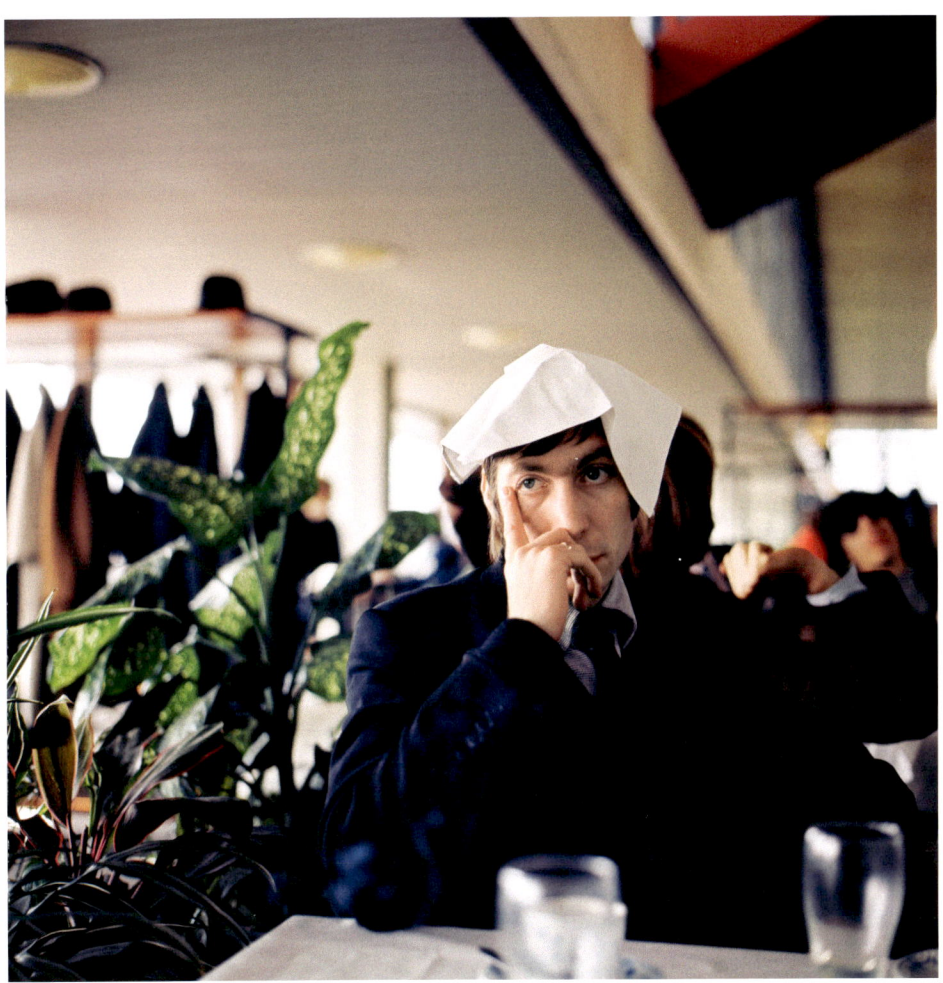

Bent Rej
With wife Shirley at their flat in central London, 1965.
"Whenever Charlie settles down with his records, Shirley settles down to her art. She will go into her studio to work on her sculptures. So far she hasn't tried to live from being a sculptress; all of her pieces of modern art go to friends and family – or *stay at home. It's because they not only love each other, but they also love art."* Bent Rej, *The Rolling Stones: In The Beginning*, 2006

Bent Rej
After lunch at the Hotel Marina, Copenhagen, 26 June 1965.

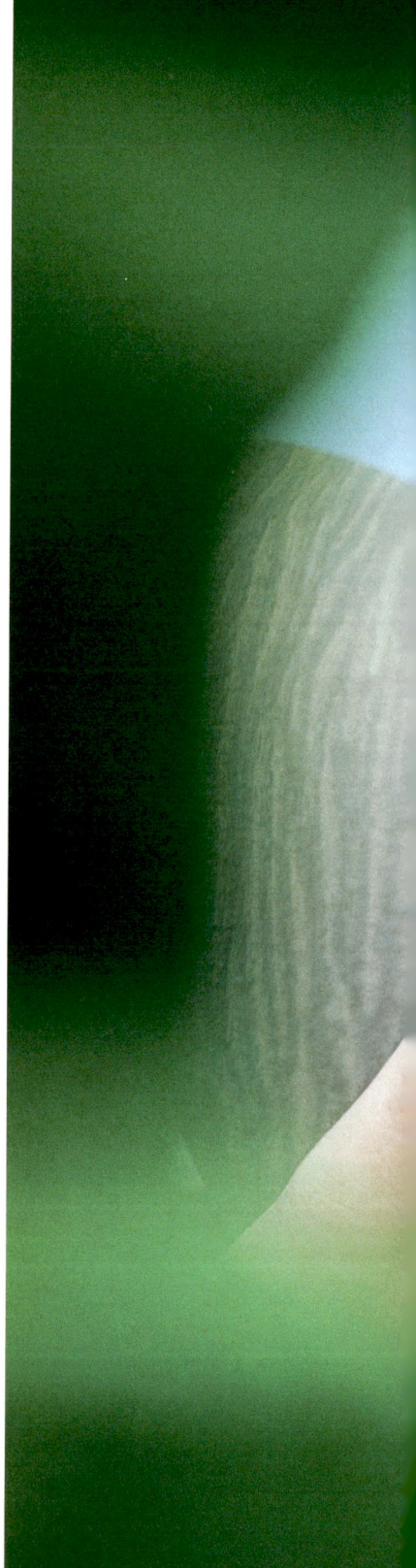

Bent Rej
Royal Hotel, Copenhagen, 26 March 1965.
*"When a reporter or interviewer gets the impres-
sion that I'm being sullen or unhelpful, it upsets
me; for the reason there are a hundred and
one things on my mind about my music while
he is talking to me. I'm one of those people
who just can't make small talk."* Charlie Watts,
Rave, December 1965

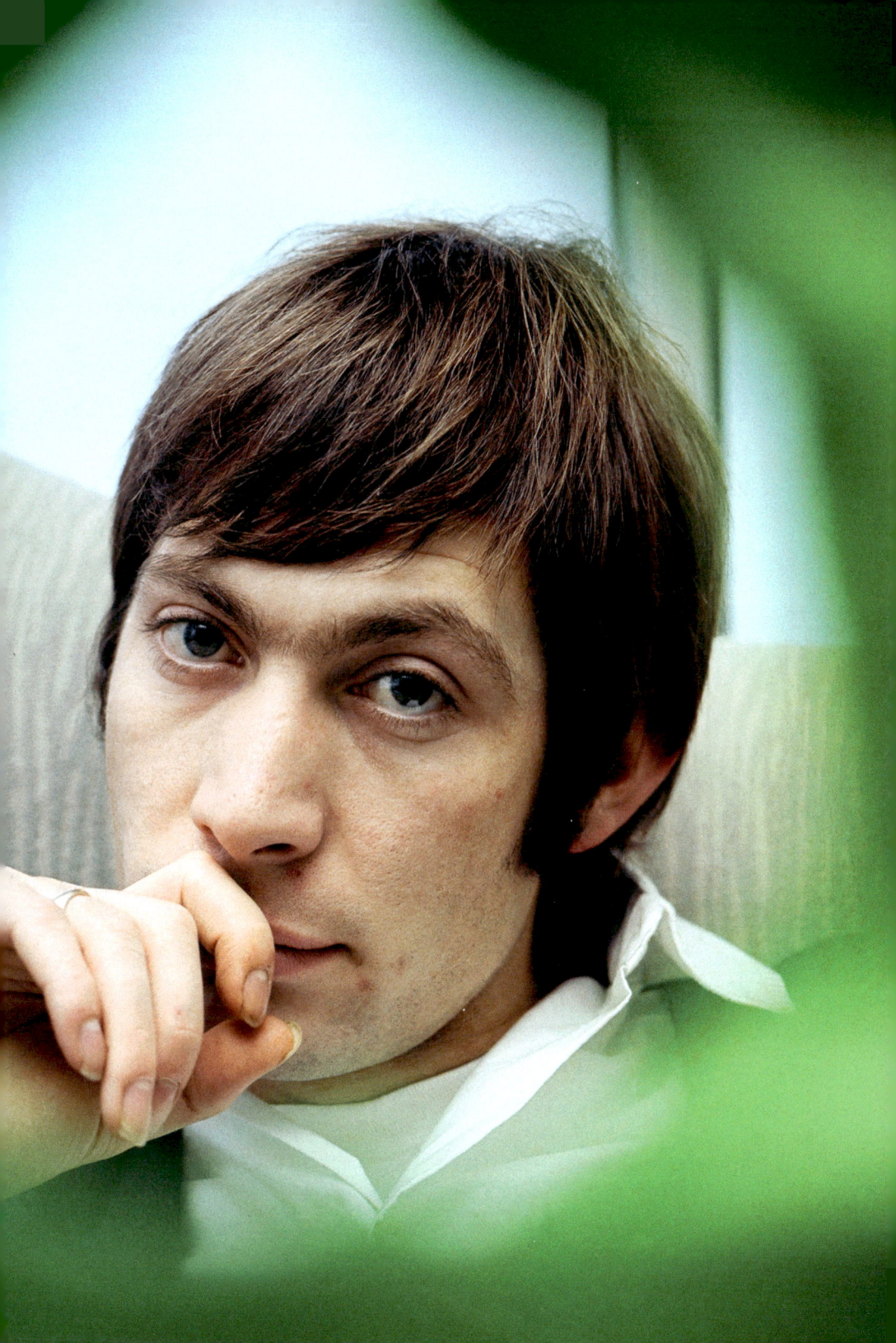

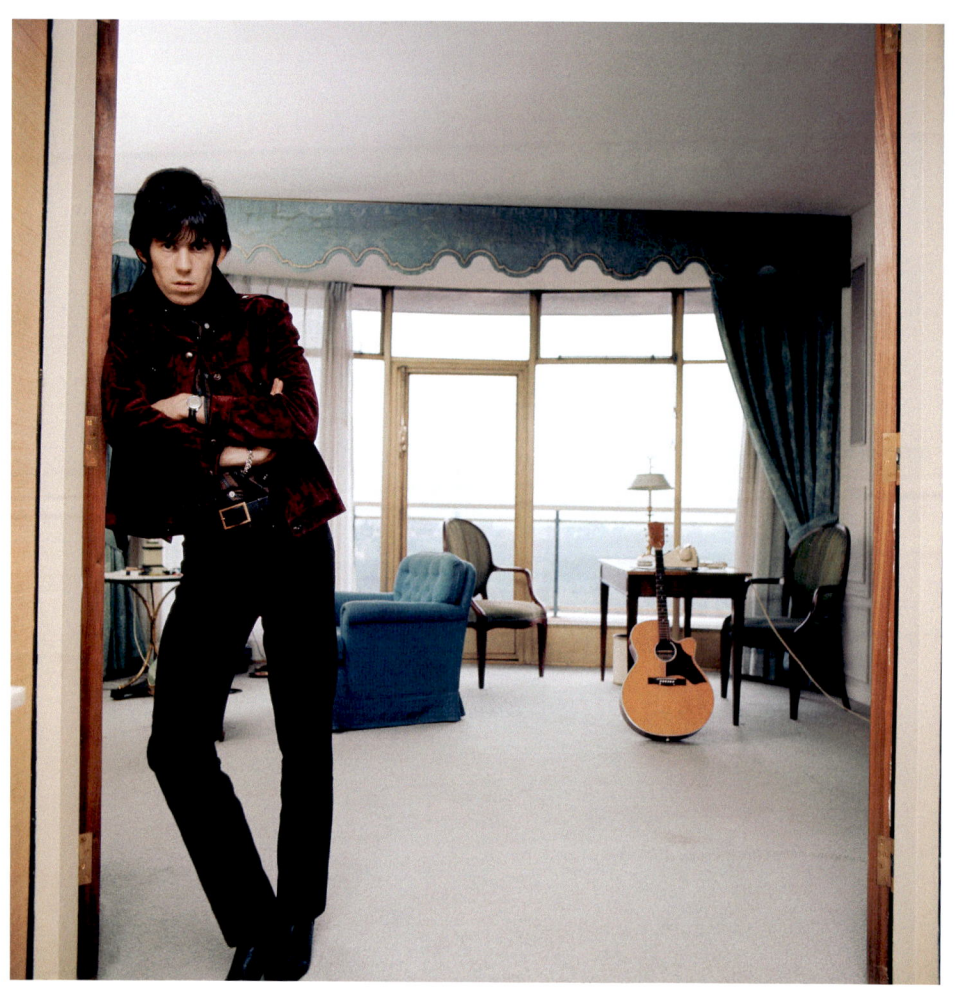

Bent Rej

Continually on the road, permanent living space wasn't of prime importance to Keith during the Stones' early days of fame. While he had previously maintained small flats and shared houses around London, a serviced room in London's swanky Hilton Hotel overlooking Hyde Park was a convenient base during June 1965, until he found somewhere more permanent.

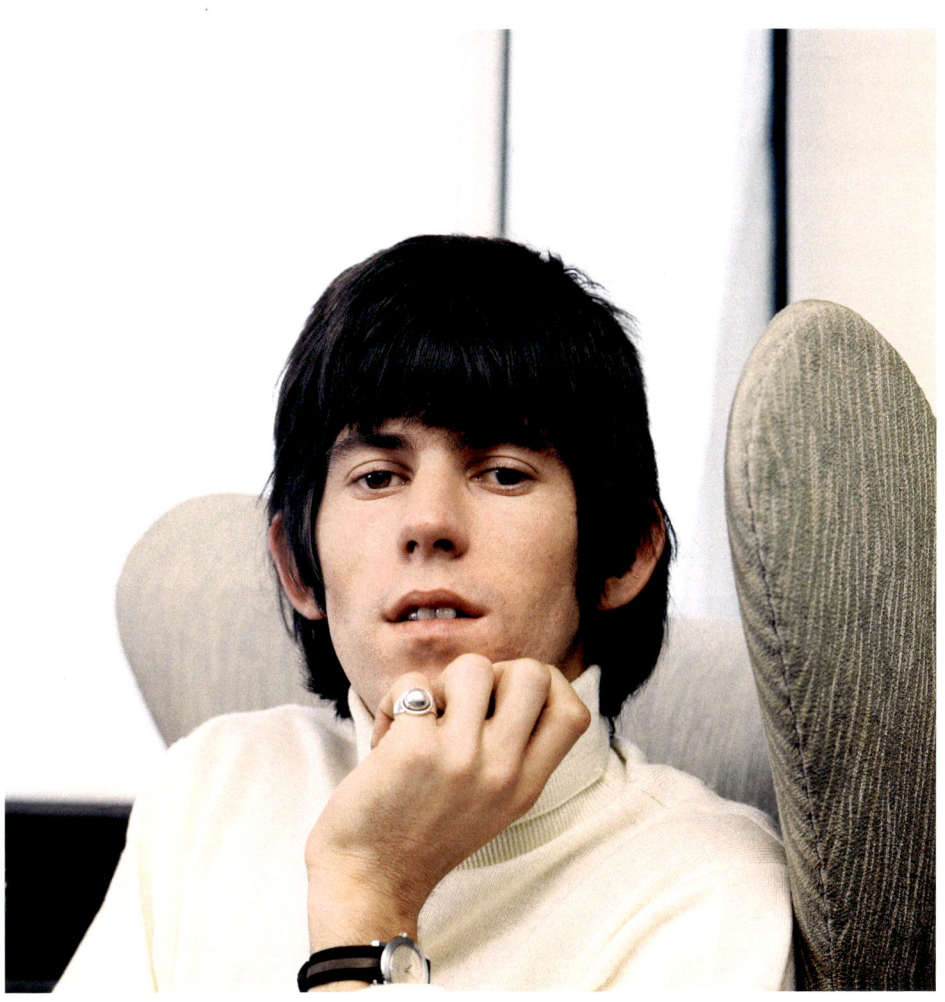

Bent Rej
Keith at the Royal Hotel, Copenhagen, 1965.
*"We belong to a generation that's separate from
any other. We believe in what we are doing. We're
happy to have the kids screaming for us. It gets*
*me down to think that a lot of them will one day
disappear into the drab nest. I hope all of them
won't. If only the whole world could stay young."*
Keith Richards, *Sunday People*, 9 October 1966

Bent Rej

With time to kill in Copenhagen on 26 March 1965, Keith indulged in some keyboard-playing. *"We get a kick from every song for a while and then we get fed up with it and write another one. But we get the horrors in a discothèque when they play something of ours – usually a whole LP or something. At first a lot of the songs we wrote were for other people, but now everything we write we can do for ourselves."* Keith Richards, *Melody Maker*, 24 September 1966

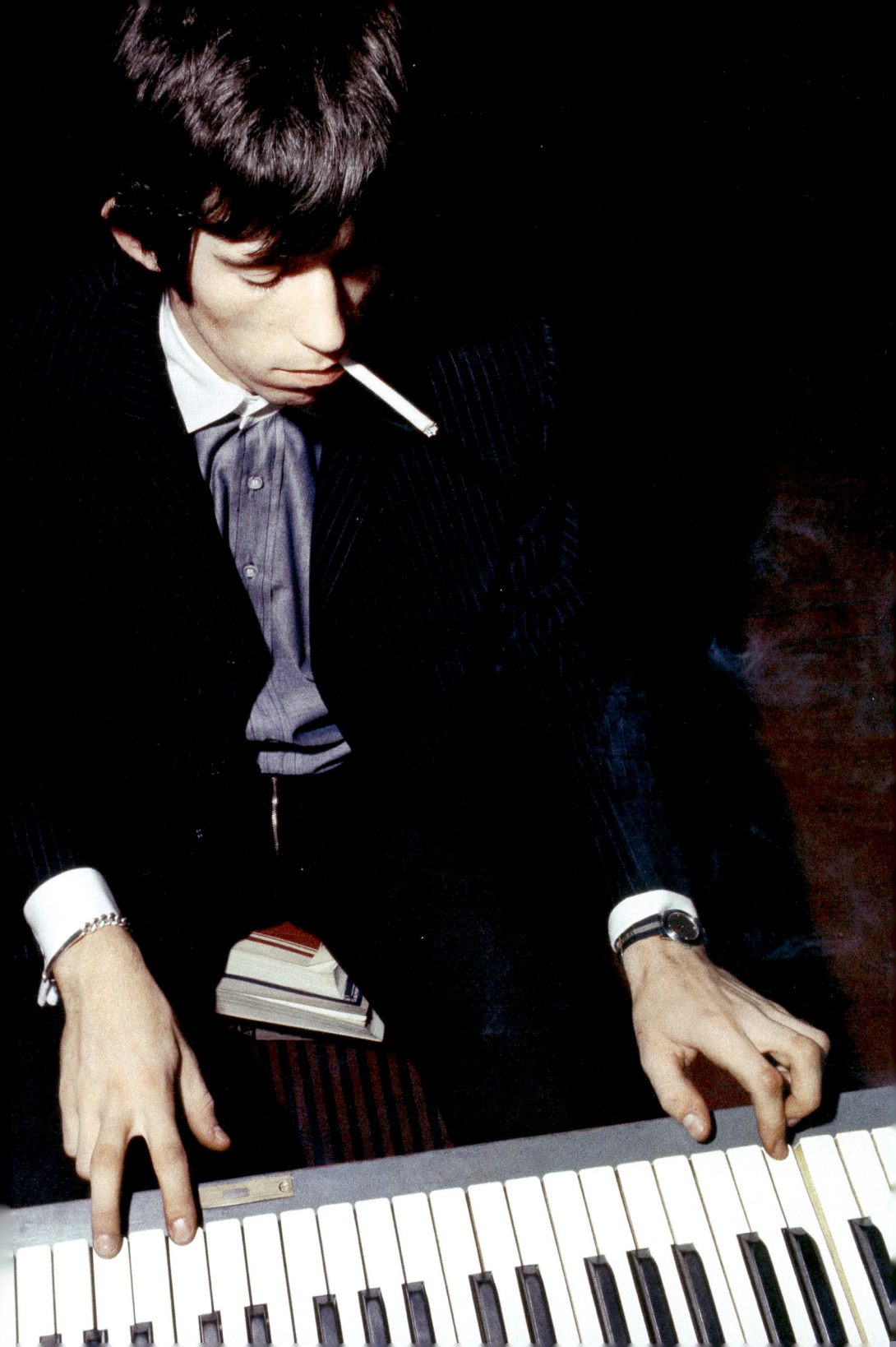

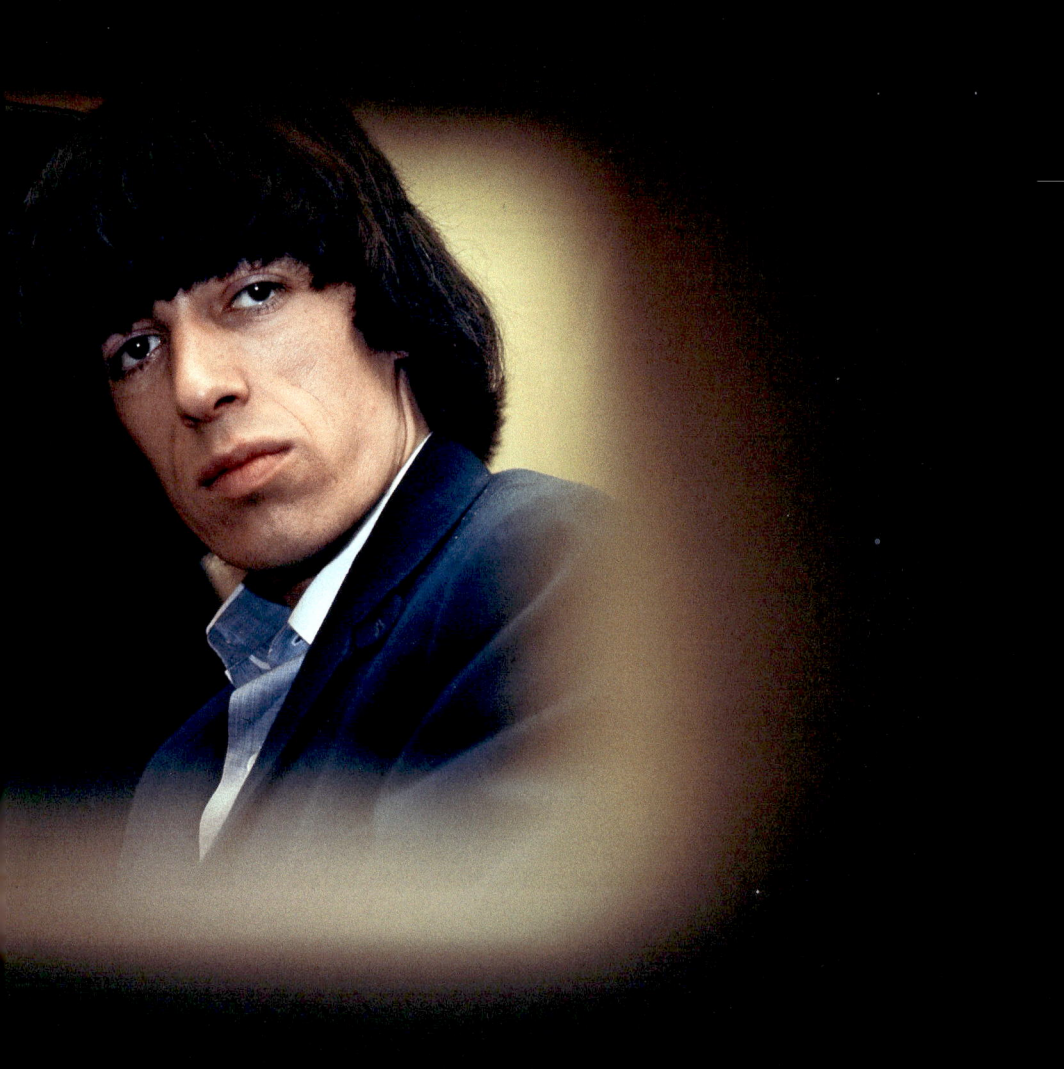

Bent Rej

Bill's impenetrable persona was obviously a focal point for photographers. Malmö, Sweden, 29 June 1965.

"When I left Beckenham grammar school I hadn't the faintest idea what I wanted to do. I didn't excel at anything, except maths ... I went to work for a big department store in Penge. That was ok for a time. I had a good future and they all asked me not to leave when I began to get on with The Rolling Stones. Eventually it got so bad with my hair that the management said I would have to make up my mind between the firm or The Rolling Stones. I chose the Stones. That surprised the boss." Bill Wyman, *New Musical Express*, 1 May 1964

Bent Rej

Larking around in Scandinavia, June 1965.

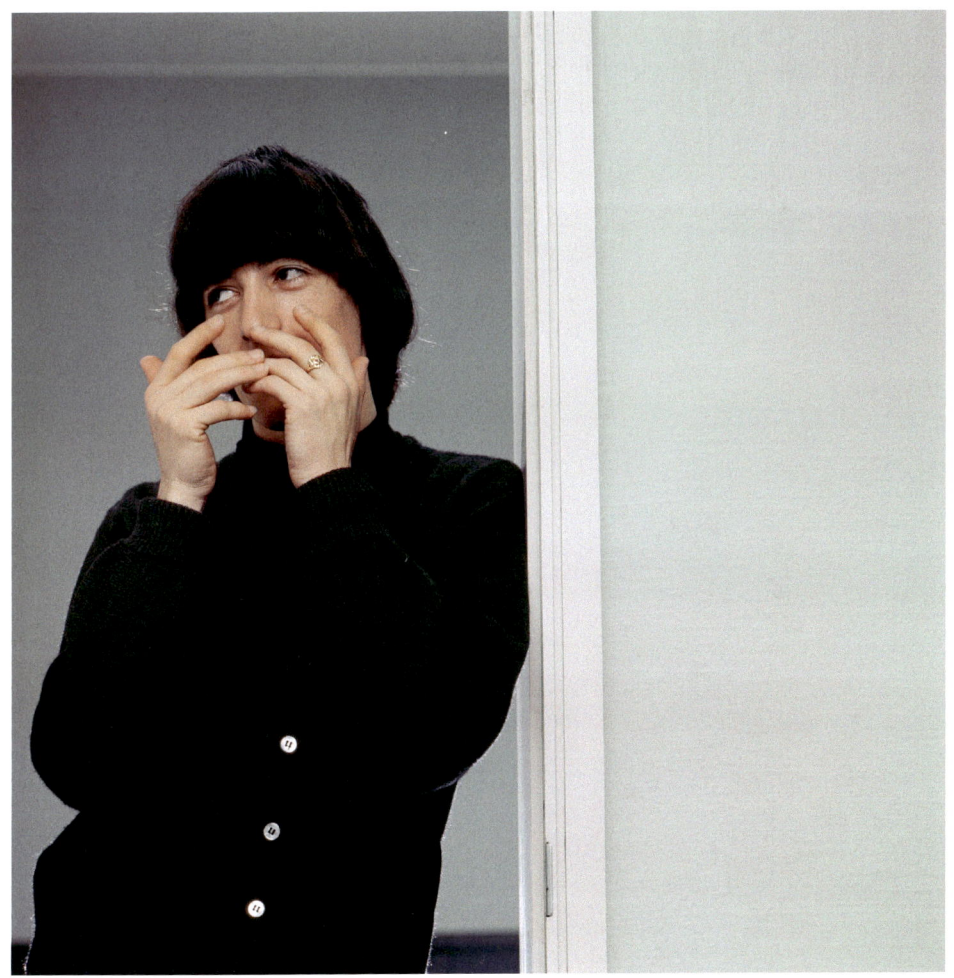

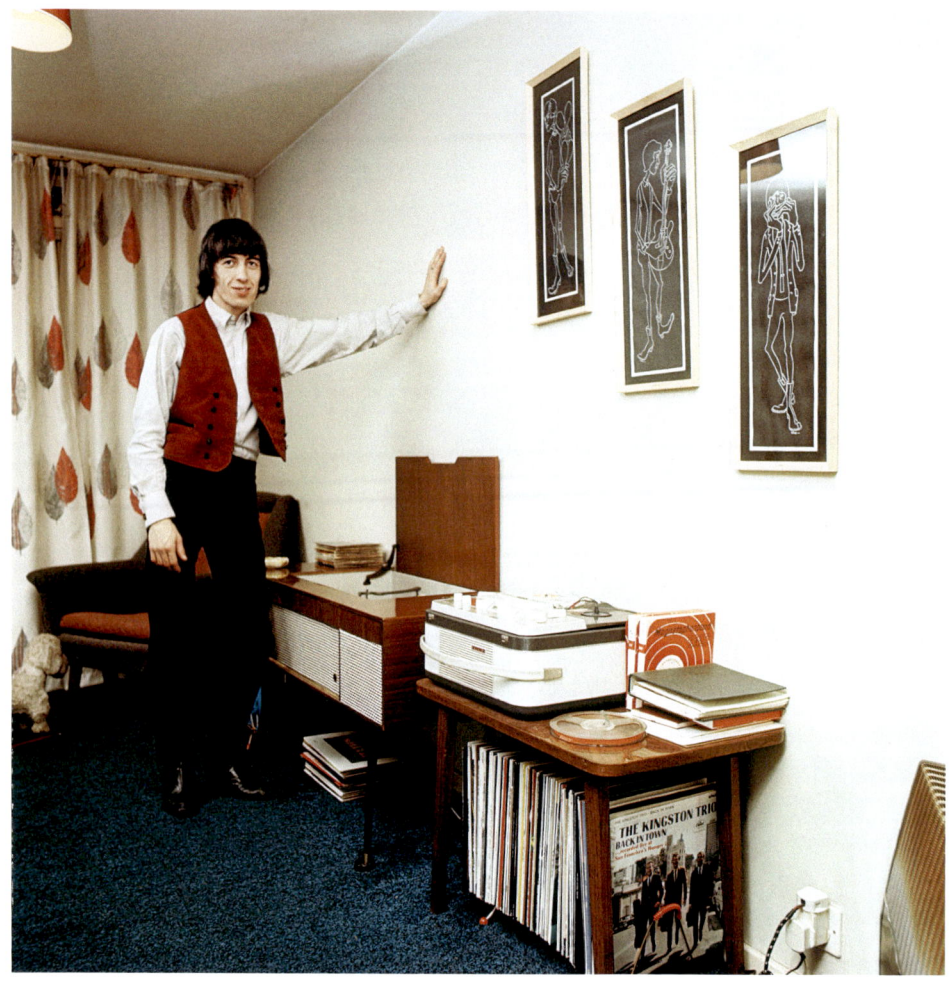

Bent Rej
Bill's tastes were largely conservative, as shown
by the décor in his south London home. June 1965.

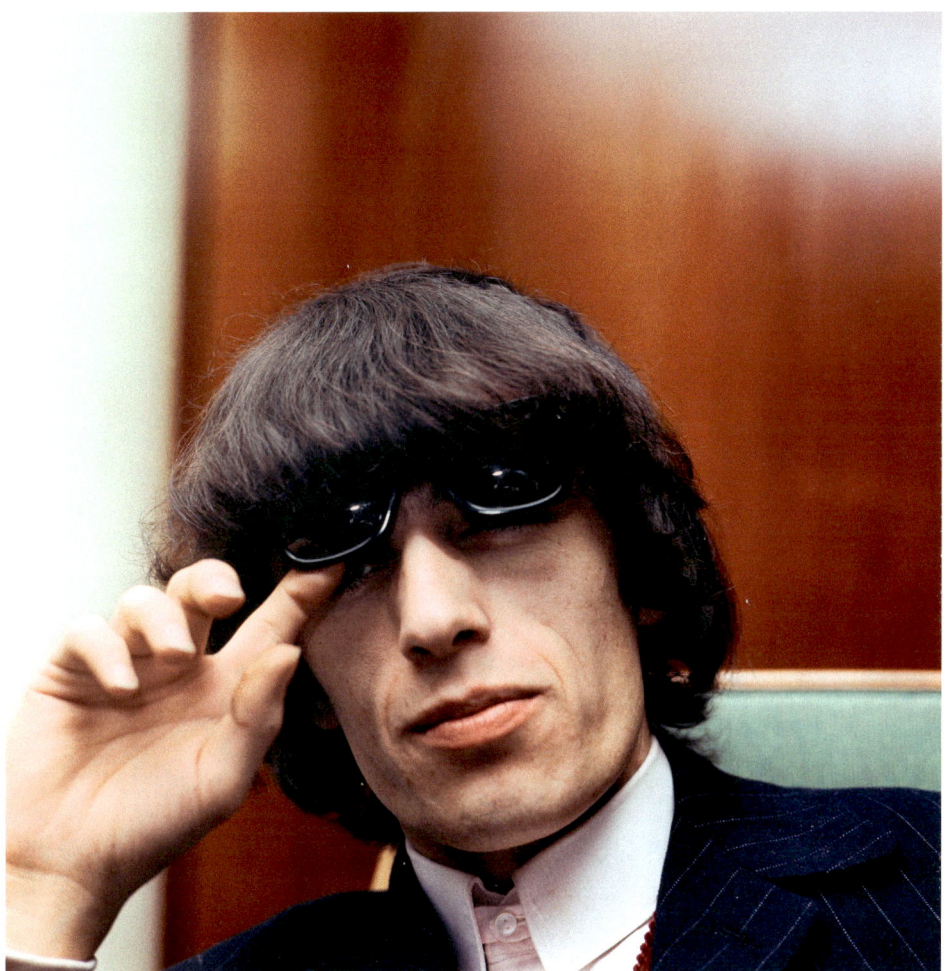

Bent Rej
Bill at a Copenhagen press conference on 25 March 1965, revealing his current eye infection.

PP. 158–159
Bent Rej
The Stones had good reason to celebrate their arrival in Copenhagen on 25 March 1965. Their sixth single, "The Last Time", was sitting at the top of the British pop charts, their third disc to achieve the coveted position.

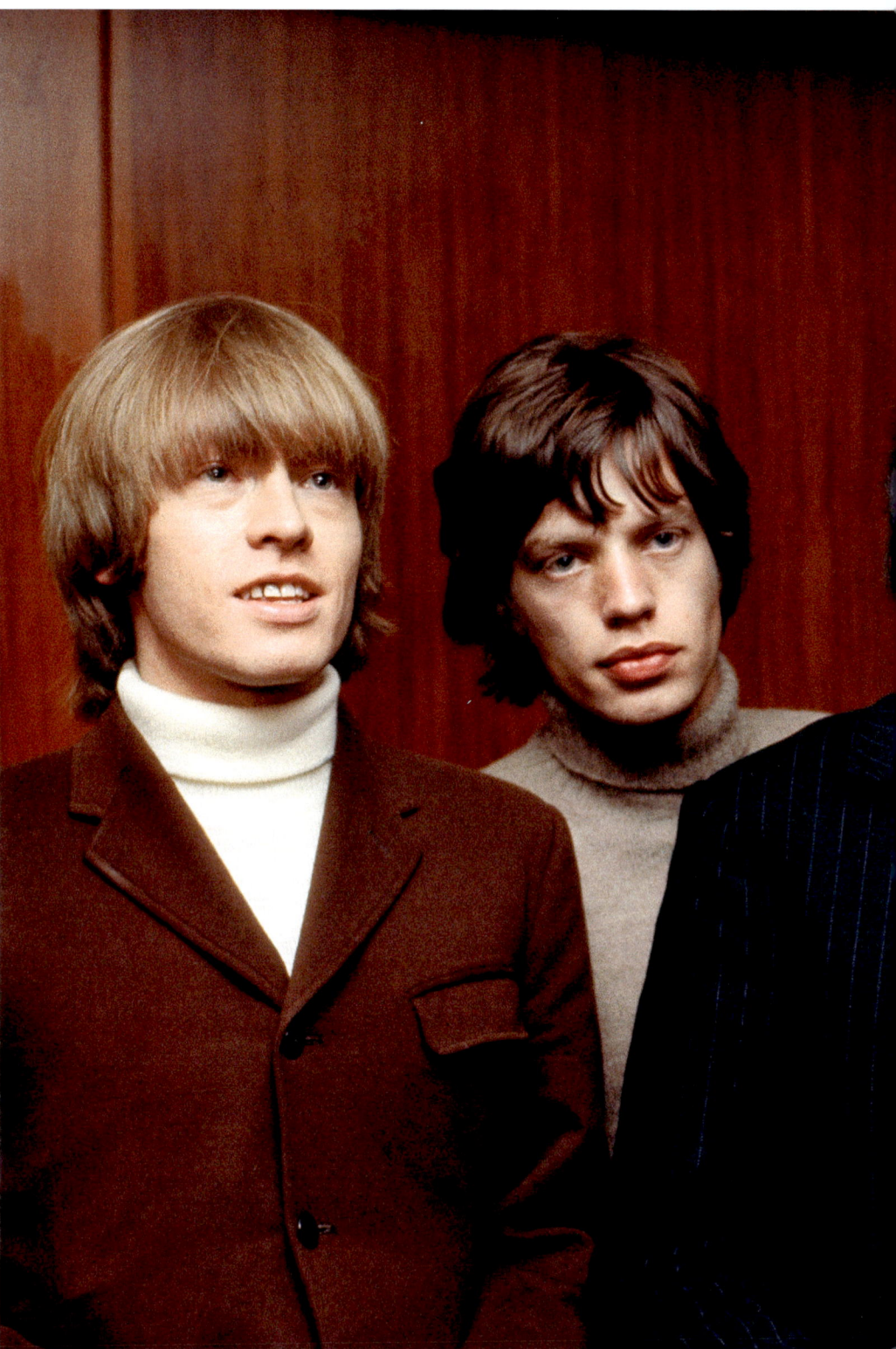

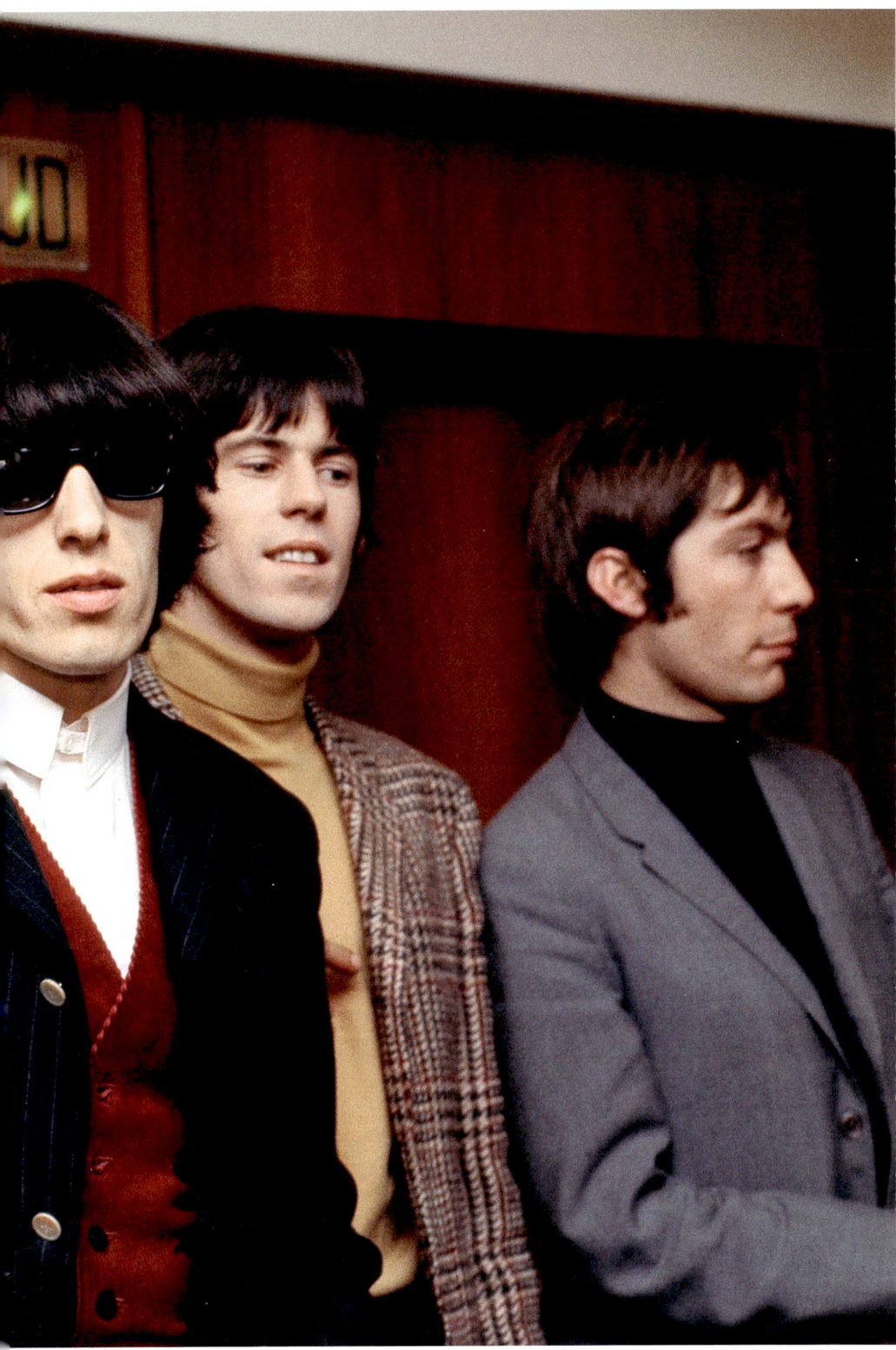

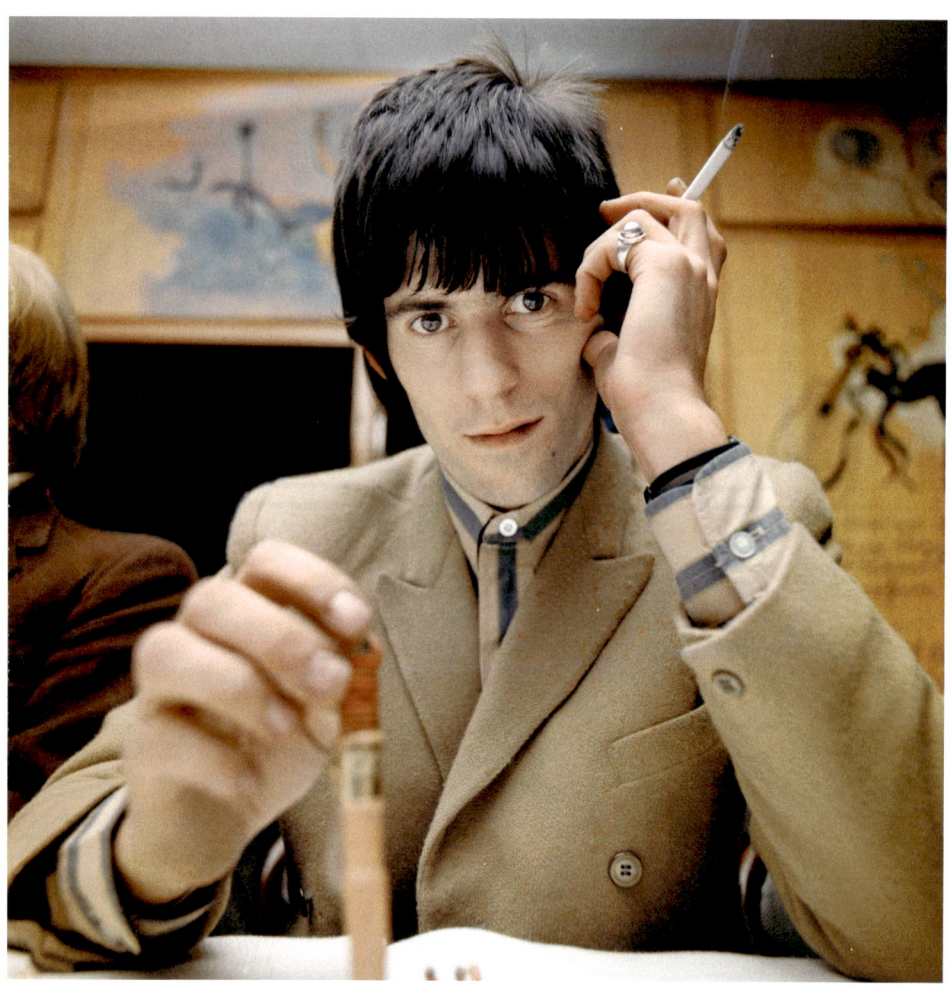

Bent Rej

A thoughtful, if slightly tired-looking Keith in Copenhagen, 25 March 1965.
"I still don't know what he's thinking about at any time, and he really is one of my closest friends ... *people find it difficult to know Keith. Sometimes he's shy and other times he can't be bothered to take an interest in people."* Mick Jagger, *Disc Weekly*, February 1966

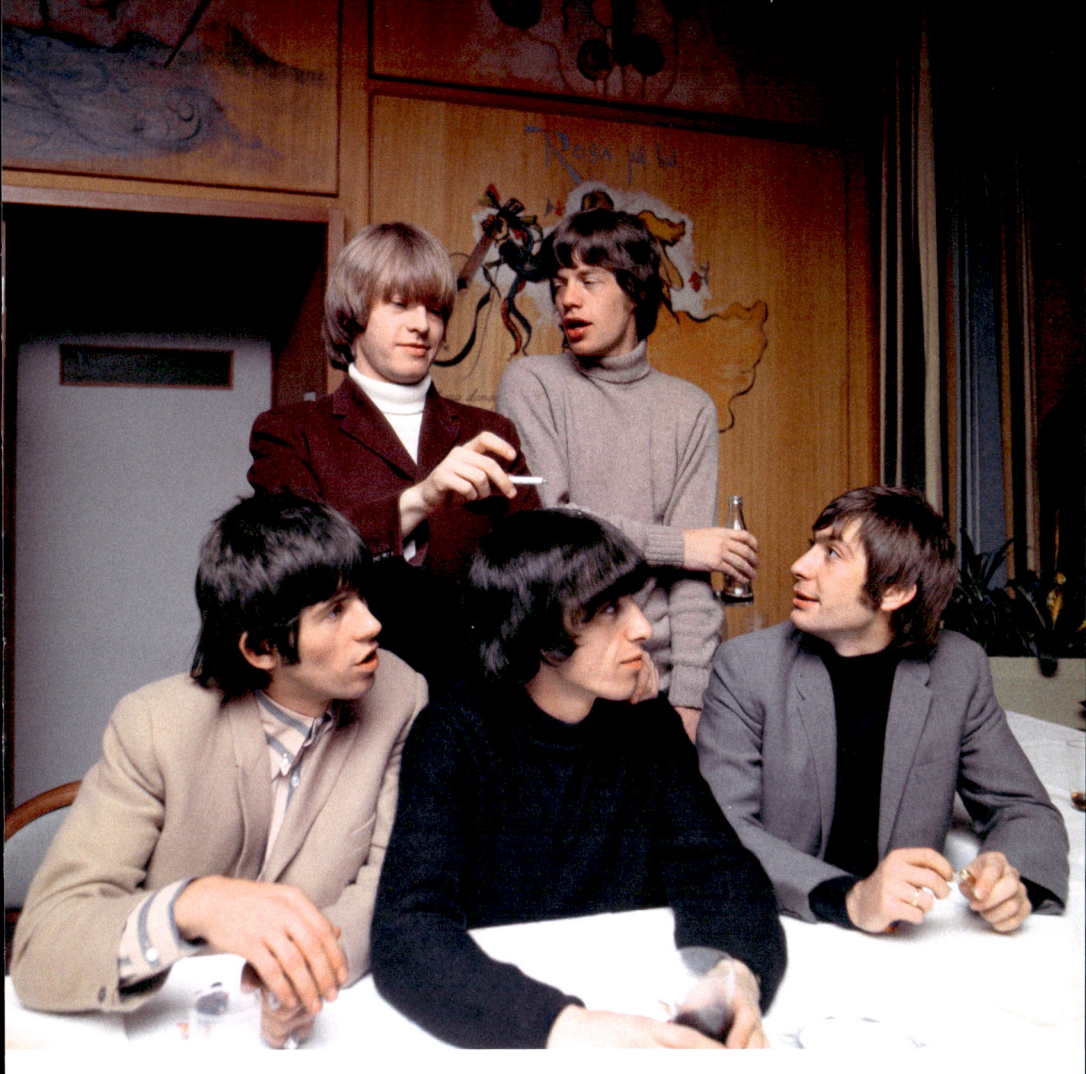

Bent Rej
Brian in mildly antagonistic mode at a press
conference in Copenhagen, 25 March 1965.

Jerry Schatzberg

In New York for an *Ed Sullivan Show* appearance
during early September 1966, the band were
togged up in conservative women's clothes
and driven to a side alley for a photo shoot on
Saturday, 10 September 1966.
*"This extraordinary photograph was taken last
Saturday afternoon in a back street off New
York's Third Avenue, and Mr. Andrew Loog Oldham
was a little worried about it at first." Daily Mirror*,
15 September 1966

PP. 164–165
Gered Mankowitz

En route from JFK airport to their New York hotel
for the start of their fourth North American tour,
27 October 1965. After just one day's preparation,
the group flew on from New York to Montreal
to begin their tour: covering 37 venues in 38 days,
often with two shows a night, it would prove to be
their most gruelling US tour to date.

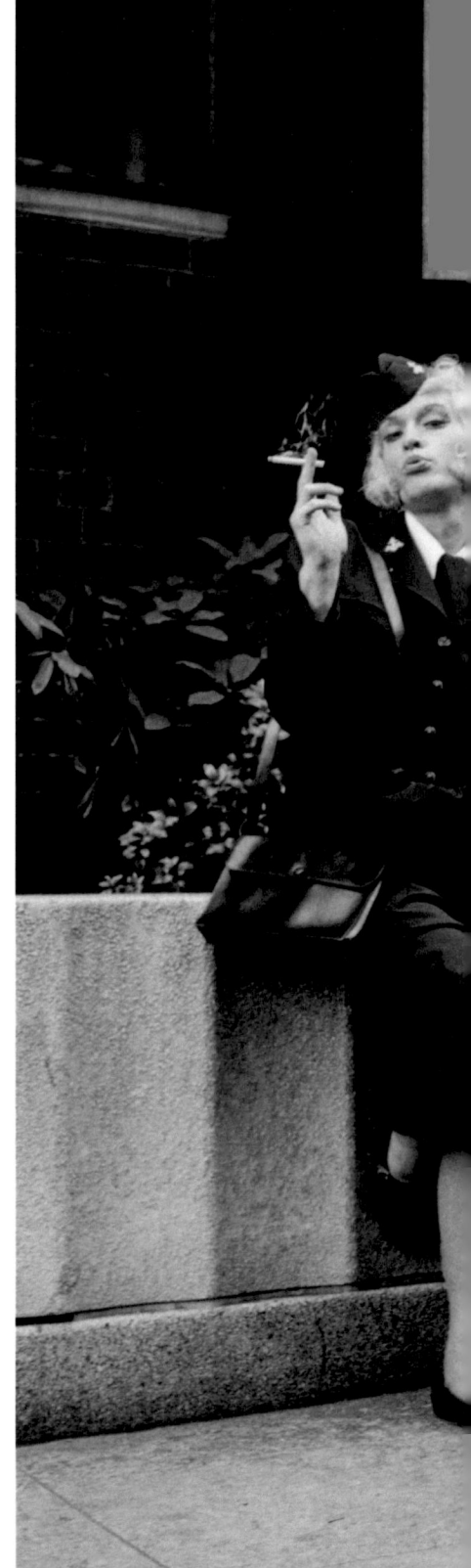

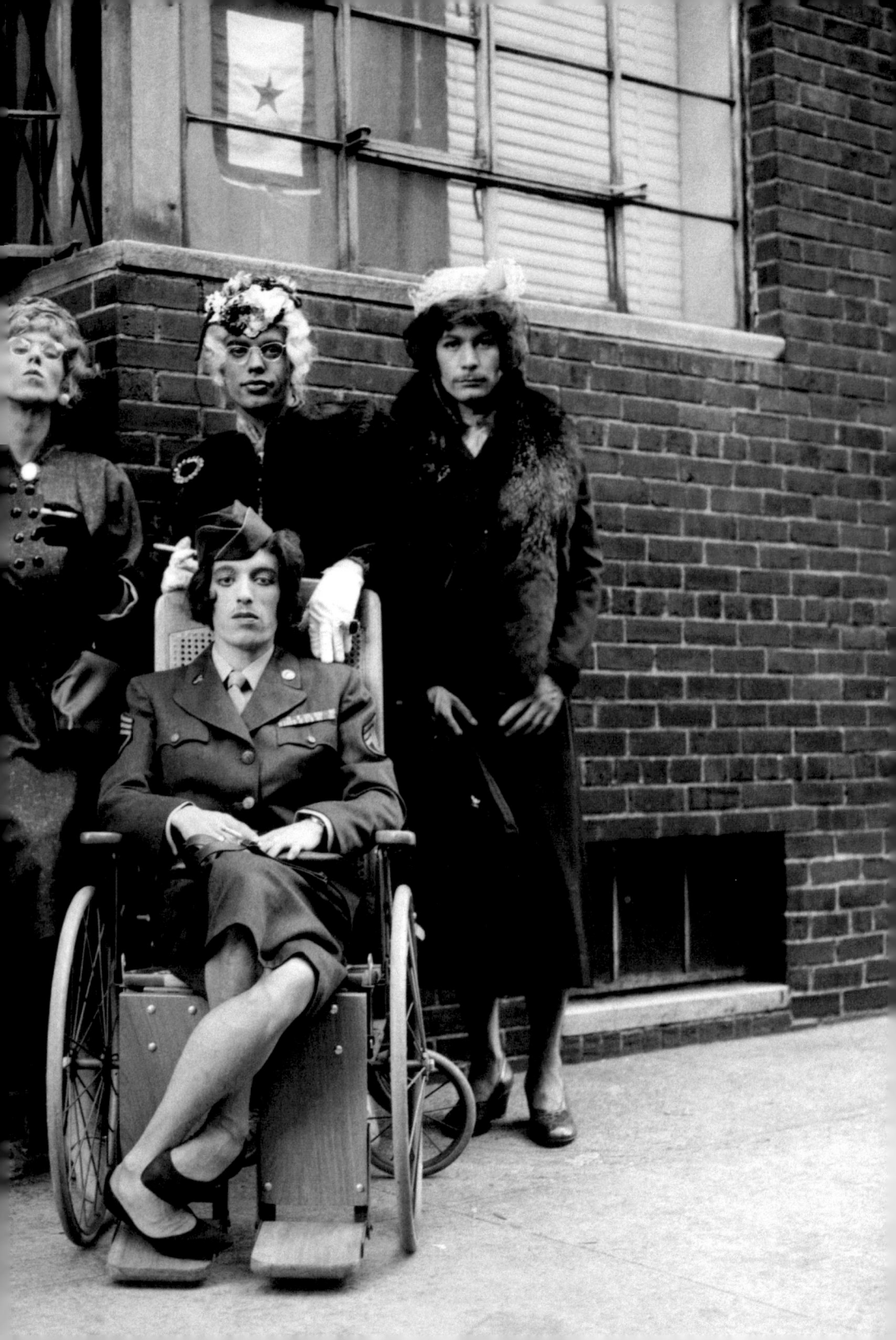

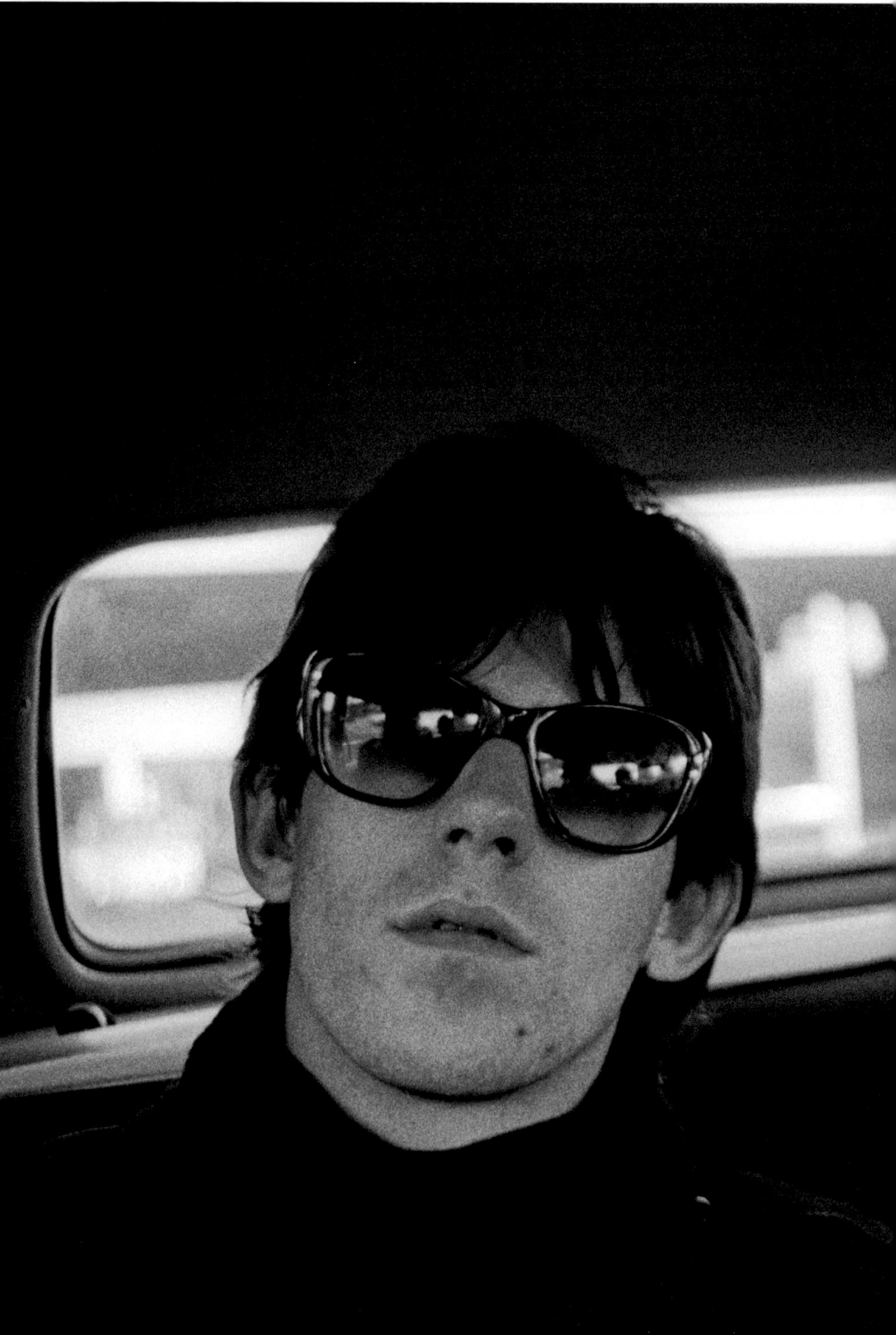

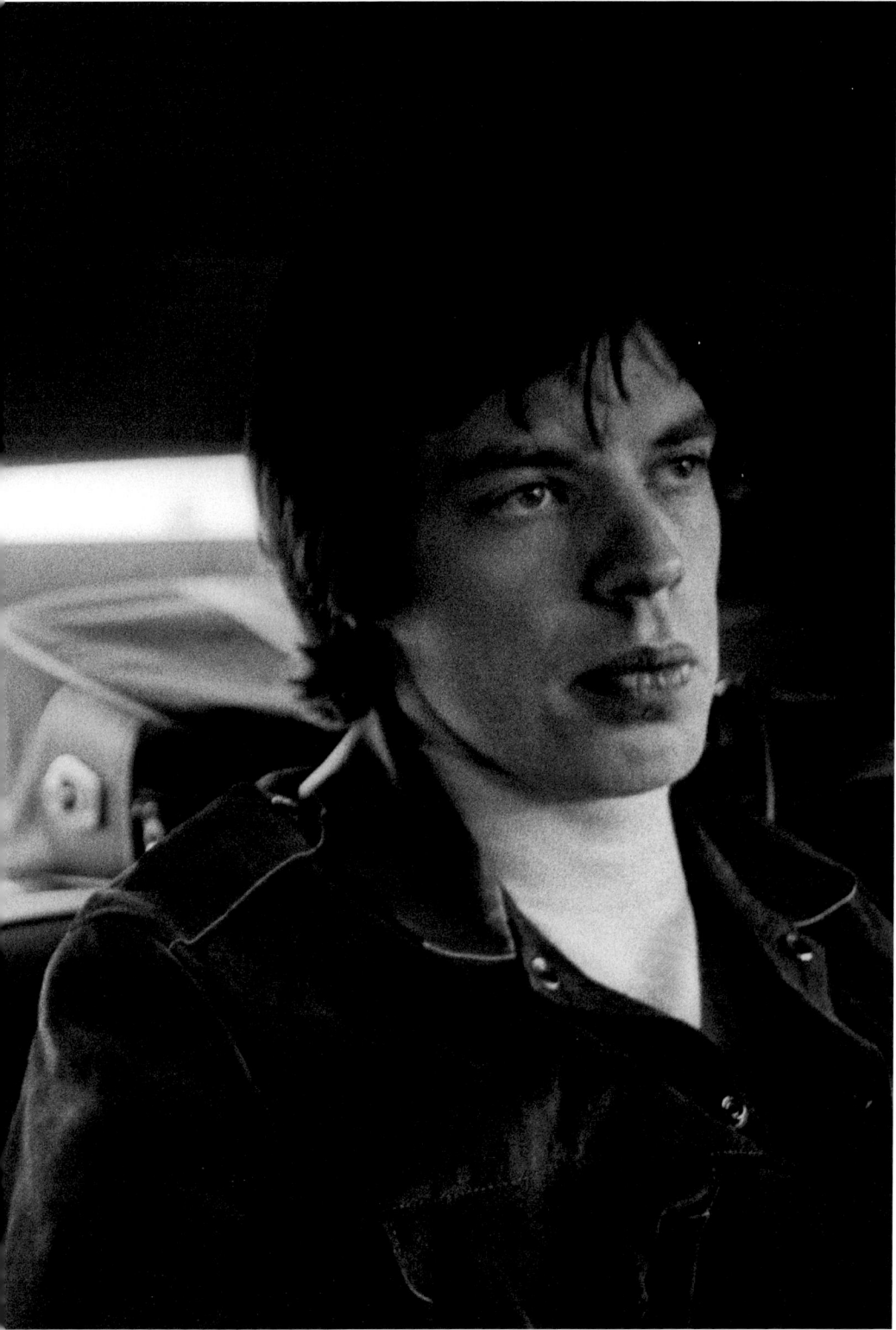

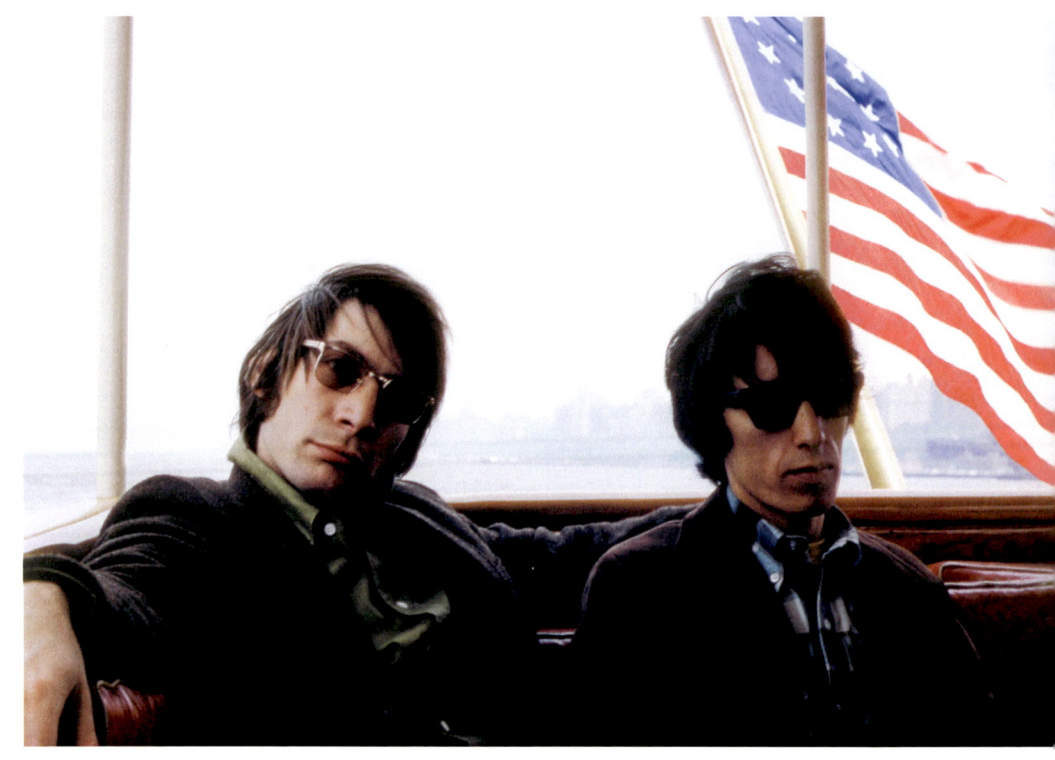

Linda McCartney
Aboard manager Allen Klein's 110-foot yacht,
the SS *Sea Panther*, on New York's Hudson River,
24 June 1966. A strictly invite-only affair, the
yacht circled Manhattan Island playing host to a
few select journalists. While no photographers
were allowed, McCartney (née Eastman) brought
a camera on board and managed to take several
photographs of the group.

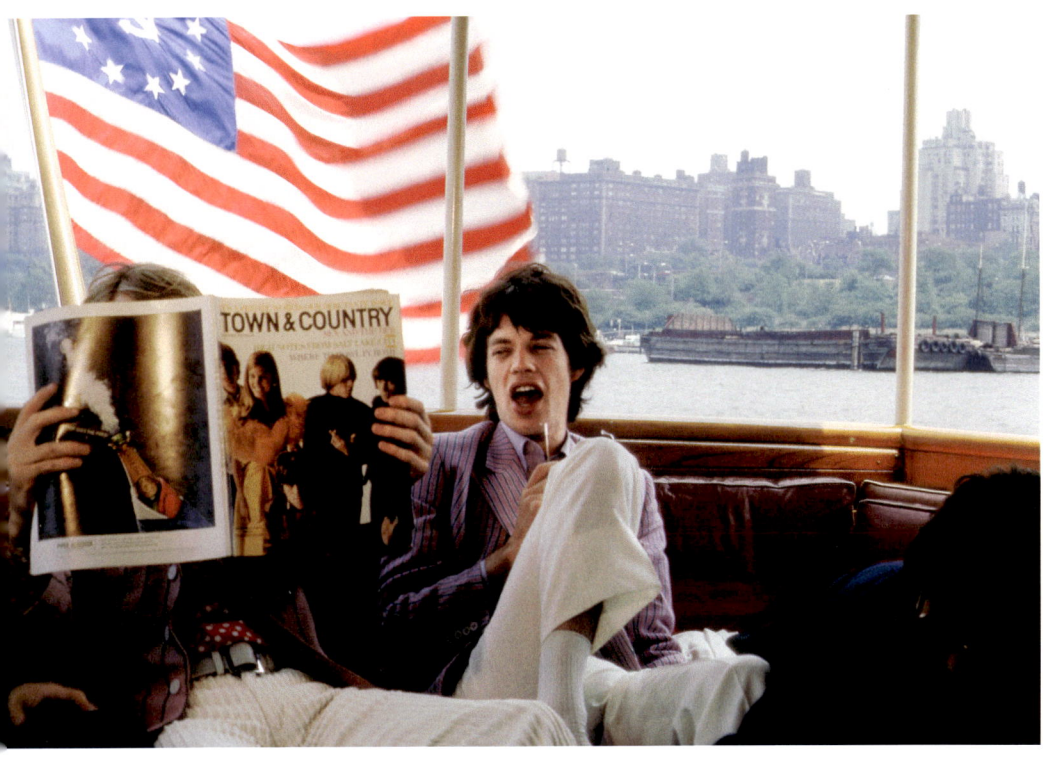

Linda McCartney
Following the press event on the Hudson River,
the group flew to Massachusetts for a show
at the Manning Bowl in Lynn.

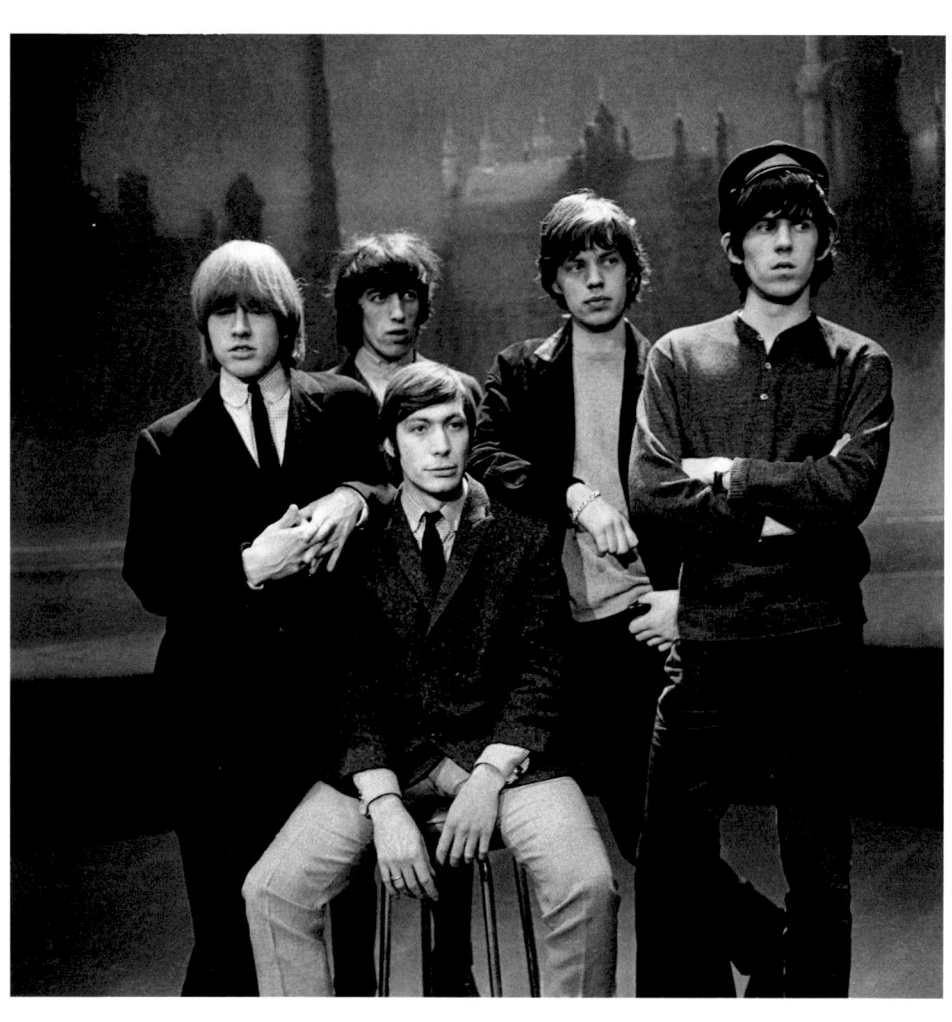

Pierre Fournier
Paris, October 1964.

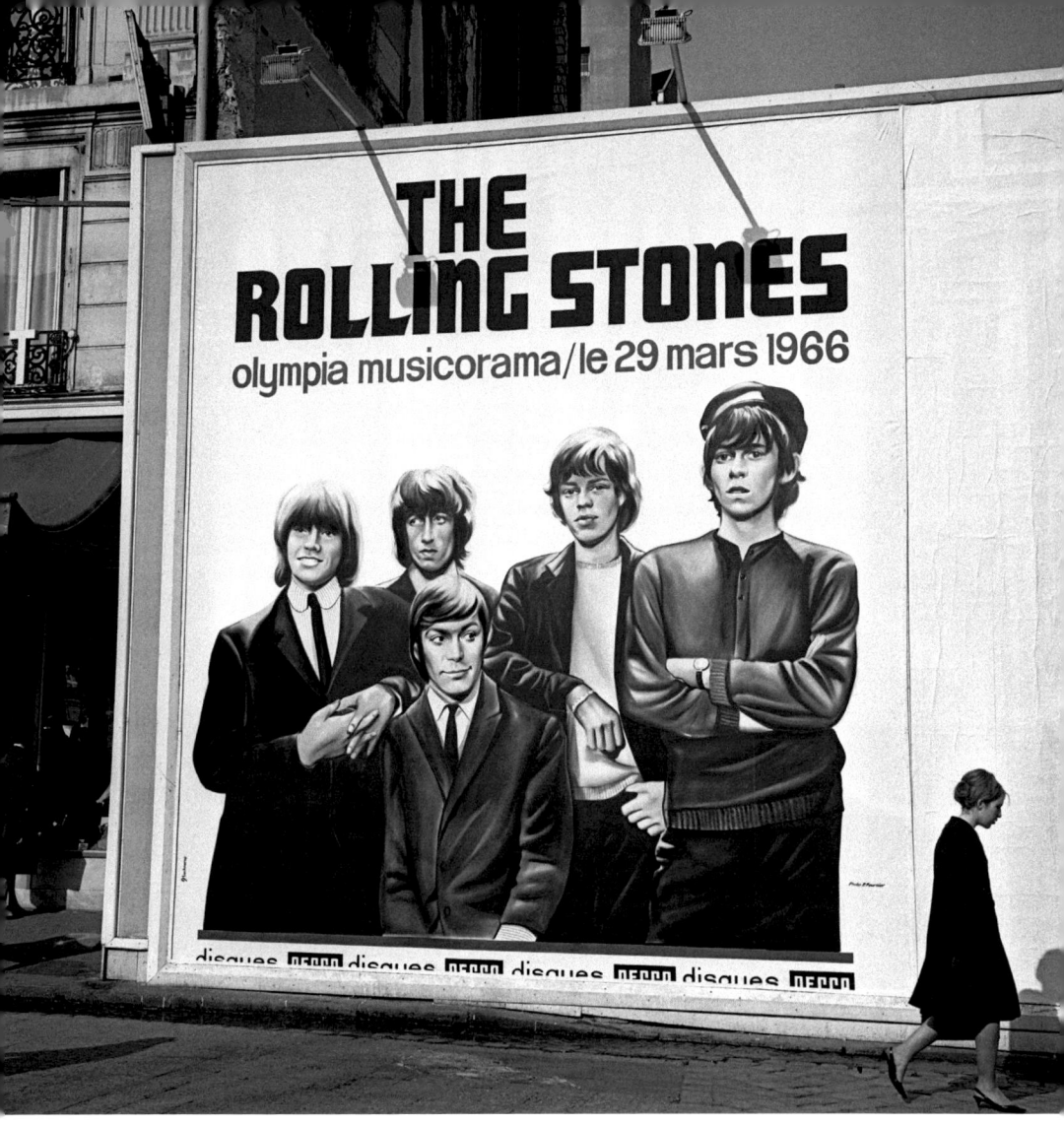

Pierre Fournier
Paris, 29 March 1966.

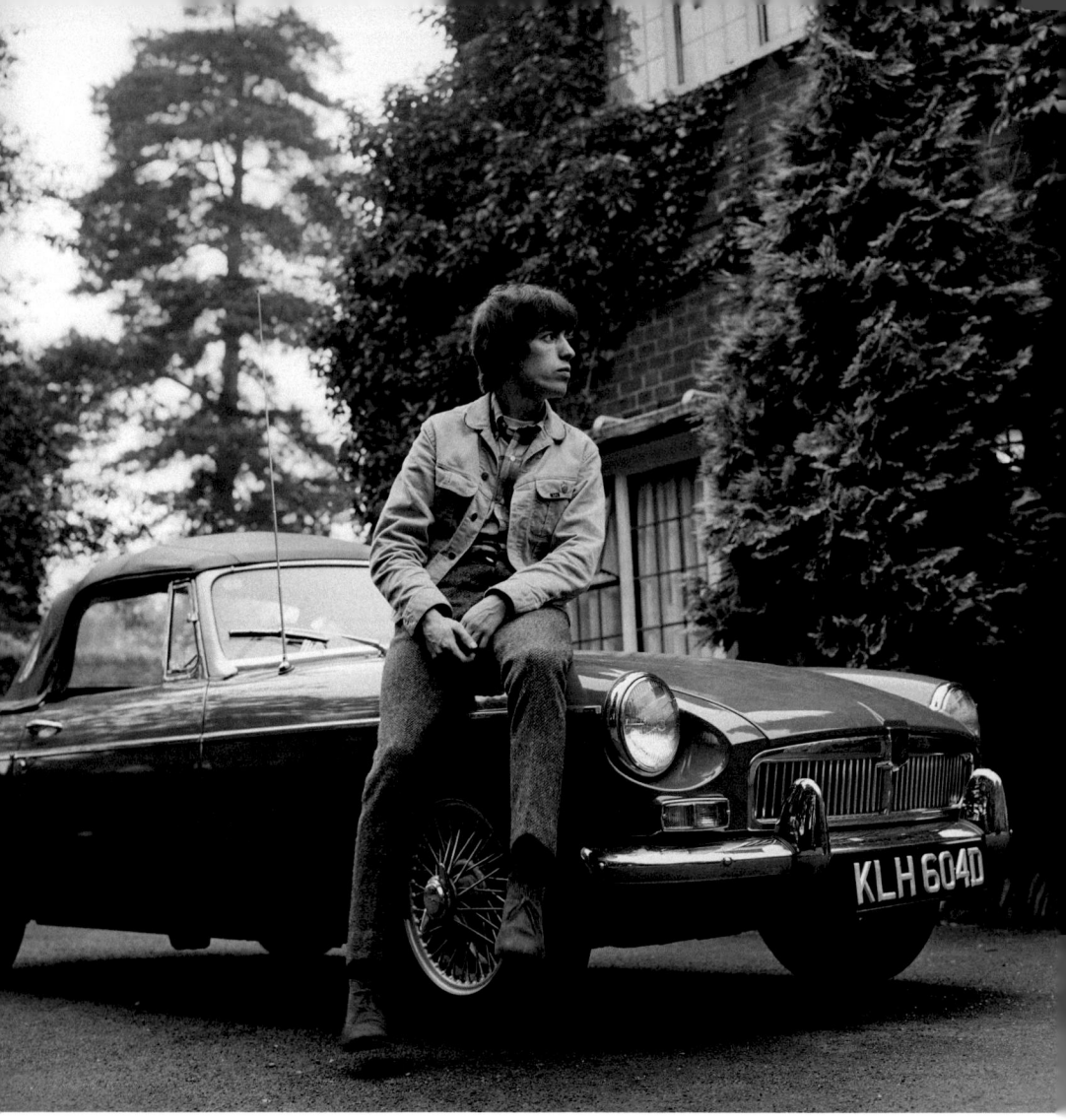

Gered Mankowitz
Despite his modest start in life, by 1966 Bill was
starting to enjoy some of the riches of his position – such as a brand-new MGB. Pictured at his
home in Keston, Kent, June 1966.

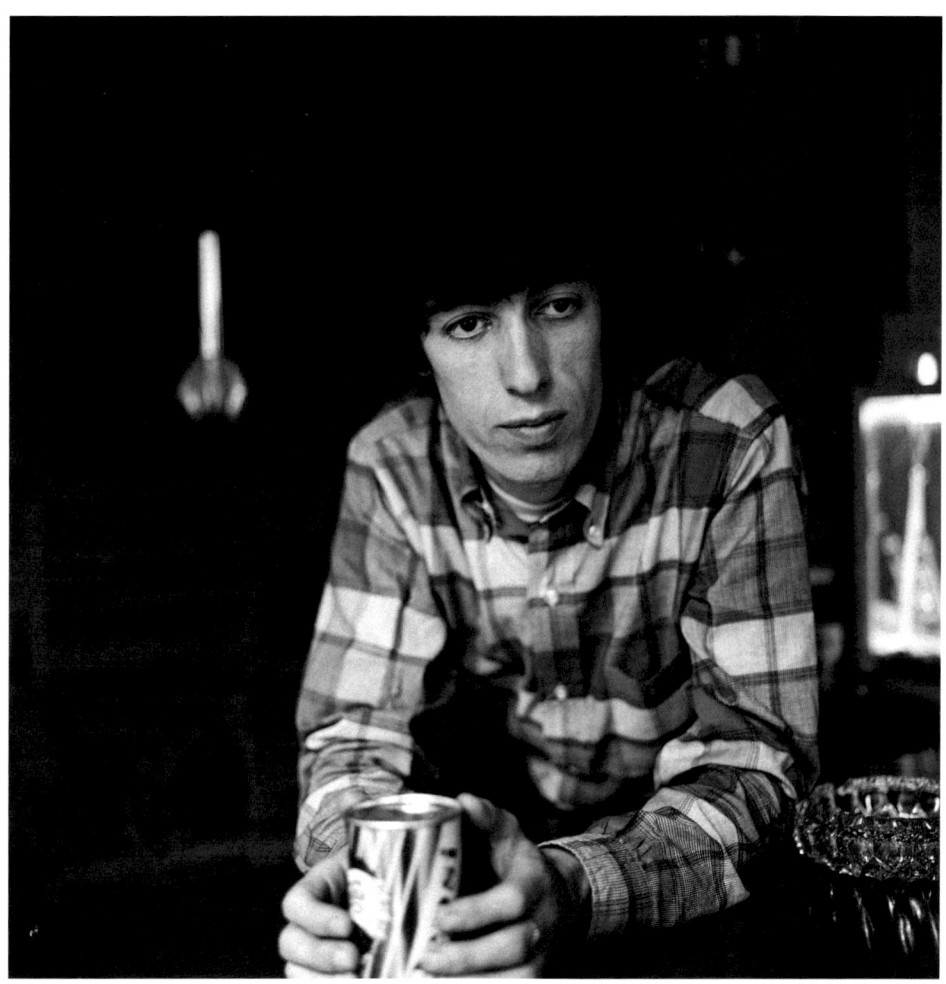

Gered Mankowitz
Bill at his Kent home in June 1966.
"I'm very fond of him. In fact, I often feel very paternal towards him ... He's more difficult to understand because he's married and until *recently lived a very reserved home life ... He's older than the rest of us and more stable, rather matter-of-fact."* Brian Jones, *Disc Weekly*, February 1966

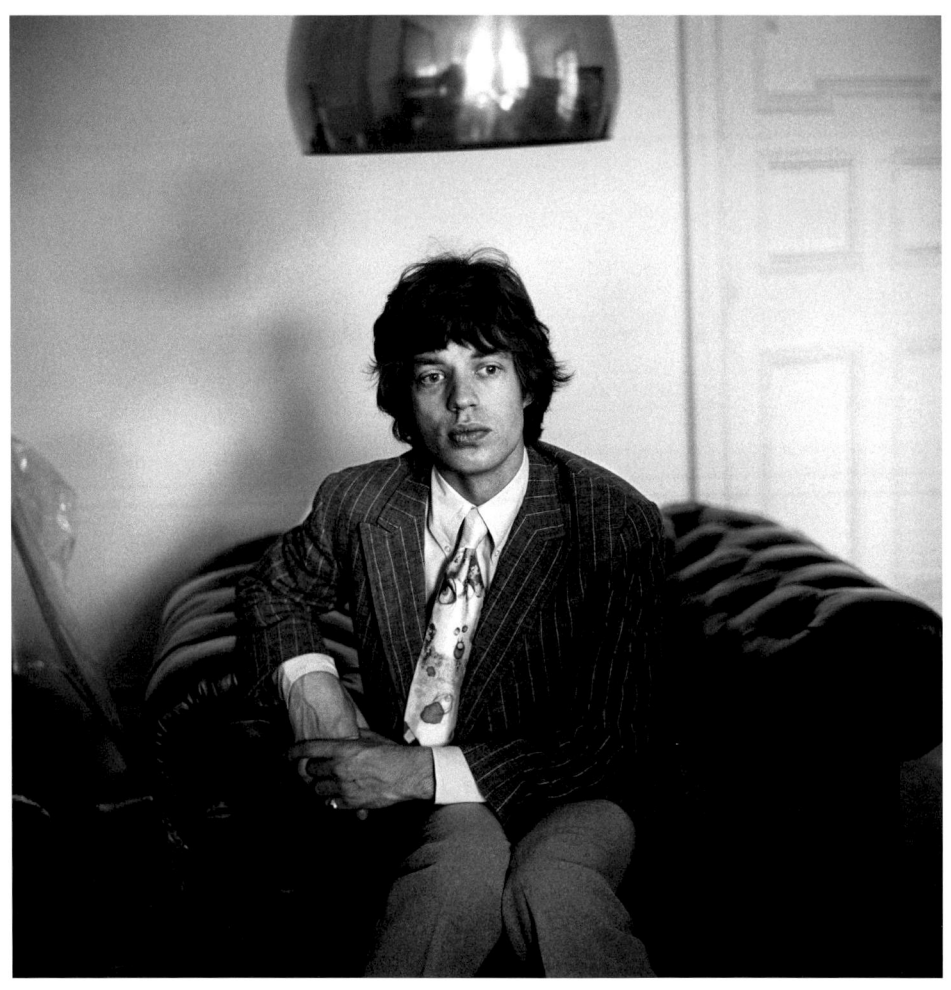

Gered Mankowitz
In June 1966 Mick took possession of a serviced
flat at 52, Harley House, on London's Marylebone
Road – at £50 a week, the property benefitted
from 24-hour security.

Gered Mankowitz
After two years of consistent work, the Stones
were at last able to enjoy the fruits of their labour
and start to put down their own roots in a manner
that suited them best. London, June 1966.

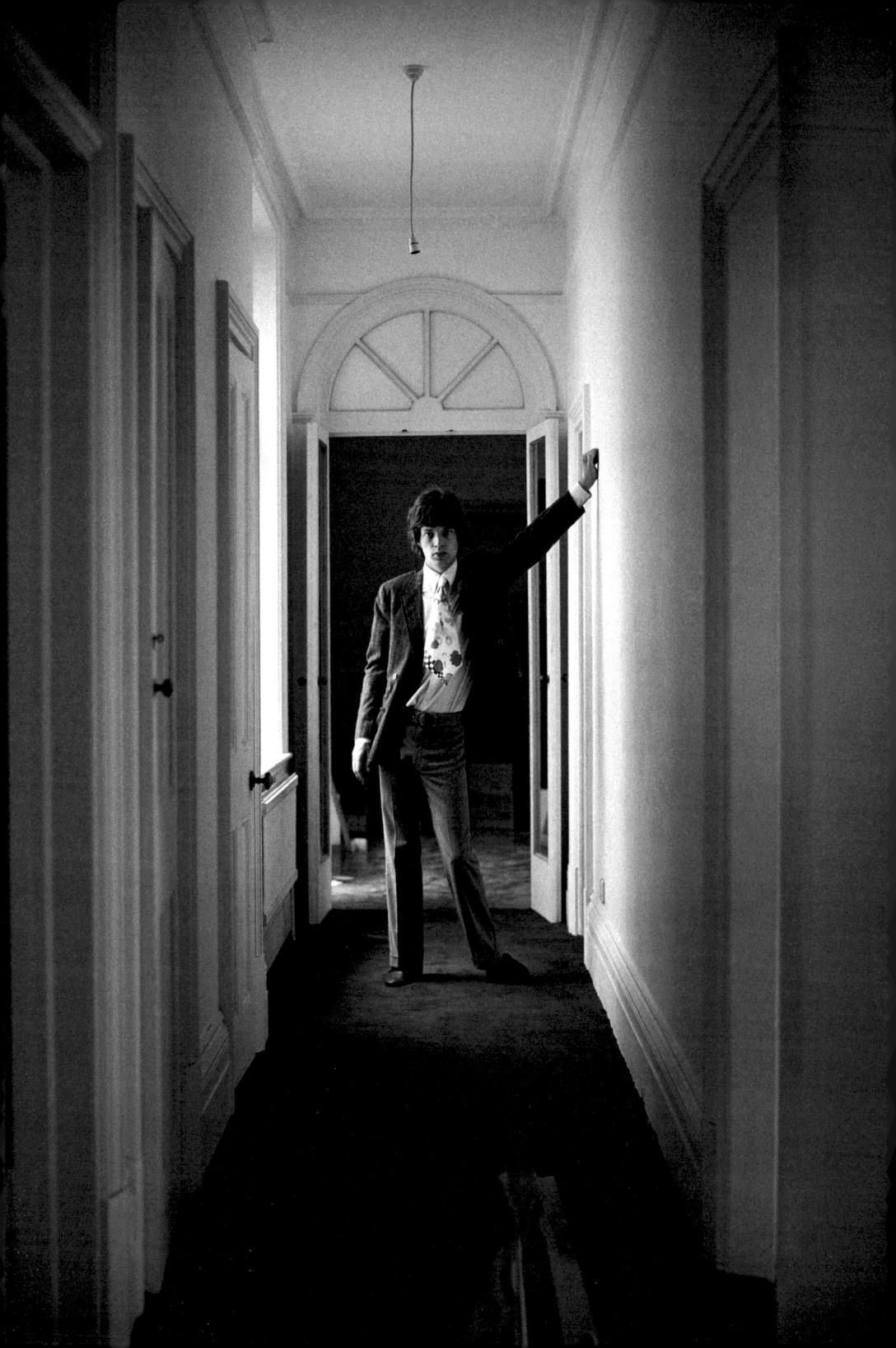

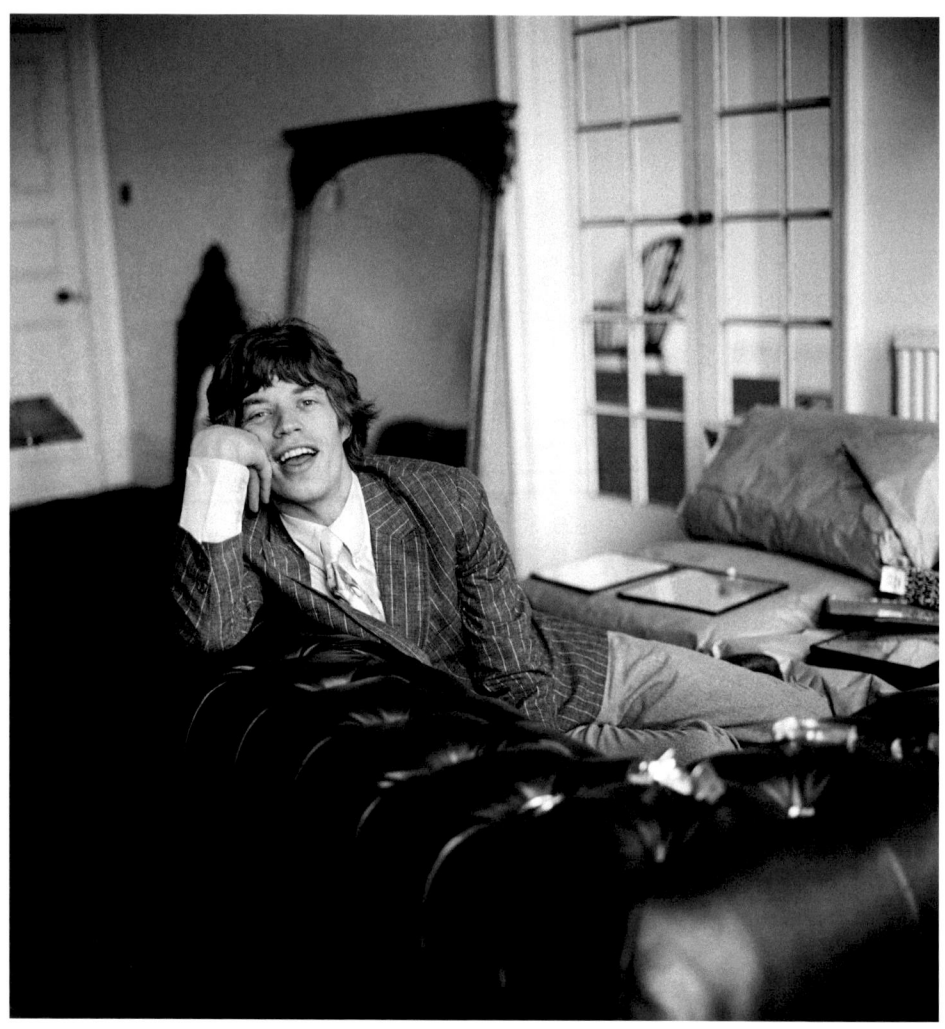

Gered Mankowitz

London, June 1966.

"We're the first generation not to worry about the material things. Because if you are hungry, you haven't got much time to worry about morals. When I say morals, I mean like fighting wars and *whether this is right or whether it's right for this society to do that."* Mick Jagger, filmed interview with Peter Whitehead for *Charlie Is My Darling*, October 1966

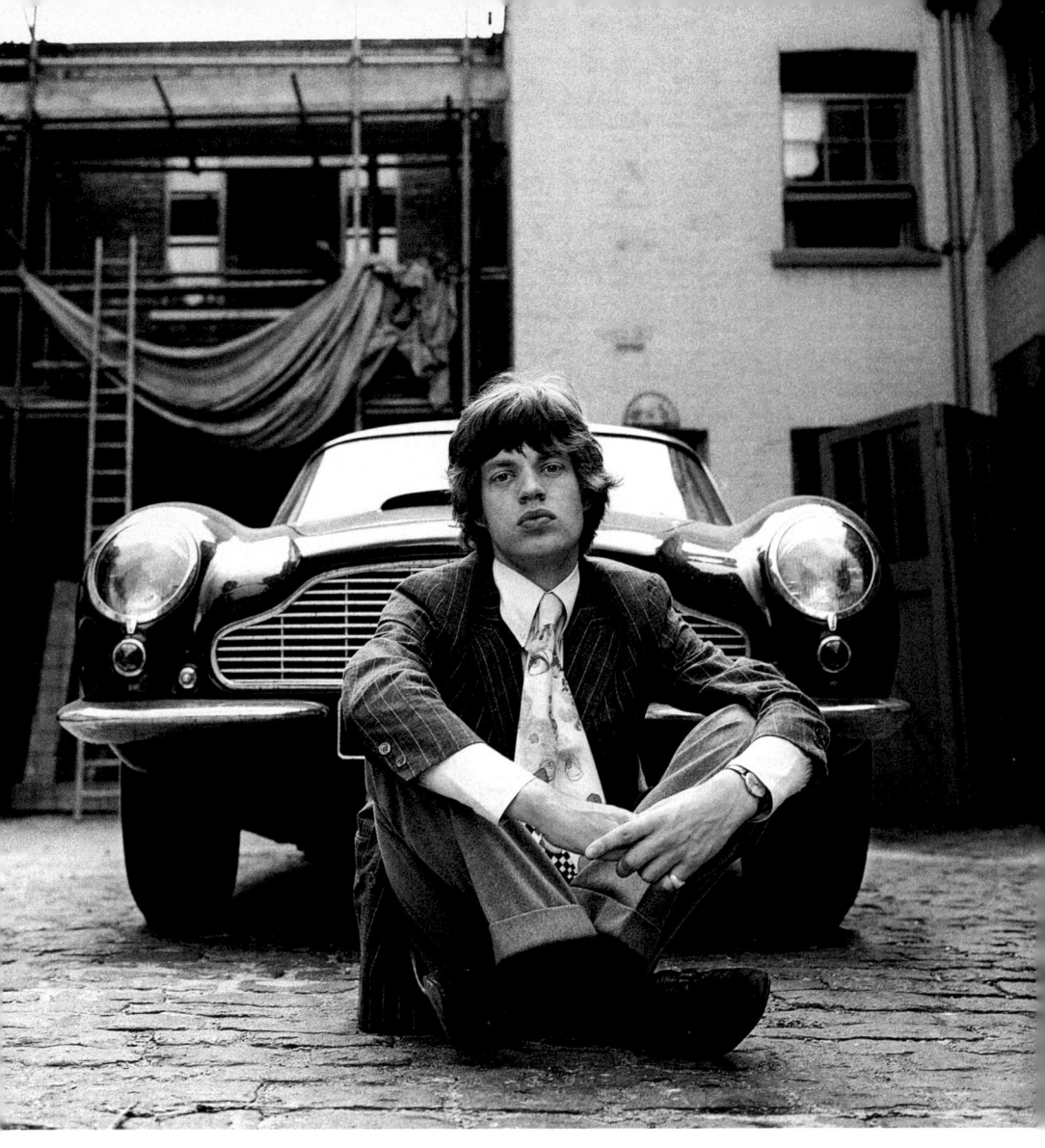

Gered Mankowitz
Seen here outside his soon-to-be-vacated
mews accommodation in central London,
Mick's gleaming Aston Martin was a symbol
of new-found wealth. June 1966.

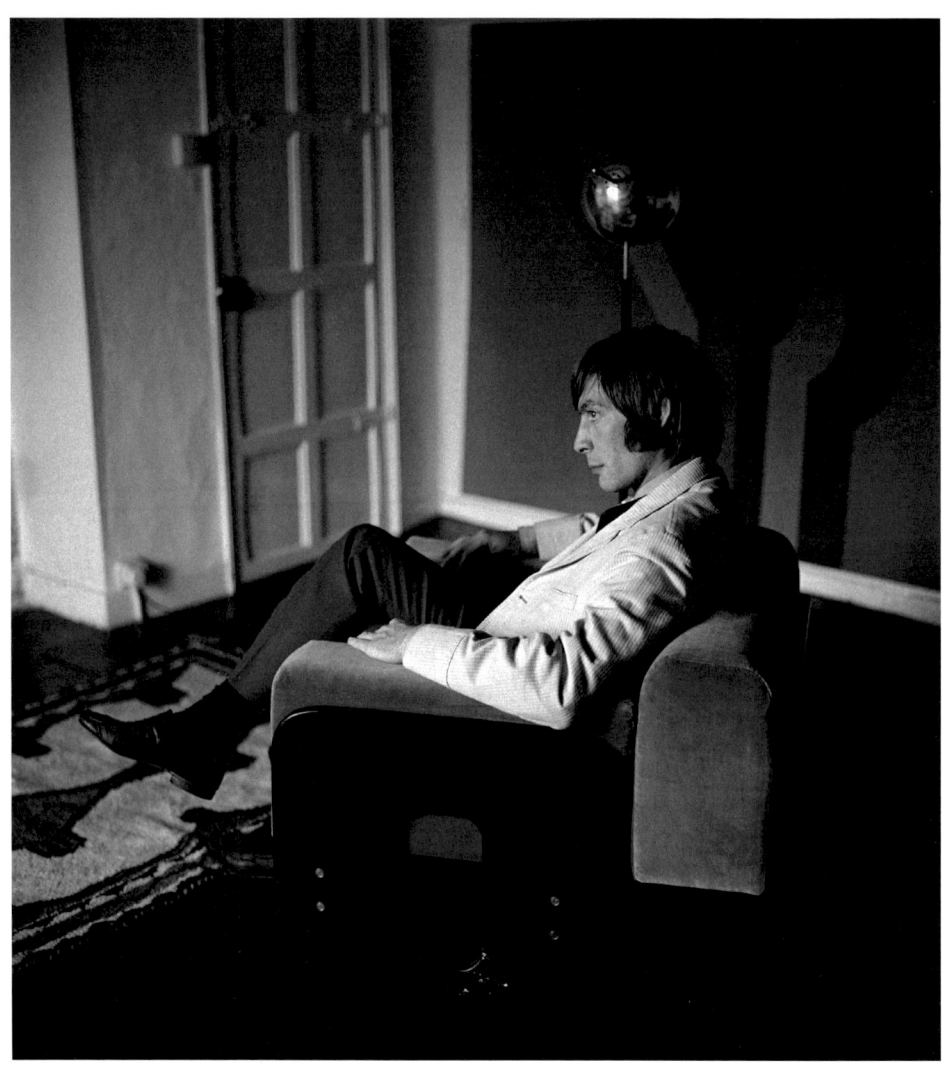

Gered Mankowitz
Charlie would leave London in 1966 for a
16th-century property in Lewes, near Brighton.
June 1966.

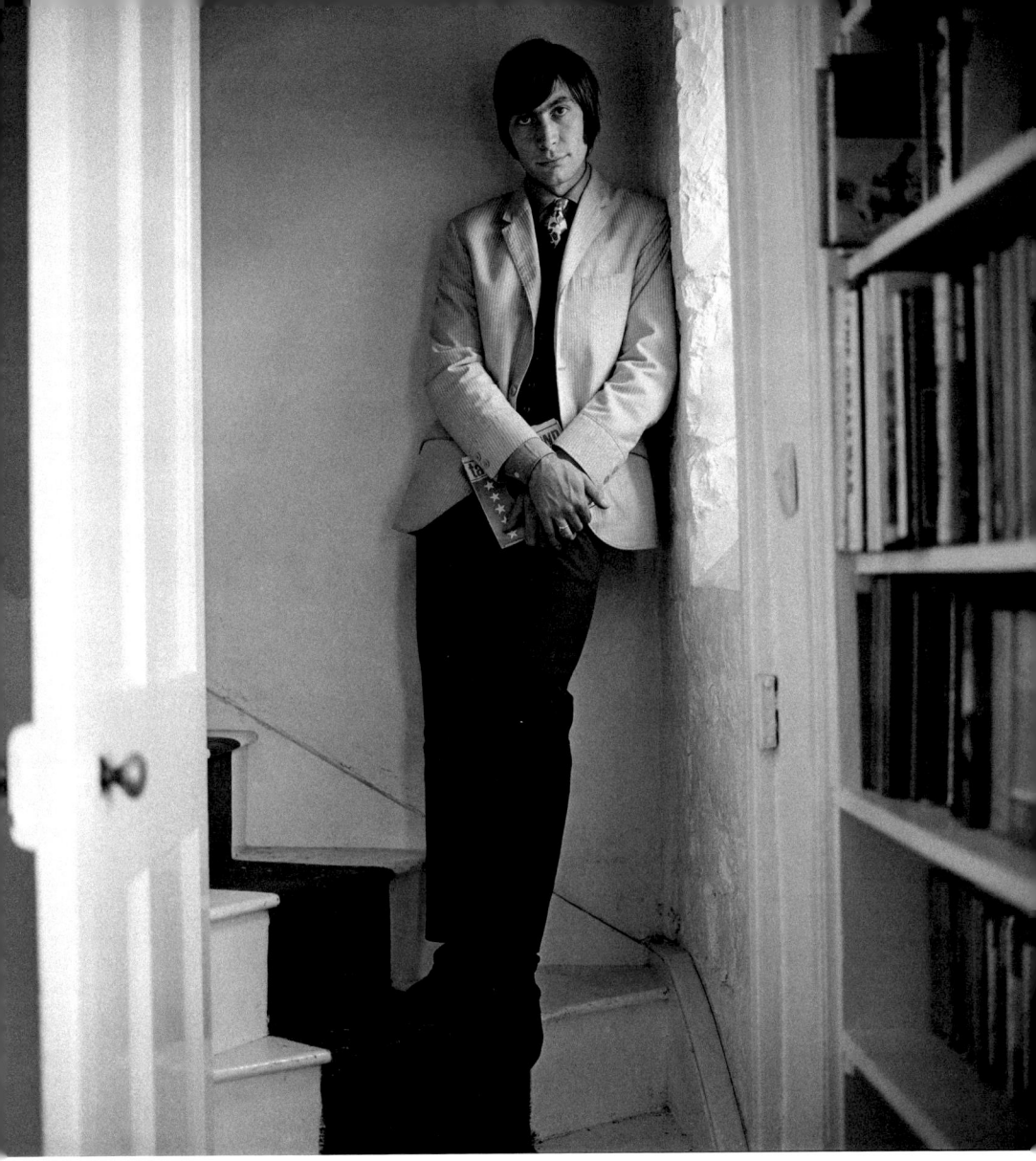

Gered Mankowitz
Charlie, June 1966.

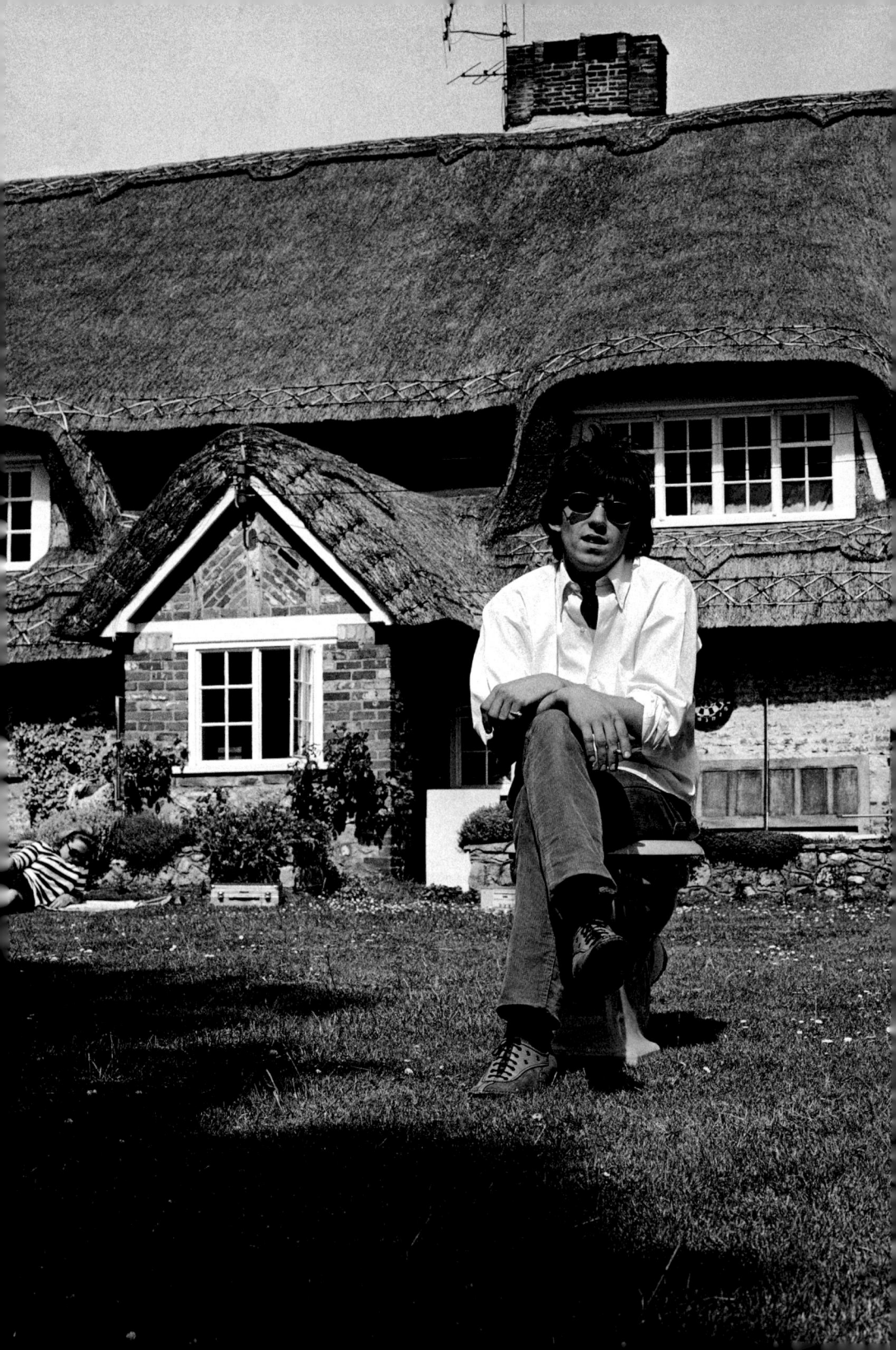

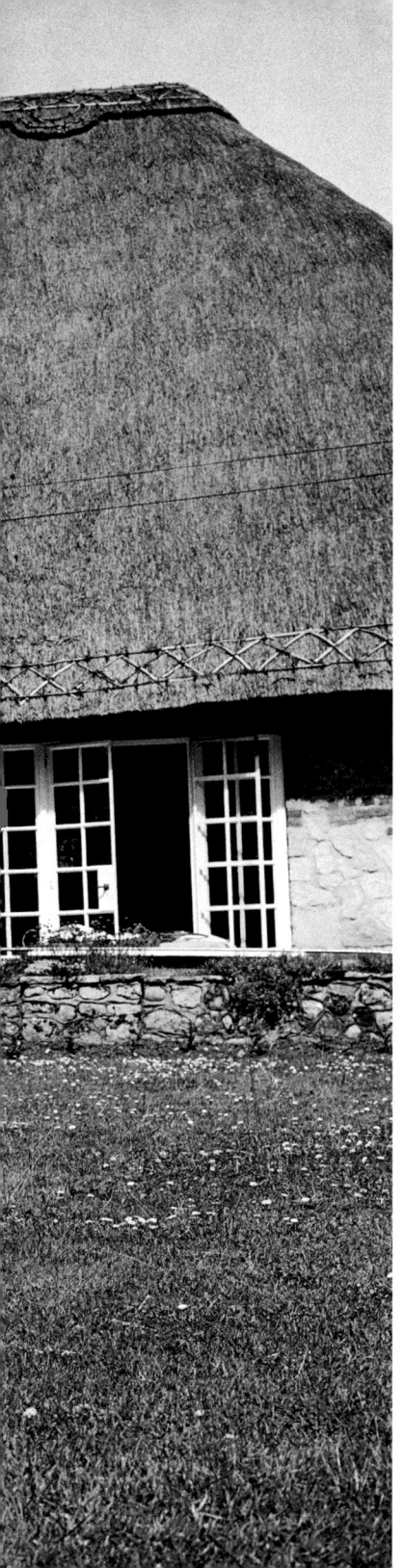

Gered Mankowitz
Keith pictured outside Redlands, his West Sussex home, June 1966. In search of a retreat outside London, Richards purchased this farmhouse in February 1966 for a paltry £17,500. It became a much-loved retreat that has endured for over five decades. Later infamous as the location for the drugs bust of February 1967, the 13th-century thatched building has a much older provenance, as it was referenced in the Domesday Book and was once (reportedly) a residence of Anne Boleyn, albeit briefly.
"On a rare day off between tours I did manage to buy Redlands, the house I still own in West Sussex, near Chichester Harbour; the house where we were busted, which burned down twice, the house I still love. We just spoke to each other the minute we saw each other ... I fell in love with Redlands the minute I saw it. Nobody's going to let this thing go, it's too picturesque." Keith Richards, *Life*, 2011

Gered Mankowitz
Keith alongside his adored Bentley S3
Continental in the driveway at Redlands,
June 1966.

PP. 182–183
Gered Mankowitz
A windy morning atop north London's Primrose
Hill was a choice location for the proposed cover
shot for the Stones' album *Between The Buttons*.
The group took off in Andrew Loog Oldham's
Rolls-Royce for the dawn shoot straight after an
all-night session at Olympic Studios in November
1966. To achieve the misty look he wanted, the
photographer smeared Vaseline over one of the
glass filters.

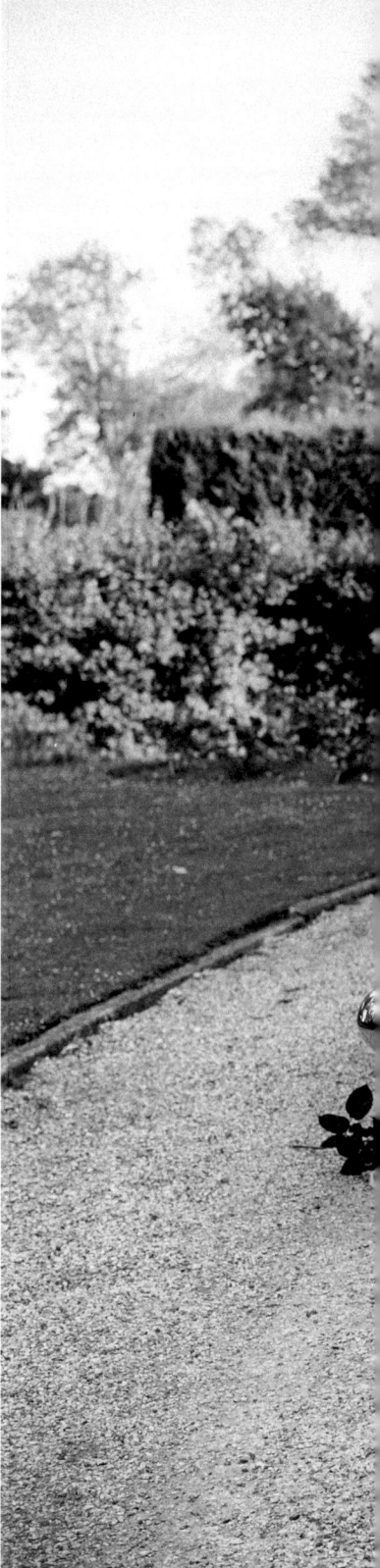

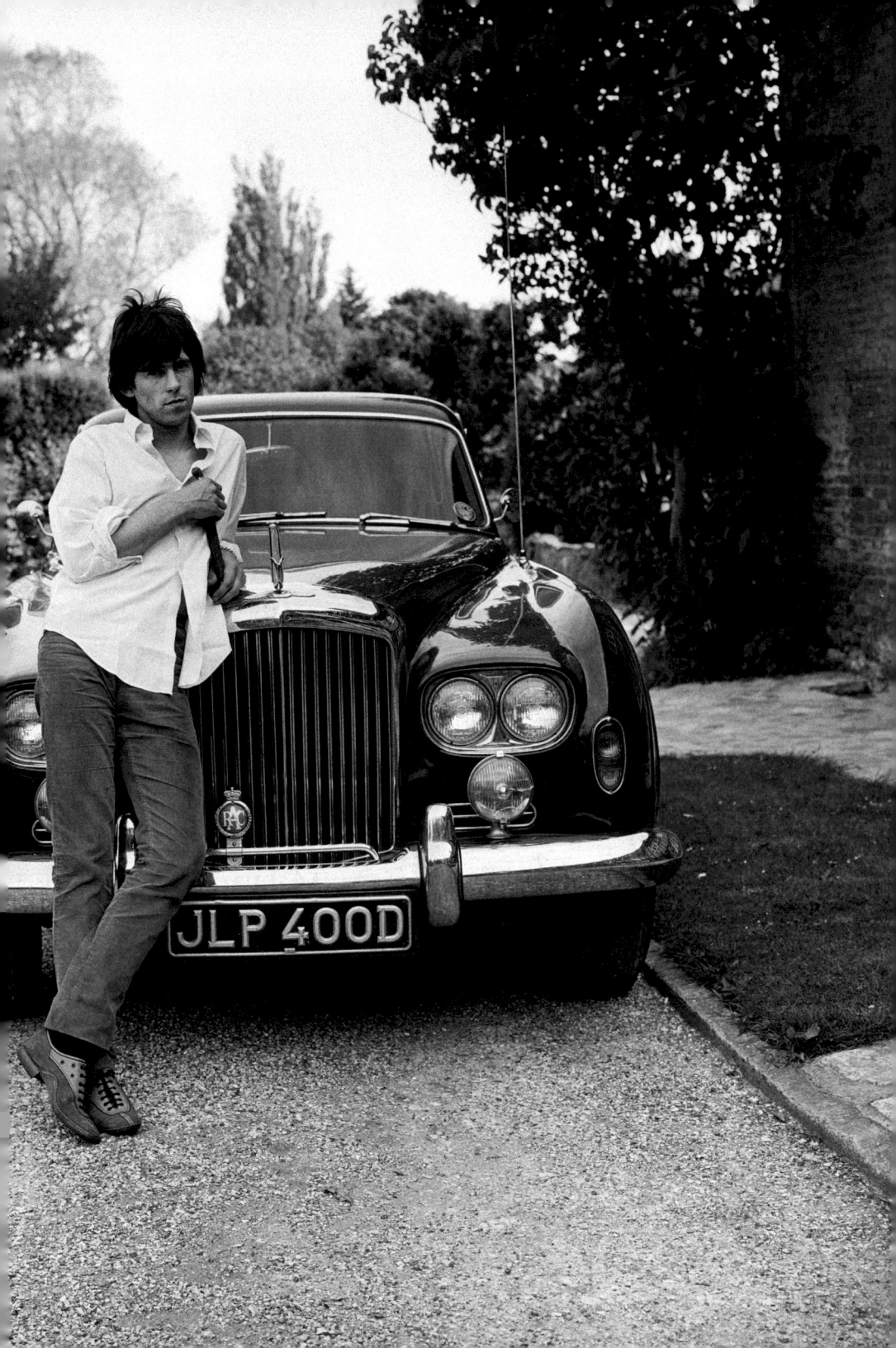

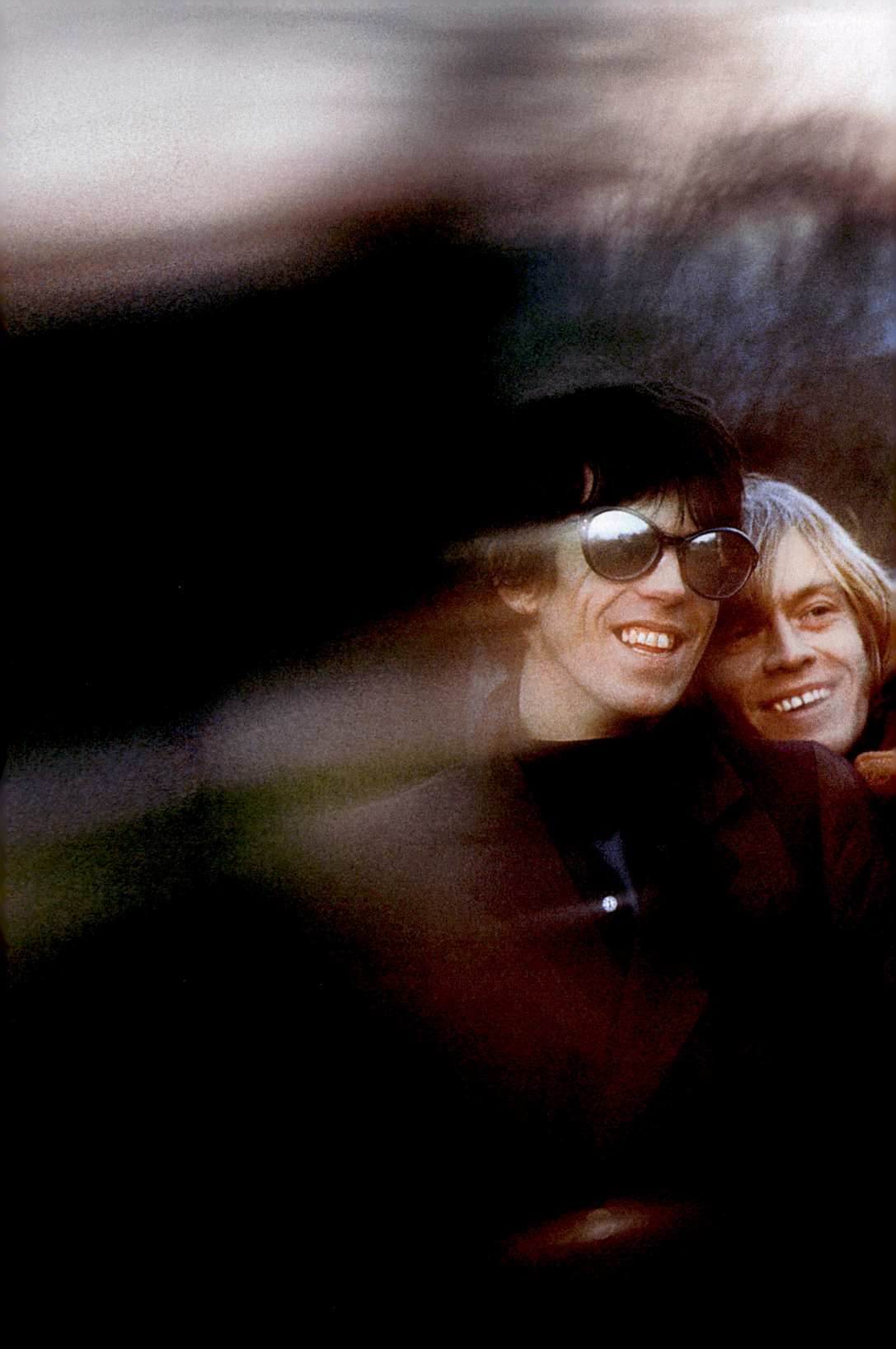

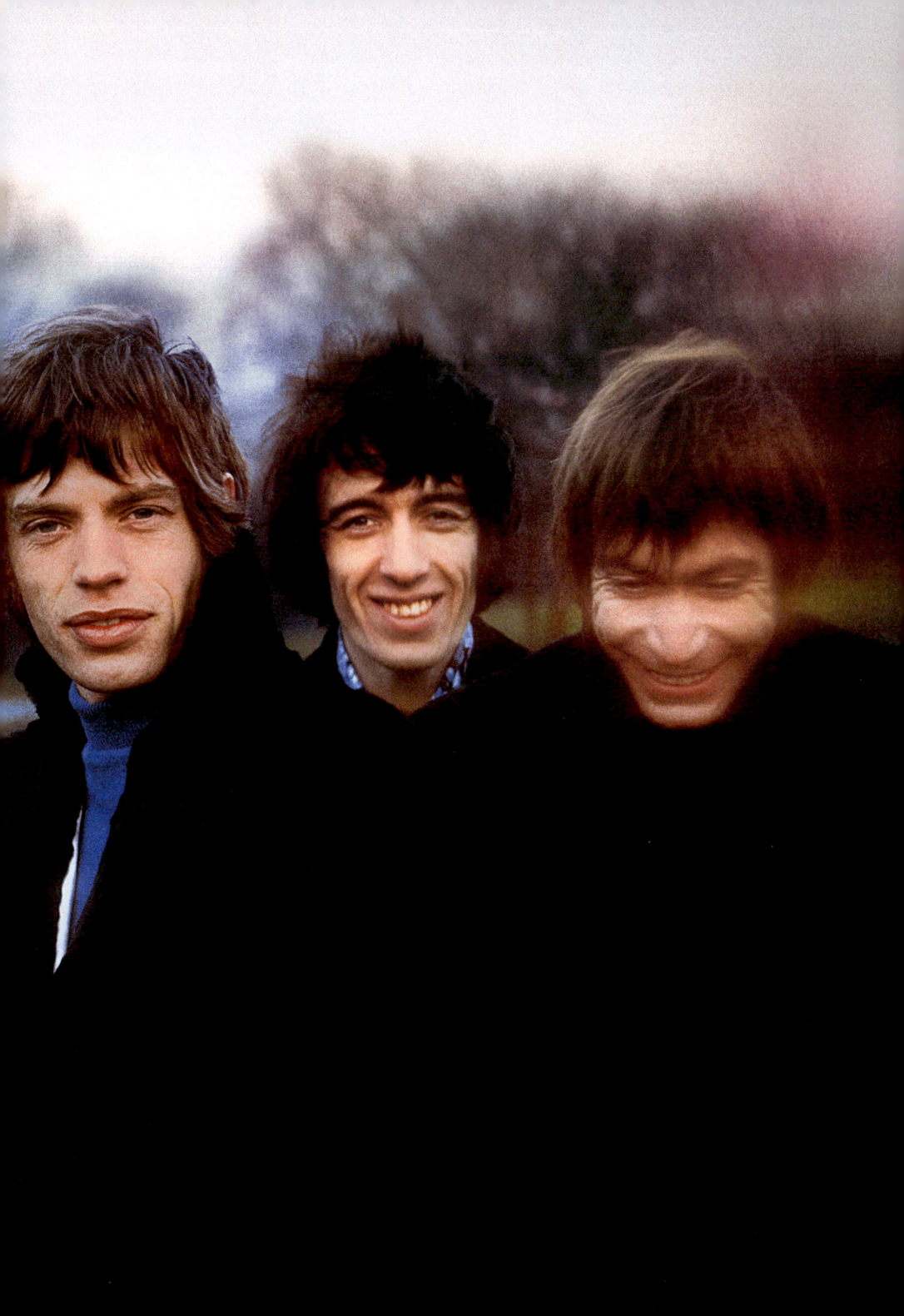

Gered Mankowitz

Primrose Hill, London, November 1966. The record cover evoked the druggy vibe swirling around Swinging London.

"When we reached the top of the hill, there was this well-known London character called 'Maxie' [sic] – a sort of prototype hippy – just standing on his own playing the flute. Mick walked up to him and offered him a joint and his only response was 'Ah – breakfast!'" Gered Mankowitz, *The Stones: 65–67*, 2002

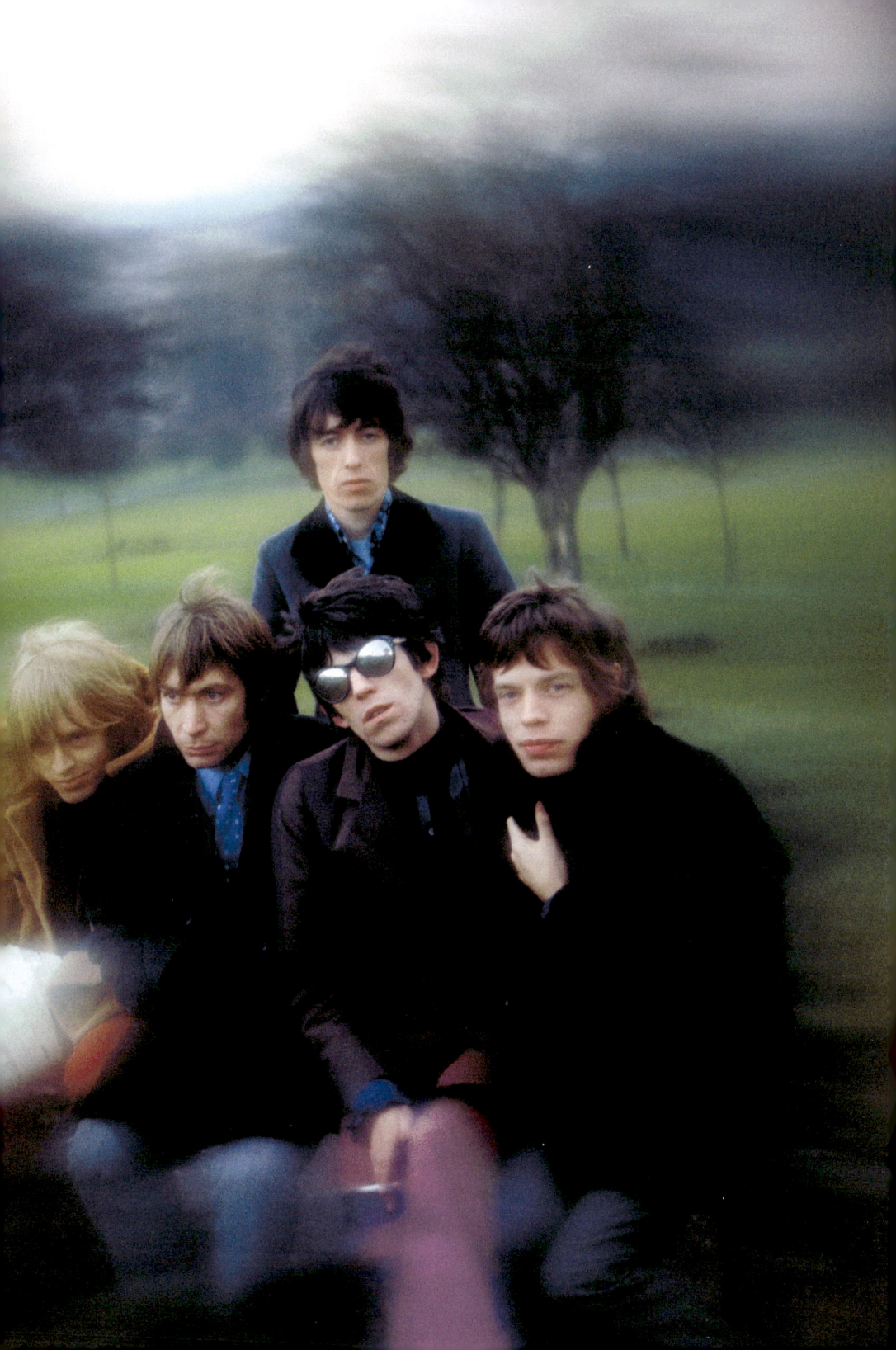

Gered Mankowitz
Primrose Hill, London, November 1966.
"The Stones' sleeves never seem to look very much different, but this one is more subtle than the rest. The back of the sleeve is far more unpretentious than is the current group trend." Record Mirror, 28 January 1967

PP. 188–189
Gered Mankowitz
Primrose Hill, London, November 1966. Despite the early-morning mist it is evident that Brian had been burning the candle at both ends. His shattered appearance shows him clearly in decline, marginalised and on the fringes of the frame.

PP. 190–191
Gered Mankowitz
Between The Buttons would serve as a curtain call to the Stones' first chapter. Released in January 1967, just as psychedelia was about to dawn, the album's highlights were songs such as "Yesterday's Papers", "Back Street Girl" and "Cool, Calm And Collected". American record buyers would find the package enlivened by the inclusion of current singles "Let's Spend The Night Together" and "Ruby Tuesday".

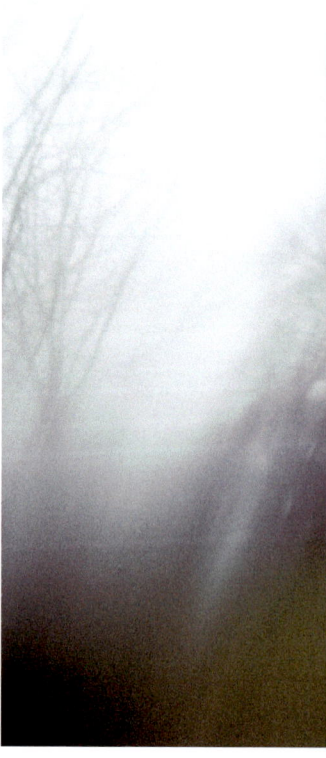

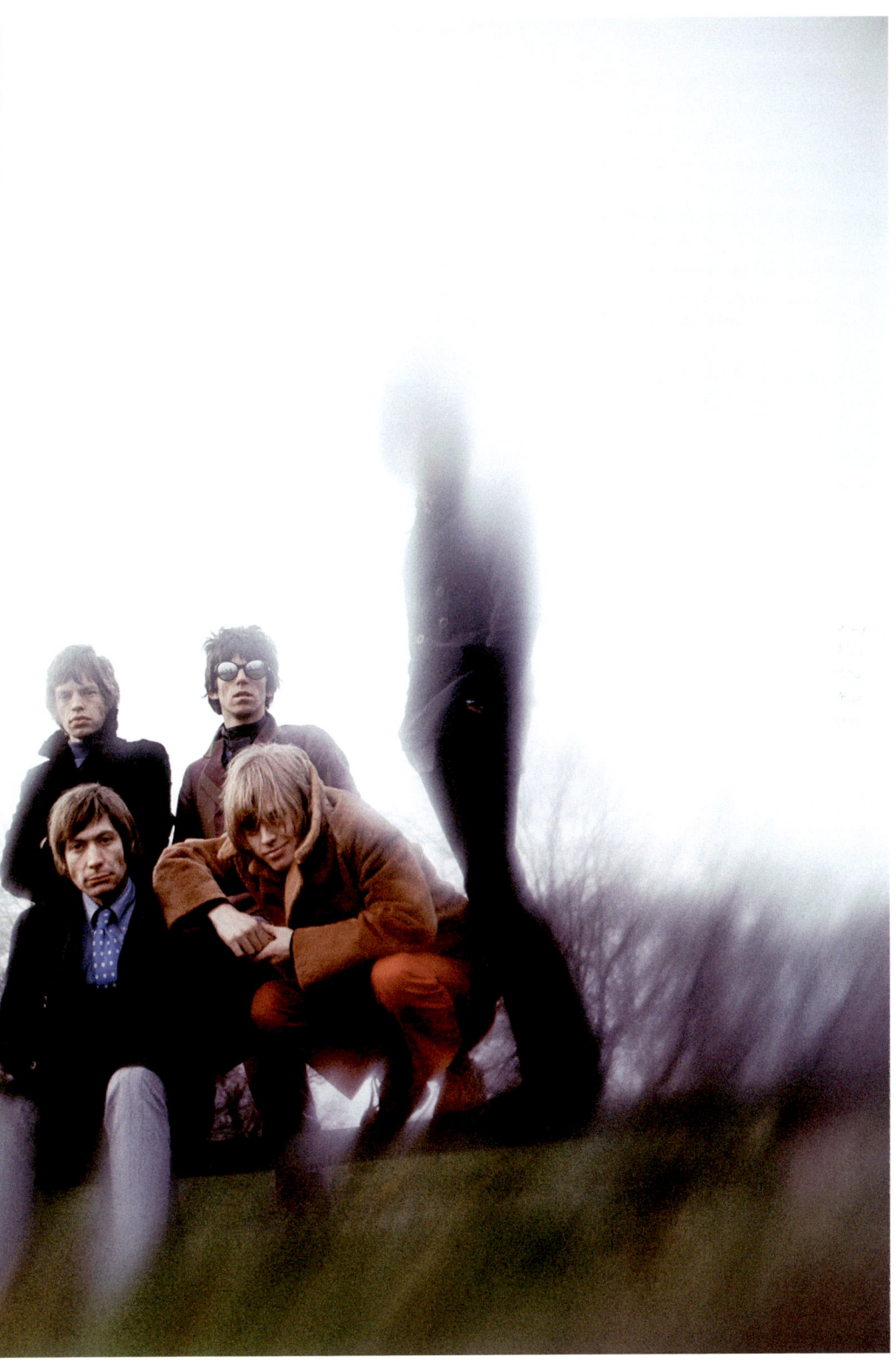

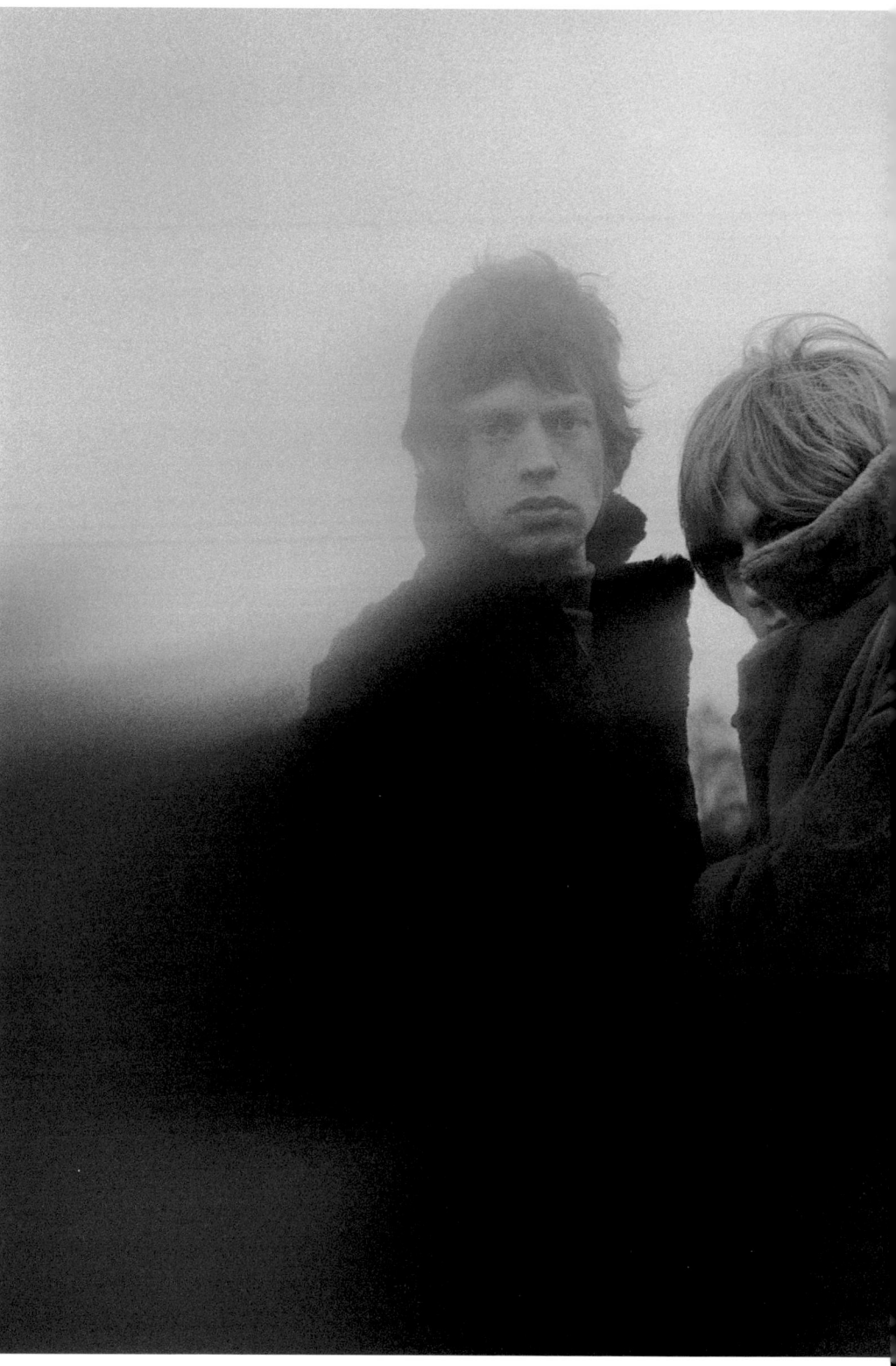

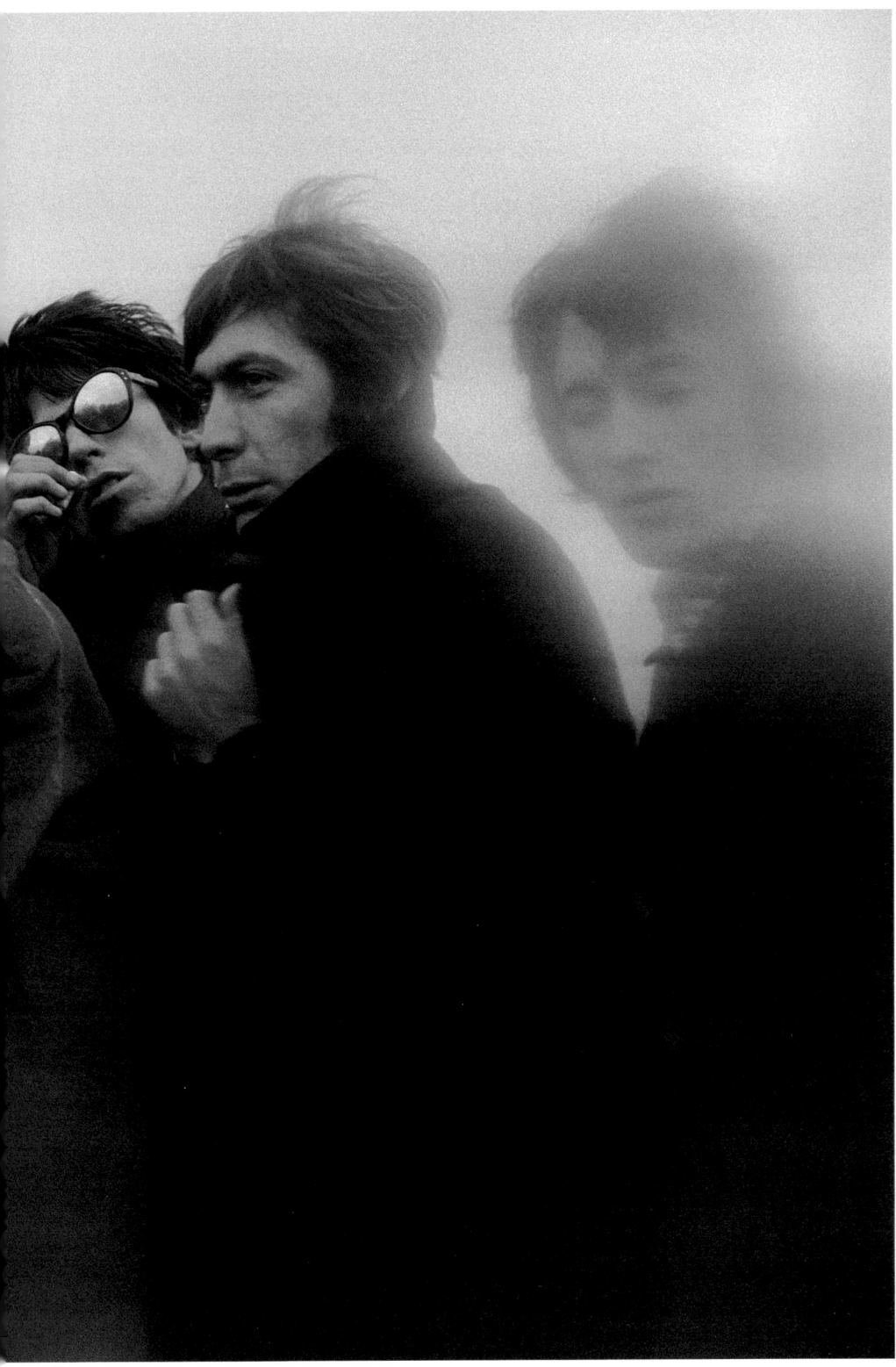

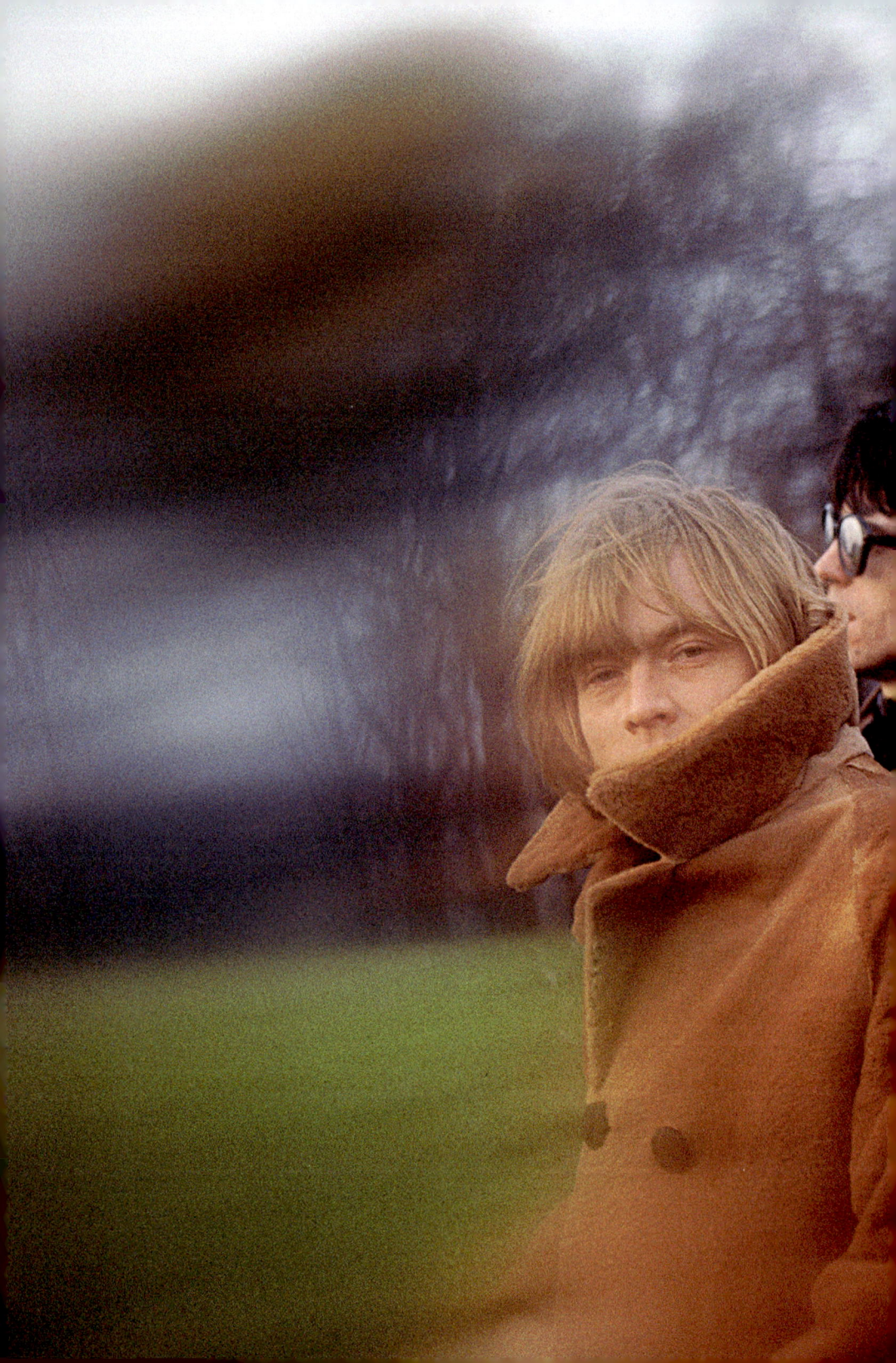

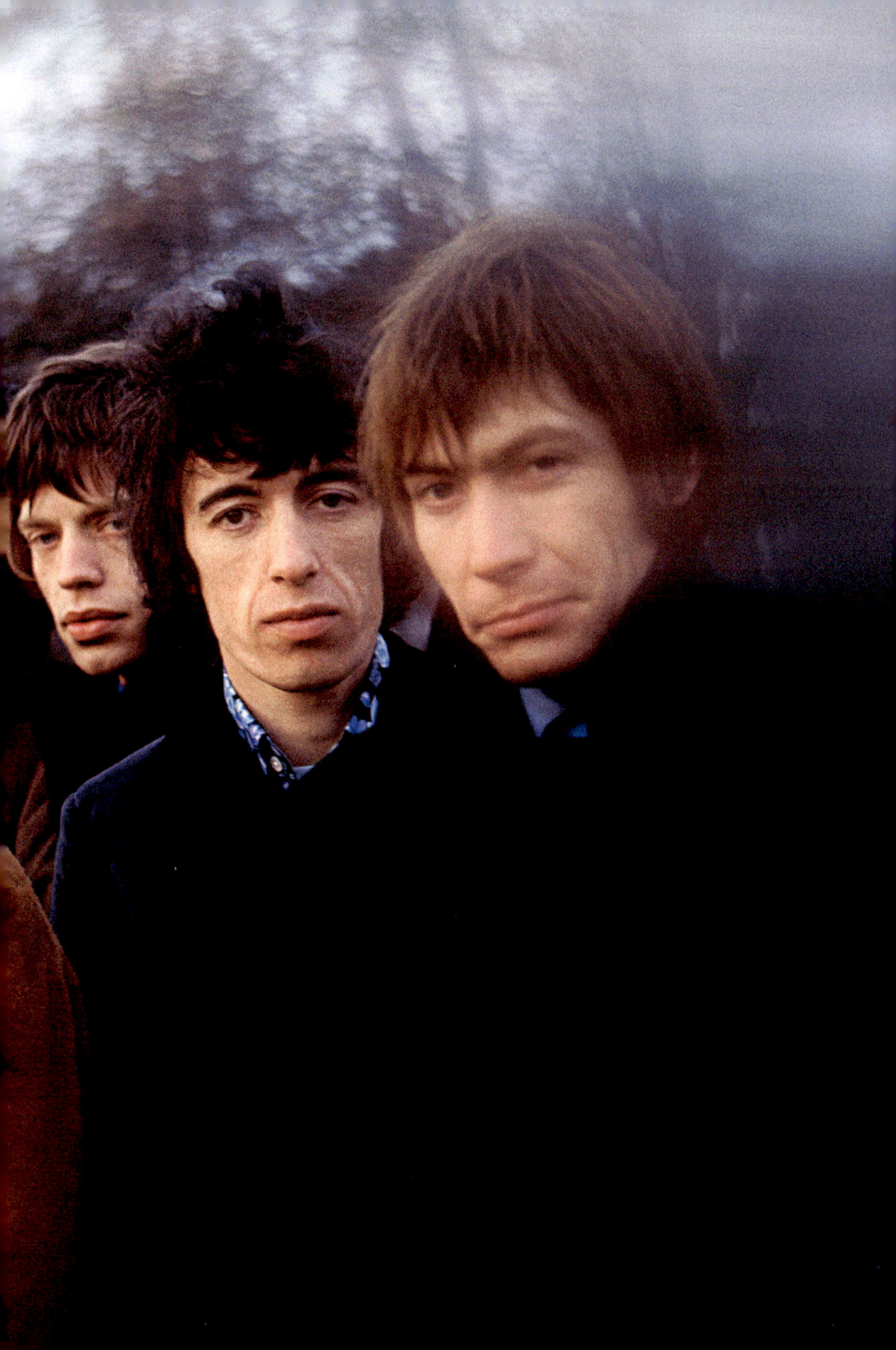

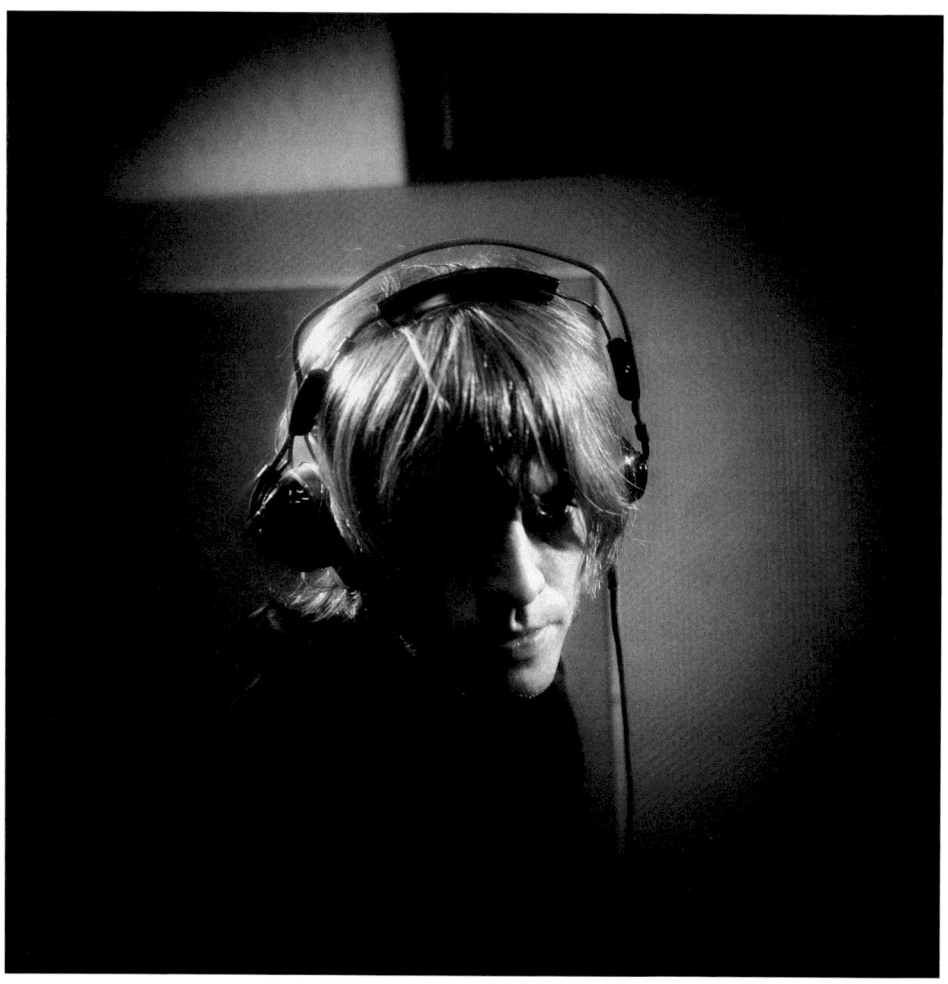

Gered Mankowitz

While he could appear lost on stage, the studio elevated Brian to achieve new levels of creativity. The studio was a far more receptive arena than concert venues, and recording *Between The Buttons* revealed the peak of his creative input. Olympic Studios, London, December 1966.

"It's important to be in the studio rather than in crappy baseball halls and stadiums around the country ... It's a question about what's about to be gained by going around again, but there's a hell of a lot to be gained from letting them share our progression, because we are progressing very fast." Brian Jones, *Beat* magazine, 15 July 1967

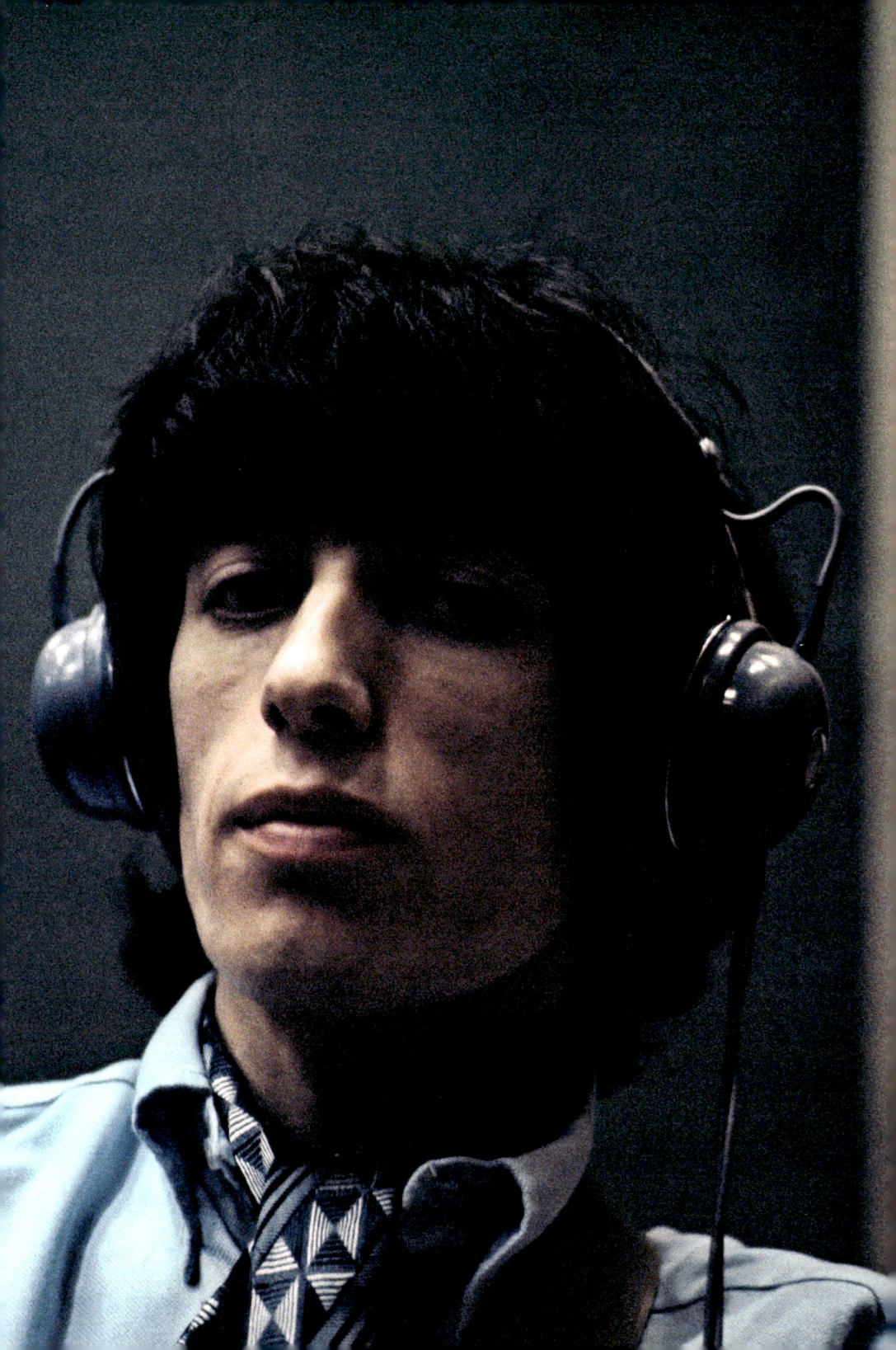

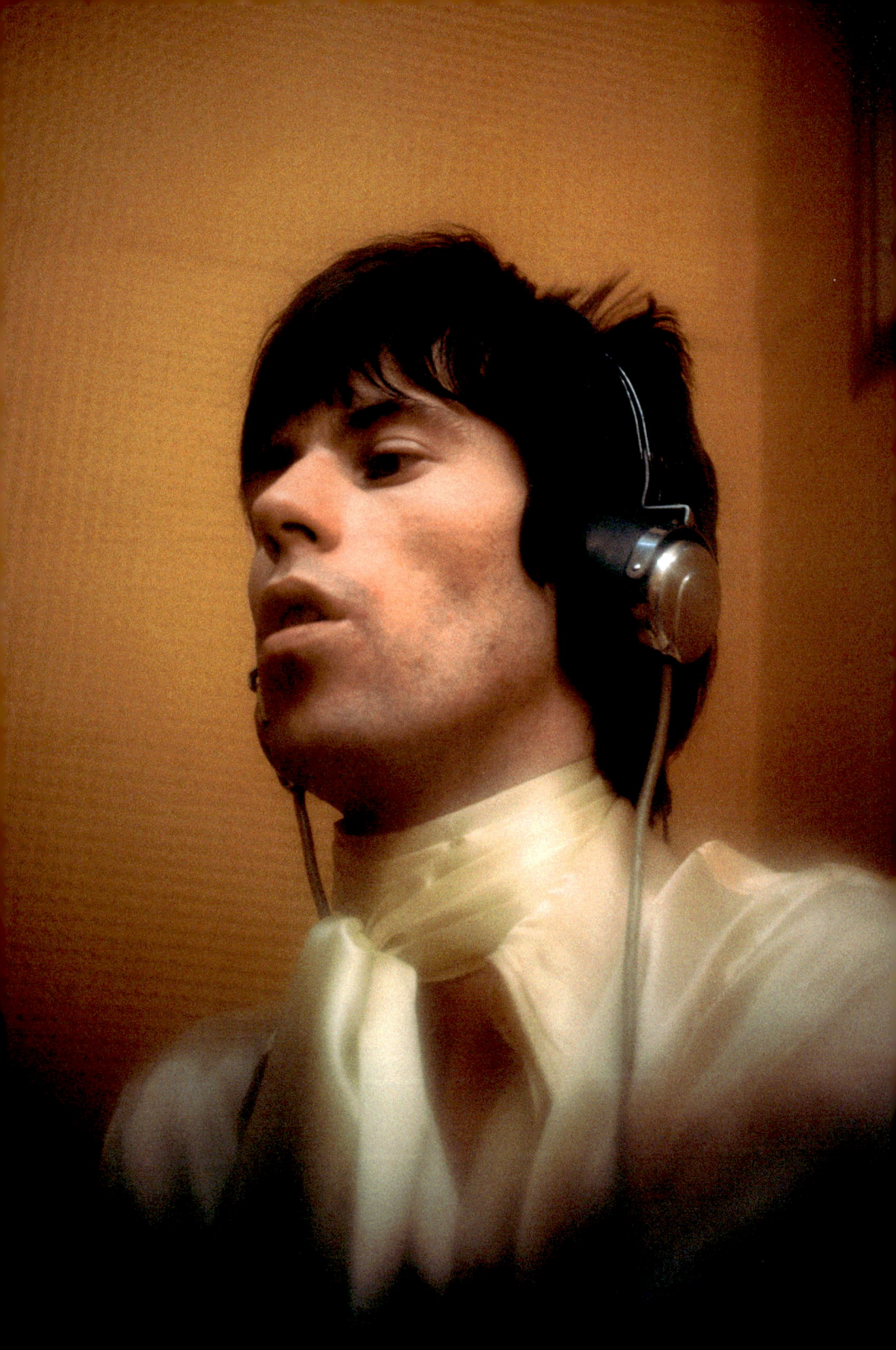

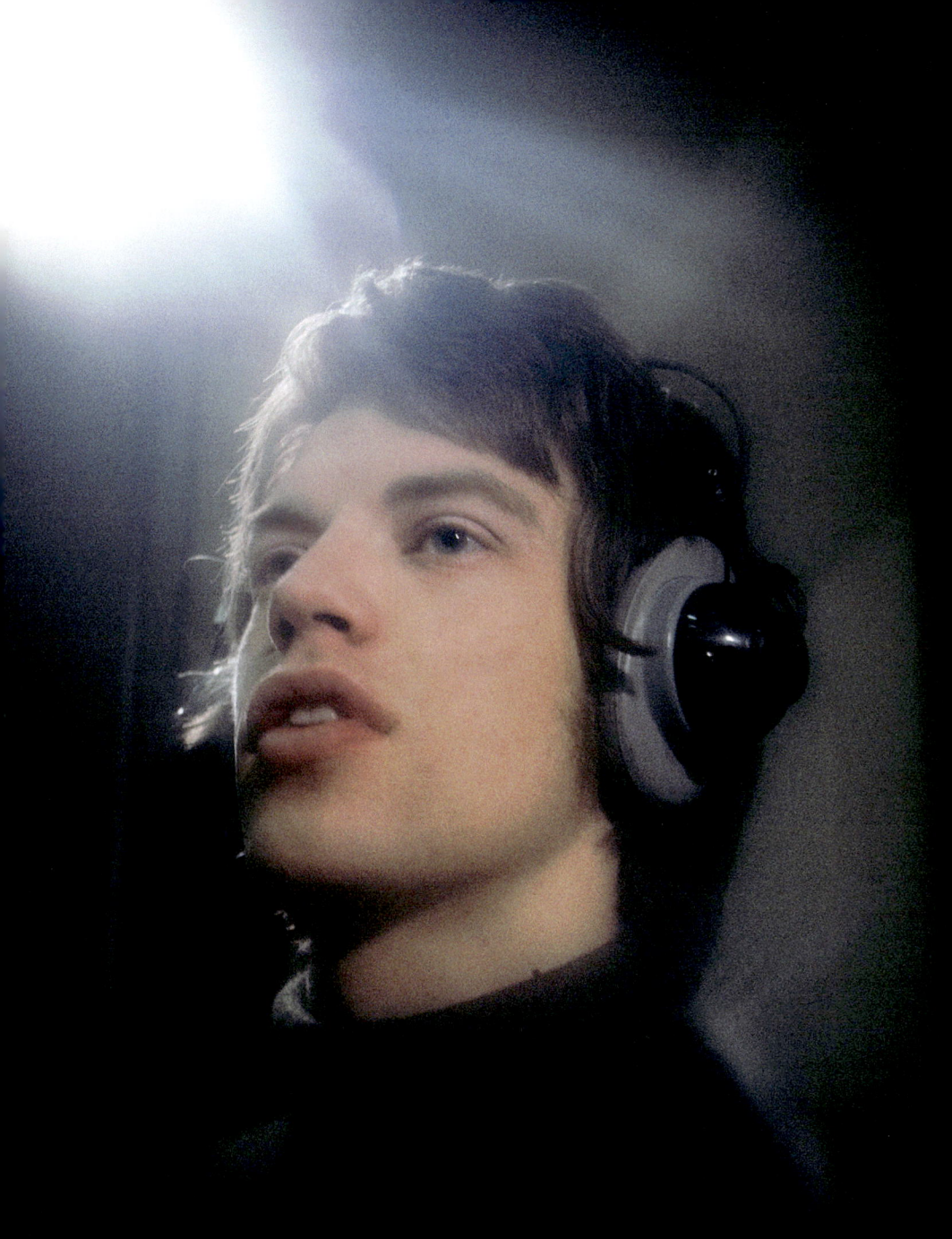

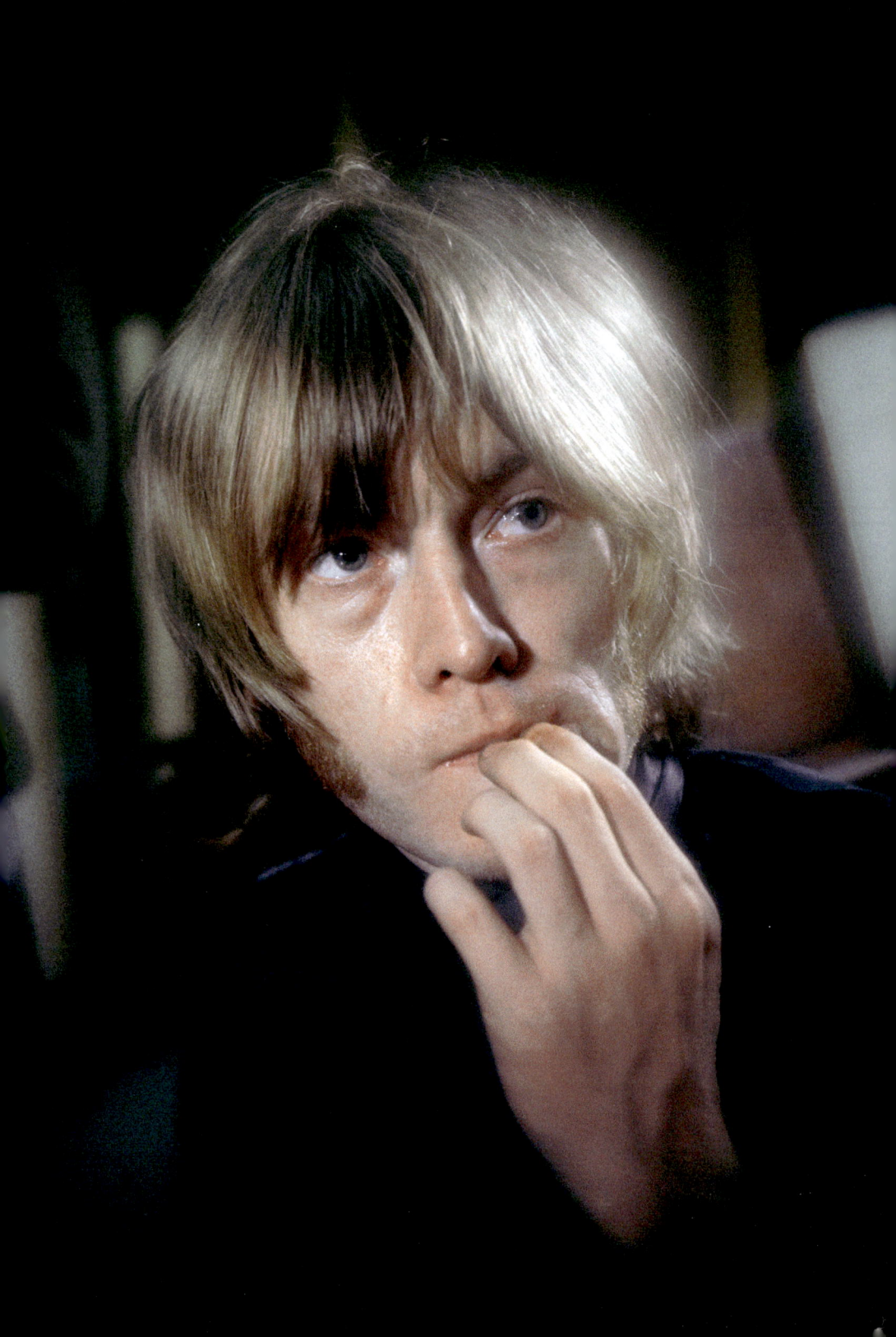

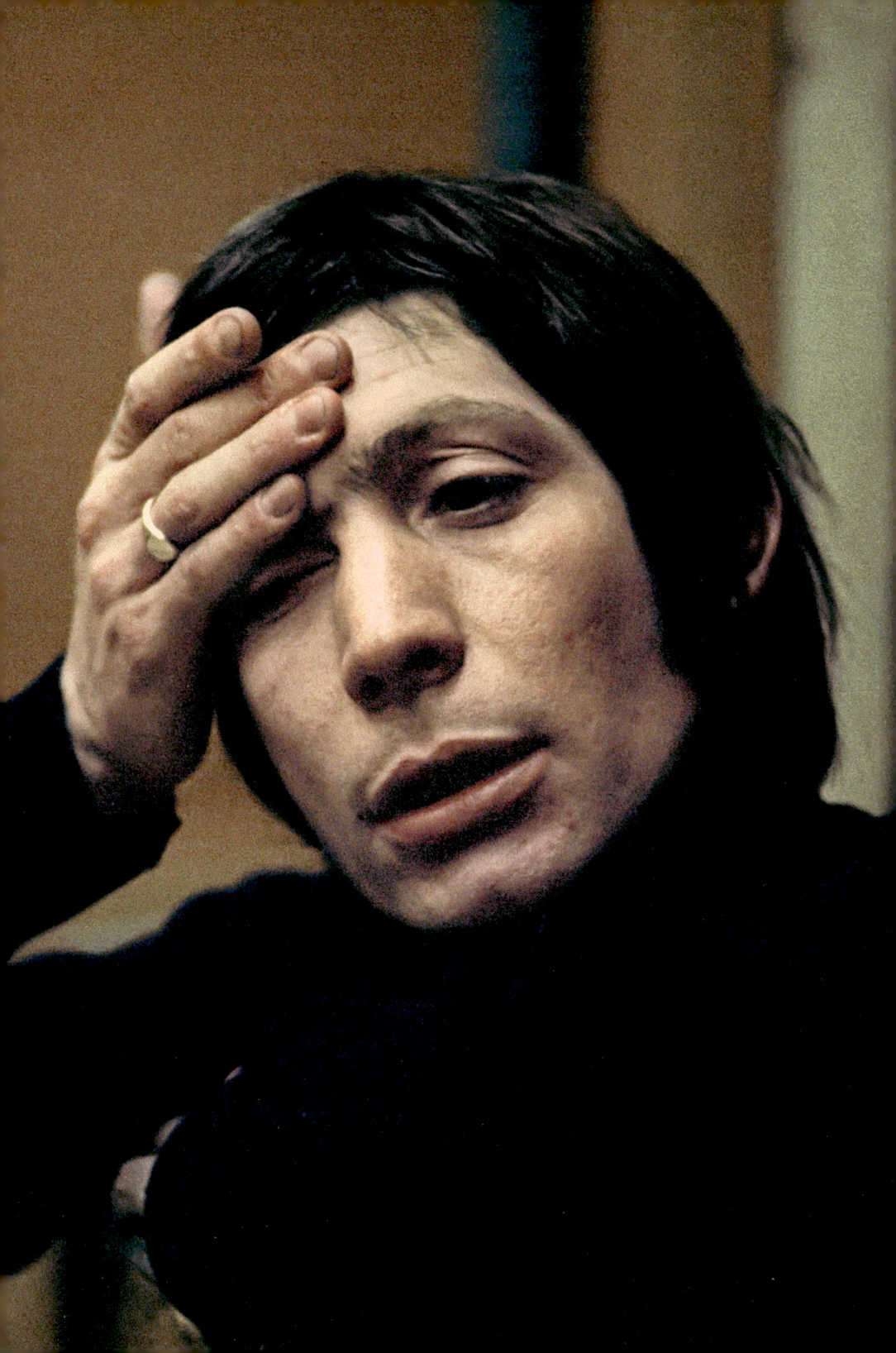

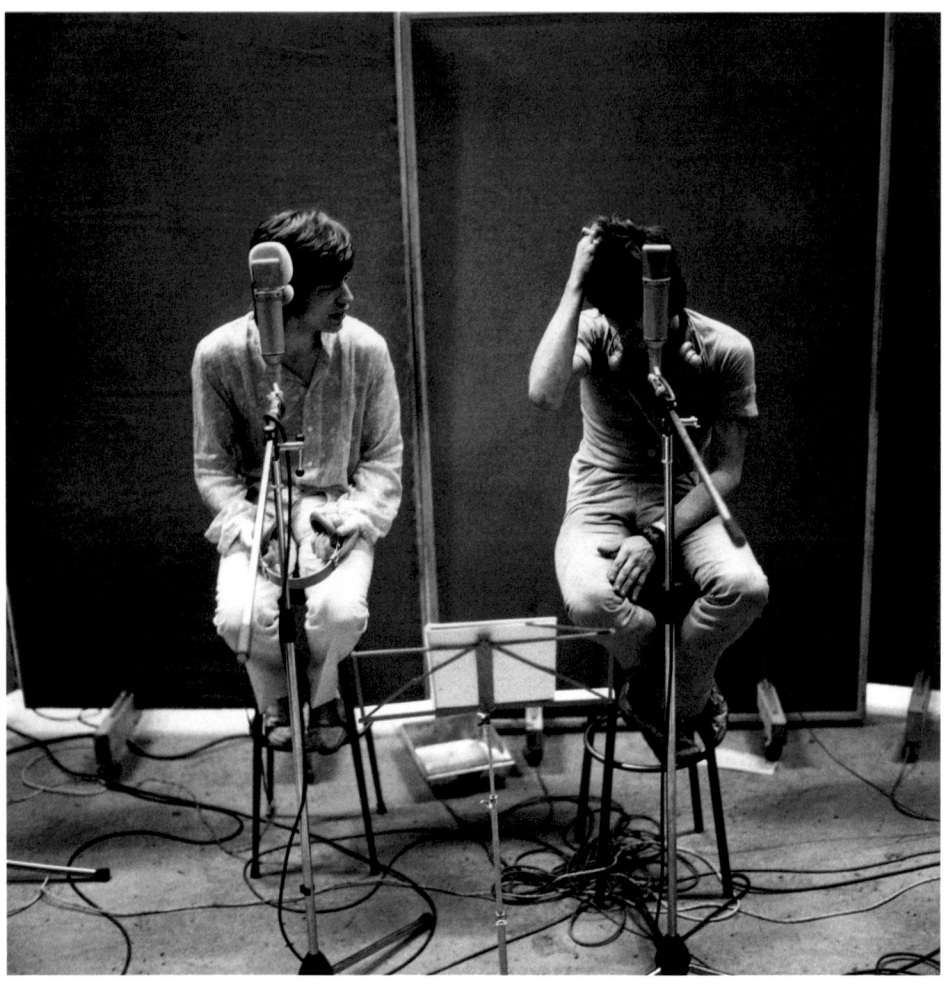

PP. 193–197

Gered Mankowitz

Olympic Studios, London, May 1967. Their profile raised by the drug bust at Redlands in February 1967, the embattled Stones – particularly Keith – found the security of the recording studio much to their liking. The group was exploring new musical dimensions and *Their Satanic Majesties Request* was in embryonic form.

"In a once sedate world of faded splendour, everything new, uninhibited and kinky is blooming at the top of London life … The Rolling Stones, whose music is most 'in' right now, reign as a new breed of royalty." Time magazine, 15 April 1966

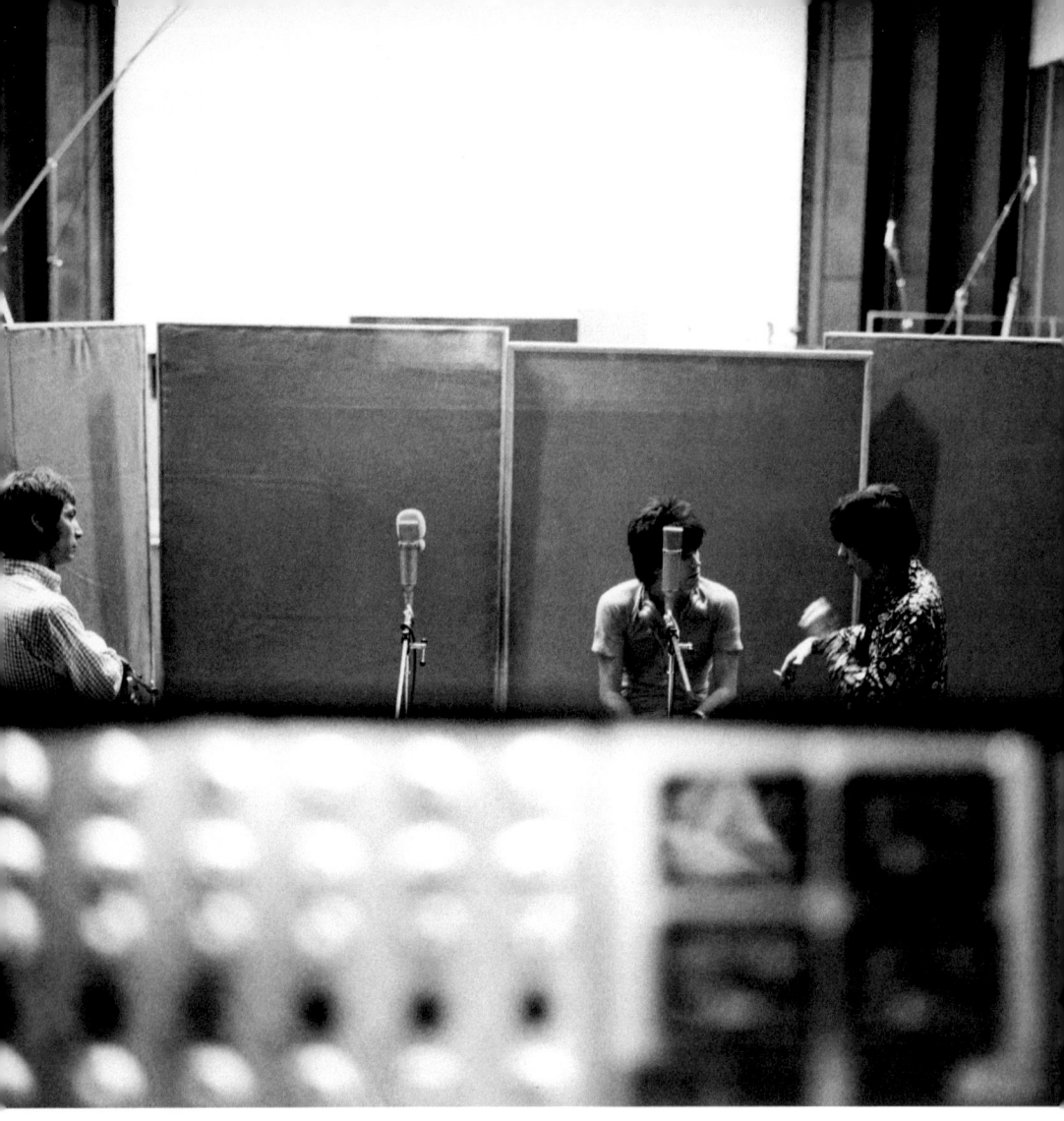

Thomas Beyl
Olympic Studios, Barnes, London, offering state-of-the-art equipment, the studio became their preferred working environment from 1966 to 1970. The group allowed more time for recording in the studio than ever before. The current music scene demanded far greater experimentation, so considerable time was spent developing new sounds, spring–summer 1967.

Thomas Beyl
Charlie, Keith and Glyn Johns: a view from the mixing desk at Olympic Studios during the making of *Their Satanic Majesties Request*, spring–summer 1967.

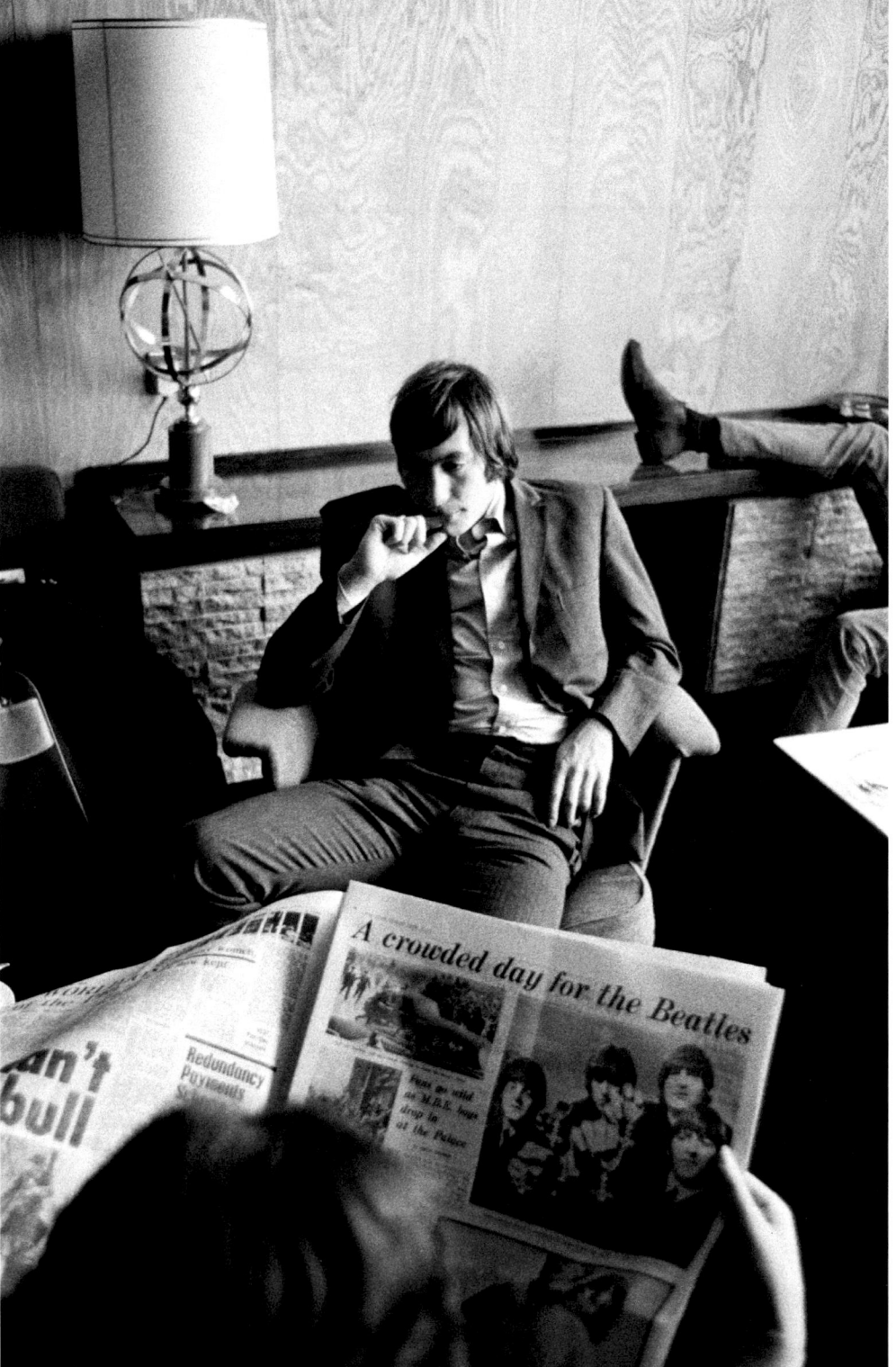

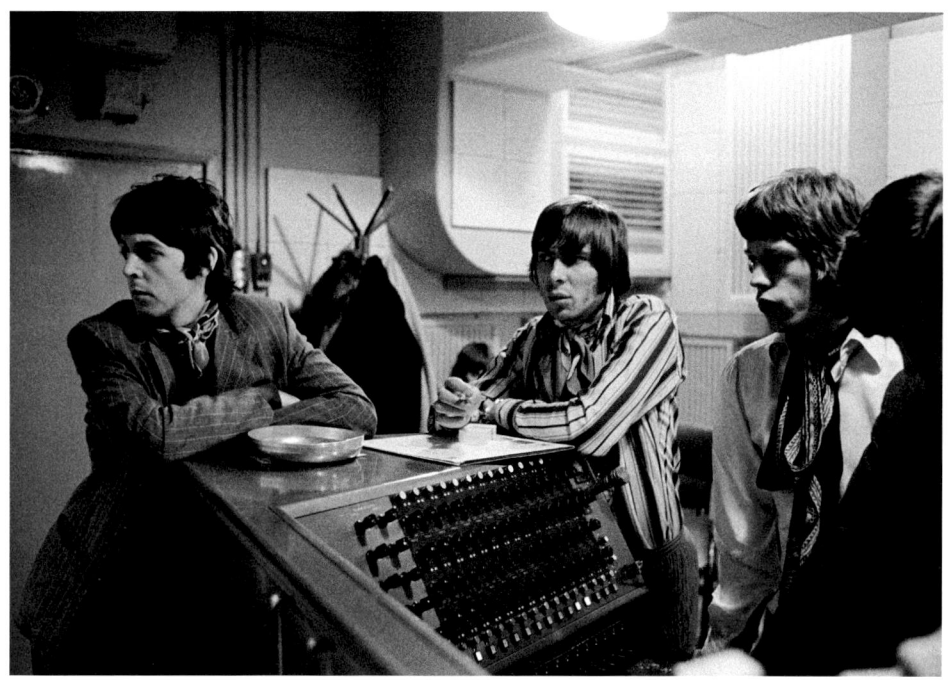

Gered Mankowitz

While waiting for a delayed flight to New York on 27 October 1965, the group was ushered into London Airport's VIP lounge. The day after The Beatles received their MBEs at Buckingham Palace, the Stones were getting their own ascension to rock royalty.

Gered Mankowitz

Despite rivalries that were played up by the media, The Beatles maintained a close friendship with the Stones during the 1960s, and mutual drop-ins on recording sessions were frequent. Of all The Beatles, Paul McCartney seemed the most interested in the Stones' output in the mid-1960s. During a Marianne Faithfull recording session at Decca Records in north London in May 1967, McCartney popped in to watch proceedings, alongside Mick and engineer Glyn Johns. *"As it went on we'd call up John, Paul or George about the single releases. Everybody was talking about The Beatles versus the Stones and all that crap, and yet between us, it would be, 'You come out first and we'll wait two weeks.' We would try never to clash; there was plenty of room for both of us. ... There would be surreptitious phone calls. It was 'Ok, ours is ready, yours ain't?' ... 'All right, you go first.'"* Keith Richards, quoted in *According To The Rolling Stones*, 2003

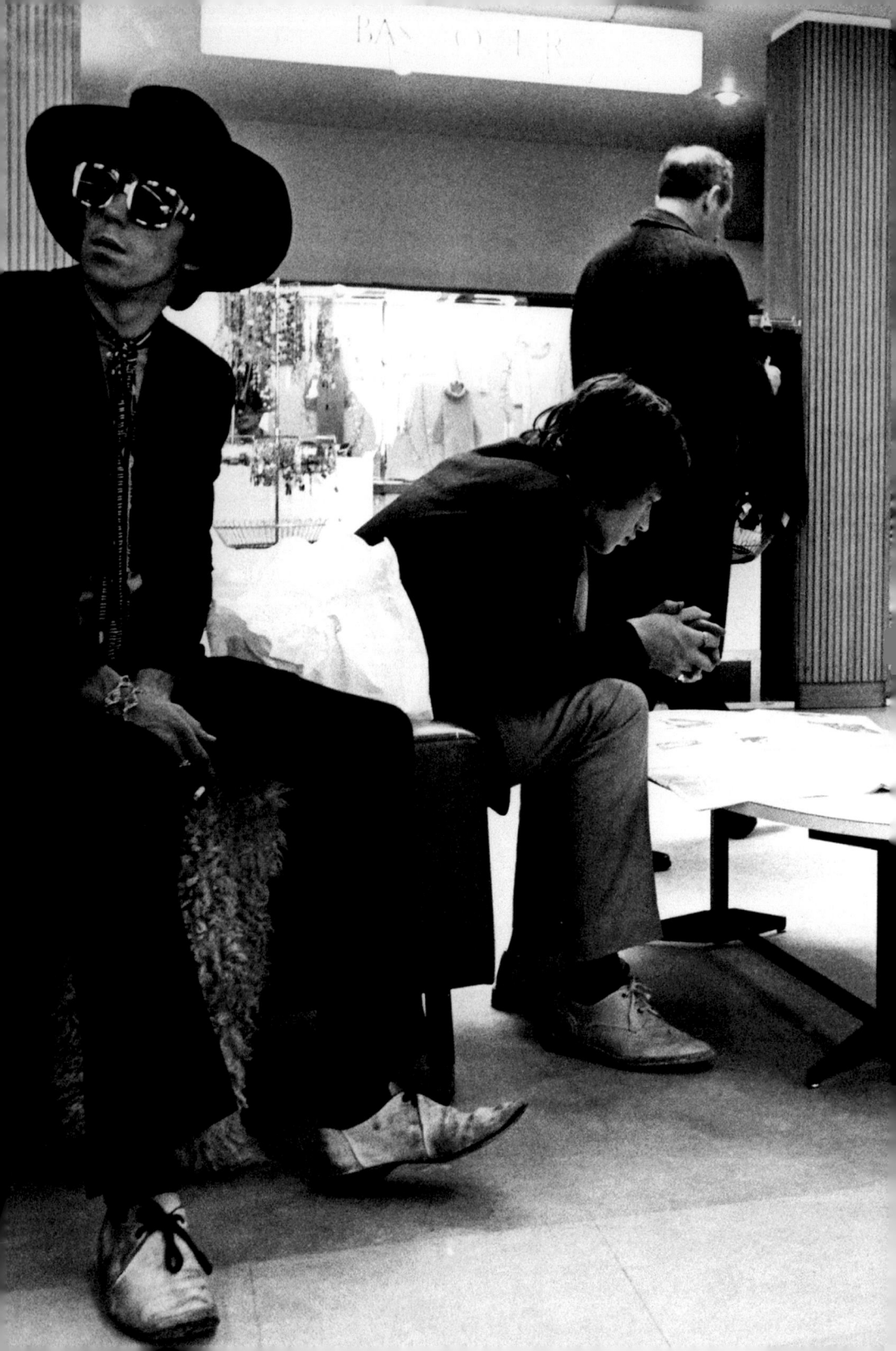

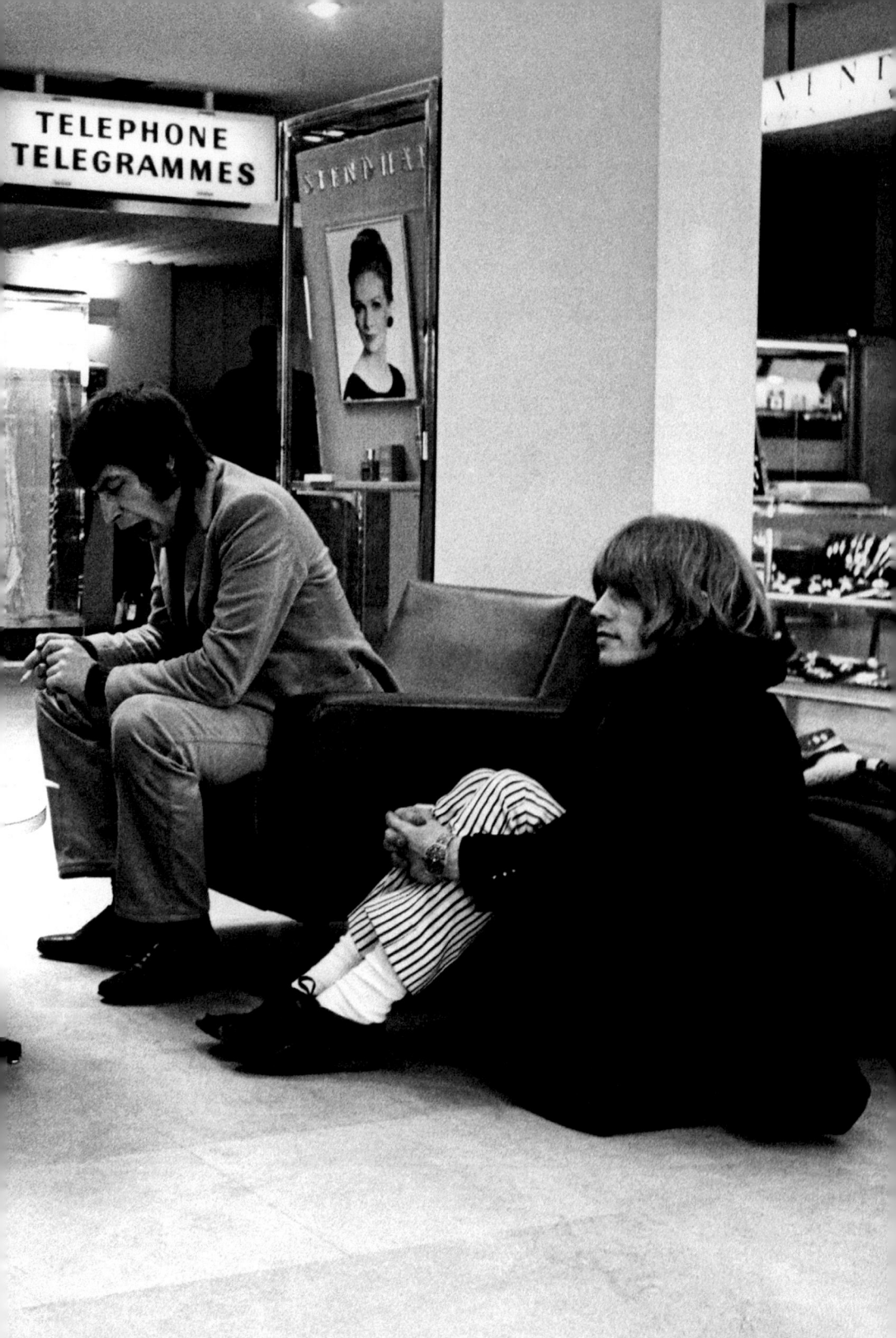

Anonymous
Between airport, concert and hotel, the Stones
take a breather during their European tour,
March–April 1967.

Günter Zint
Meeting the press in Bremen, West Germany,
29 March 1967. That day, the Stones would play
two shows at the Stadthalle, with support acts
including The Creation and The Easybeats.

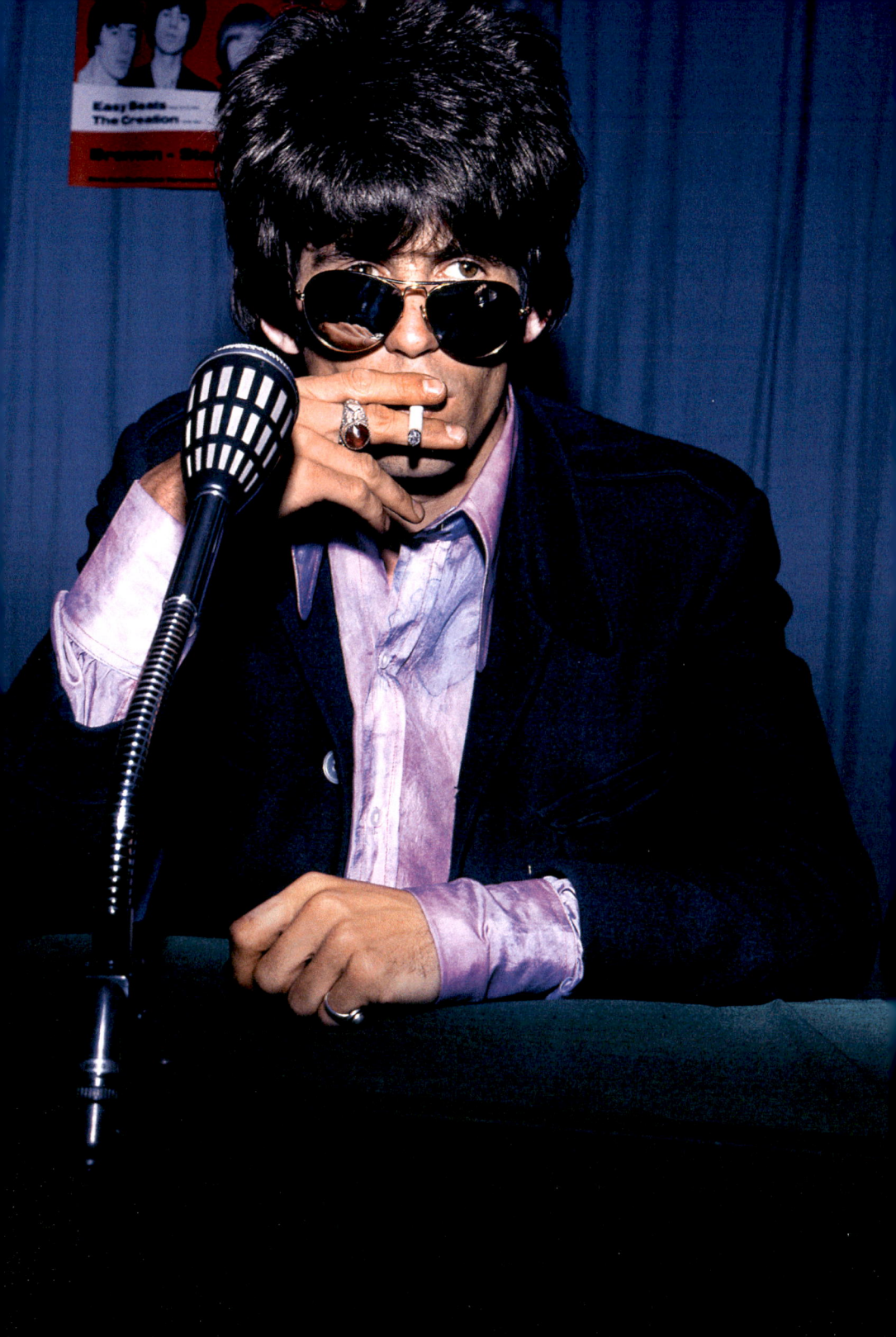

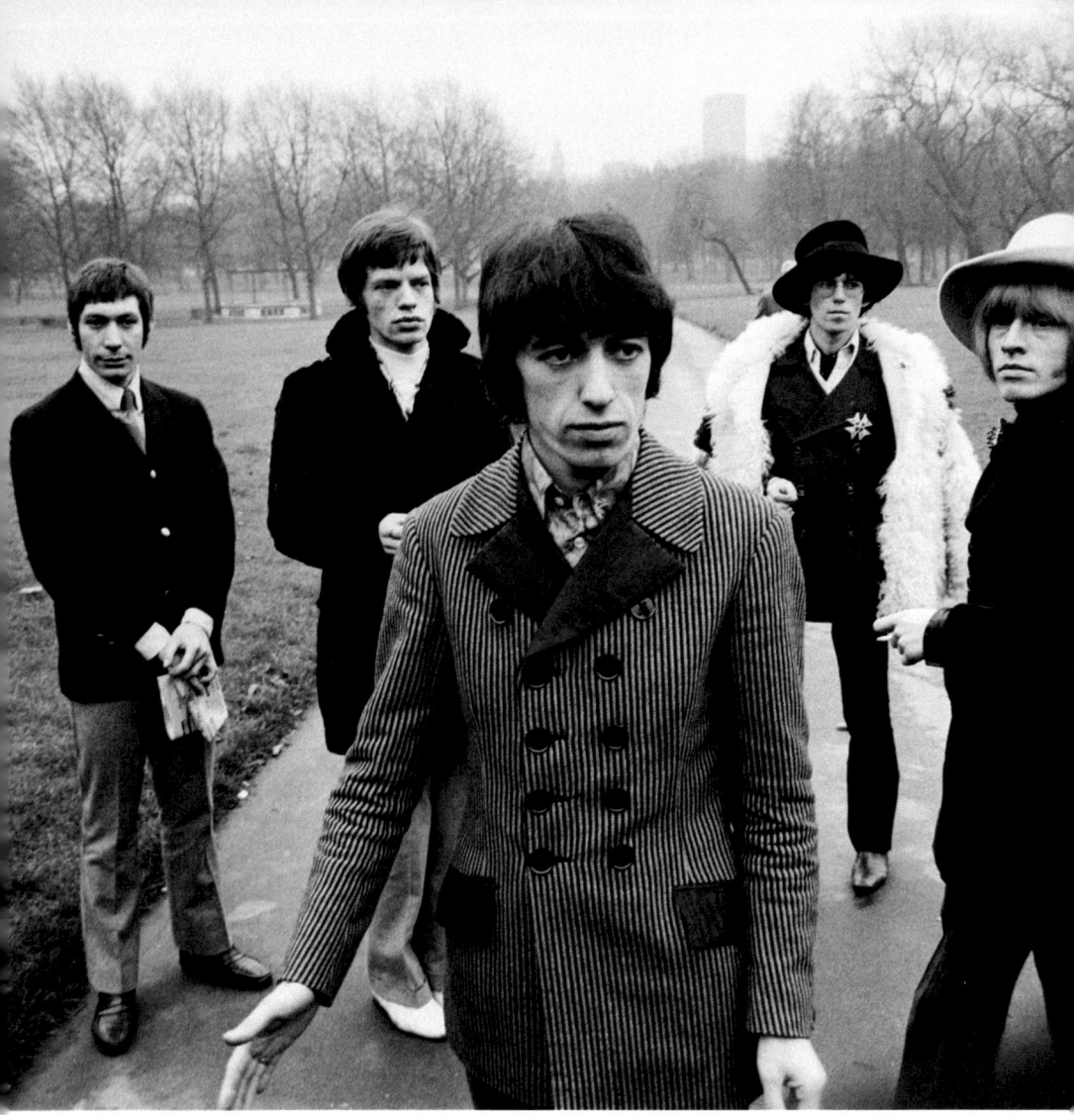

Peter Stone
A famous photo session held on 11 January 1967
prior to their trip to the States to appear on
The Ed Sullivan Show. It is a grim London morning, but nevertheless the Stones in all their
1960s finery are clearly the lords of the manor.

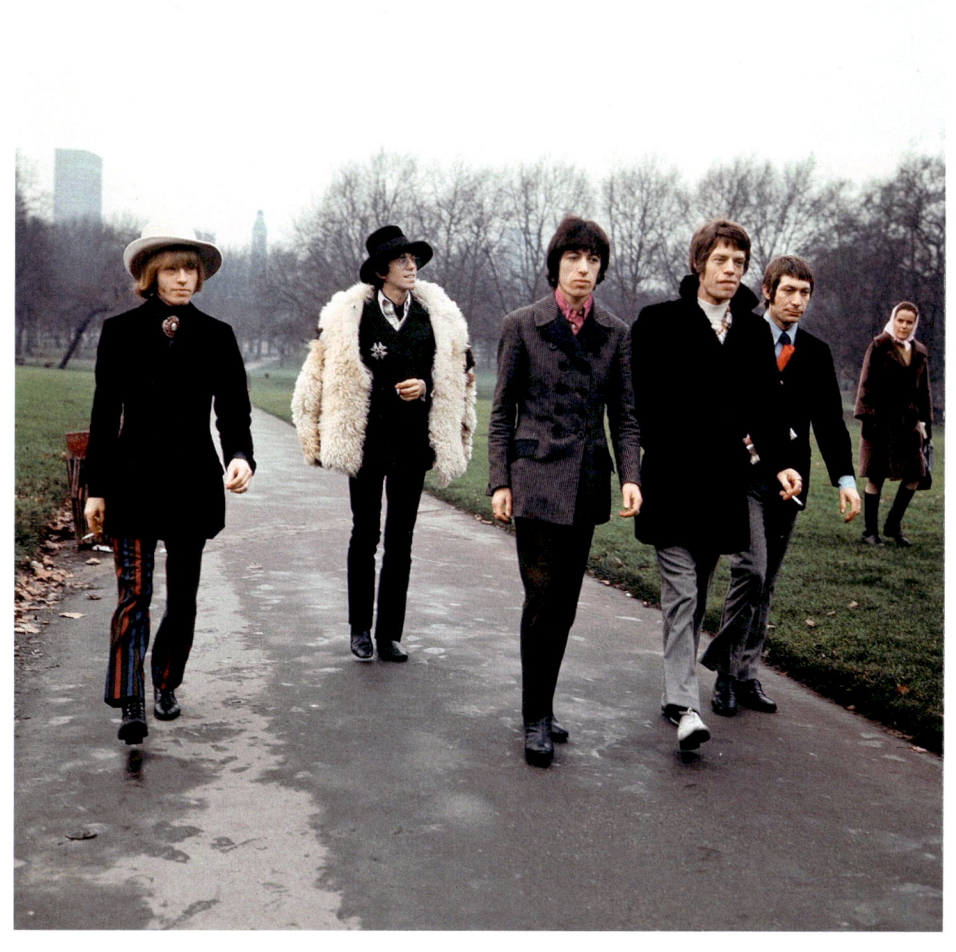

Anonymous
Green Park, London, 11 January 1967.

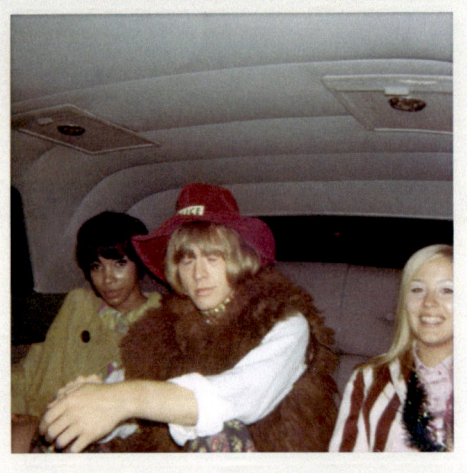
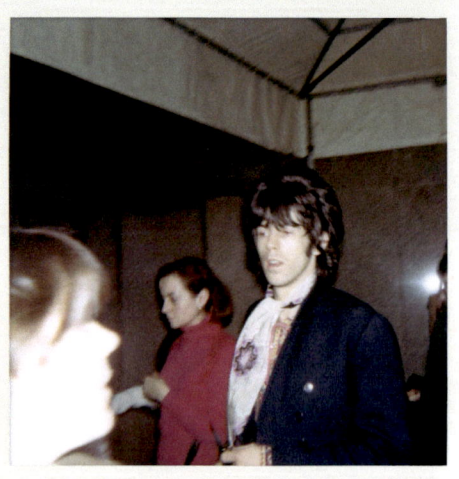
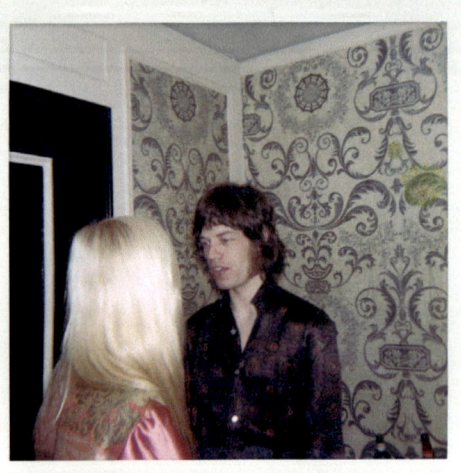
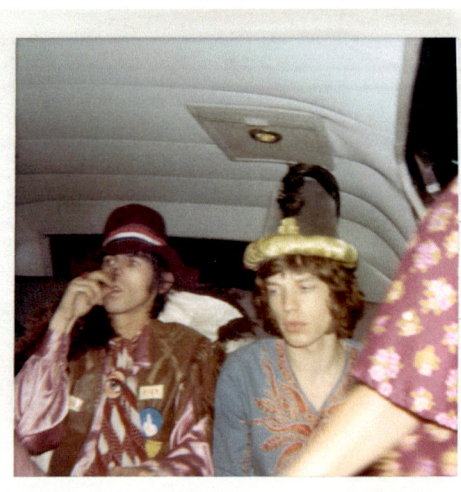
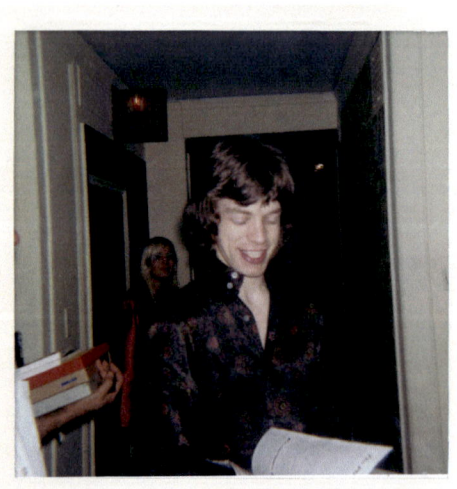
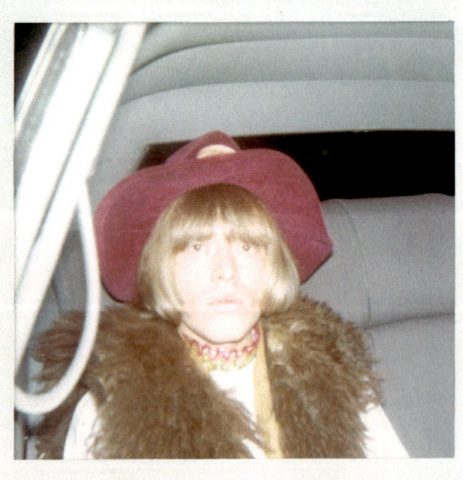

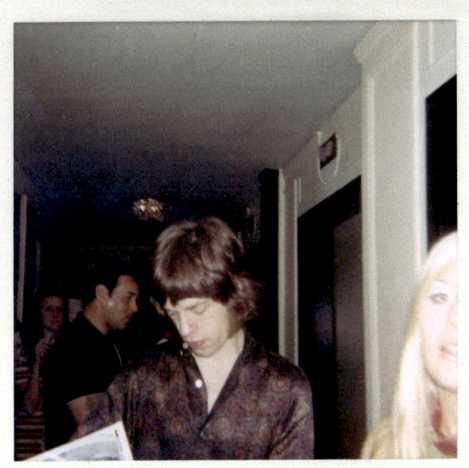

Michael Geary
Taken from a fan's-eye view, these Polaroid pictures capture the Stones at the height of their psychedelic period and were taken around the photo shoot in New York for *Their Satanic Majesties Request* album sleeve over the weekend of 16–17 September 1967.

PP. 210–211
Shepard Sherbell
Brian and mushroom, September 1967.

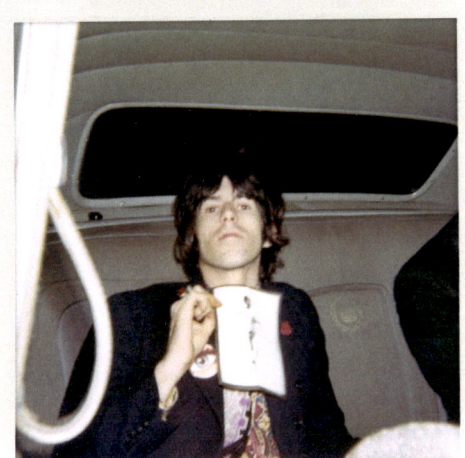

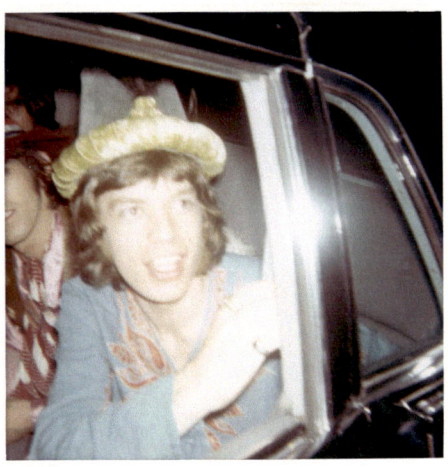

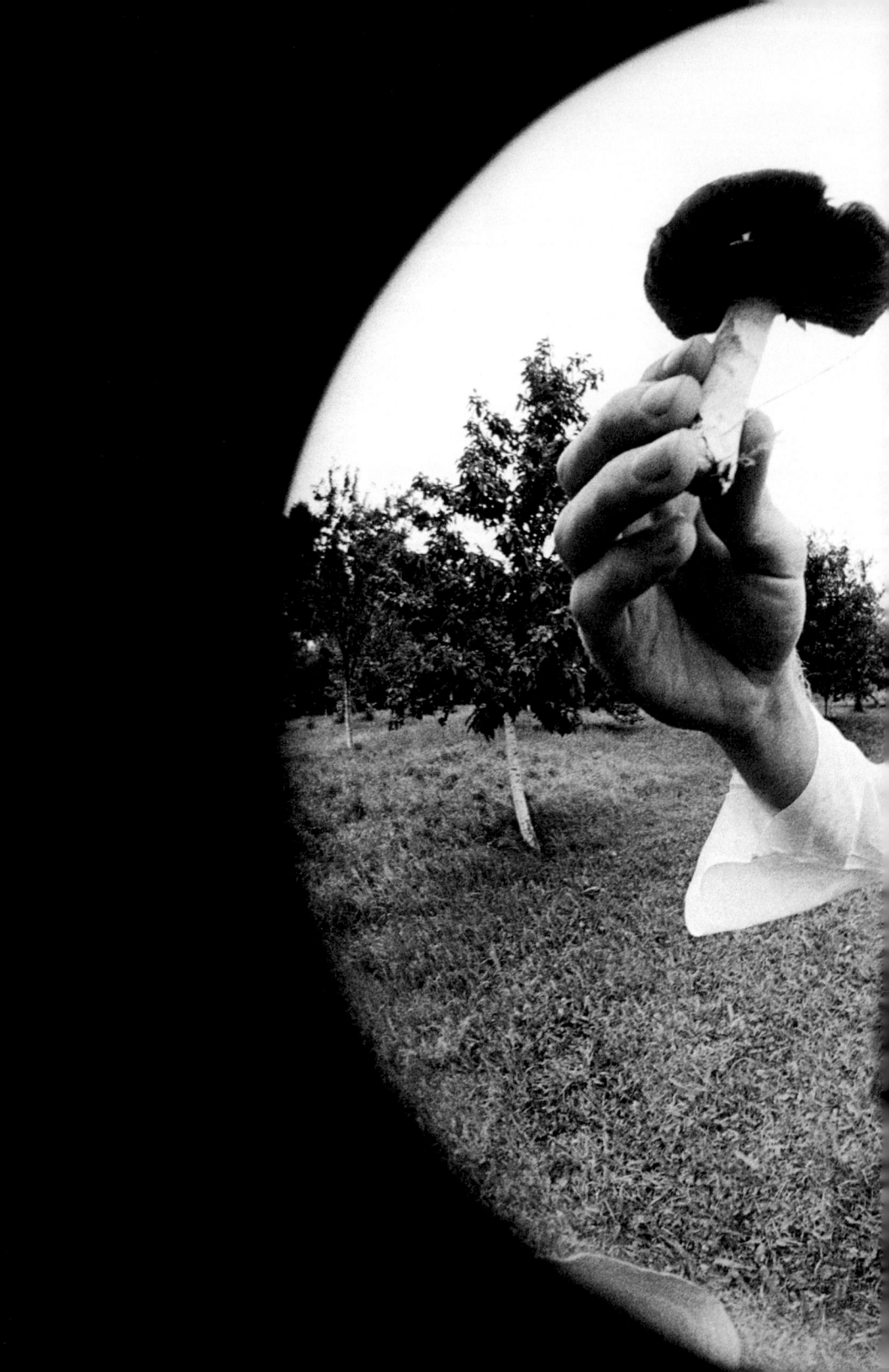

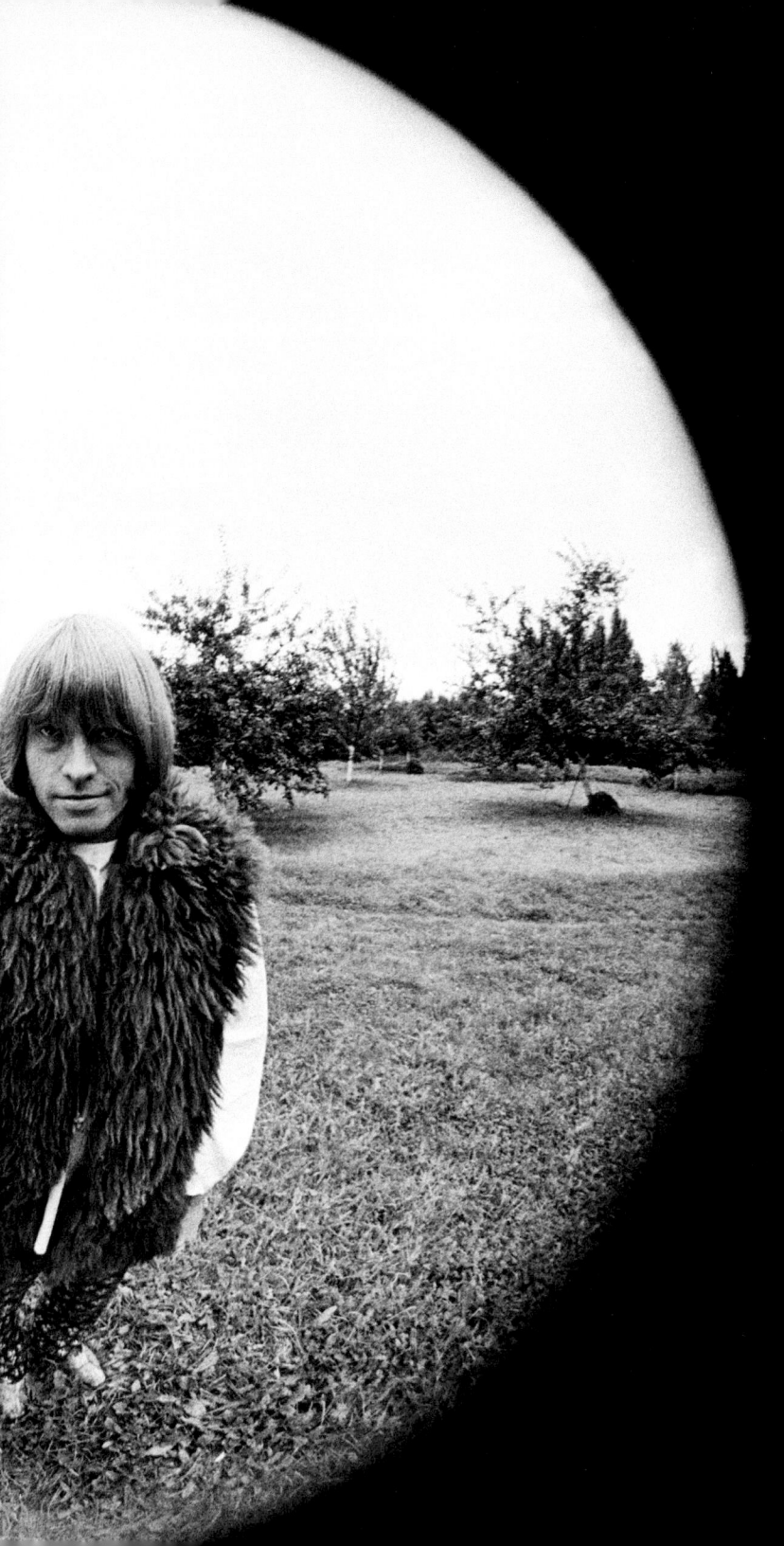

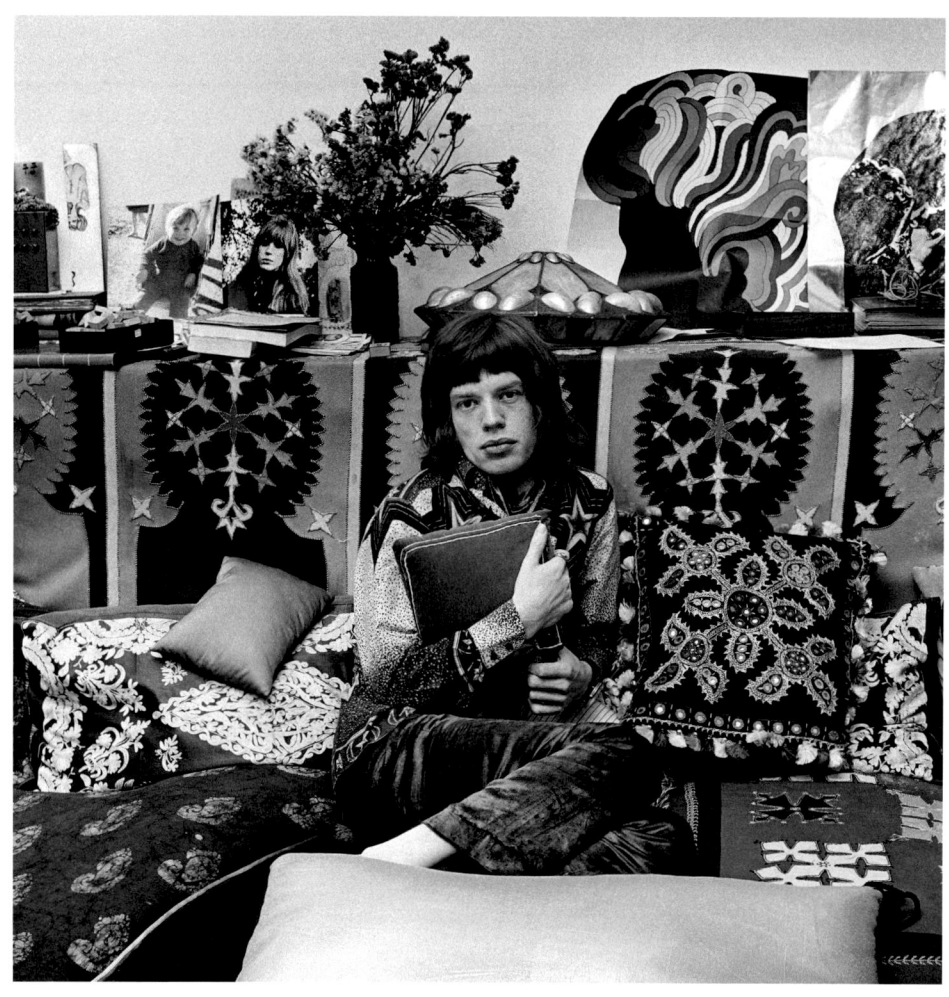

Gered Mankowitz
Harley House, Marylebone, London. Among all the
"Summer of Love" home furnishings is a simple
portrait of Marianne Faithfull, autumn 1967.

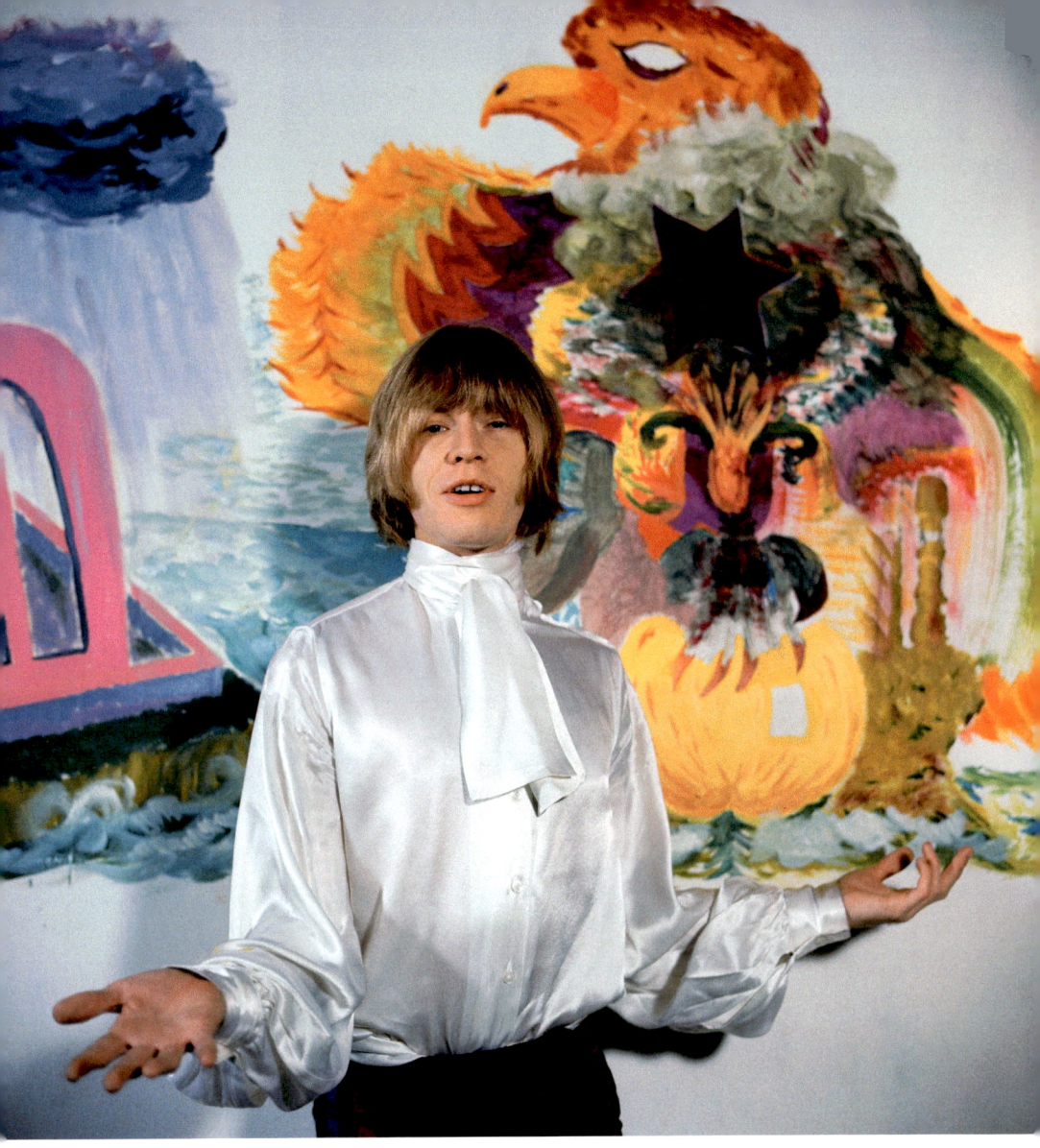

Gered Mankowitz
1 Courtfield Road, Kensington, London. Absorbed
by the psychedelic movement, Brian branched
out in numerous directions – including painting
this piece of art on the wall of the flat, late 1966.

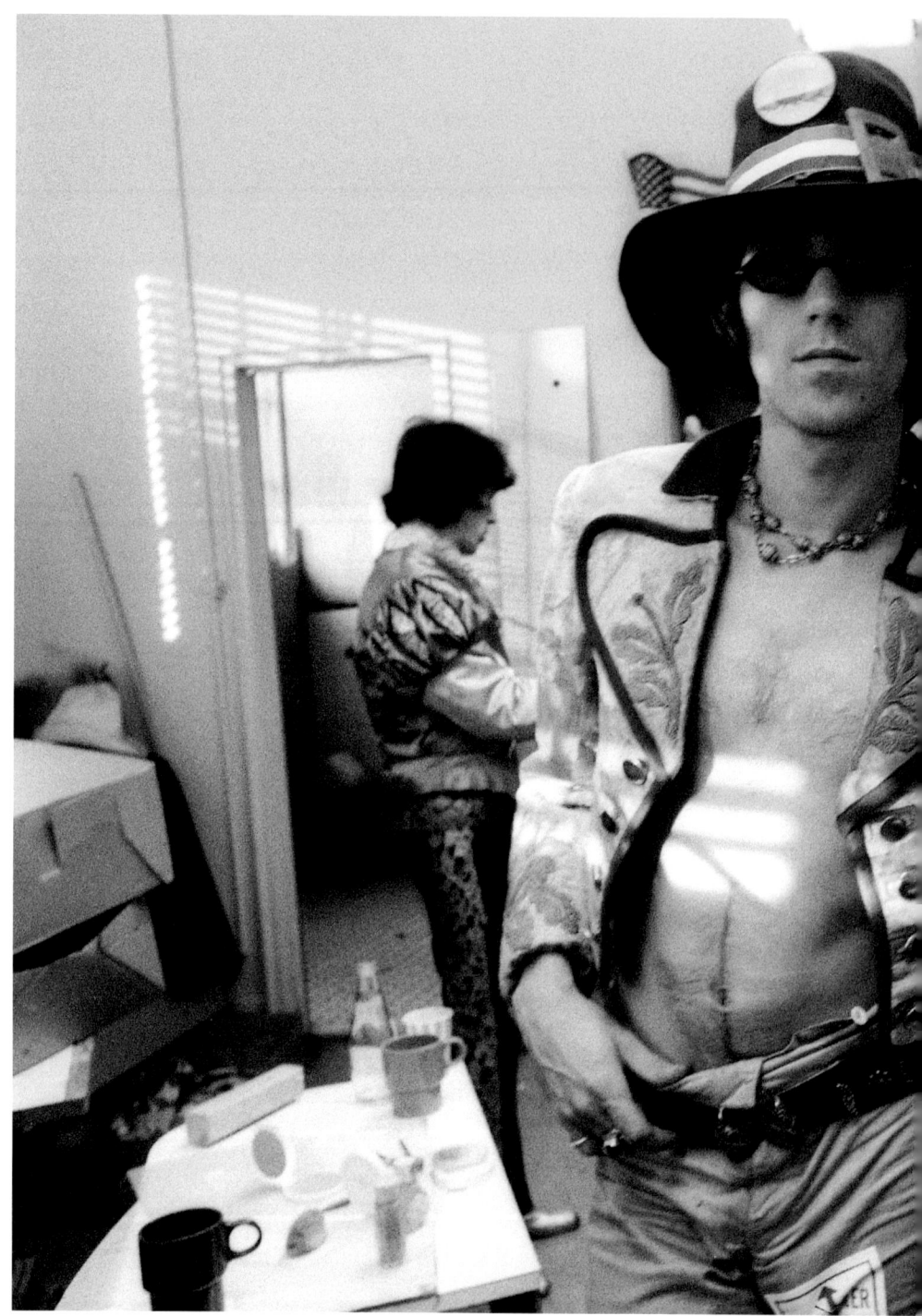

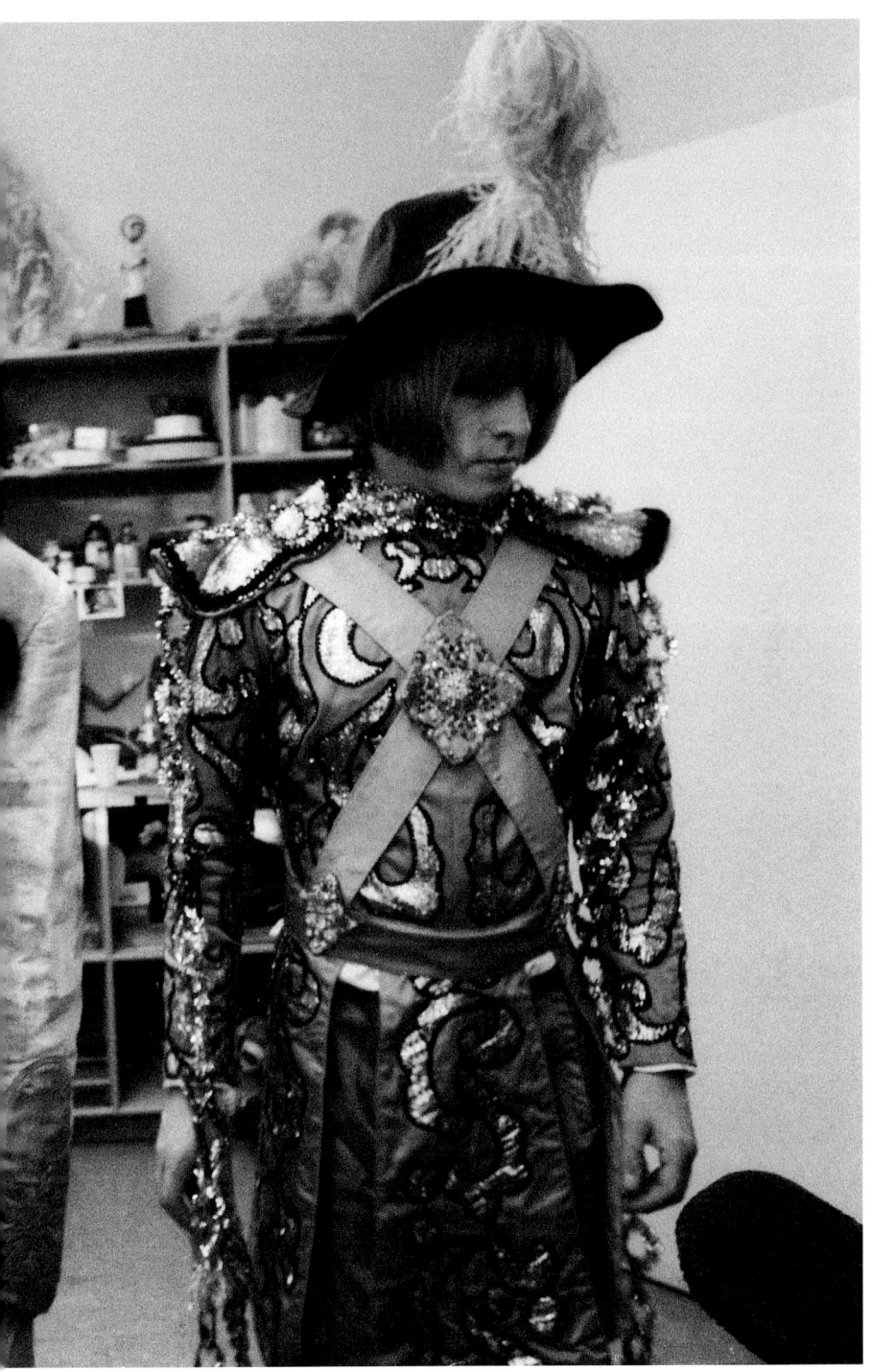

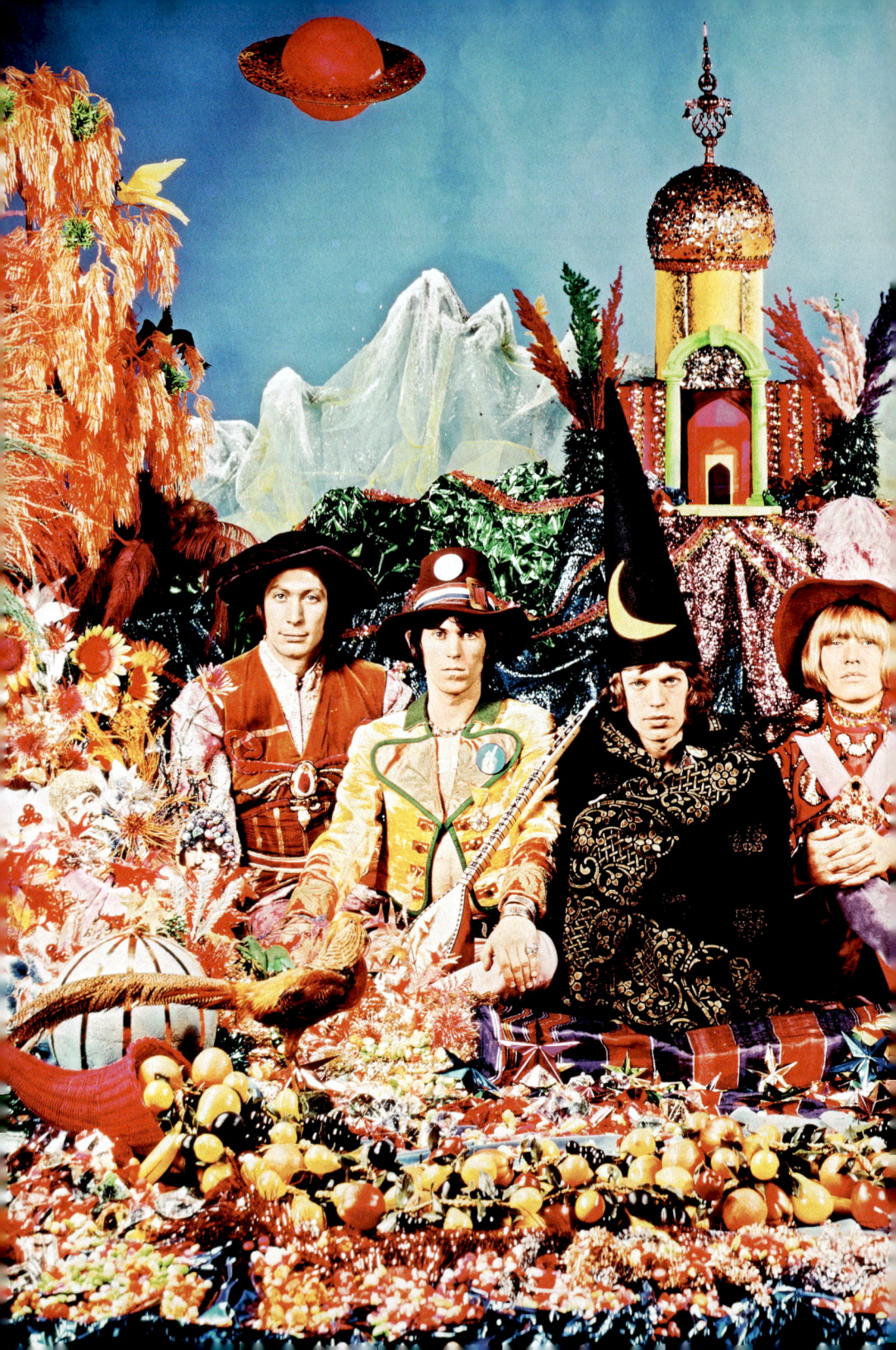

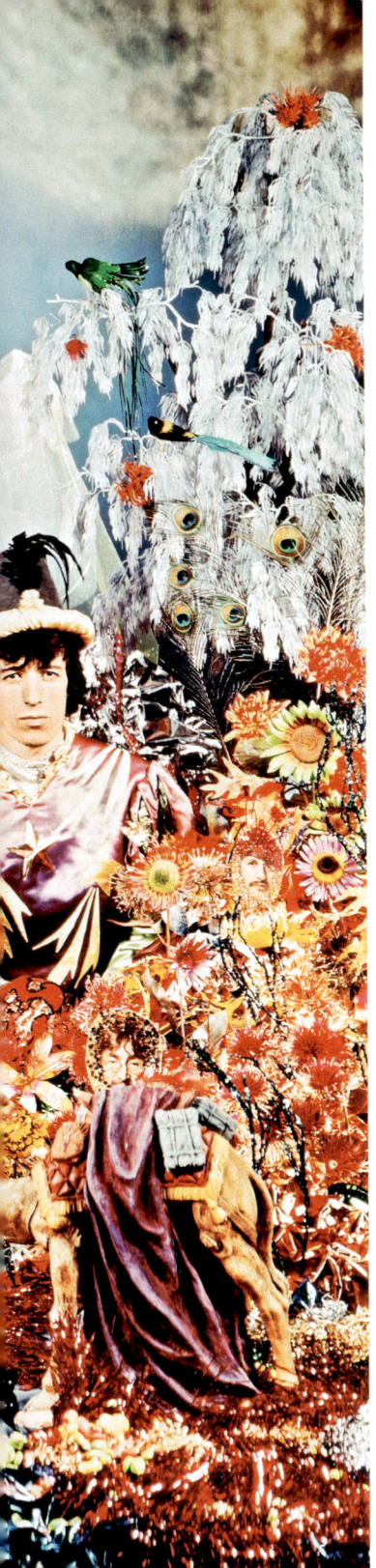

PP. 214–215
Michael Cooper
On Sunday, 17 September 1967, the group arrived at a New York studio hired by the photographer and decked themselves out in an array of psychedelic clothing for the cover shot for *Their Satanic Majesties Request*.

Michael Cooper
The cover image photographed by Cooper, who also shot the sleeve for The Beatles' *Sgt Pepper's Lonely Hearts Club Band*.
"Their Satanic Majesties Request, *despite moments of unquestionable brilliance, put the status of the Rolling Stones in jeopardy.*" Jon Landau, *Rolling Stone* magazine, 8 December 1967

PP. 218–219
Michael Cooper
Photograph taken during the cover shoot for *Their Satanic Majesties Request* in New York, 17 September 1967. The person whose hand is on top of Charlie's head has never identified themselves.
"This is the 'Too Many Hands' photo. I've actually gone to the trouble of counting all the hands … That's the kind of thing Michael is inclined to do, five people and the eleventh hand there." Keith Richards in Michael Cooper, *Blinds And Shutters*, 1990

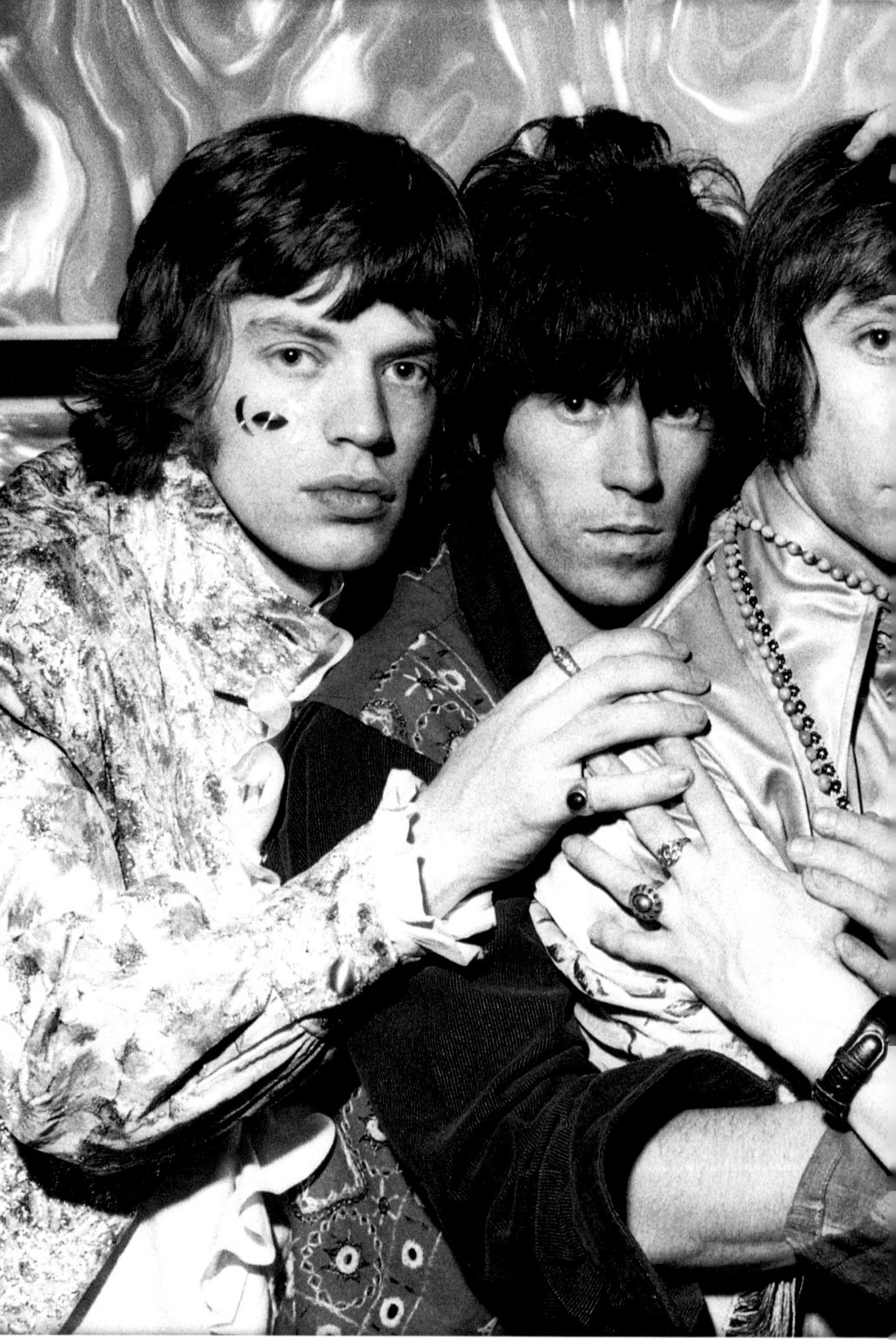

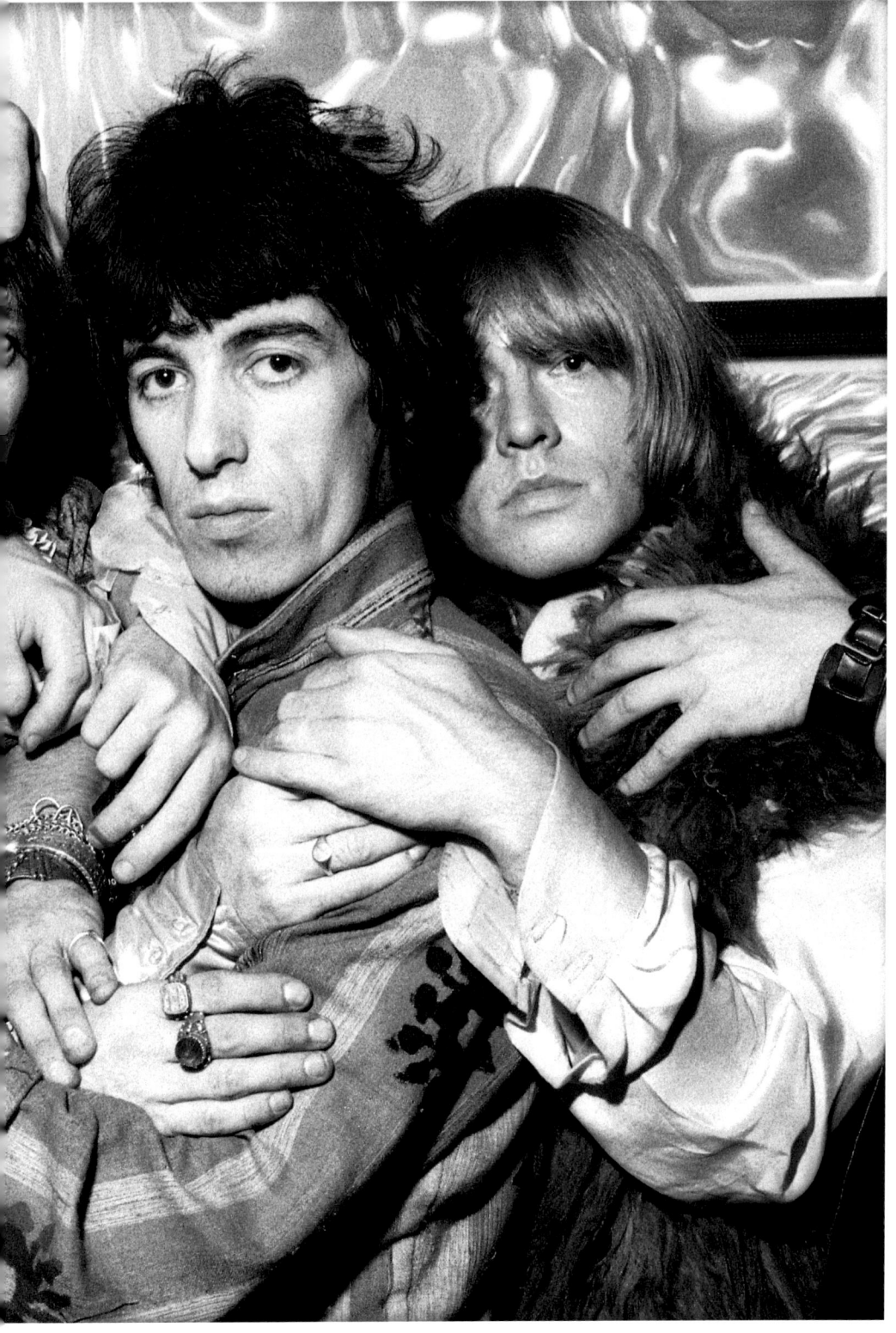

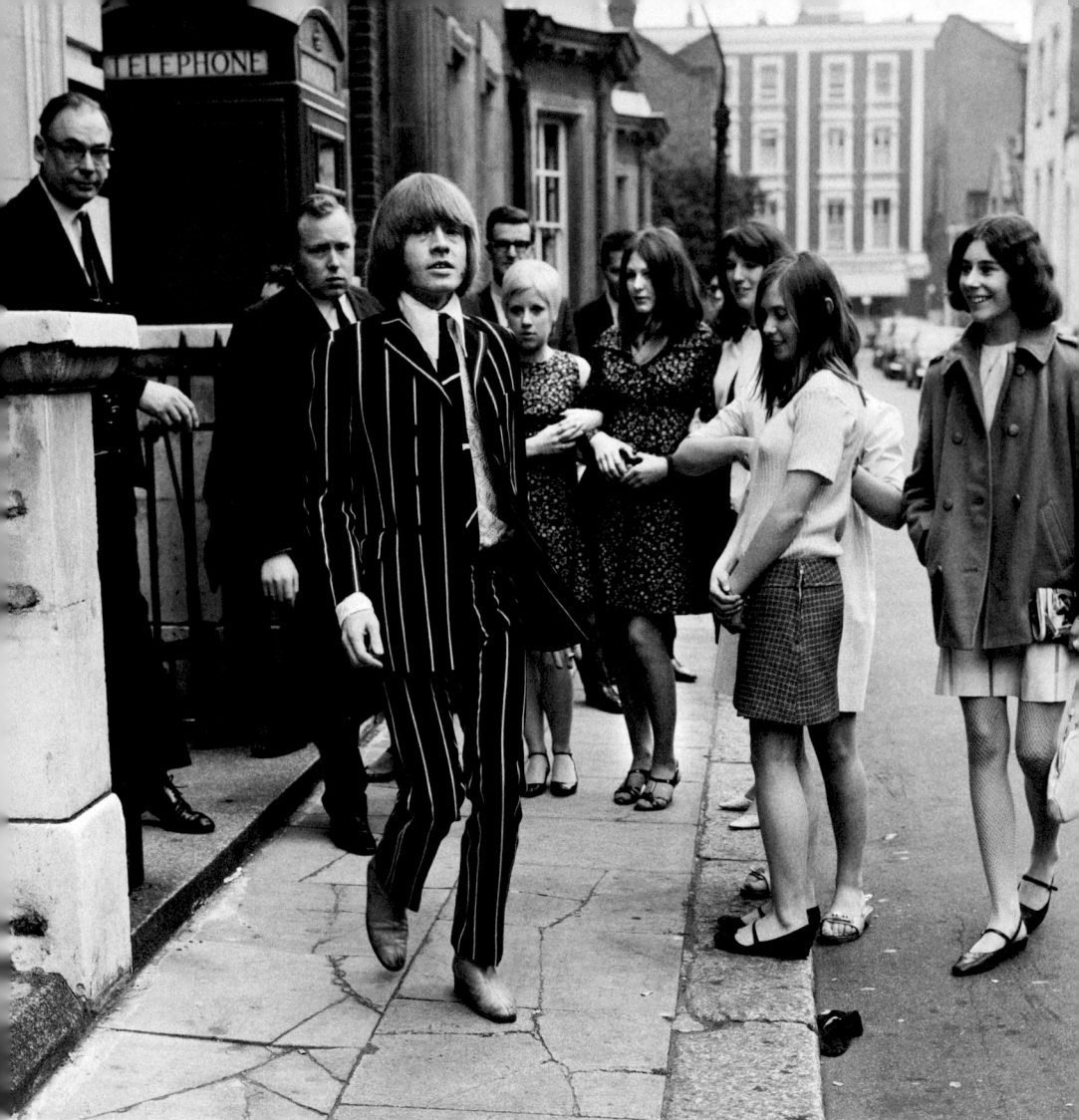

Anonymous

Flanked by his solicitors, Brian leaves West London Magistrates Court on 2 June 1967 following a hearing on drugs charges. Open season had evidently been declared on pop stars and Brian's careless behaviour around drugs made him an easy target for a vindictive police force. Brian's arrests prompted banner headlines around the world, and he cabled his parents in Cheltenham to reassure them that all was well: "Please don't worry. Don't jump to hasty conclusions and don't judge me too harshly. All my love, Brian."

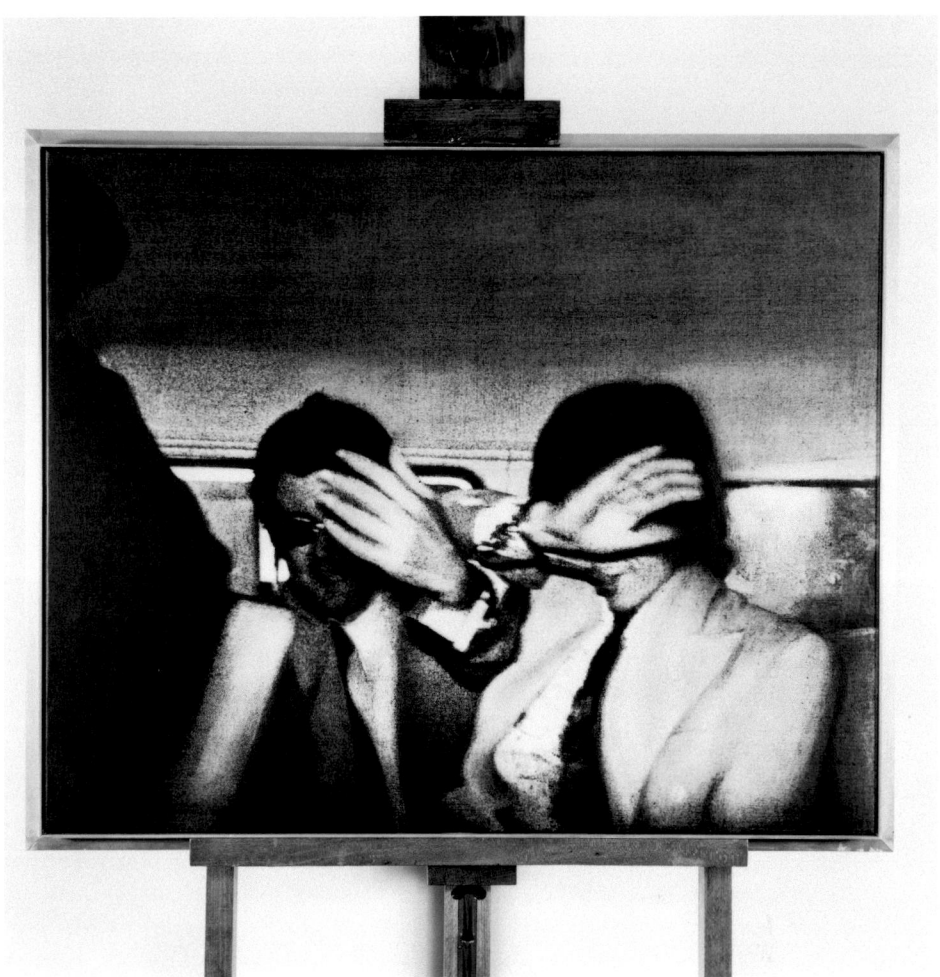

Michael Cooper

The prison sentences passed on Mick, Keith and art dealer Robert Fraser in June 1967 served as a call to arms for London's artistic community. Keen to commit the demeaning situation to canvas, Pop artist Richard Hamilton transformed a paparazzi shot of Jagger and Fraser in handcuffs into a remarkable series of garish lithographs. Entitled "Swingeing London", the embellished imagery highlighted the pair's

hugely indignant moment. *"Why did I call it 'Swingeing London'? There was a phrase that struck me very forcibly, a remark made by the judge in the case, who said, 'There are times when a swingeing sentence should be administered.' … So it was a pun on Swinging London and the swingeing sentence."* Richard Hamilton, quoted in Harriet Vyner, *Groovy Bob: The Life And Times Of Robert Fraser*, 1999

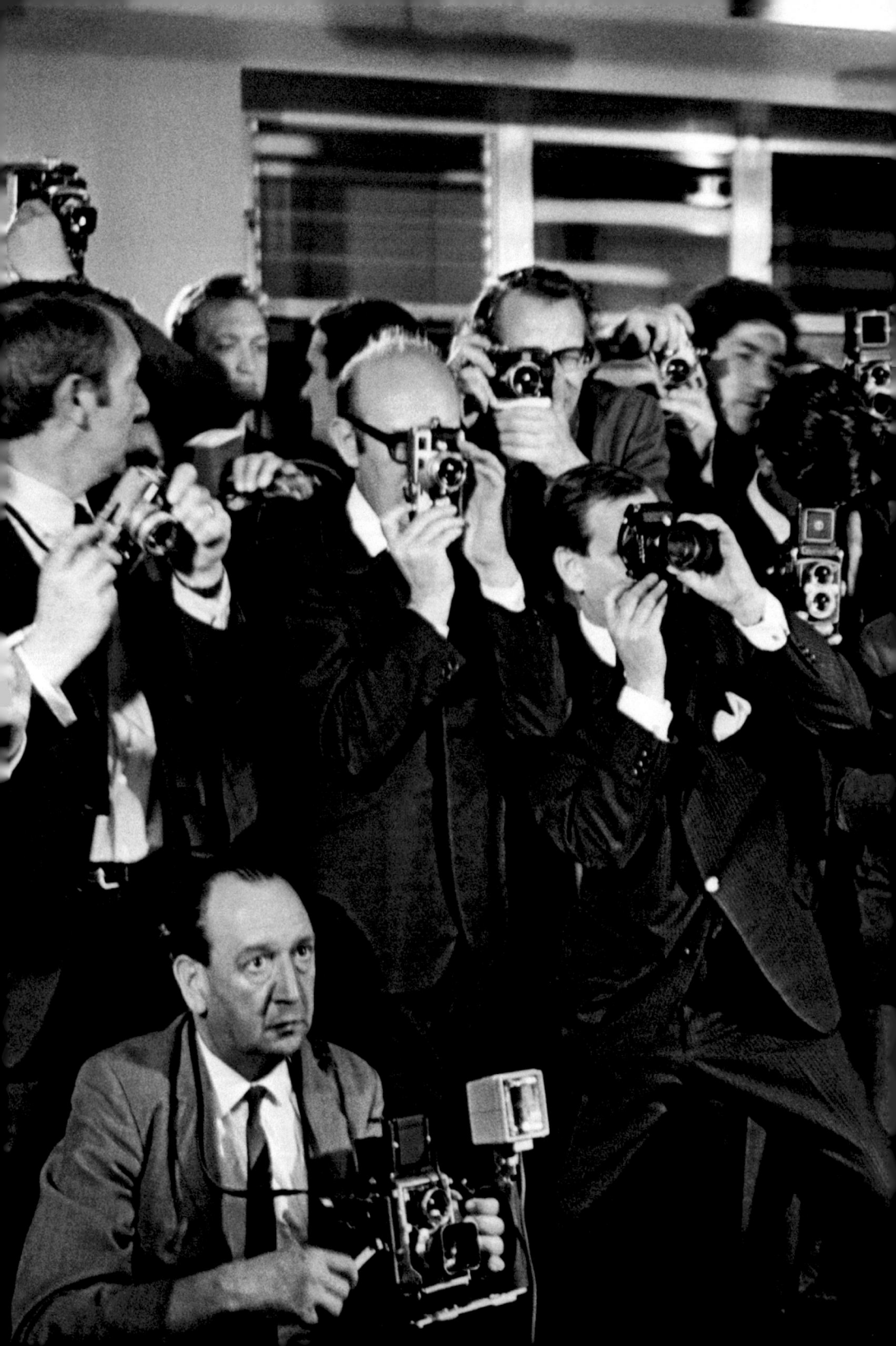

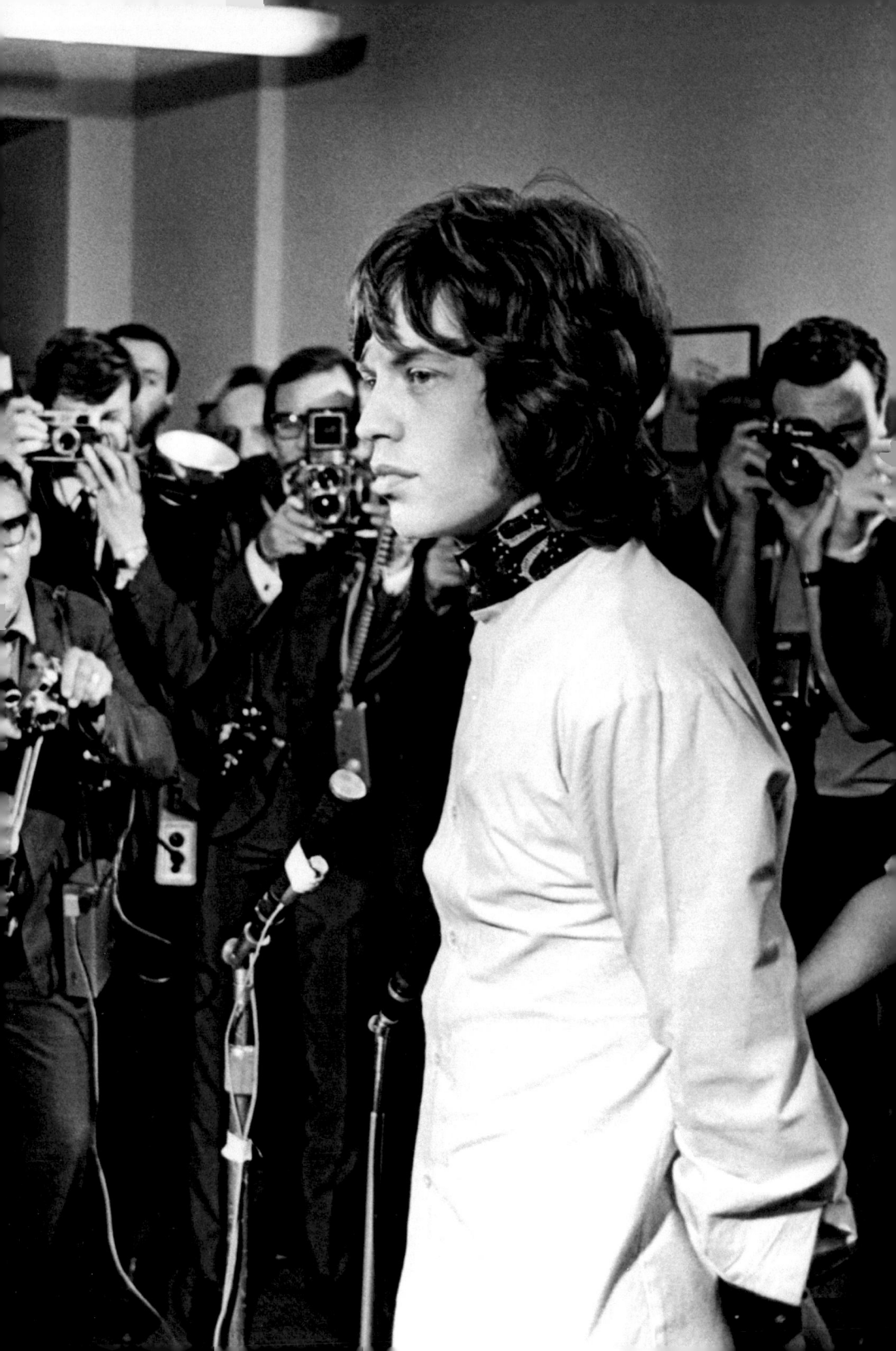

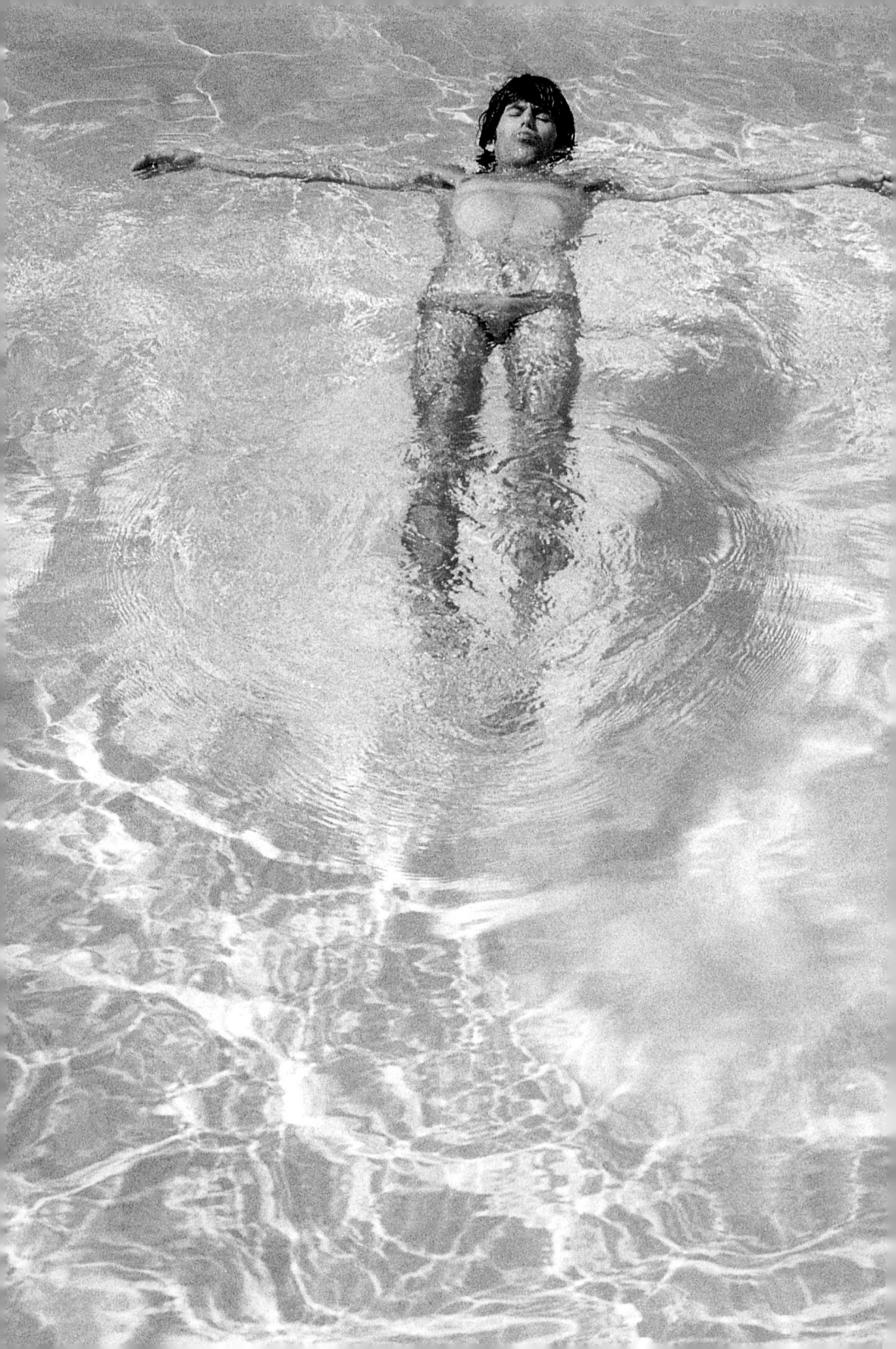

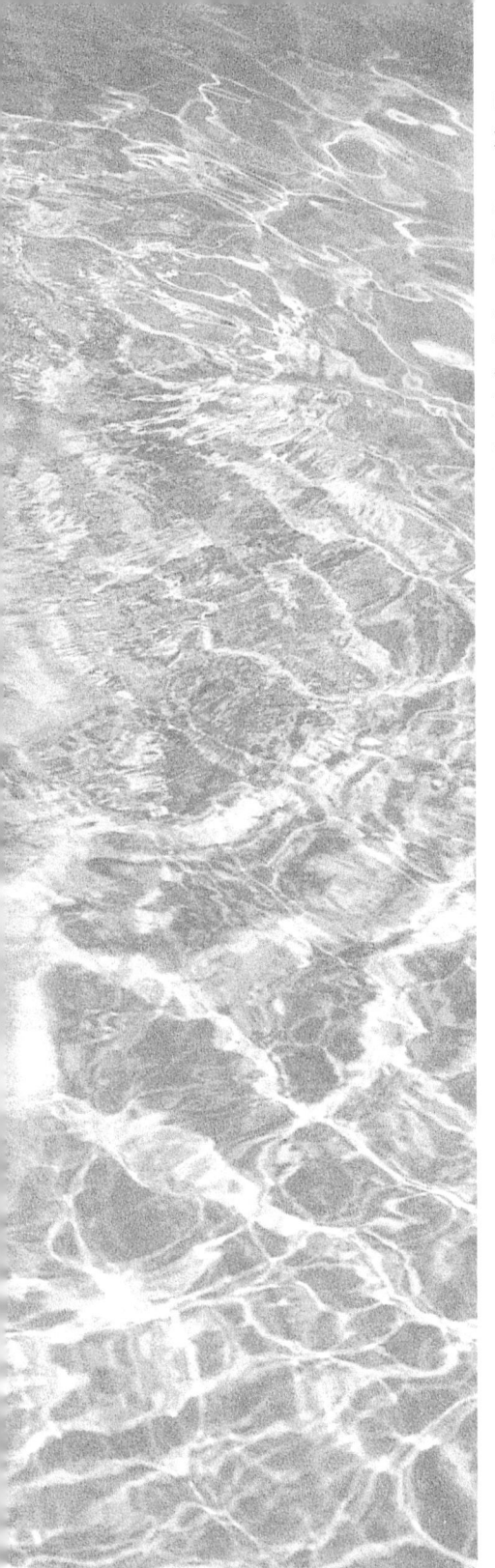

PP. 222–223
Anonymous
The whole world wants to know: moments after
having his sentence for possession of four
amphetamine pills reduced to a conditional
discharge, Mick faced the press at the offices of
Granada Television, in Soho, London, 31 July 1967.
*"My responsibilities, as far as that goes, are
only to myself. The responsibility, which as one
of my friends has said before me, is also on the
gentlemen of the press who create those responsibilities, perhaps for themselves, and by trying
to report every personal detail of one's life, which
one doesn't wish to be made public, which one
tries to keep private."* Mick Jagger, *ITN* interview,
31 July 1967

Michael Cooper
At the Hotel Es Saadi in Marrakesh, 1967.

PP. 226–227
Michael Cooper
At the fashionable Hotel Es Saadi in Marrakesh,
where photographer Cecil Beaton was on hand
to shoot the band. While legend has it that his
lenses were mostly trained on Mick, Beaton did
find the other Stones worthy of photographing,
March 1967.
*"The drummer [sic], Keith of the Stones, an eight-
eenth-century suit, long black velvet coat and
the tightest pants ... Everything is shoddy, poorly
made, the seams burst. Keith himself had sewn
his trousers, lavender and dull rose, with a band
of badly stitched leather dividing the two colours.
Brian appears in white pants with a huge black
square applied at the back. It is very smart in spite
of the fact that the seams are giving way."* Cecil
Beaton, *The Selected Diaries Of Cecil Beaton,
1926–1974*, 2004

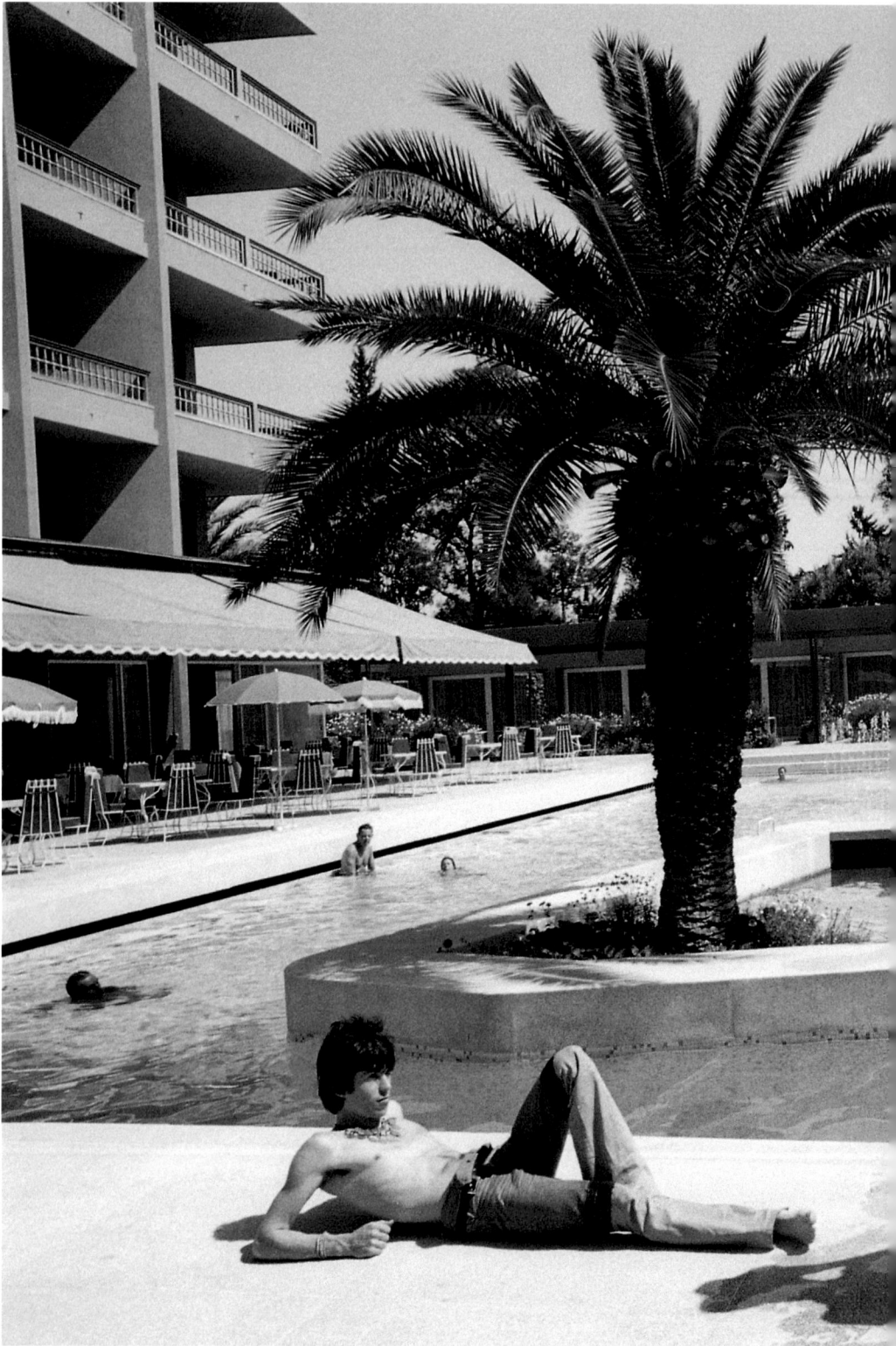

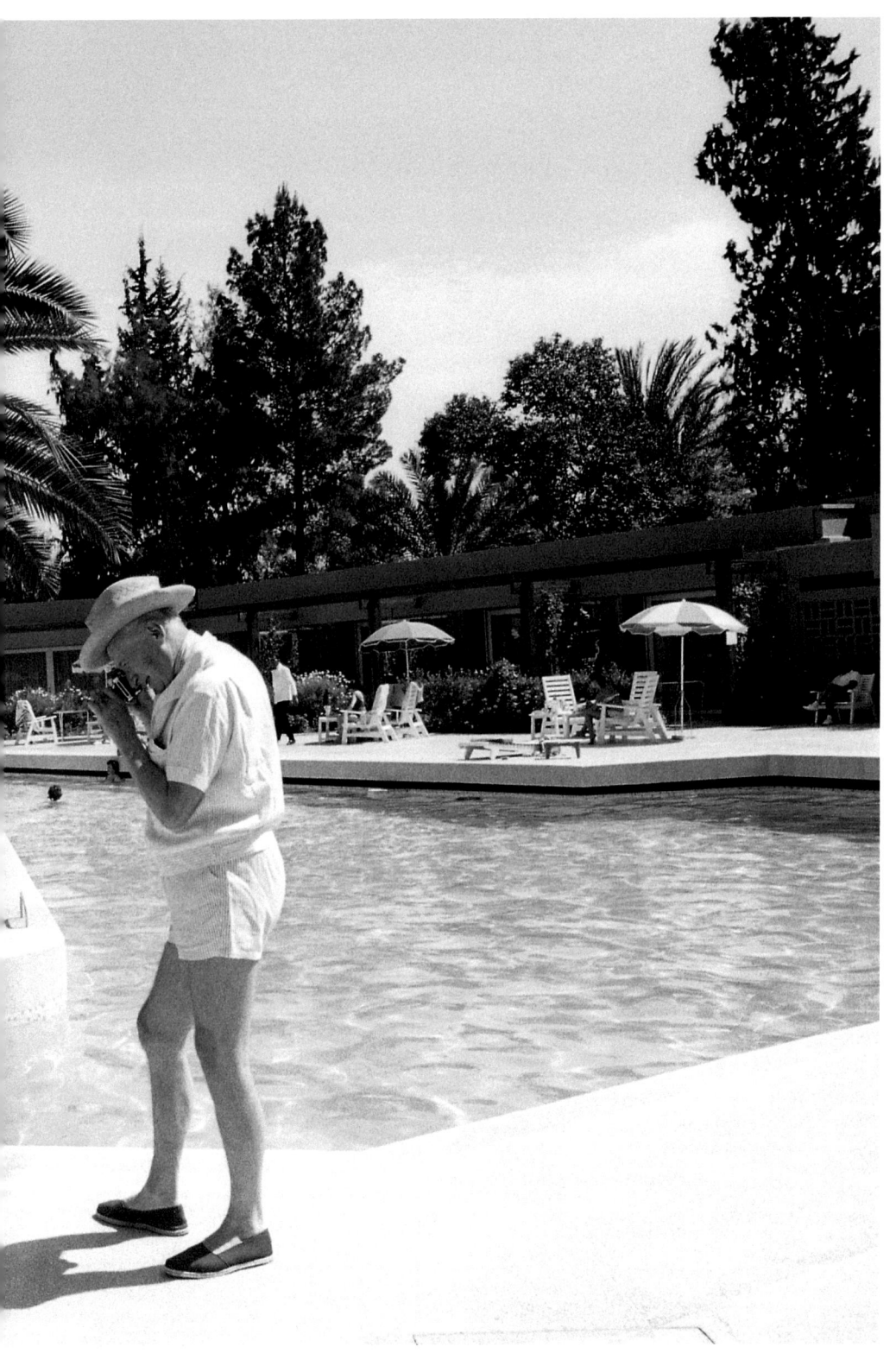

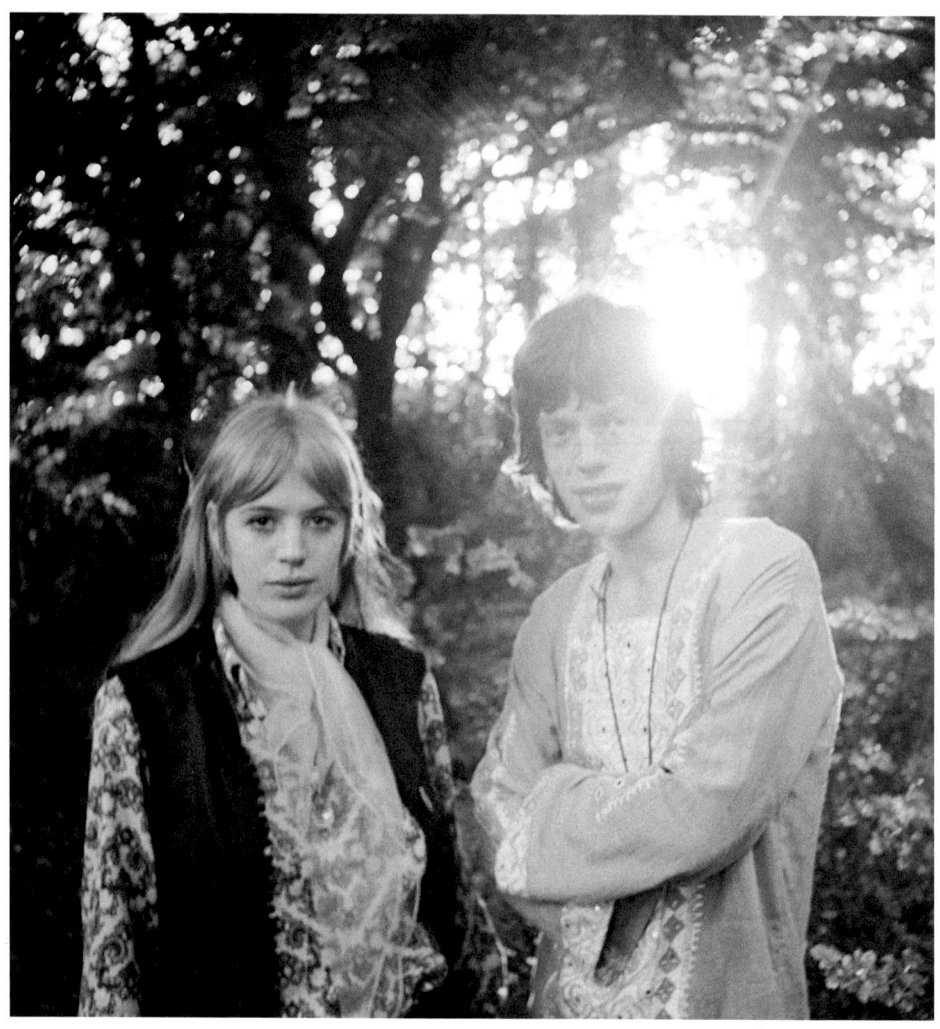

Michael Cooper

The long series of trials relating to the Redlands' bust finally came to a halt at the end of July 1967, and Mick was able to find some solace with Marianne Faithfull at Braziers Park in rural Oxfordshire.

"We'd just got off the bust, they'd let Mick out. So we thought that the place to go and hide at first was Braziers, my father's place, which was a country house in Oxfordshire. And indeed, they never found us." Marianne Faithfull, quoted in Michael Cooper, *Blinds And Shutters*, 1990

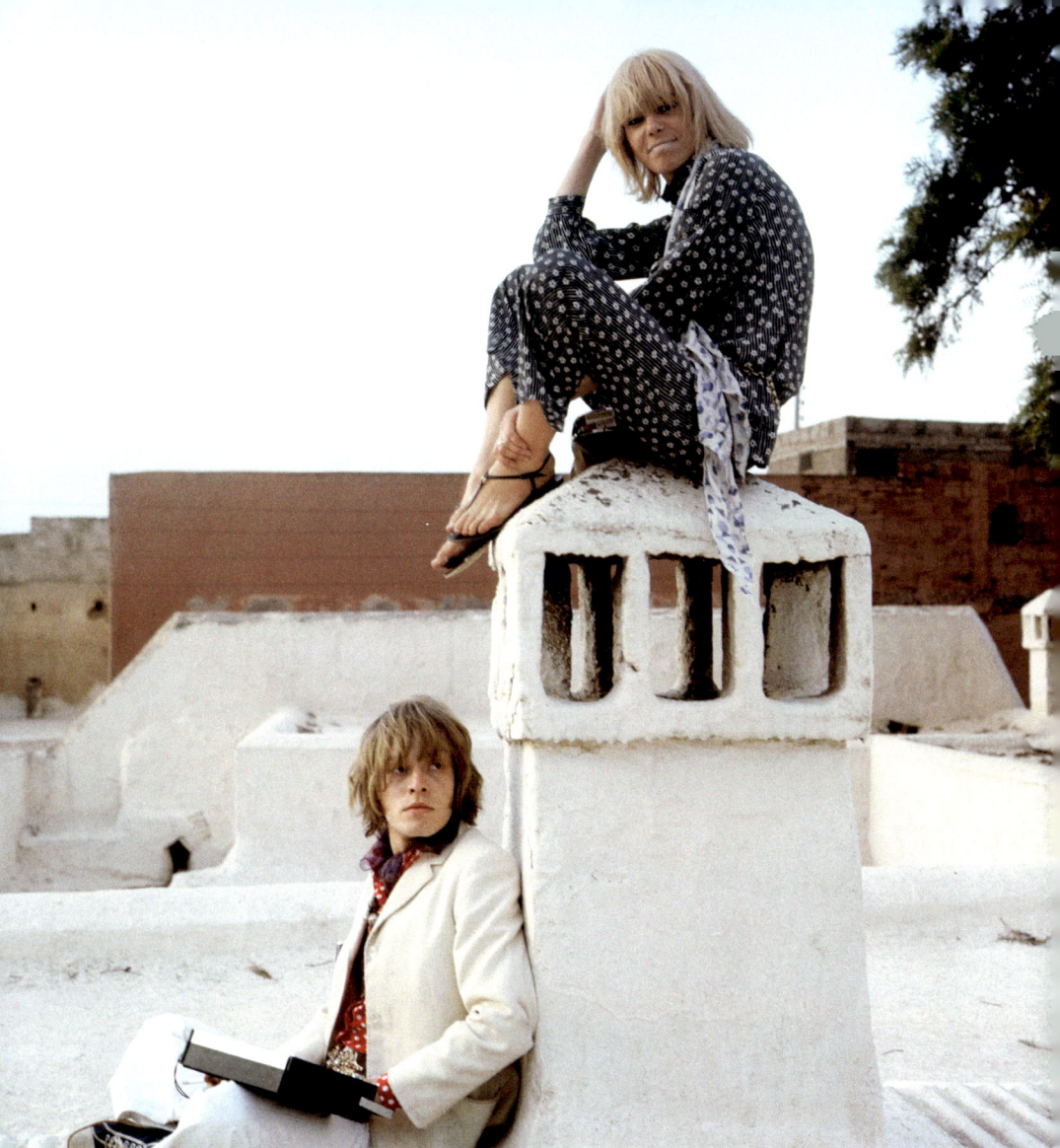

Cecil Beaton
With the sun high in the Moroccan sky during
March 1967, Brian and Anita pose for Cecil
Beaton. The couple's volatile relationship would
conclude in Marrakesh, allowing Pallenberg to
find solace with Keith.

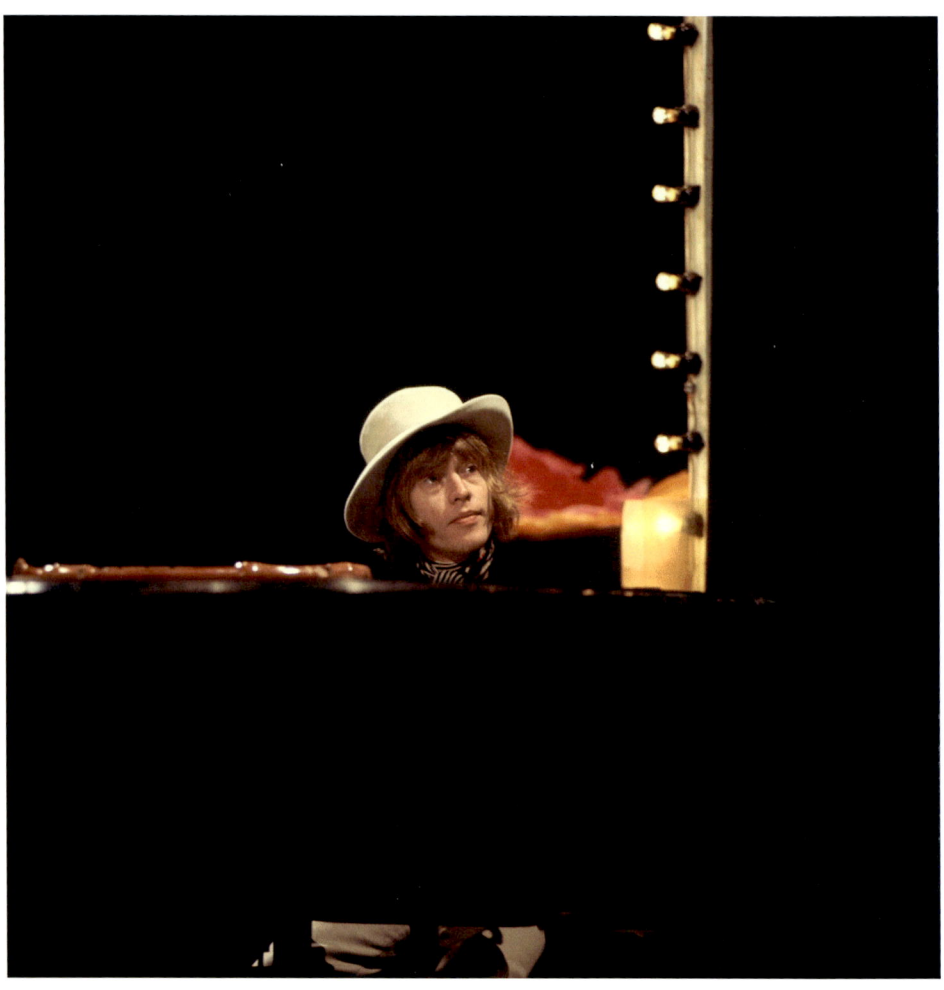

David Redfern
Brian as seen during camera rehearsals for
the Stones' appearance on the top-rated BBC
TV show *Top Of The Pops*, Lime Grove, London,
25 January 1967. The group were there to promote their current single "Let's Spend The Night
Together"/"Ruby Tuesday".

Michael Cooper
Brian in full psychedelic livery as photographed
in Chelsea, London, June 1967.

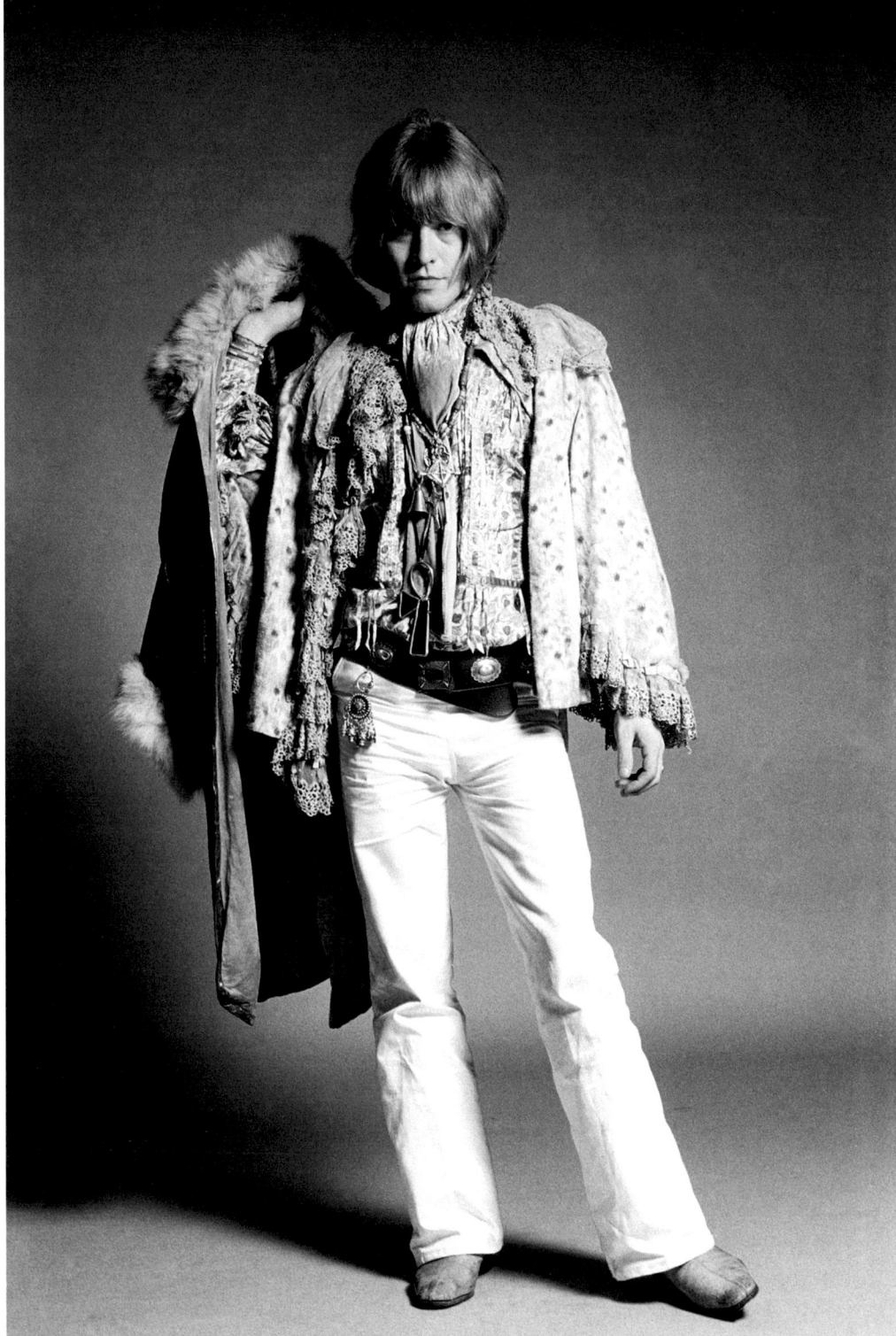

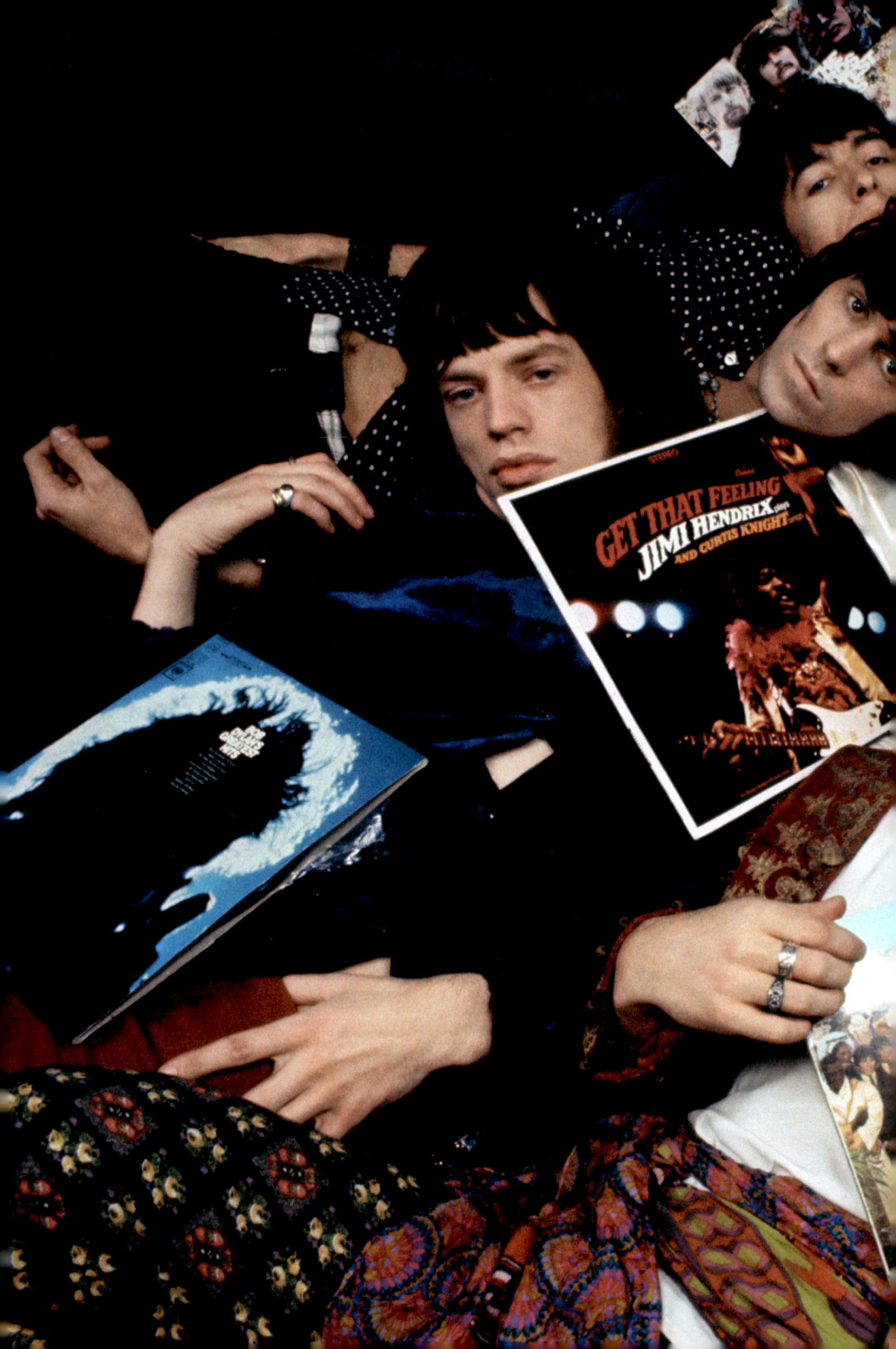

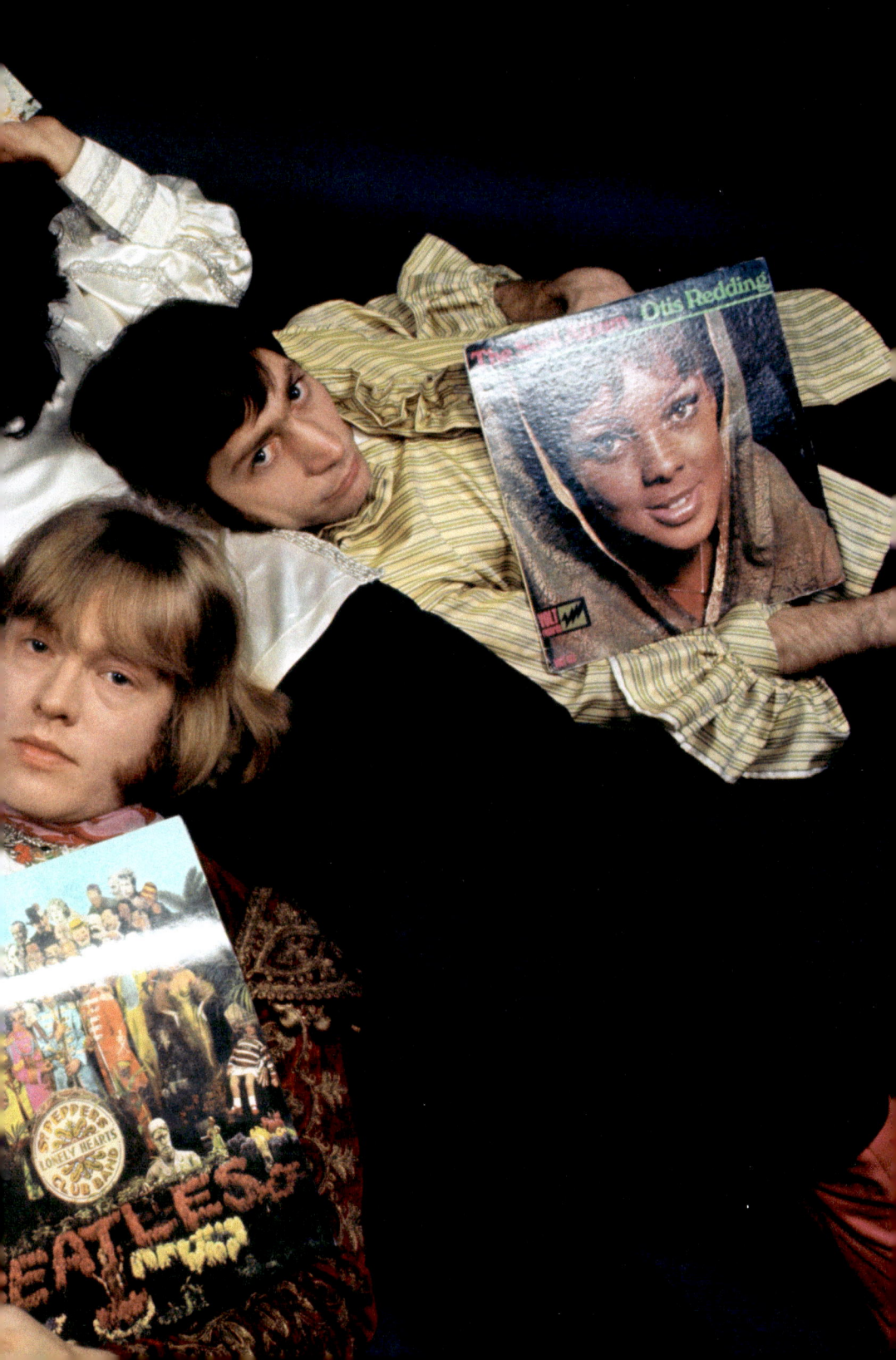

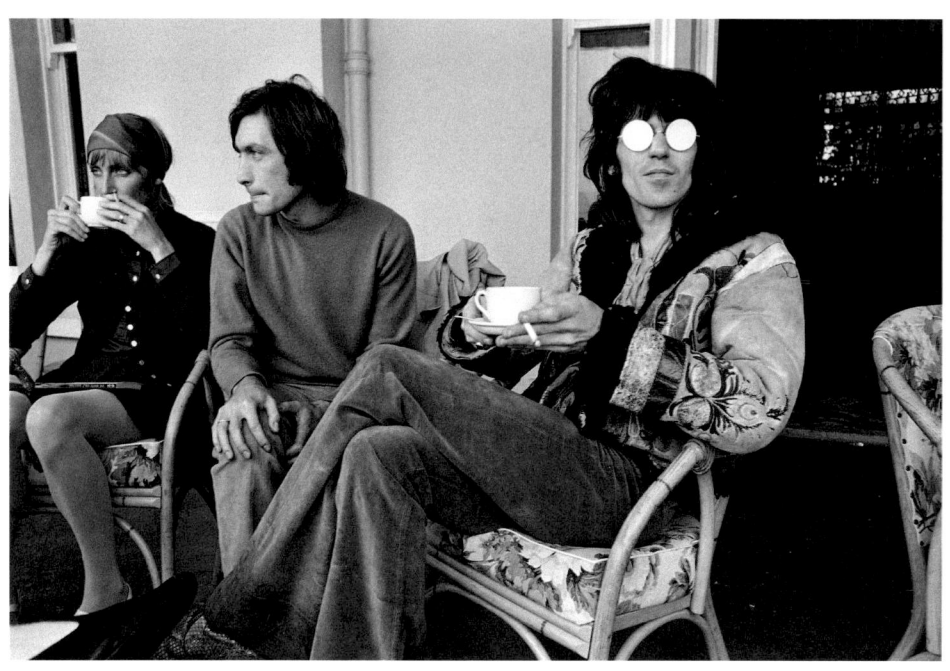

PP. 232–233

Thomas Beyl

Surrounded by sleeves from The Beatles, Bob Dylan, Jimi Hendrix, The Byrds and Otis Redding, the Stones reveal their favourite records of the moment. Late 1967.

"To learn about the early days of our religions we waited for Moses to descend from Mount Sinai with the two tablets which made up the Ten Commandments. We look to Shakespeare and Dickens and Chaucer for accounts of other times in our history, and we feel that tomorrow we will on many occasions look to the gramophone records of The Rolling Stones who act as a mirror for today's mind, action and happenings." Decca Records press release – early 1967

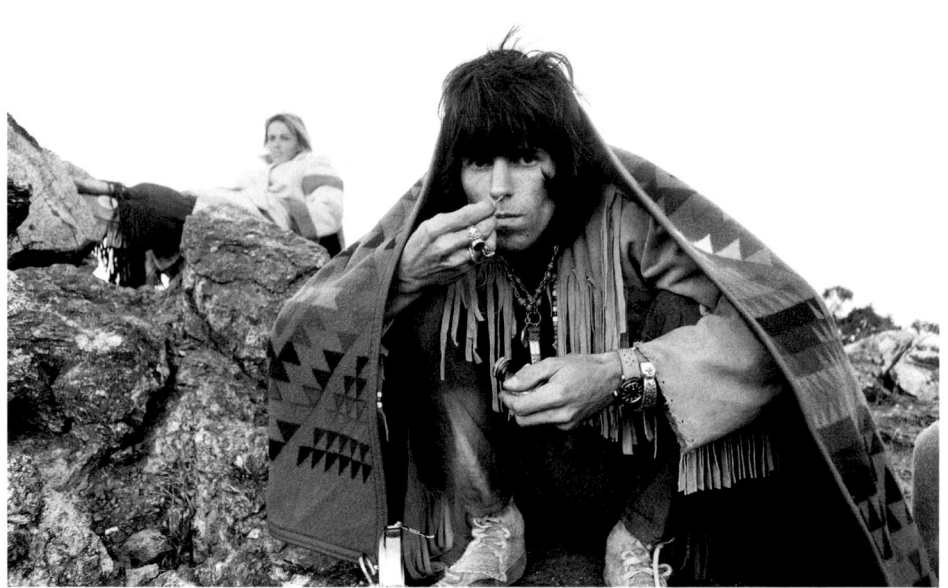

Michael Cooper
Bob Dylan's rare appearance at the Isle of Wight Festival on 31 August 1969 served as a call to arms for Britain's higher echelons of rock. Several Beatles attended, and Keith and Charlie were present for the historic event, as well as Charlie's wife Shirley.

Michael Cooper
Keith indulging in some relaxation at the Joshua Tree Memorial Park in southern California. In the summer of 1968, Keith, Anita Pallenberg, Marianne Faithfull and photographer Cooper joined Gram Parsons and roadie Phil Kaufman for a mystical road trip into the Californian desert.

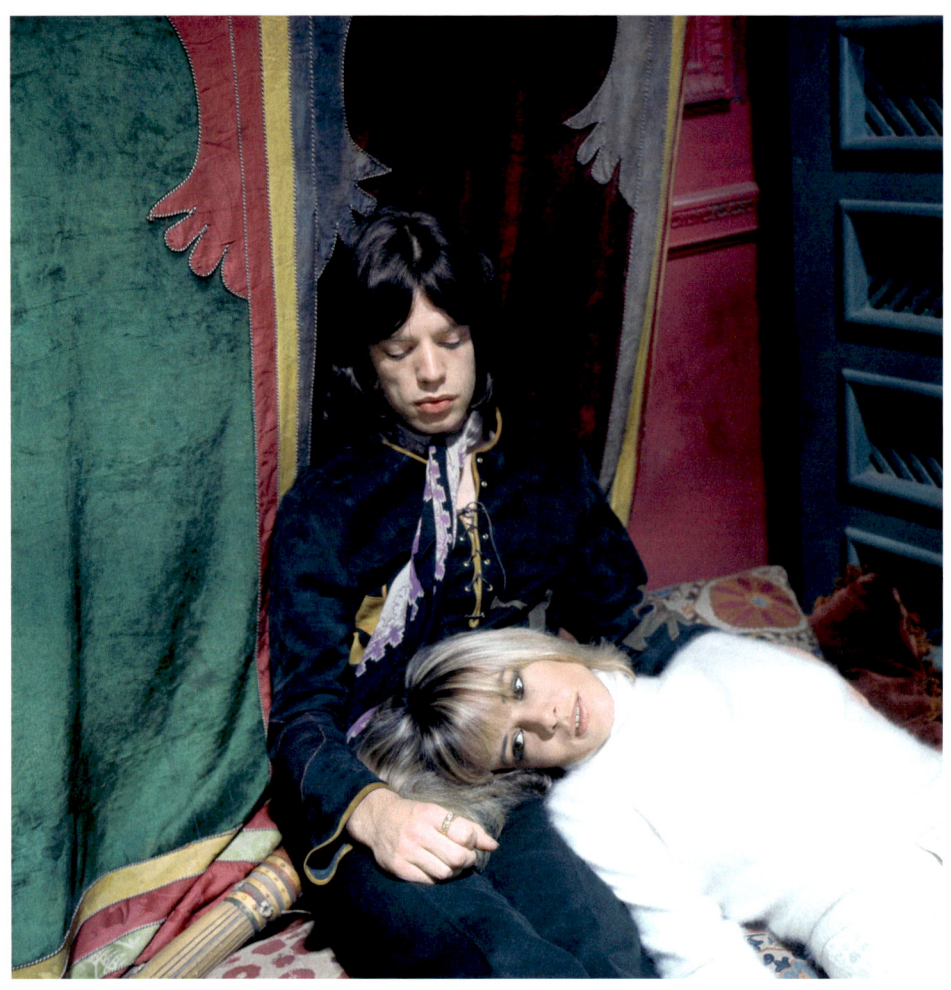

Cecil Beaton

Mick and Anita Pallenberg on the Knightsbridge, London, set of *Performance*, September 1968. The complex energies emanating from *Performance*'s cast couldn't help but drip into Donald Cammell's quirky film. While now considered a bona fide cult classic, initially the movie's financiers were eager to excise some of the more controversial moments to maximise the film's commercial appeal. An edict ordering numerous cuts to the film produced a terse response by telegram from Donald Cammell and Mick: *"You seem to want to emasculate the most savage and most affectionate scenes in our movie. If Performance doesn't upset audiences, it's nothing. If this fact upsets you, the alternative is to sell it fast and no more bullshit!"*

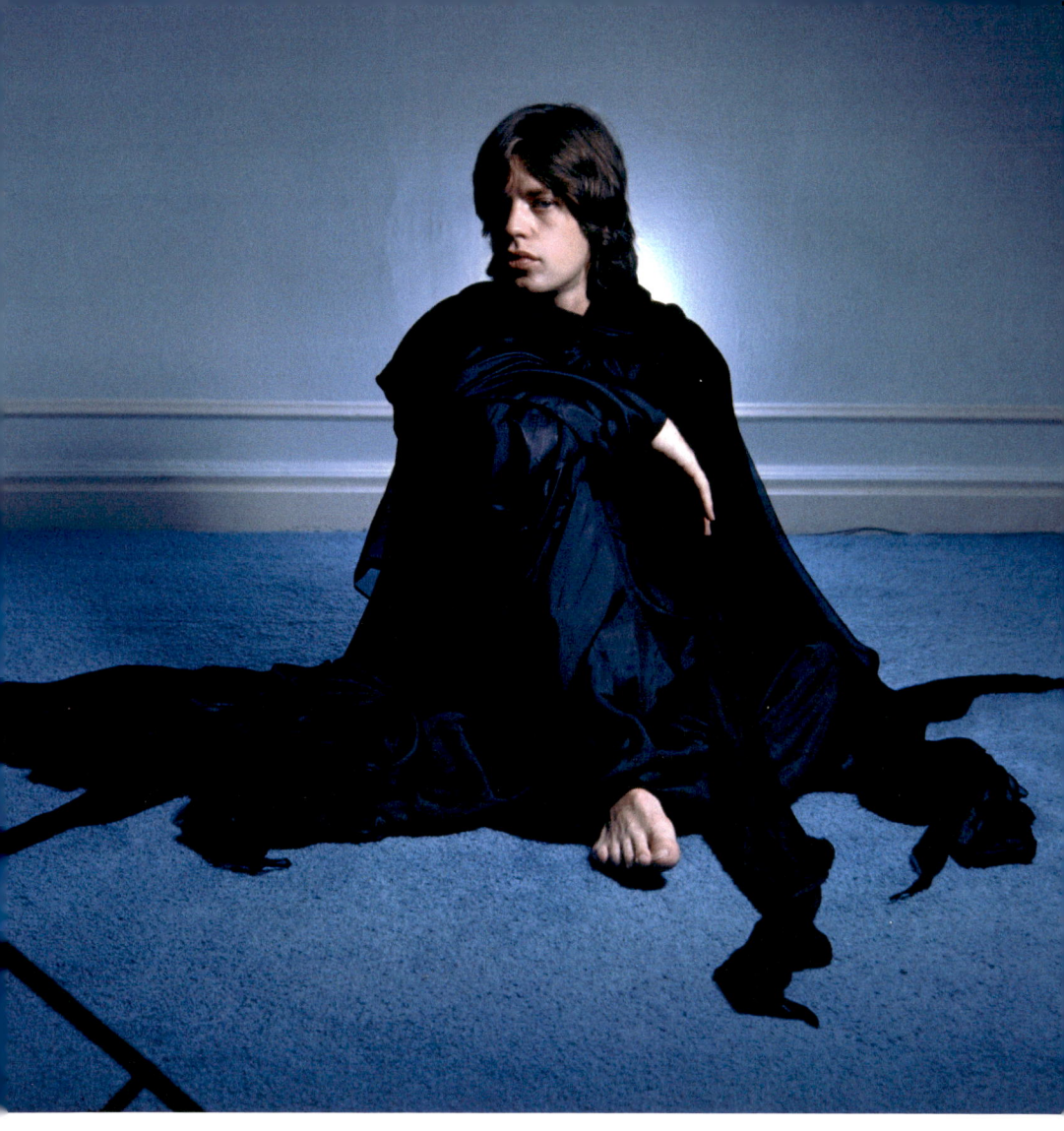

Cecil Beaton

Mick between takes on the set of *Performance*,
London, September 1968.
*"[Mick] is very gentle and with perfect manners.
He has much appreciation and his small albino-
fringed eyes notice everything."* Cecil Beaton,
*Beaton In The Sixties: The Cecil Beaton Diaries
As He Wrote Them, 1965–1969*, 2004

David Bailey

A promotional shoot for new release 'Jumpin' Jack Flash". Psychedelia consigned to the past, the Stones' May 1968 single signalled a revival of fortunes. Strident, punchy and uncomplicated, the single tore up the charts, igniting critics and fans. *"The Stones have taken a step back. This new single takes them back to the era of 'Satisfaction', nearly three years ago. Welcome back."* Daily Sketch, 21 May 1968

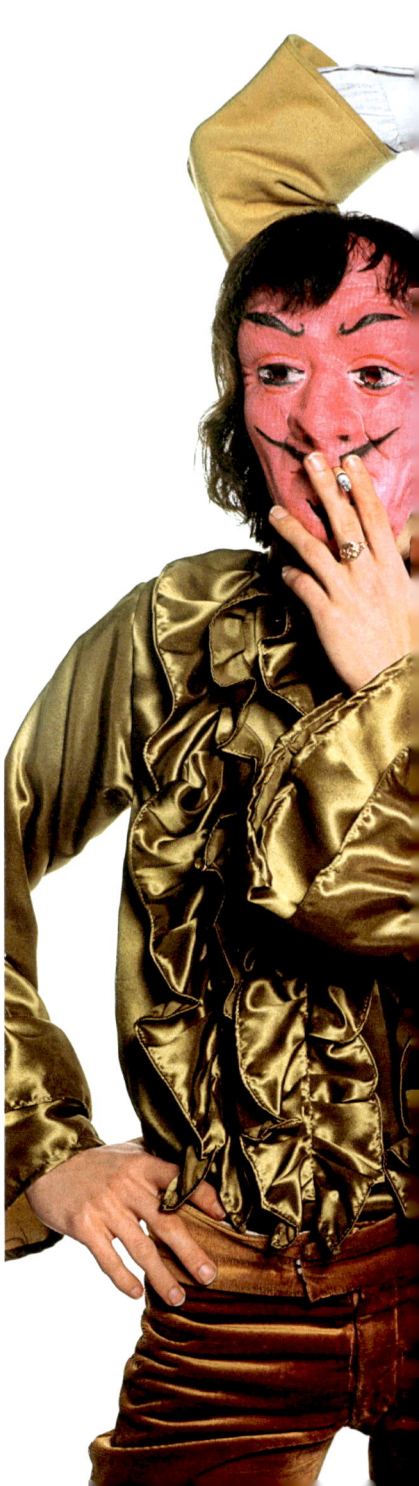

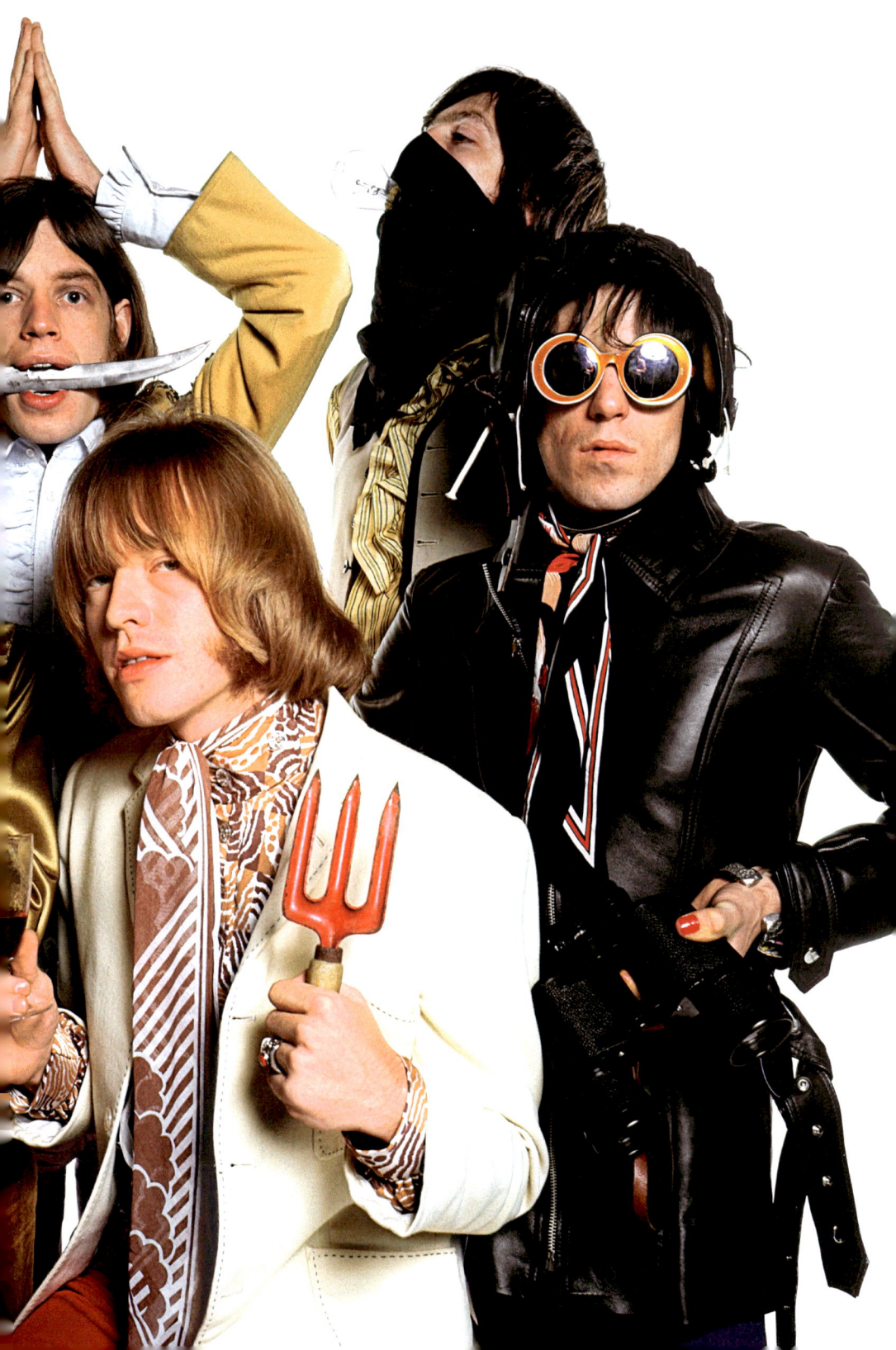

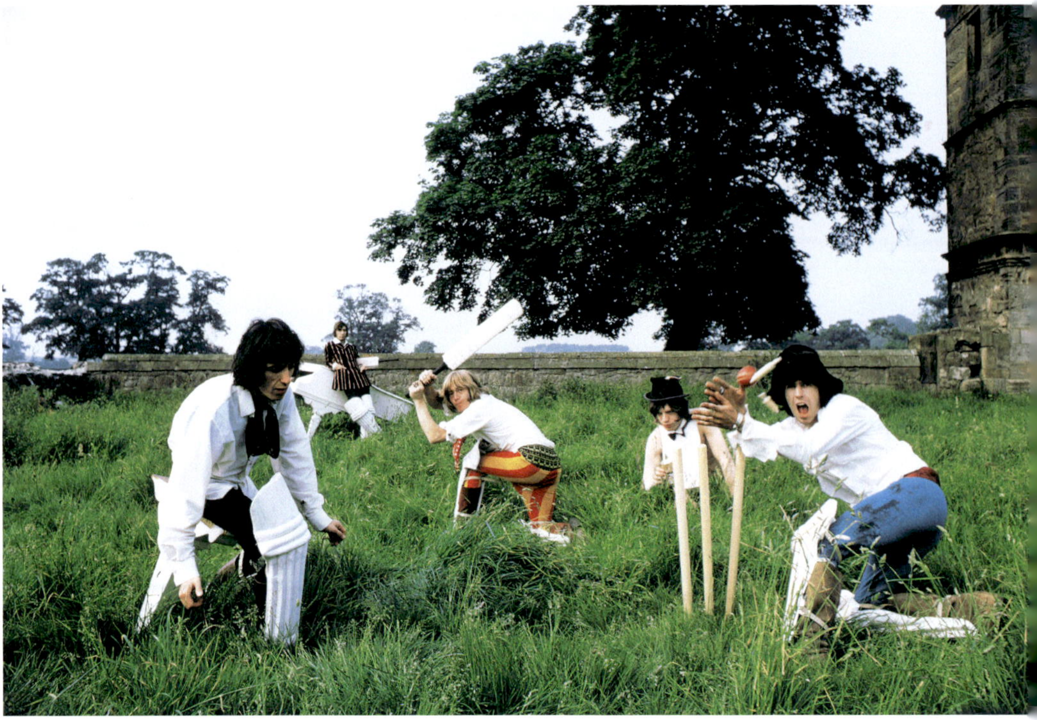

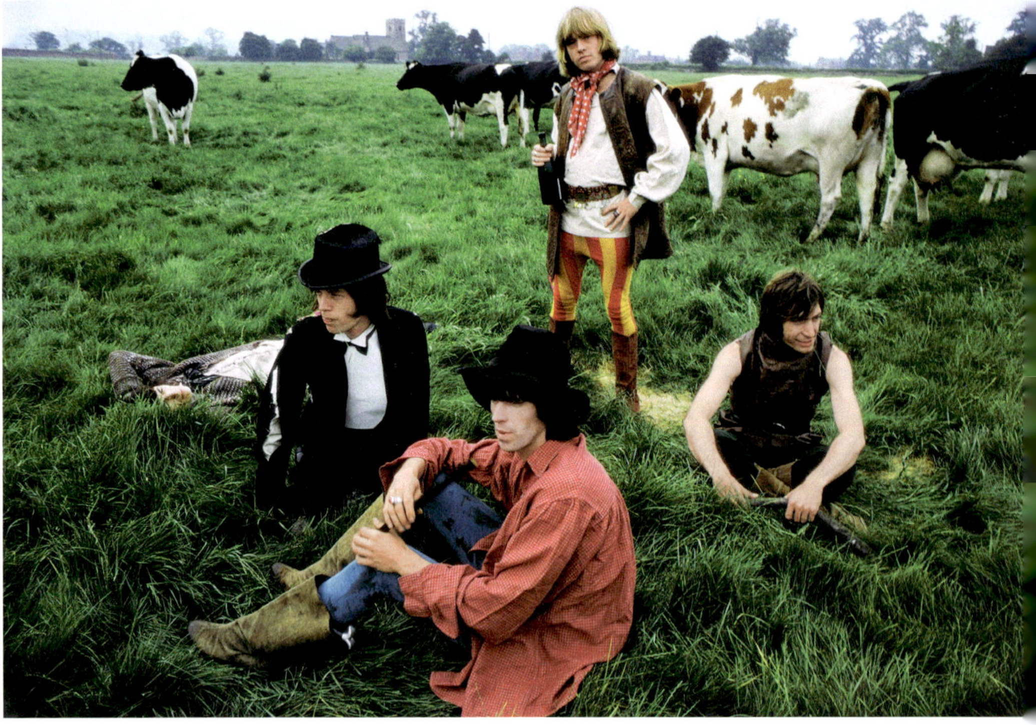

TOP

Michael Joseph

The Stones were happy to engage in an impromptu game of cricket at Swarkestone Hall, Derbyshire, 8 June 1968.

BOTTOM

Michael Joseph

Communing with nature in the long grass at Swarkestone Hall, Derbyshire, 8 June 1968. A series of locations were found to take suitable photographs for the sleeve of *Beggars Banquet*. The first was an interior at Sarum Chase, Hampstead, London, on 7 June 1968. The following day, exterior shots were taken in the grounds of Swarkestone Hall in Derbyshire, a derelict 17th-century property. On the morning of 8 June 1968, the Stones raced up the M1 motorway to the Derbyshire location, taking along the clothes they had used for the interior shots the previous day.

PP. 242–243

Michael Joseph

The concept of *Beggars Banquet* suggests larger-than-life imagery requiring elaborate sets and props, and the skills of an advertising photographer.

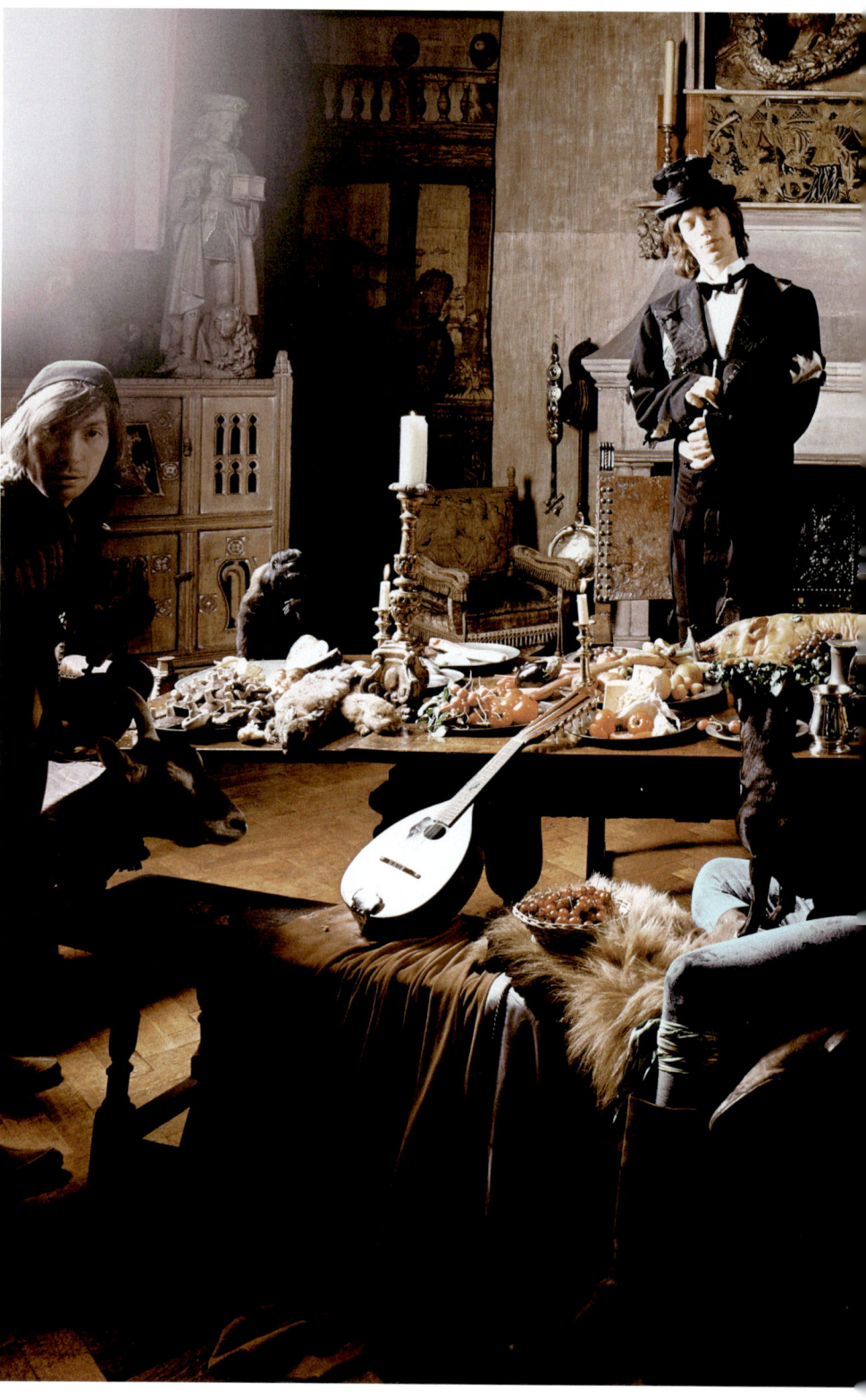

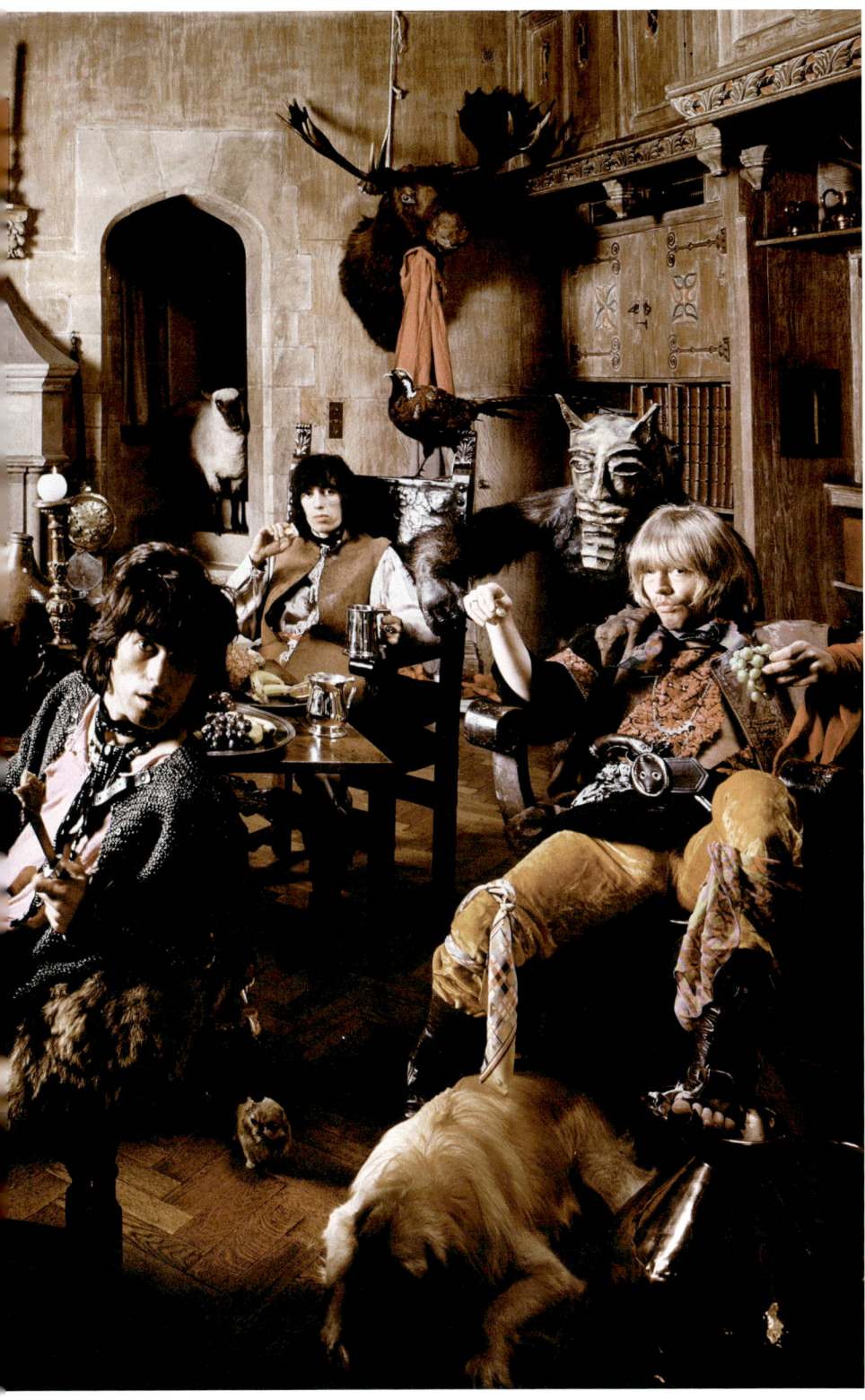

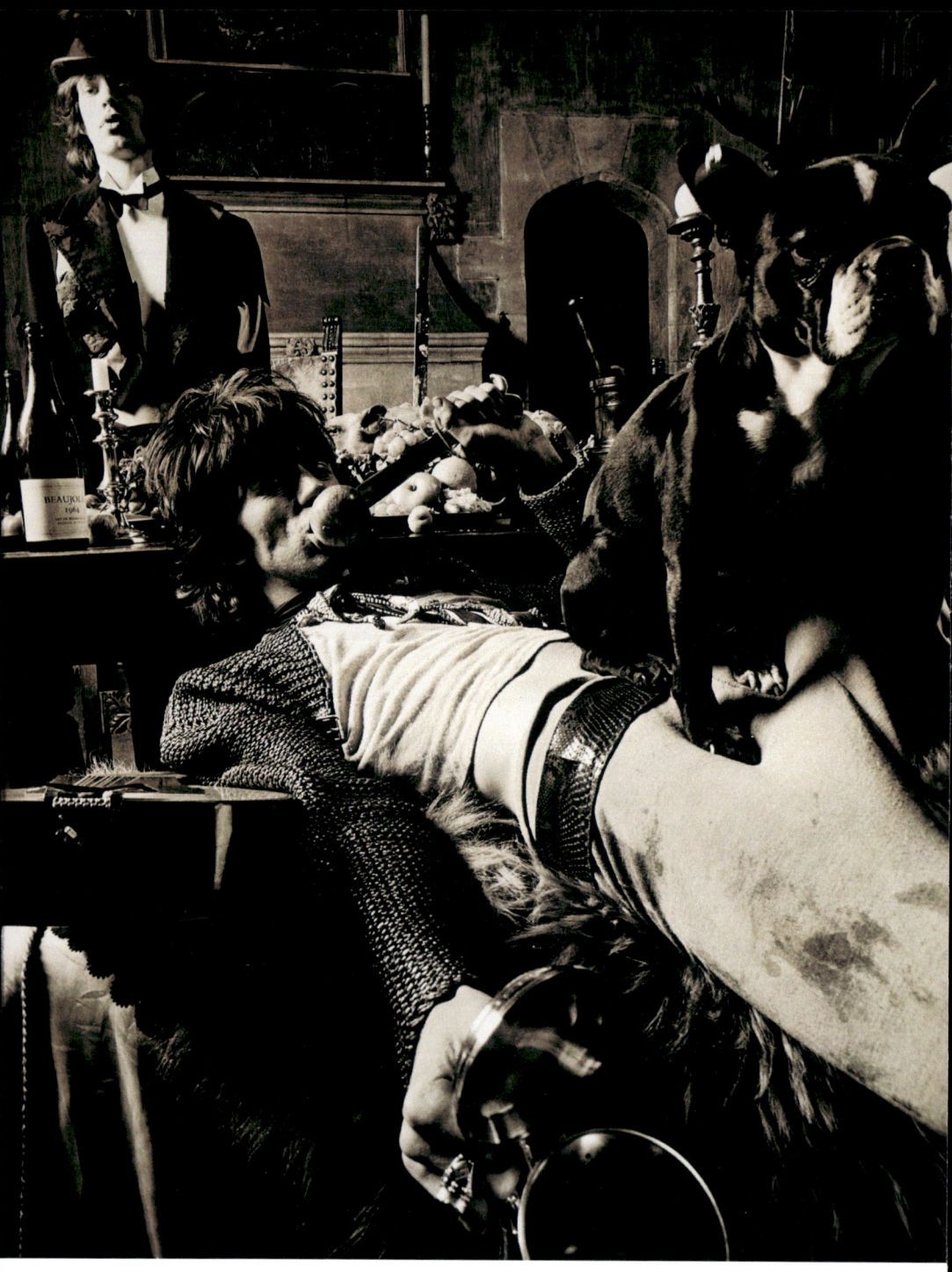

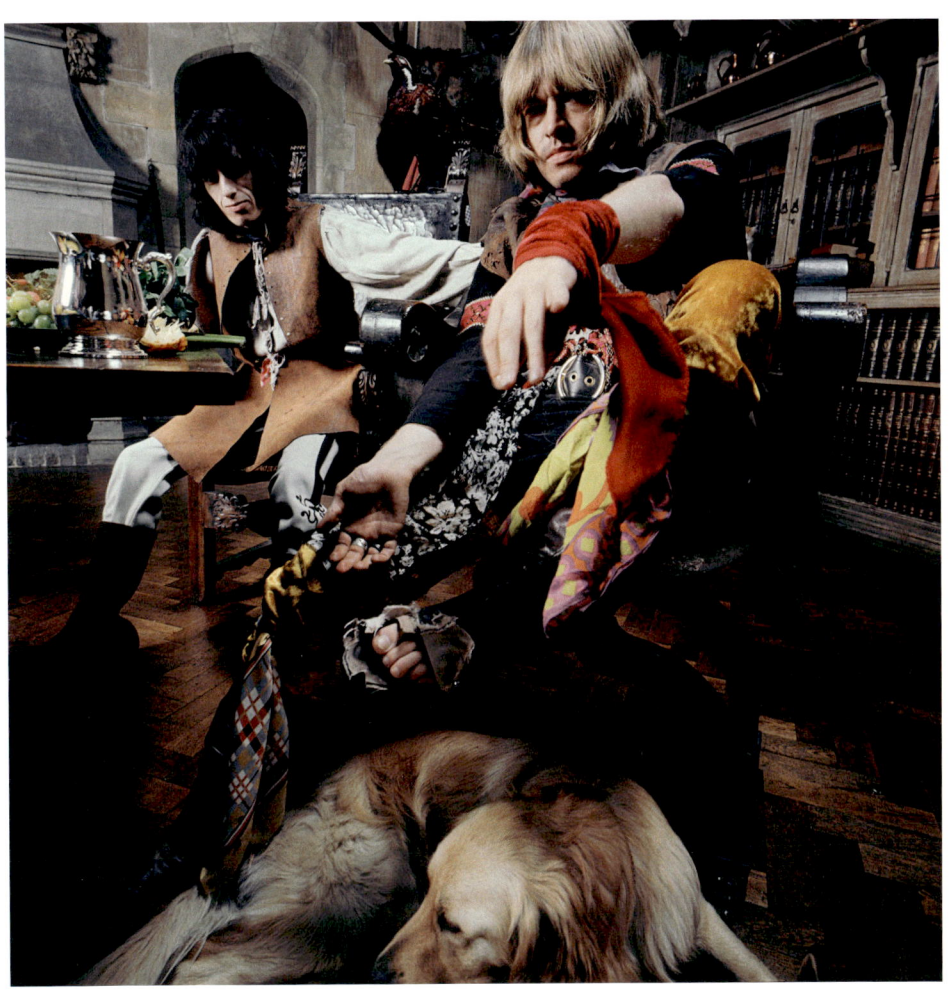

Michael Joseph
Inside the *Beggars Banquet*,
London, 7 June 1968.

Michael Joseph
London, 7 June 1968.
*"The album bristles with the brand of hard,
raunchy rock that has helped to establish the
Stones as England's most subversive roisterers
since Fagin's gang in* Oliver Twist.*" Time* magazine, 11 October 1968

Bill Wyman

A moment from *The Rolling Stones Rock And Roll Circus*, filmed (mostly) on the evening of 11 December 1968 as a counterpoint to The Beatles' *Magical Mystery Tour* television film of December 1967. The Stones were hardly doing any live work and Mick was keen for them to conceive their own TV special to keep them in the public eye.

Thomas Beyl

Initially envisaged as a fun experience, filming *The Rolling Stones Rock And Roll Circus* proved a major endurance test. It was well past midnight when the Stones made their appearance on stage at InterTel Studios in London's Stonebridge Park on 11 December 1968.

"Mick gave a performance I've never seen repeated, even by him. Like a great actor, he became another person, or maybe just more of himself; seductive, sly, ingratiating, tantalis-ing, cruel, violent, ecstatic, and finally spent." Michael Lindsay-Hogg (director), quoted in Mike Randolph, *The Rolling Stones' Rock And Roll Circus*, 1991

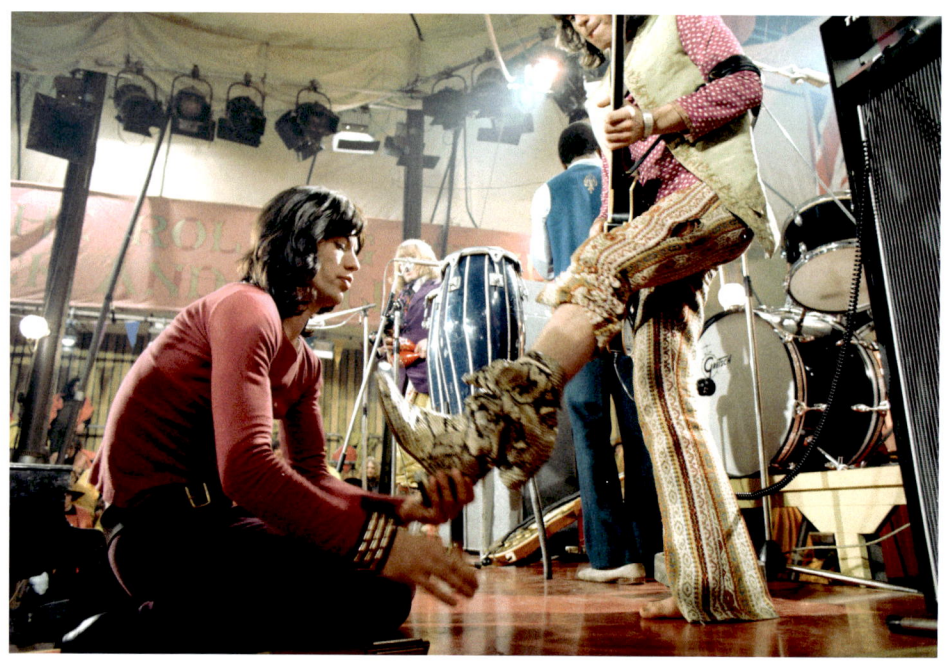

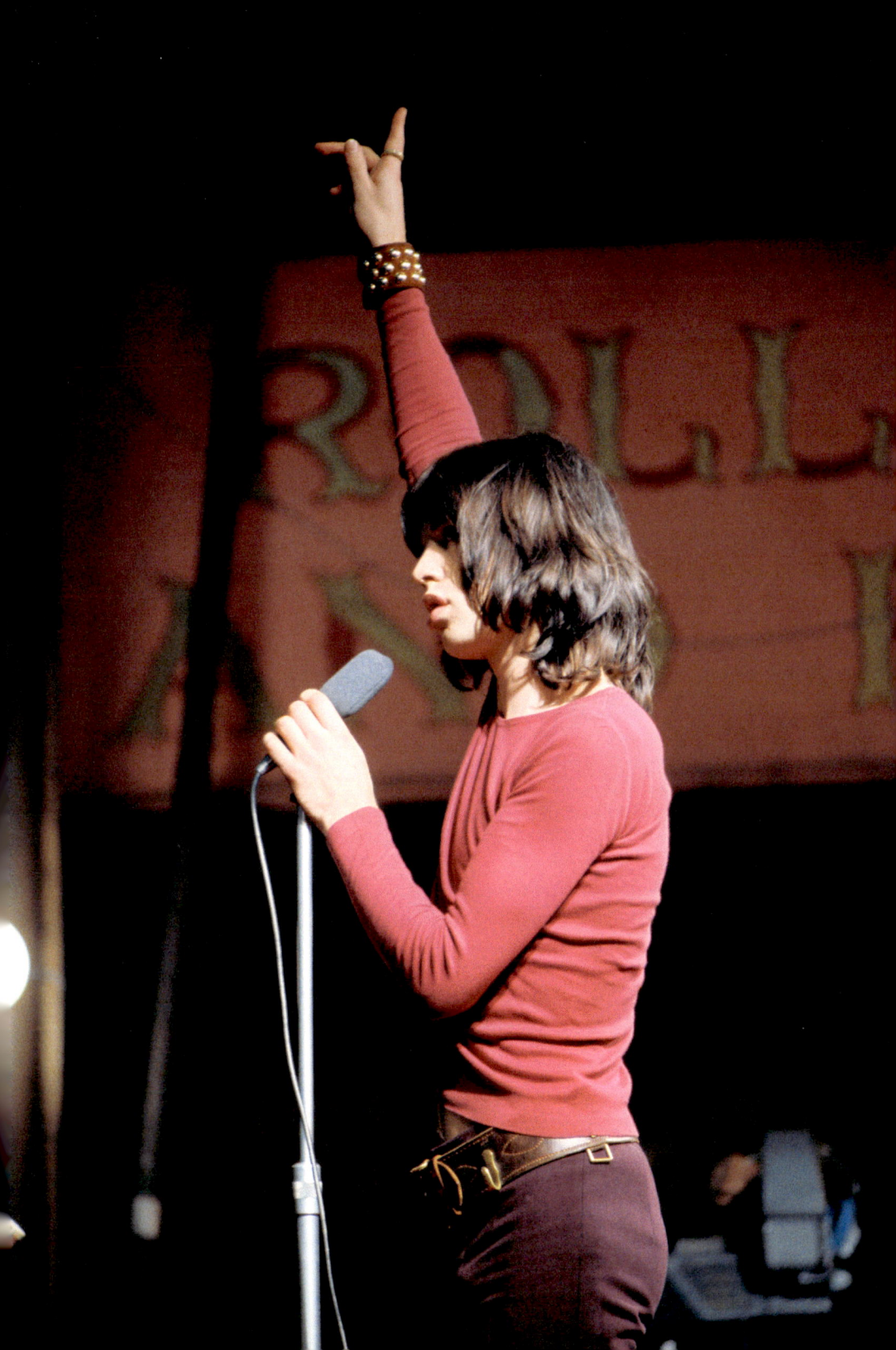

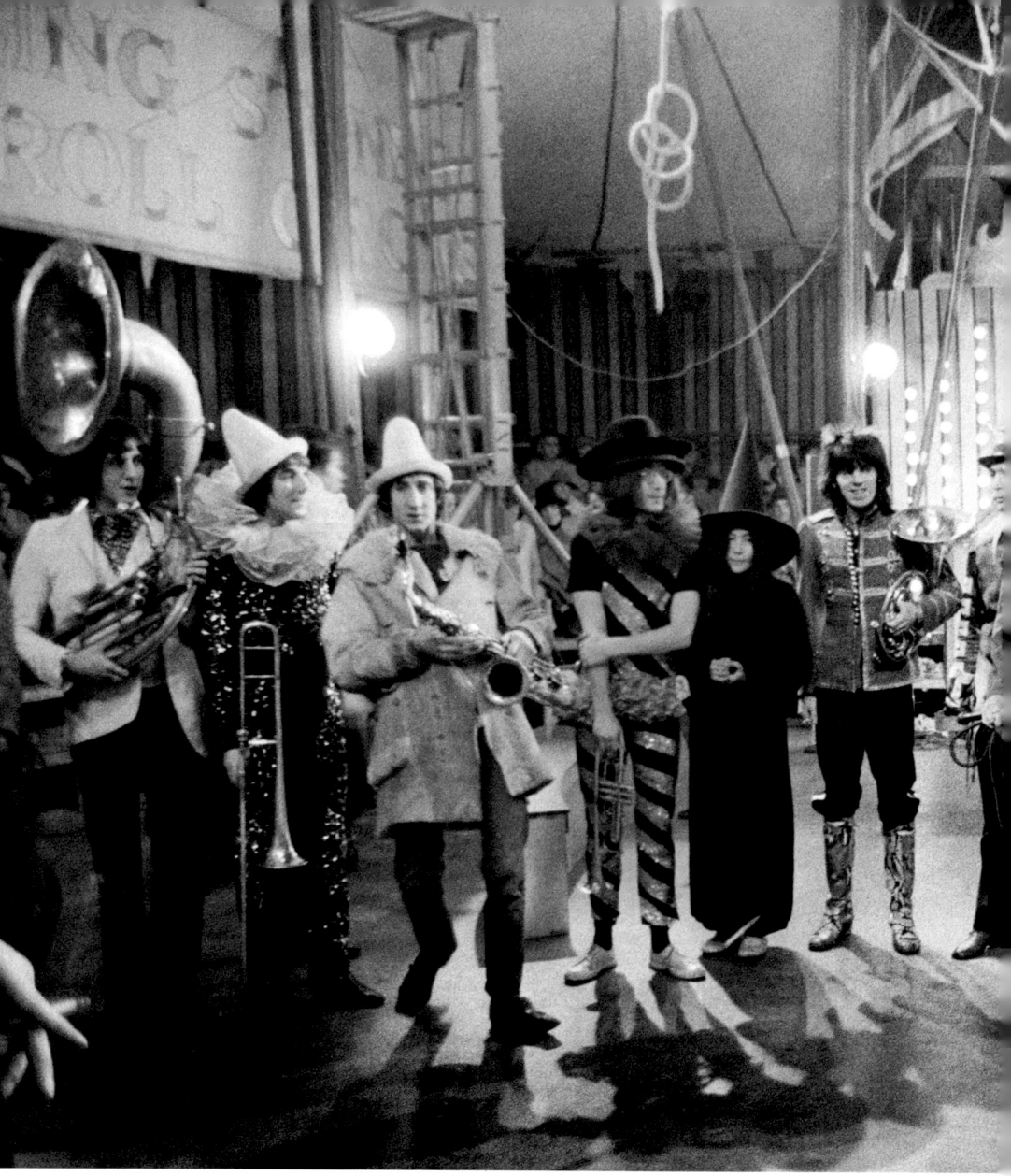

Peter Stone

InterTel Studios, Stonebridge Park, London,
11 December 1968.
The line-up for *The Rolling Stones Rock And Roll
Circus* was a "Who's Who" of rock talent, with
appearances from Jethro Tull, Marianne Faithfull,

Taj Mahal, The Who and a super-group called
"The Dirty Mac" comprising Keith, Eric Clapton,
Mitch Mitchell, John Lennon and Yoko Ono. The
show was topped off with a spirited six-track
finale by the Stones. With the gamut of circus

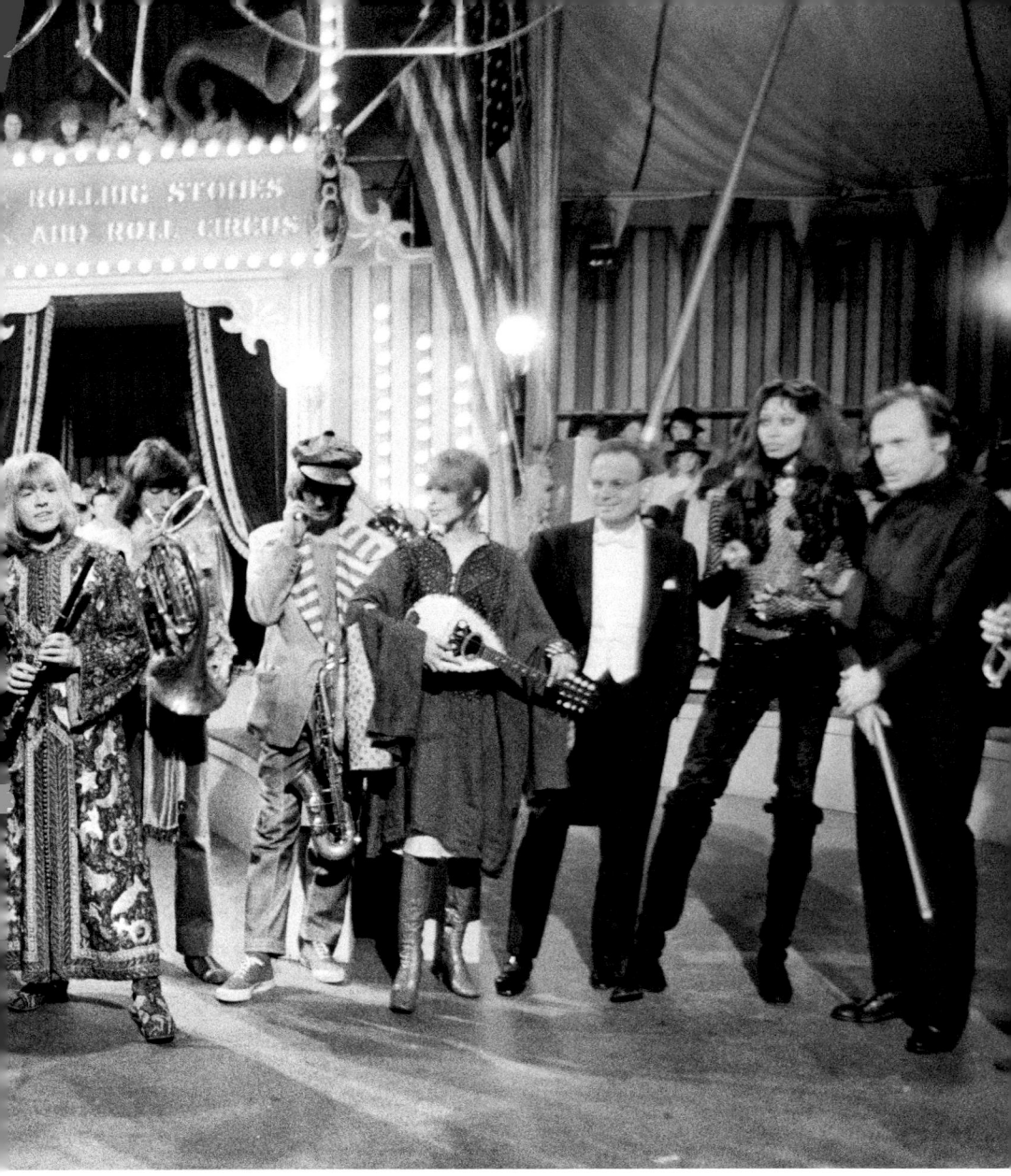

performers acting as interludes to the music, it added up to an extraordinary spectacle.
"If anyone had told me we would have been doing this sort of thing six years ago I would have said they were mad. But here we all are, thoroughly enjoying ourselves with clowns, midgets, acrobats and classical musicians." Brian Jones, *Rave* magazine, February 1969

Ethan Russell
Keith at the *Through The Past, Darkly* album
sleeve shoot, London, 21 May 1969.

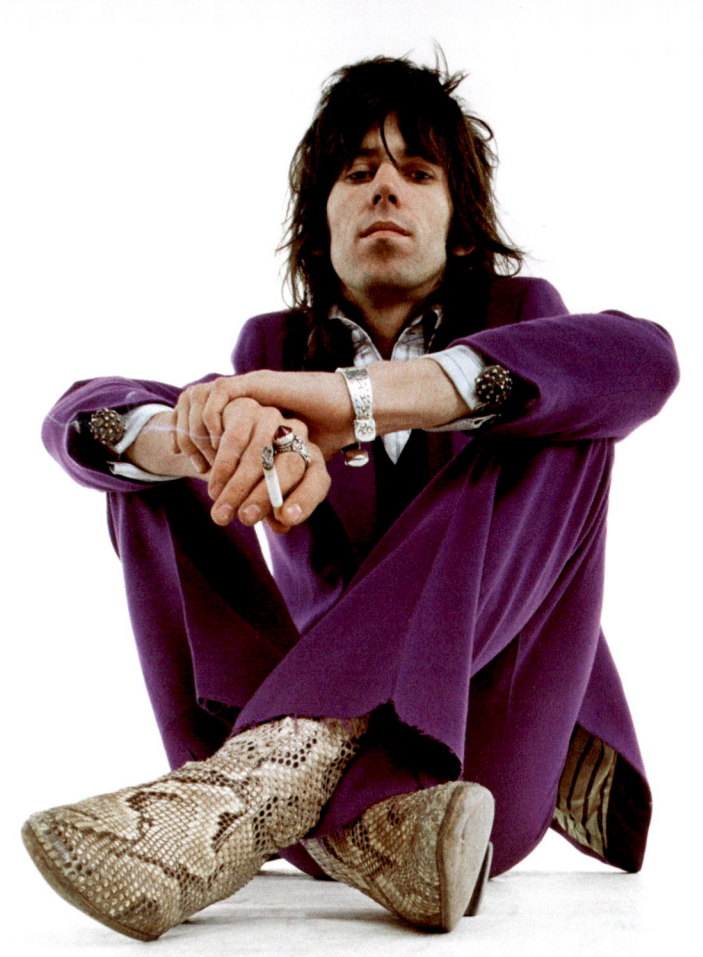

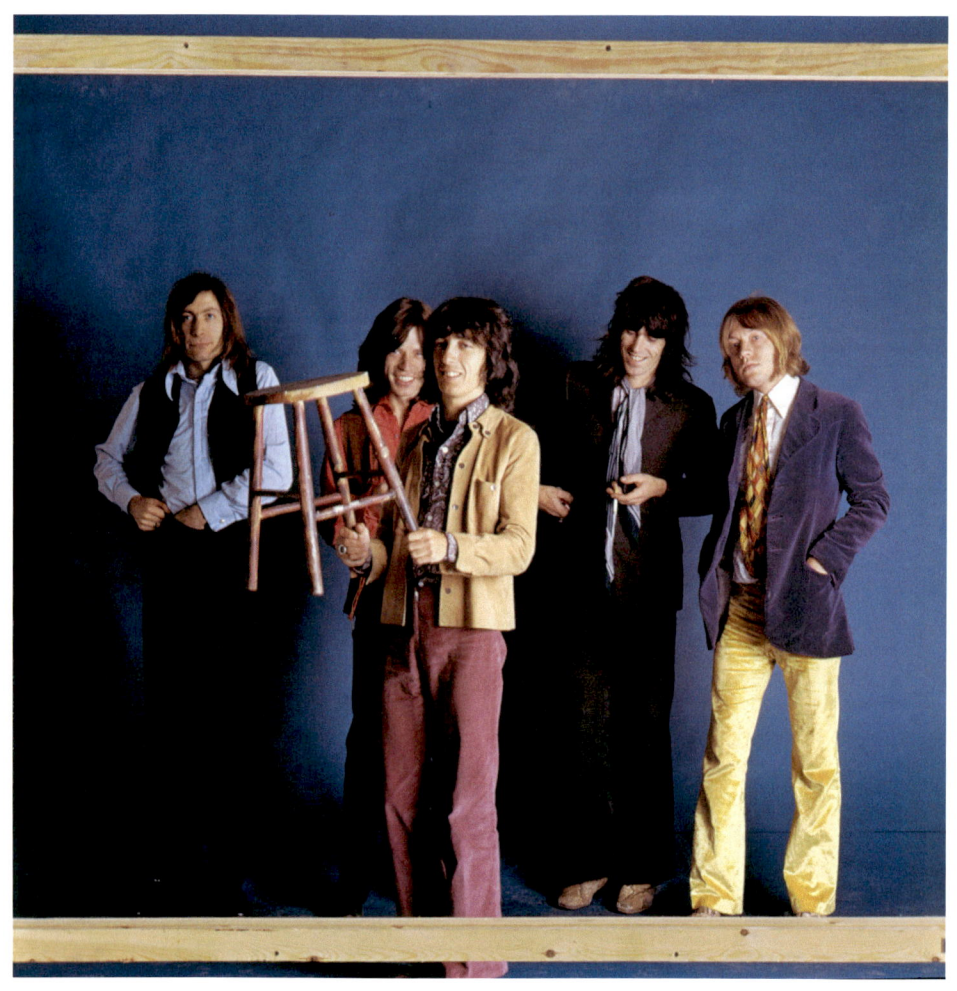

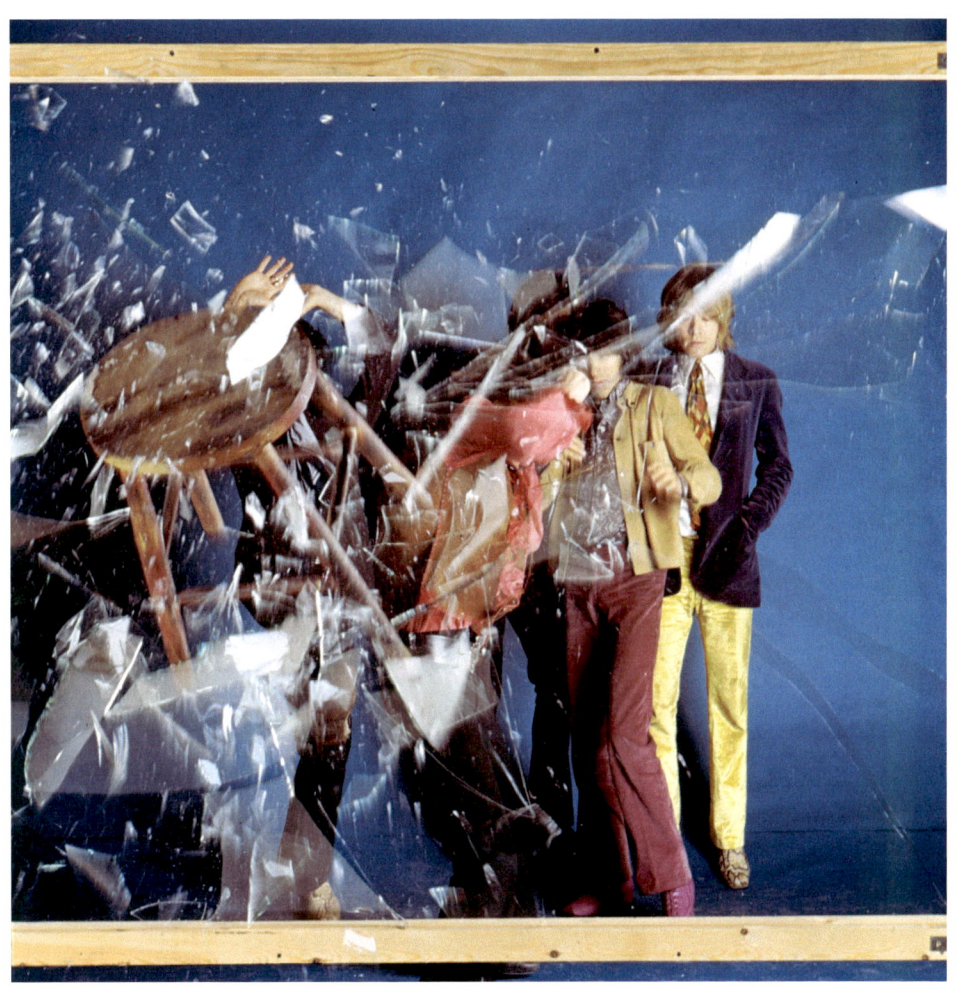

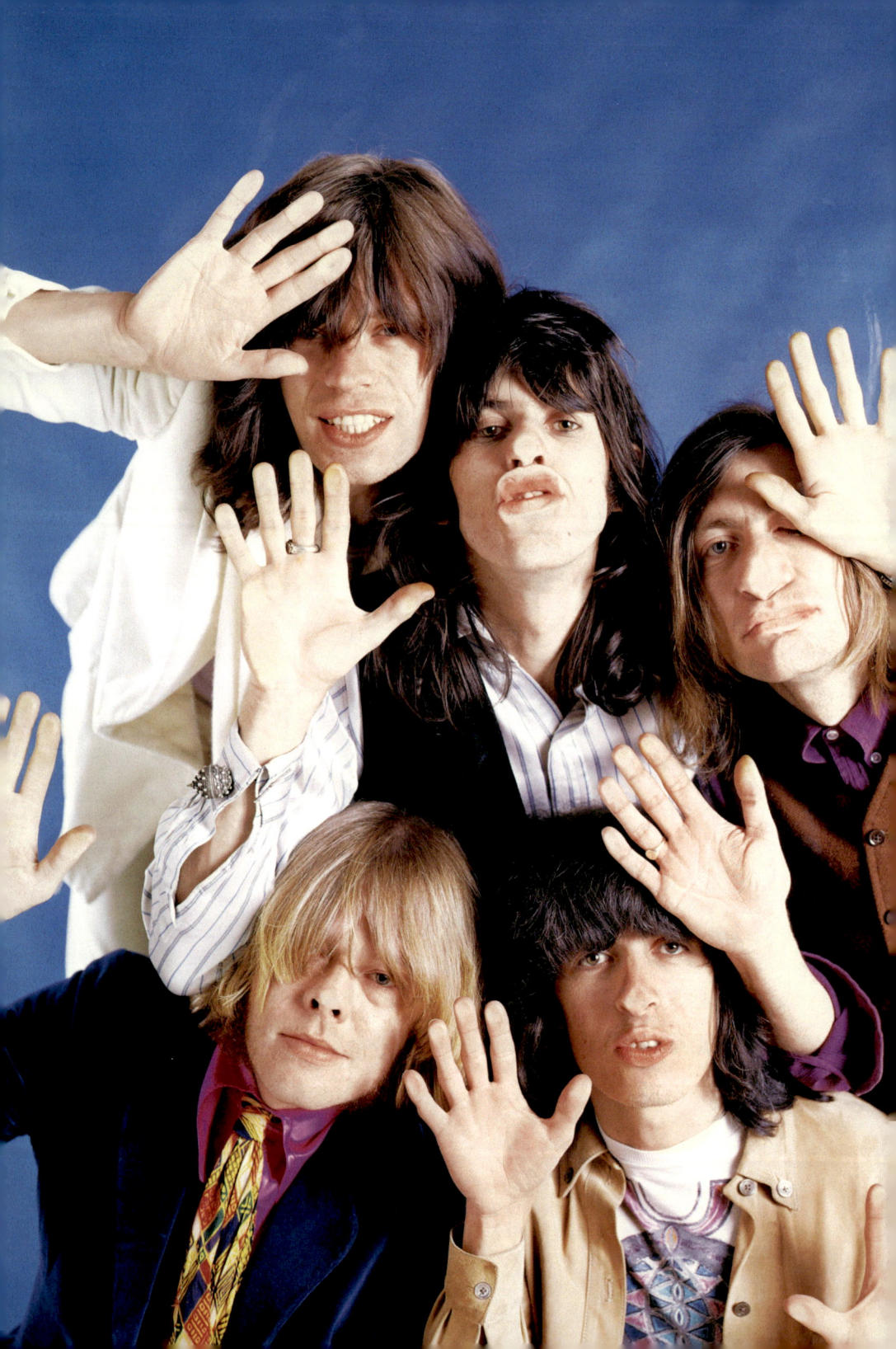

PP. 252–253

Ethan Russell

London, 21 May 1969. As a curtain was drawn over the 1960s, it was deemed timely to issue a second compilation of the Stones' greatest hits to signify the closing of a chapter. *Through The Past, Darkly (Big Hits Vol. 2)* was prepared for release in September 1969. Collecting 12 tracks (11 in the US), mostly from the period 1966–69, the album signified the end of Brian's contribution to the Stones. The album's cover shoot would prove to be his last official photo session with the band.

Ethan Russell

London, 21 May 1969. The title of the collection was inspired partly by Ingmar Bergman's 1961 film *Through A Glass Darkly* and the sleeve was a radical departure from the norm, presented in an octagonal design.

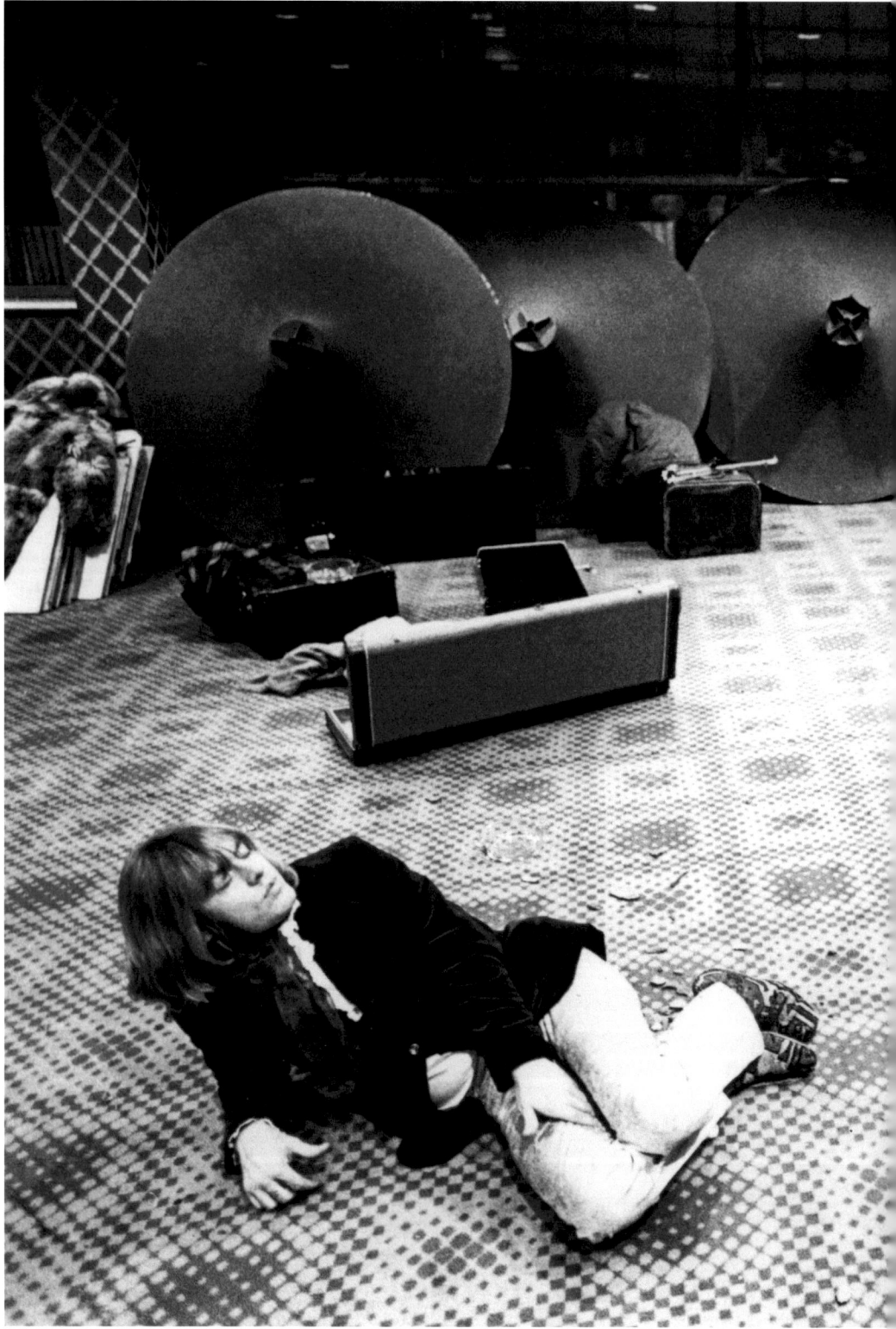

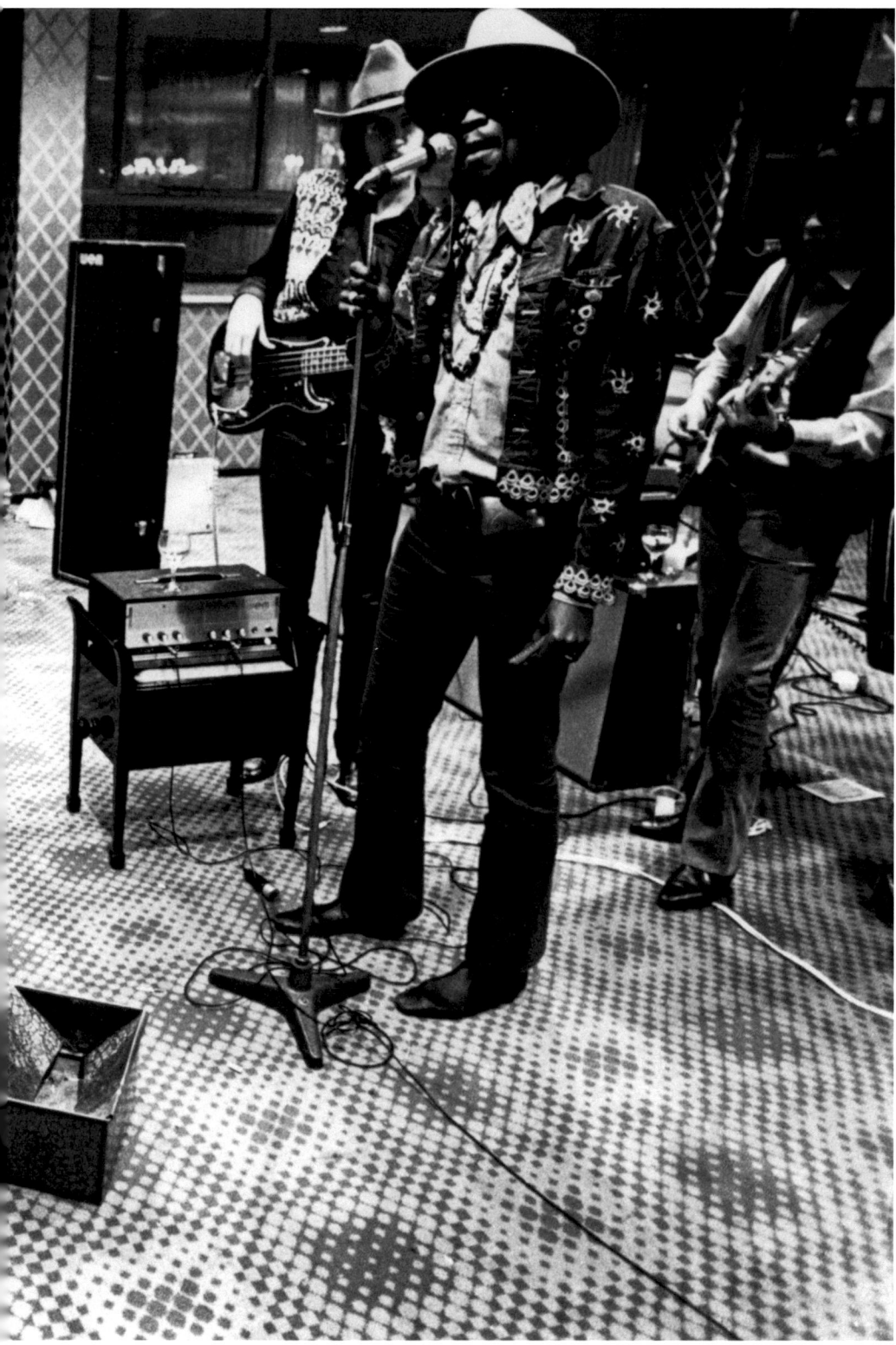

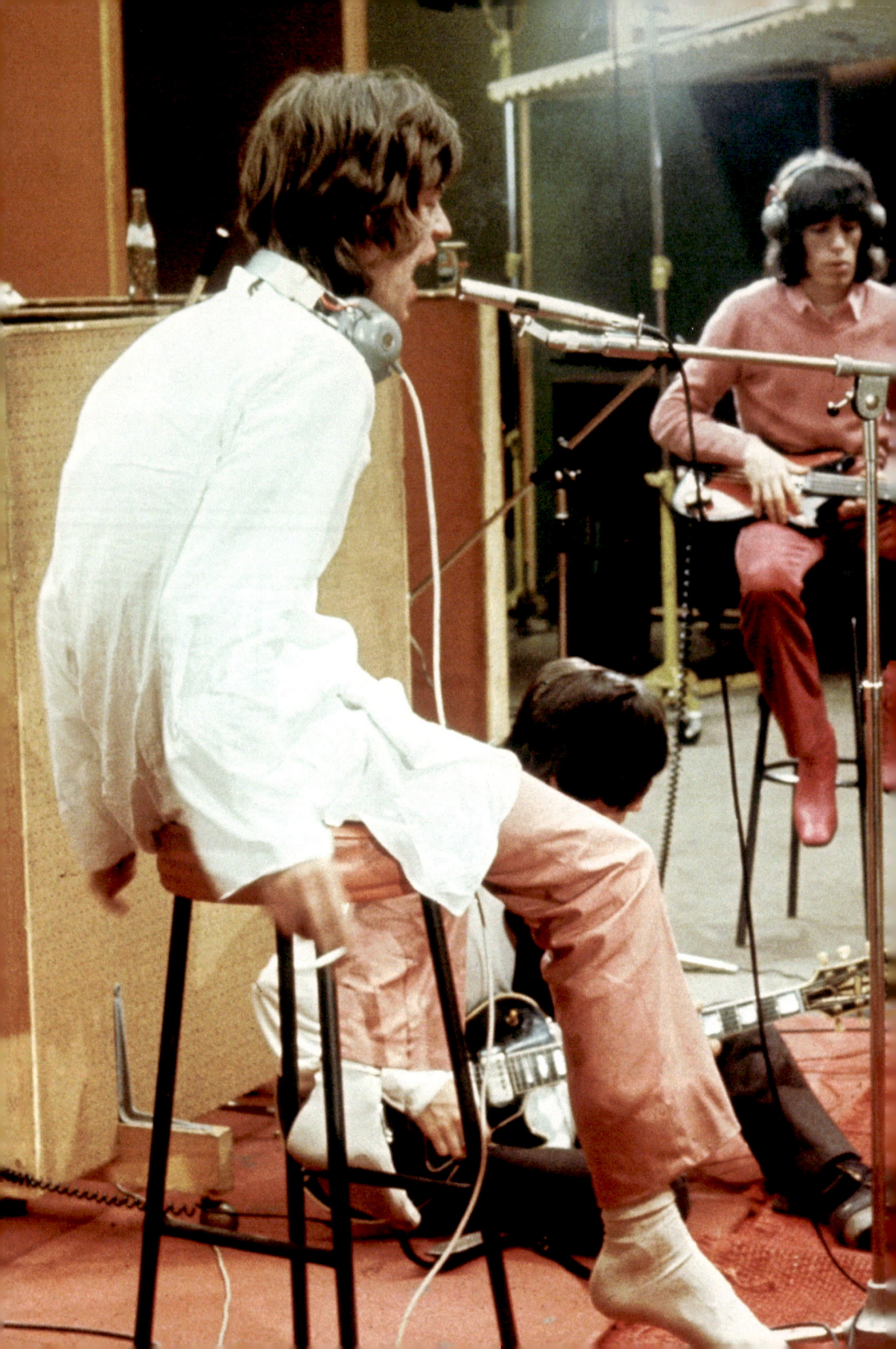

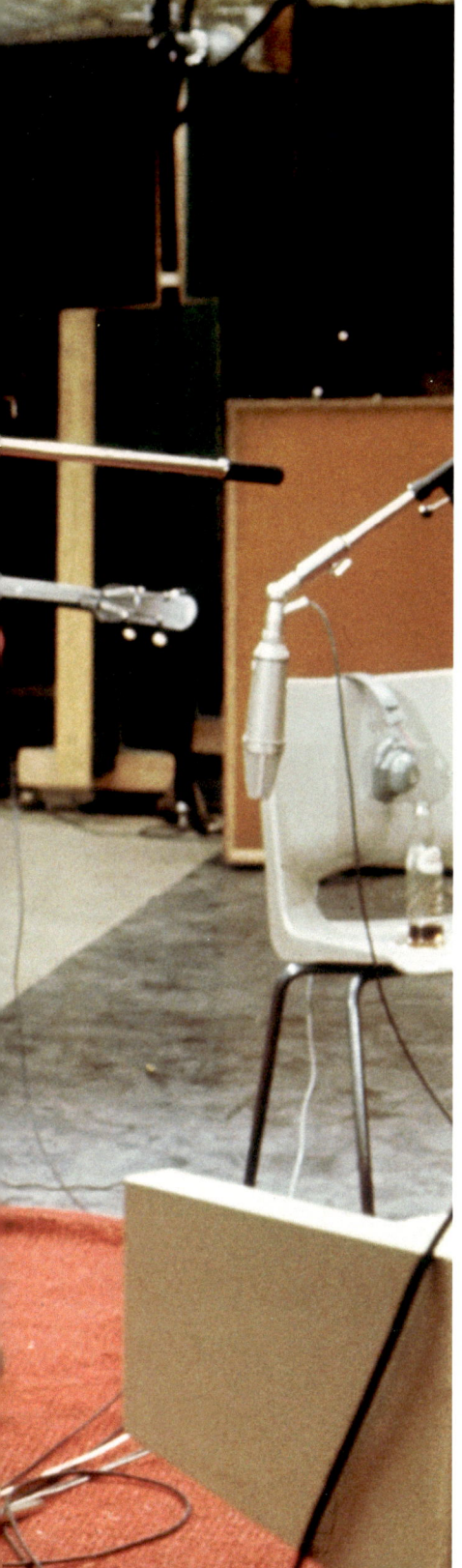

PP. 256–257

Ethan Russell
Brian on the floor watching Taj Mahal during rehearsals at the Londonderry Hotel on Park Lane for *The Rolling Stones Rock And Roll Circus*, 8 December 1968. *The Rock And Roll Circus* also saw the first public unveiling of the newly recorded "You Can't Always Get What You Want".
"Jimmy Miller sat down at the drums and remained there playing on the take. Charlie was not happy but was graceful about it. Mick and Keith played acoustic guitars, I played piano, Bill was on bass and Brian lay on his stomach in the corner reading an article on botany throughout the proceedings. I then overdubbed the organ." Al Kooper, *Backstage Passes: Rock 'N' Roll Life In The Sixties*, 1977

Tony Gale
Working on "Sympathy For The Devil" in early June 1968, the Stones shared Olympic Studios, London, with film director Jean-Luc Godard. The resulting footage of the band rehearsing cut into the film *One Plus One* (aka *Sympathy For The Devil*) is far more interesting than the muddled storyline.
"I think that ['Sympathy For The Devil'] was taken from an old idea of Baudelaire's, but I could be wrong. Sometimes when I look at my Baudelaire books, I can't see it in there. But it was an idea I got from French writing. And I just took a couple of lines and expanded on it. I wrote it as sort of like a Bob Dylan song." Mick Jagger, *Rolling Stone* magazine, December 1995

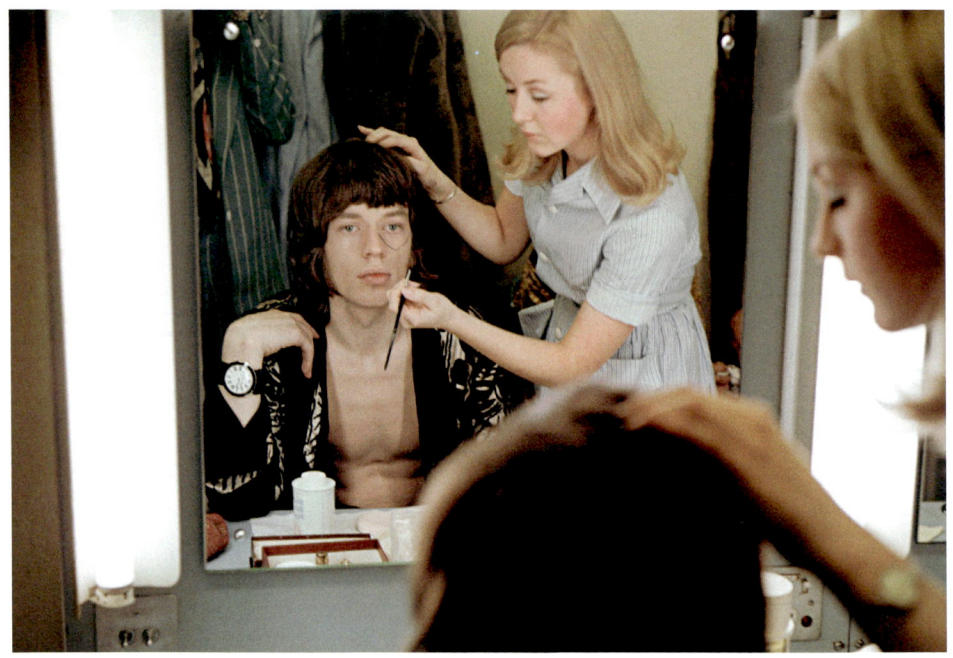

Thomas Beyl
Applying the war paint on Mick moments before the video shoot for the US single "2000 Light Years From Home" in late 1967. Still dabbling with psychedelia, the group turned in an otherworldly promotional film that complemented the song perfectly.

Baron Wolman
Mick and Anita Pallenberg on the Knightsbridge, London set of Donald Cammell's movie *Performance*, September 1968.

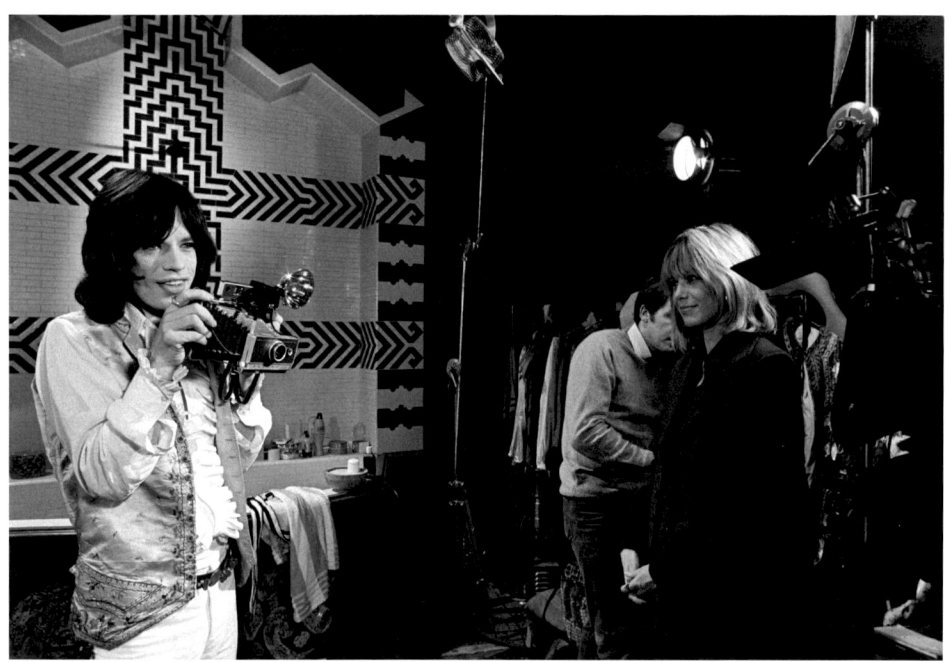

PP. 262–263
David Bailey

Alongside a host of issues, Brian's mental frailty, lack of focus and litany of drug convictions would prove untenable for overseas touring and he'd find himself exiled from the band in June 1969. He had plans for a solo musical career, but was found dead at the bottom of his swimming pool on 3 July 1969.

"He died when he was happier than he had ever been. I hope that people give him a better deal in death than they did in life." Alexis Korner, *Daily Express*, 4 July 1969

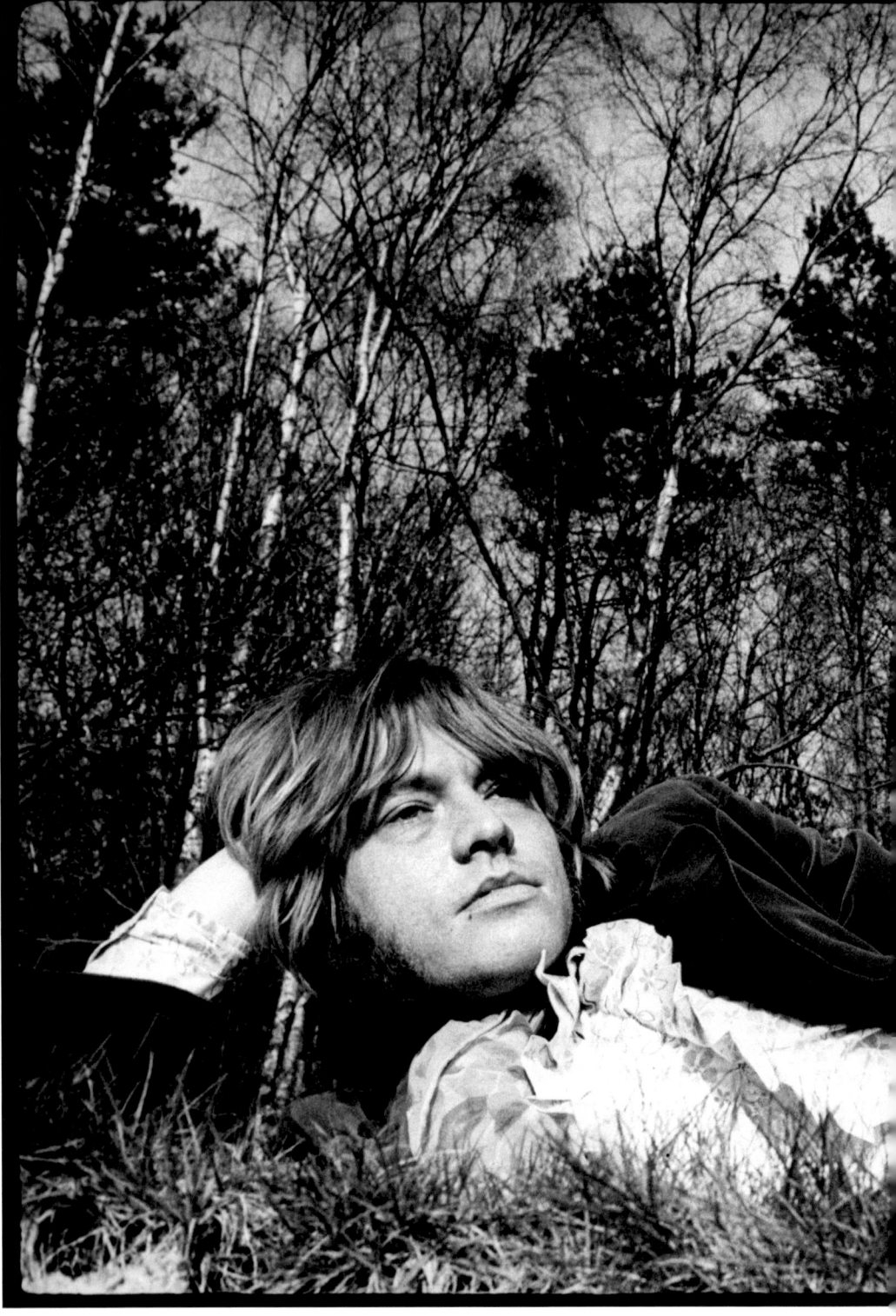

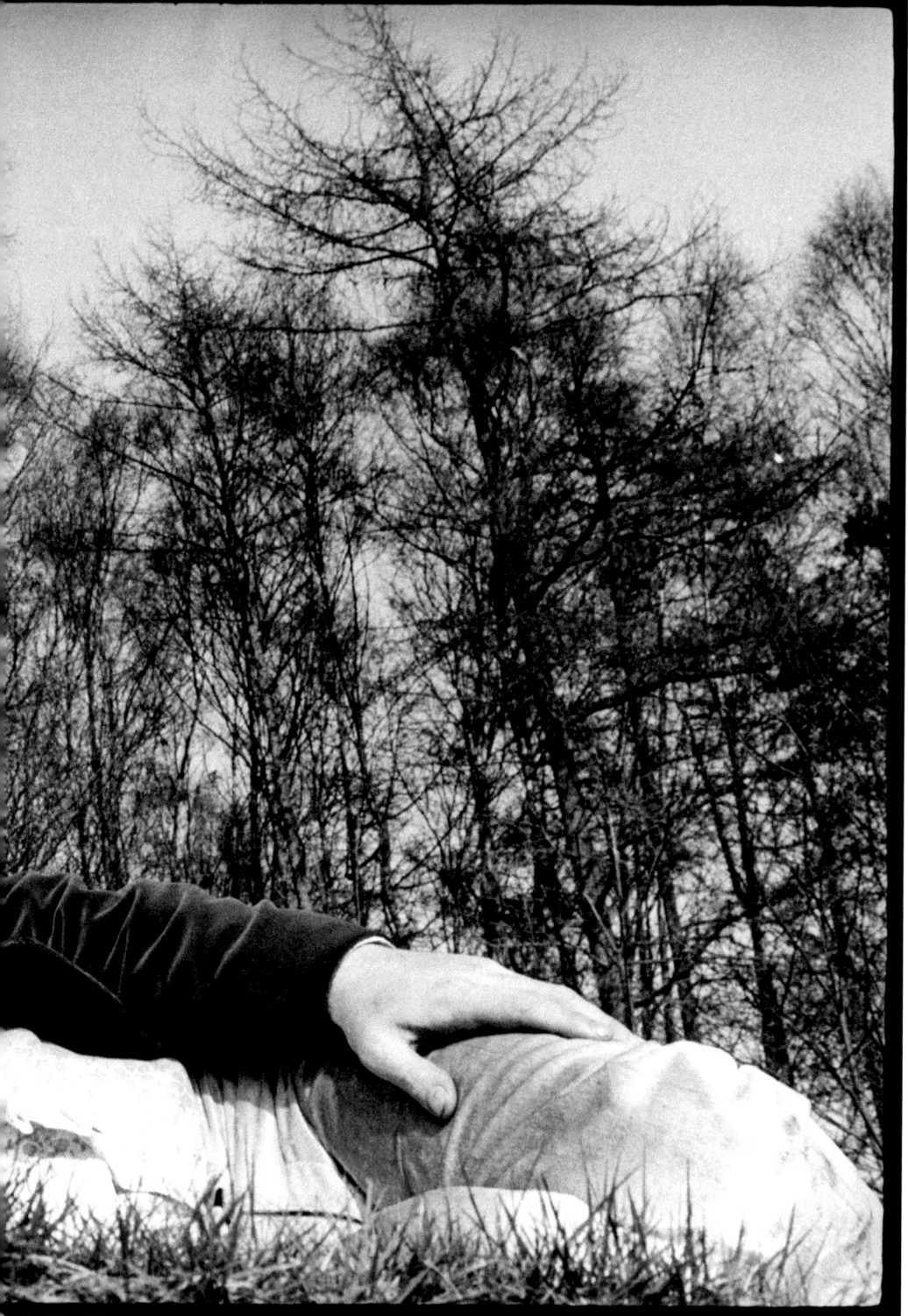

The Soundtrack to Our Lives: The Music of The Rolling Stones

By David Dalton

Let's say you've decided to put *Aftermath* (The American version) on for the first time. You plunge right in at full throttle to the first album The Rolling Stones wrote entirely by themselves – dark, cynical, eccentric and as unstoppable as a rhythm & blues freight train. Starting with the modal lament of "Paint It, Black" (still the #1 Stones song on iTunes). Following this comes a vituperative new genre they've recently honed to a fine art, the girlfriend revenge song – "Stupid Girl" (there are two more on the album, "Under My Thumb" and "Think") – and then, without a fare-thee-well, on to a lilting Elizabethan song played on the dulcimer ("Lady Jane"); a bit of black humour ("Flight 505"); and, when you least expect it, your actual morbid introspection ("I Am Waiting"). It's a giddy-making sequence of mood swings all held together by the Stones' trademark blend of irony, sophistication, cynicism and camp.

> *"('Satisfaction') has a very catchy title. It has a very catchy guitar riff. It has a great guitar sound, which was original at that time. And it captures a spirit of the times, which is very important in those kind of songs."*
>
> Mick Jagger, *Rolling Stone* magazine, December 14, 1995

To begin at the beginning: England after the war was shabby, drab, dull and depressing. In contrast to the dowdy post-war UK, there was the widescreen, Technicolor fantasy kingdom of the USA – cowboys, gangsters, movie stars, pulsing with rock 'n' roll's boogie-woogie flu.

Soon, suburban English kids – all right, Keith Richards, Mick Jagger and Brian Jones – began to discover the blues, a music so earthy, ancient and melancholy it sounded like the music God must've hummed when he made the world. They identified with the ferocious, ironic, doom-drenched laments of Delta sharecroppers as a weapon with which they could prise themselves and their generation loose from the smugness and hypocrisy of suburban England. By and by, they all subscribed to an exclusive club of blues cognoscenti. "It was almost a theological dispute with us," says Mick. Their taste wasn't for the folky blues then popular, but for the raunchy, ominous, electric Chicago blues. The Stones awakened the revolutionary energy latent in blues by igniting its charged particles, setting off a chain reaction that would set the 1960s alight.

That flash is felt through the Stones' early albums – *England's Newest Hit Makers*, *12 x 5*, *The Rolling Stones, Now!* and *Out Of Our Heads*. They communicated their inspired reimagining of the blues and R&B with such wry ferocity it became contagious. Americans heard their own lost music with new ears and fell in love with it all over again. And before you knew it, they were actually *exporting* this stuff to the USA. They did it so convincingly that they ended up realigning the history of American pop music so that we now look to blues, country, gospel and soul music as our sole primal roots.

They are serious musicians dedicated to the blues, but they aren't purists, and, early on, Keith, the Stones' mojo mechanic, saw that Chuck Berry's motivatin' over-the-hill V8 engine was their key to the highway. Chuck Berry himself was an ingenious guitar player: he took his chops from Carl Hogan of Louis Jordan's Tympany Five, his chords from boogie-woogie piano player Johnnie Johnson's left hand and hammered his accents on the second and fourth beats. Berry's double-string licks made the guitar more percussive and gave it a sweet, fat sound. Keith, in essence, simply doubled that. He describes the Stones as the way two guitars sound together. Not only did he blur the distinction between rhythm and lead guitars, but playing with Brian Jones (1962–68) and Ronnie Wood (1975–the present), Keith's inspiration was to weave the two guitars together in such a way that it was more of a conversation between the two instruments than a rhythm and lead guitar.

> "To me, 'Lady Jane' is very Elizabethan. There are a few places in England where people still speak that way, Chaucer English."
>
> Keith Richards, *Rolling Stone* magazine, August 19, 1971

Keith's pile-driving raunch and Mick's stream-of-consciousness lyrics are the glory of the band, but they were only able to pull it off because they had the bedrock of the Stones' rhythm section – Charlie Watts and Bill Wyman – behind them.

Charlie Watts started out as a subtle jazz drummer who hated rock 'n' roll but got seduced into playing it by way of an artful dodge, saying: "We [are] a blues band, serious, very serious." With Charlie, there are no paradiddles or drum solos, no gongs or bells, no sprawling drum kits, just a three-piece set. He called his approach "march-snare-drum style", but what he brought with him from jazz is *swing* – meaning an ability to go with the rhythmic groove of the band.

Bill Wyman, true to his gothic image – the stony face, his stiff manner, his habit of holding the bass vertically (his small hands are the reason) – is the one who brought electricity to the Stones. An early example of his ingenuity is his "dive-bombing" bass in "19th Nervous Breakdown", but, for the most part, his style is cool and slow, and so embedded in the Stones' sound it's almost invisible. But, like breathing, it's the vital pulse that keeps the runaway train steady as she goes.

As songwriters, Mick and Keith started out using pared-down generic chords and lyrics ("Tell Me", "The Last Time"), but rapidly developed their own style, composing intimate ballads ("Play With Fire"). They soon extended the code language of rock with their quintessential anthem "(I Can't Get No) Satisfaction", blending a whiff of social protest with naughty sexual innuendo. The menace of Keith's fuzz guitar and insinuation of Mick's whispered vocals were tantamount to a devastating double assault, producing their first US #1 hit.

The way they'd built their chassis out of R&B spare parts proved very adaptable in incorporating other forms of pop music into their sound, such as their quirky 1966 hits "Mother's Little Helper", "19th Nervous Breakdown" and "Have You Seen Your Mother, Baby, Standing In The Shadow?" By the time you get to 1967s "Let's Spend The Night Together" and "Ruby Tuesday", the Stones are no longer quite the angry young men. But then came the sensational drugs bust, at Redlands, Keith's country estate. Nothing could have been better for the Stones' bad-boy reputation, but the disruption of Mick and Keith being thrown into jail, lawyers and court cases (and their eventual dismissal) took its toll on their next album, the psychedelically noodling *Their Satanic Majesties Request* with its wizard-on-Alpha-Centauri 3D cover.

> "(Their Satanic Majesties Request) *is really like got-together chaos... Whatever people might think about that album, I think it is very valid as a comment on The Rolling Stones as they were in 1967... We were a little freaked out.*"
>
> Brian Jones, KRLA Radio *The Pop Chronicles*, (recorded) January 1968

By 1968, it was time to rebuild the Stones' war wagon, not the least of which was Keith's inspired retooling of his guitar, making it into a gear-shifting percussion instrument with which to lob the Stones' formidable ordnance. He did this through an act of acoustic surgery, by removing the lowest (E) string from his guitar because, if accidentally struck, it could cause complications. One of the first songs he used the five-string open G tuning on was the Stones' re-emergence anthem, 'Jumpin' Jack Flash" (which he describes as "Satisfaction" backwards). You can hear the swashbuckling raunch of his open tuning all over "Honky Tonk Women", "Brown Sugar", "Can't You Hear Me Knocking", "Gimme Shelter" and "Start Me Up". Open tuning had a subtle, unexpected side effect: a drone quality similar to the sympathetic ringing tones on a sitar. The advantage (of the open G tuning) is that you really only use three notes.

The Stones delved back into their blues roots, but now tinged their sound with rock, country, gospel, and R&B. And with this mix, they produced the first of their four classic albums of the late 1960s and early 1970s: *Beggars Banquet*, *Let It Bleed*, *Sticky Fingers* and *Exile On Main St.* Their smokestack lightning careened down the track on the mock satanic "Sympathy For The Devil", the wet-dream Delta fantasy of "Parachute Woman", the Doppler sound shift of the British police siren in "Street Fighting Man" and the lubricious "Stray Cat Blues". Where *Beggars Banquet* was pared down and bluesy, *Let It Bleed* came off as epic and vaudevillian. *Sticky Fingers*, despite its opening salvo (the big, brash, blousy mock minstrelsy of "Brown Sugar"), is ruminative and reflective.

By the late 1960s, Mick and Keith's songwriting had evolved into a seismograph for recording elusive mental states (in songs like "Sway"). Like griot novelists, they sprinkled their songs with titillating tales about themselves and their fictional haute Bohemian playmates in much the same way Dickens or Balzac presented an ongoing cast of characters they'd invented. Keith's dirty, grinding sound pumped adrenaline into these songs, while Mick's images: *plastic boots … cocaine eyes … speed-freak jive …* distilled them into an addictive brew that insinuated their music into our heads. By the time we get to *Sticky Fingers*, the transmission is subliminal; the whole album is so heady you can almost get a contact high from it.

Virtuoso blues guitarist Mick Taylor had played on a couple of tracks on *Let It Bleed*, but on *Sticky Fingers*, he really comes into his own. His spacey guitar spirals sensuously out of Keith's rhythmic riffs like a spectral echo, while his solos mirror the inflection of Mick's voice, etherealising the lyrics into pure sound. Mick Taylor's improvisations along with the textured layers of the horns, organ and piano give *Sticky Fingers* an extended jazzy feel, allowing the Stones to focus on the mood of their albums, rather than singles.

In 1972 came the Stones' double-album masterpiece *Exile On Main St.* It's a subterranean bunker album like Bob Dylan's *Blonde on Blonde*, a hermetically sealed world – the planet Stoned – situated in this case in the basement of Nellcôte, Keith's tax-exile hideaway in the south of France. *Exile* is a prolonged reflection on where the blues, country and R&B had taken the band and transformed them into something rich and strange. Around the mesmerising drone of Slim Harpo's voodoo blues in "Shake Your Hips", the Stones would spin their ragtag, torn and frayed hoard of funky American music – tawdry gems picked up on the road and off records, or thought up in their heads.

"A lot of those songs like 'Miss You' on Some Girls *and later 'Undercover' and things like that, were heavily influenced by going to the discos. You can hear it in a lot of those 'four on the floor' rhythms and the Philadelphia-style drumming."*

Charlie Watts, *According To The Rolling Stones*, 2003

Through *Exile*, the Stones had become rock gods, but the psychic weather had changed and they needed to acclimatise to it. Deeper into the 1970s, they became almost chameleon-like in their synthesis of different genres as they absorbed different trends.

Mick and Keith were following their own instincts and leading their own lives. Mick, a natural creature of the zeitgeist, became more and more involved with the contemporary scene, while Keith succumbed to a hard living rock 'n' roll lifestyle. What got the Stones' juices flowing again was relocating to New York and getting inspired by the raw energy of the streets, the nightlife, and punk. The new stripped down sound re-emerges with a vengeance on the brain-jolting "Shattered". Turning self-referential is the fate of all successful rock groups – after all these years of fame, they were no longer singing about us, exactly – it was more about them. But on "Miss You", a rueful cry of loss and regret, Mick's hypnotic vocals make us forget all that as he conjures his disco-dusted moan into a form of cultural nostalgia.

Mick's voice *is* the Stones, it's the way the Stones talk to us, an instrument of such subtle, insinuating power that it can simultaneously seduce and taunt you. It's an art Mick practised from the very beginning. In that aching, breathy first syllable of "Tell Me", "*Iuh* want you *back* again…", you can hear Mick transform a riff into a classic double-entendre Stones song with the timbre of his voice alone. Yeah, he wants her back, but, as the rhythm picks up and the emotion intensifies, the voice becomes manic and starts to imply something else, something ambivalent. Eight years later, in the spoken opening of "Let It Loose", Mick slides into your consciousness. He's confiding something to you and, as he does so, he imperceptibly shifts emotional gears and, suddenly, you're caught up in the turmoil of a love affair gone awry. Mick, through these vocal sleights of hand, implants these songs indelibly inside our heads.

"'Start Me Up' became a Mick- and Keith-welded song with contributions from both of them. It was one of those genuine collaborations between the two of them, with a little magic from both sides happening instantly."

Ronnie Wood, *According To The Rolling Stones*, 2003

By the 1980s, the Stones had become legendary presences, descending to earth every three years or so to perform in raunchy extravaganzas and put out a new brew of pungent tracks. *Emotional Rescue* rocked because the Stones in 1980 were coming off their *Some Girls* high. *Tattoo You*, the following year, was another great album, but it doesn't really count since it was a compilation album – they had their '81 and '82 tours of the US and Europe coming up – and you need vinyl to hustle. But by the time they were making 1983's *Undercover*, there were well-documented tensions within the band – a situation that began to affect their charts. *Undercover* made it only to #4 on the US charts, breaking a run of eight #1 albums in a row. On account of these infamous feuds and more significantly their staying power, there has been some grumbling about the Stones' albums of the past three decades. Weren't they punk enough, funk enough, grunge enough, in love enough for you? They can still crank their firepower at maximum velocity. You want hard rock? It's all over these albums. If you wanted something a little more soulful, there were always the plaintive, wistful ballads "All About You", "Waiting On A Friend", "Sleep Tonight", "Slipping Away", "Out Of Tears" and the remarkable "Laugh, I Nearly Died".

The Stones have outlasted all their peers and prospered for more than 60 years. The power of the songs and the hypnotic performances are fantasies dreamed up by the dark princes of rock 'n' roll. They embody their songs so totally, thus creating rock's most sensual and compelling theatre.

PP. 270–271
Dick Barnatt
Earls Court Arena, London, May 1976.
The six concerts at the west London arena broke box-office records for the venue. With over a million ticket applications received, the initial schedule of three concerts was extended to six over the period 21–27 May 1976.

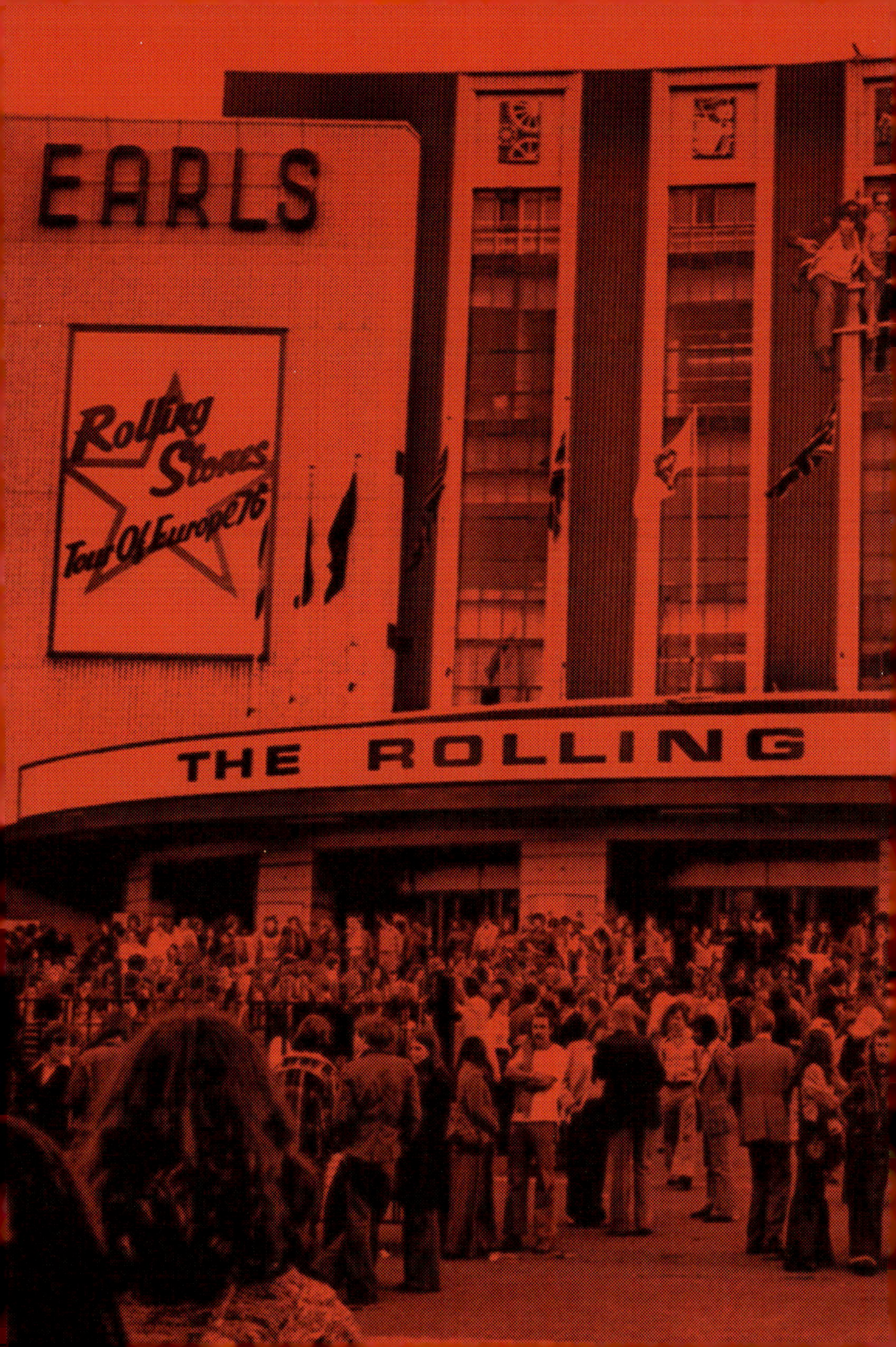
EARLS
Rolling Stones
Tour Of Europe 76
THE ROLLING

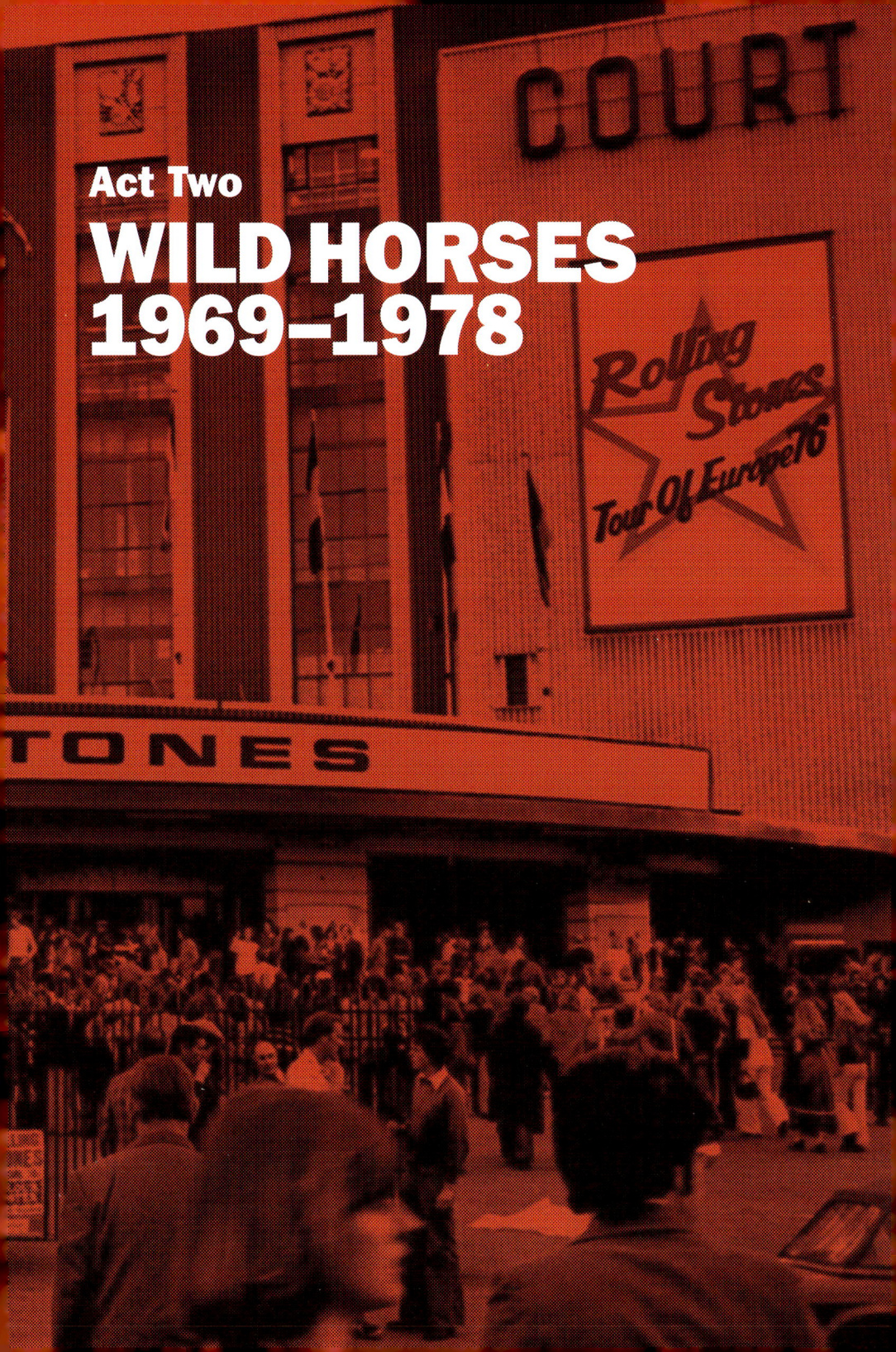

Act Two

WILD HORSES
1969–1978

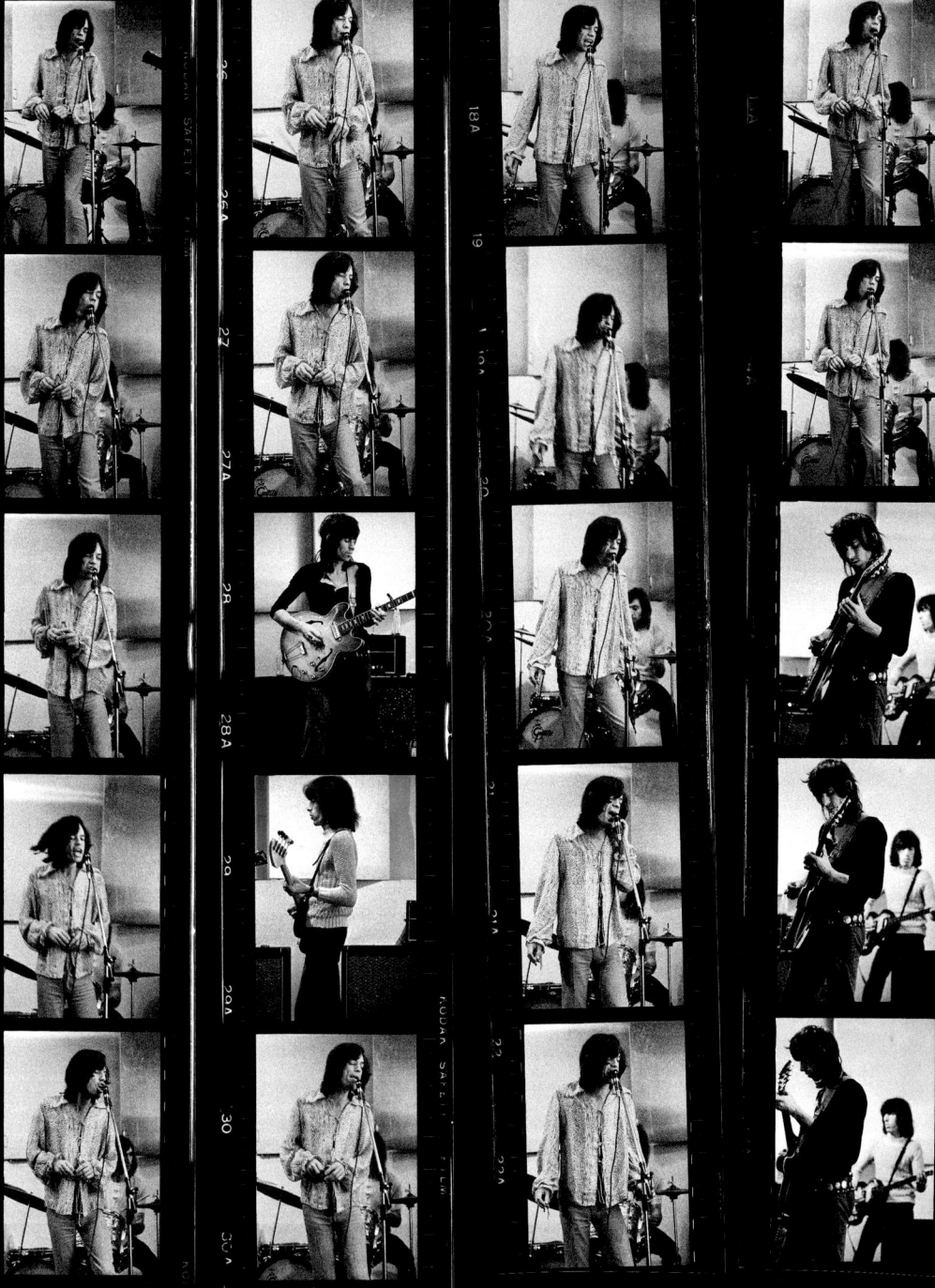

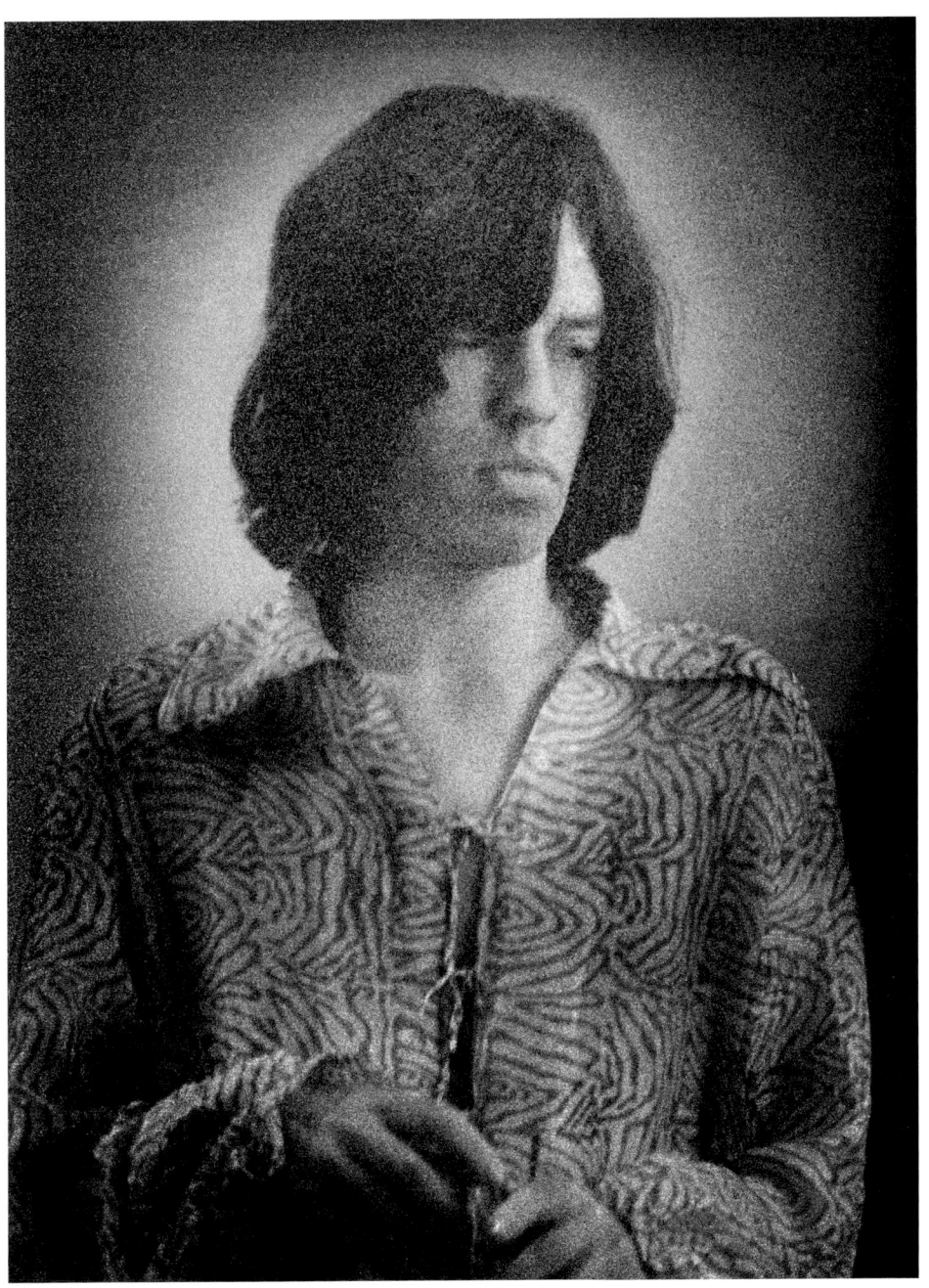

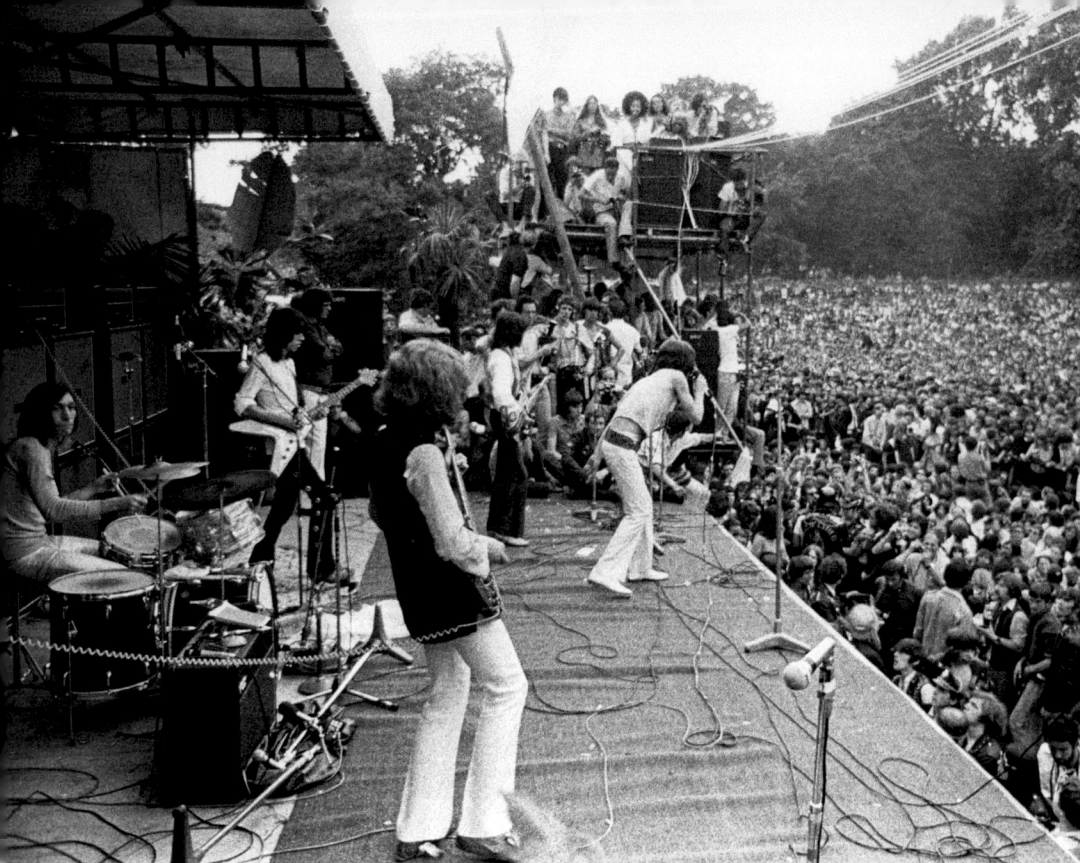

PP. 272–273
Willie Christie
The band hadn't toured since the spring of 1967
and Mick Taylor's recent arrival plus the looming
Hyde Park concert meant that there was an
urgent need for rehearsal time. To this end,
the Stones made use of The Beatles' expansive
basement studio in central London at 3 Savile
Row – an arrangement they maintained between
late June and early July 1969.

Barrie Wentzell
Planned to reintroduce the Stones back into
live work after a two-year hiatus, the Hyde Park
free concert on 5 July 1969, just two days after
Brian's death, turned into a memorial for him.
The gig was preceded by a reading from Shelley's
"Adonaïs" by Mick, dressed in a white frock.
*"Brian will be at the concert. I mean, he'll be
there ... I don't believe in Western bereavement.
I can't suddenly drape a long black veil and walk
the hills. But it is still very upsetting. I want to
make it so that Brian's send-off from the world is
filled with as much happiness as possible."* Mick
Jagger, interview, *The Stones In The Park*, 1969

274

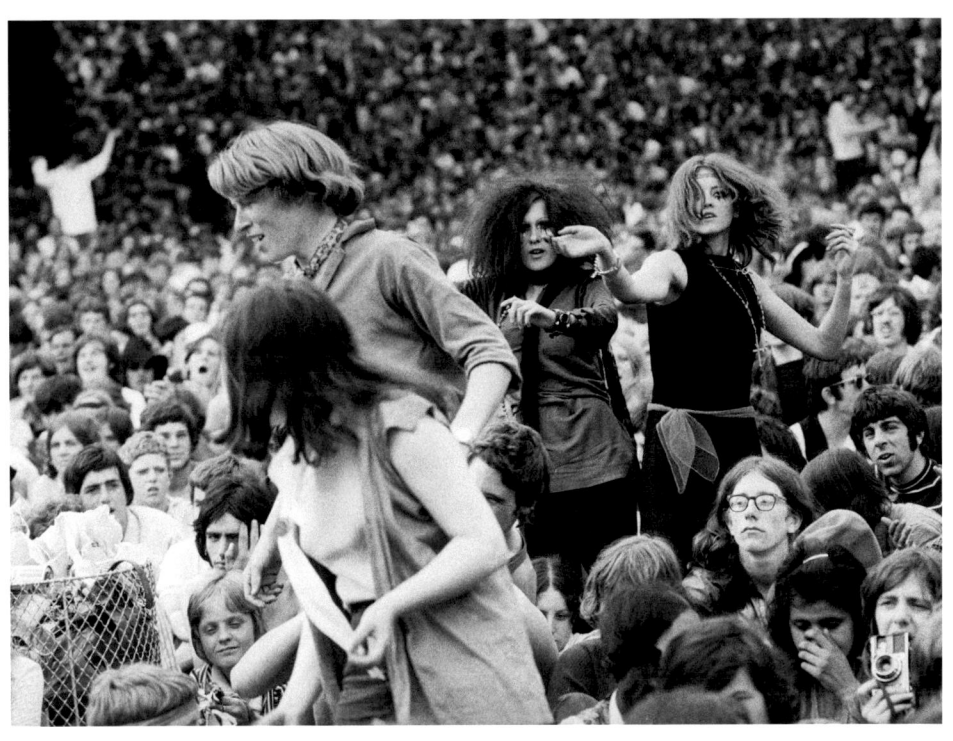

Wolfgang Heilemann
Hyde Park, London, 5 July 1969.
The enormous crowd at Hyde Park was the epitome of peaceful coexistence. In charge of security were a chapter of London's Hells Angels who, despite their dubious reputation, handled the situation without any controversy. Later in the year, however, the San Francisco chapter of the gang would present a far greater challenge. *"The Stones are real-life people. Not like The Beatles with this seven days in bed; they're true to life."* Hells Angel comment, *The Stones In The Park*, 1969

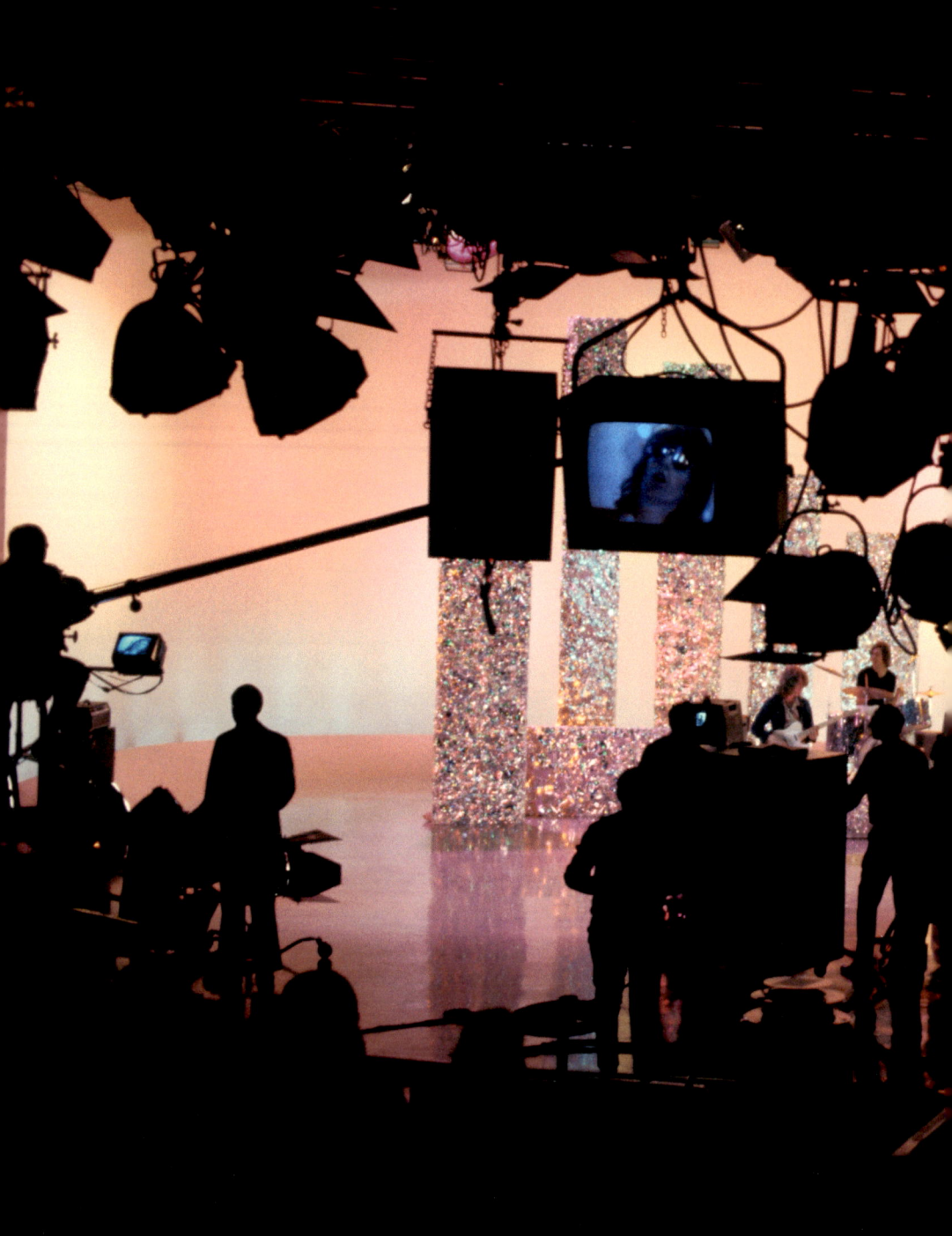

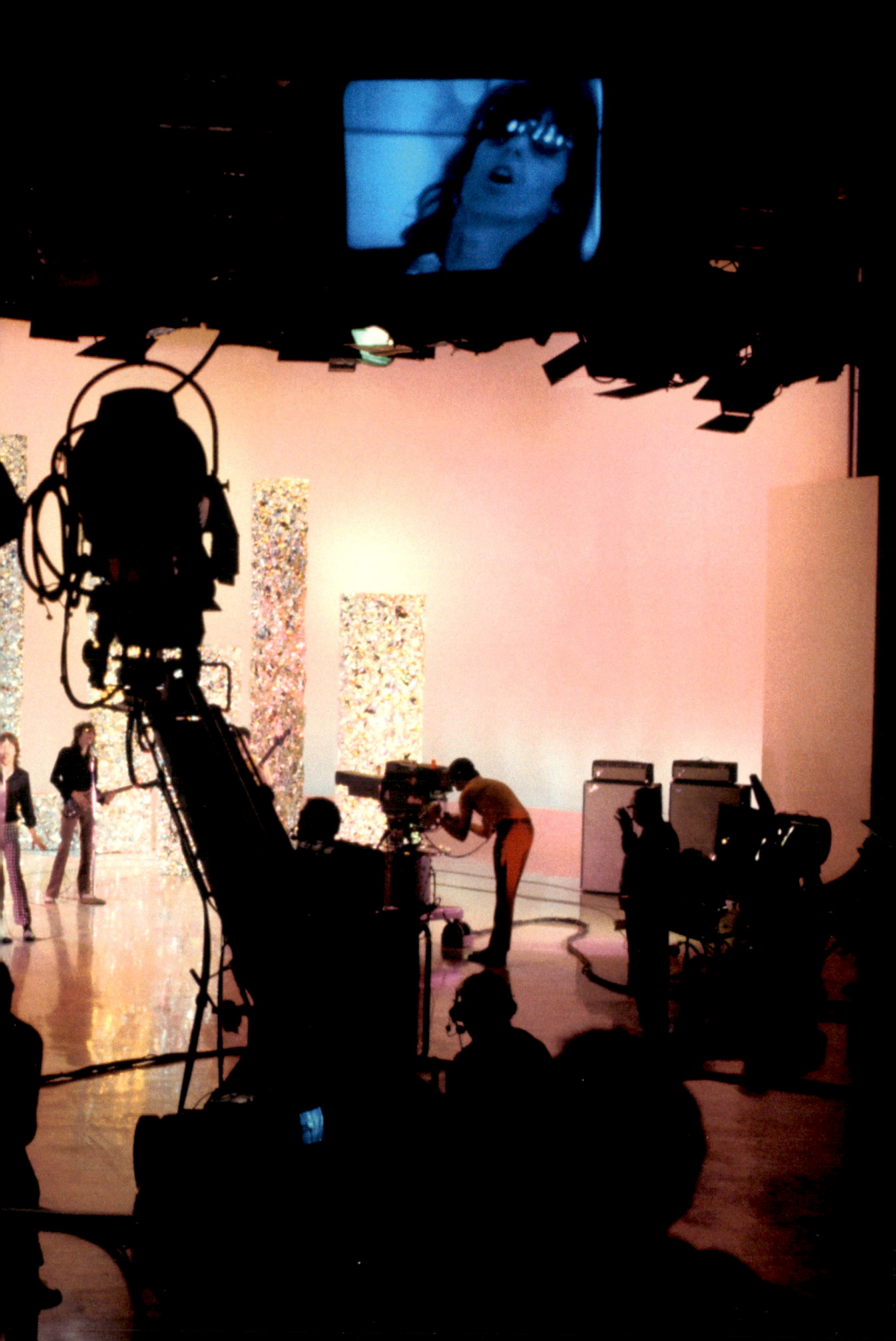

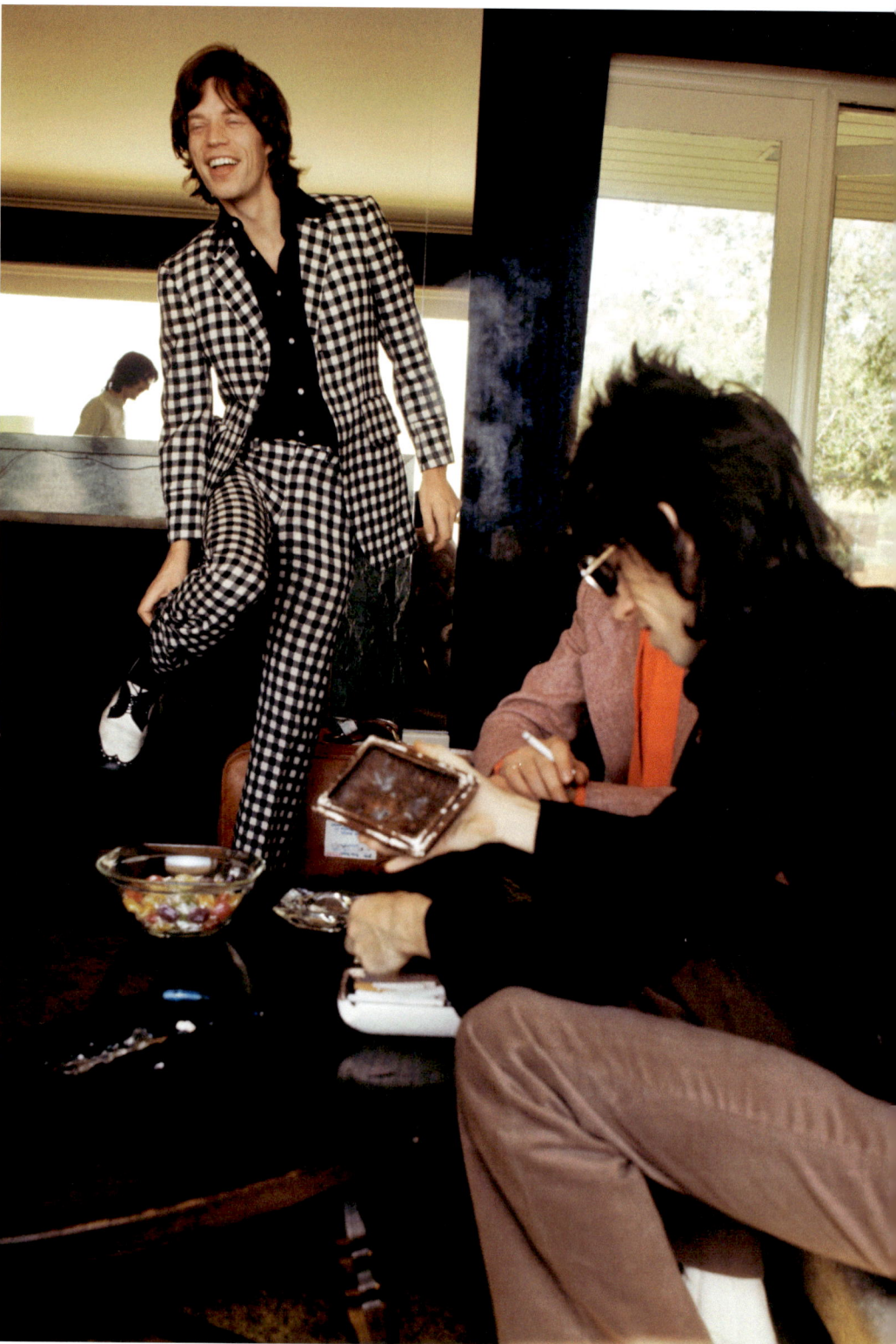

PP. 276–277

Ethan Russell

Taping a pre-recorded appearance on 18 November 1969 for *The Ed Sullivan Show* at 1697–99 Broadway, New York, where the band mimed (with live vocals) to three tracks, "Gimme Shelter", "Love In Vain" and "Honky Tonk Women".

Ethan Russell

A few laughs between rehearsals at Stephen Stills' house, October 1969. Designed by the composer Carmen Dragon, and previously owned by Monkee Peter Tork, the property had a distinct musical heritage – The Mamas & the Papas, Neil Young, Joni Mitchell and Gram Parsons were just some of the artists who had used the basement studio. Just a few months previously, Crosby, Stills and Nash held their first rehearsals in the same studio.

Ethan Russell

In preparation for their landmark tour of the United States of late 1969, the Stones flew into Los Angeles on 13 October to begin rehearsals. Mick, Keith and Mick Taylor took up residence in Stephen Stills' Laurel Canyon property at 3615 Shady Oak Road. Credited with the successful stewarding of the Hyde Park concert, Sam Cutler (in a tie-dyed shirt, his back to the camera) was employed as US tour manager.

"Sharing a house with Mick, Keith and Mick Taylor sometimes felt like living with three English gentlemen in a sedate country hotel. Most of the time the house was very quiet and that was the way everyone liked it." Sam Cutler, *You Can't Always Get What You Want: My Life With The Rolling Stones*, 2010

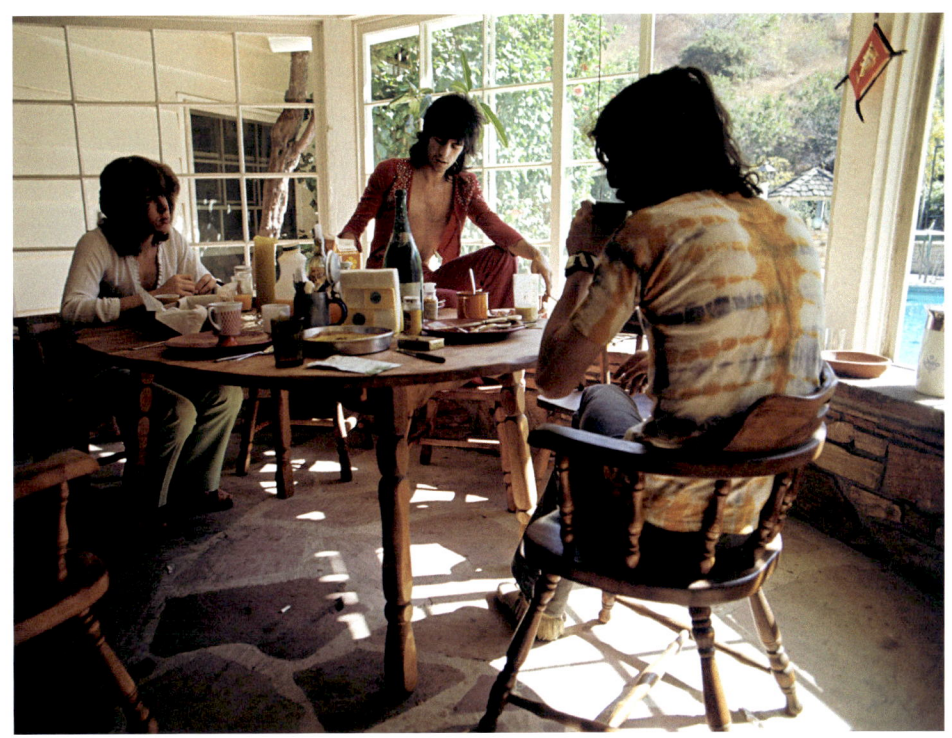

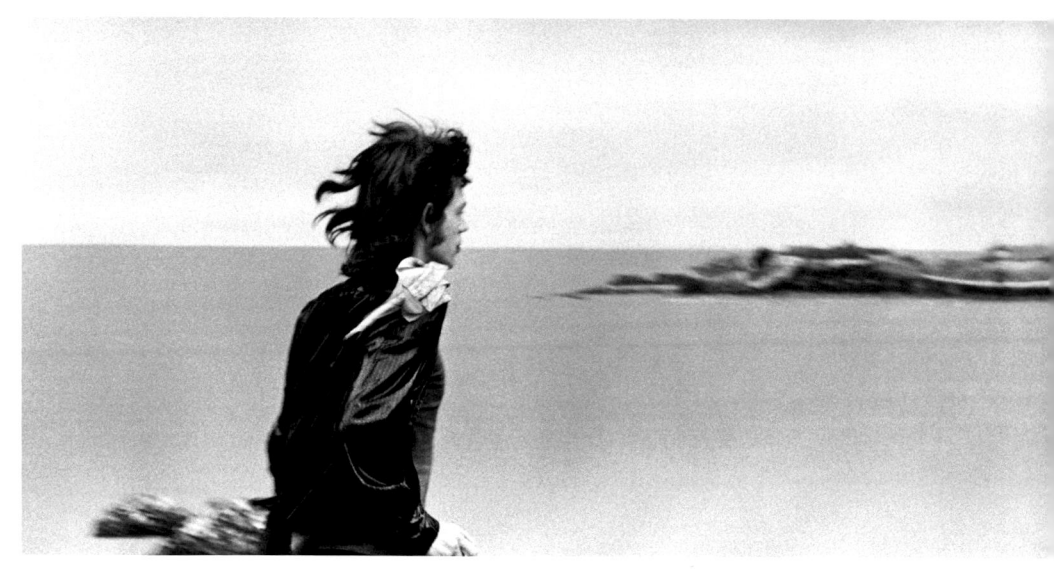

Andee Nathanson

Hollywood, 1969. Preparations in Los Angeles for the 1969 US tour allowed for plenty of socialising and sightseeing around the locale. One sojourn found Mick in the grounds of a palatial Hollywood property where, alongside a swimming pool, a large mural inspired by Asian art had been created.

Andee Nathanson

The Joshua Tree Memorial Park proved enticing, and several trips were made to indulge in the park's breathtaking expanse during October 1969. On this particular visit, Mick and Marianne Faithfull were joined by scriptwriter Tony Foutz, photographer Nathanson and tour guide Ted Markland. The party stayed overnight, wrapping themselves in blankets to await the majestic dawn.

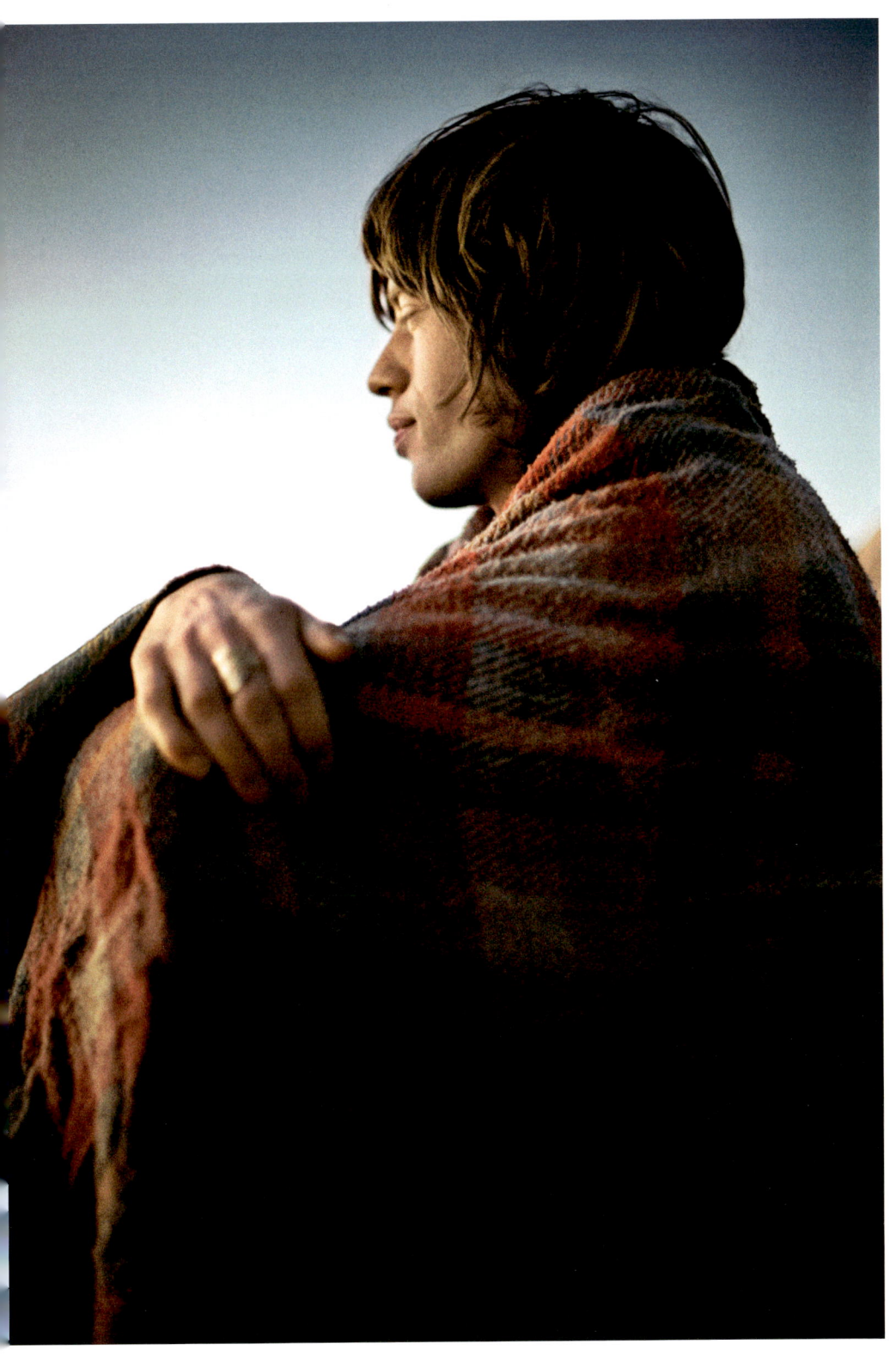

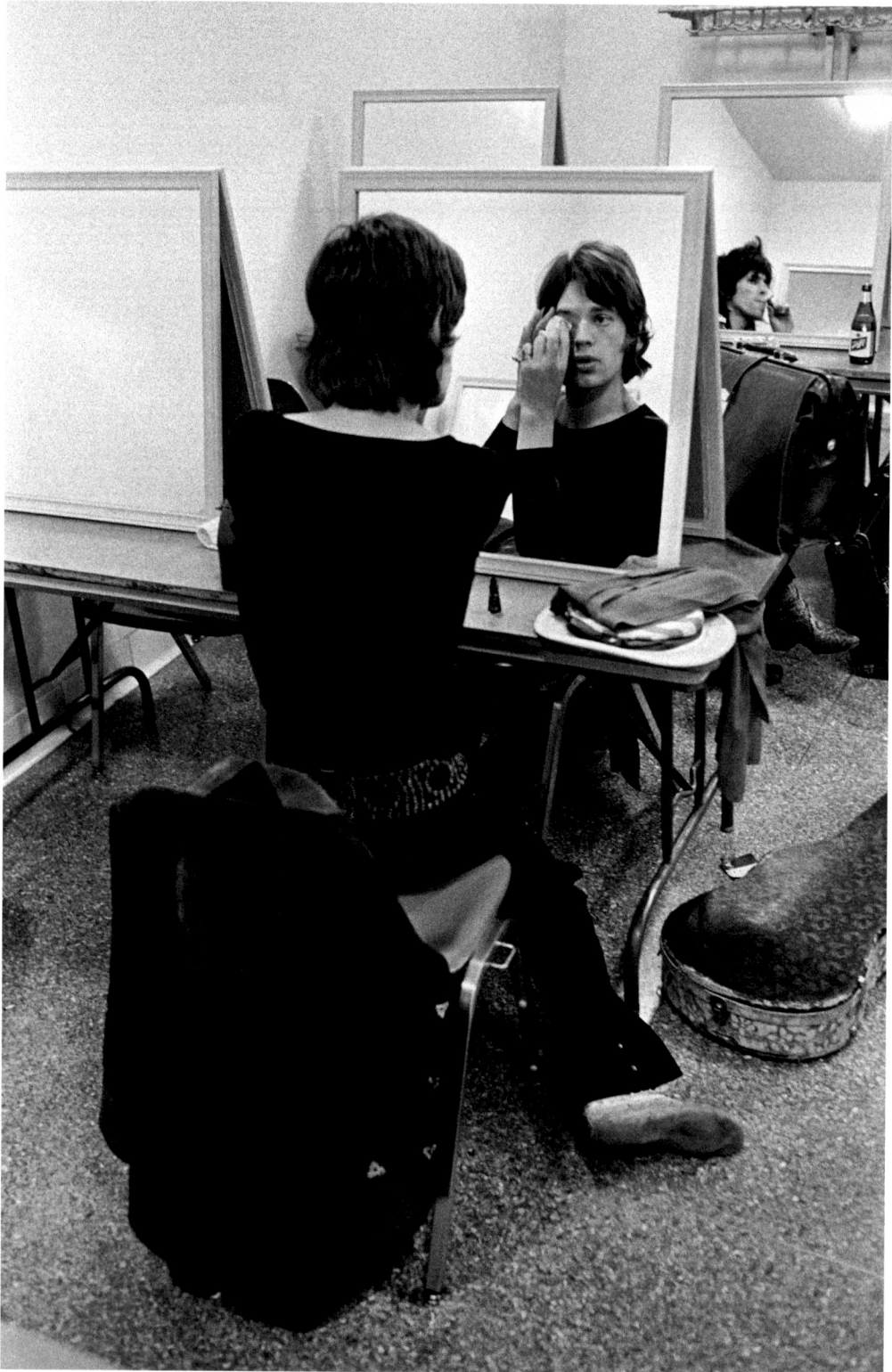

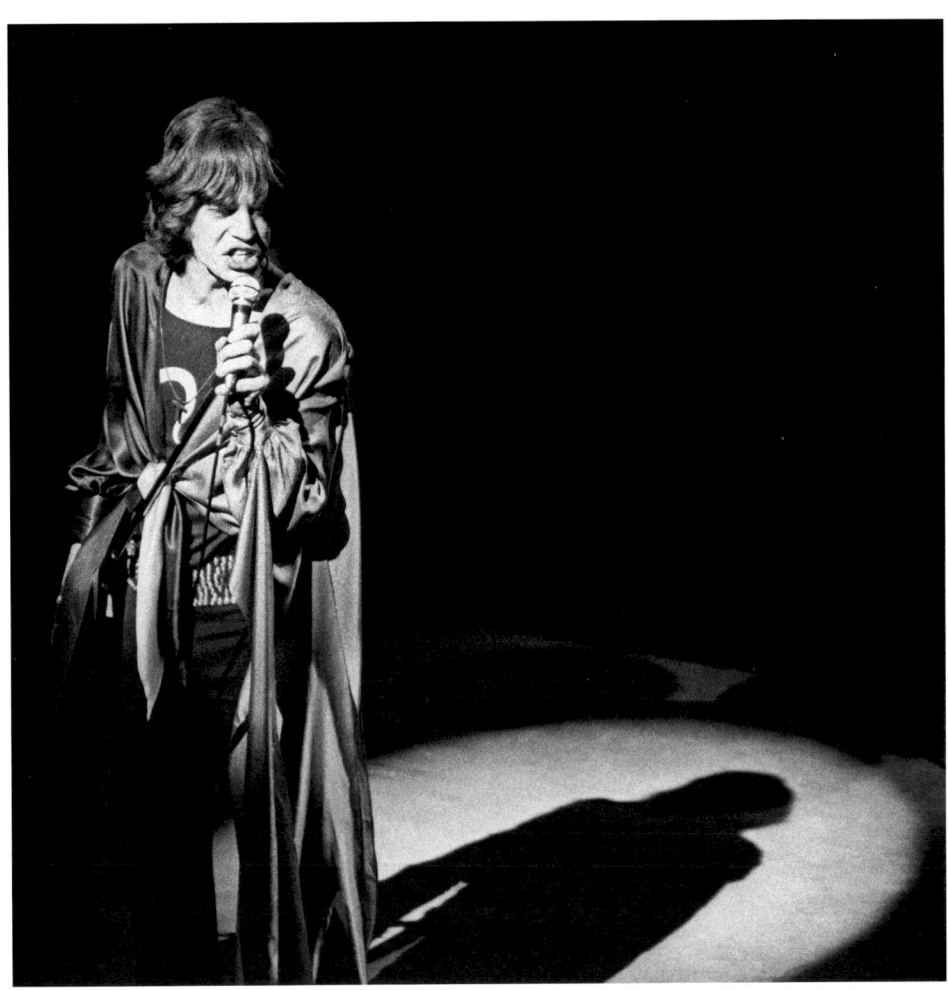

Ethan Russell

Backstage on the US tour, November 1969. Reinvigorated and rebranded, their tour of the States found the Stones looking firmly forward. *"I don't want to go back to the womb. We want to do something new. We're not interested in repeating ourselves. The new band isn't going to be like [the] early Stones. This thing is to go on, doing something new."* Mick Jagger, *Melody Maker*, 21 June 1969

Barrie Wentzell

With their mammoth US tour behind them, the group played some relatively modest shows in London – the first at the Saville Theatre on 14 December 1969. Seven days later they played two further shows in one evening in front of a larger crowd at the Lyceum Ballroom, just off London's Strand.

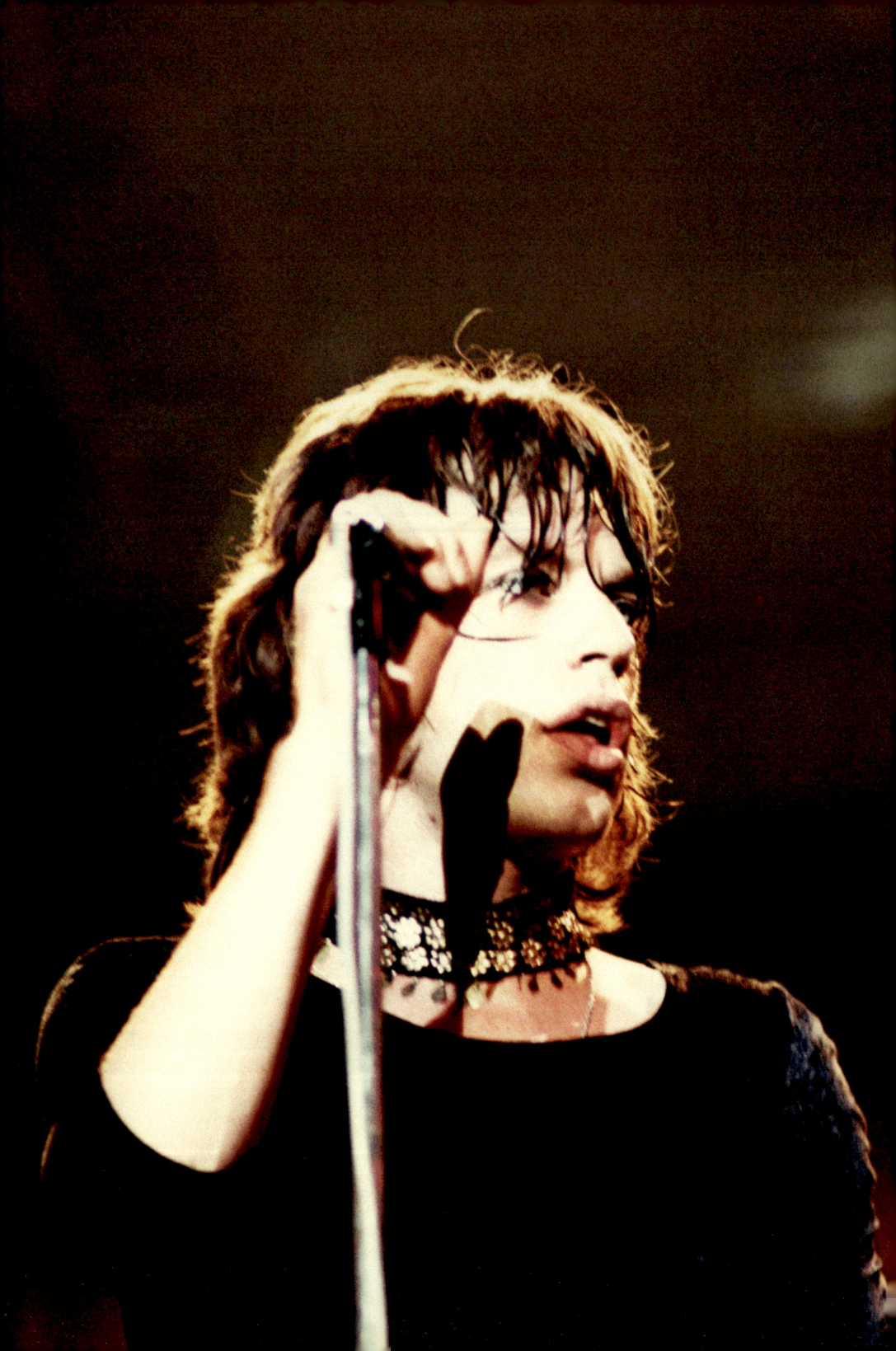

Harm Botman

A moment from the last show of The Rolling Stones' 1970 European Tour at Amsterdam's RAI Amstelhal on 9 October. The gig was enlivened by a special guest appearance by Stephen Stills on piano during the 14-song set.

Eddie Kramer

The Rolling Stones' return to American stages attracted a slew of fellow musicians to mingle backstage. Jimi Hendrix was one such personality, appearing when the group played Madison Square Garden on 27 November 1969. To be as close to the action as possible, Hendrix, who was celebrating his 27th birthday, viewed the concert from behind Keith's amplifier.
"Hendrix was smiling, as if saying, 'This is it – the real rock 'n' roll soup.' I couldn't see anyone that wasn't smiling." Stanley Booth, *The True Adventures Of The Rolling Stones*, 2000

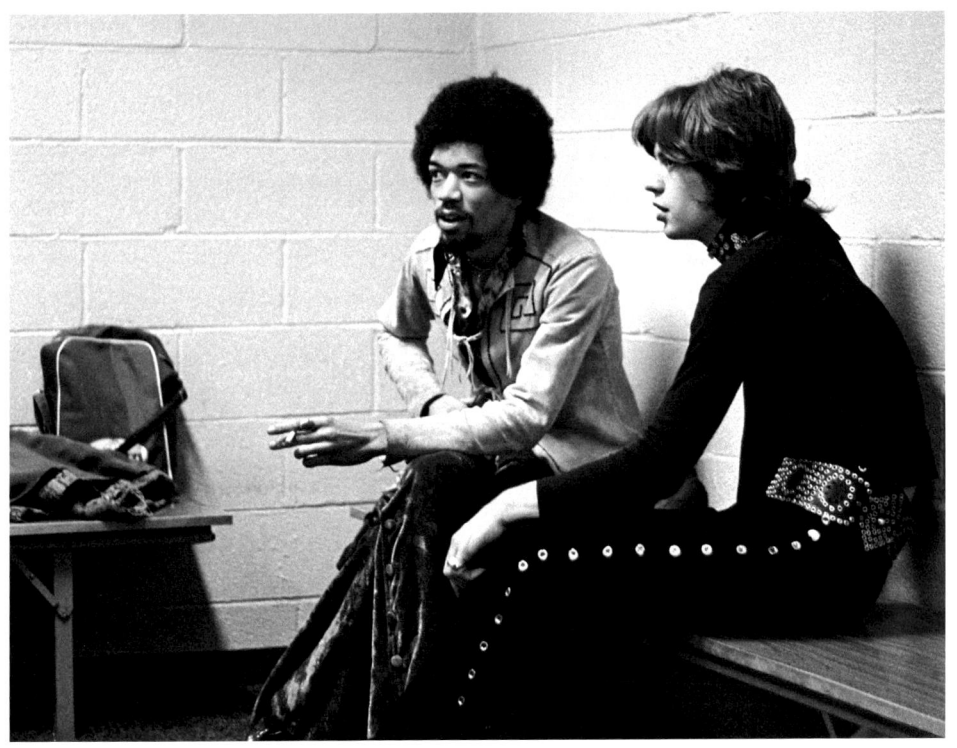

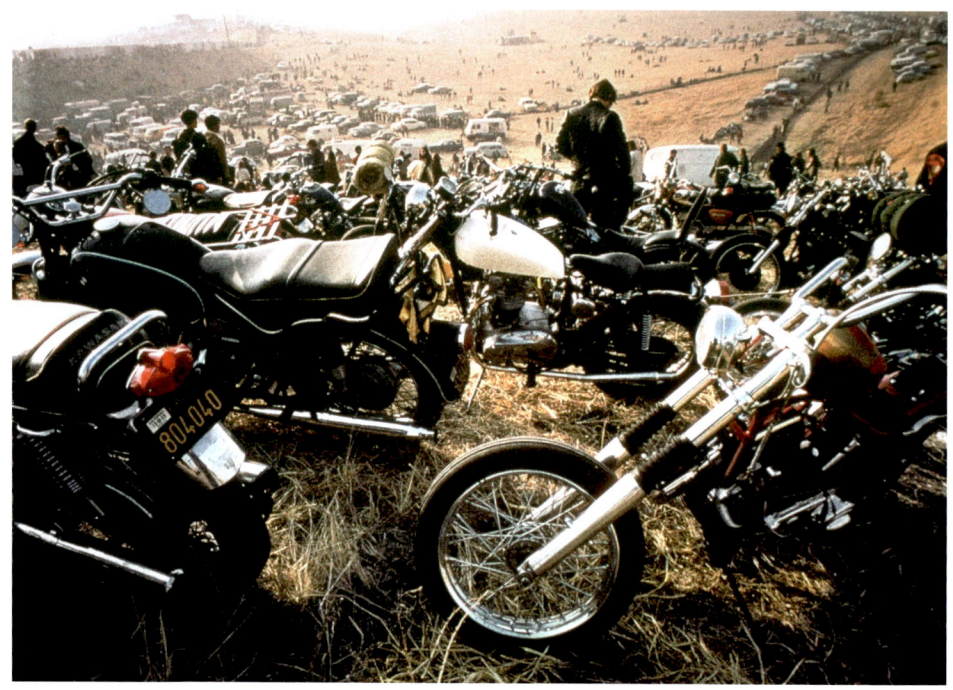

Anonymous

Despite the best of intentions, the free concert on 6 December 1969 at Altamont Speedway, near San Francisco, was a very dark moment in rock history, and a grisly curtain call for the Stones' otherwise joyous return to American stages. To some it symbolised the end of the 1960s hippy idealism.

"Many of the people at Altamont are blank or frightened, but are in thrall to the music, or perhaps just to being there; some twitch and jerk to the beat in an apocalyptic parody of dancing; others strip or crawl on the heads of the crowd; and we can see tormented trippers' faces, close to the stage, near the angry Angels." Pauline Kael, *The New Yorker*, reviewing the film *Gimme Shelter*, 1970

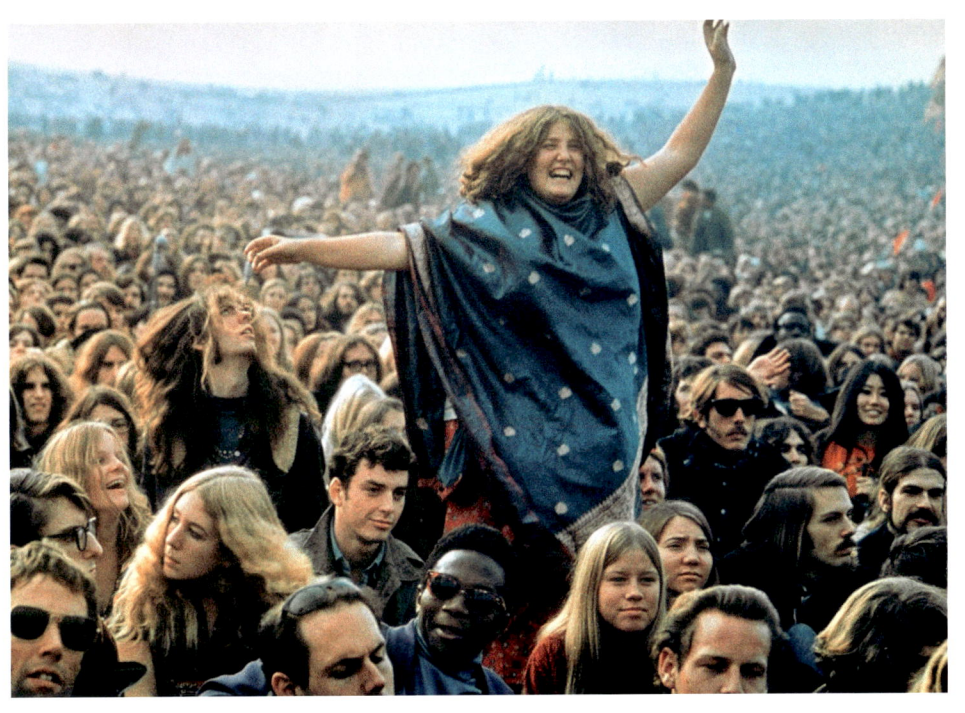

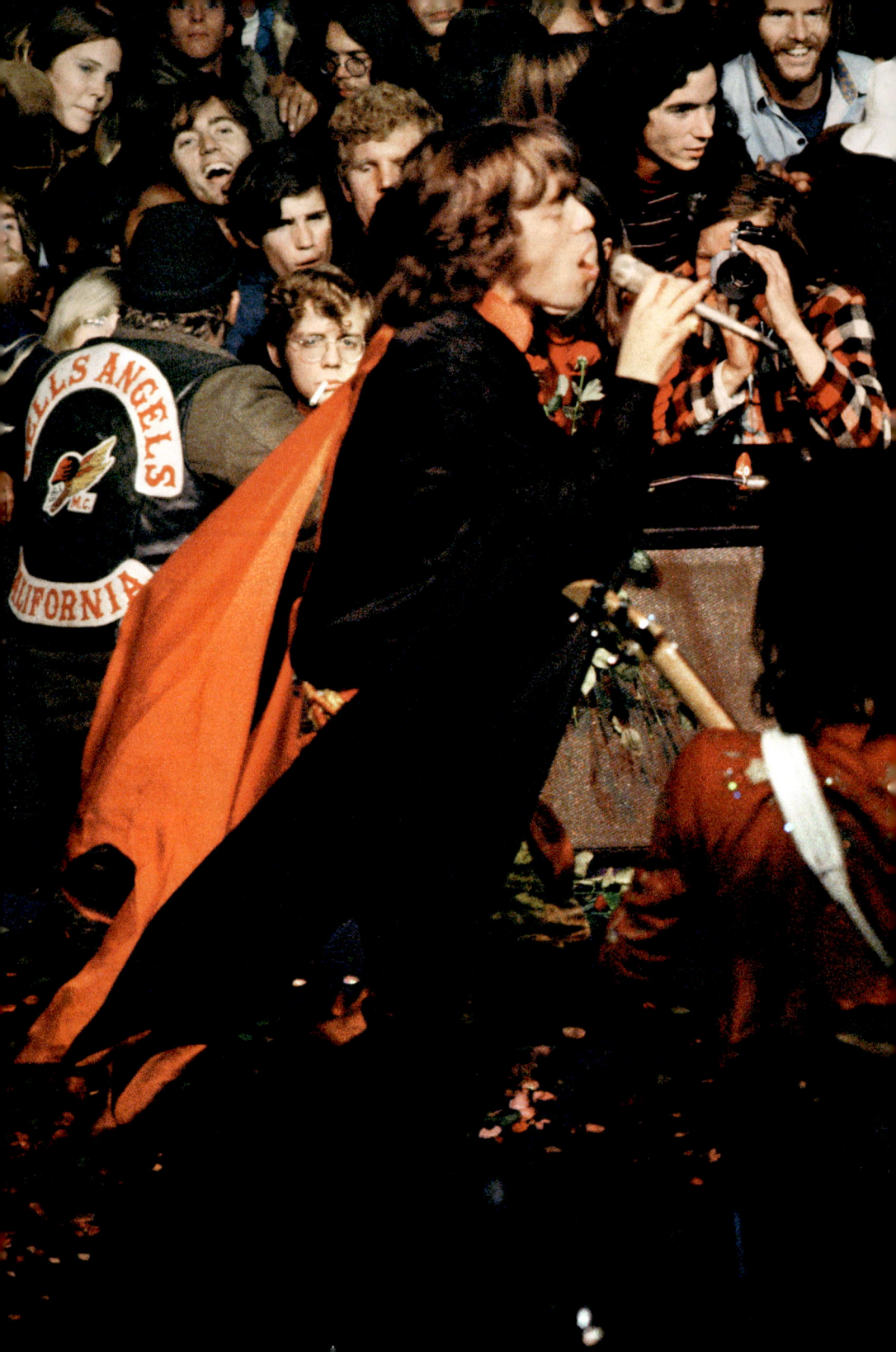

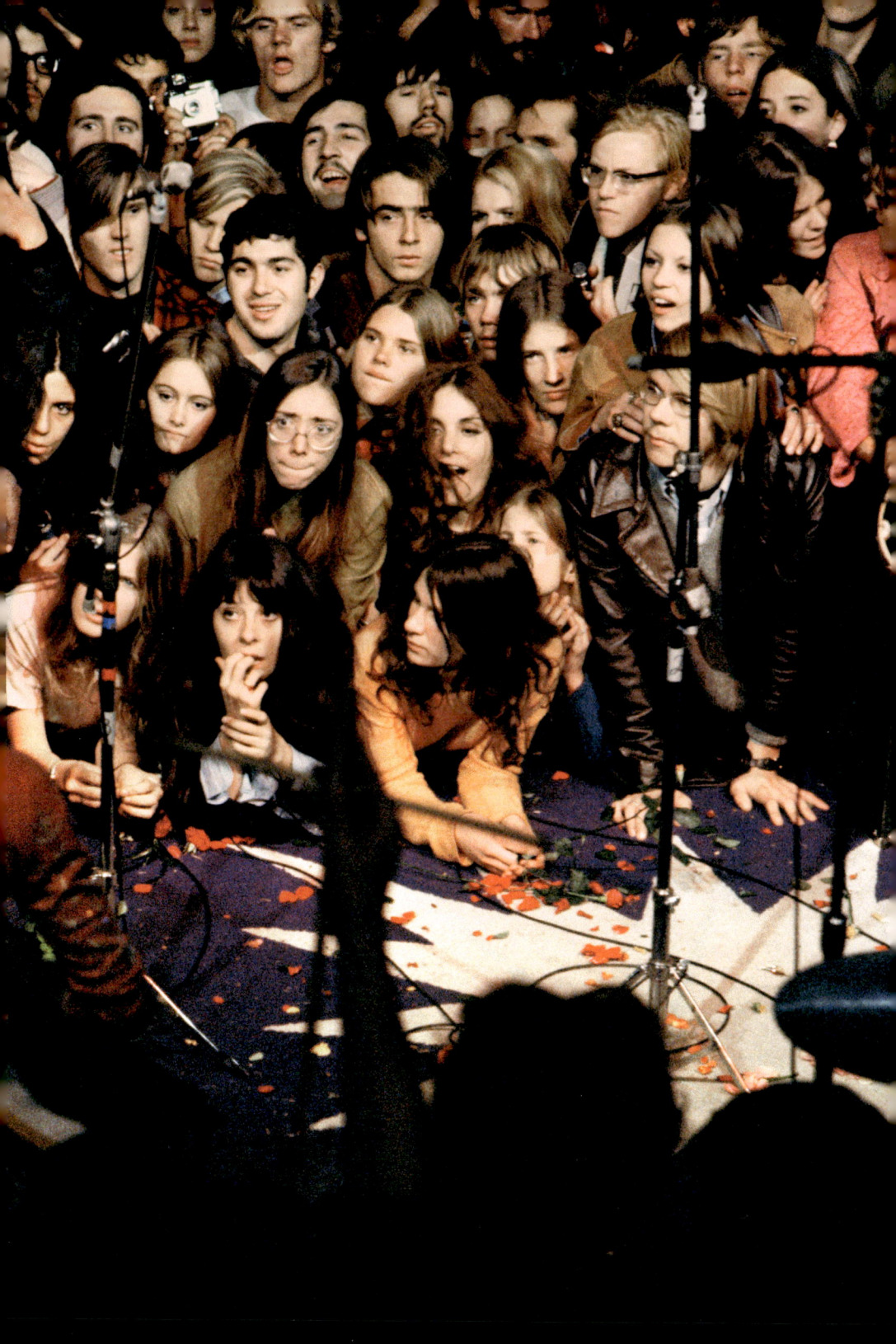

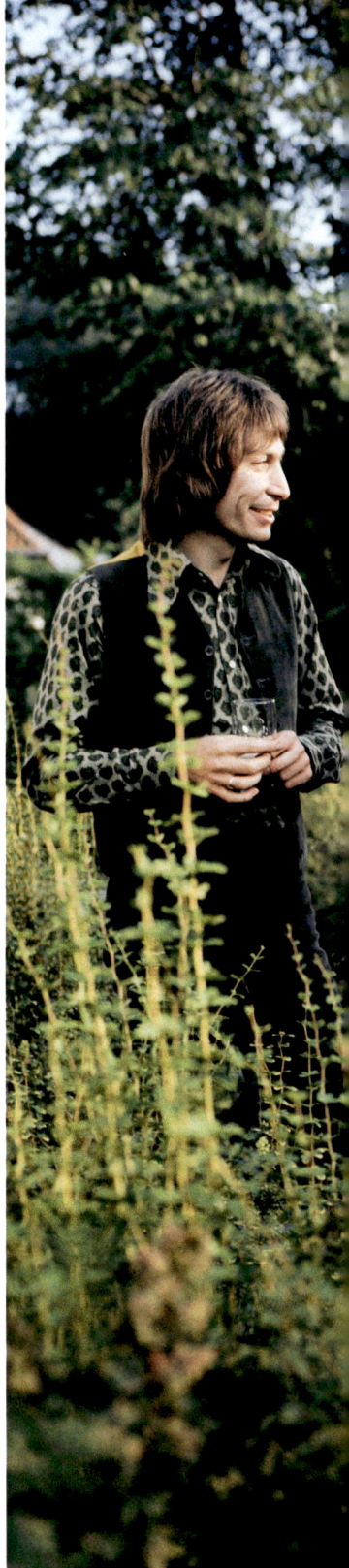

PP. 288–289
Ethan Russell
Altamont, 1969.

Bent Rej
Back on the road in Europe during 1970.
Revisiting Scandinavia for the first time in over
three years, the group held an impromptu press
conference and photo session after alighting from their ferry to Helsingborg, Sweden,
30 August 1970.

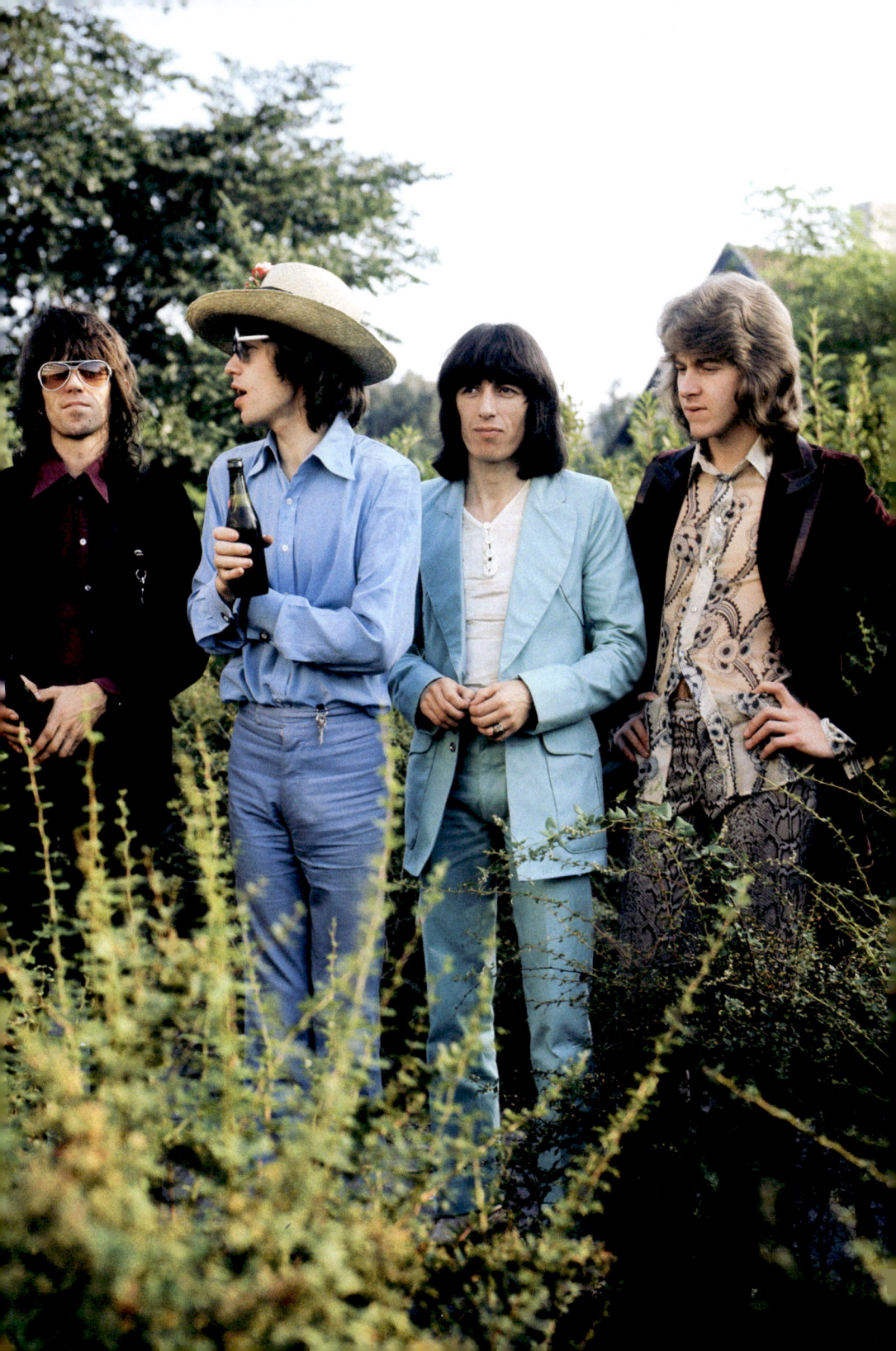

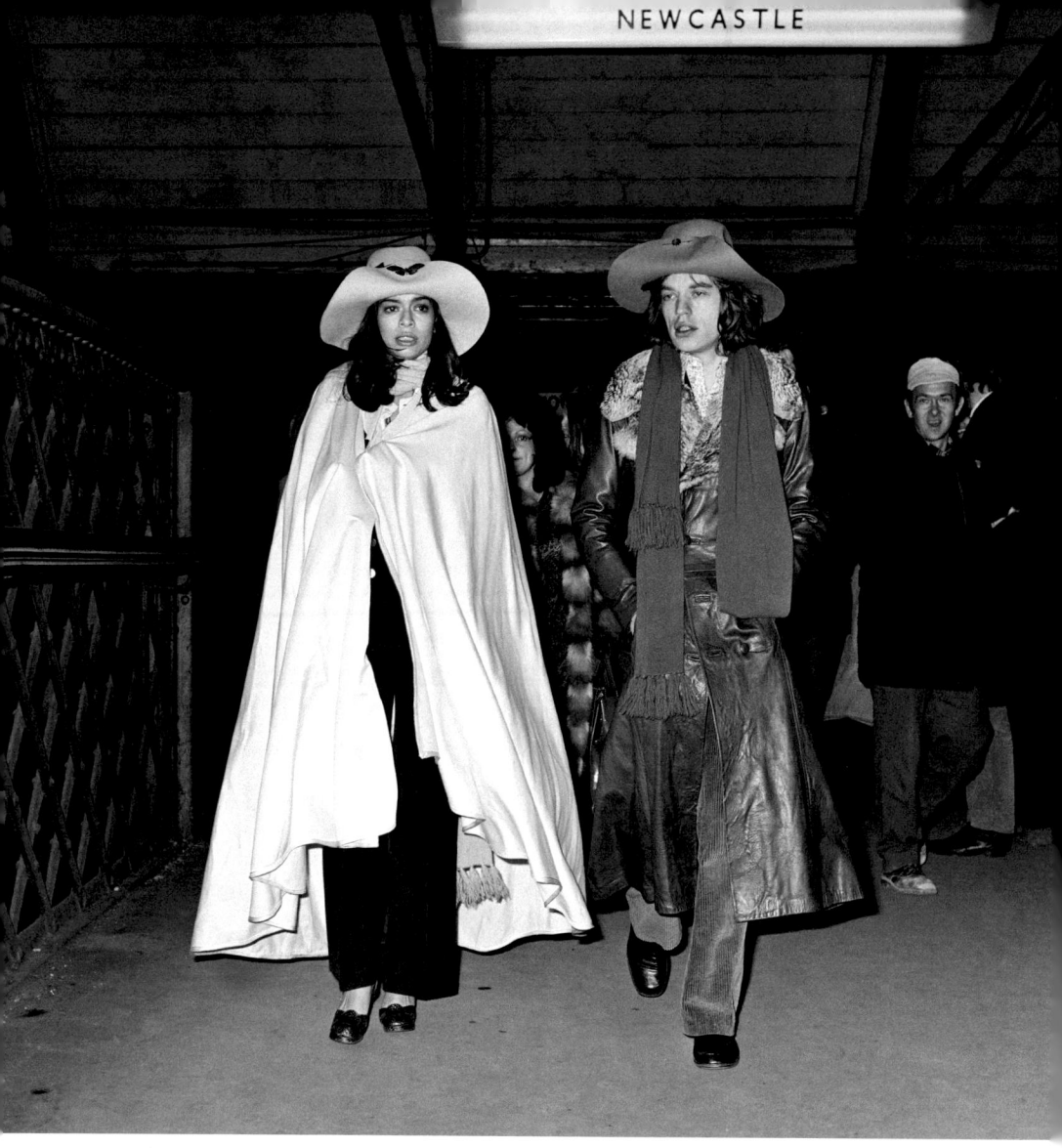

Anonymous

The Stones' appearance at Newcastle City Hall on 4 March 1971 was a modest gig for the band, and – with a capacity of just over 2,000 – an immediate sell-out. Predictably, the press were waiting to catch Mick's arrival by train with partner Bianca Pérez-Mora Macías.

"This tour should reassert their extraordinary talents as showmen, and remind the public of their great contribution to British rock. Above all, the Stones still mean excitement and fun."
Duncan Fallowell, reviewing the Newcastle show, *The Guardian*, 5 March 1971

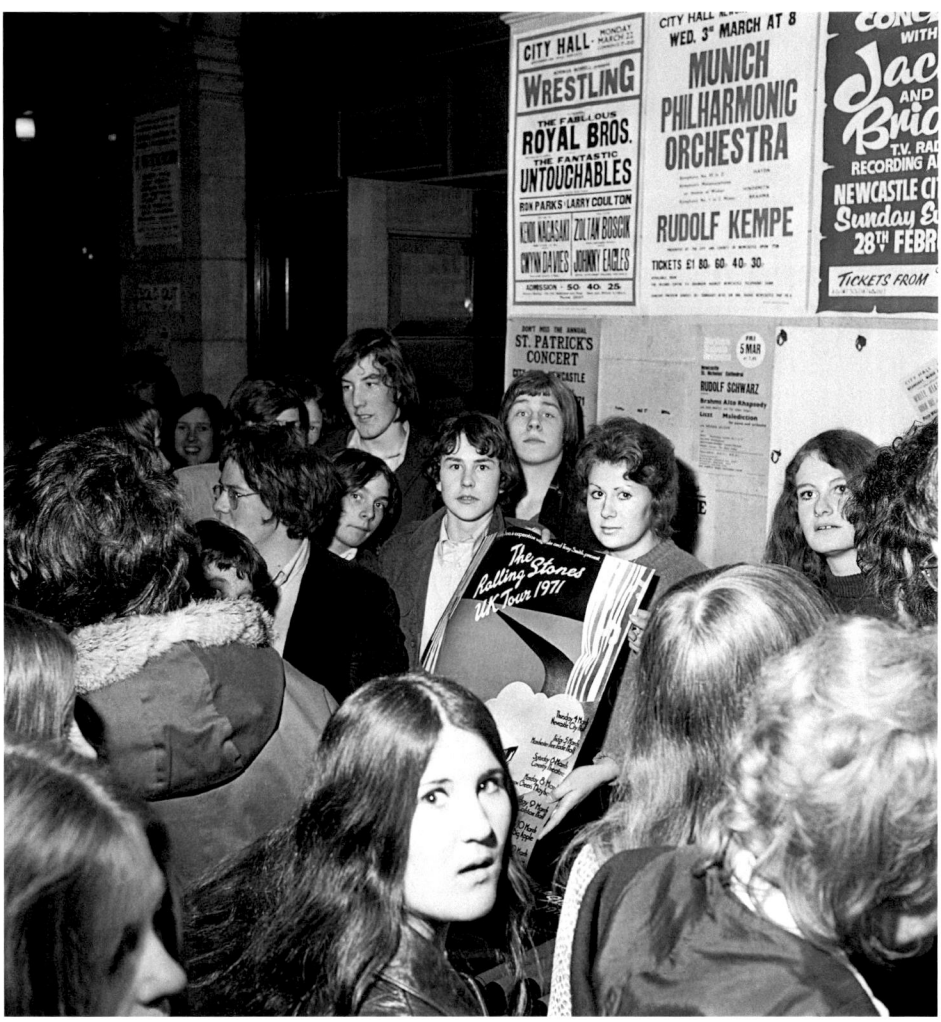

Anonymous

The Stones' 1971 appearance at Newcastle City Hall enlivened the otherwise cold modernity of the northern English city. Extra publicity surrounded the show as word got out that the group was set to relocate abroad because of the state of their finances.

"We did this farewell tour of England which was quite short and kind of sad. I remember it so vividly; everyone thought we were never coming back." Mick Jagger, interviewed in *Stones In Exile*, 2010

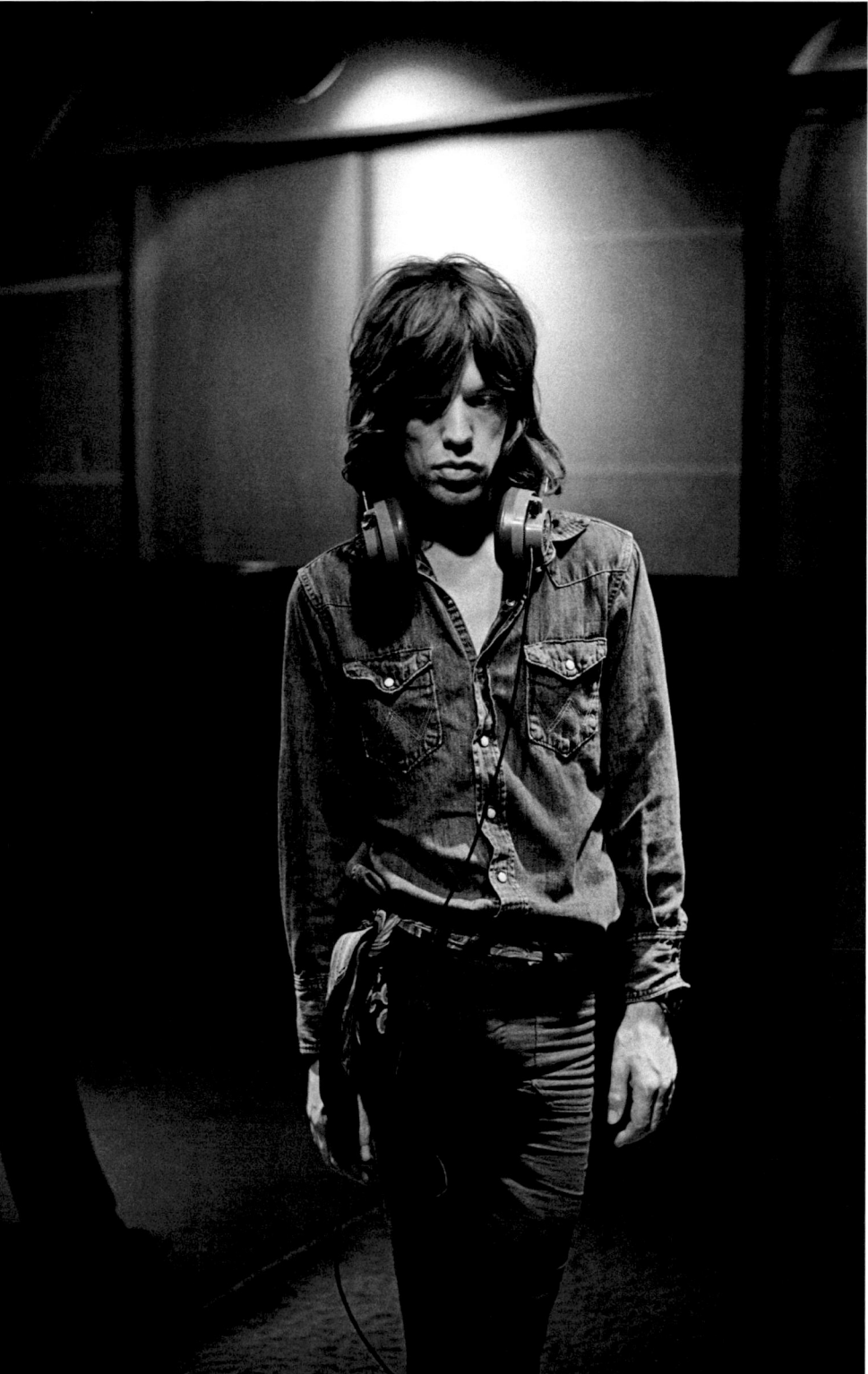

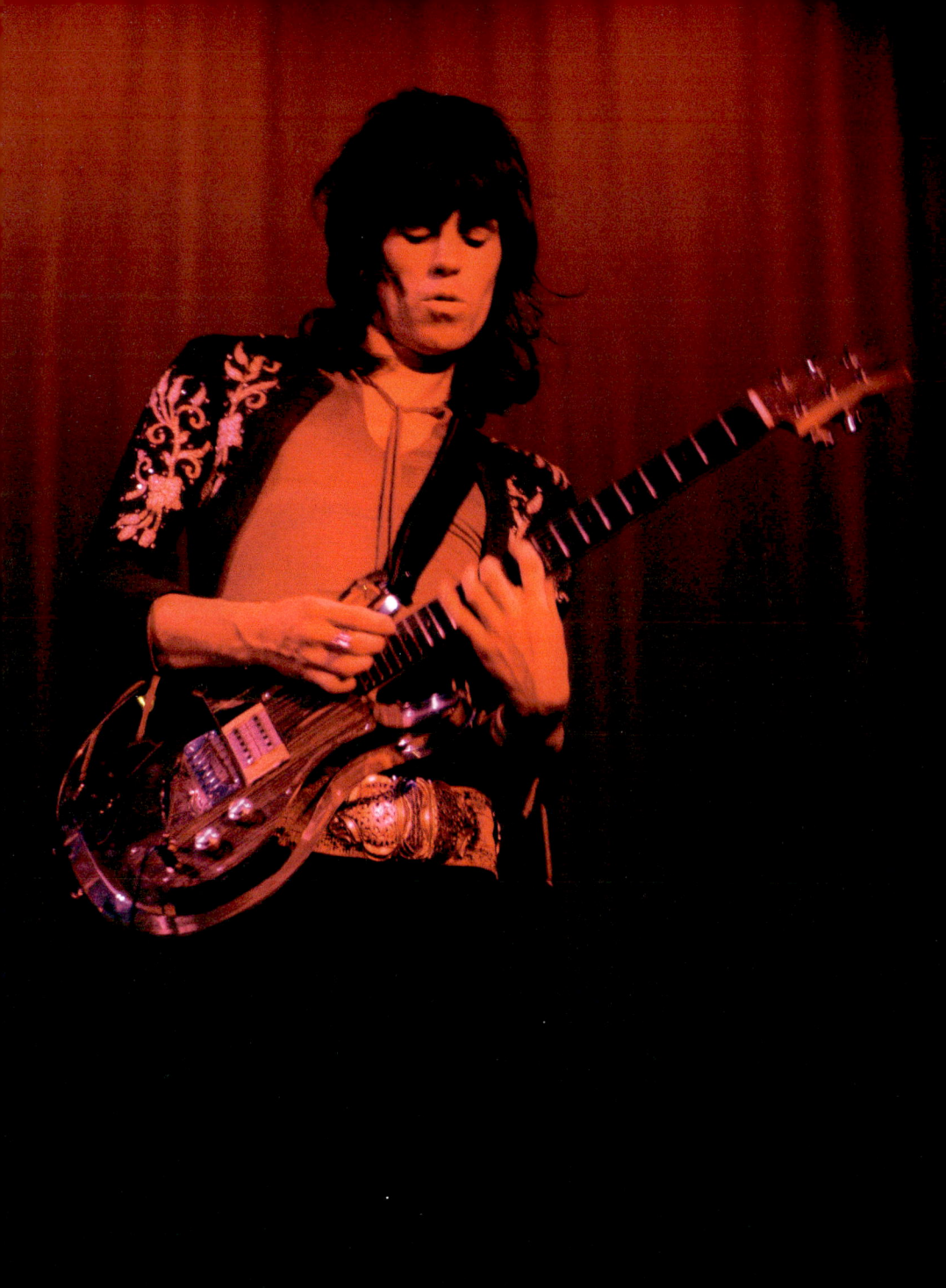

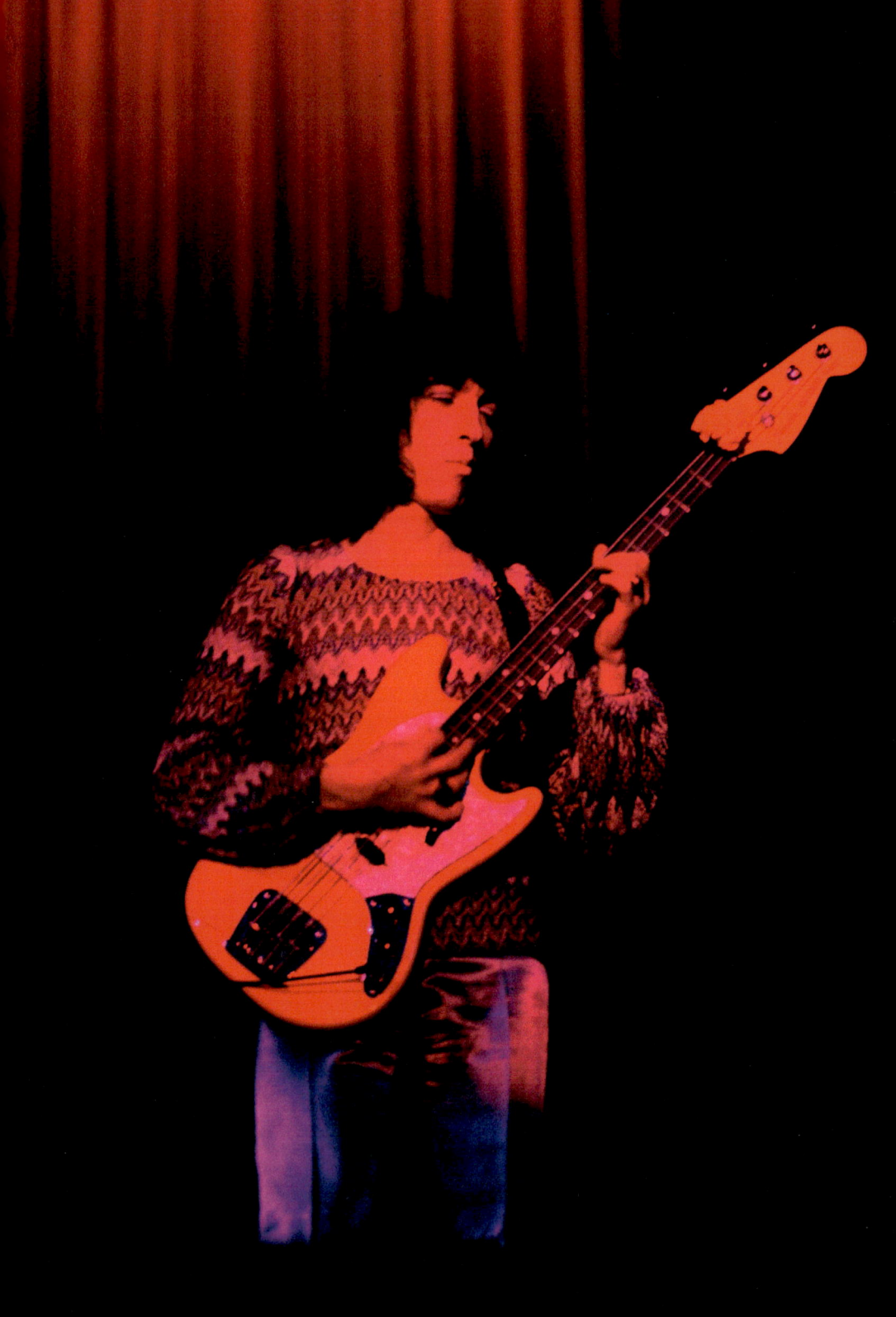

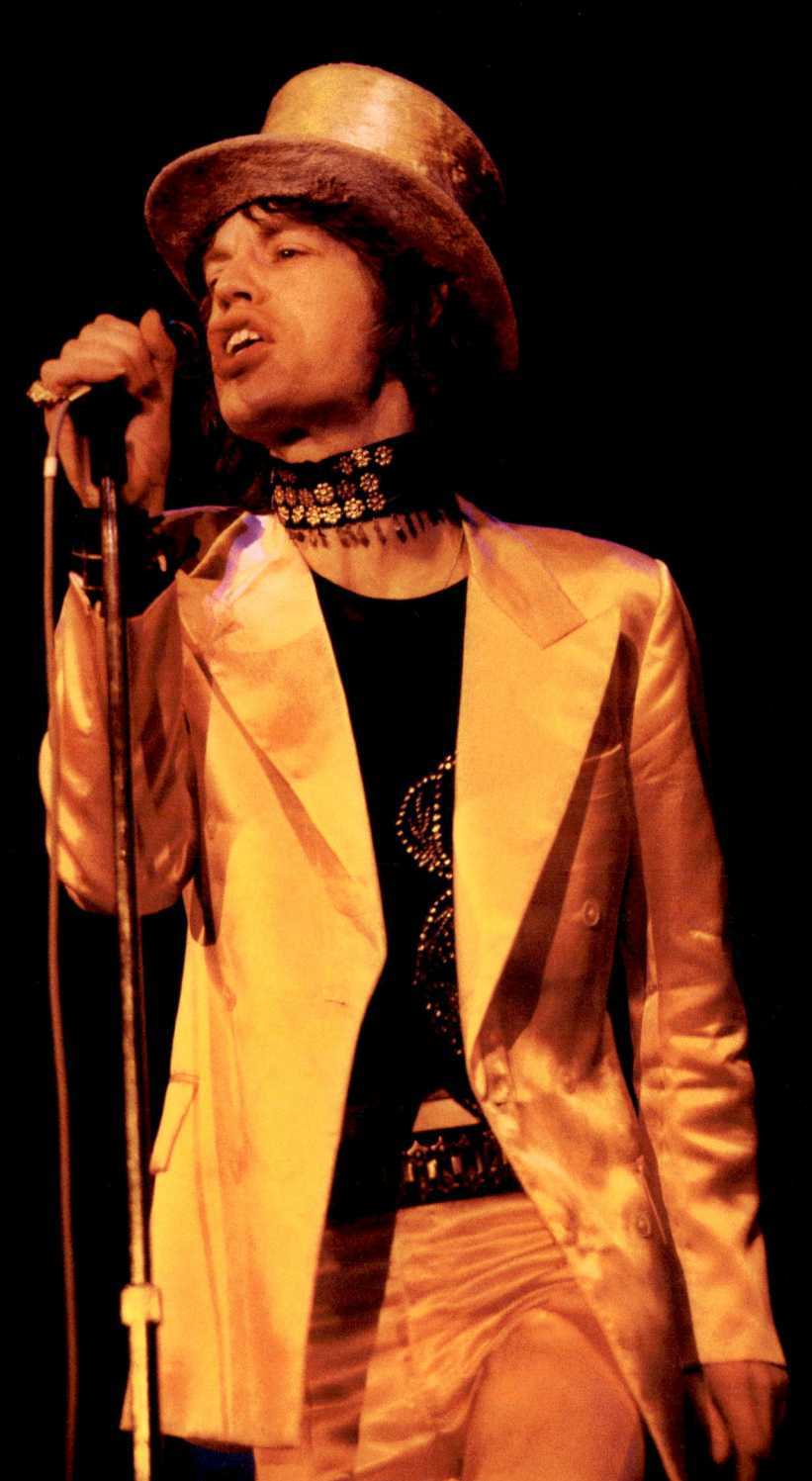

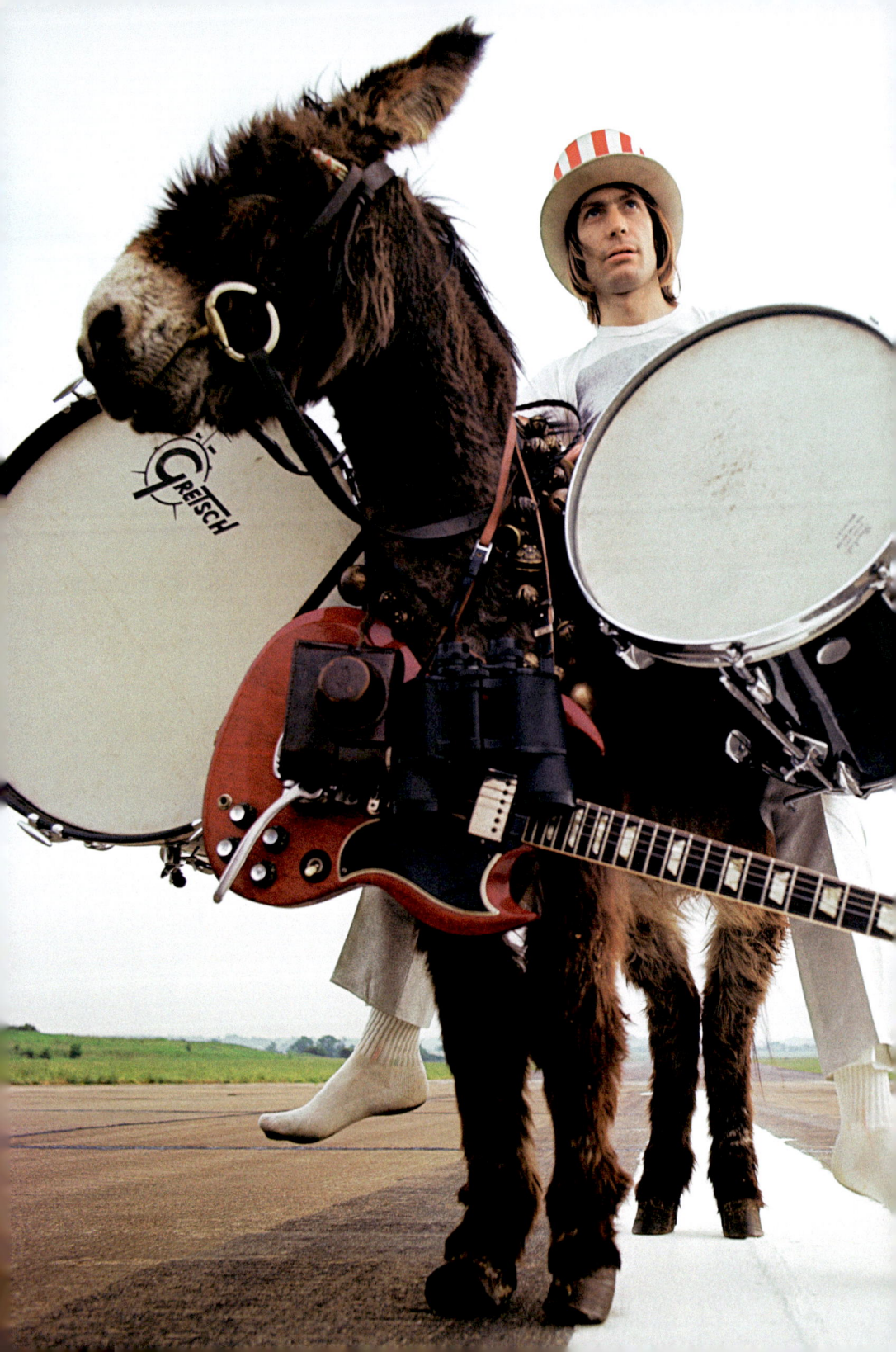

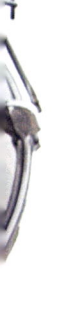

P. 294
Jim Marshall
With *Exile On Main St* requiring overdubs and mixing on numerous tracks, the Stones convened at Los Angeles' Sunset Sound Studios during late 1971/early 1972. Mick laid down some of his final vocal tracks for the album here.

P. 295
Bent Rej
Keith on stage at Copenhagen's Forum, 12 September 1970. The transparency of Richards' Dan Armstrong Plexiglas guitar gave his stage presence a whole new dimension. The group's two shows at the Forum saw a return to form in a set that featured 14 songs, with only a cover of Chuck Berry's "Roll Over Beethoven" mining their deeper past.

PP. 296–297
Bent Rej
Bill and Mick caught on stage at Copenhagen's Forum, 12 September 1970.

David Bailey
The cover shoot for the live album *Get Yer Ya's Out!,* 7 June 1970.
With no audio record of the Stones' current live show to purchase (and with a bootleg album *Live'r Than You'll Ever Be* doing brisk business), the release of *Get Yer Ya-Ya's Out!* in 1970 was warmly received by both fans and critics.
"I have no doubt that Get Yer Ya-Ya's Out! *is the best rock concert ever put on record. The Stones, alone among their generation of groups, are not about to fall by the wayside. And as long as they continue to thrive this way, the era of true rock-and-roll music will remain alive and kicking with them."* Lester Bangs, *Rolling Stone* magazine, 12 November 1970

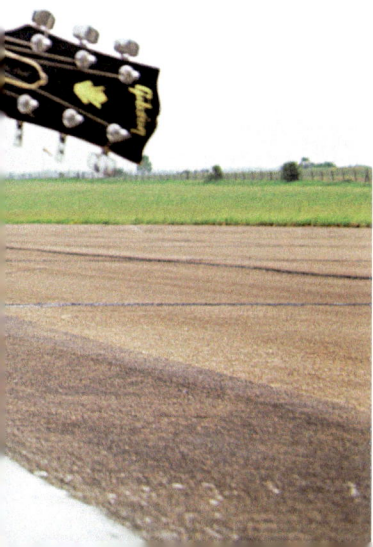

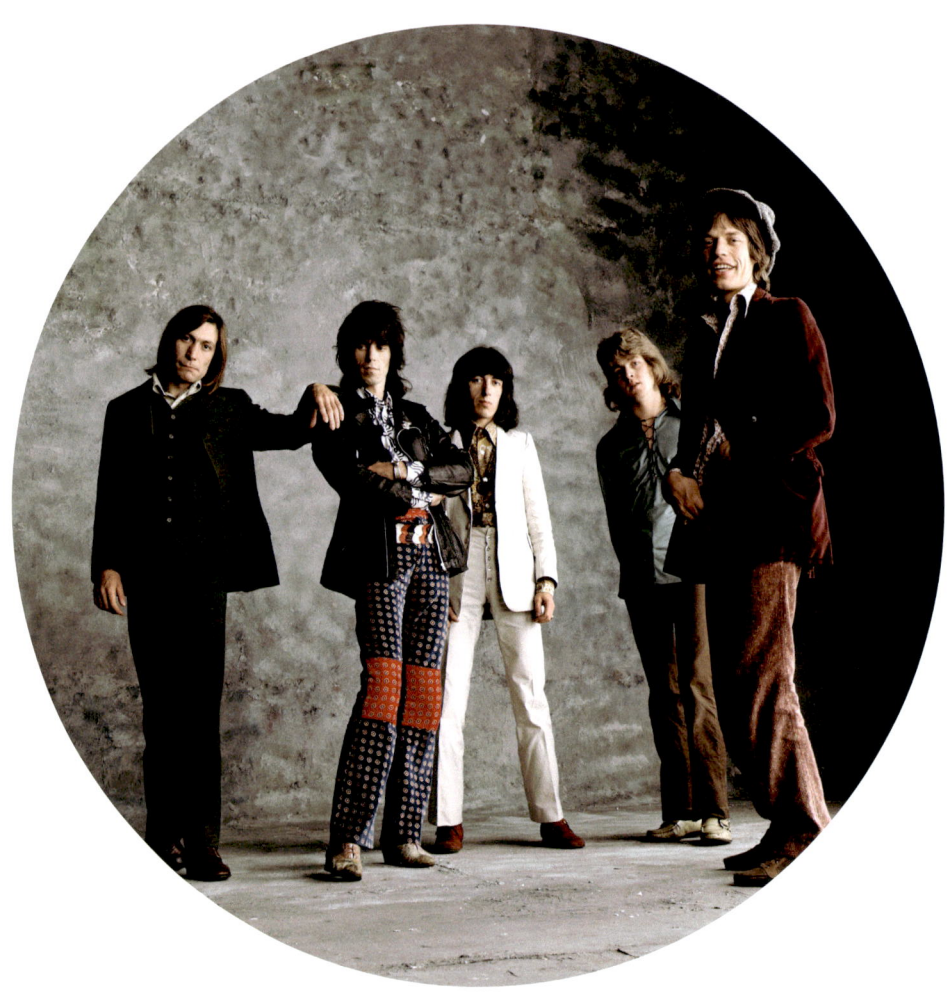

Peter Webb

In tandem with their musical metamorphosis, Stones' album sleeves continued their tradition of breaking new territory. For the cover of the *Sticky Fingers* album, various ideas were thrown around before Andy Warhol's iconic design finally made the cut. At an earlier session in 1971, the photographer used a monochrome background for the shots in his London studio. Ultimately, only one black-and-white photo from the session would be used on the album's insert.

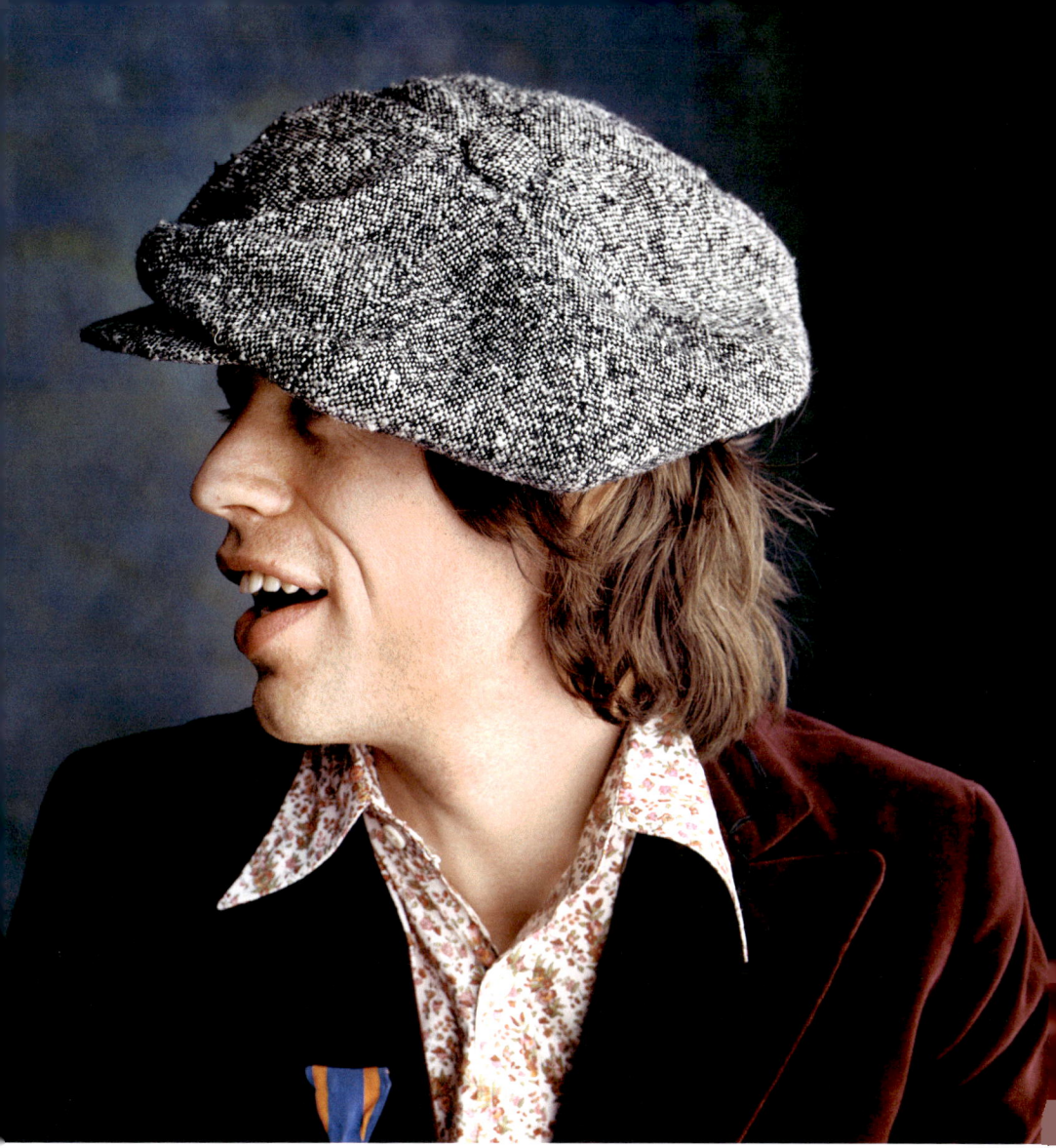

Peter Webb
Mick in profile for the aborted *Sticky Fingers*
photo shoot. London, 1971.

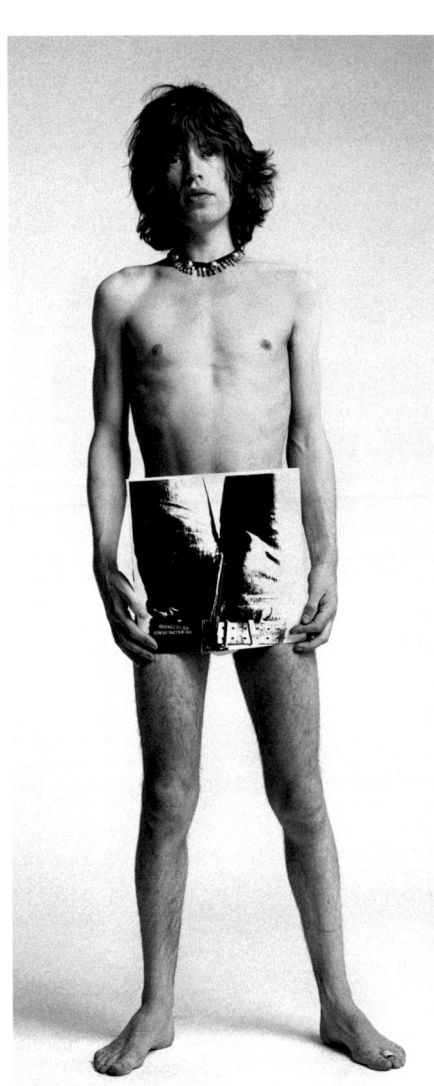
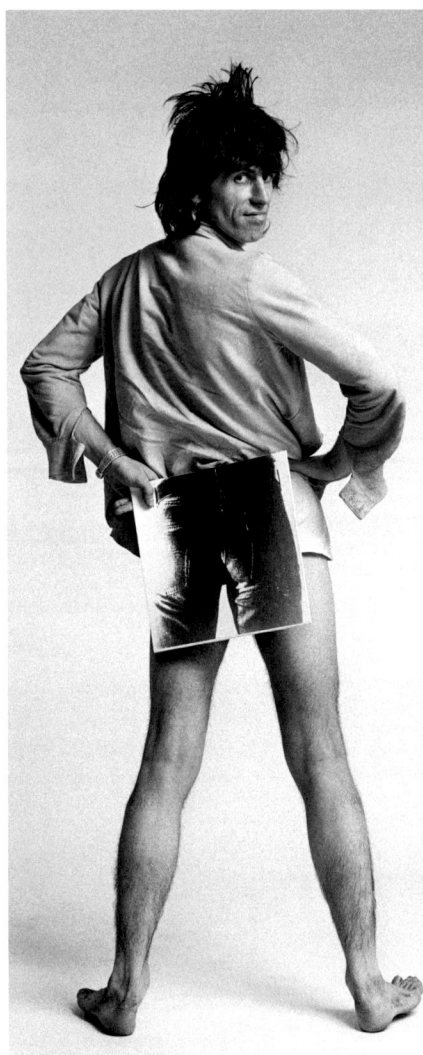
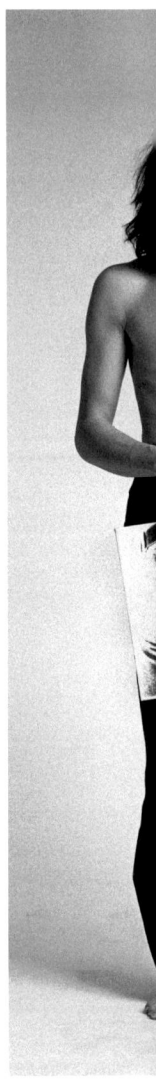

David Montgomery
Chelsea, London, February 1971.
While Andy Warhol's design for *Sticky Fingers*
proved a benchmark in rock music sleeve design,
more traditional promotional material was
required to identify the group with the product.
Most famously, a colour shot from this session
would adorn the single release of "Brown Sugar"
in April 1971.

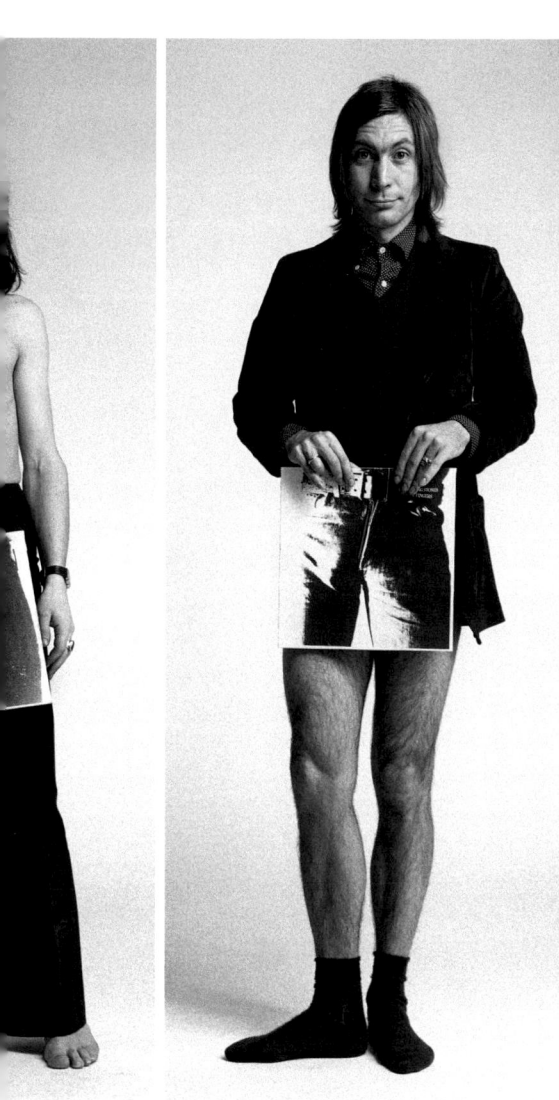
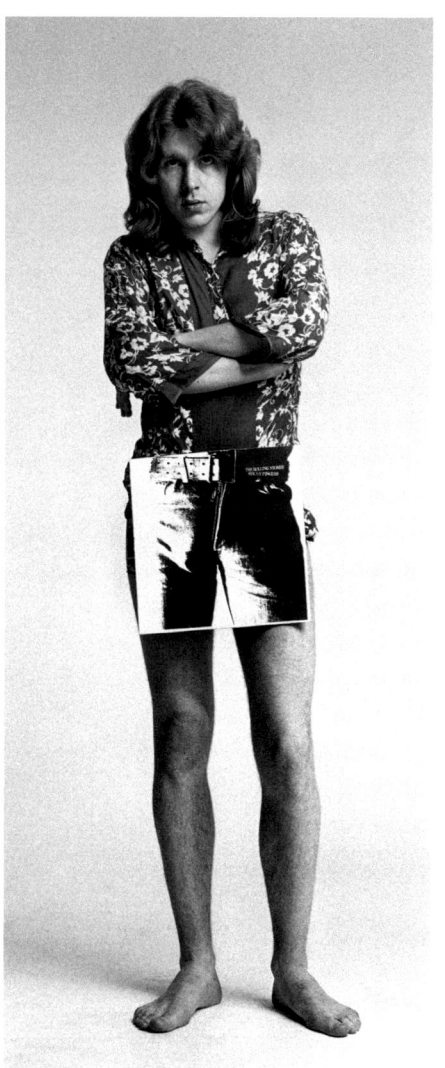

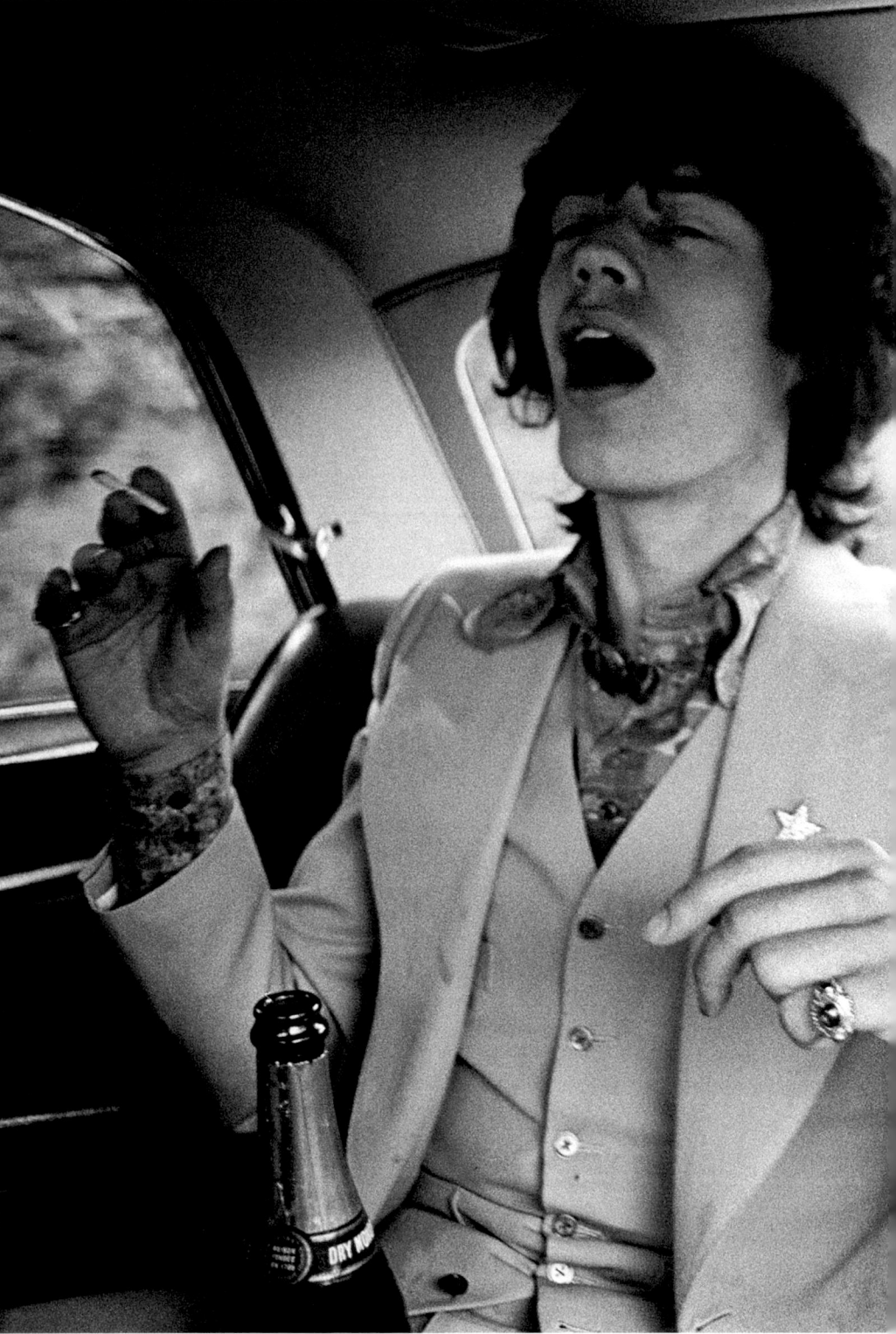

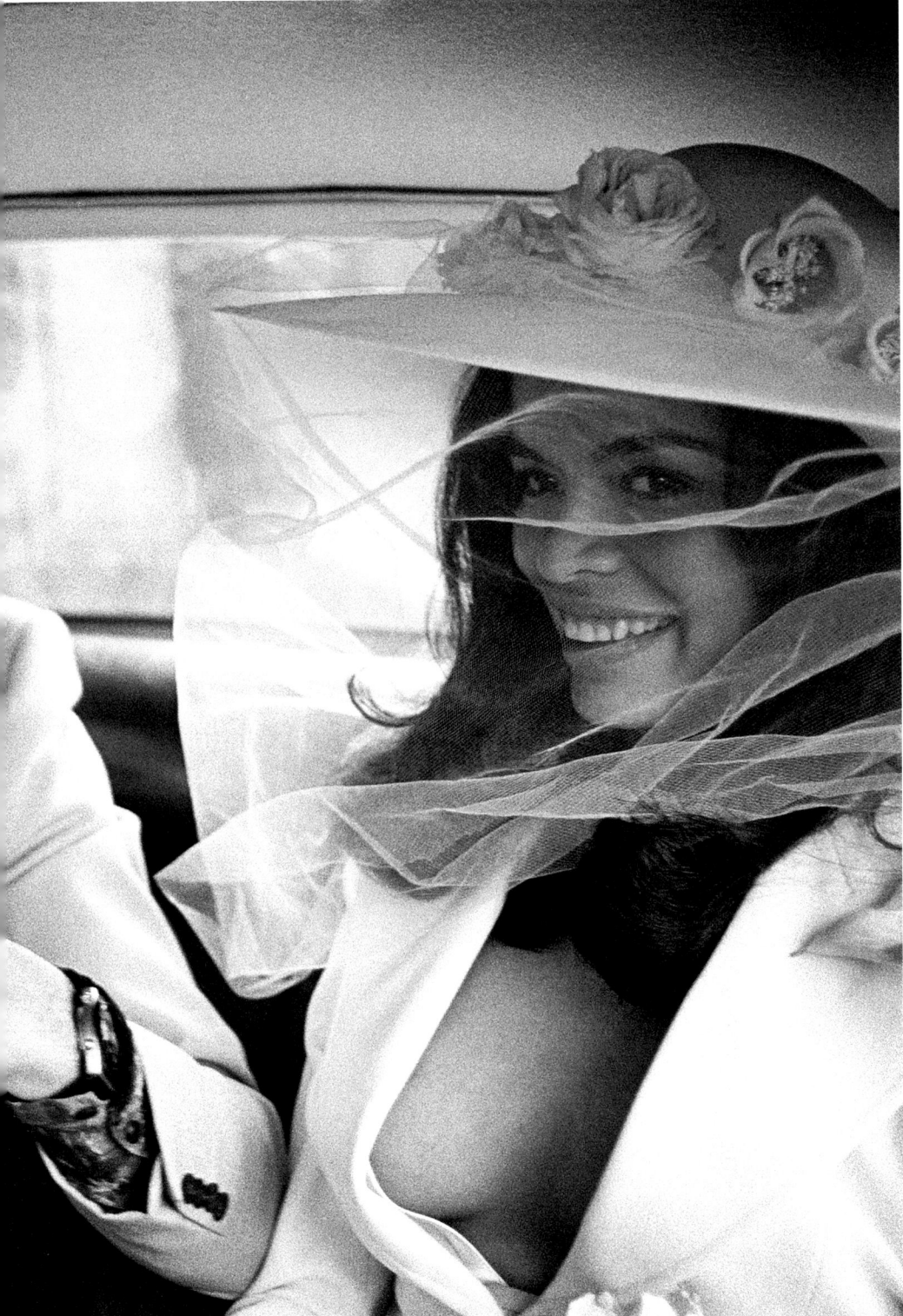

PP. 304–305
Patrick Lichfield

A brief moment of calm when Mick married
Bianca Pérez-Mora Macías in Saint-Tropez on
12 May 1971. The day was – even by Stones'
standards – hectic, the small town on the French
Côte d'Azur being ill equipped to deal with the
magnitude of the event.

*"Mick Jagger and his Nicaraguan-born wife-to-be
eventually arrived at 5:00 p.m. Police and journalists exchanged blows in the frenzy. Hippies turned
up on foot and bicycles, mingling with members
of the international jet set, who arrived in Rolls-
Royces for the wedding."* BBC News report, 1971

Dominique Tarlé

Keith evidently enjoyed his Mediterranean existence in Villa Nellcôte's sun-kissed ambience,
with plenty of periods of relaxation by day. 1971.

PP. 308–309
Dominique Tarlé

Villa Nellcôte's previous incarnation as an
ambassadorial palace showed in its fading grandeur, which created a decadent atmosphere.

*"I remember vividly: late afternoon, early evening
one meal a day, we'd all sit at this long, long table.
We would all smoke joints and hash in between
courses. It was a whole new* La Dolce Vita
Fellini-esque lifestyle." Marshall Chess, interviewed in *Stones In Exile*, 2010

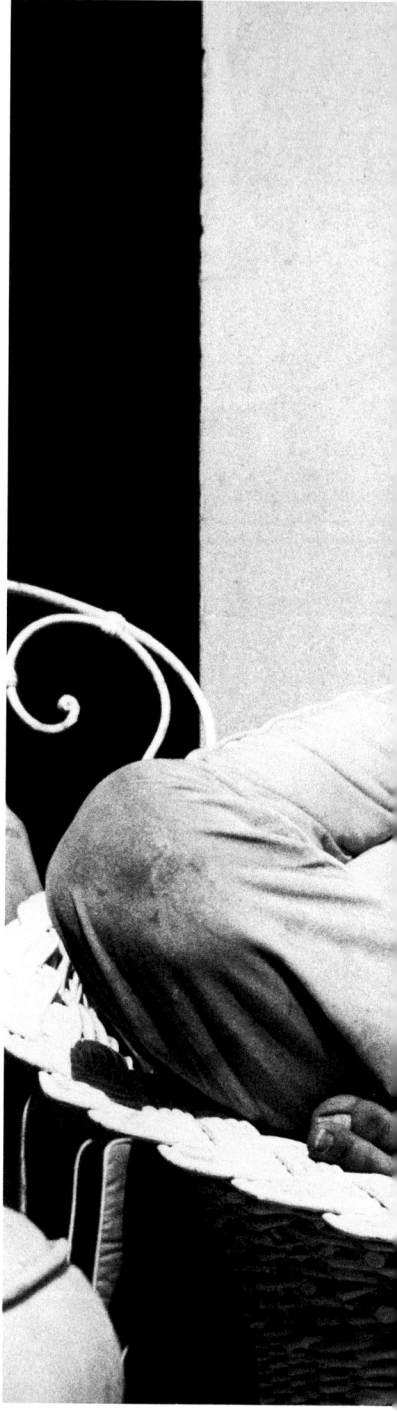

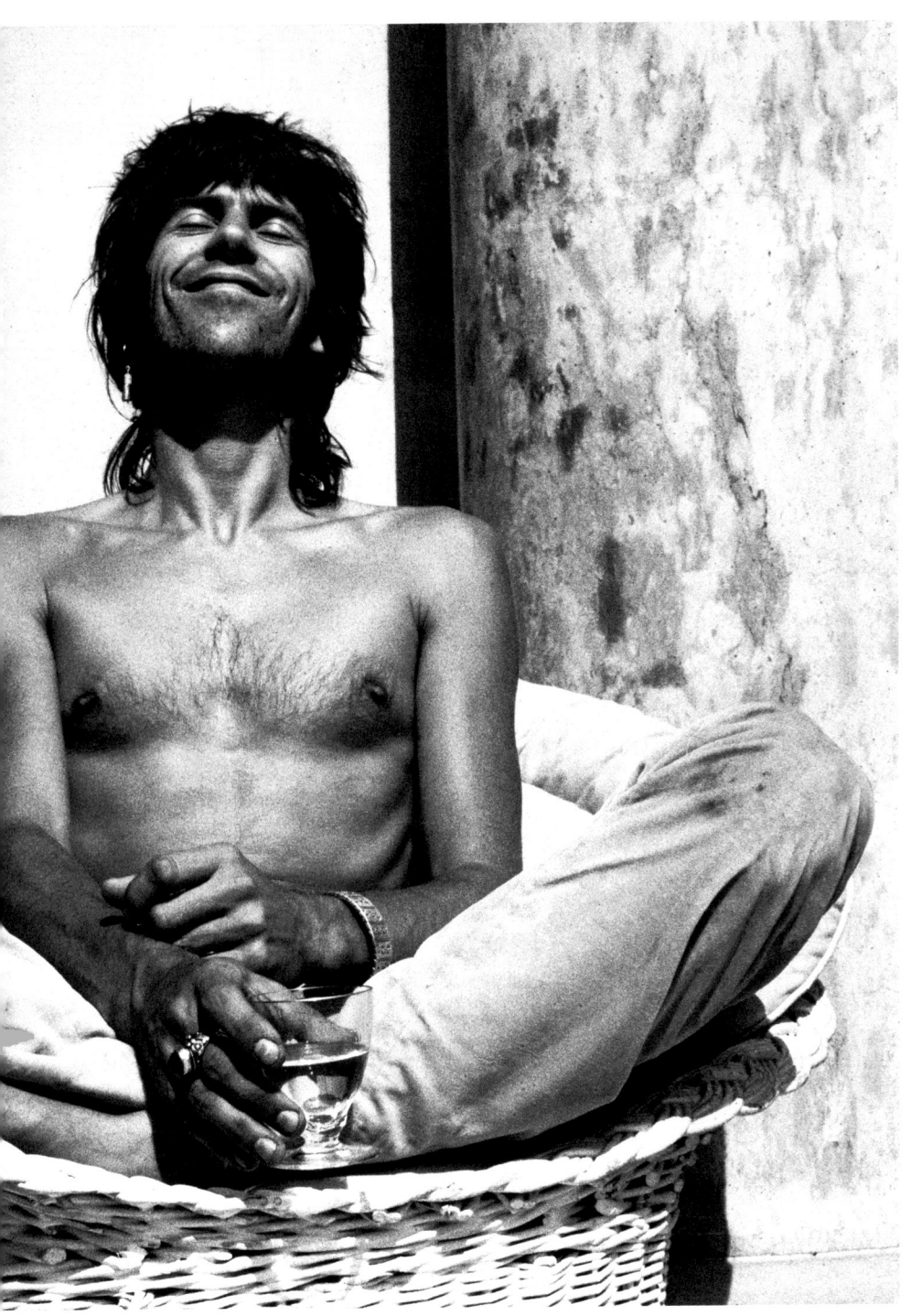

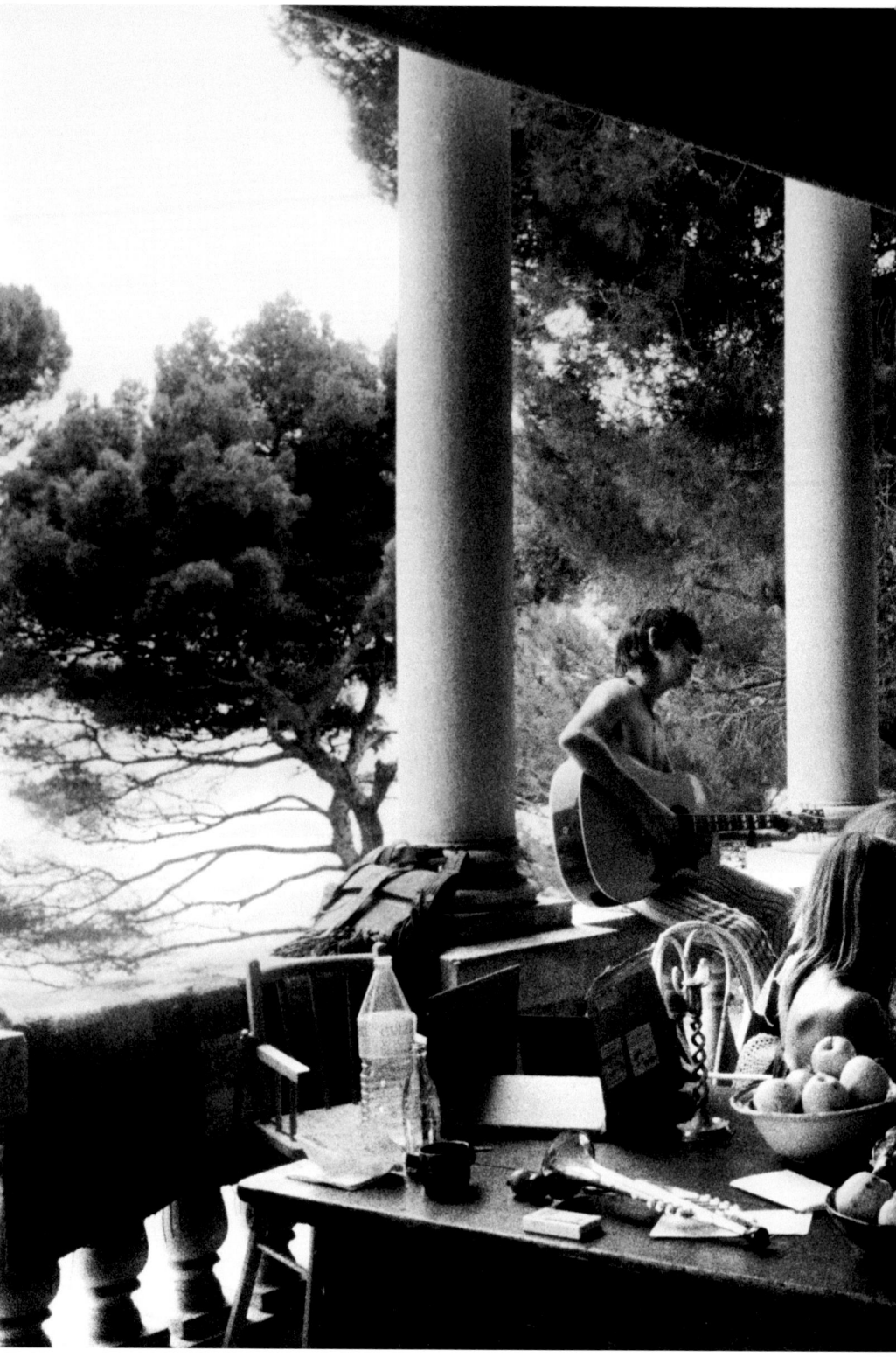

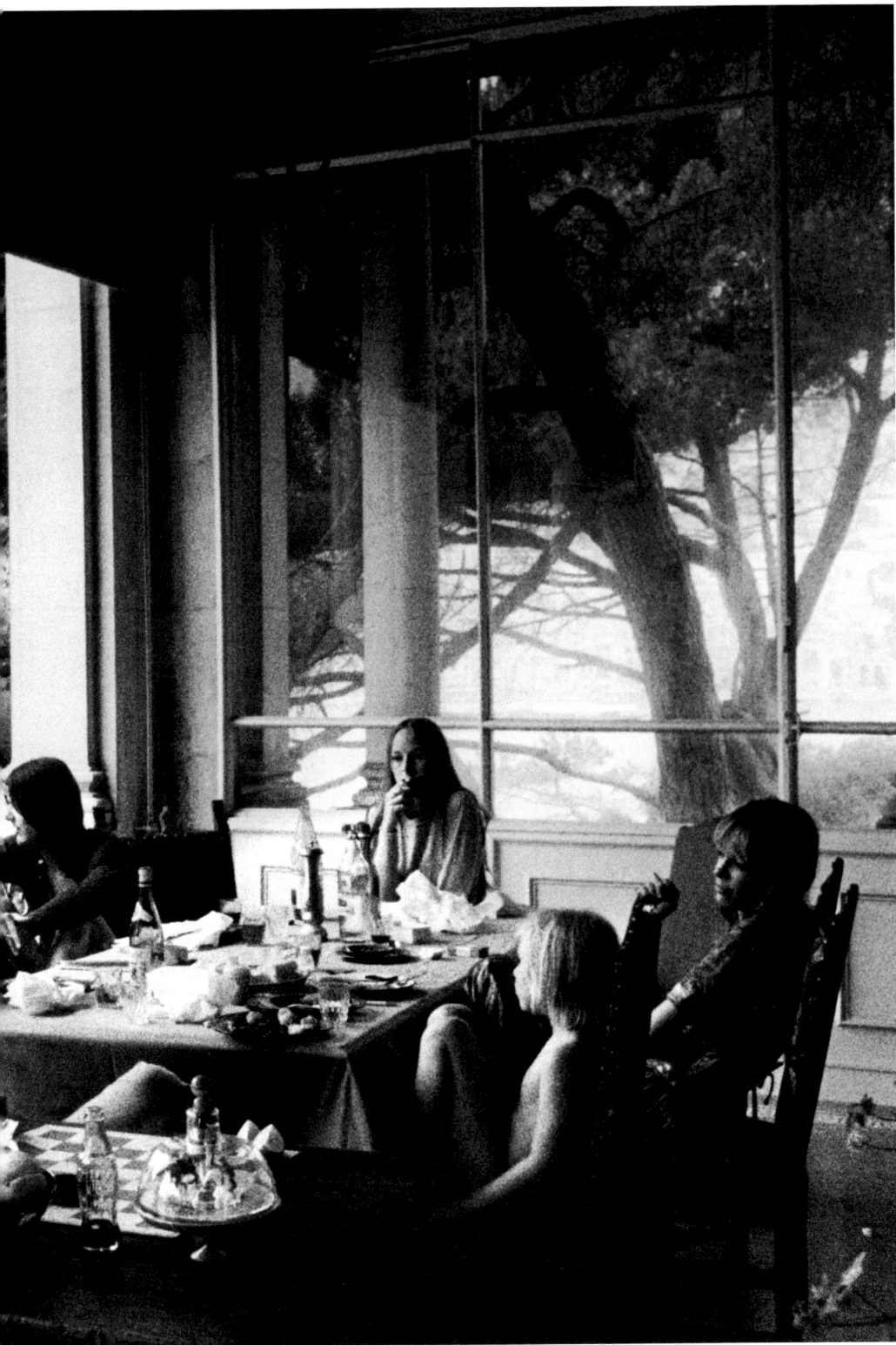

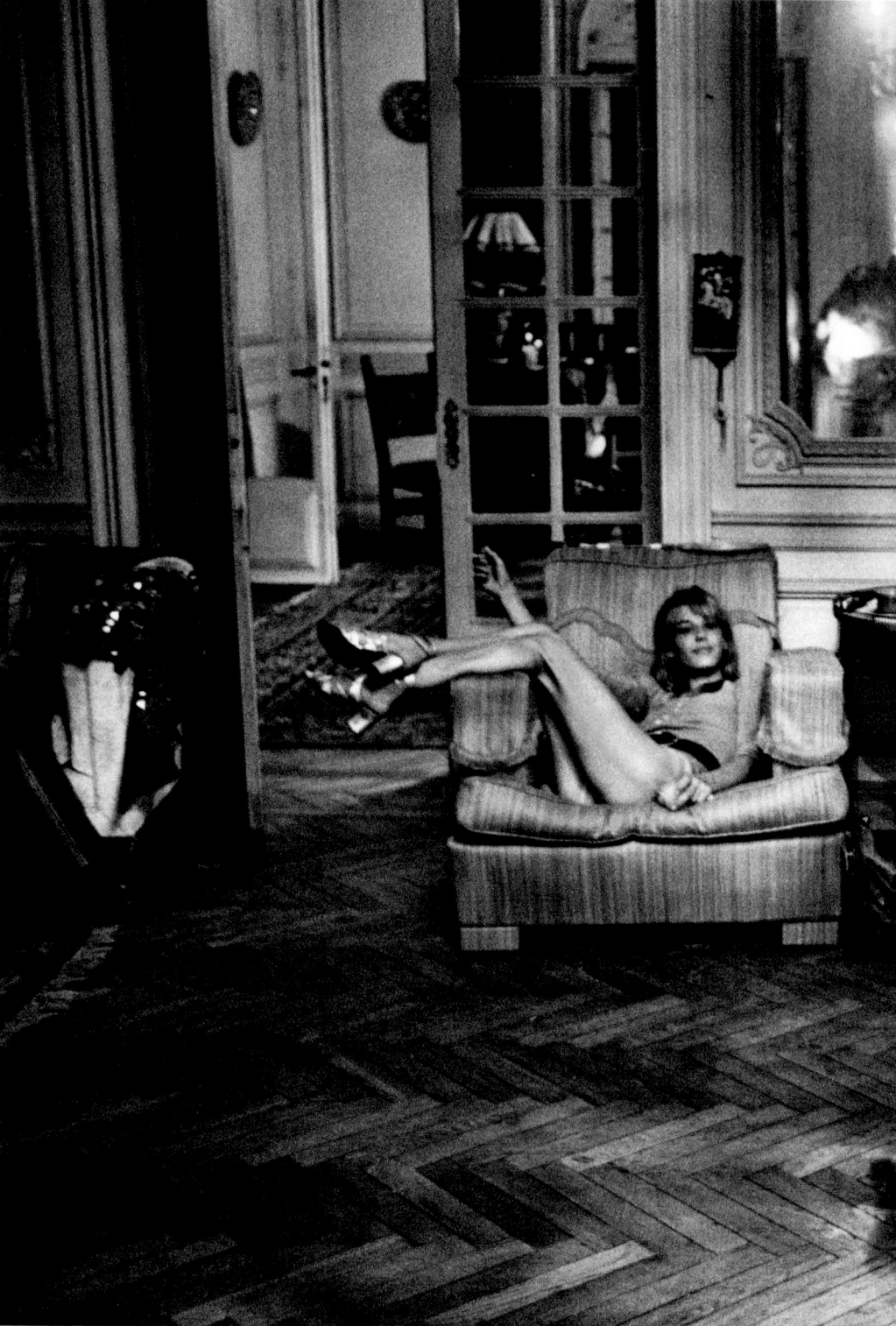

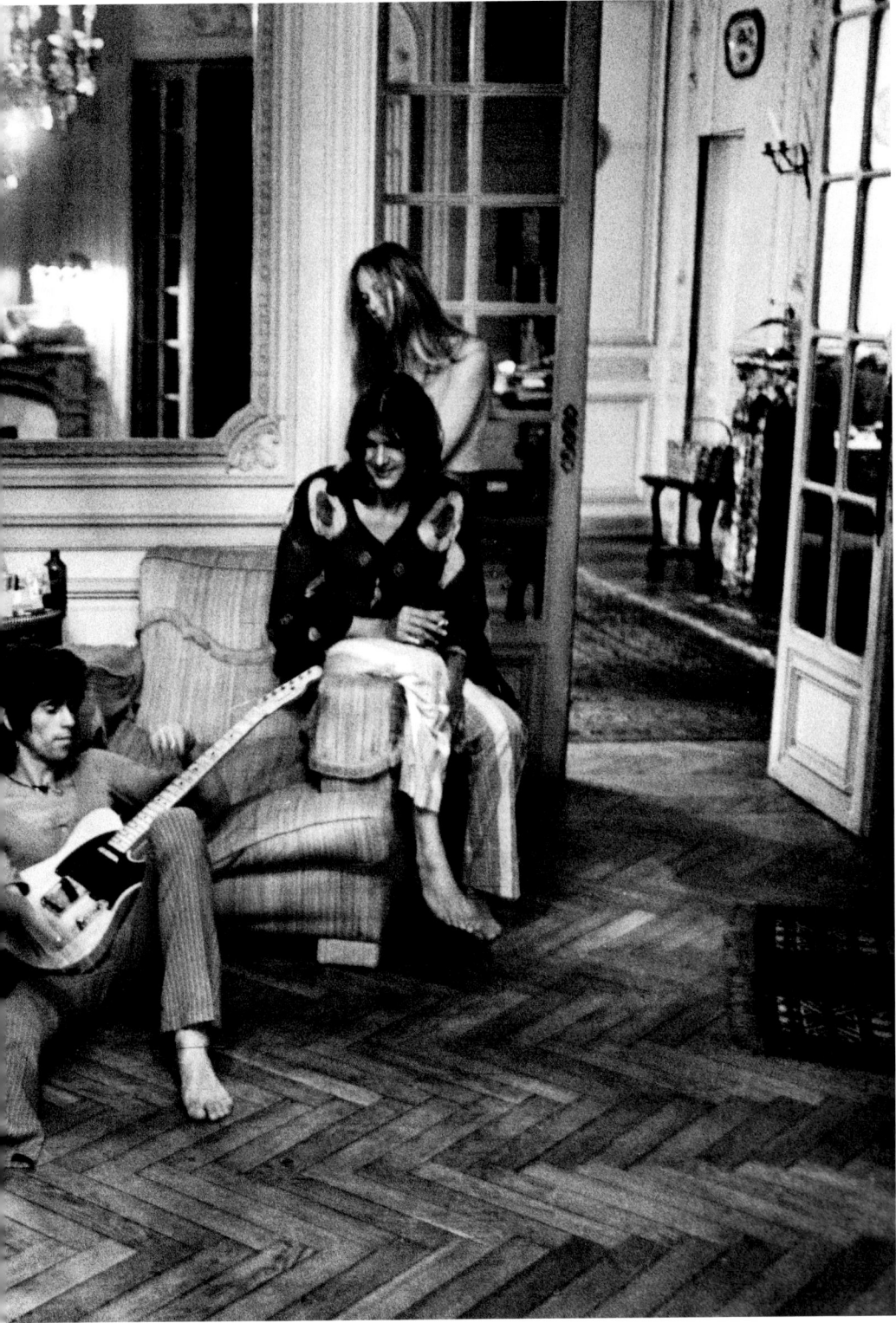

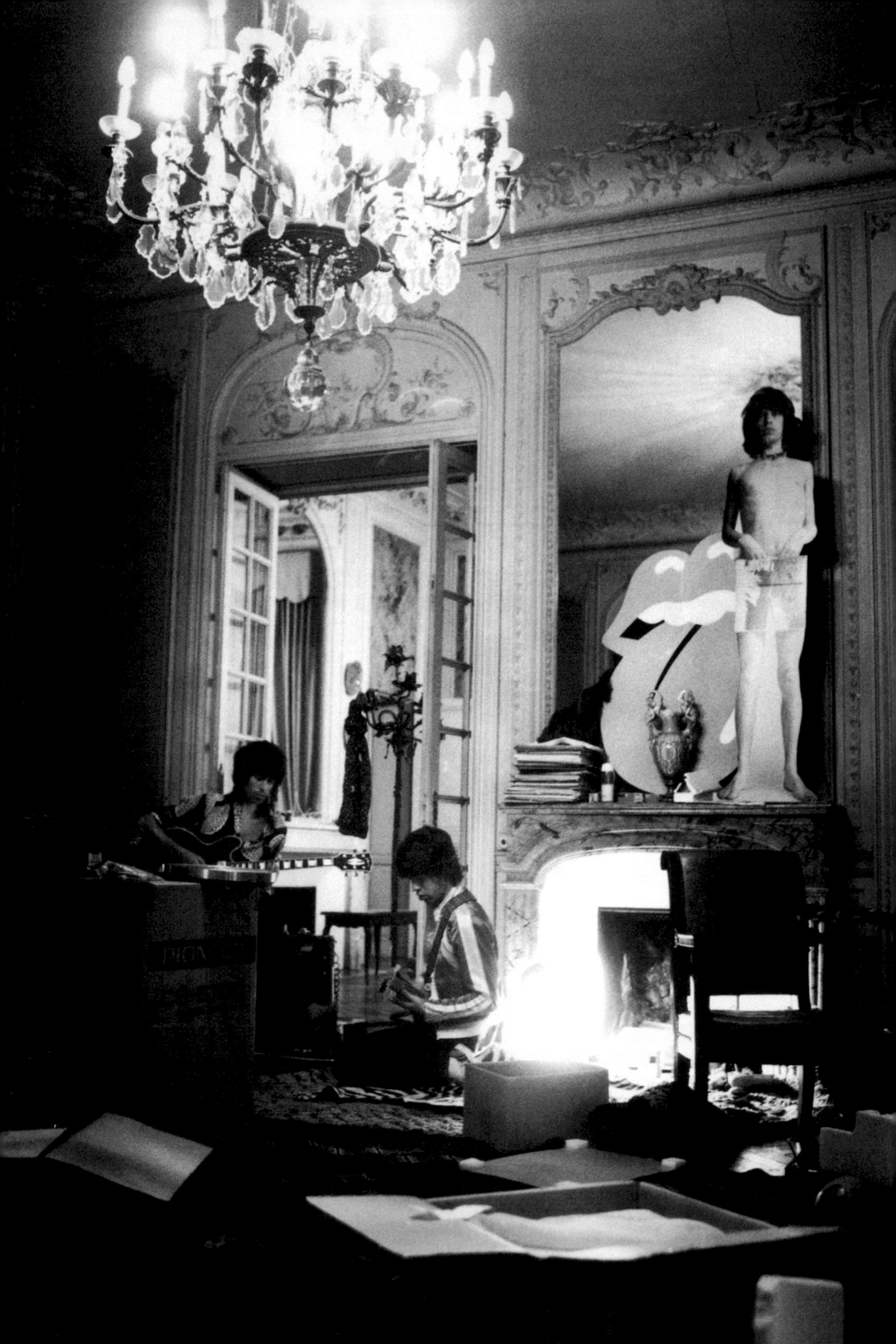

PP. 310–311
Dominique Tarlé
Anita Pallenberg, Keith, Gram and Gretchen
Parsons enjoy some late-night entertainment
at Villa Nellcôte.
*"Mick and Keith liked a few of my songs and
we gotta lotta kicks outta just sitting around
playing together. All I did was sing and pick
with the Stones."* Gram Parsons, *Melody Maker*,
12 May 1973

OPPOSITE
Dominique Tarlé
Making music together. Villa Nellcôte, South
of France, 1971.

BELOW
Dominique Tarlé
Despite the extracurricular activity on offer, the
Jagger/Richards partnership endured as best it
could at Villa Nellcôte.

*"We'd say, 'We haven't got a song for tomorrow
yet.' We were scrambling writing them on the spot.
'Happy' came like that one afternoon and several
others. 'Tumbling Dice', that came quick. Started
as a song called 'Good Time Women'. The only
difference was that we still didn't have the lyrics,
but it's the same riff."* Keith Richards, interviewed
in *Stones In Exile*, 2010

PP. 314–315
Dominique Tarlé
A touching image of eight-year-old Jake Weber
watching Mick in one of Villa Nellcôte's rooms.
*"We were allowed to wander freely around.
There was no such thing as 'bedtime' – you just
took yourself off when you felt tired. The days
were endlessly sunny. We had a series of chefs
who would cook you anything you wanted."* Jake
Weber, *Daily Mail*, 10 July 2010

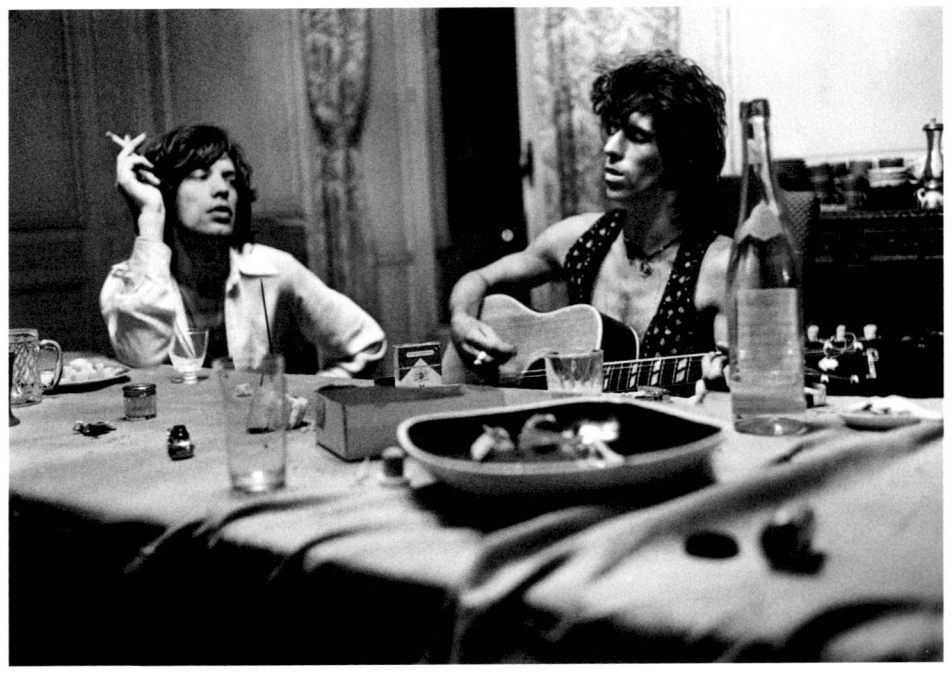

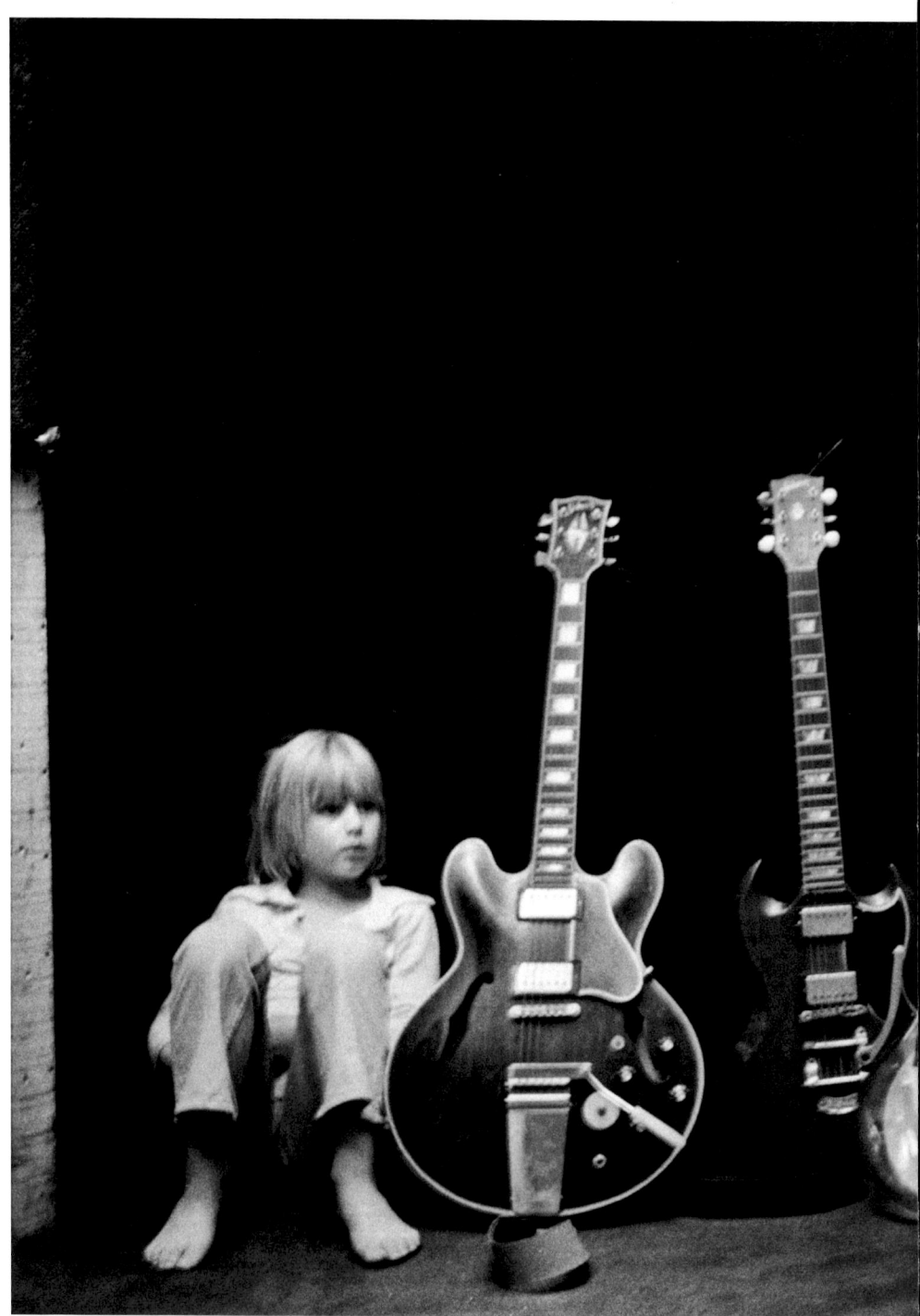

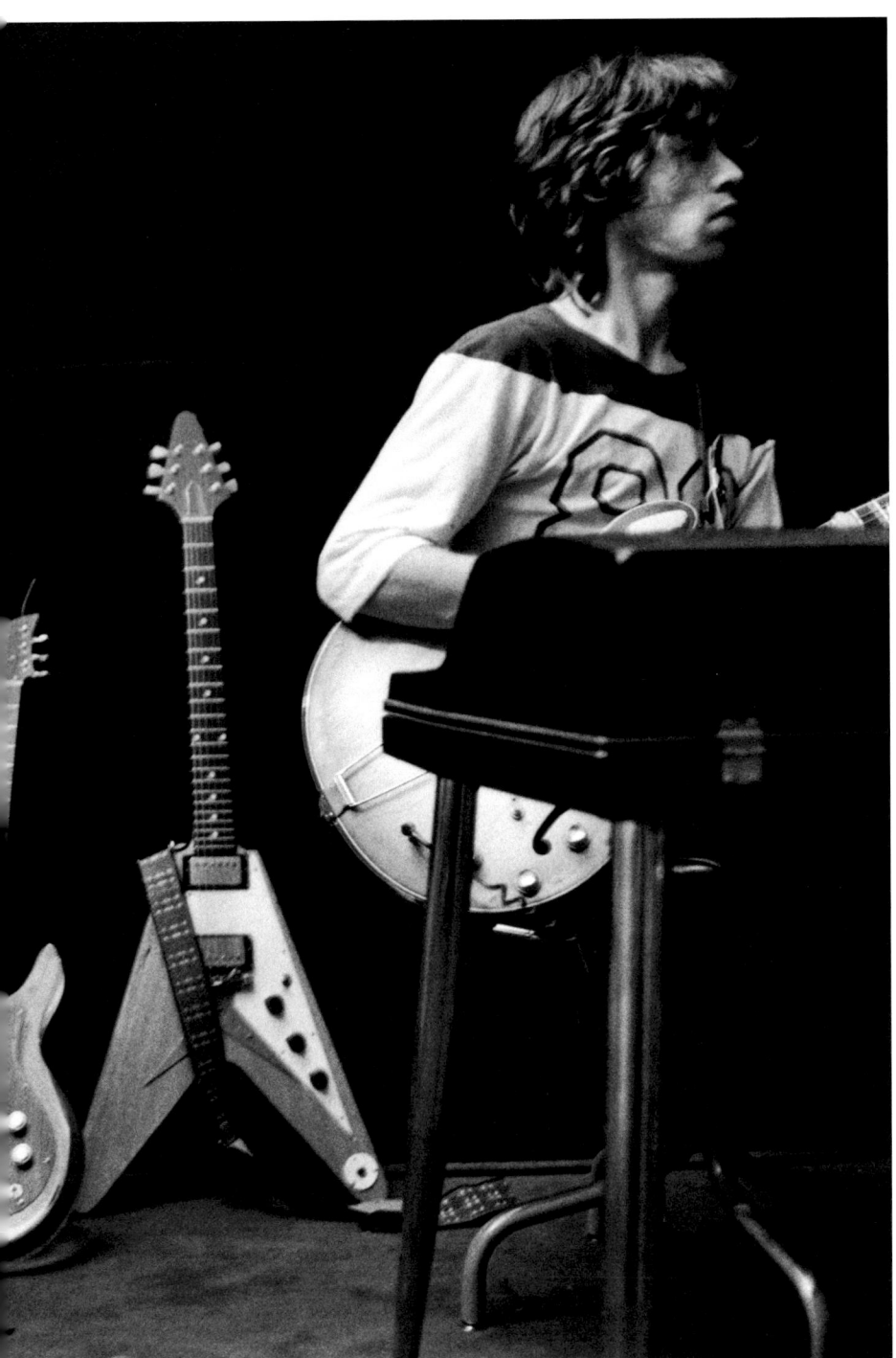

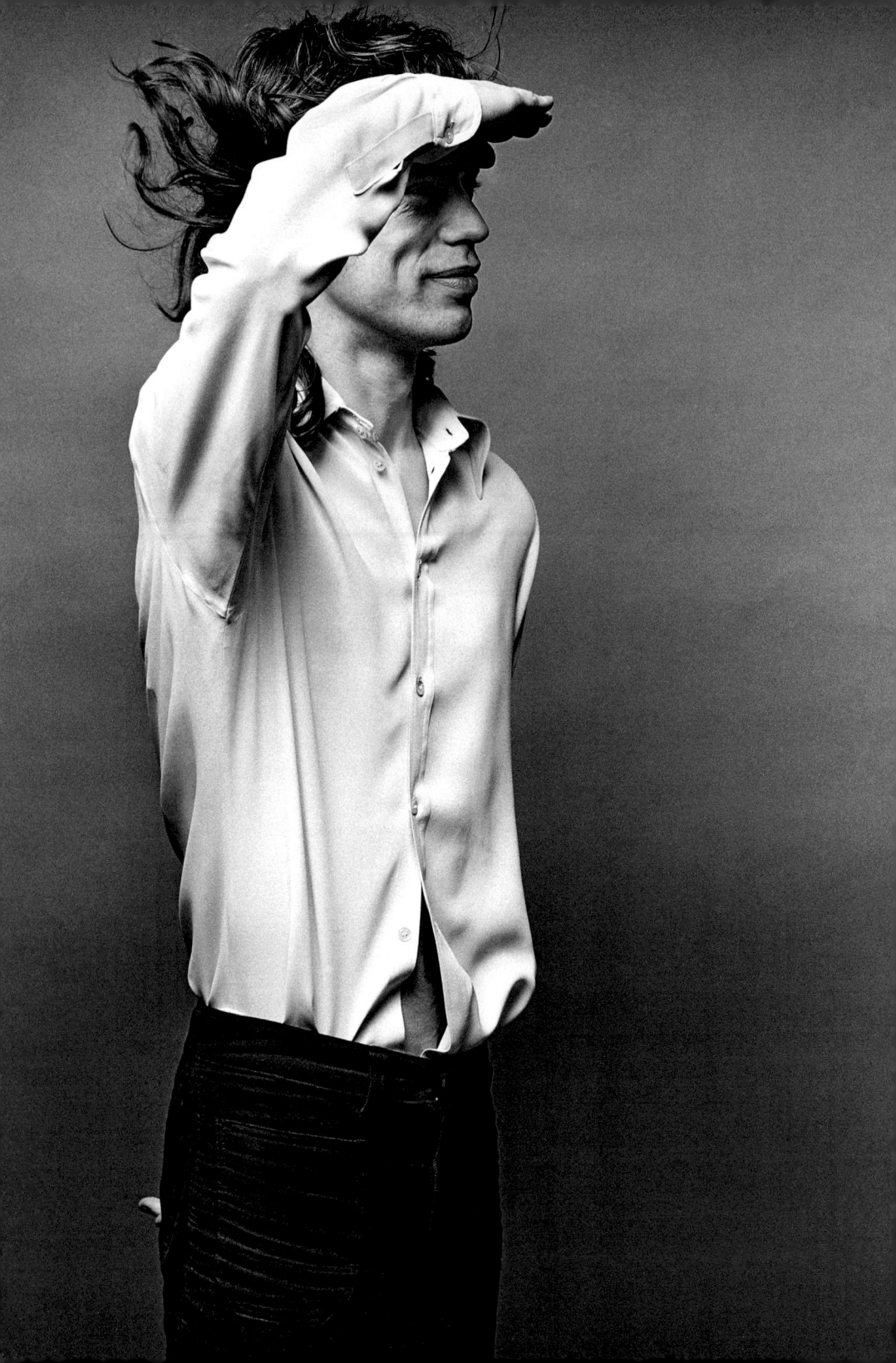

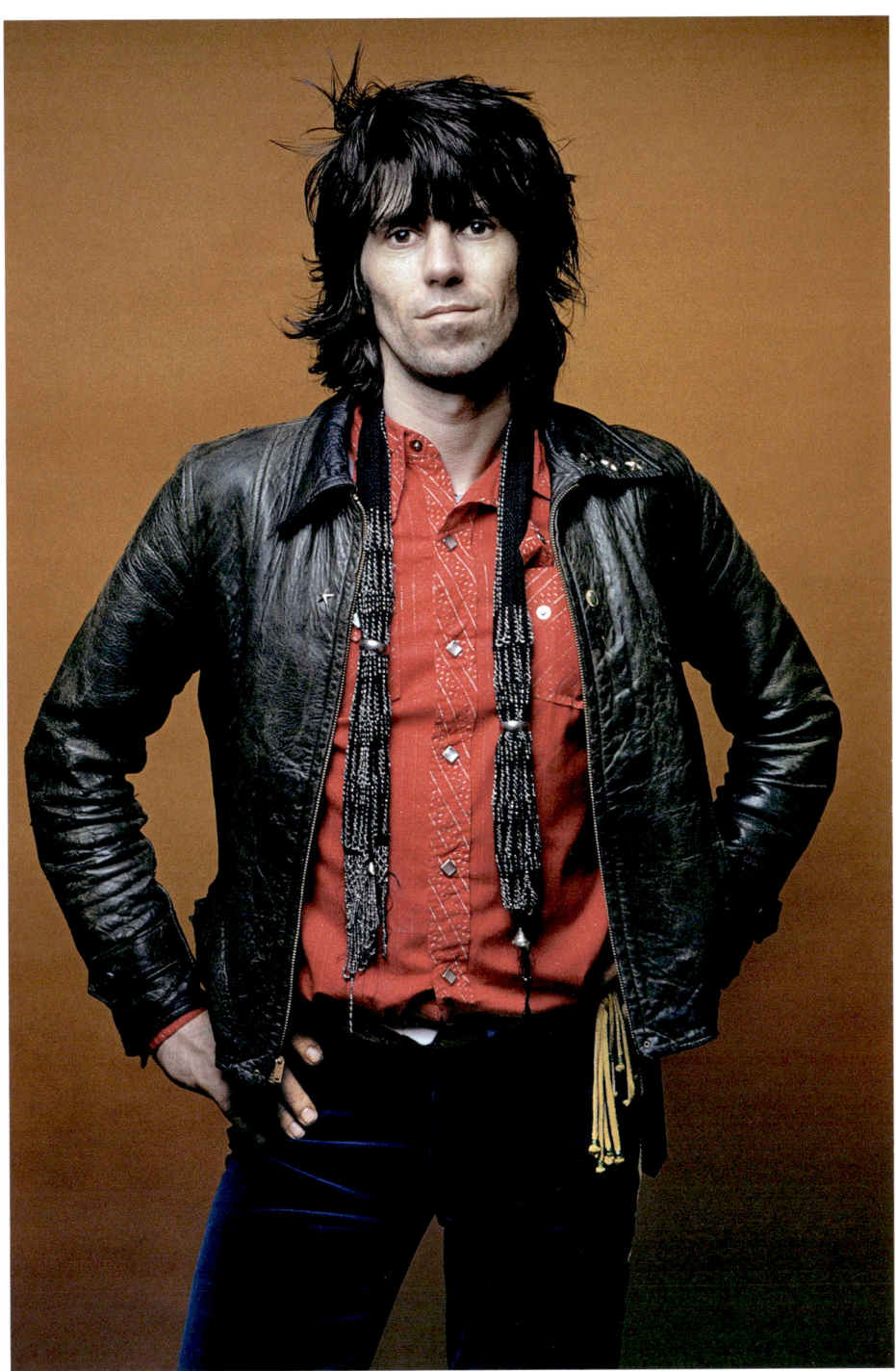

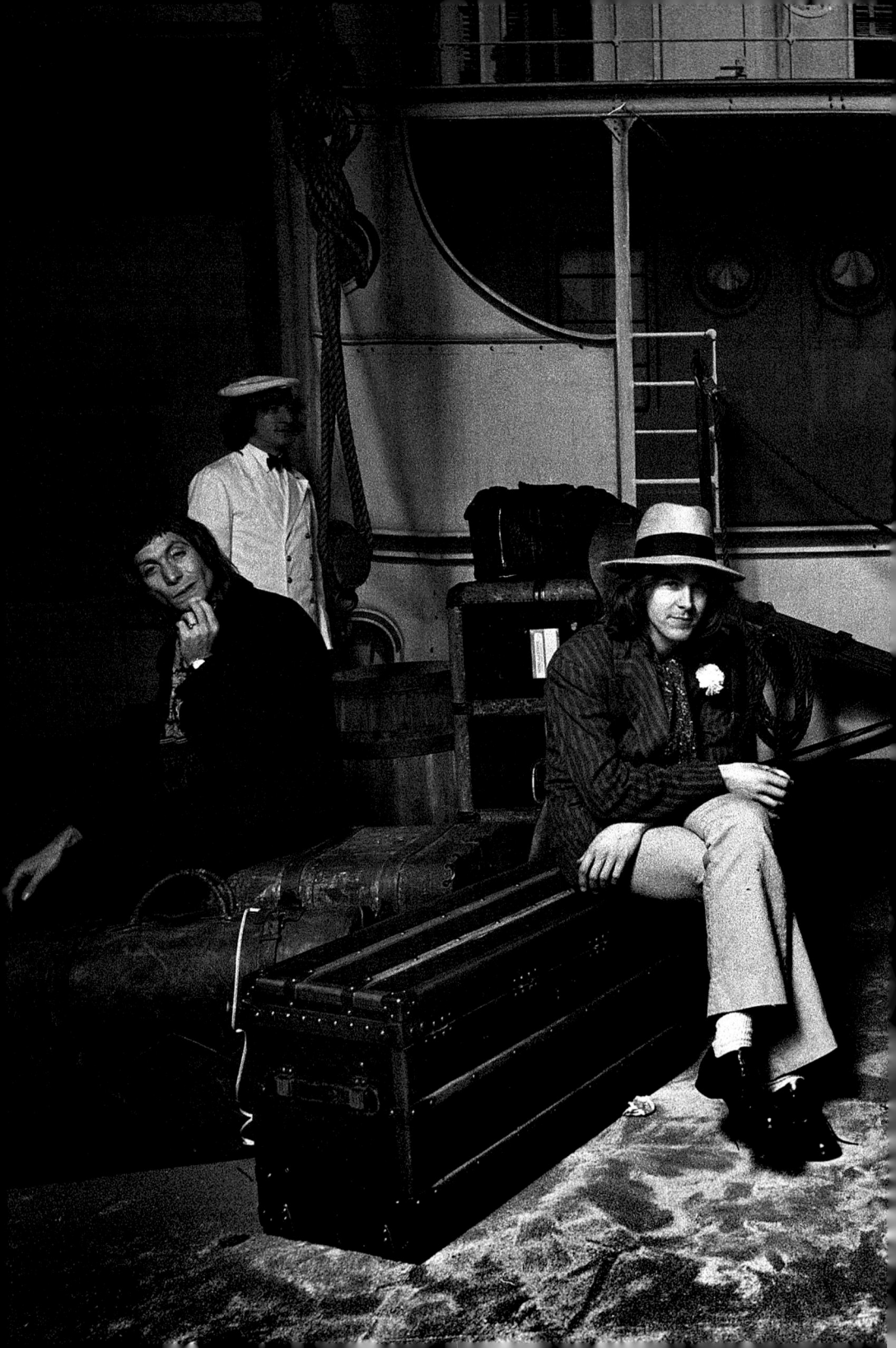

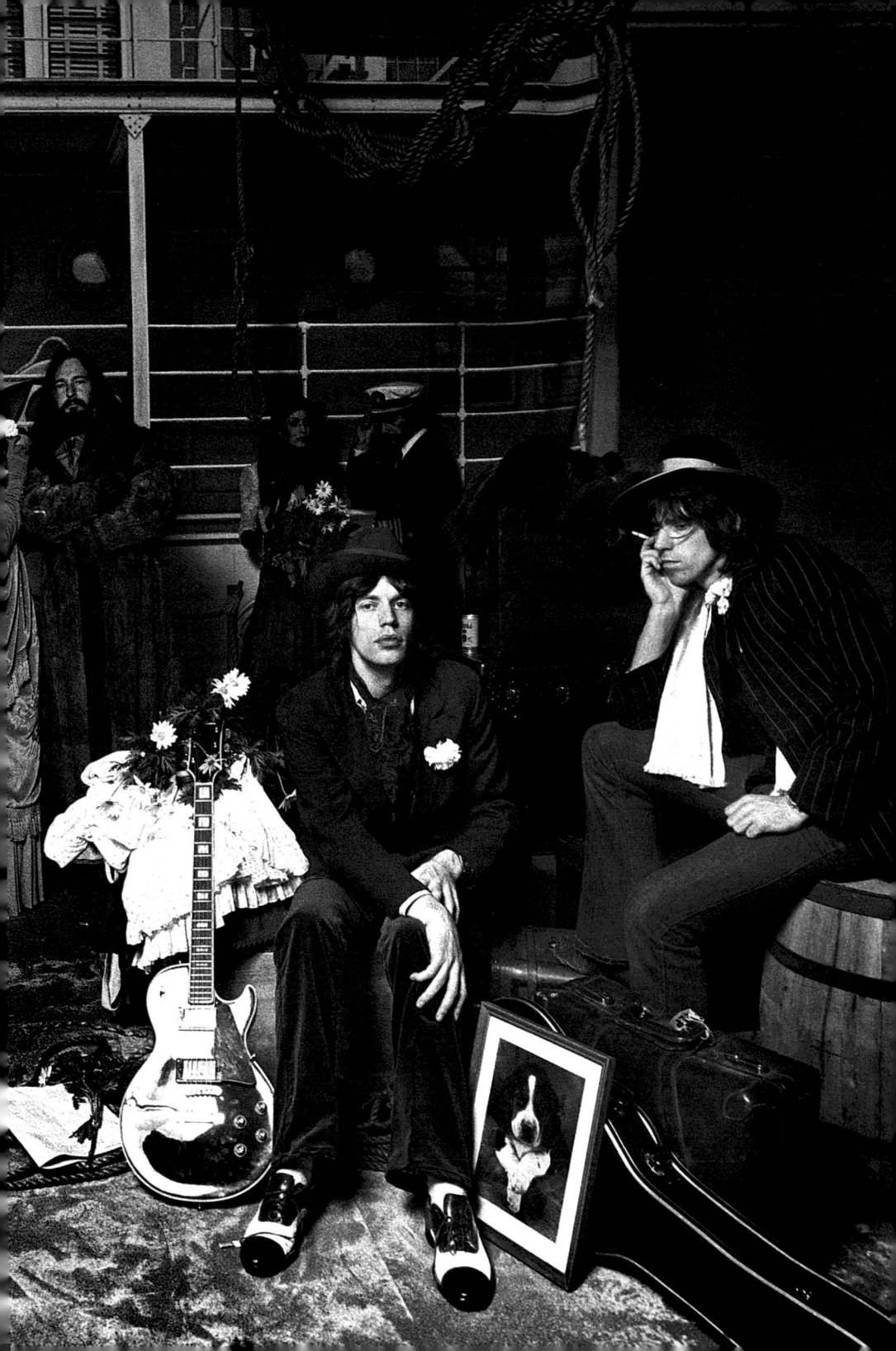

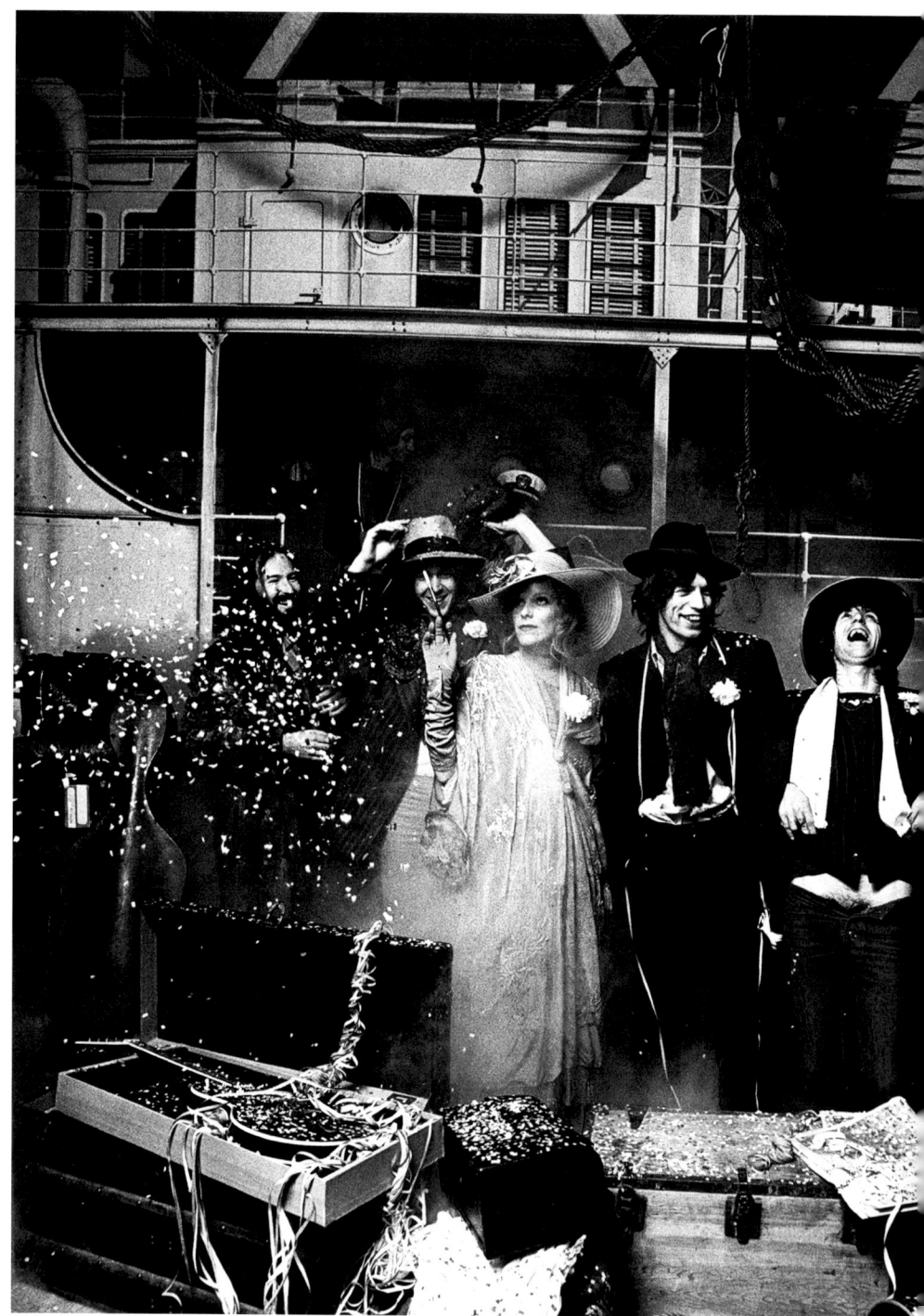

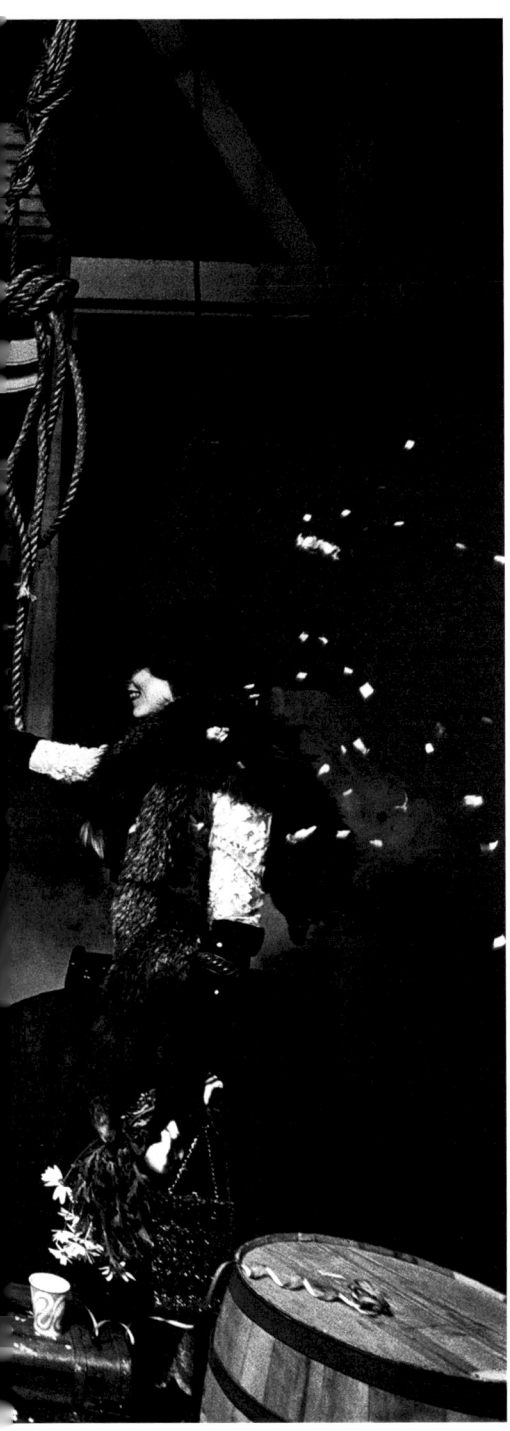

P. 316
Norman Seeff
While in Los Angeles during February and March 1972 for the overdubbing and mixing of *Exile On Main St*, Mick and Keith held several meetings with Norman Seeff, designer John Van Hamersveld and photographer Robert Frank at a Bel Air villa to determine the concept and execution of the album's sleeve. When time allowed, they also posed for a few photographs.

P. 317
Norman Seeff
Keith in Bel Air, February–March 1972.

PP. 318–319
Norman Seeff
While a collage of Robert Frank stills would adorn the front cover of *Exile On Main St*, following a suggestion from Keith, a series of 12 period-style postcards were shot to accompany the album. The shoot took place at a session convened at midnight on 6 December 1971 on a Hollywood sound stage. The lady in the centre is Mick's assistant Chris O'Dell, who went on to work for George Harrison and Ringo Starr.

Norman Seeff
Only four Stones attended the "postcard" photo session in Hollywood for *Exile On Main St.* A stand-in was provided for Bill and his face was superimposed later.

PP. 322–323
Annie Leibovitz
Los Angeles, May 1972.
Preparations for the *Exile* tour of the States required extensive rehearsals to bring the group and accompanying musicians up to speed on the new material. Following a few cramped days in a small studio in Bel Air, the group moved to a sound stage at Warner Bros. Studios in Burbank where, with assistance from the likes of saxophonist Bobby Keys and pianist Nicky Hopkins, shows for the imminent tour could be perfected before things started in earnest on 3 June 1972.

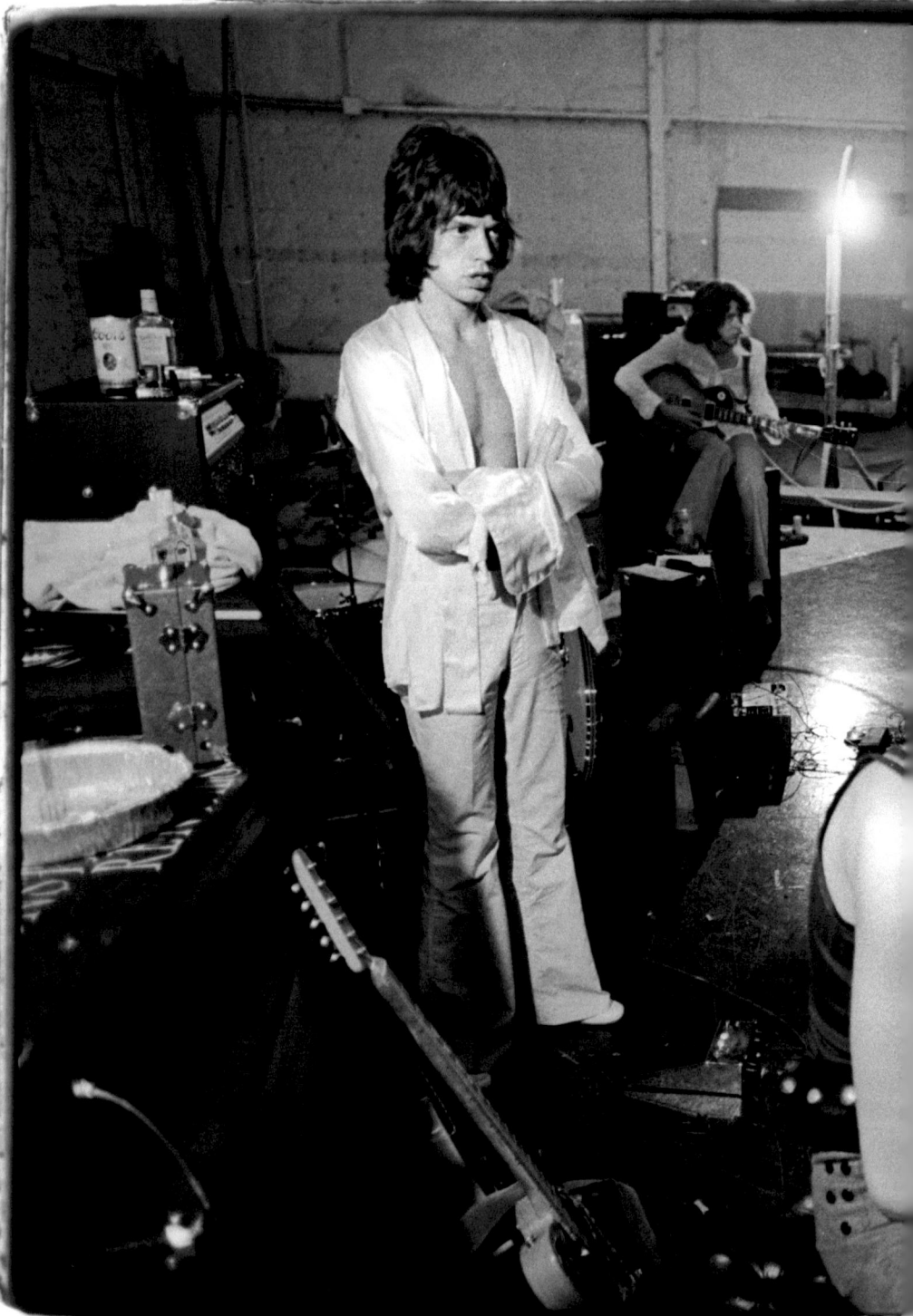

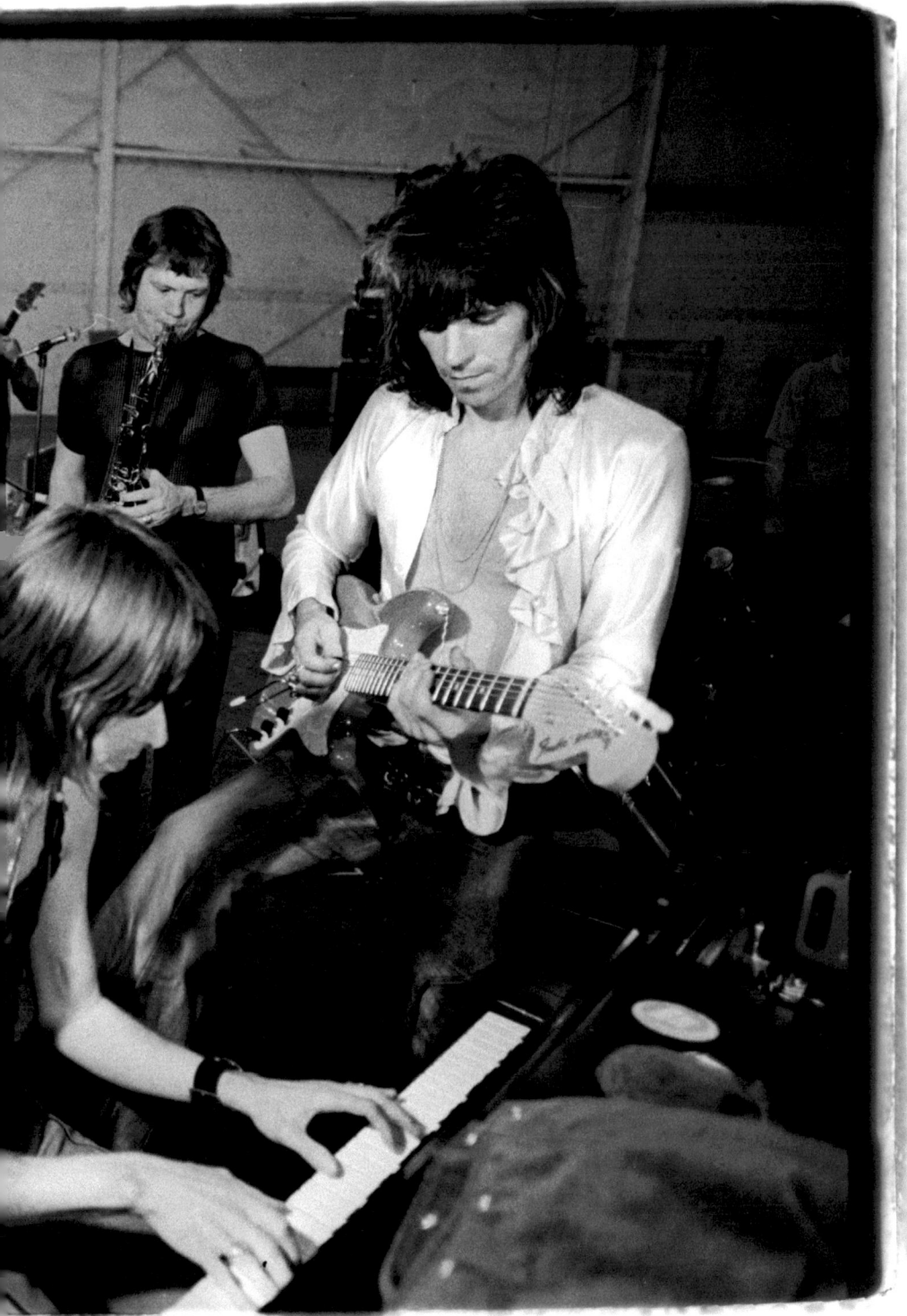

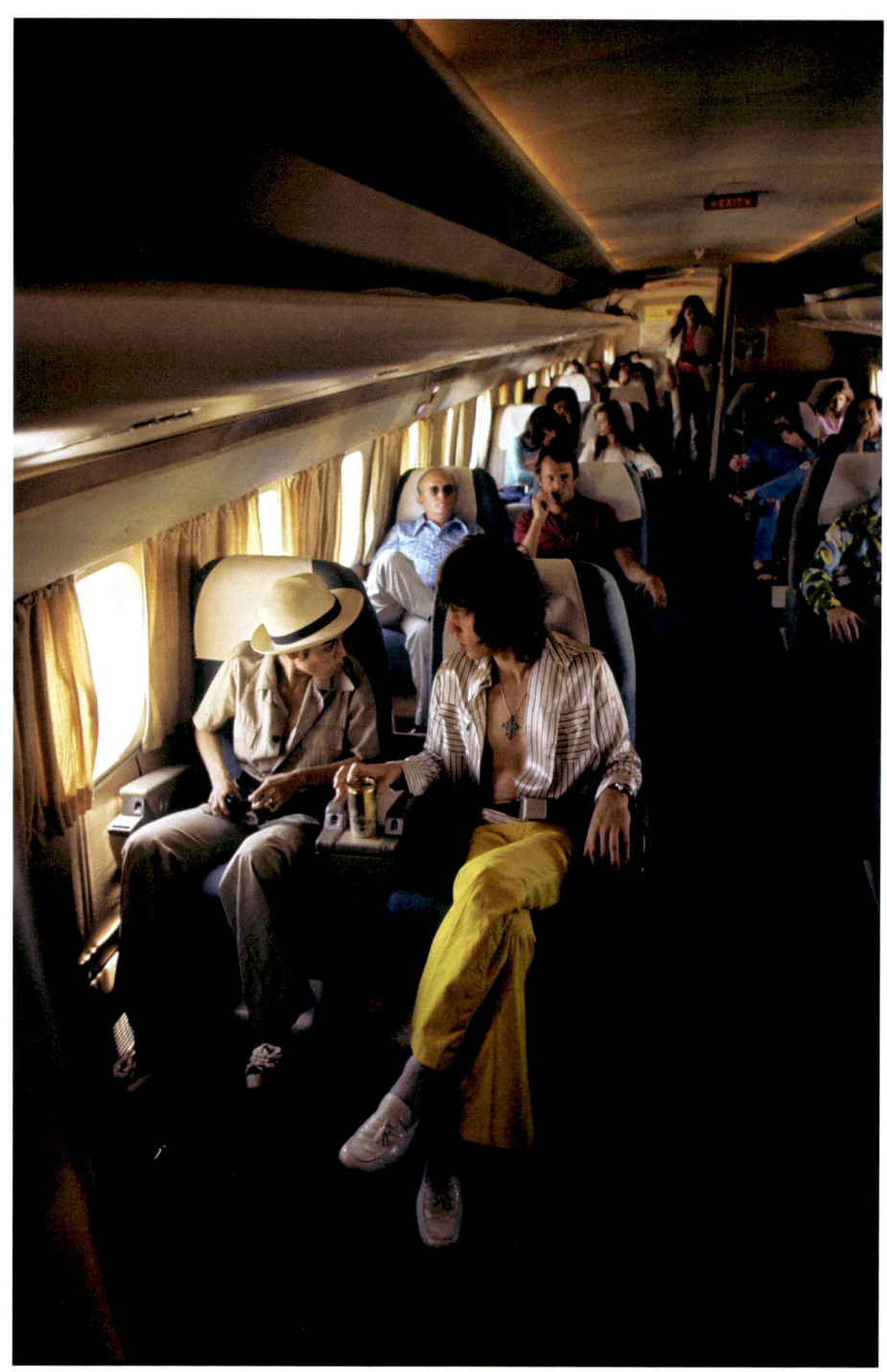

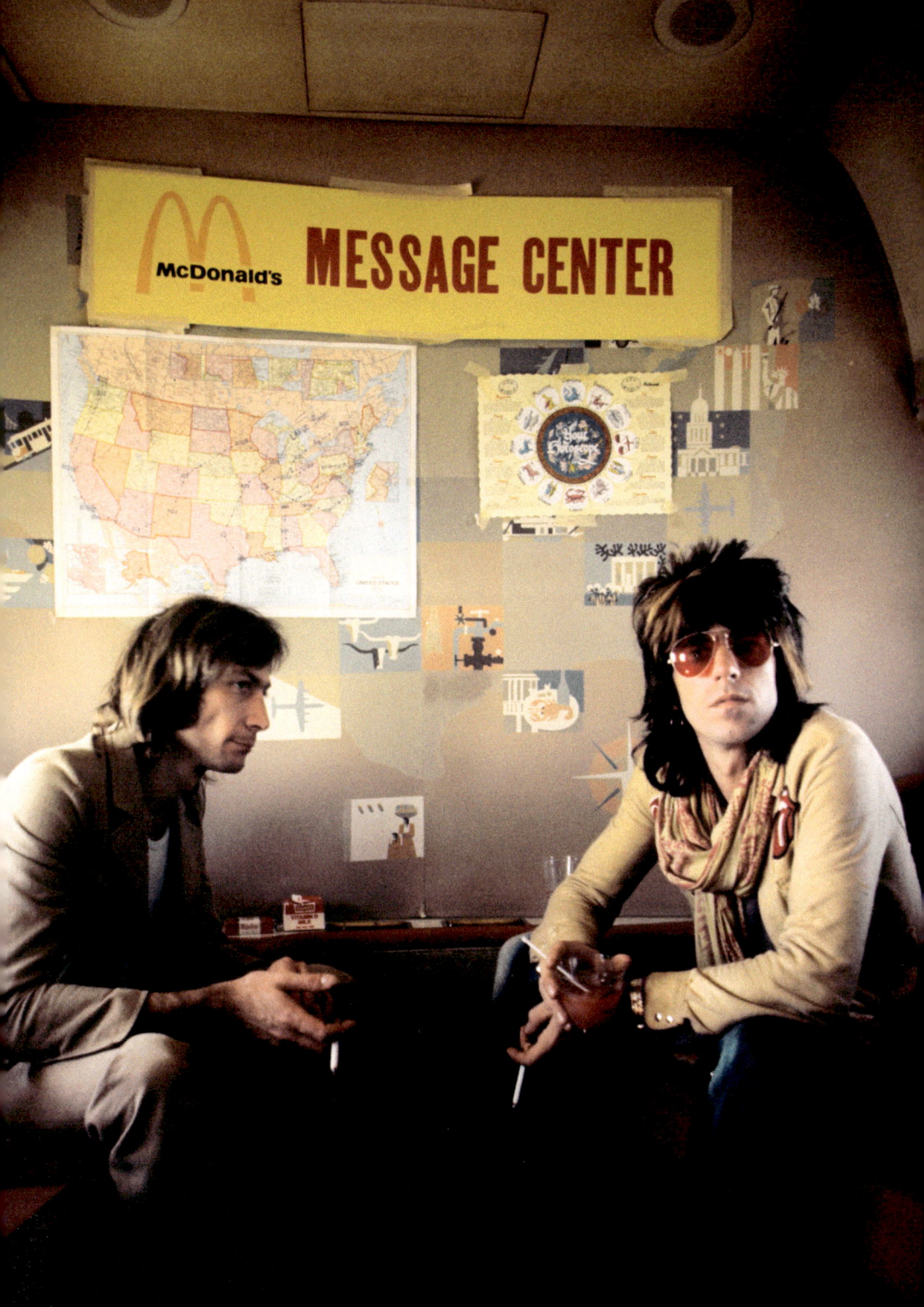

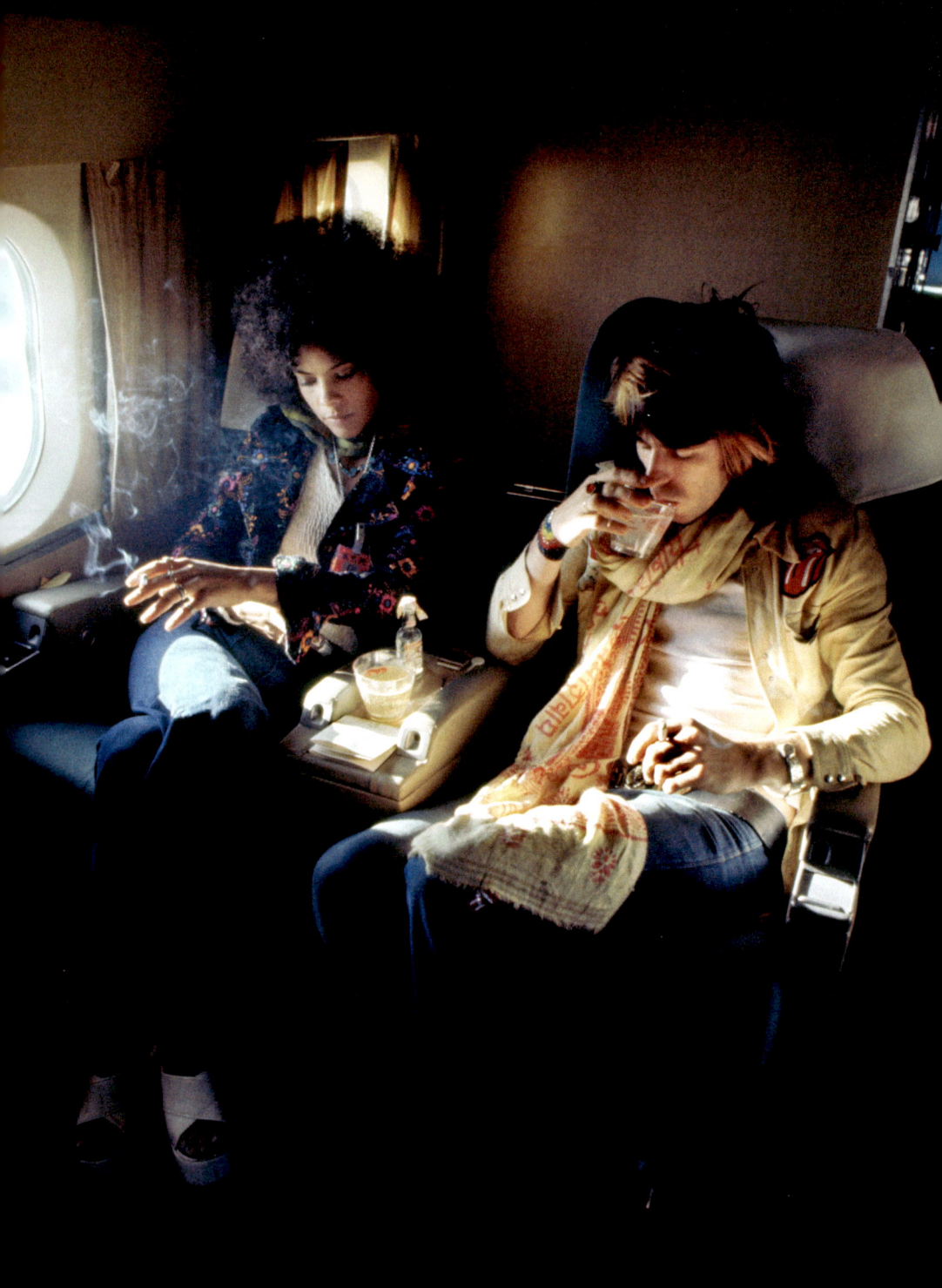

P. 324
Ethan Russell

The 48 shows that made up the *Exile* tour of the States during June and July of 1972 redefined touring for rock musicians. Coined S.T.P. (euphemistic for "Stones Touring Party"), the excess of action offstage was possibly best exemplified aboard the Stones' chartered jet. With a film crew under the direction of Robert Frank present, many of the more riotous moments were captured in the notorious movie *Cocksucker Blues*. Along for the ride were renowned author Truman Capote and photographer/artist Peter Beard sitting behind Mick and Bianca.

P. 325
Ethan Russell

Charlie and Keith grab a few moments' peace at the rear of their chartered jet between gigs during the Stones' groundbreaking 1972 tour.

Jim Marshall

Keith and Jolie Jones captured on the Stones' jet en route to Los Angeles on 9 June 1972. Jolie, eldest daughter of producer Quincy Jones, tagged along during the Stones' visits to the West Coast of America that year.

Jim Marshall

A contemplative Mick aboard the Stones' chartered jet during the 1972 tour of the United States and Canada.

"One thing I'll say about Mick Jagger. He's fascinating in the sense that he's one of the most total actors I've ever seen. He has this remarkable quality of being absolutely able to be totally extroverted. ... But what makes it more remarkable is that the moment it's done, it's over. And he reverts to quite a private, sensible, and a more emotionally mature person than most actors and intellectuals are capable of being." Truman Capote, *Rolling Stone* magazine, 12 April 1973

PP. 330–331
Ethan Russell

Keith alighting from the Stones' chartered plane at Los Angeles, 9 June 1972.

"Some of the finest moments were aboard this plane. Sunrise in hand, hopping from one gig to the next – Fort Worth to Houston, Houston to Nashville, Nashville to New Orleans – short flights, and, like the dressing rooms, a boss groove and comfort to us all." Terry Southern, *Saturday Review*, 12 August 1972

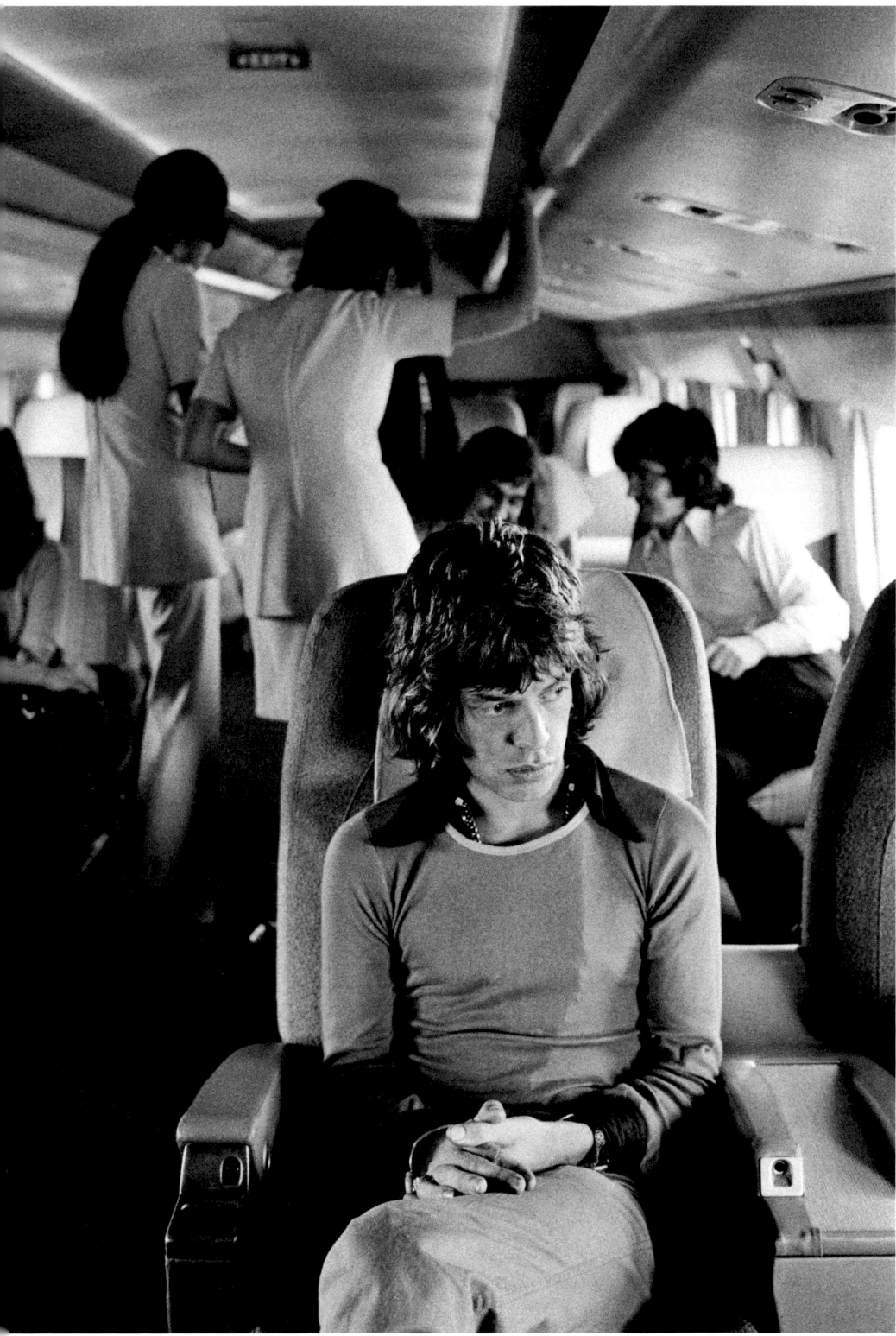

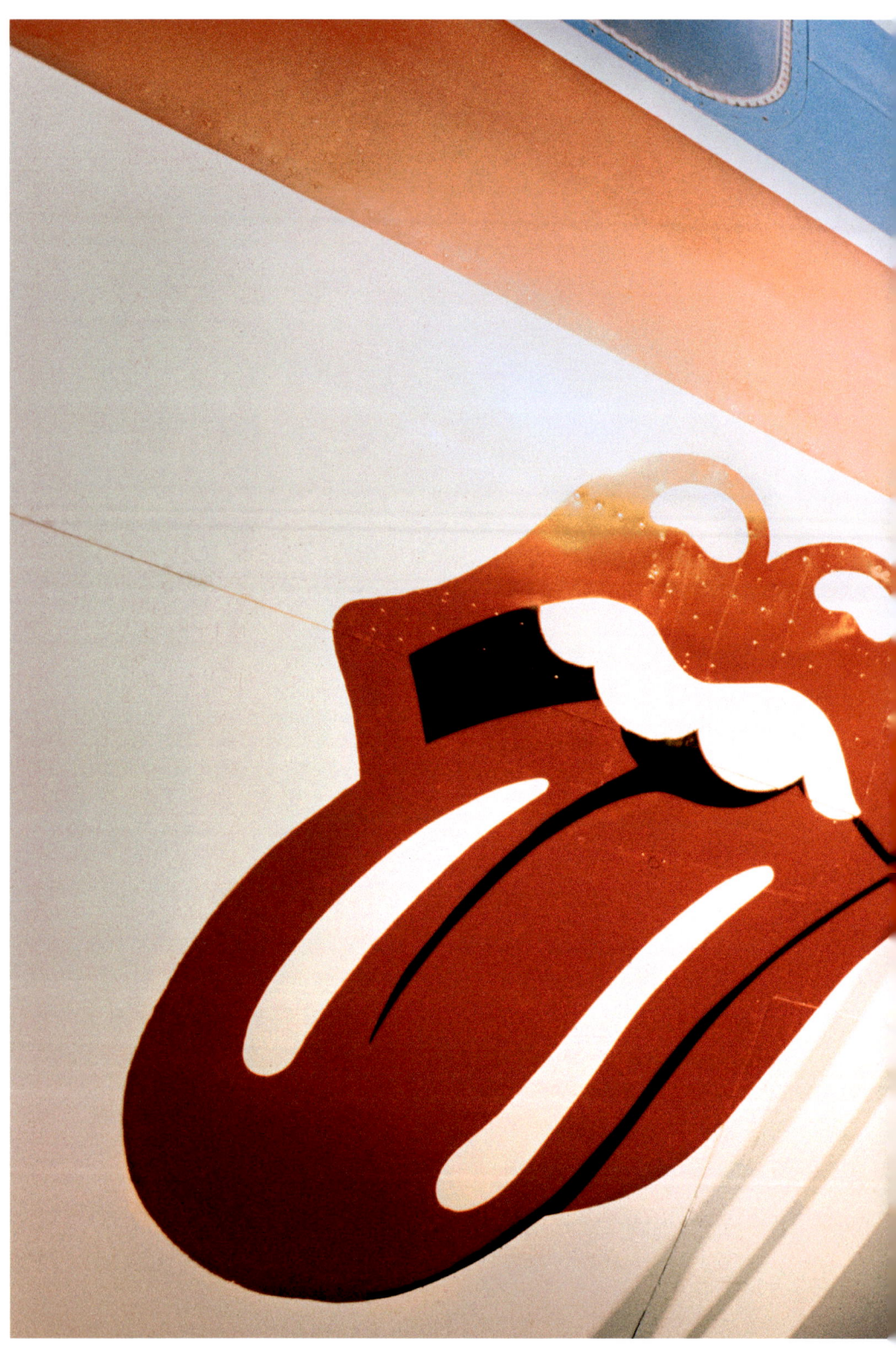

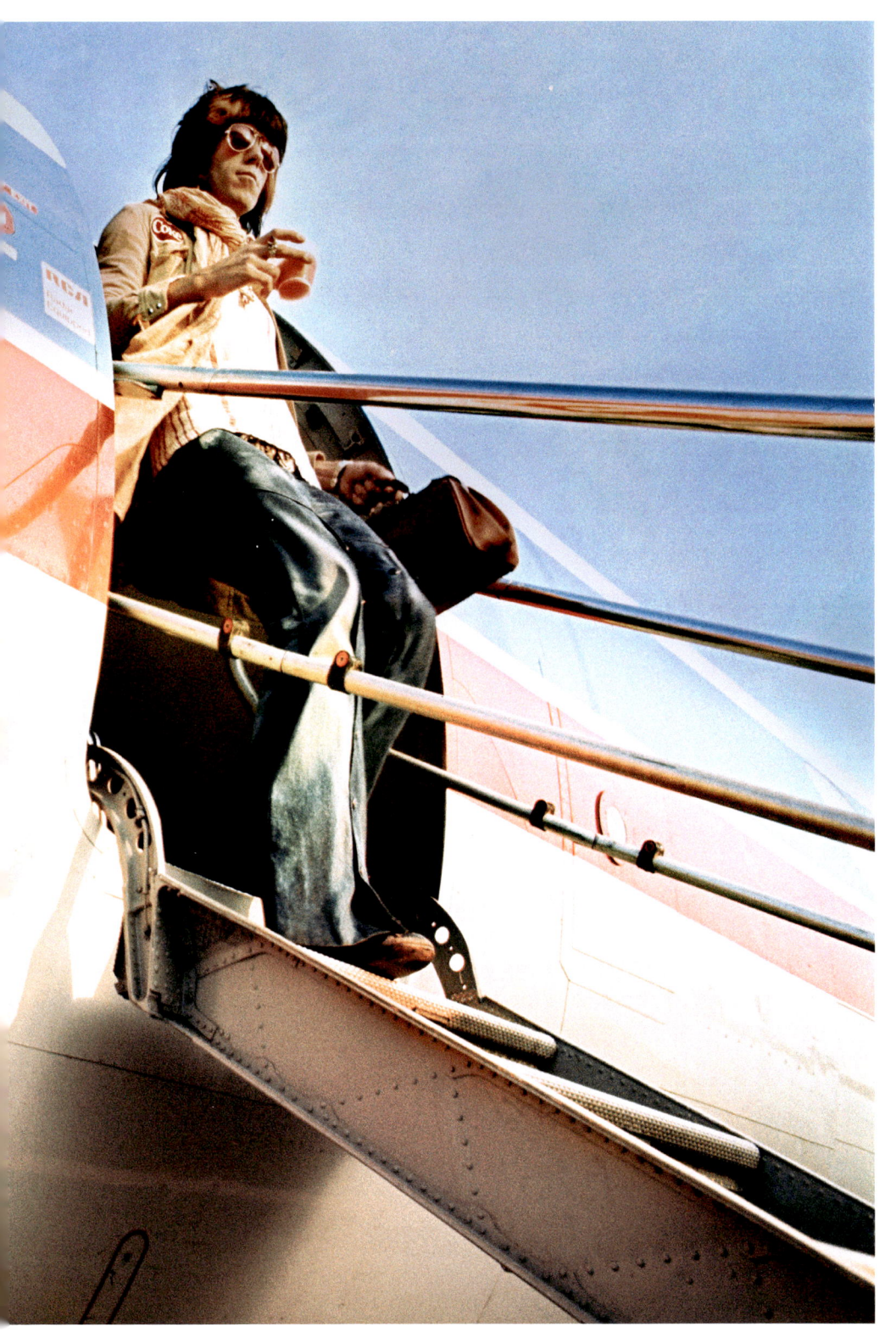

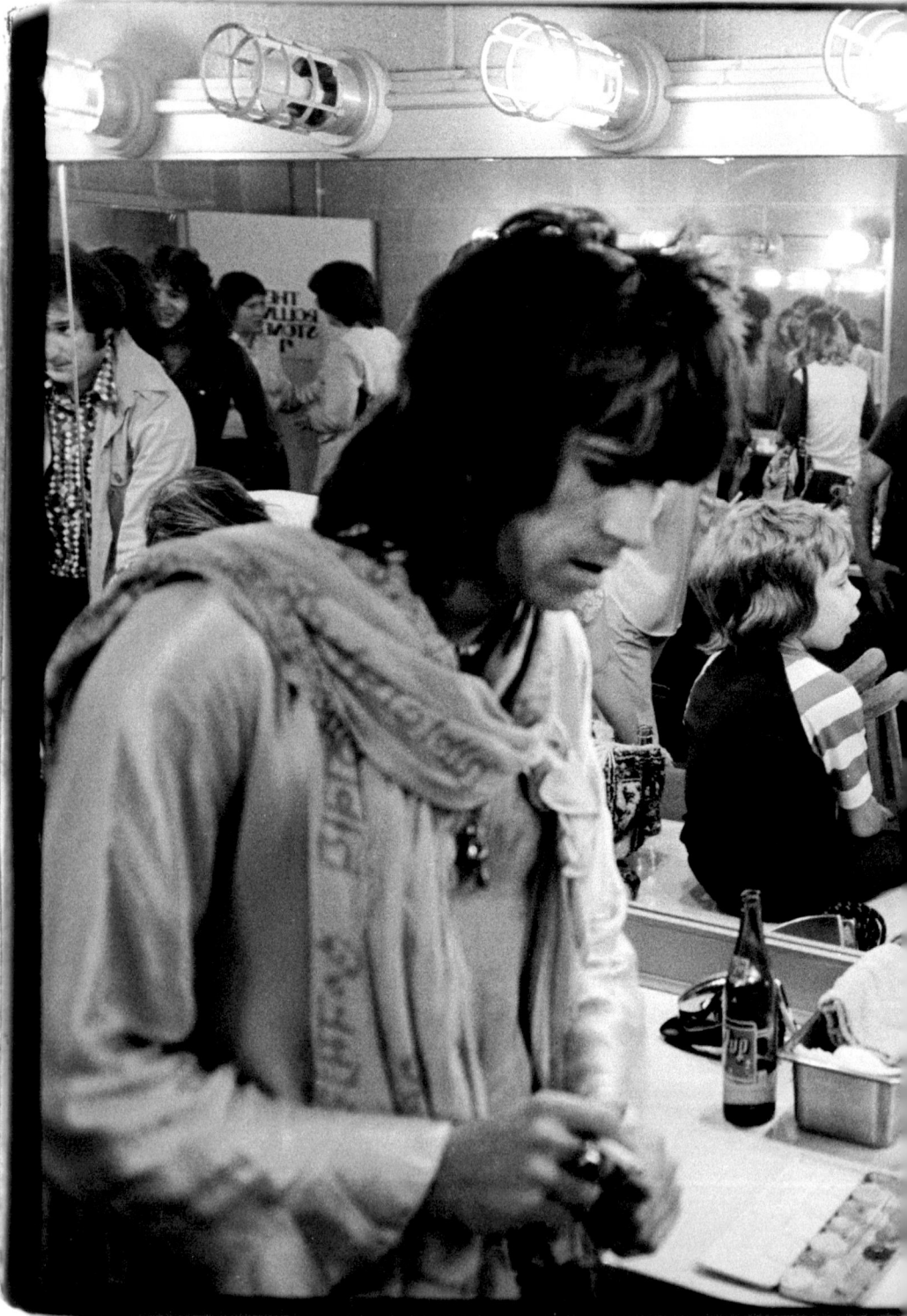

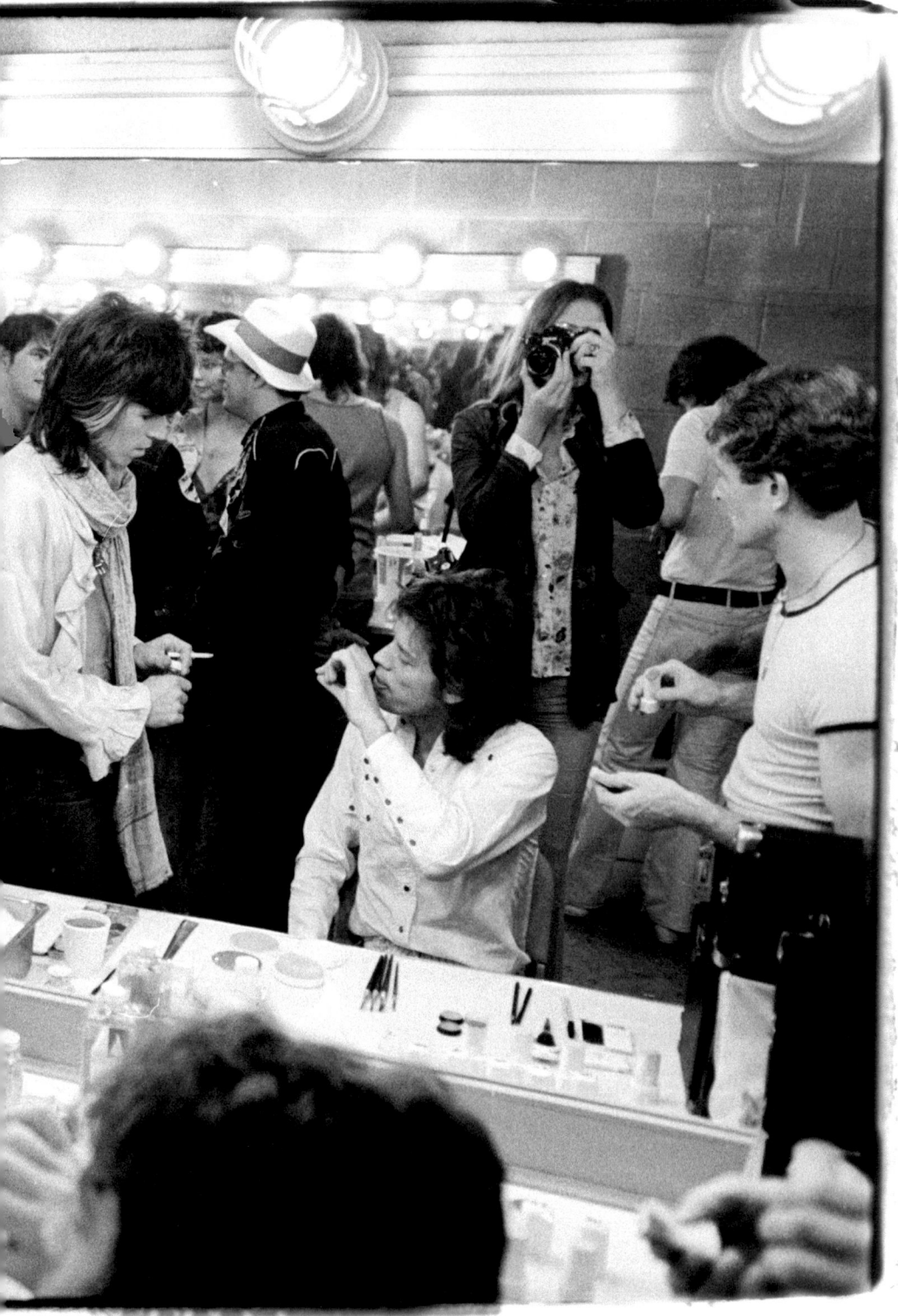

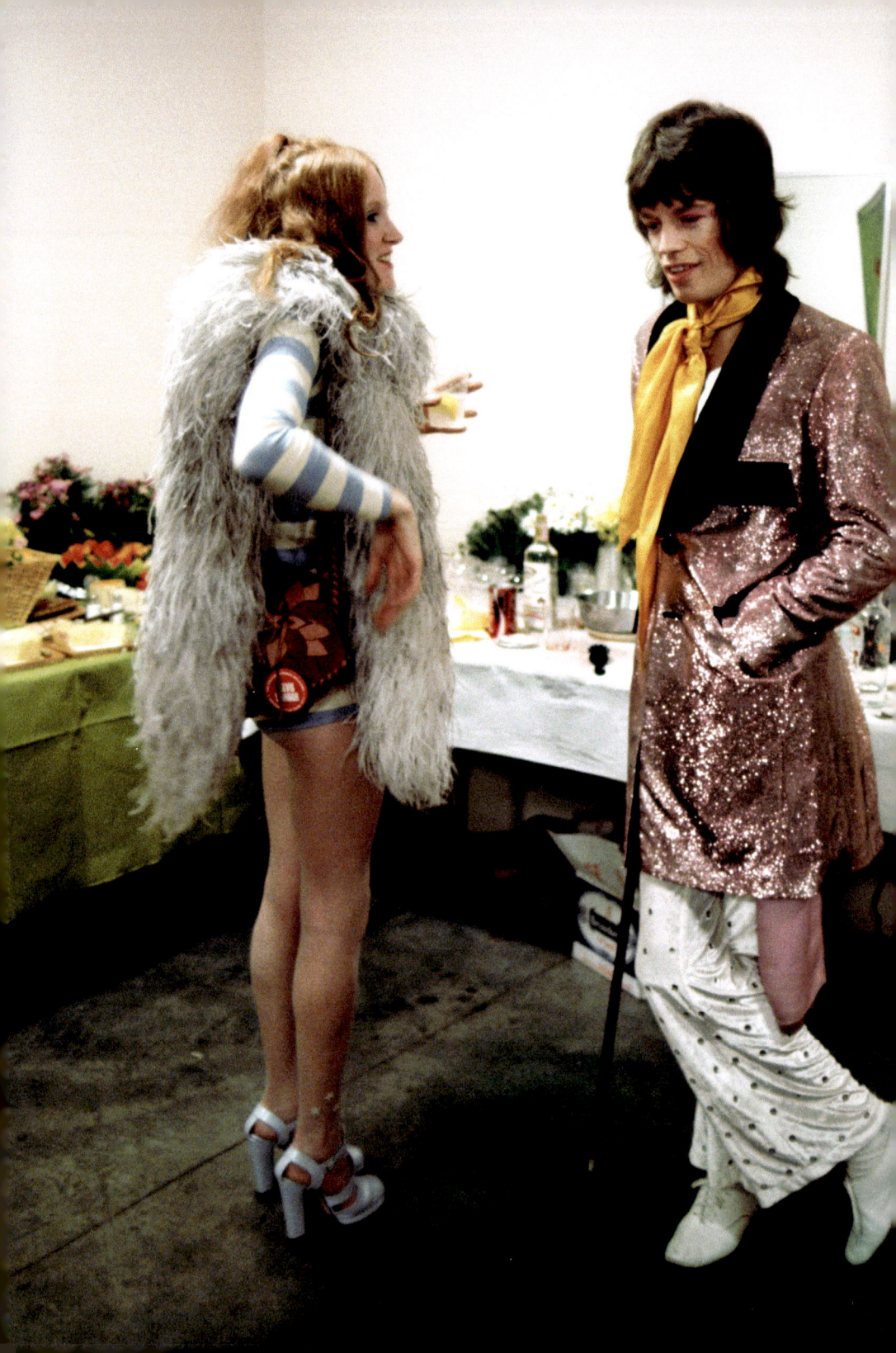

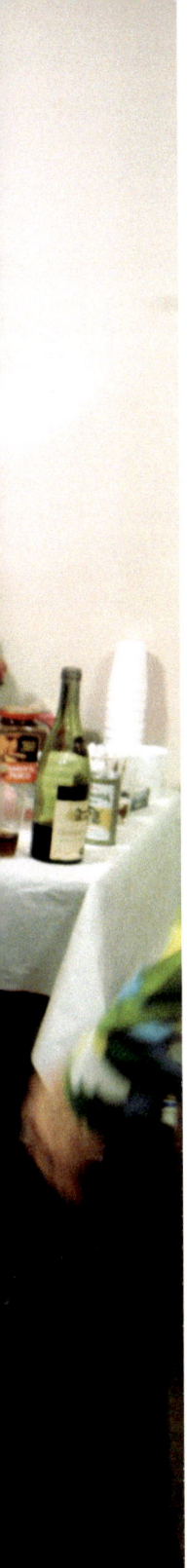

PP. 332–333
Annie Leibovitz
Backstage on the *Exile* tour of the States. Annie Leibovitz (in reflection) was covering the tour for *Rolling Stone* magazine with filmmaker Robert Frank (to the left of Keith).

Jim Marshall
Mick and Mick Taylor's wife Rose before a show at the Los Angeles Forum, 11 June 1972.

PP. 336–337
Jim Marshall
The Stones plus Mick Taylor's wife Rose backstage at the Los Angeles Forum. Stones fever had engulfed Los Angeles prior to the group's two appearances at the venue, with over 350,000 unlucky ticket applicants being disappointed. Nonetheless, those who gained entry saw the Stones on superb form, delivering a 90-minute set of 16 songs starting with "Brown Sugar" and encoring with "Honky Tonk Women".

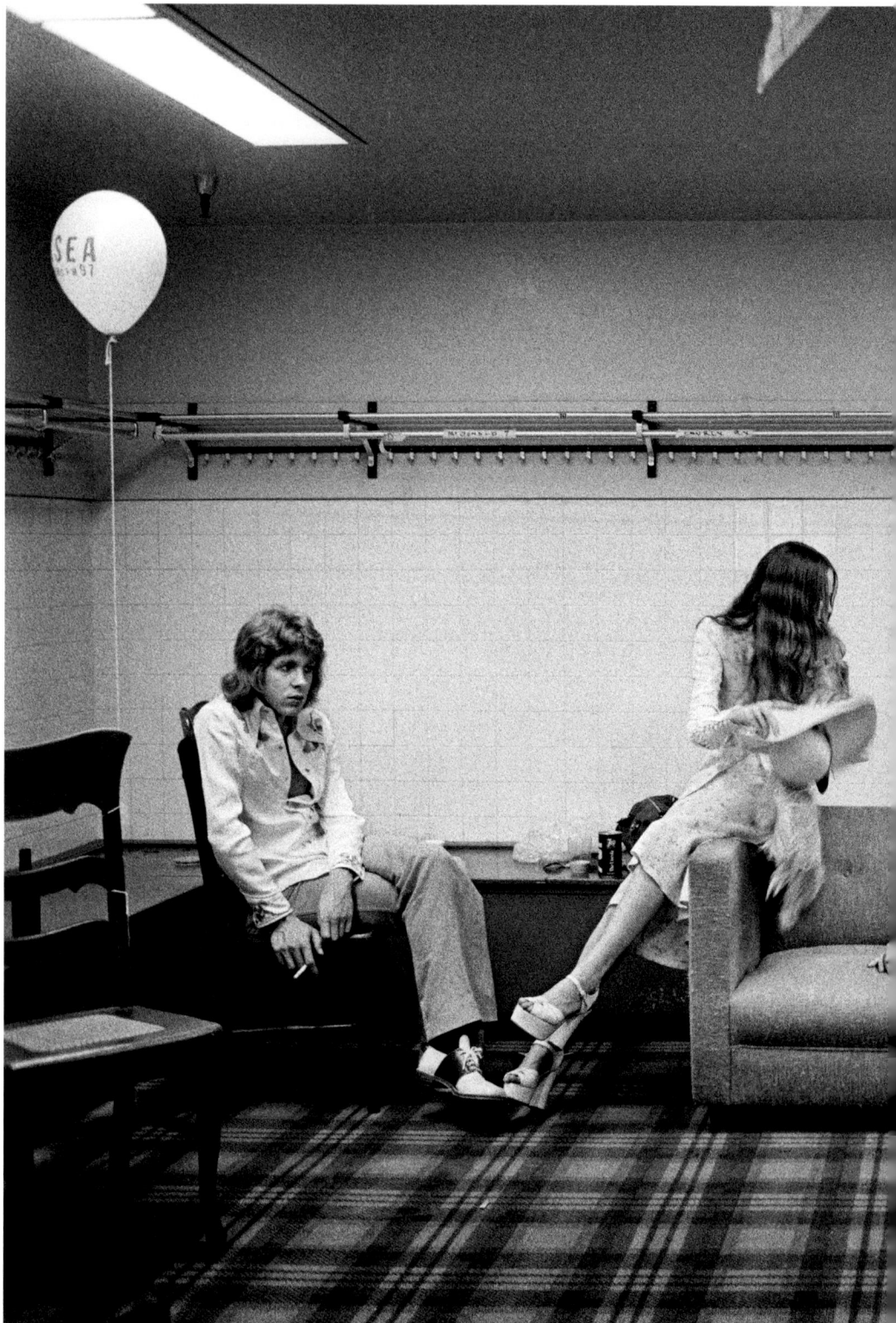

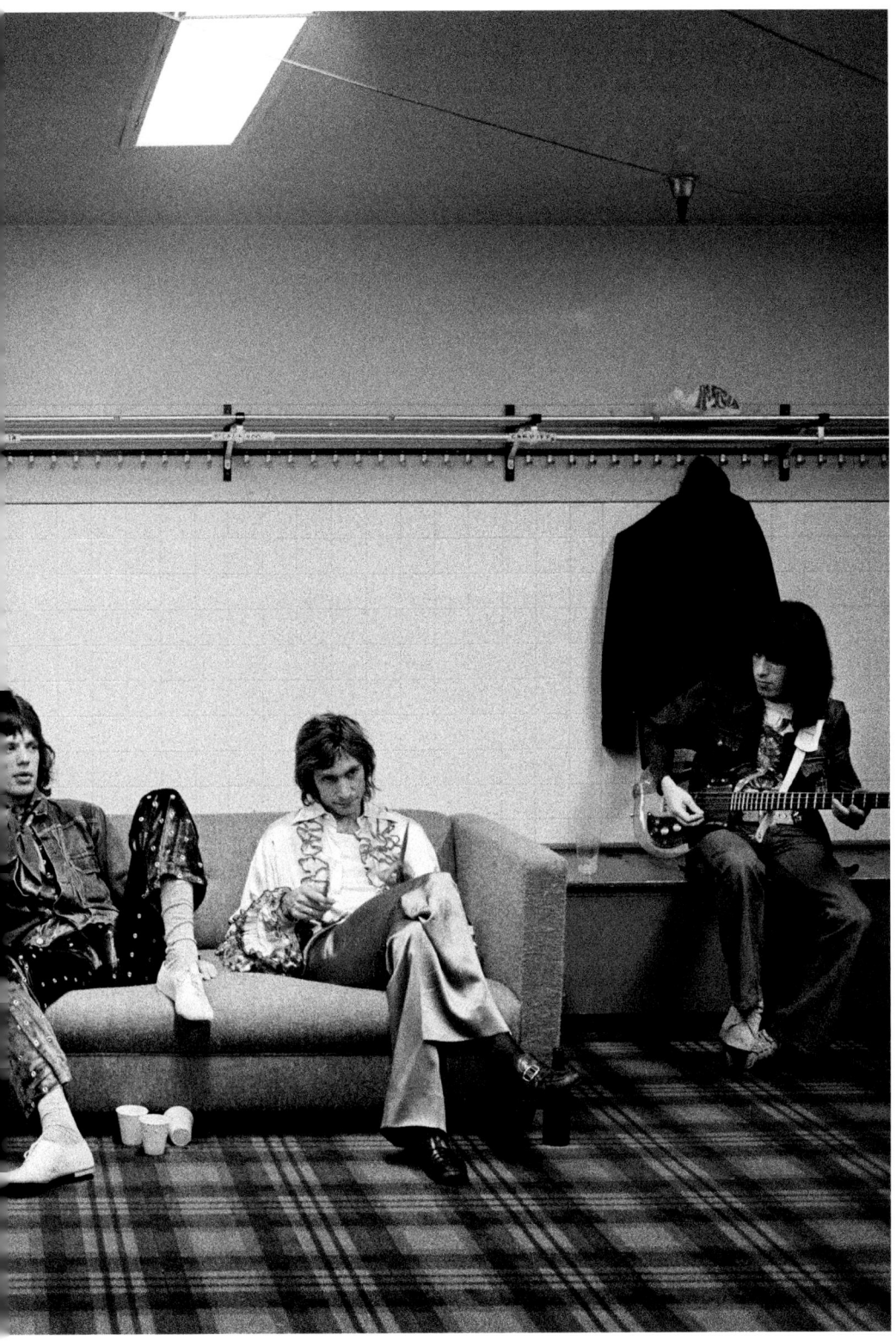

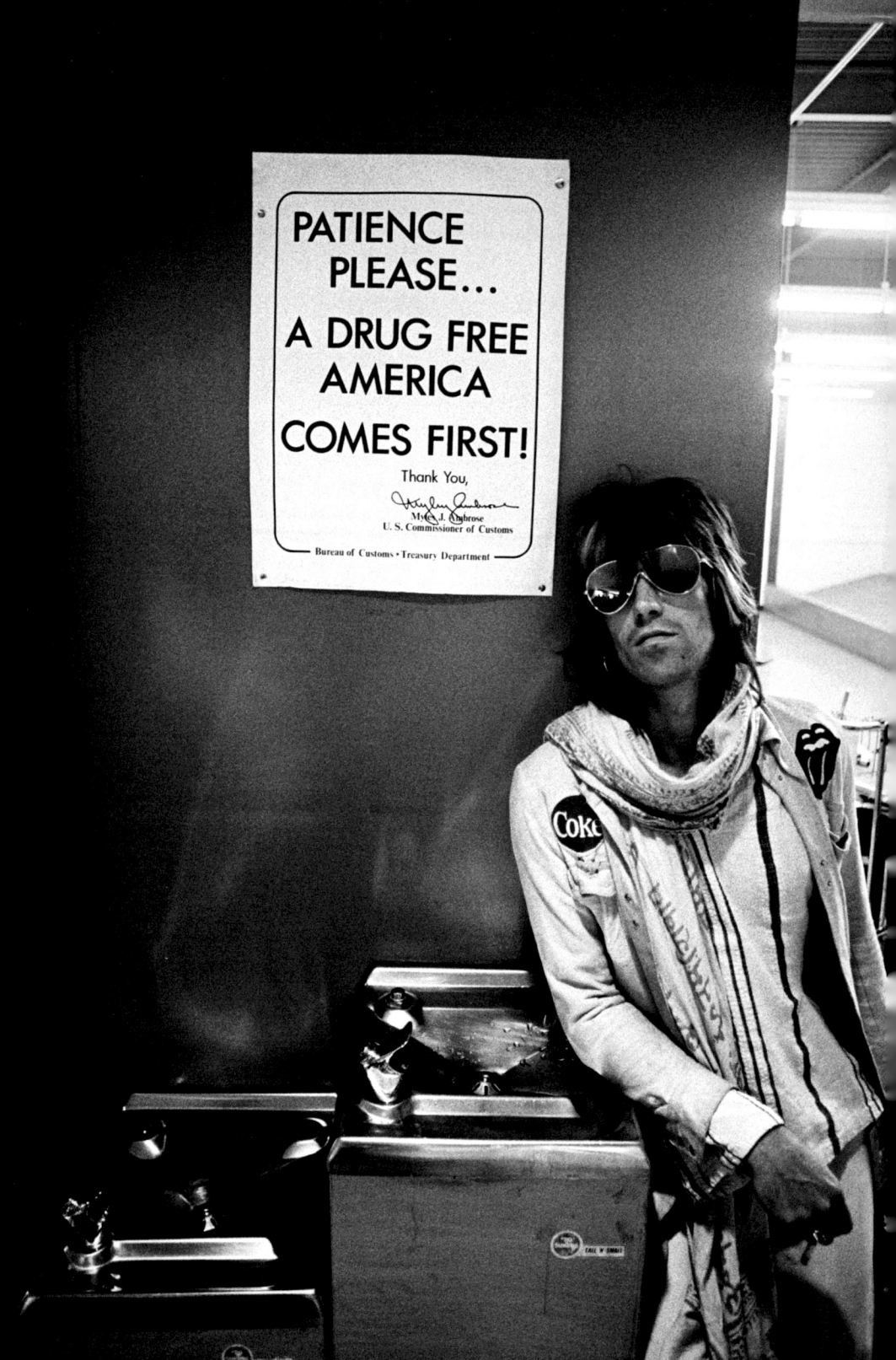

Ethan Russell

The exhaustive *Exile* tour of the States did have its lighter moments, such as here, en route from Vancouver to Seattle, 4 June 1972. The *San Francisco Chronicle* described the image as "one of the great rock photos of all time".

Ethan Russell

Exile tour, June–July 1972.

"At certain moments he [Jagger] wanders dazed like Frankenstein's monster, dying for a recharge. He gulps for air, hands twitching, legs crumbling, body bending, waving kisses and shaking fingers, whirling sweat like a lawn sprinkler." Newsweek, 7 August 1972

PP. 342–343
Ethan Russell

Keith and Mick backstage at the Los Angeles Forum, 11 June 1972.

PP. 344–345
Ethan Russell

On stage during the *Exile* tour of the States, June–July 1972. Jack Daniels, Keith's preferred bourbon: the symbiosis between musician and alcohol has never been better defined.

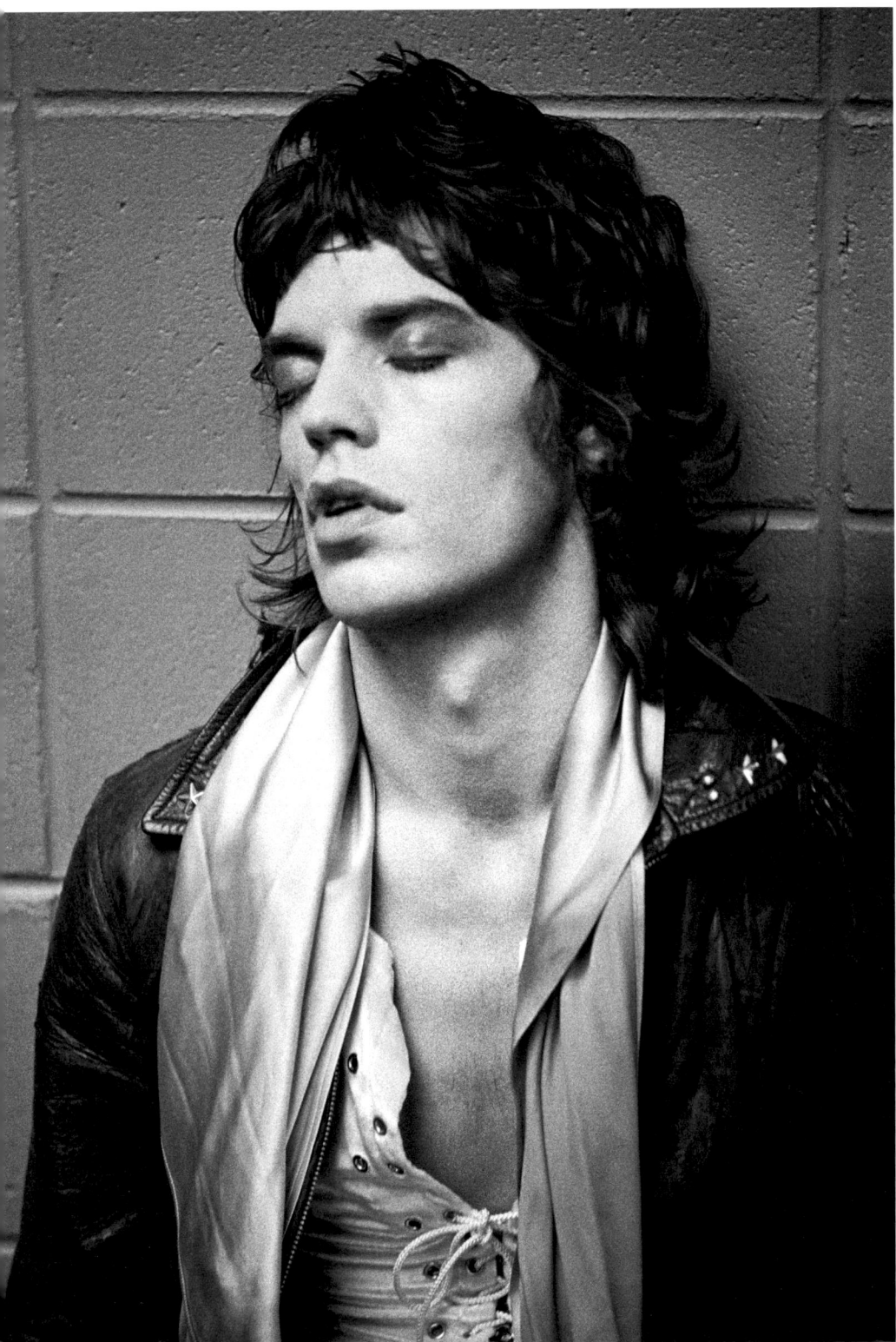

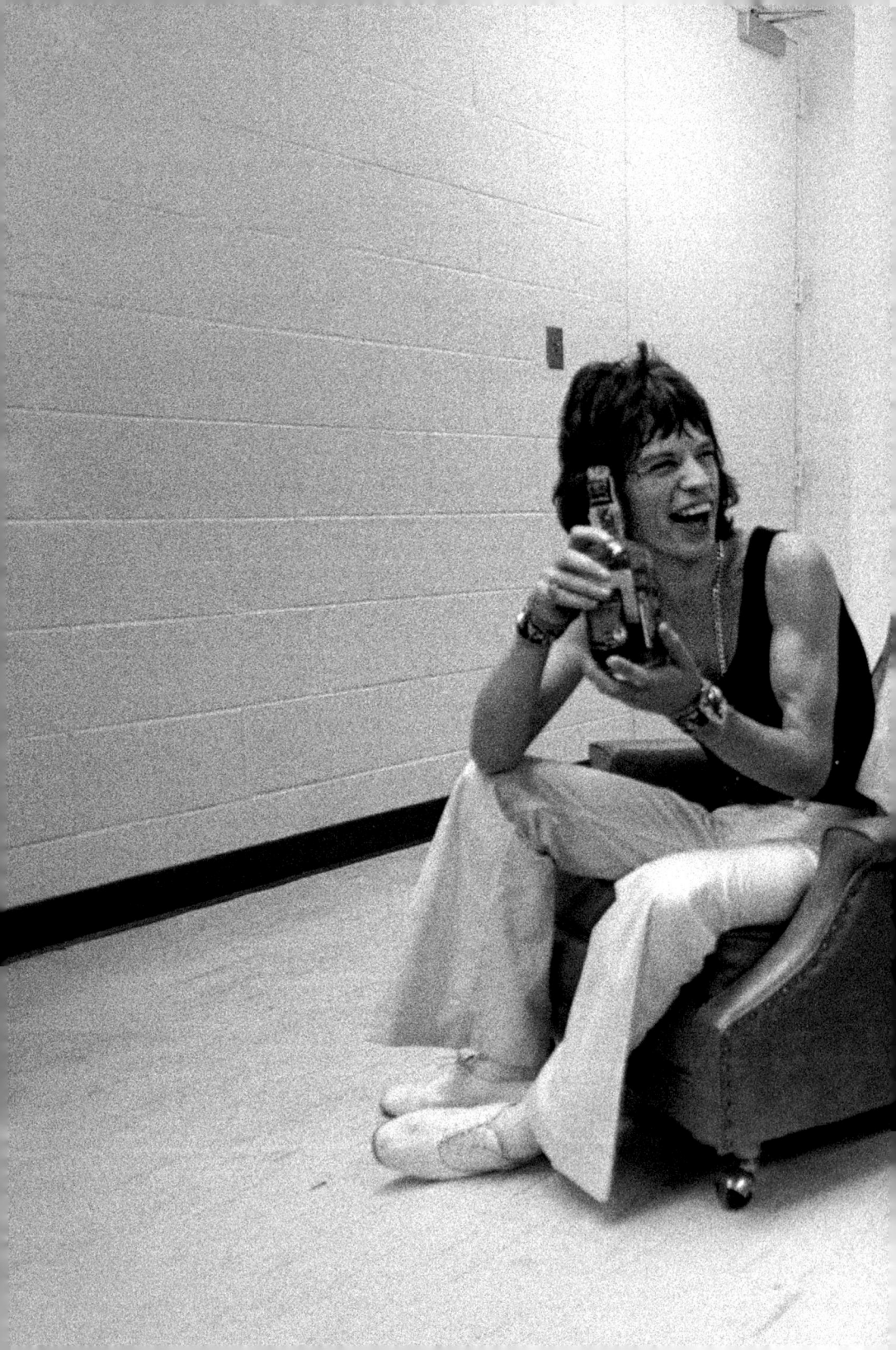

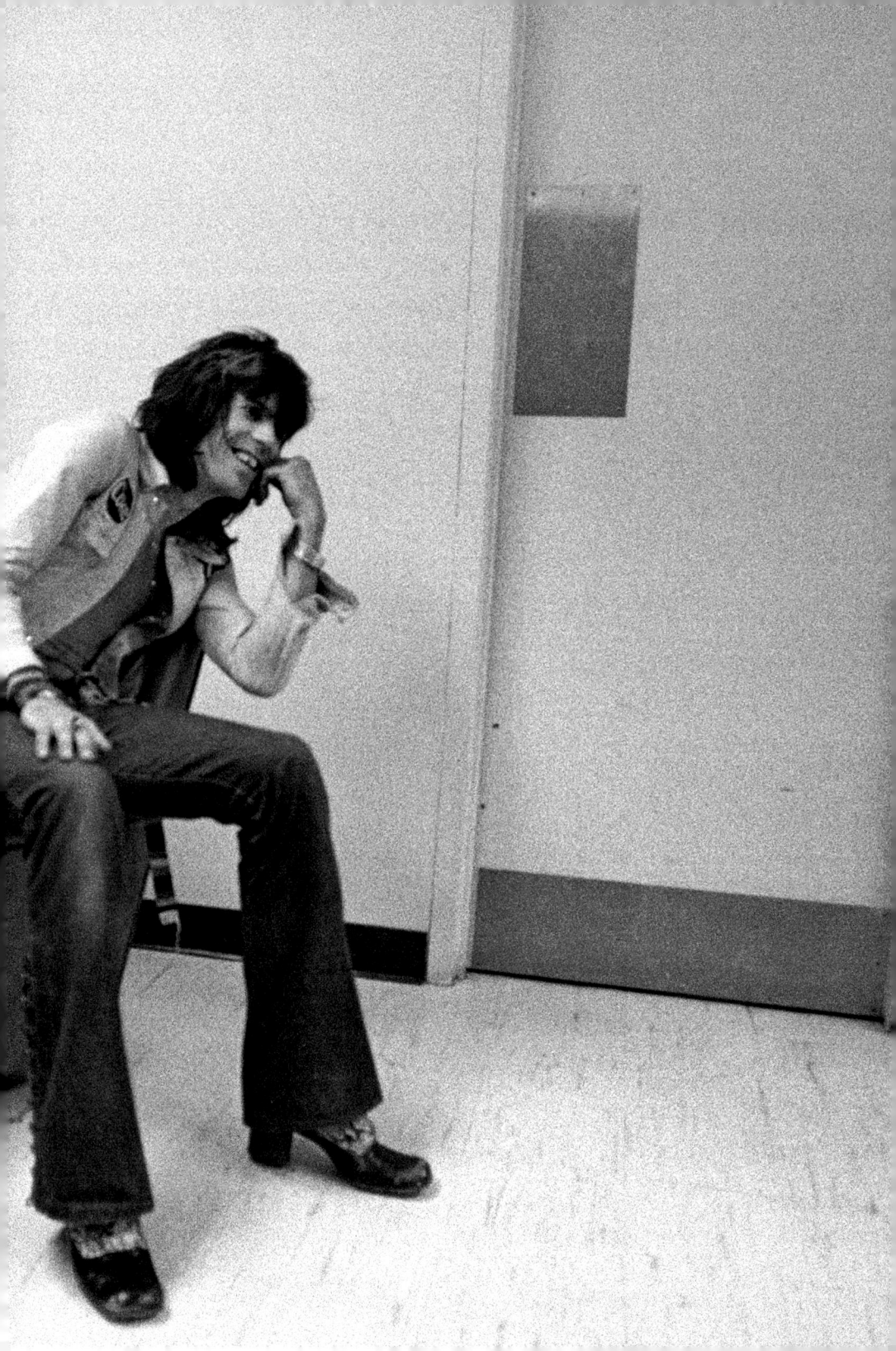

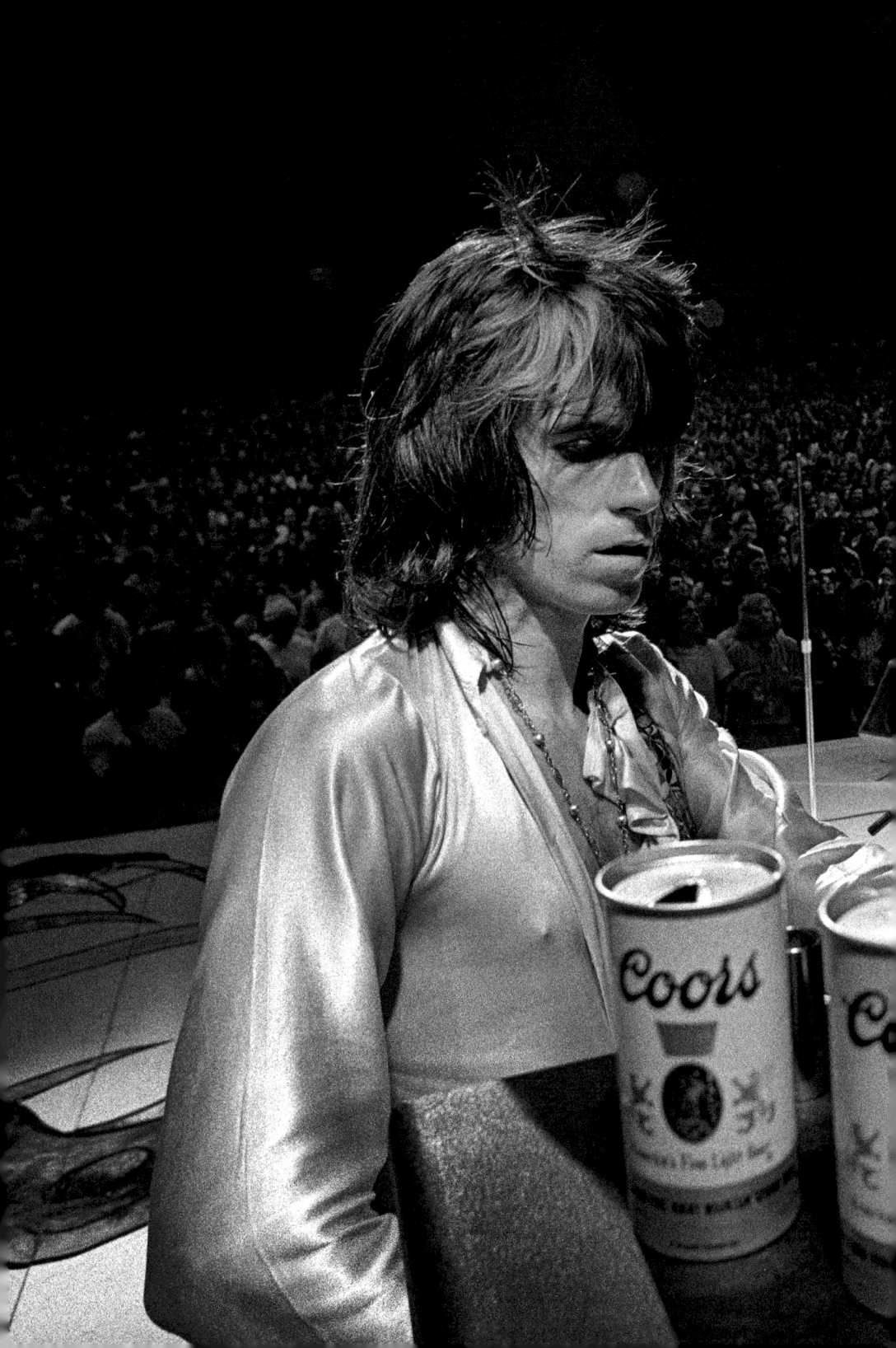

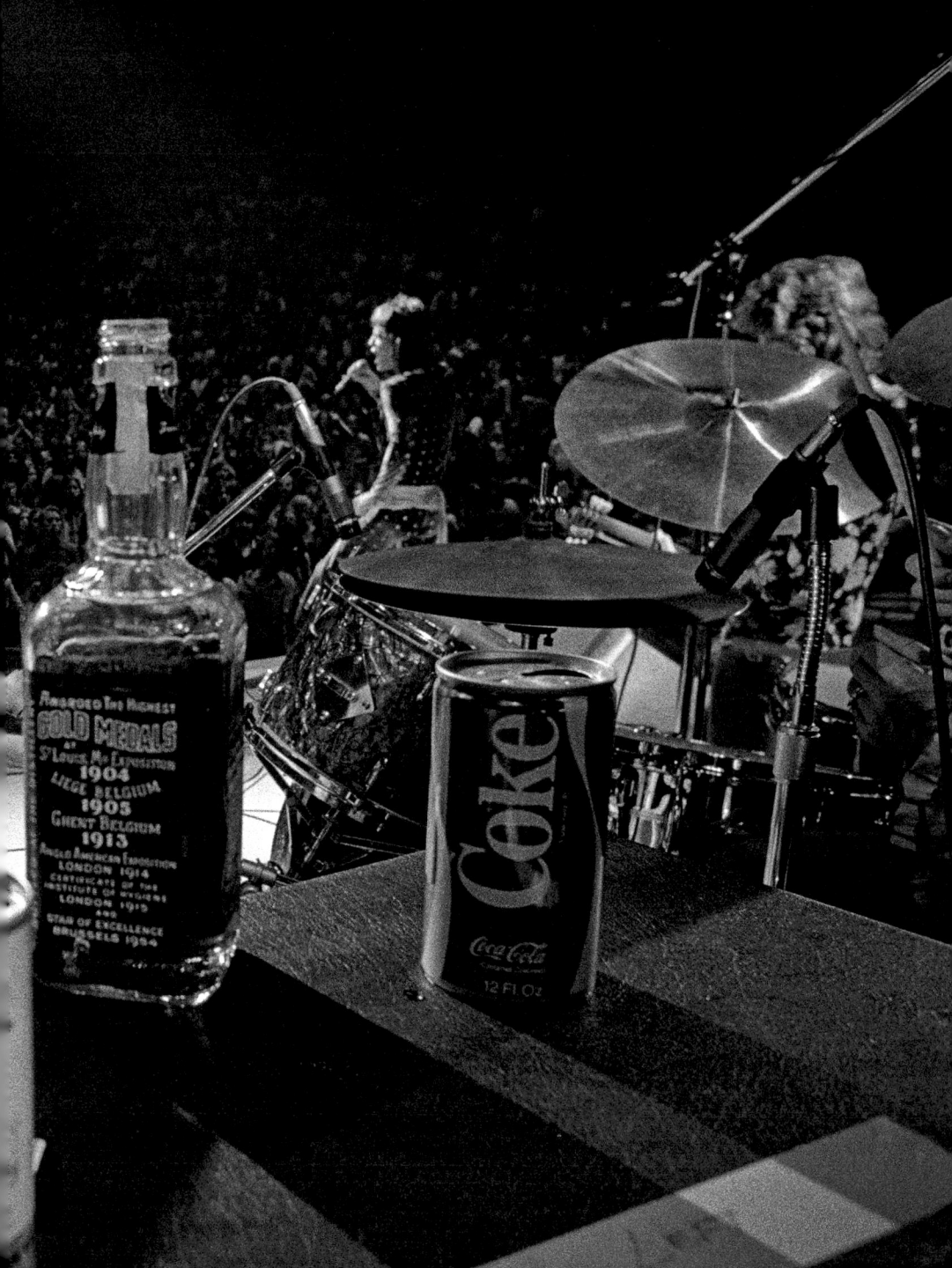

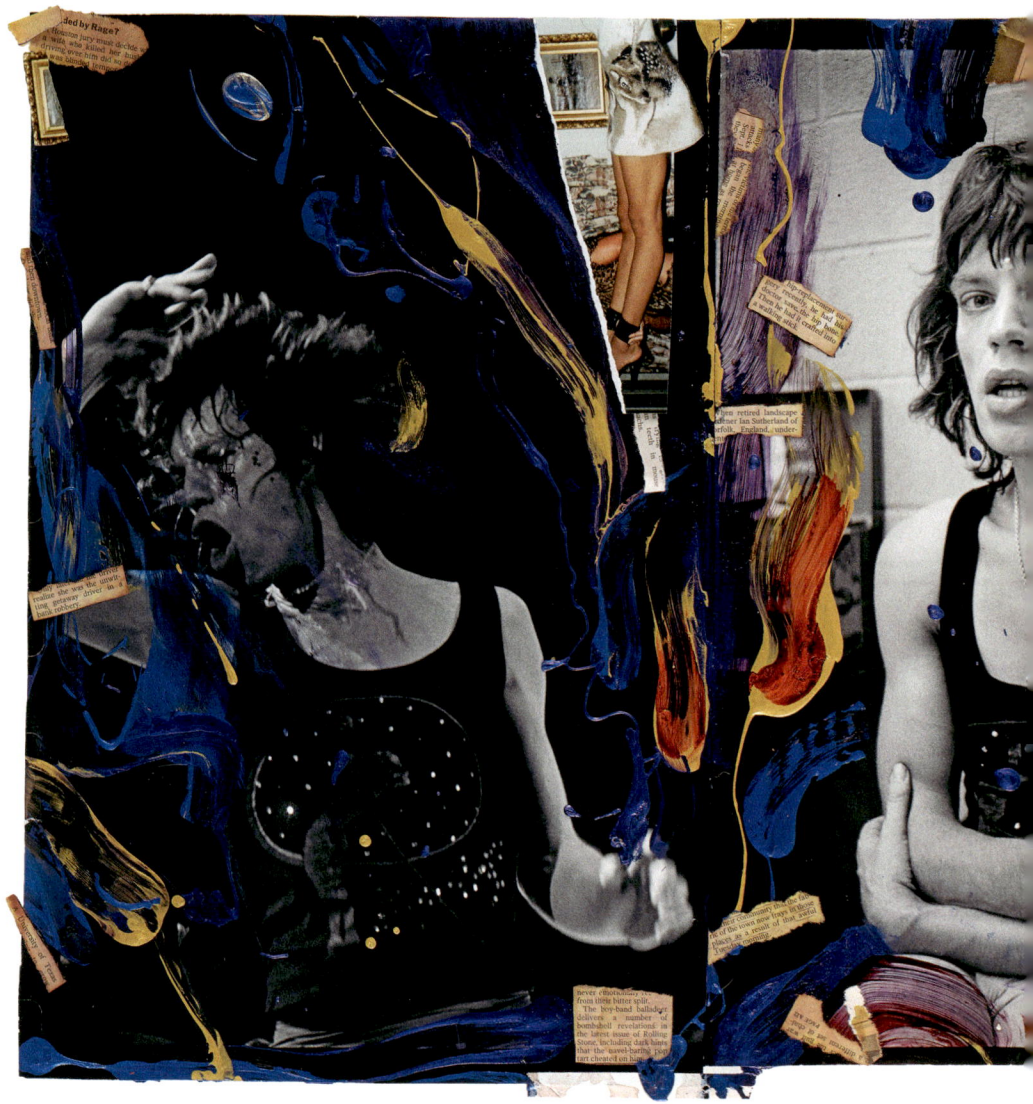

Peter Beard

Peter Beard and Truman Capote's brief was to document the action as it unfolded for *Rolling Stone* magazine, June–July 1972.
"*Somewhere in Illinois, we have seen an array of folk art representing a dark storm threatening farmers in full harvest. It was titled 'It Shall Soon Be Here,' literally, 'It will not be long.' Truman told me: 'This is our way.' It was rather appropriate, because when you think about it, all the states where the Stones were due to visit were also waiting impatiently.*" Peter Beard, *PB2*, 2006

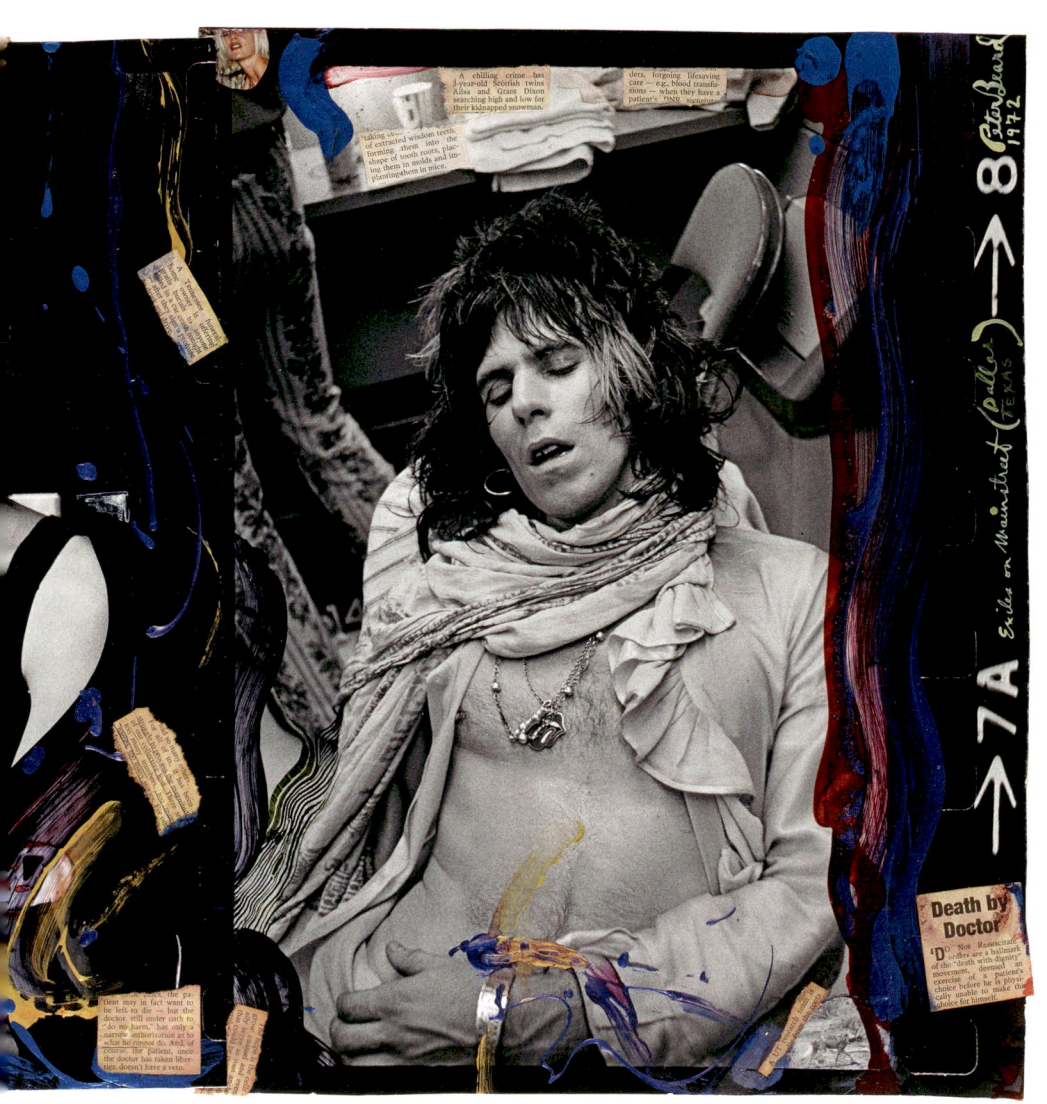

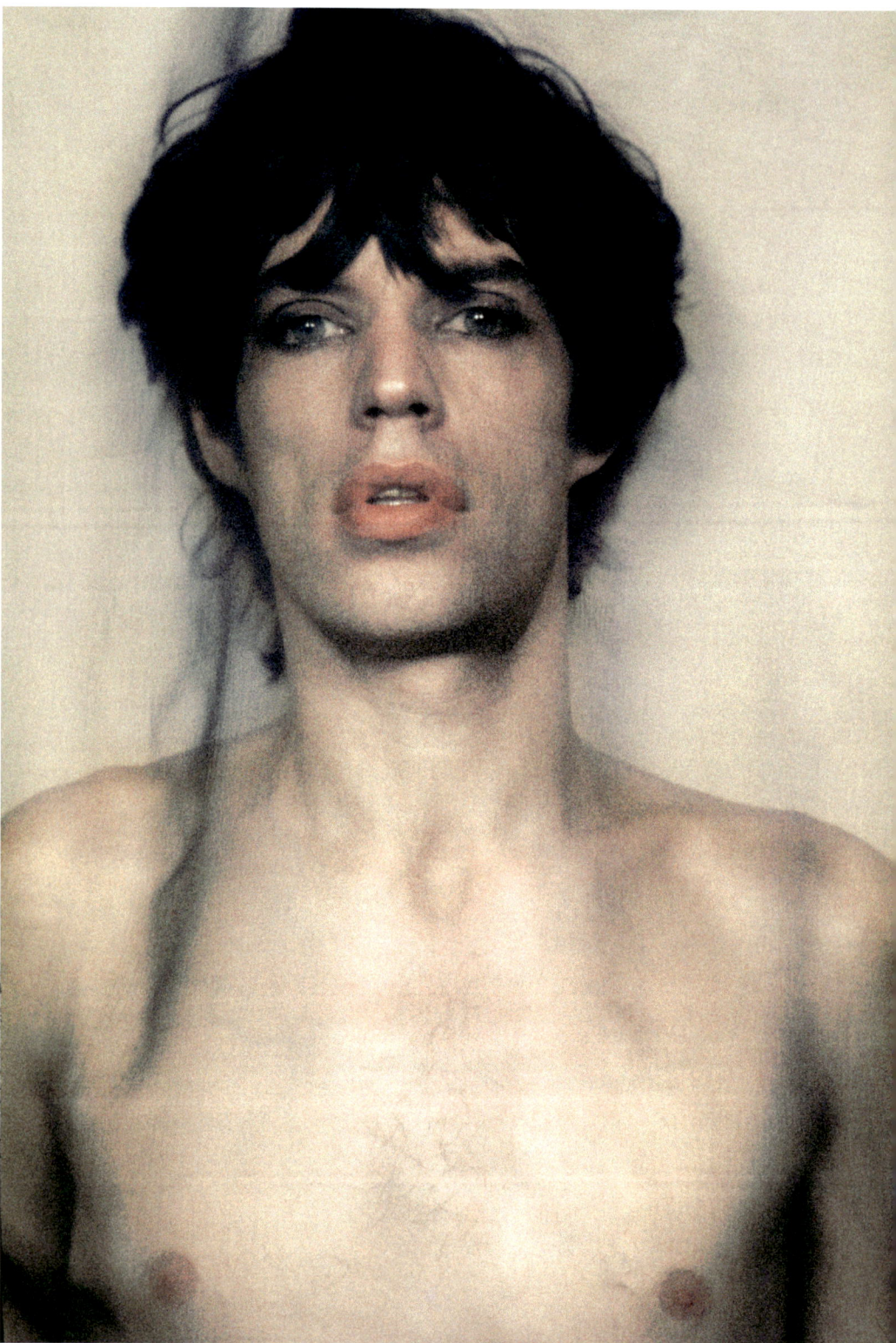

David Bailey
Hampstead, London, 6 June 1973.
With convoluted tax issues still requiring exile
from the UK, in November 1972 the decision was
taken to record in Jamaica. Its edgy ambience
proved conducive for capturing the diverse
sounds on *Goats Head Soup*. Unlike the pro-
tracted sessions for *Exile On Main St*, recording
Goats Head Soup was swift and productive –
requiring a minimum of post-production work.
*"It amazed me, as an old-time record guy, that
the Stones might not have played together for six
or eight months, but within an hour of jamming,
the synergy that is their strength would come
into play and they would lock it together as one."*
Marshall Chess, quoted in *According To The
Rolling Stones*, 2003

PP. 350–351
David Bailey
On 6 June 1973 the Stones arrived at Bailey's
studio in Hampstead, north London for a shoot;
the images would later adorn the *Goats Head
Soup* gatefold album sleeve.

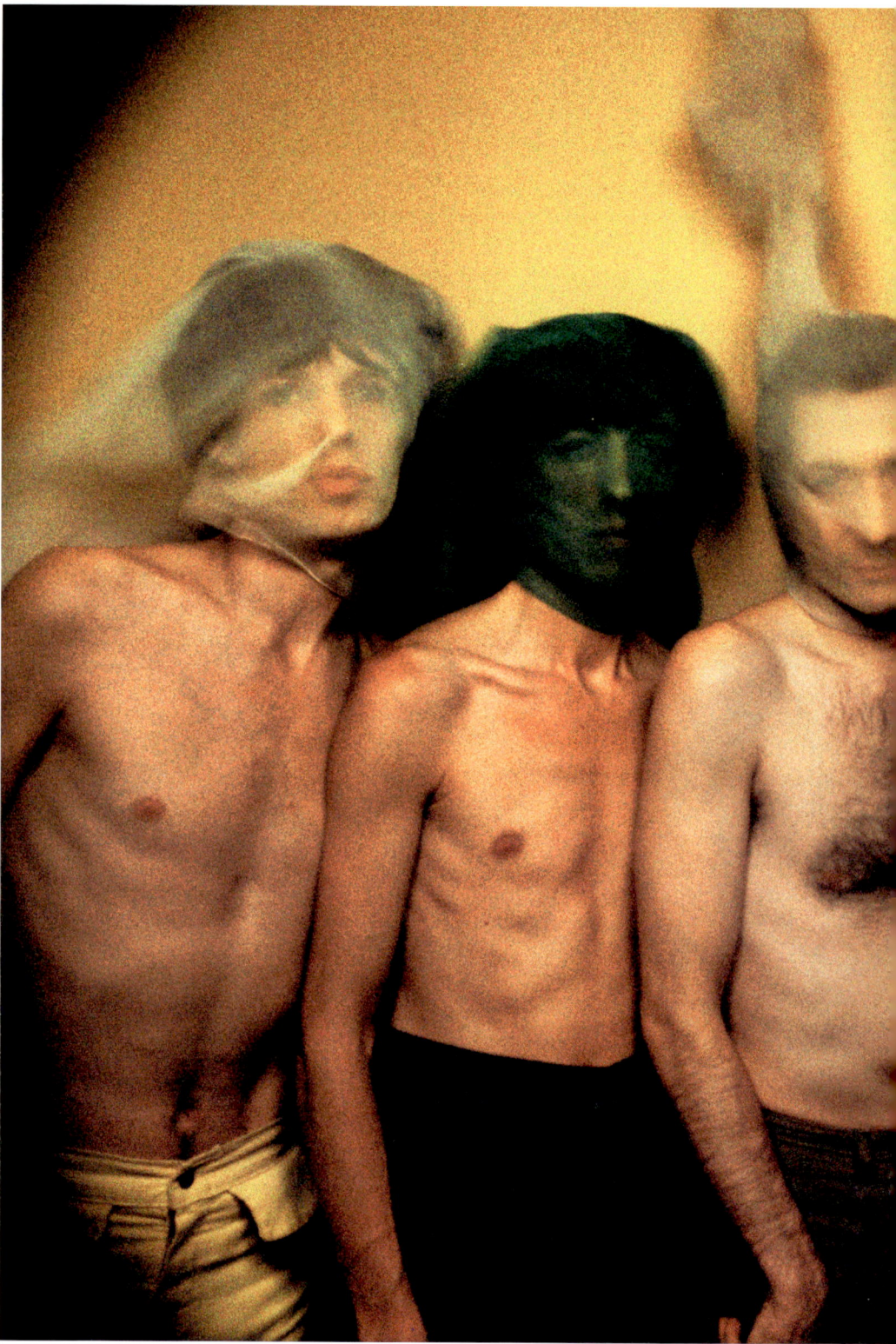

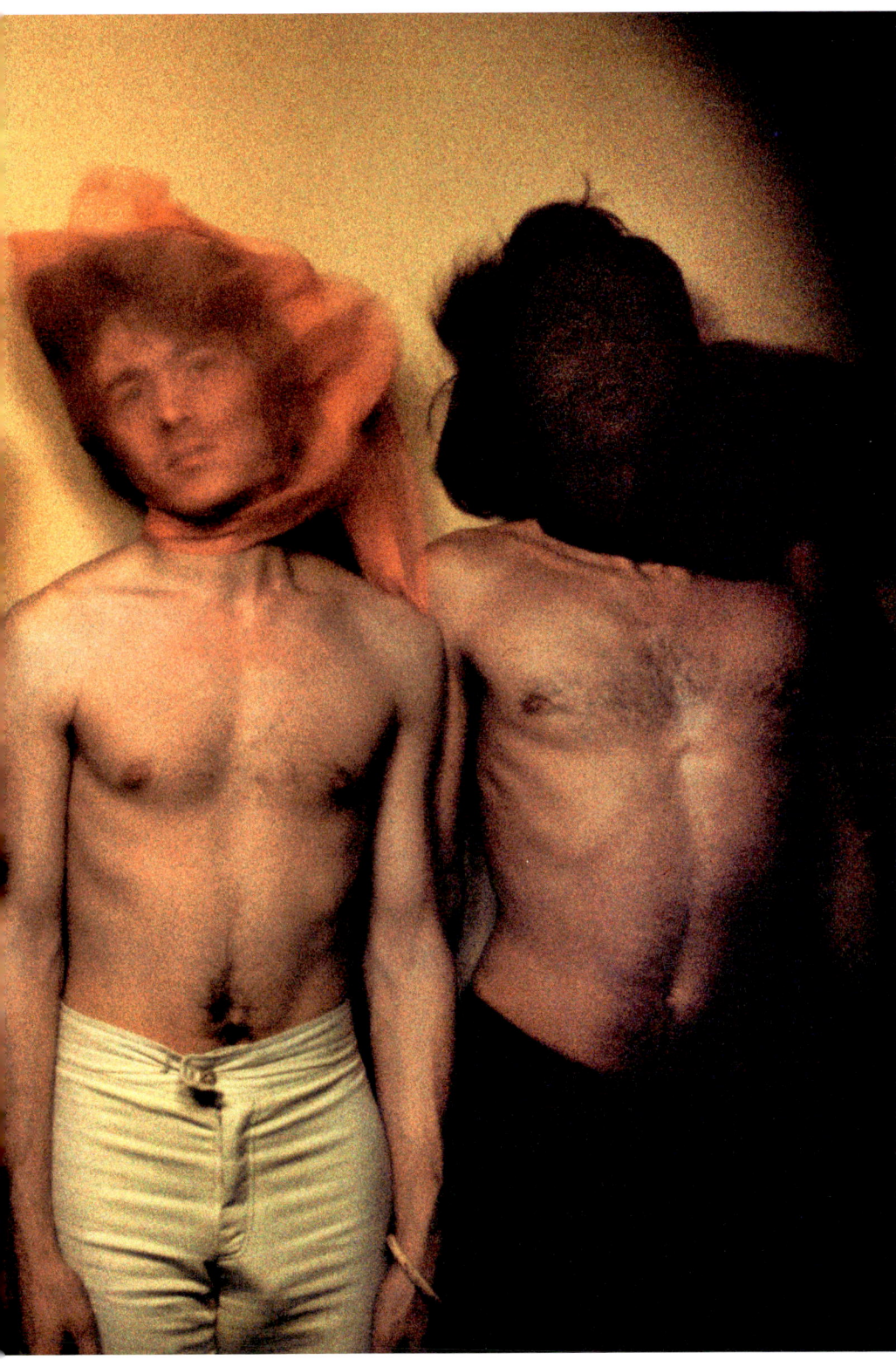

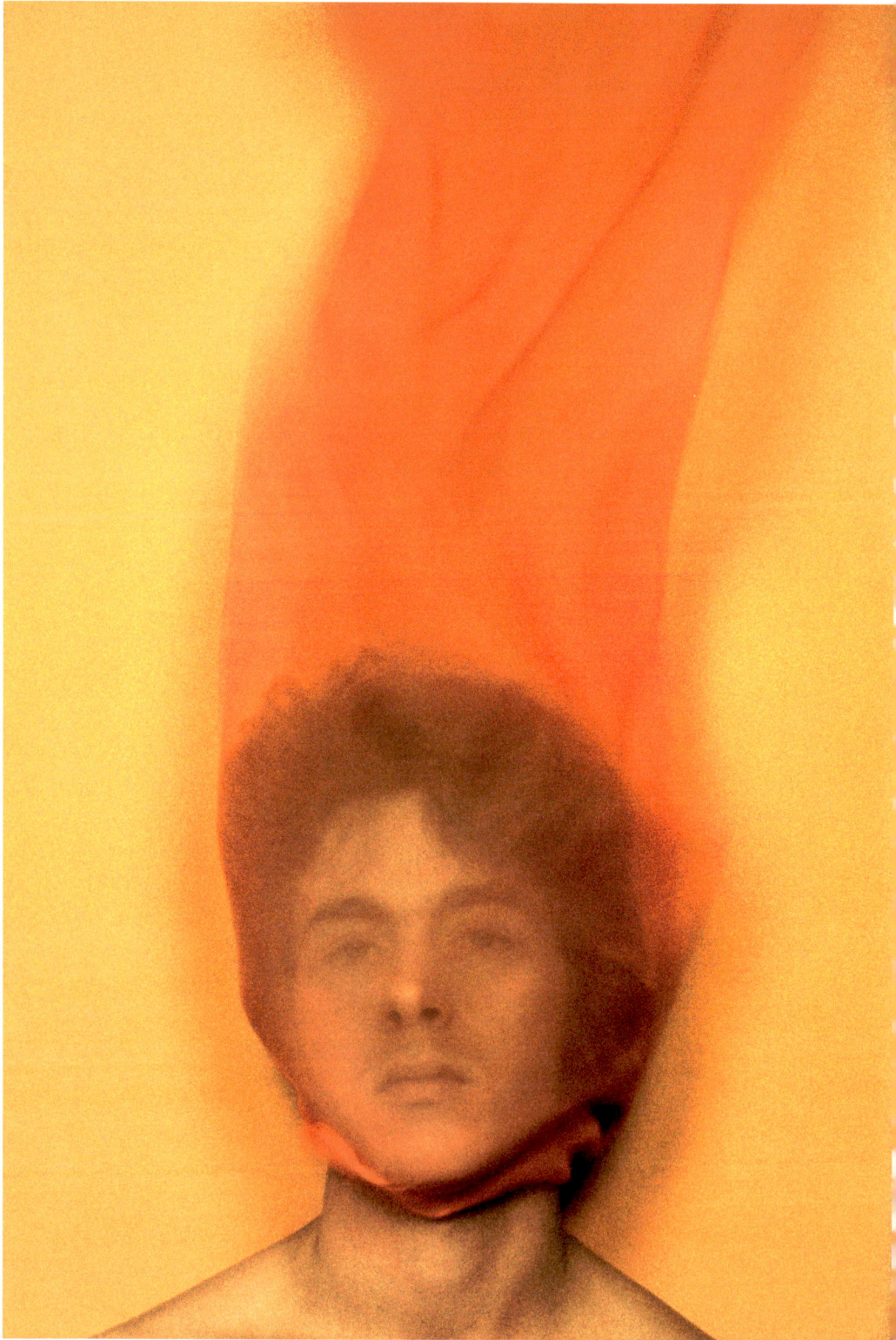

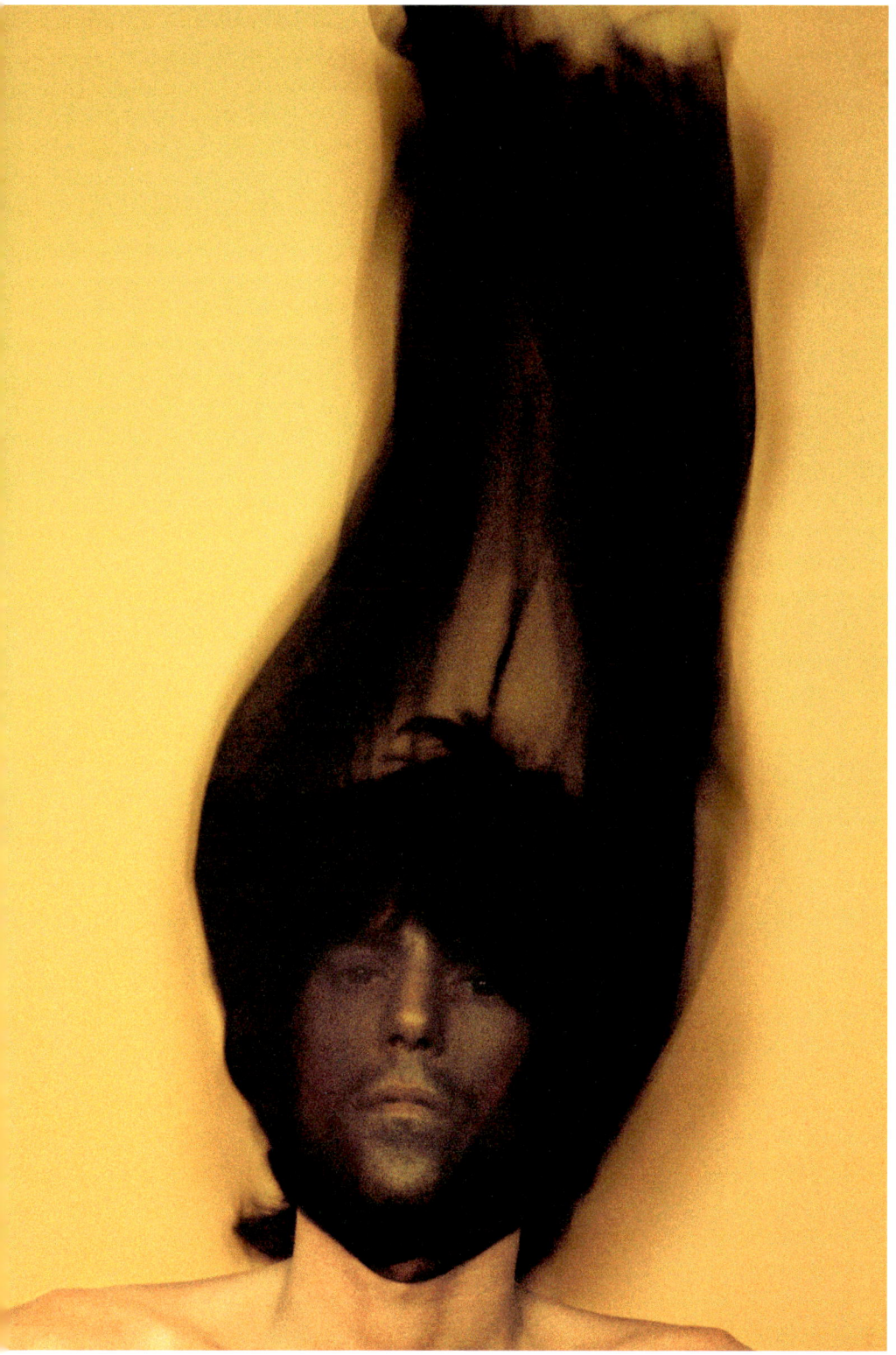

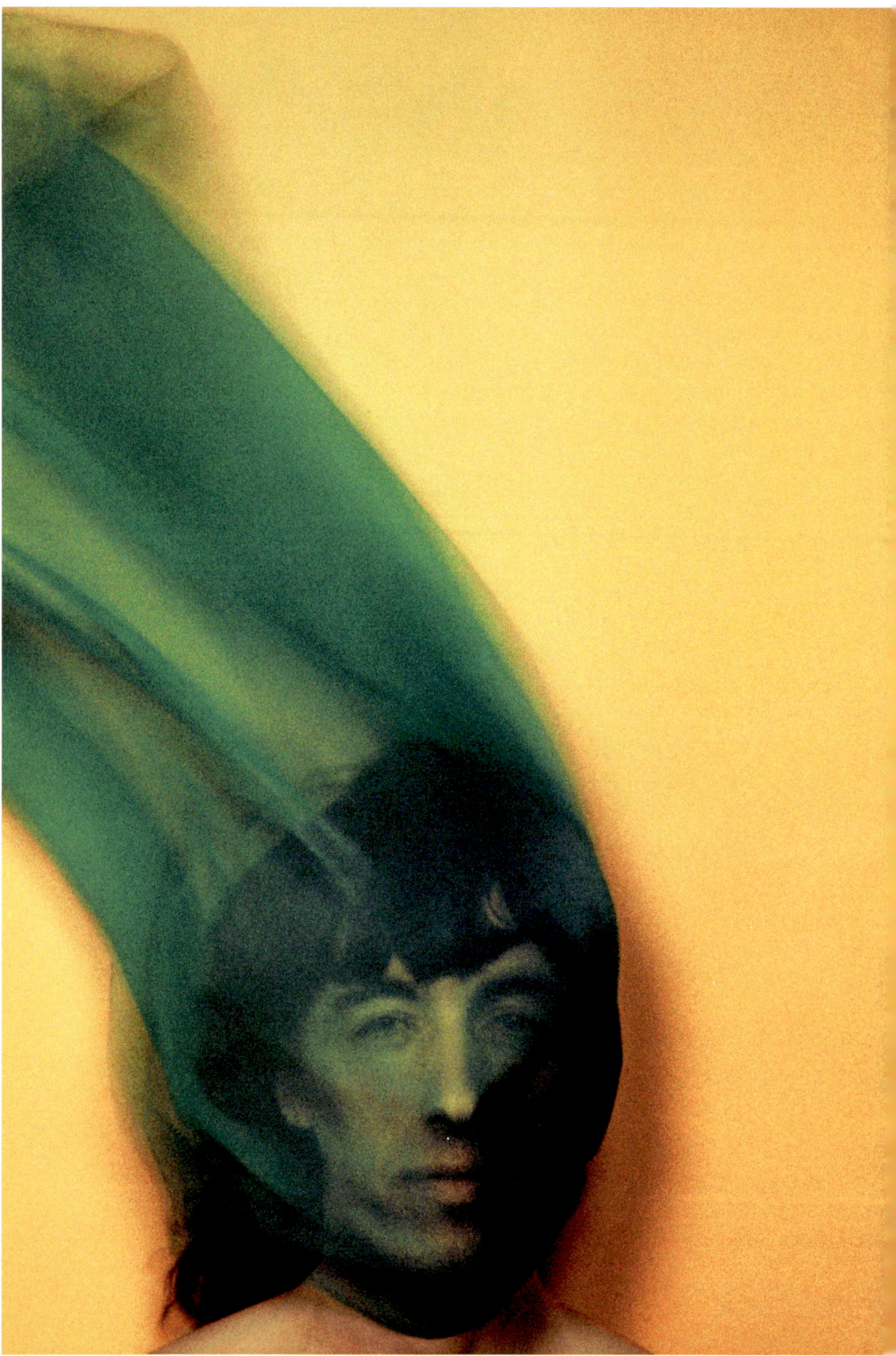

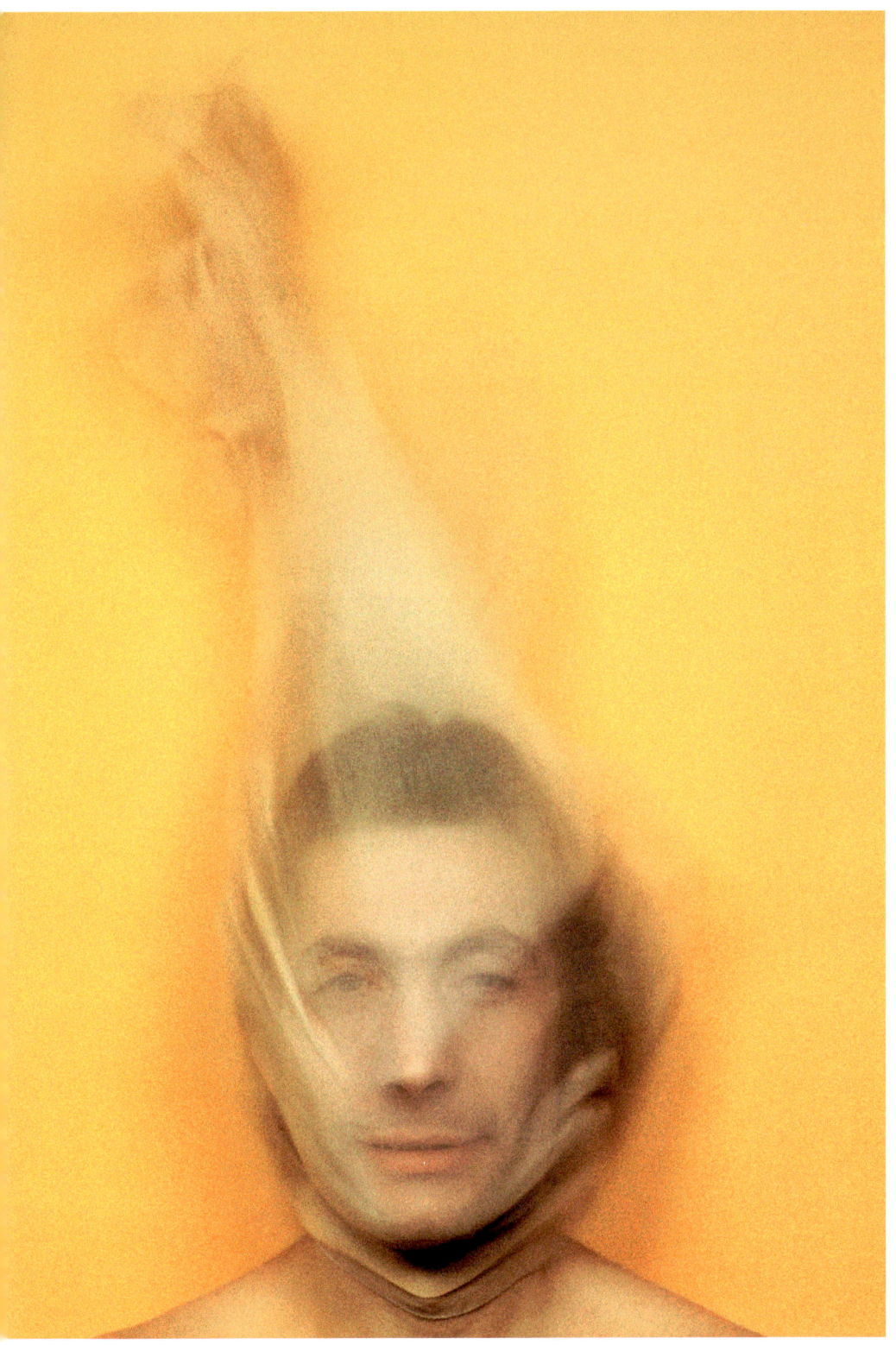

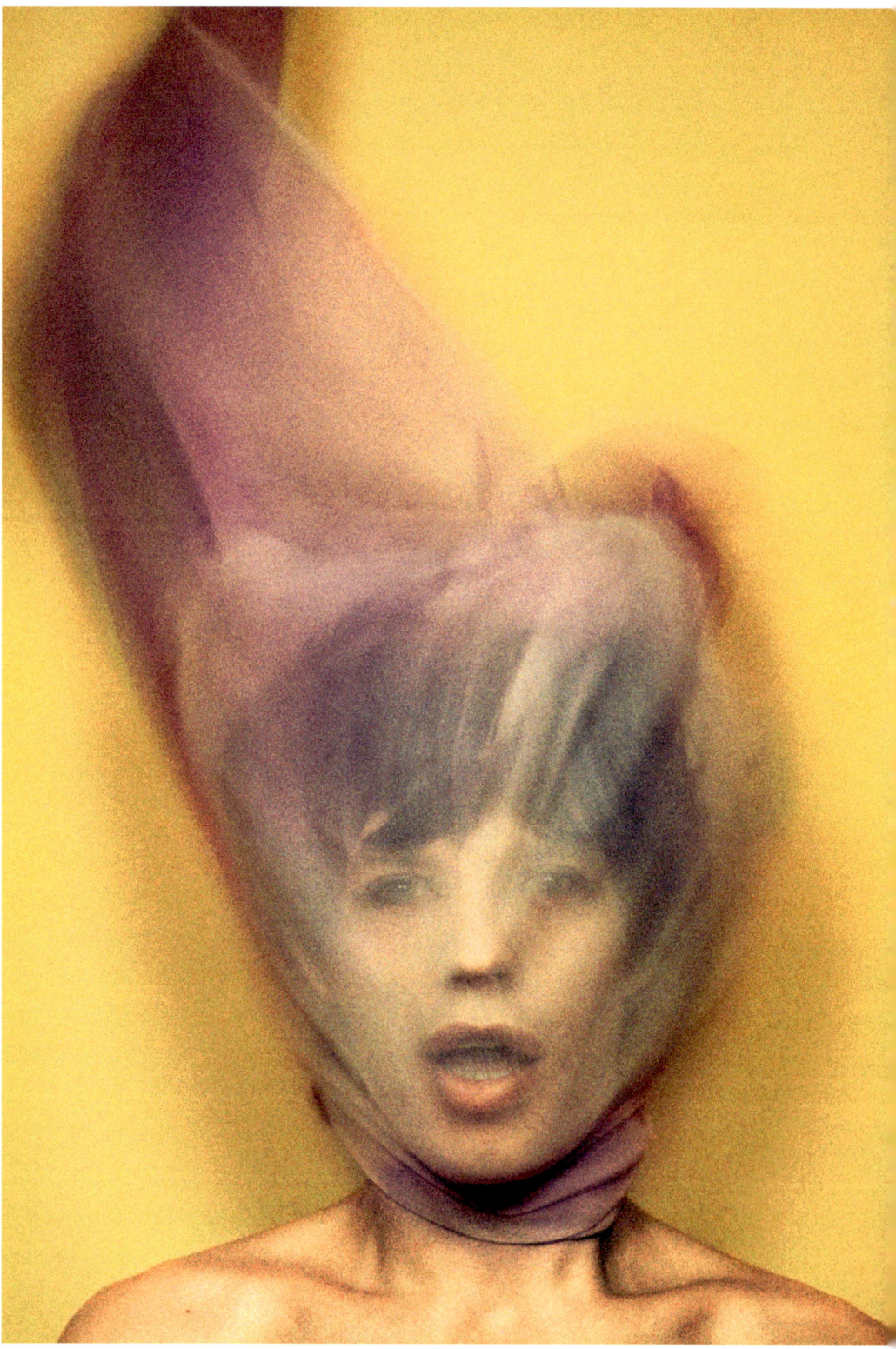

PP. 352–356
David Bailey
Led by the haunting ballad "Angie", *Goats Head Soup* proved a slight departure from the sound most associated with the band. Following sessions in Kingston, Jamaica, during late 1972, the band completed the recordings in London and Los Angeles with the aid of trusted session men such as Bobby Keys, Billy Preston and Nicky Hopkins.
"On the strength of this album, there seems no more reason to dispute the Stones' title as the 'Greatest Rock'n'Roll Band in the World' than to dispute the pre-eminence of the Rolls-Royce motor car." Sounds magazine, 8 September 1973

PP. 358–359
Christopher Simon Sykes
Dallas, 6 July 1975, during the *Tour of the Americas*. With temperatures hovering over the 100-degree mark, the 51,000 fans at the Cotton Bowl were in for a highly charged evening.

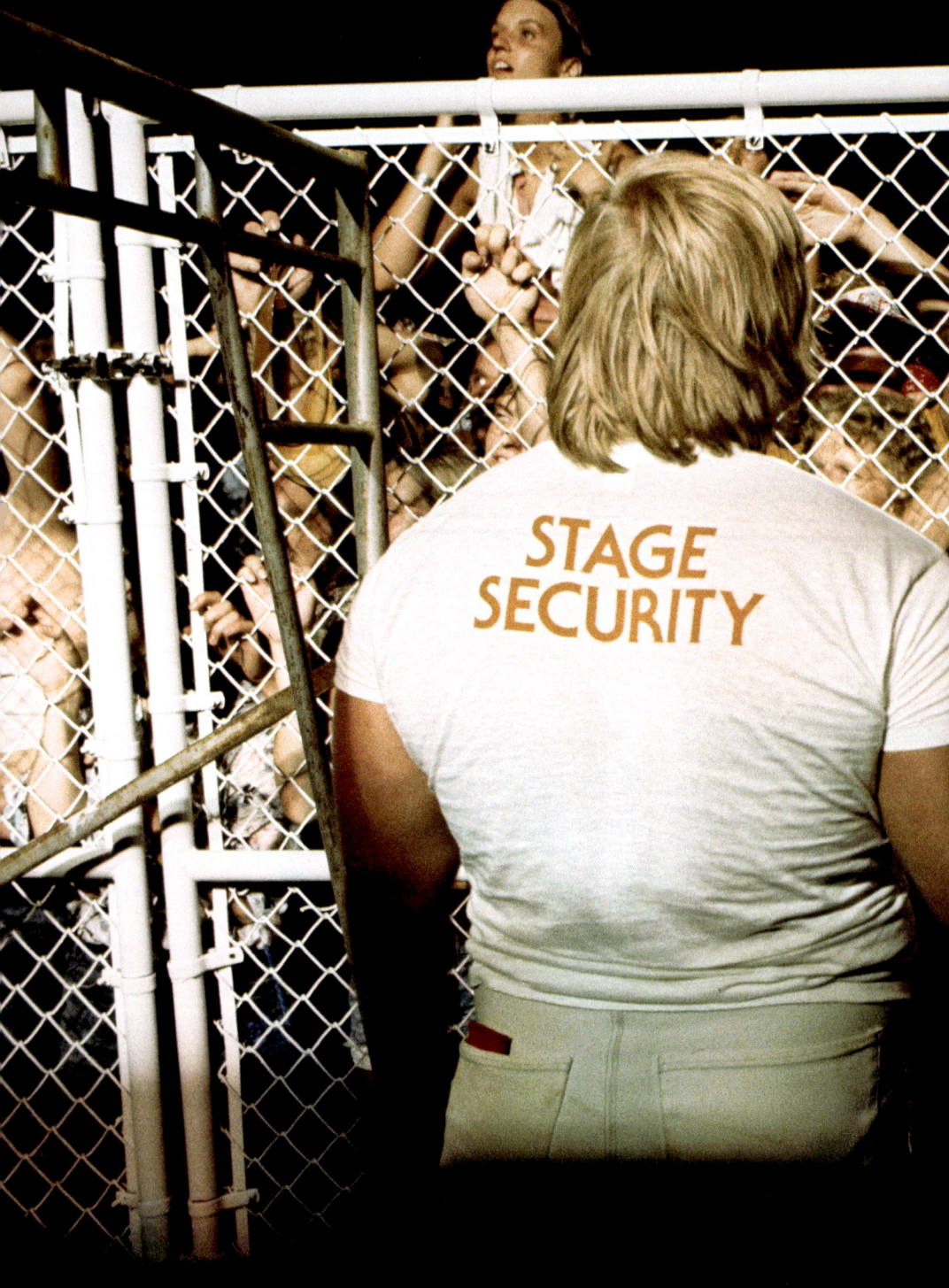

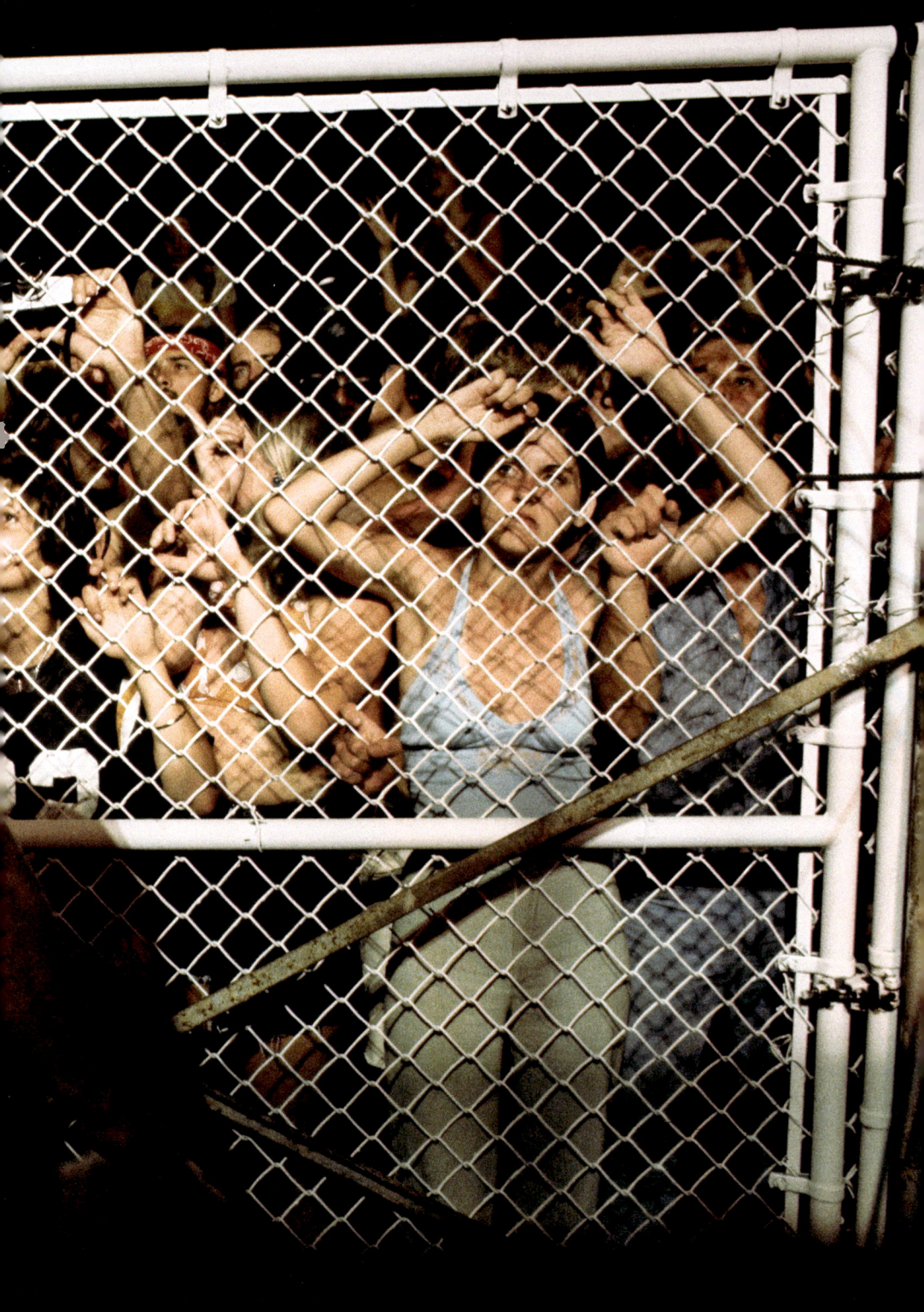

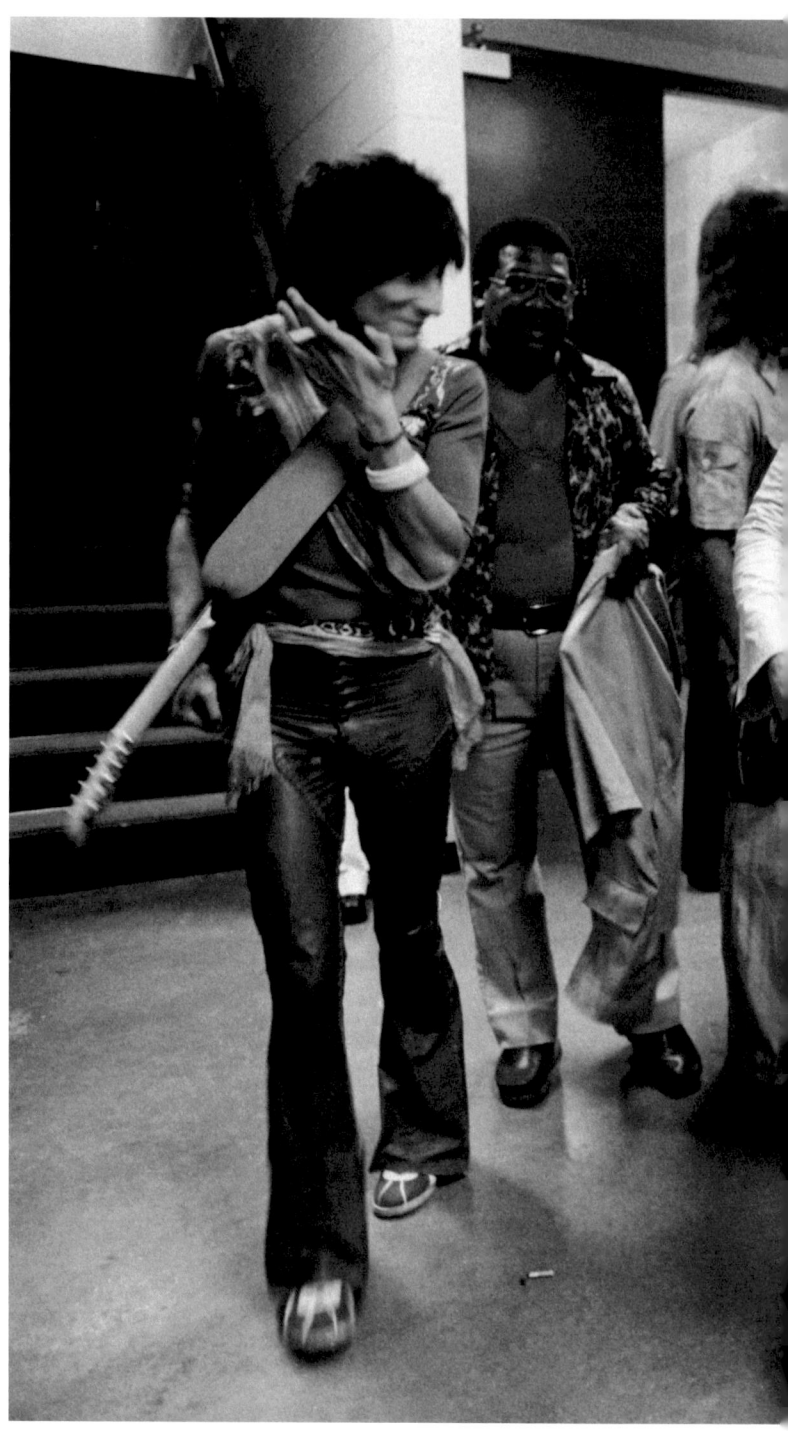

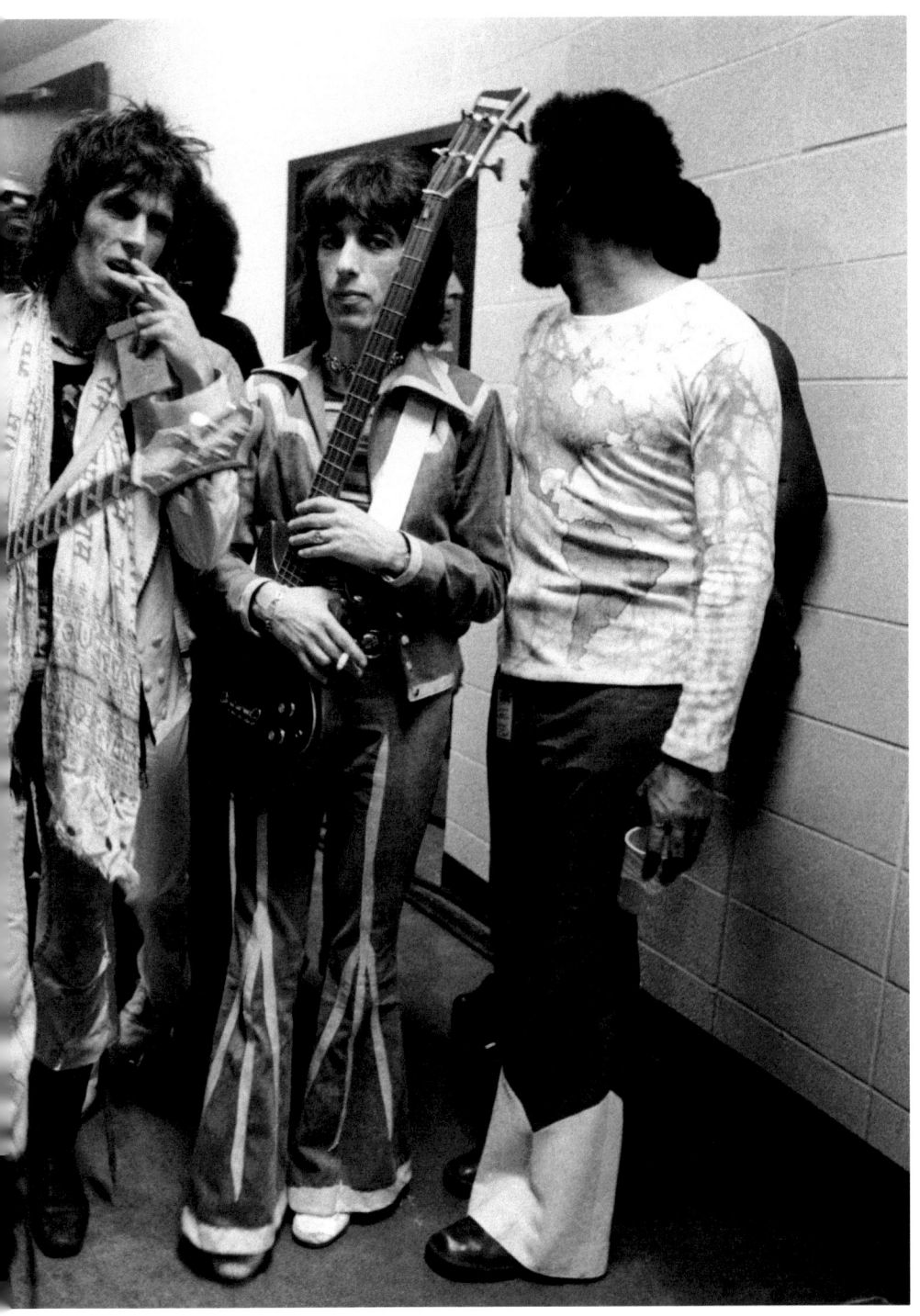

PP. 360–361

Christopher Simon Sykes
Emerging from the dressing room before
hitting the stage for another date on the 1975
Tour of the Americas.

Christopher Simon Sykes
Mick enacting a cricket bowling stance back-
stage at the Chicago Stadium on 23 July 1975.
Grossing in excess of $10 million, the 1975 North
American tour upstaged all expectations.

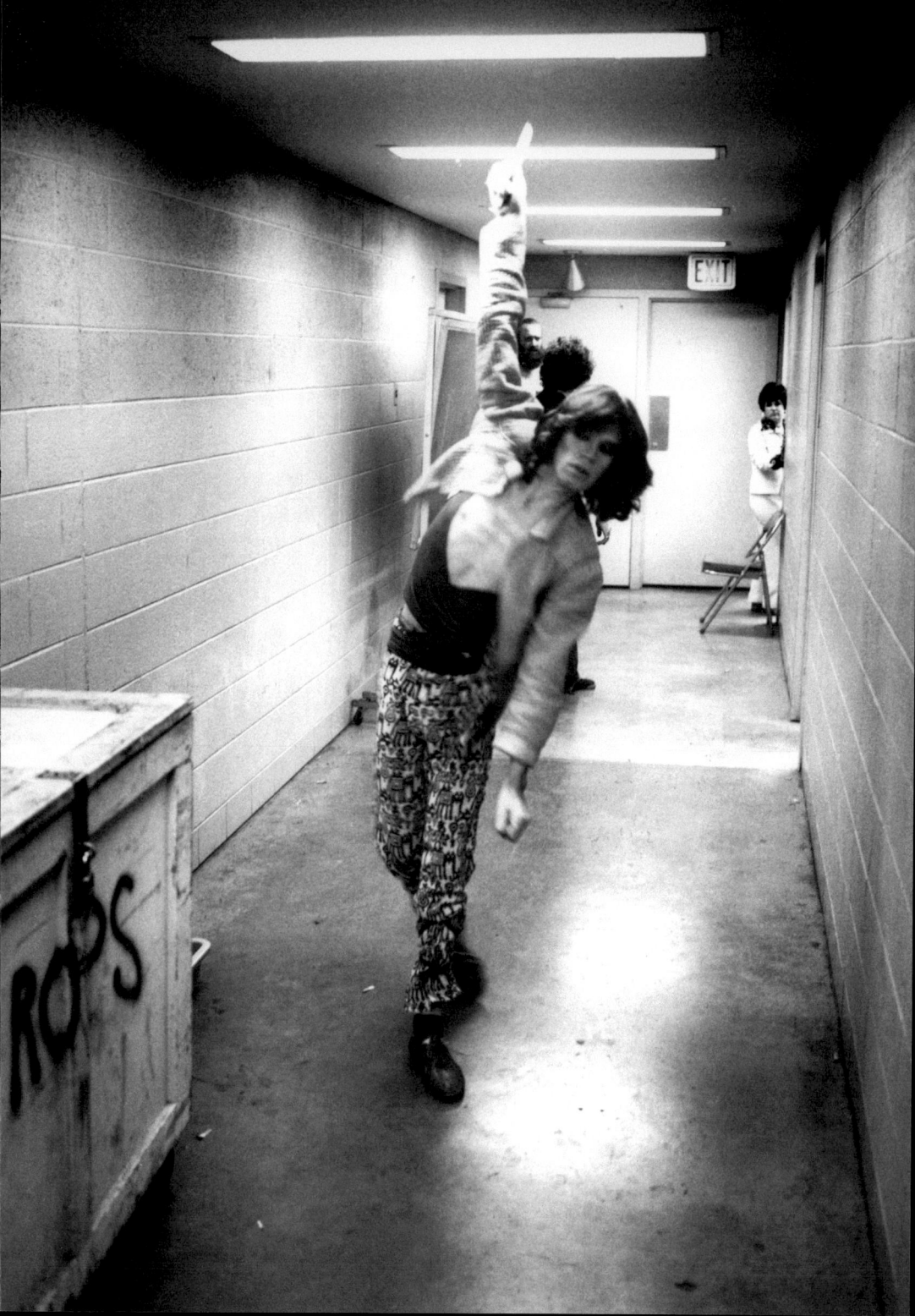

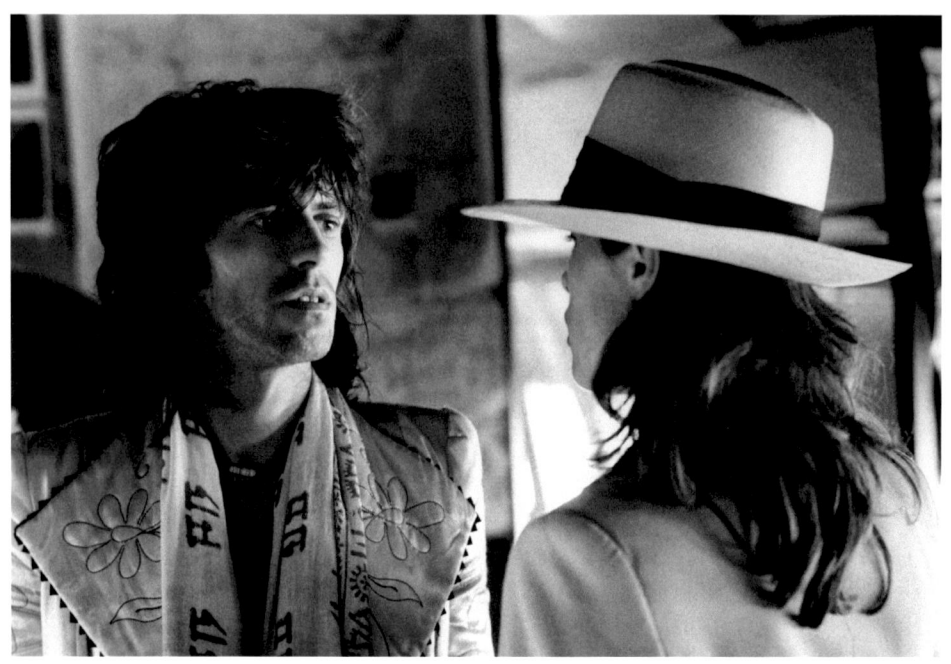

Christopher Simon Sykes
Keith publicly pronounced Bianca to be "a groovy chick", but she would remain an aloof presence during the 1975 tour.

Annie Leibovitz
A candid moment captured on 8 August 1975. That night, the Stones played Rich Stadium (now the Ralph Wilson Stadium) in Buffalo, New York, to a capacity audience.

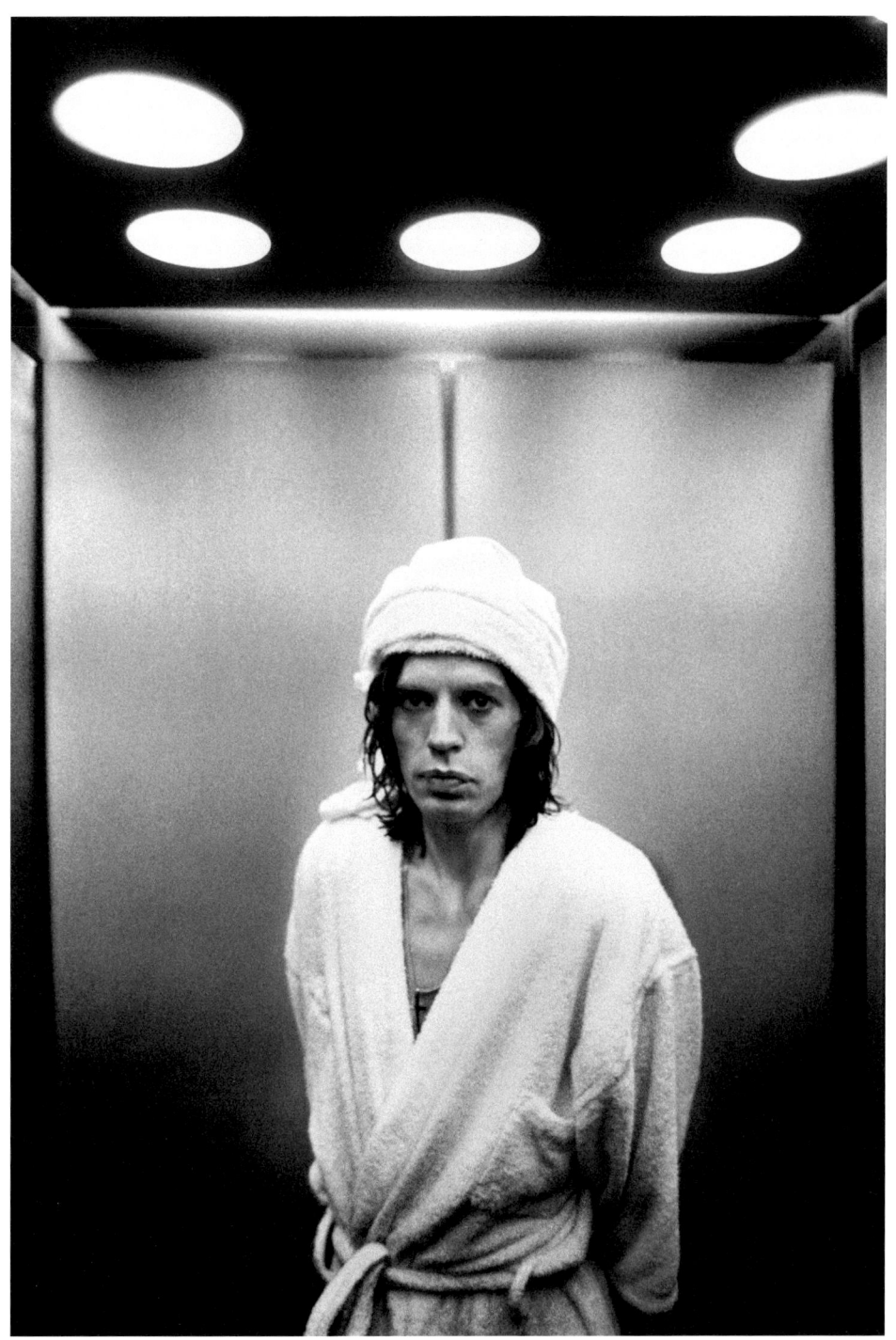

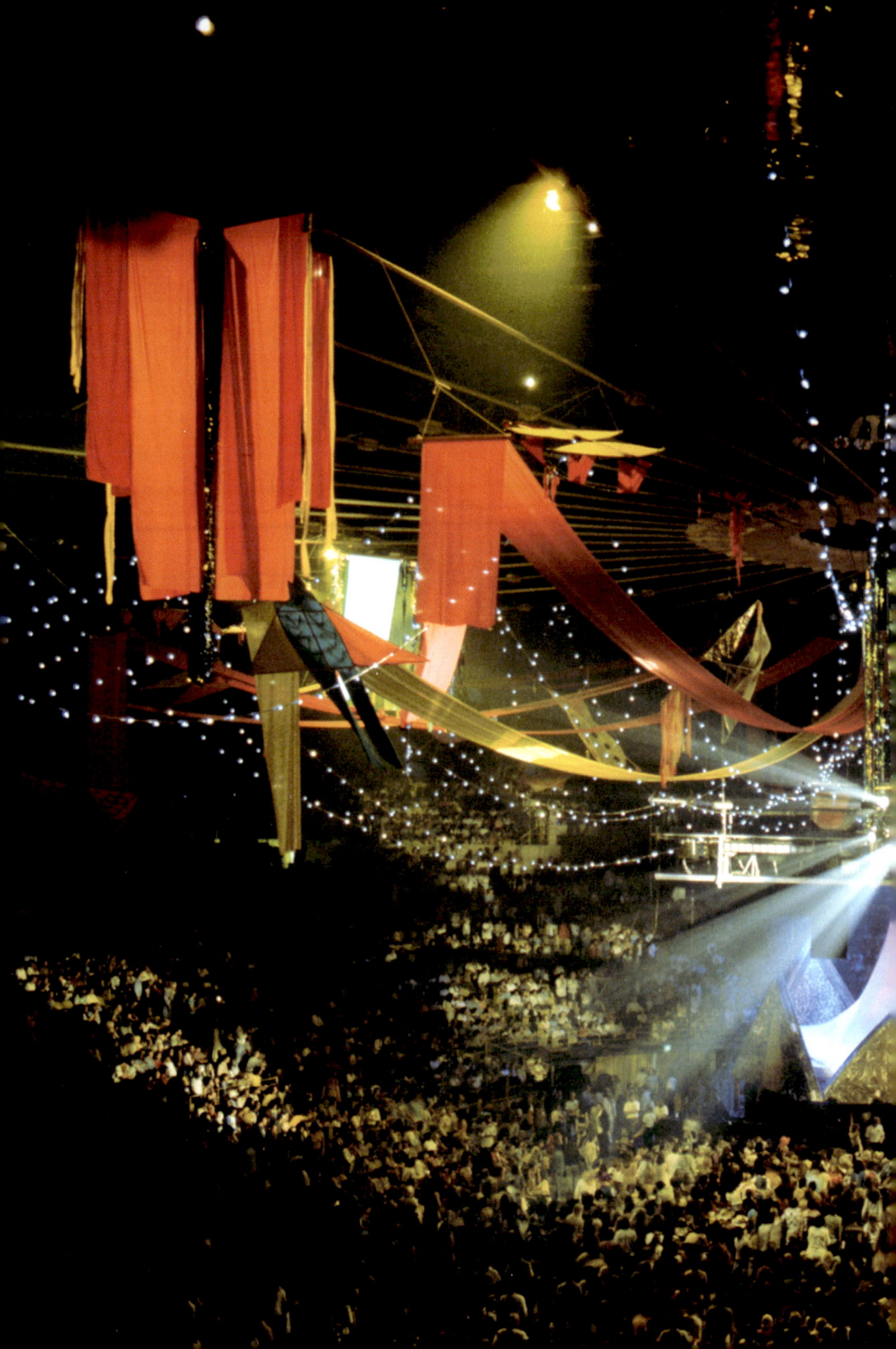

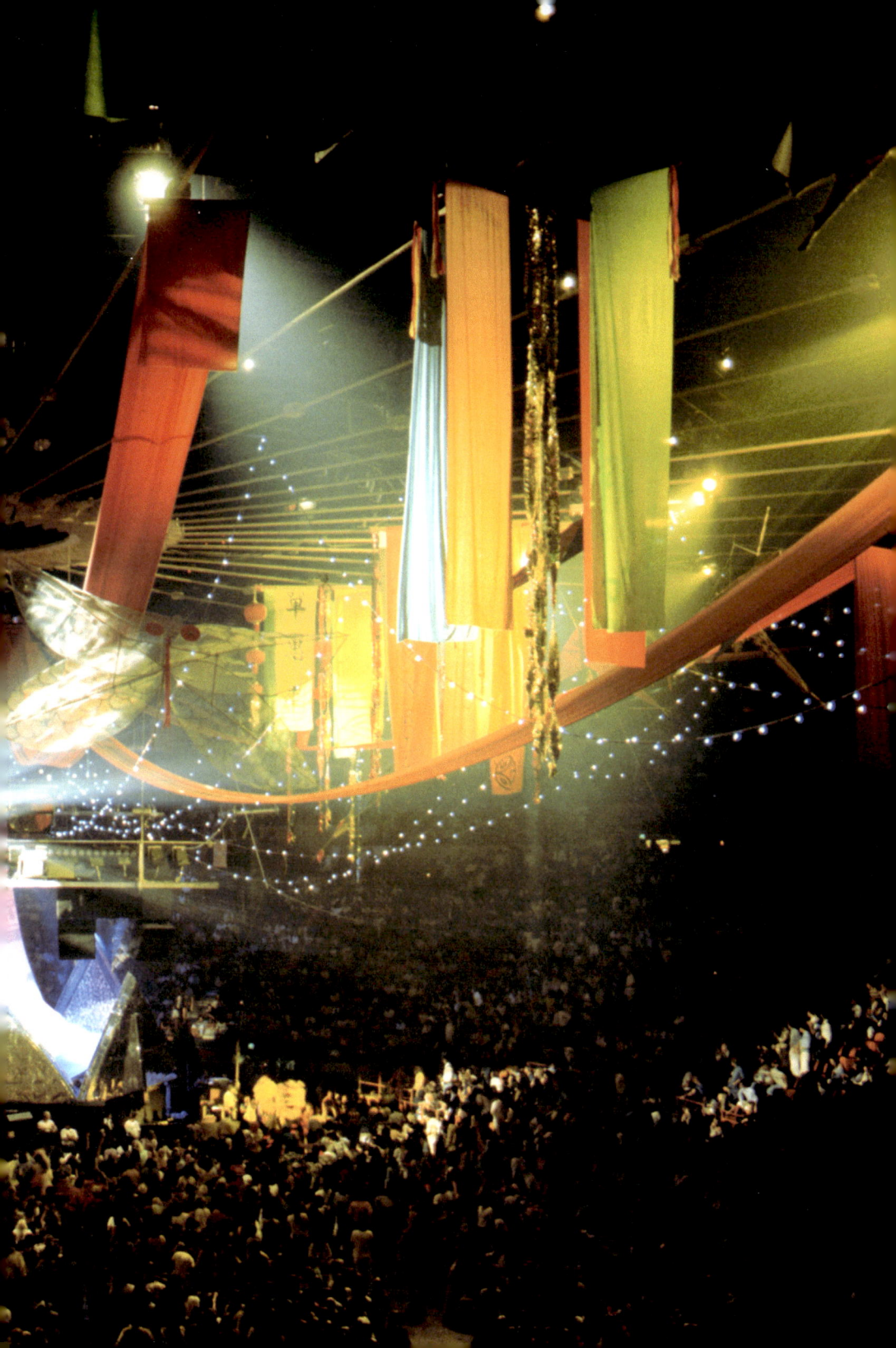

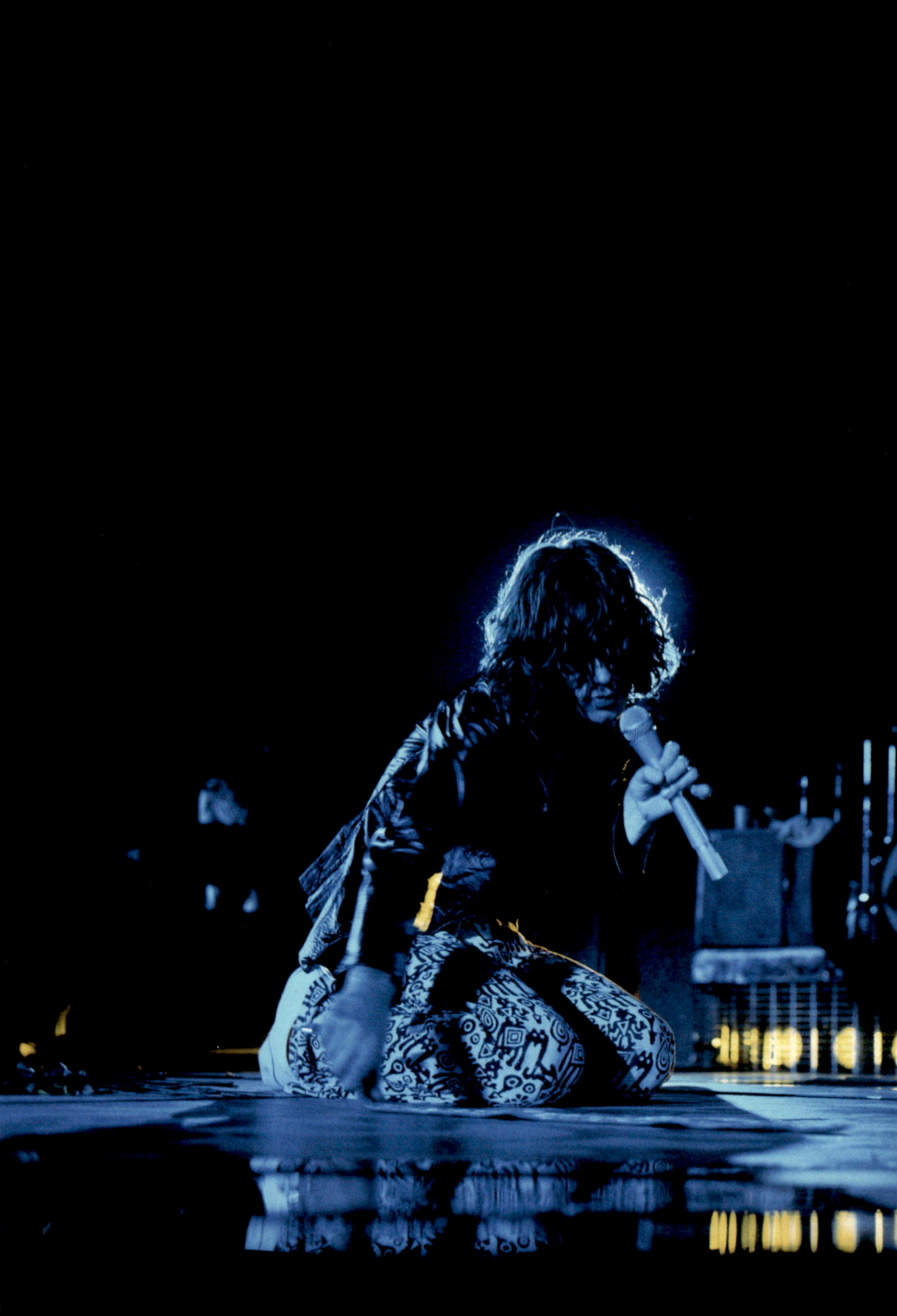

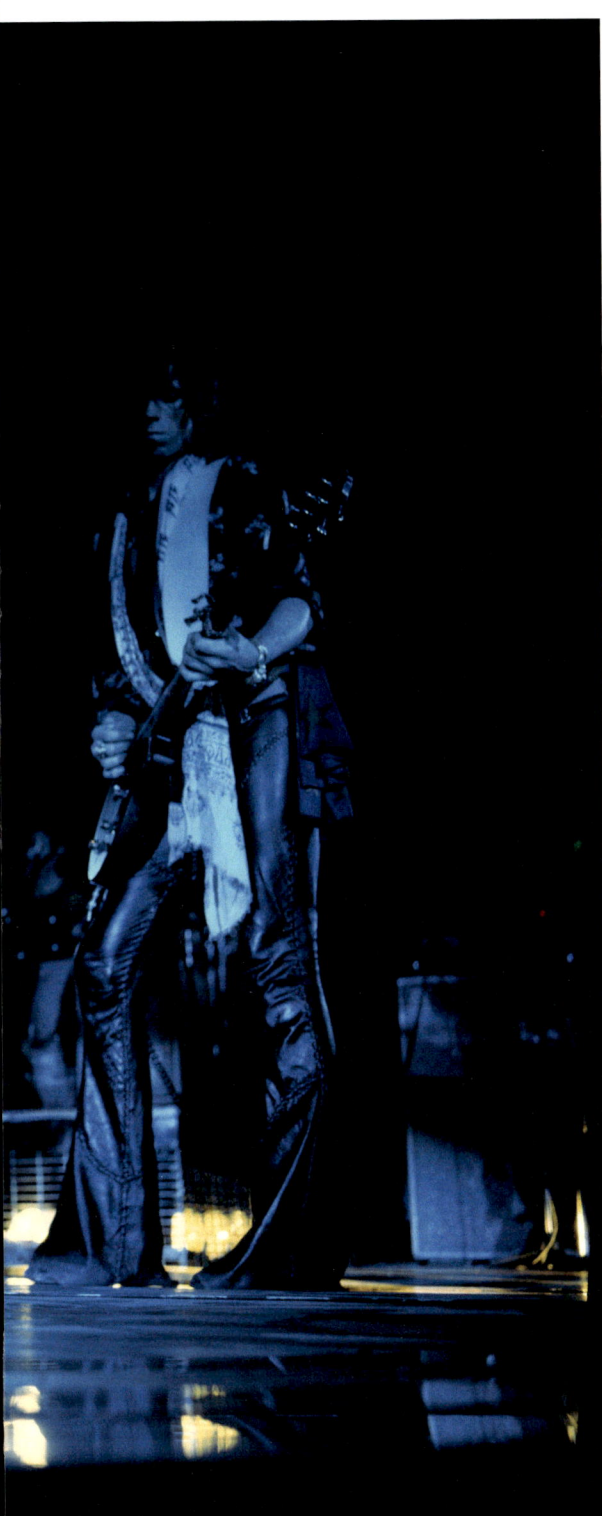

PP. 366–367
Christopher Simon Sykes
The 1970s saw stage design, lights
and elaborate props becoming as
important as the music. Way ahead
of the pack were the Stones, viewing
each new tour as an opportunity to
build a bigger and more adventurous
set. For their 1975 visit to the States
they played at far larger venues than
before, and a unique stage shaped
like a lotus leaf (conceived by Charlie)
was used. Construction of the stage
required advance riggers to start work
in venues four days before the actual
concert.

Christopher Simon Sykes
On stage during the 1975 *Tour of the
Americas*.
*"I like entertaining ... I suppose
performing is an aid. It helps me as
a person, an individual, to get rid of my
ego. It's a better process than others.
If I get rid of my ego on stage, then the
problem ceases to exist when I have
left there. I no longer have a need to
prove myself continually to myself."*
Mick Jagger in David Dalton, *Rolling
Stones: In Their Own Words*, 1980

P. 370
Christopher Simon Sykes
Tour of Europe, April–June 1976.

P. 371
Christopher Simon Sykes
Tour of Europe, April–June 1976.
*"Richards struck me as being in some
weird almost mystical way ... someone
who gave himself up so completely to
the rock life, who identified with it so
completely, who did so little to protect
himself from its dangers and its traps,
that he eventually developed a strange
purity amidst filth. He obtained a
kind of blessedness in the gutter."*
Albert Goldman in Victor Bockris,
Keith Richards: The Biography, 1992

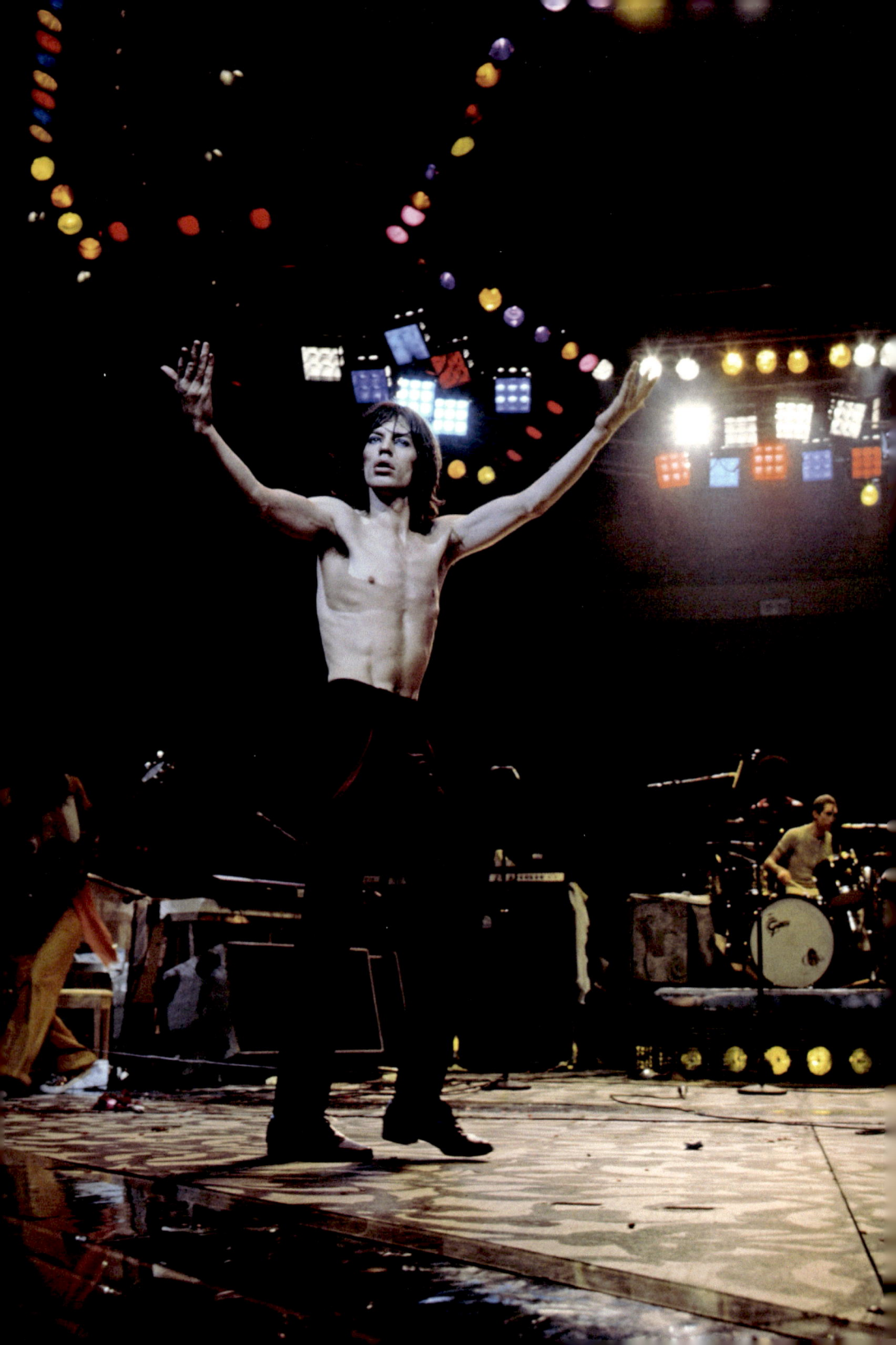

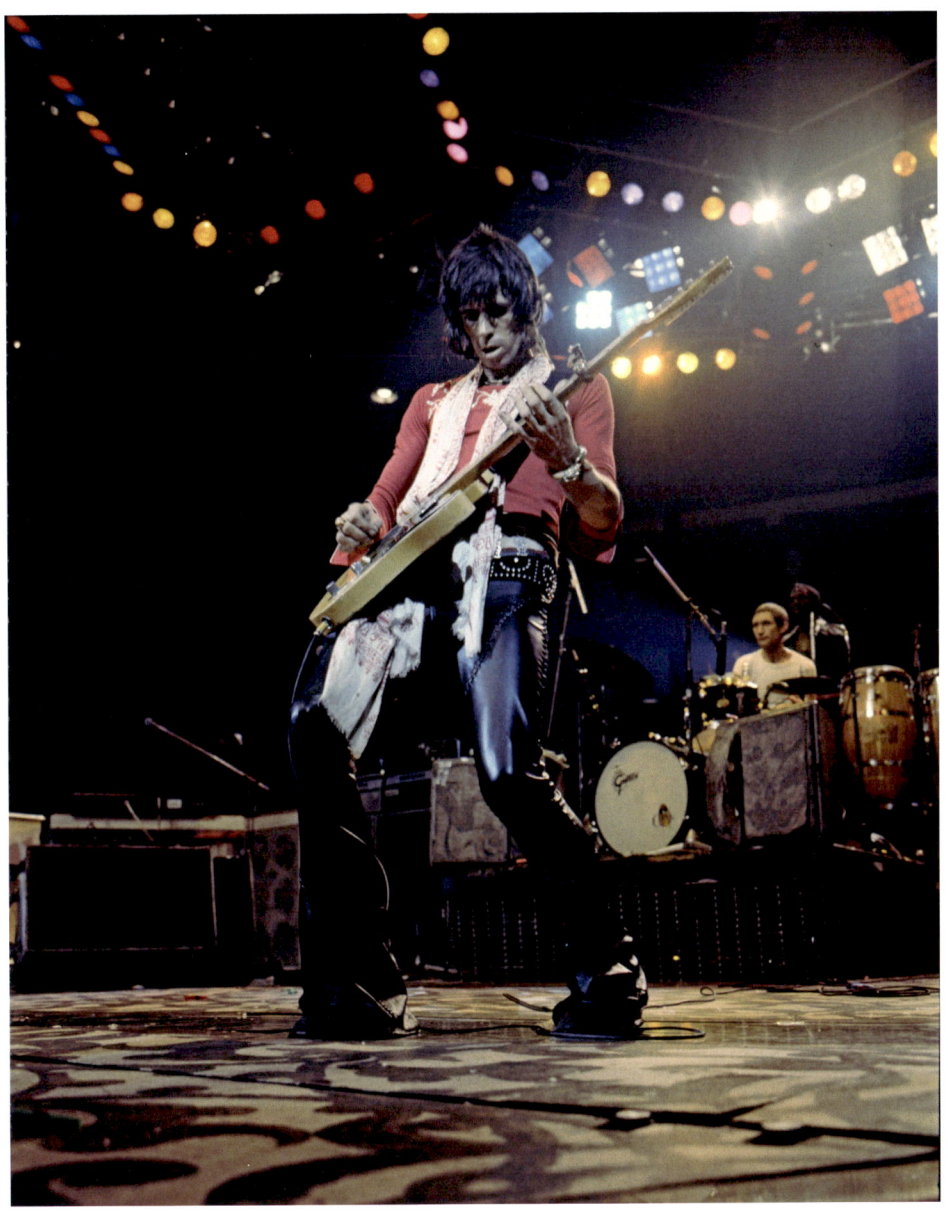

PP. 372–373

Christopher Simon Sykes / Anonymous

Intimate and candid Polaroid snaps from the Stones' 1975 tour of the States. Their extraordinary 40-show *Tour of the Americas*, more simply known as "T.O.T.A. '75" raised, yet again, the benchmark of rock 'n' roll extravagance.

371

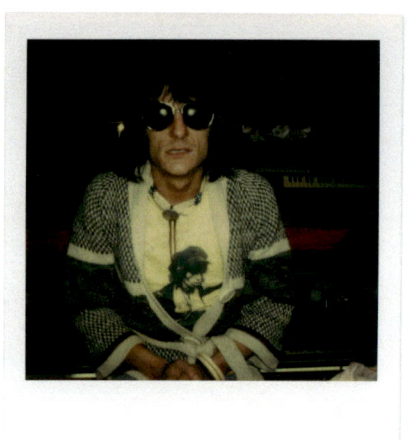

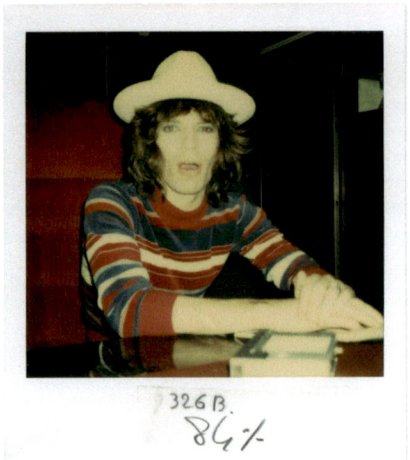

326 B.
84%

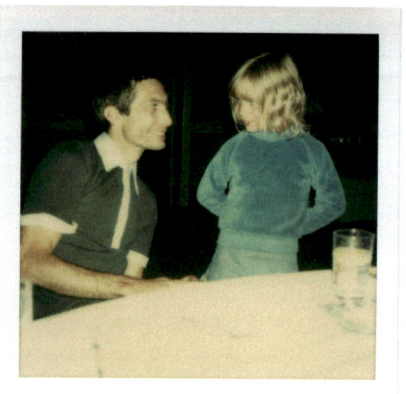

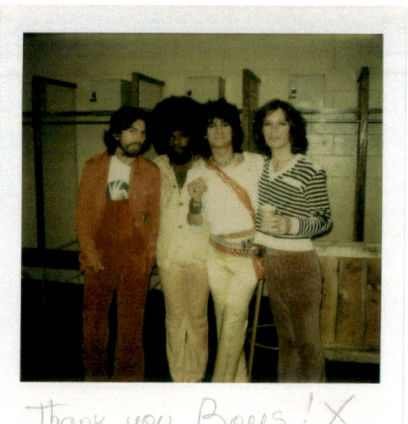

Thank you Boys! X

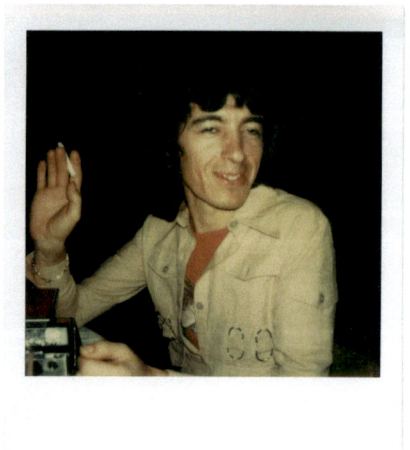

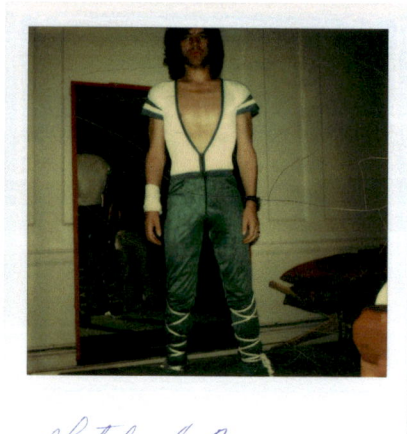

Sketch # 2

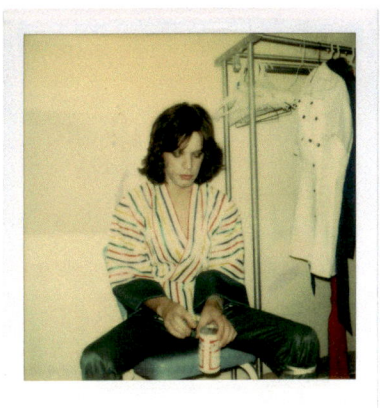

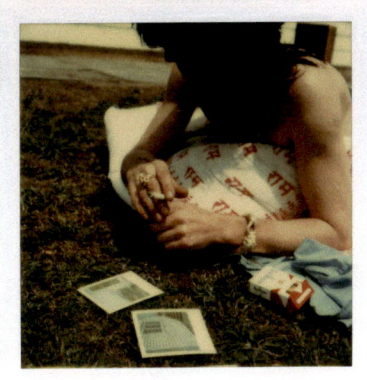

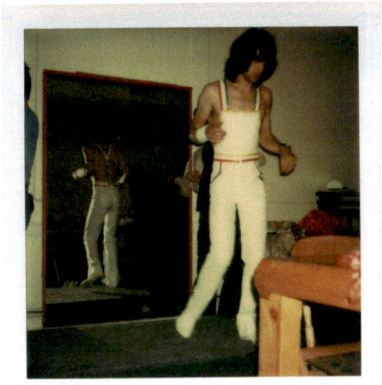

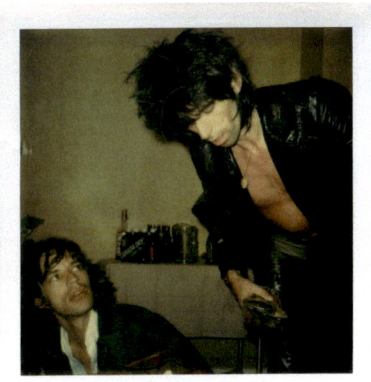

Sketch #6

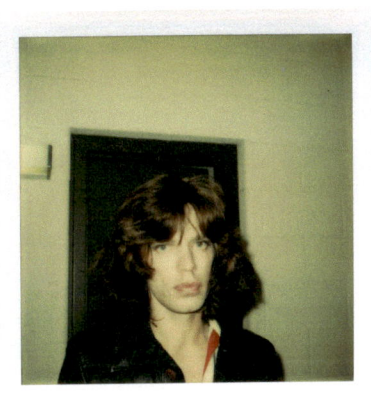

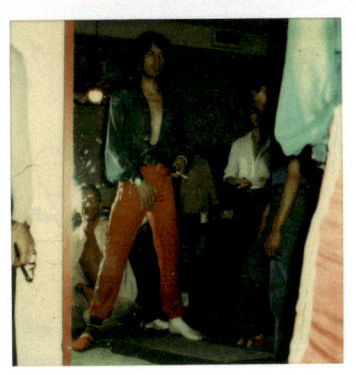

Sketch # 11

373

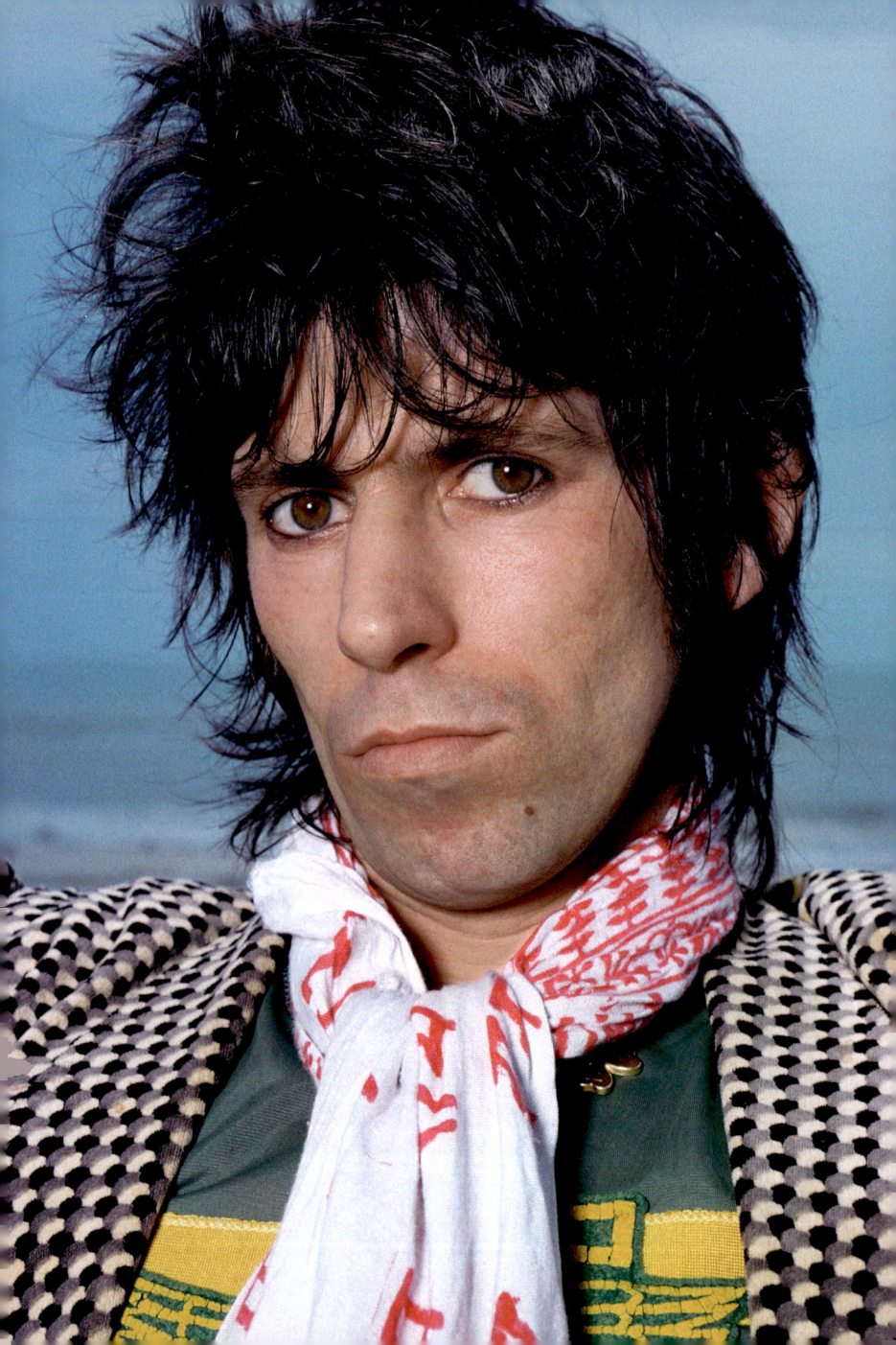

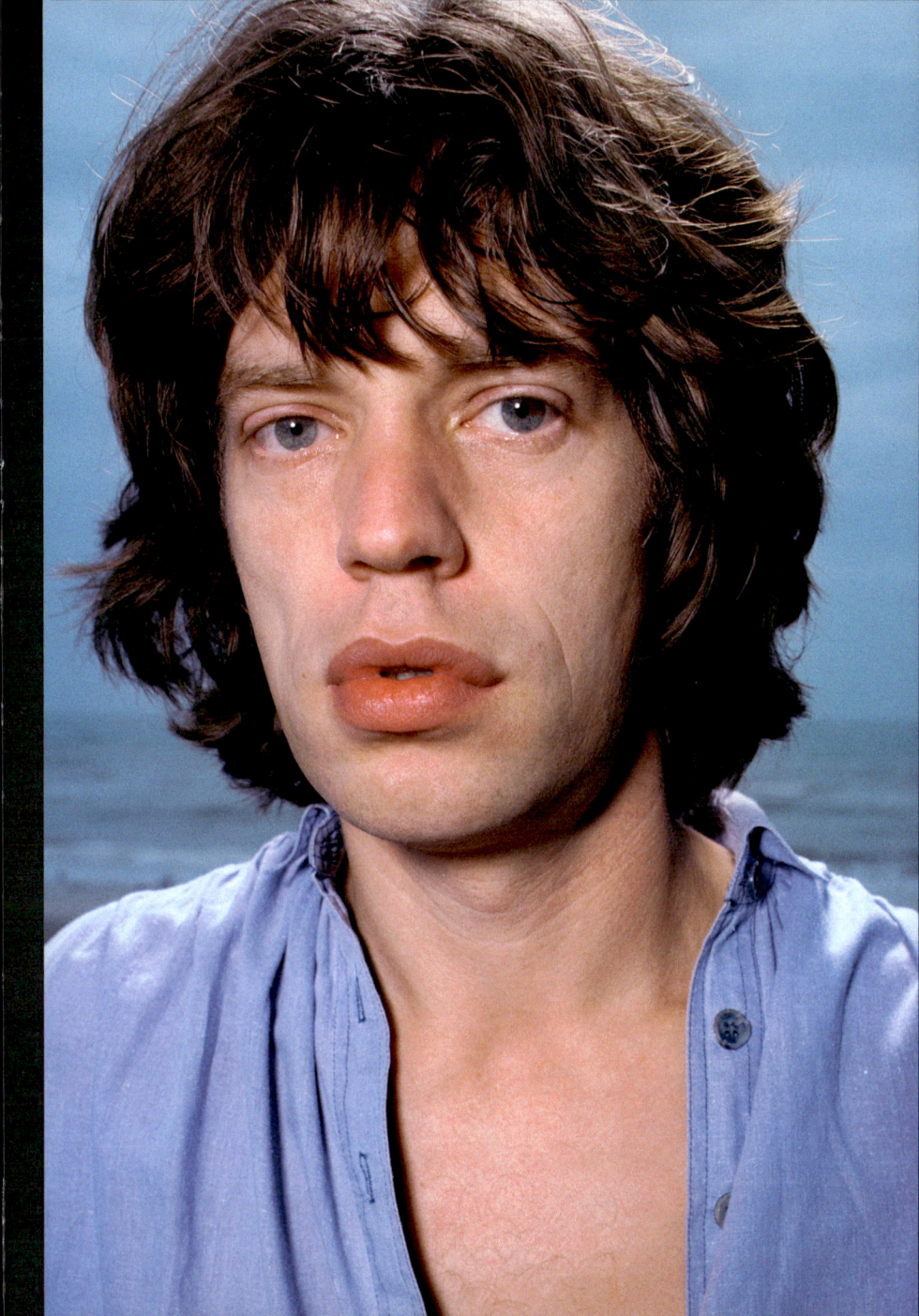

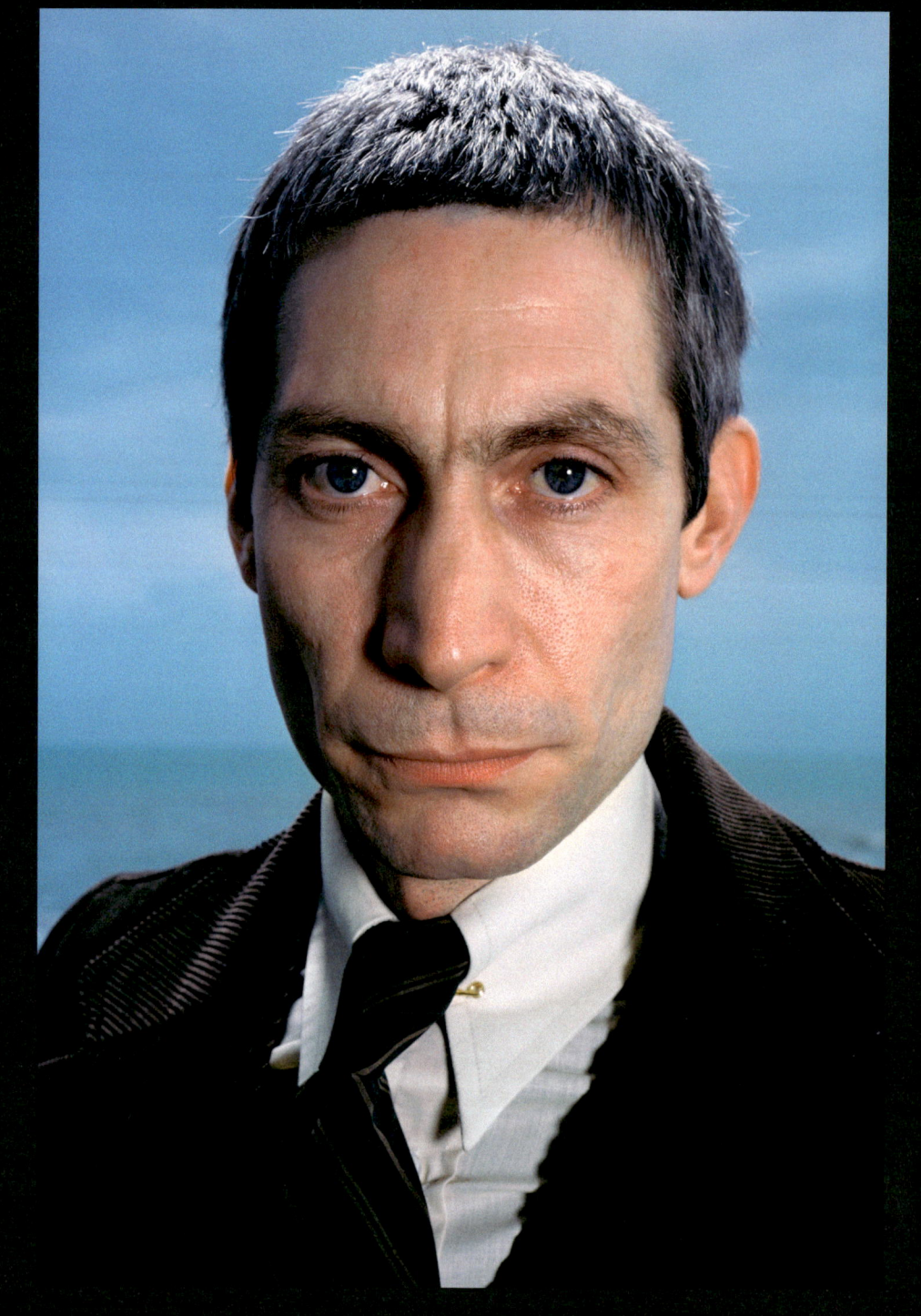

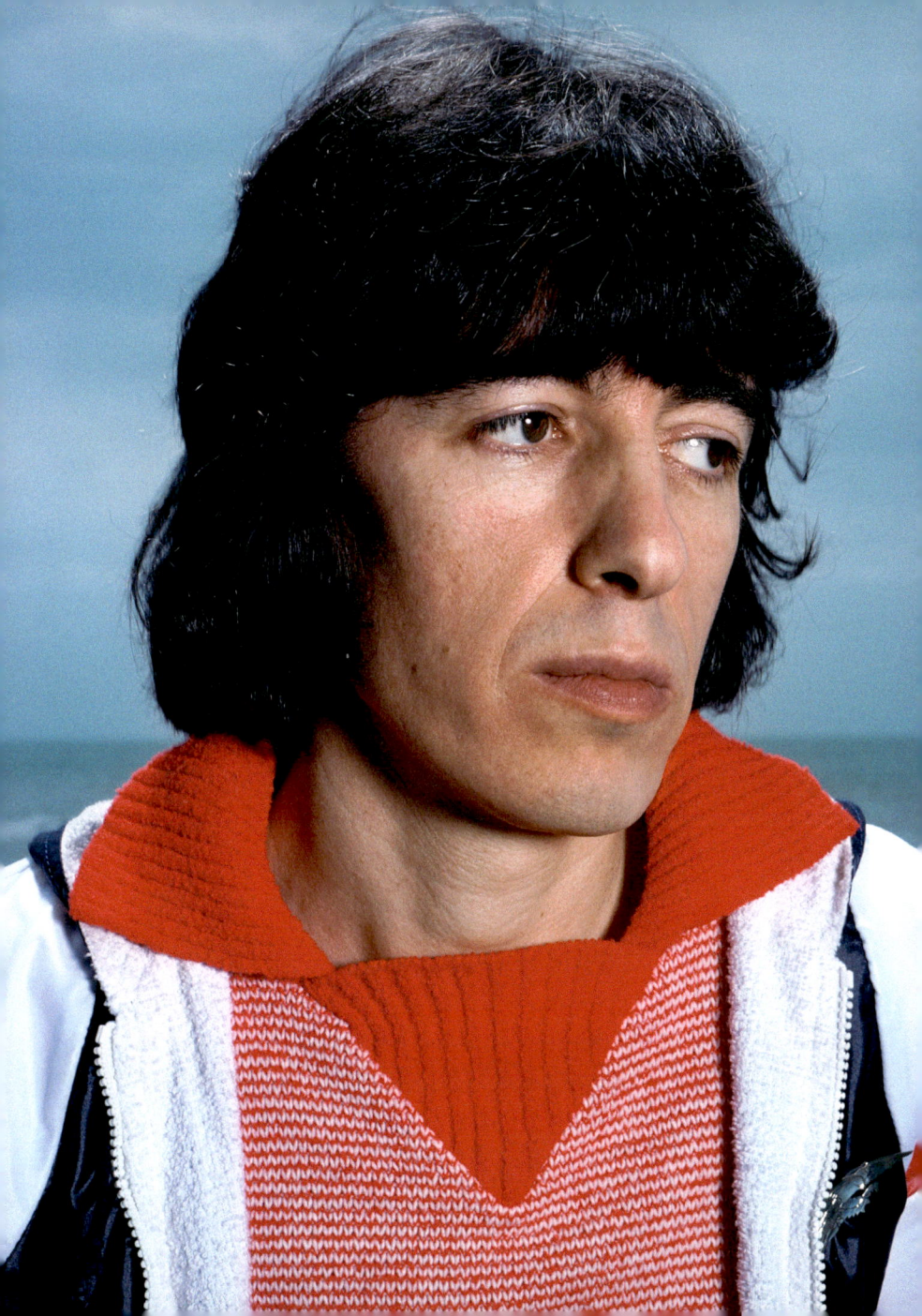

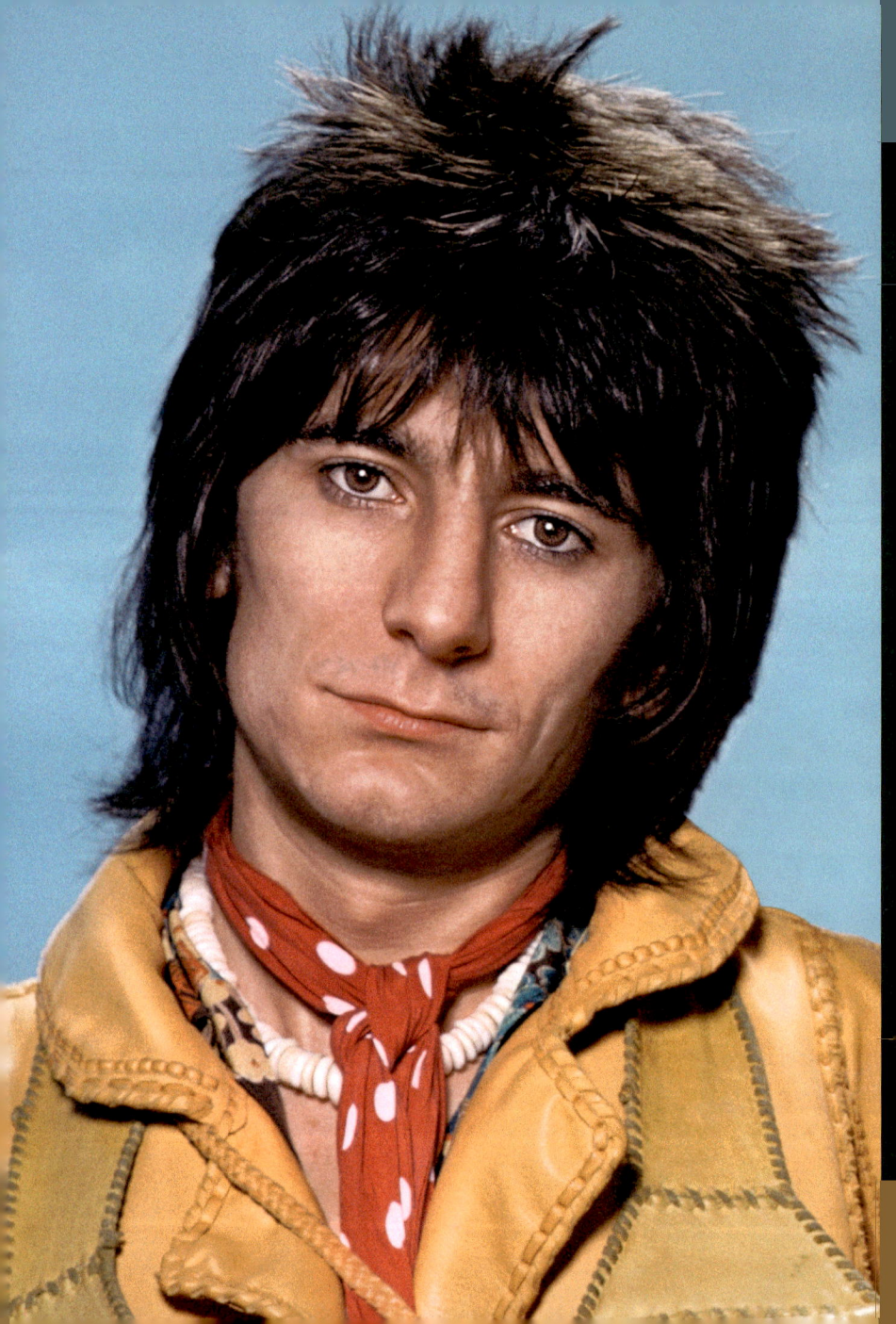

PP. 374–378
Hiro
Sanibel Island, February 1976. *Black And Blue* maintained a Stones tradition of recording in several different countries, with sessions in Germany, Holland and Switzerland, before the final work in New York City. Despite comprising just eight tracks, the final album included such memorable songs as "Hot Stuff", "Memory Motel" and "Fool To Cry", with influences spanning gospel, reggae and funk.

PP. 380–381
Andy Warhol
Warhol's Polaroid pictures would form the basis for the cover of *Love You Live*, the group's 1977 double live album. Selected from 24 photos, the artist embellished the imagery across the gatefold sleeve, producing an aesthetic and design that was in line with the New Wave look. The solo shot of Mick is from a 1975 session unrelated to the record.

"Let the neighbours be damned as you shut your eyes and astro project yourself to wherever you may fantasise about seeing the Stones perform. That's all you gotta do, 'cause right from the introduction, you can actually feel when the band materialises on stage, and then you are off, right there with the crowd." Love You Live review, *Sounds*, 24 September 1977

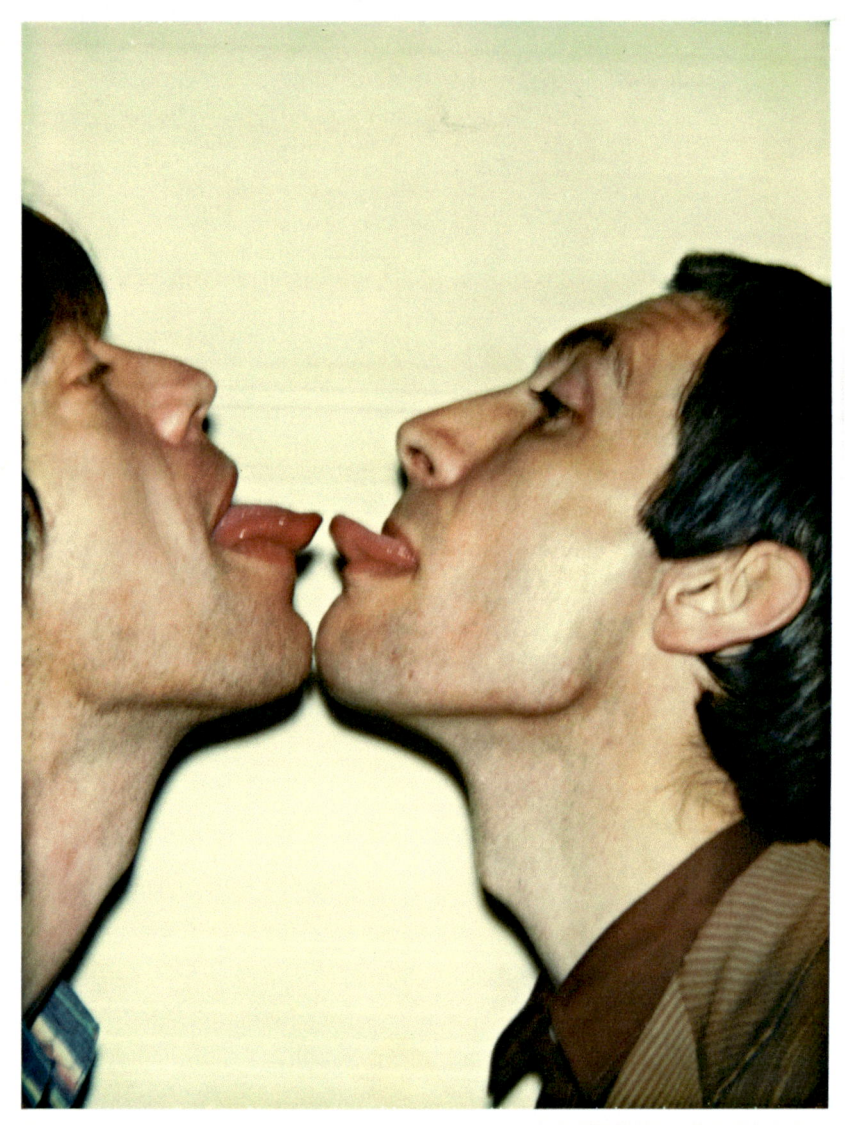

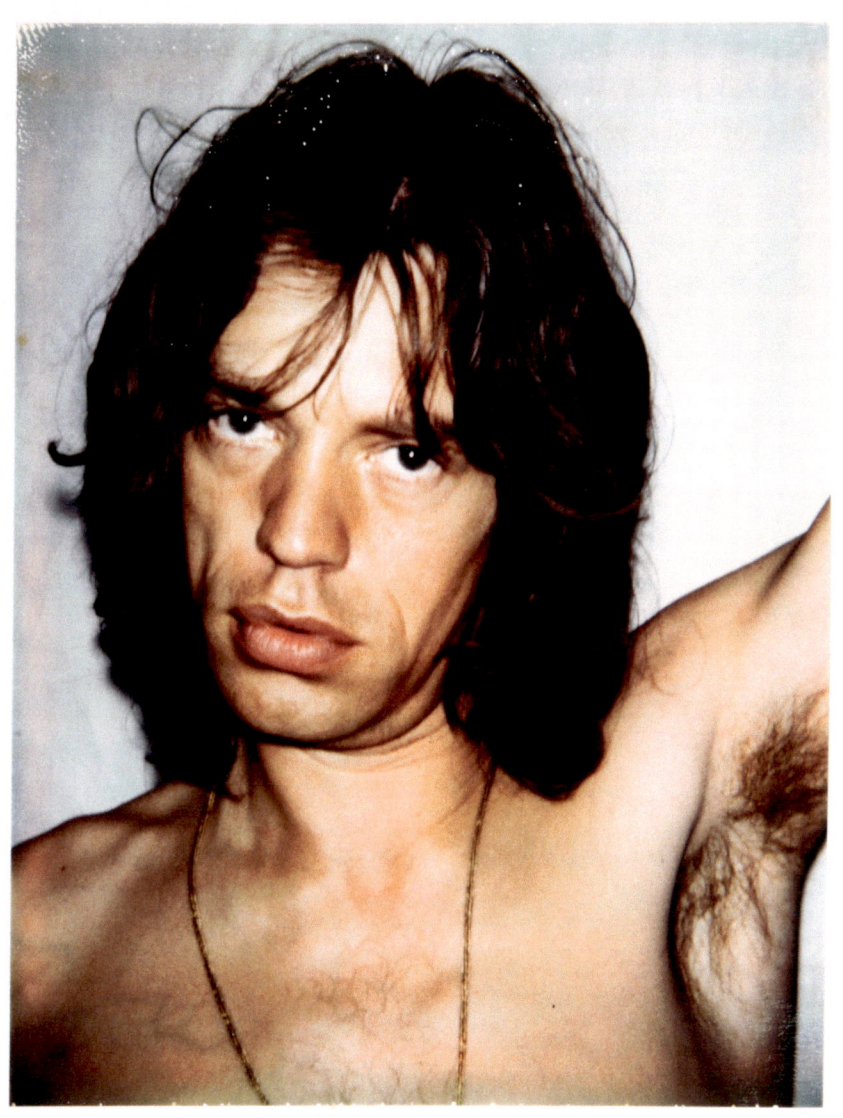

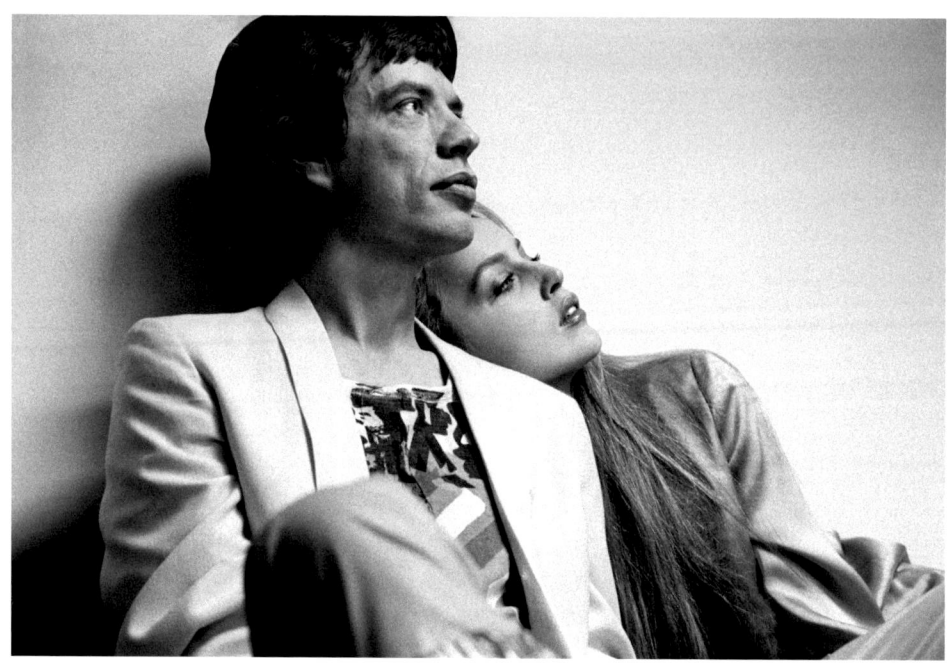

Jean Pigozzi
Mick and Jerry Hall backstage during rehearsals for *Saturday Night Live* on 7 October 1978.
The Stones were to appear on NBC's top-rated
show playing three songs from the *Some Girls*
album: "Beast Of Burden", "Respectable" and
"Shattered".

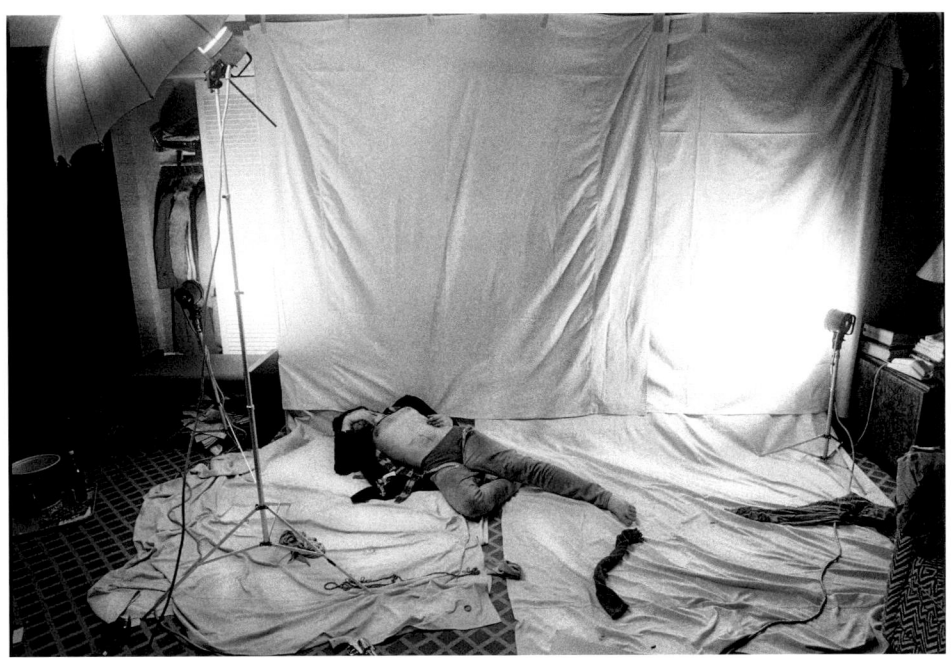

Annie Leibovitz
Keith, Toronto, 1977.
"Some of my most outrageous nights – I can only
believe actually happened because of corroborat-
ing evidence. No wonder I'm famous for partying!
The ultimate party – if it's any good – you can't
remember it." Keith Richards, *Life*, 2010

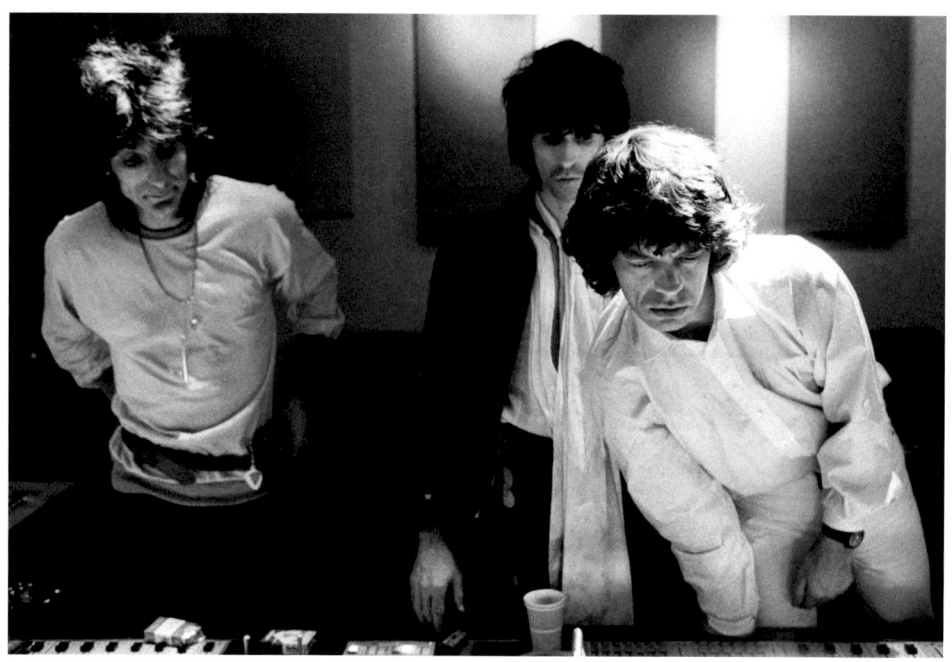

Jean Pigozzi

Sessions for *Some Girls* maintained the Stones' tradition of recording outside Britain – this time at EMI's Pathé Marconi Studios in Boulogne-Billancourt, near Paris. During January–March 1978 the tracks "Far Away Eyes", "Some Girls",

"Before They Make Me Run" and "Start Me Up" were committed to tape. These prolific sessions would also furnish part of the 1981 album *Tattoo You*.

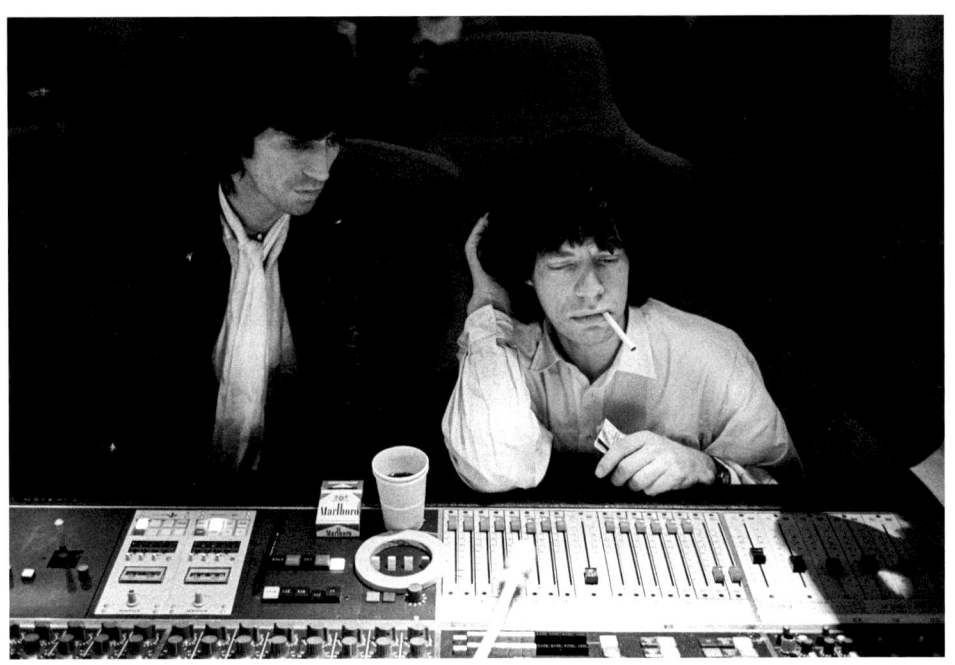

Jean Pigozzi

Some Girls sessions in Pathé Marconi Studios, January–March 1978.
"*I think it was pretty conscious of living in the day ... You had sort of a return to very basic rock music – you know, The Sex Pistols and all that – but you also had the beginning of hip-hop, the beginning of rap, and you had lots and lots of kinds of dance music. I think in some ways this album reflects some of that time, and I think that's what makes it an interesting album.*" Mick Jagger, *Some Girls* re-release promotional interview, November 2011

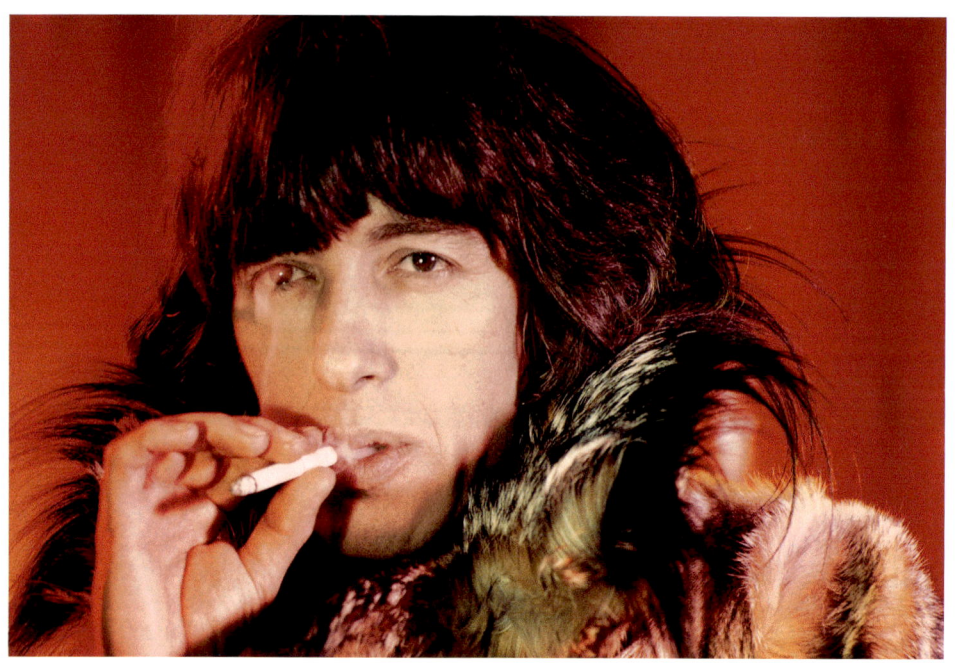

Dieter Zill
Bill captured during the Stones' *Tour of Europe*,
April–June 1976.
*"I'm a family man, I suppose. I keep myself to
myself. Mick and Keith are the only two members
of the group who go around with each other.
I'm about the only Stone who has the same
relationships with friends I had before the group
started."* Bill Wyman, quoted in David Dalton,
Rolling Stones: In Their Own Words, 1980

Dieter Zill
On stage during the Stones' *Tour of Europe*,
April–June 1976.
*"The Stones are very much Mick's creation as he
rushes around stage like a trapped butterfly, still
marvellously energetic ... It's a very reassuring
sight." Financial Times*, 26 May 1976

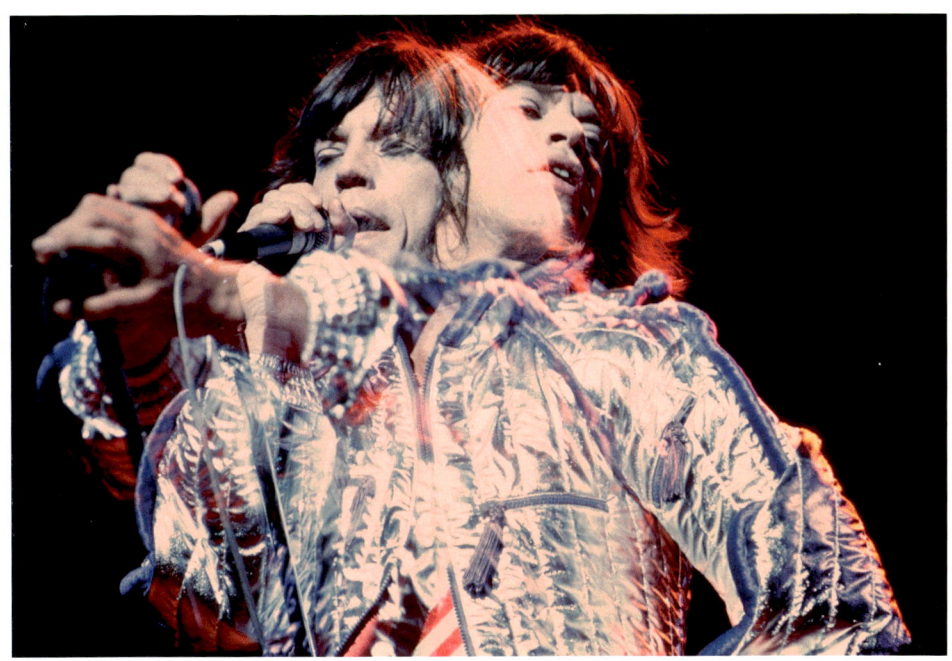

PP. 388–389
Michael Putland
Video shoot for "Miss You", 2 May 1978. A busy day, with clips also for "Respectable" and "Far Away Eyes" shot in New York City.

PP. 390–391
Michael Putland
Between takes for the video shoot, New York, 2 May 1978. Having weathered the punk explosion of 1977, the Stones returned to glory with their June 1978 album *Some Girls.* With tracks such as "Miss You", "Shattered" and "Respectable" revisiting an urgency not expressed since 1972s *Exile On Main St,* the collection was a huge financial and critical success, and the album became one of the band's biggest sellers.
"The punks had given us a kick up the ass ... It felt like we'd been sitting on our laurels for a couple of years. There'd been The Sex Pistols, the punk movement. We wanted to strip the band down so there weren't a lot of horns or extra musicians ... We decided to keep it strictly guitar." Keith Richards, *The Guardian*, 13 November 2011

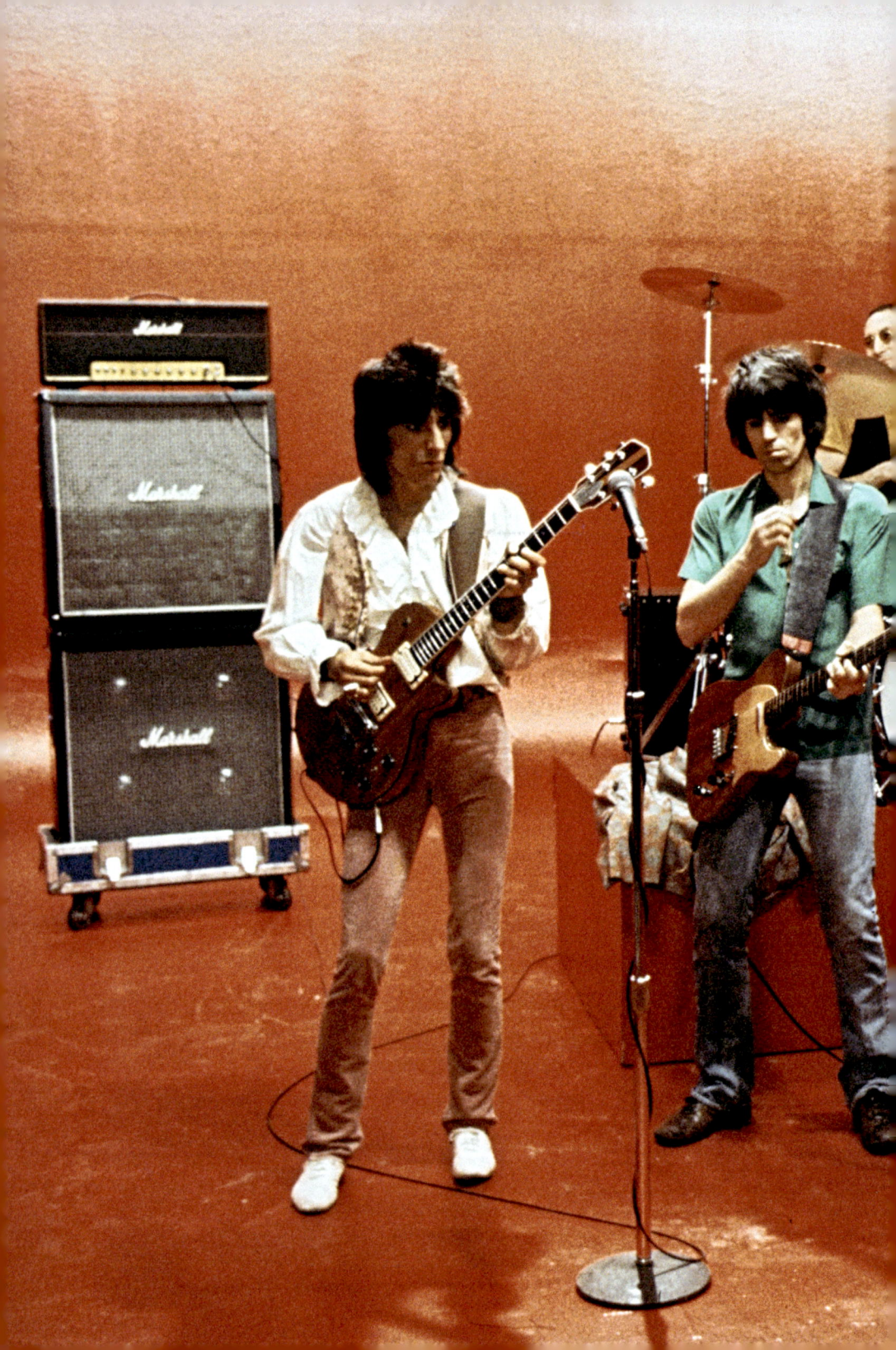

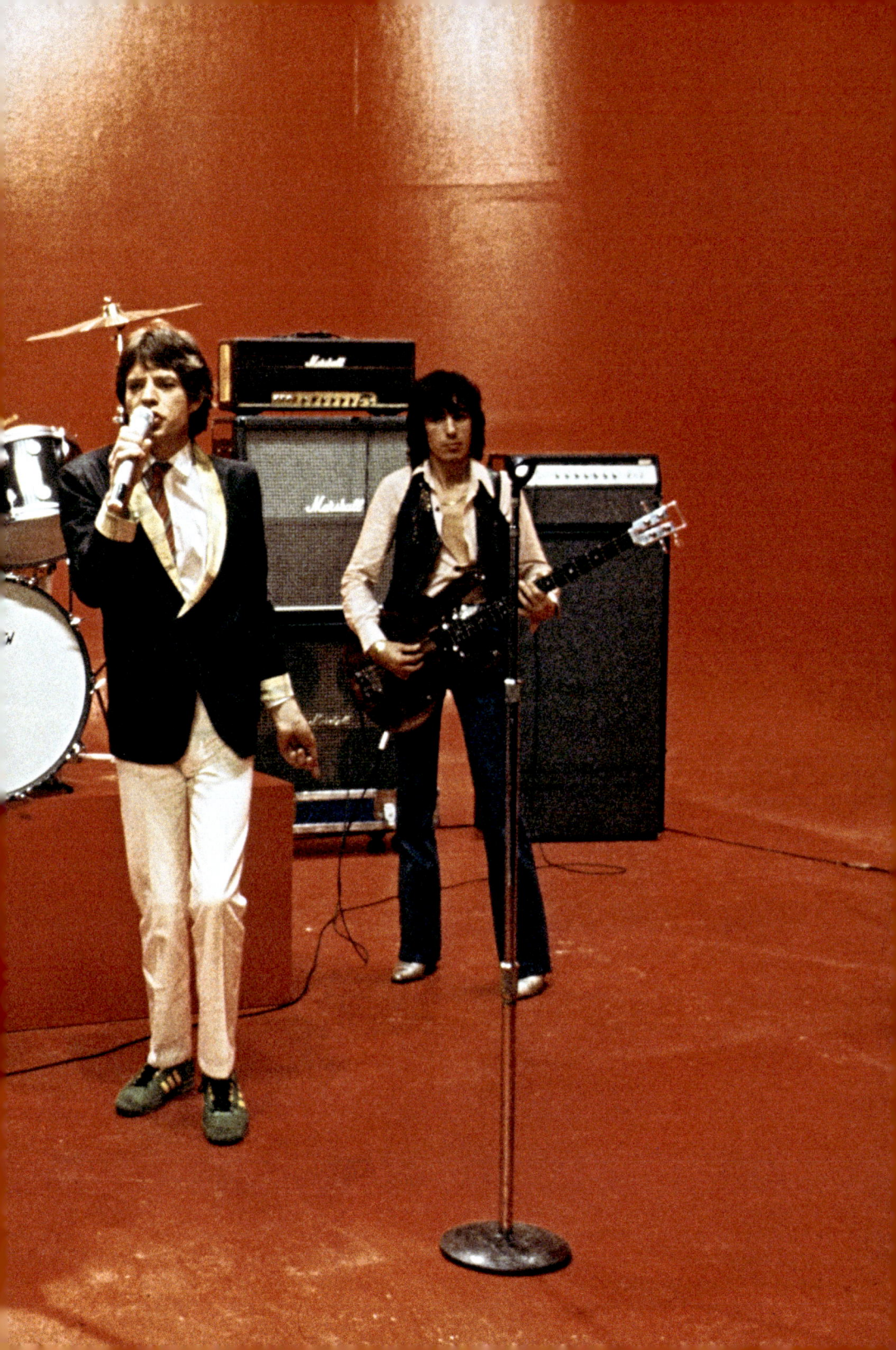

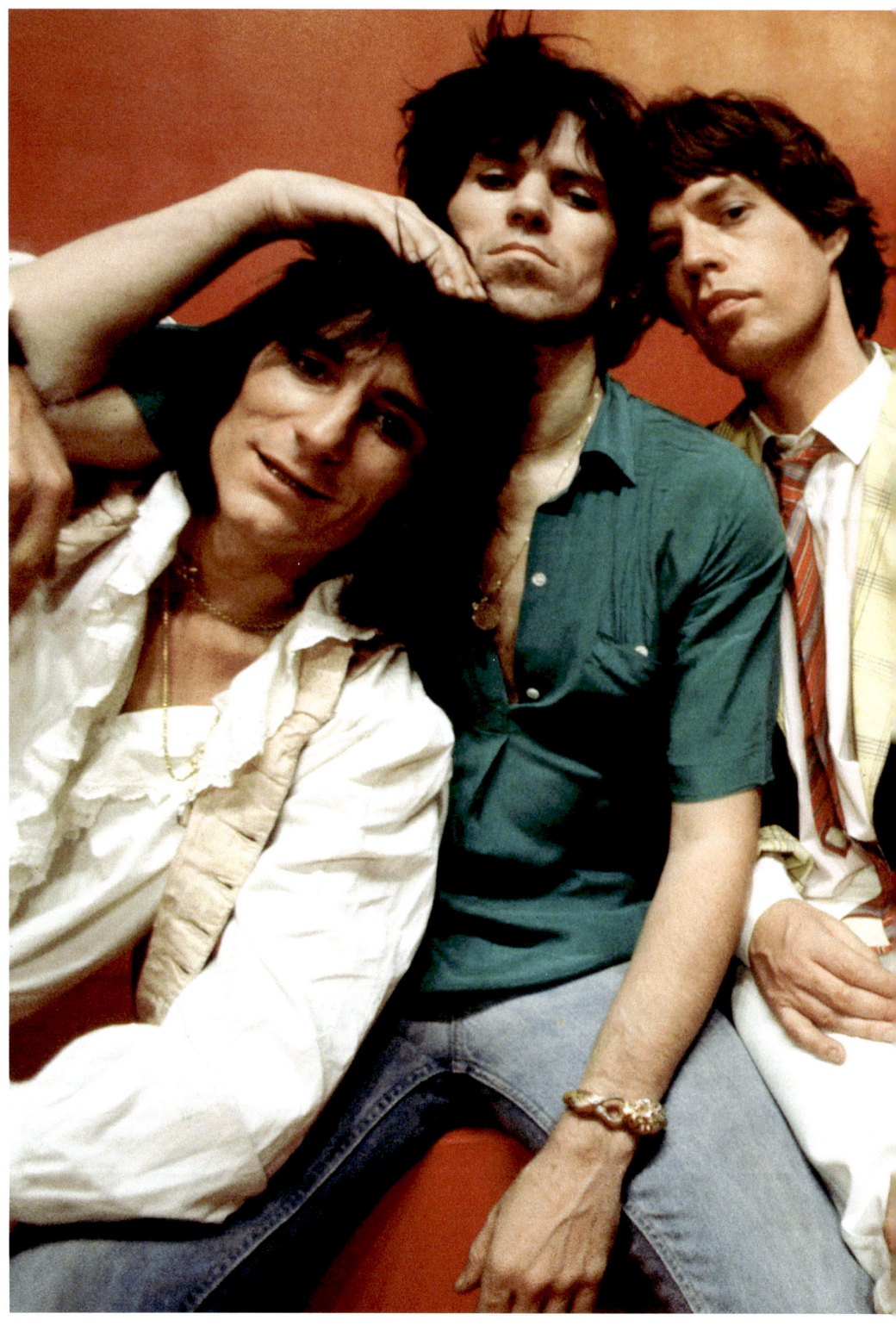

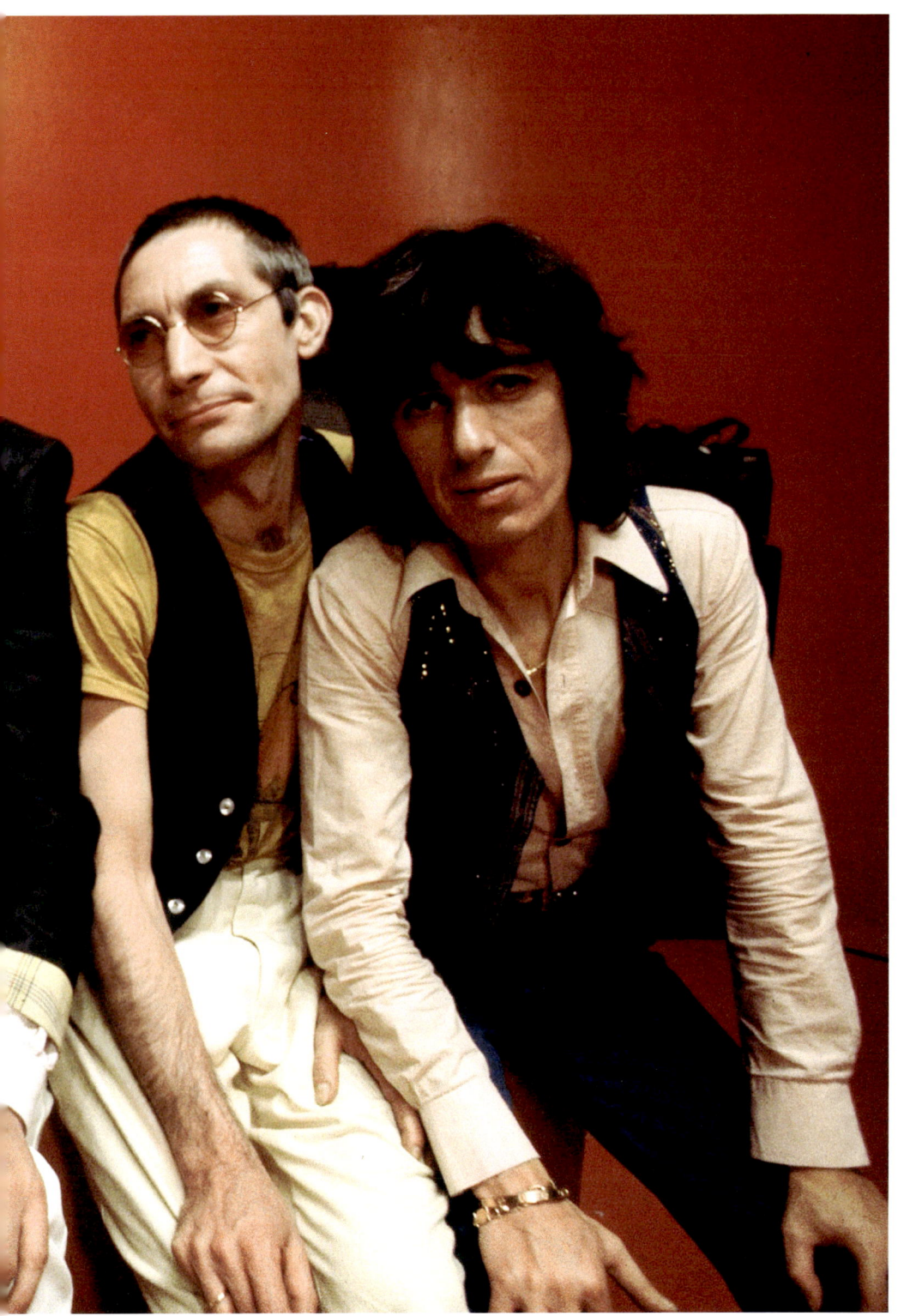

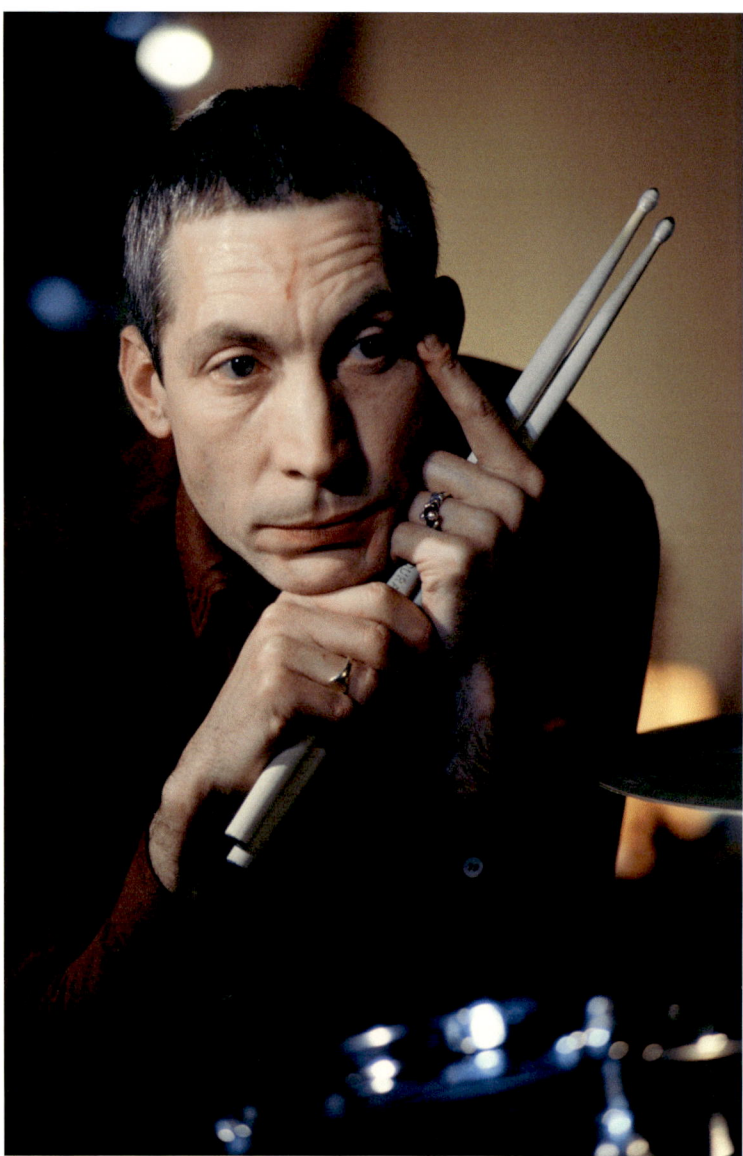

Helmut Newton
Charlie in repose during sessions for *Some Girls* at EMI's Pathé Marconi Studios, near Paris, January–March 1978.
  "It was a period that Mick and I [much to Keith's annoyance] actually liked disco records ... I was quite happy to do it because I quite liked disco music." Interview with Charlie Watts, BBC Radio 2, *Sounds Of The 70s*, 20 November 2011

Helmut Newton
Ronnie between takes at the Pathé Marconi Studios, January–March 1978.

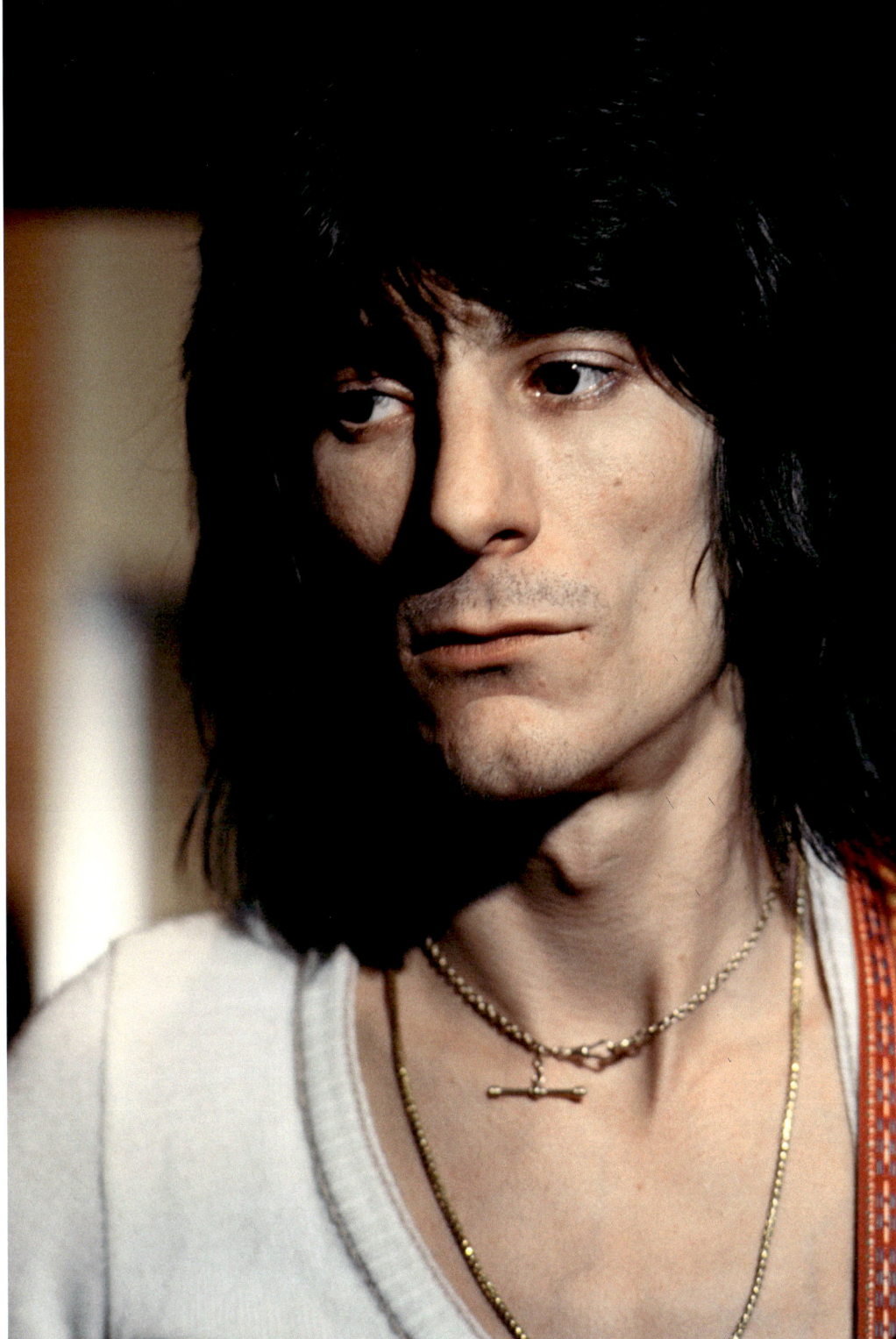

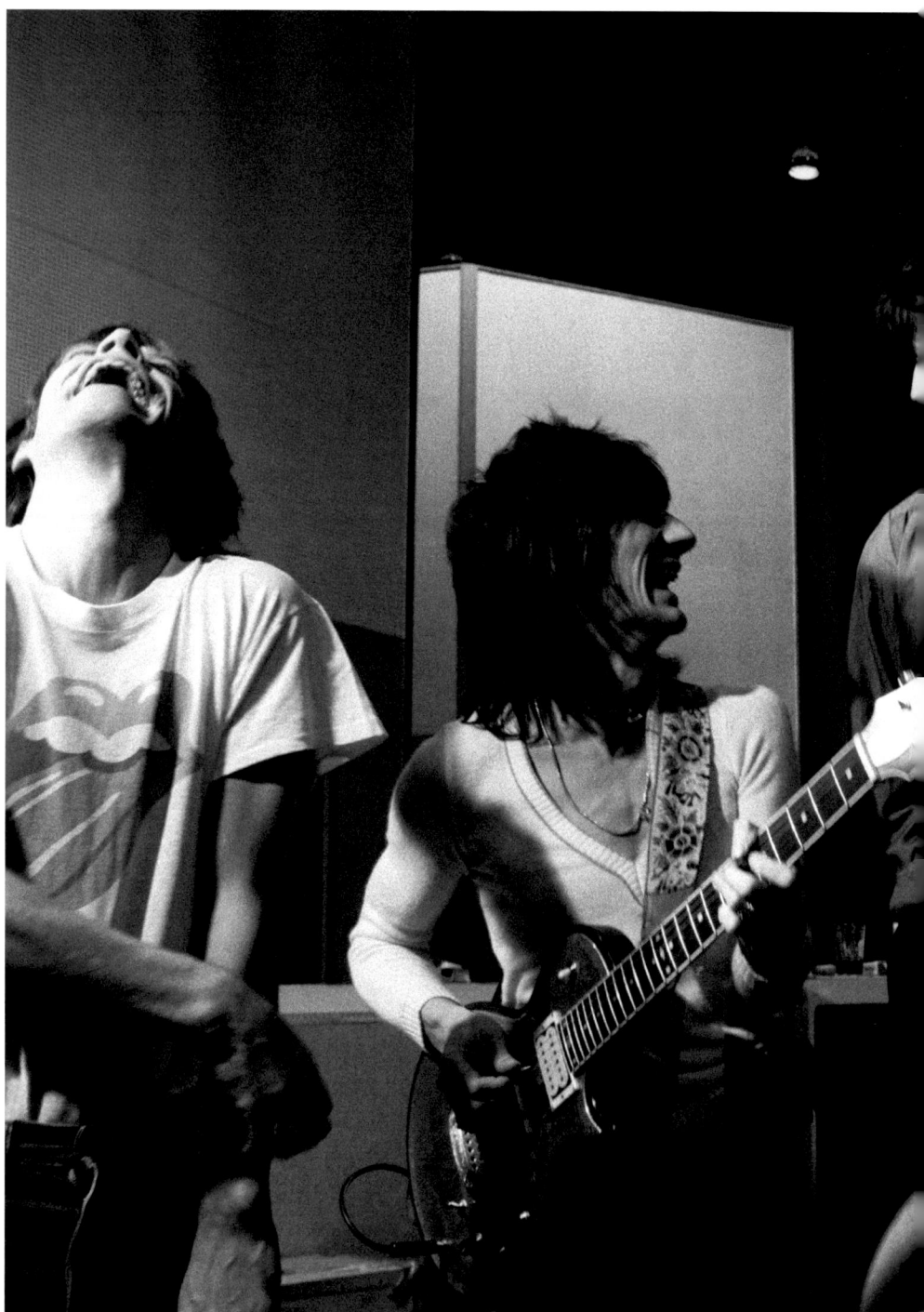

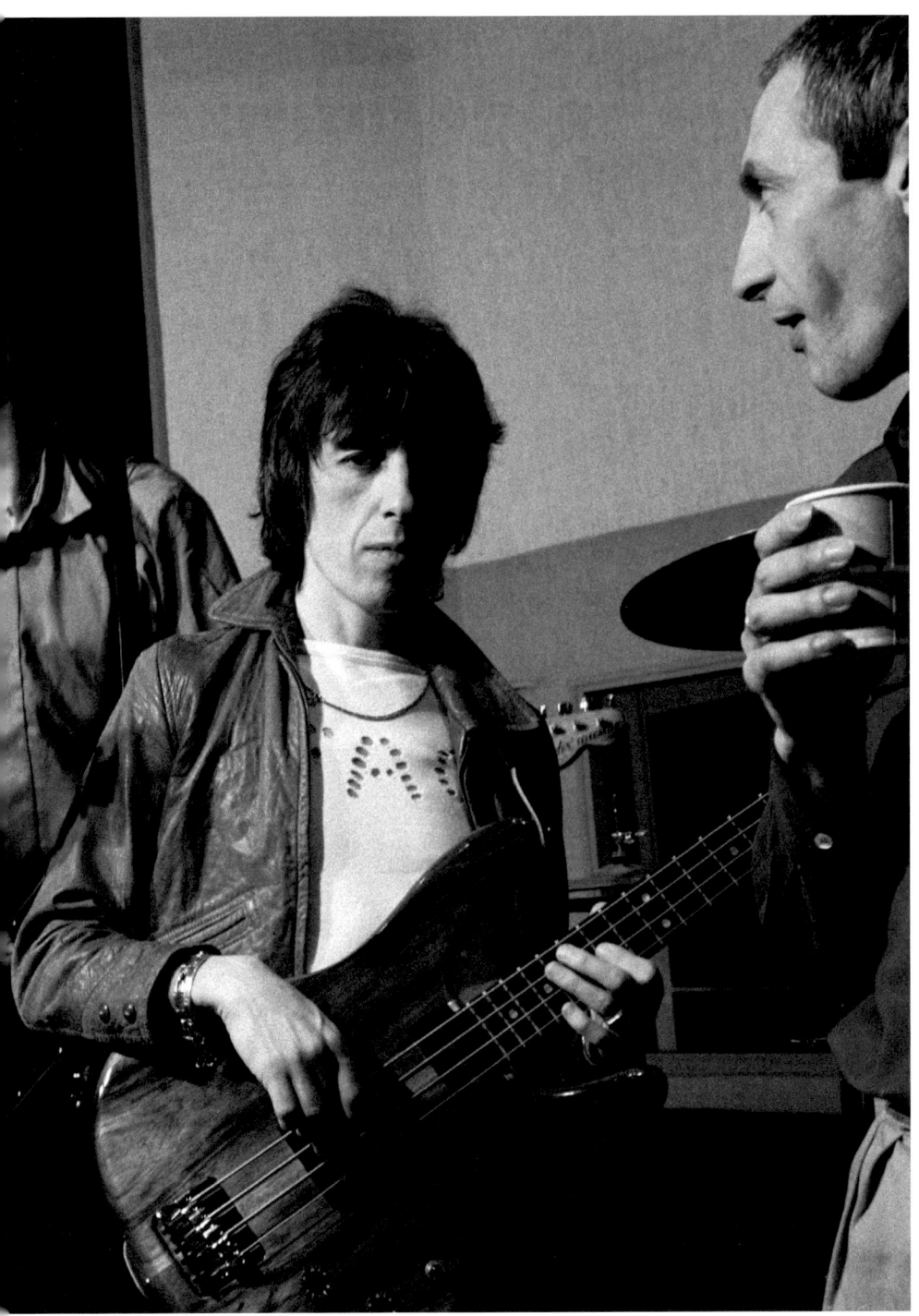

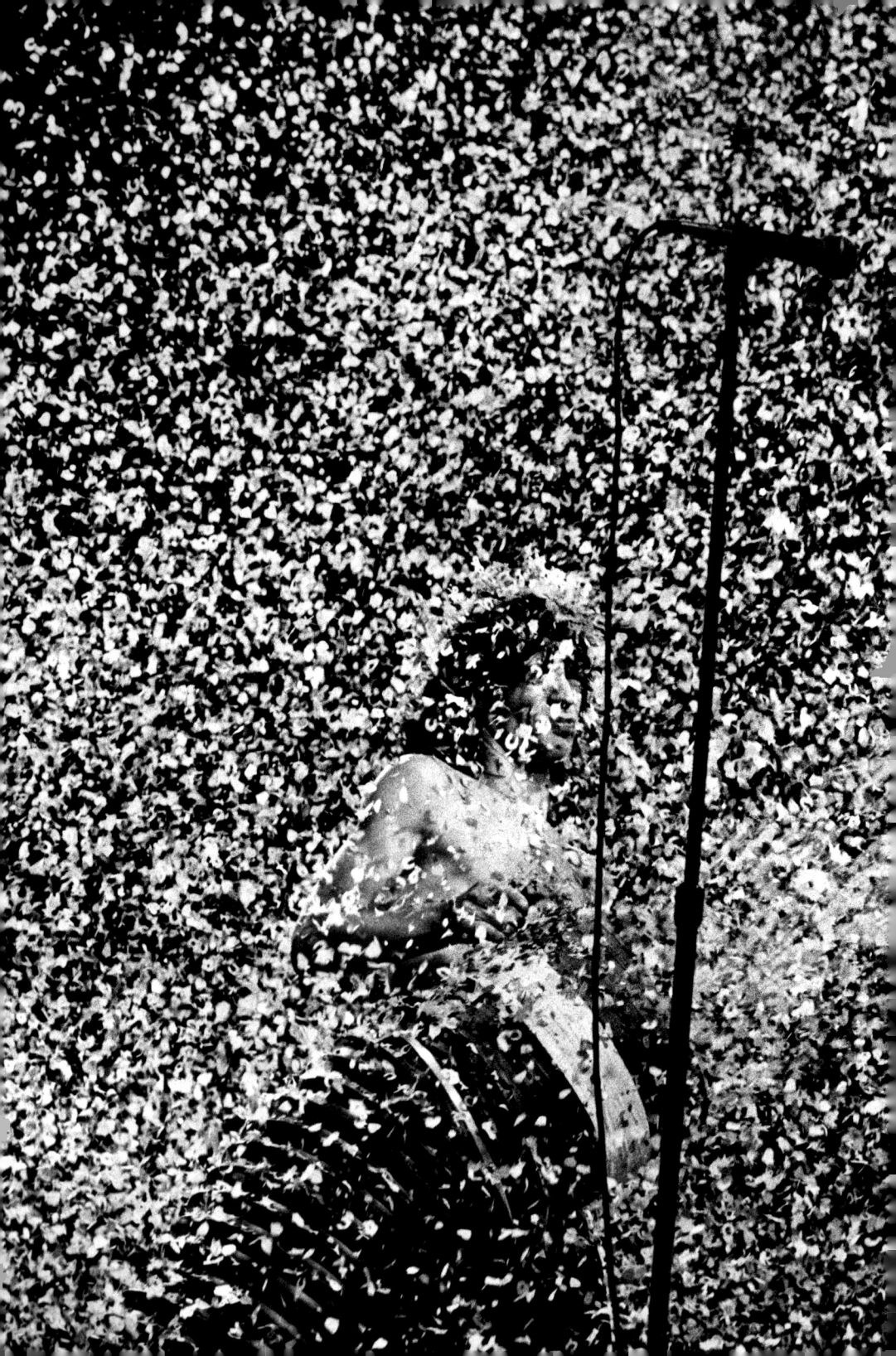

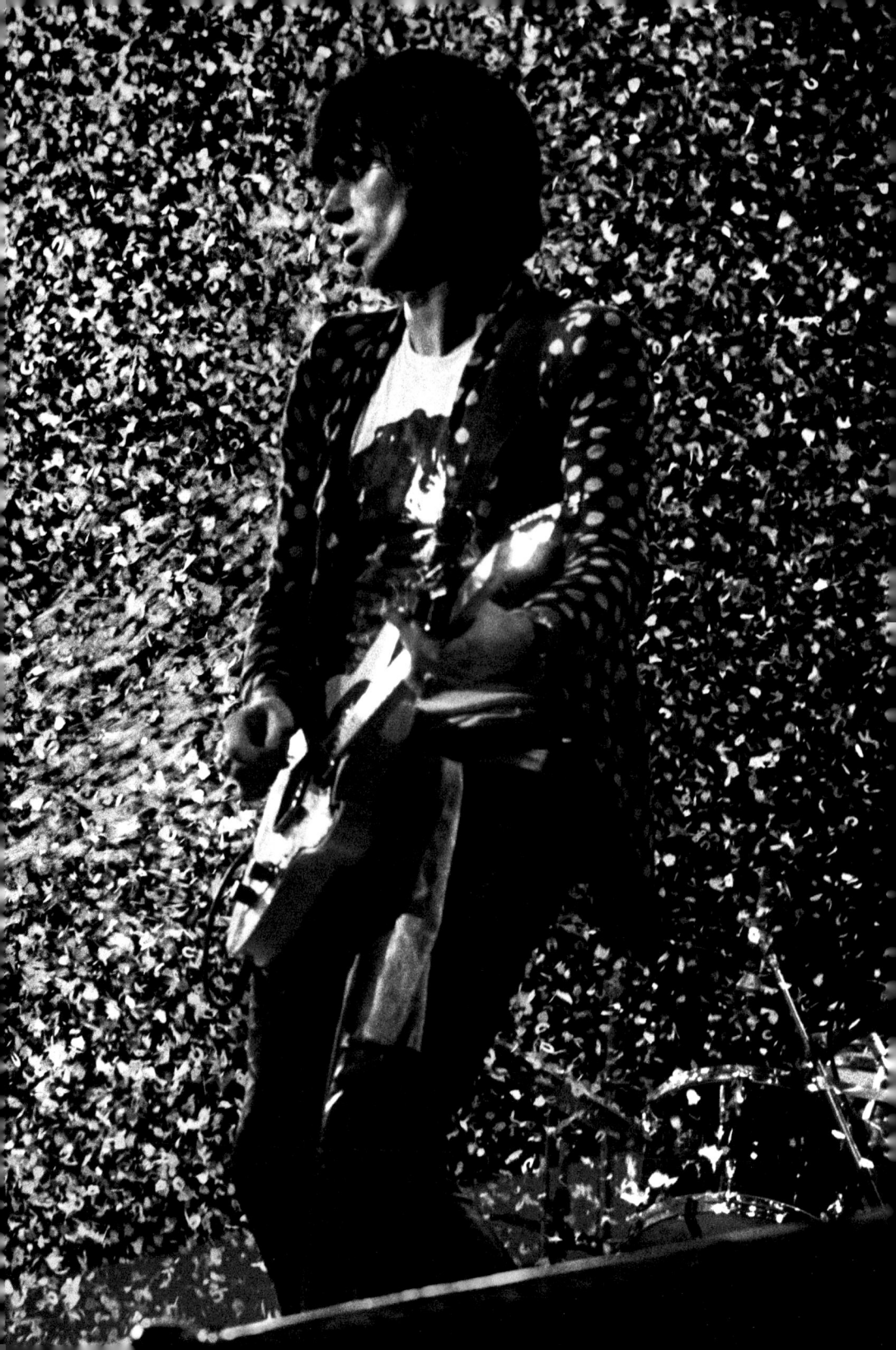

When Grey Turns to Blue: The Cultural Impact of The Rolling Stones

By Waldemar Januszczak

It's the perfect name right? In 50 BC, the Roman writer Publilius Syrus, a freed slave from Syria, wrote "Saxum volutum non obducitur musco", or that "a boulder that rolls is not covered with moss". People have known this for a long time. When The Rolling Stones chose their name, they chose international significance and universal resonance.

Not, of course, that they did it on purpose. These were wild things from the fringes of London and the pleasant pastures of middle-class England. When these boys started chasing girls, smoking and listening to Muddy Waters, the last thing on their minds was pan-continental significance. They were after the action and, as lots of people know in lots of languages, tumbling boulders cannot be tamed, or stopped, or told what to do.

The story goes that it was Brian Jones who christened them. Brian was from Cheltenham. It's two hours west of London and very genteel: a town full of old people who've gone there to die nicely in elegant Regency surroundings. Brian got out of there as soon as he could – he was never one to hang around – and it isn't a coincidence that he turned out to be so good at wearing white. The bell-bottoms. The polo neck. The hair. When you're as naughty as Brian, you pretend to be angelic. Look at the photos.

Brian took his inspiration from a record that was being played continuously in a Chelsea flat he shared with Mick and Keith, *The Best of Muddy Waters*. Track 5 on side one of this fine disc was a song that growled and wailed its way through a steamy confession about catfish and women and husbands who were away. It was called "Rollin' Stone", and the way Muddy sang it was the way the Devil might have sung it: slow, snaky and wicked.

A good way to understand the 1960s is to remember that they came after the 1950s – Britain's Greyest Decade. In Britain, tea was rationed until 1952. Sweets and sugar were rationed until 1954. For the rest of the decade, pleasure was rationed as well – or so it seemed. When the 1960s arrived, it was like being let out of jail. Most of the Stones were actually born in the 1940s, another kind of decade altogether. The

1940s were full of war. Wars aren't grey. They're black. Apart from Bill Wyman, the Stones were too young to remember it. But Bill, who was born in 1936, remembered it so well, that it seemed to freeze his expression and render him immobile on stage.

The others were born during the London Blitz. And even if they didn't remember it, its impact was in them: the destruction, the blackness. Keith once told an interviewer that whenever he hears a siren in a documentary about the war, his hair stands on end. He was just a baby, but the darkness got in. Charlie grew up in a London prefab after the rest of the houses in his street were bombed. All this seeped into their sound, and even today, when they tour the world as happy survivors, the thunder of the nighttime bombing raids can still be heard in Keith's guitar and in the darkly destructive brilliance of Mick's lyrics: "I wanna see the sun, blotted out from the sky. I wanna see it painted, painted, painted, painted black." Who in popular music had ever thought like that before?

Until the Stones appeared, British groups had sweet and innocuous names like Cliff Richard and The Shadows, or Joe Brown and The Bruvvers. Those nice boys from Liverpool, The Beatles, who had also turned up in London in the summer of 1962 to record their first single, "Love Me Do", had a fun name. They wanted to "hold your hand". The Rolling Stones wanted to hold a whole lot more than that. They wanted to spend the night together.

And they certainly knew how to dress for the occasion. Make that dangerous and ruthless. Examine those photos. Has there ever been a more alluring or irresistible musical presence than Michael Philip Jagger? When Mick Jagger strutted across Hyde Park in 1969 in *that* dress, and said goodbye to Brian in those unforgettably uncomfortable circumstances, he wasn't just blurring the divide between yin and yang, between male and female. Mick was completing the instruction book on how a rock star should look.

Where The Beatles looked sweet in their matching suits and buttoned-up empire jackets, the Stones never pulled off the we-all-look-the-same shtick. When Keith put on a suit, he messed it up, like a schoolboy messing up his uniform. Whatever they

PP. 394–395
Helmut Newton
January–March 1978.
"We were in the Pathé Marconi Studios because they were owned by EMI, with whom we'd just made a big deal. This one was way on the outskirts of town in Boulogne-Billancourt, near the Renault factory; nothing around like restaurants or bars." Keith Richards, *Life*, 2010

PP. 396–397
Claude Gassian
Paris, June 1976. In what amounted to a short residency, the band performed four dates at the Pavillon de Paris (known colloquially as Les Abattoirs) between 4 and 7 June 1976. The former slaughterhouse and meatpacking building provided excellent acoustics, allowing the band to capture nine songs on tape for their *Love You Live* album.

wore, they looked unruly, but always cool. As you flick through the fabulous fashion show, taking place in these pages, you will see all kinds of things being invented: how not to smile at a camera; how to flounce; how to ignore; how to flirt. Look at the way each of them makes a tangible and unique contribution to the whole: the way the different pieces lock together to form a band. We're used to it nowadays: the flamboyant lead singer who throws the moves; the stony bass-player who never shifts; the rhythm guitarist on the edge of chaos; the other guitarist who does the frilly bits. And then, right at the back, lurking in the shadows and keeping it solid the drummer who doesn't say much. It's the classic rock line-up, and the Stones created it.

Which brings us to their hair: a mega-important subject. The big thing about The Rolling Stones when they appeared was their long hair. It was what everyone knew about them: what everyone was afraid of. The story of long hair in Britain is loaded with significance. The divide between longhairs and shorthairs runs through English history like a Grand Canyon. Britain has only ever had one genuinely cultured monarch: Charles I, who wore pearl earrings, floppy white silks and long hair that fell to his shoulders in beautiful cascades. It was a great look. Mick and Brian, around the time of *Their Satanic Majesties Request*, adopted a kind of 1960s variation on it. Later on, Keith would do a passable approximation of Charles I after a night out on the tiles with the wenches when he popped up as Johnny Depp's dad in *Pirates of the Caribbean*.

Charles' followers, the Cavaliers, were notoriously glamorous. But the Roundheads, as they were called then, the puritan followers of Oliver Cromwell, loathed Charles I. They loathed his silk tunics, his satin doublets, his art, his wife. But most of all, they loathed his hair. So much so that in 1649, in an act of scarcely credible political brutality, they cut it off. Not just his hair – his whole head! When the Stones arrived on the doorstep of the 1960s, with their cuffs a-popping and their locks a-flouncing, that prejudice was still there. Long hair wasn't just considered effeminate or impractical: it was dangerous.

The Rolling Stones didn't just invent British rock music: they led the revolution. In 1971, they even gave us a flag to rally round when they came up with that splashy logo of theirs: the wet tongue poking out from two big lips. This famous tongue, far and away the most recognisable logo in rock music, first appeared on the cover of the *Sticky Fingers* album and was designed by an art-school kid named John Pasche who apparently based it on Mick's mouth. What an eloquent international sign it is, standing for the same things: great food, great drink, great sex and great rebellion.

If you fast-forward the story of the Stones to about 1989, you can actually see them changing the world with their hair and their tongues. Eastern Europe doesn't get much press in the story of rock. No one cares much about what was happening musically in Poland or Czechoslovakia or Russia. Whenever I went, I would take with me some bad recordings of The Rolling Stones: a cassette, a 45, a bootleg album. People out there were desperate for that music.

While we were listening to "Start Me Up", the entire Iron Curtain set-up, every kid in every grey communist tenement, was hungry for the Stones. It was the battle between the shorthairs and the longhairs all over again. But this time, with tanks. The police and the army wore short back and sides: the kids who taunted them grew as much hair as they could get away with. On street corners and pop-up markets, they sold photocopies to each other of some of the fabulous pictures in this book. It cost them all the money they had, but it was worth it because it stood for so much. In all those lonely, isolated years when the Iron Curtain fell across their lives the only truly important band ever to cross over and play for them was The Rolling Stones, in Warsaw, in 1967.

These are things people don't forget. And when the longhairs finally overthrew the shorthairs in Prague, when Václav Havel finally became president of the newly freed Czech Republic, whom did he invite to his city for a concert in 1990? The Rolling Stones. Anyone who has been to one of their gigs will know exactly why the president was so keen to have them in Prague. The Stones, live, burn it up like no one else. It isn't just that they are so damned good on stage that needs admiring. It's their commitment to it as well. See the photos. You'll never catch The Rolling Stones lip-synching at a presidential inauguration, or anywhere else. They are the bastard sons of Muddy Waters and Howlin' Wolf, so they'll go on and play whatever's happening. It's how they've been brought up.

How marvellous that they are still here for us. No rock band had ever grown old before. So how the hell do you do it? While all the others fell away – split up, gave up, died or went part-time – the Stones stayed on the job and saw it through, heroically. The tumbling boulders just keep tumbling – it's what they do. See the photos.

PP. 402–403
Anonymous
The 35-show 1982 European tour called in at Munich's Olympiastadion for two dates on 10 and 11 June 1982. Rapturously received in West Germany as elsewhere, the tour's set list ranged from "Under My Thumb" and "Satisfaction" to tracks from the then current album, *Tattoo You*.

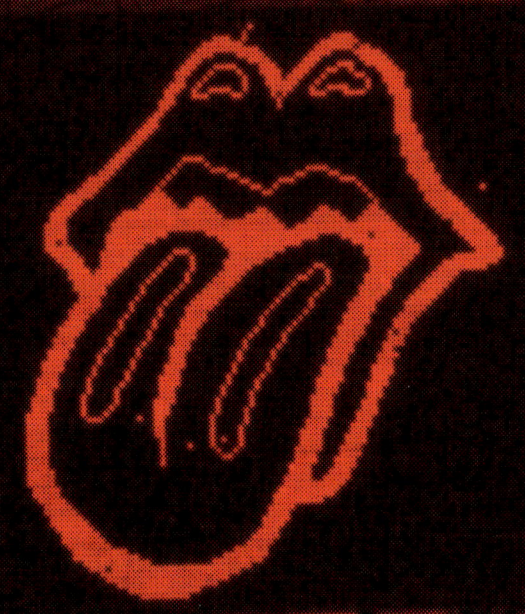

IT'S
ROCK
BUT
LIKI

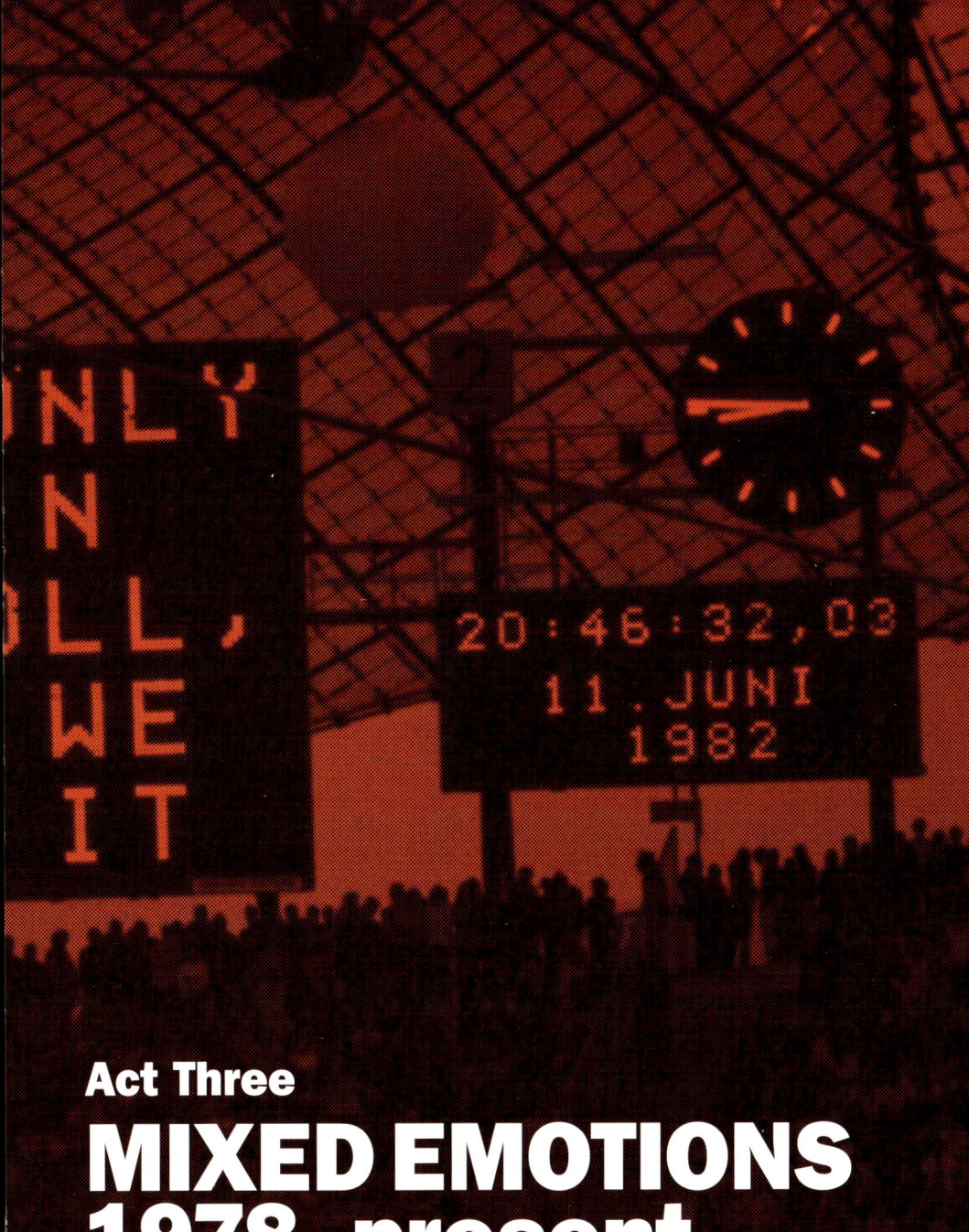

Act Three

MIXED EMOTIONS
1978–present

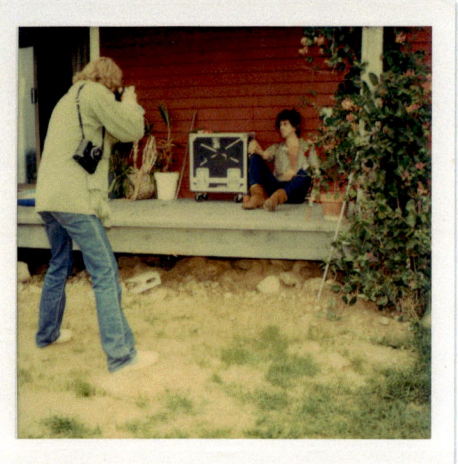
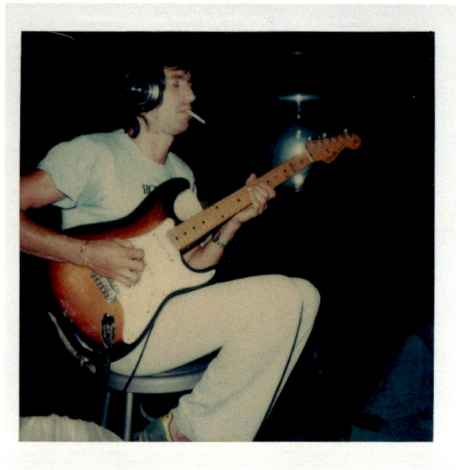
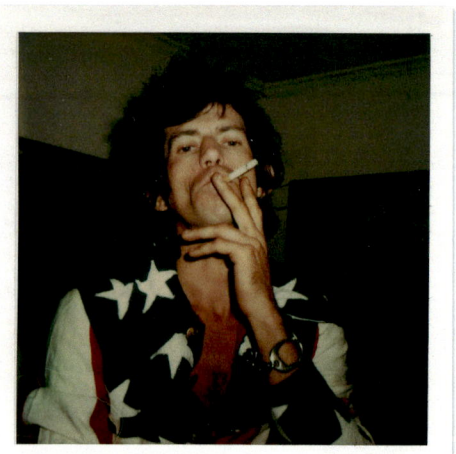
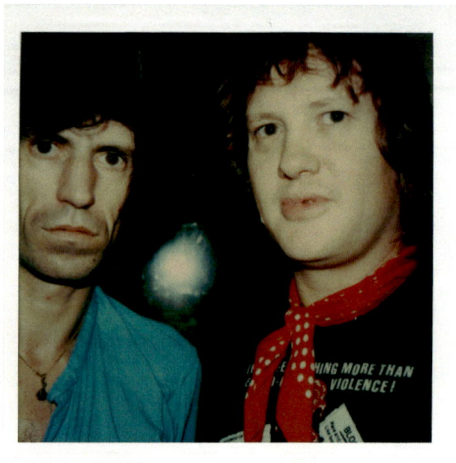
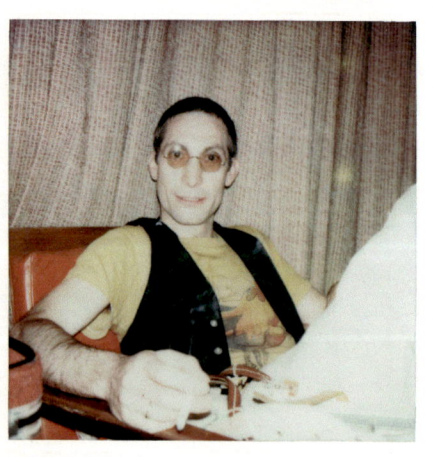
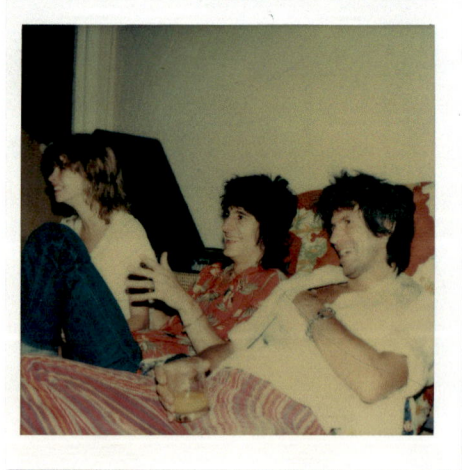

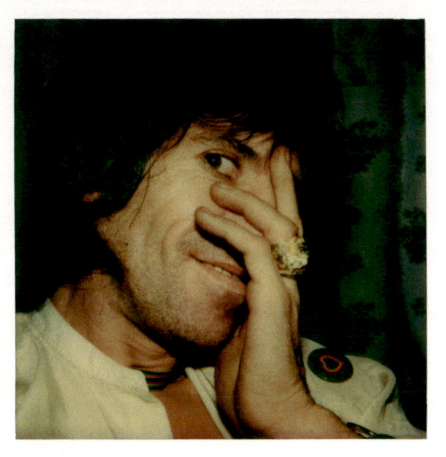
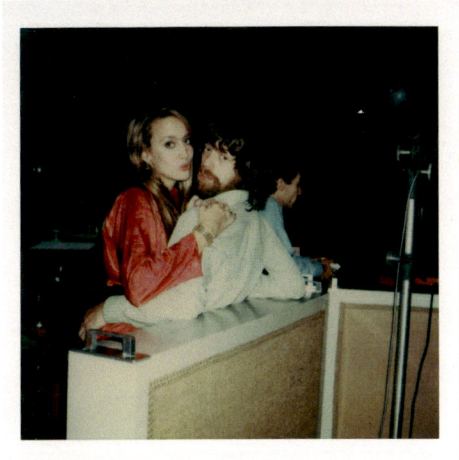
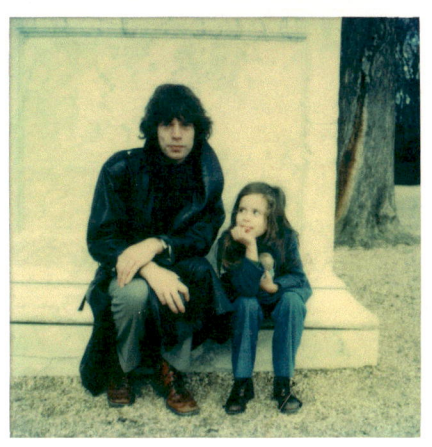
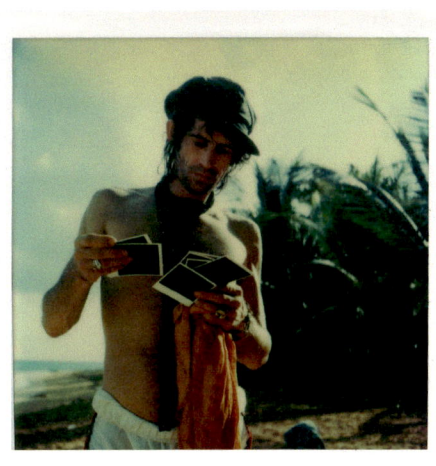
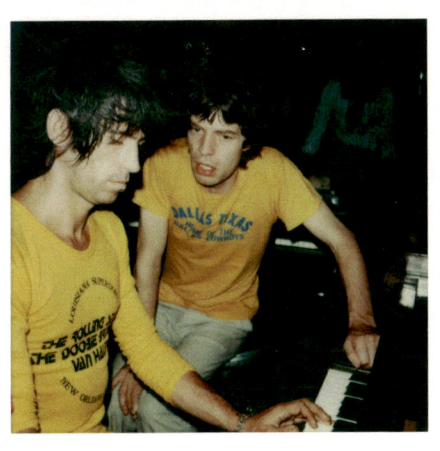
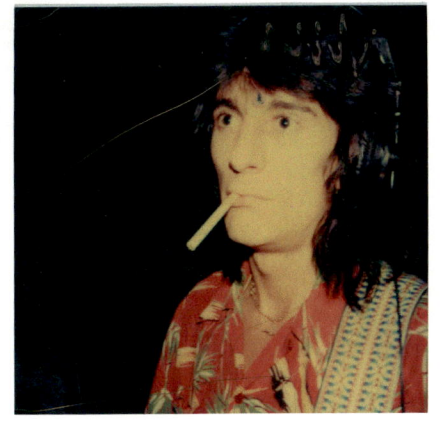

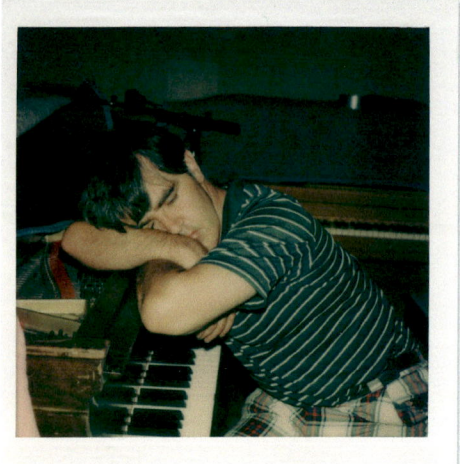
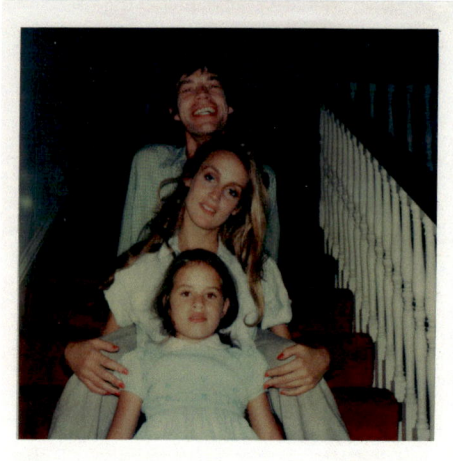
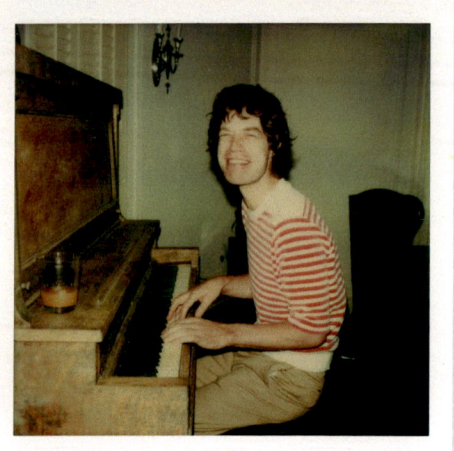
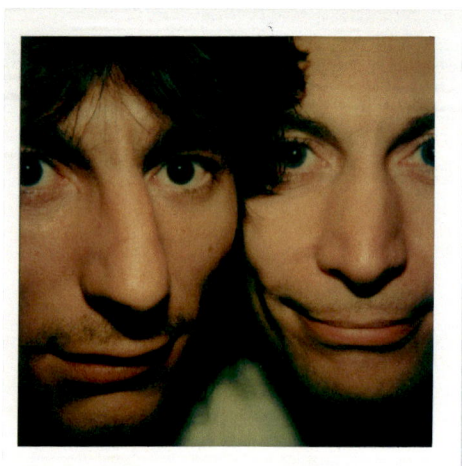
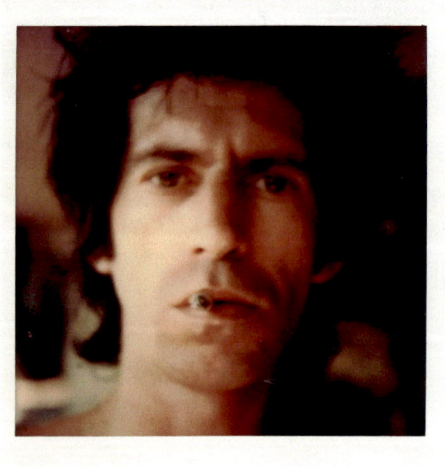
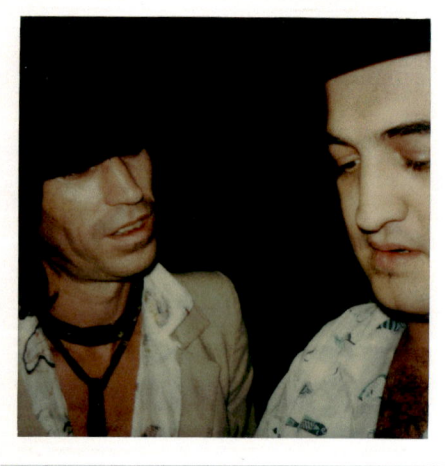

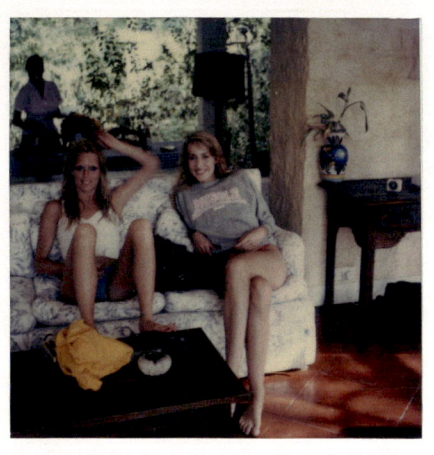
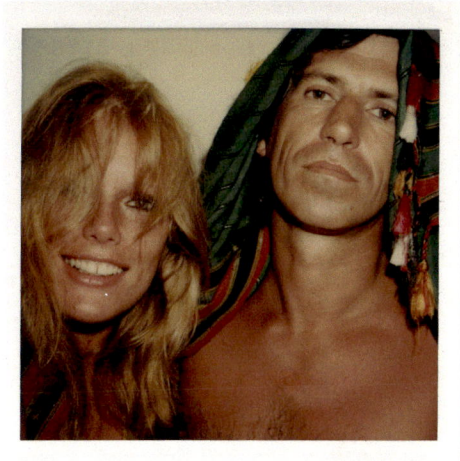
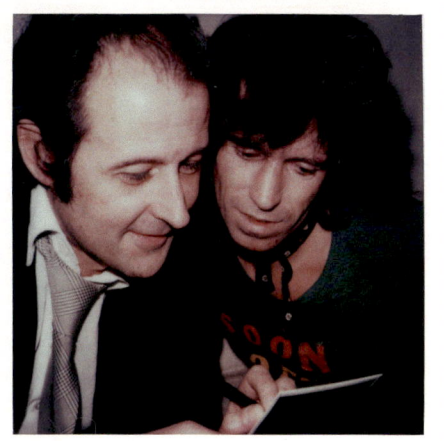
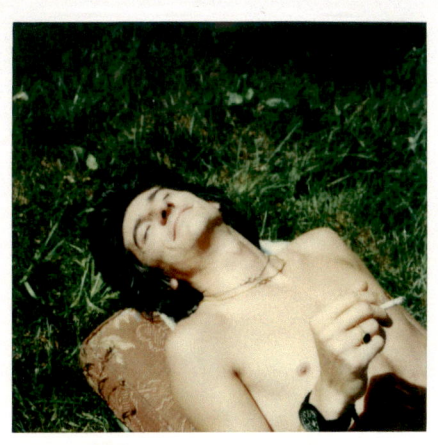
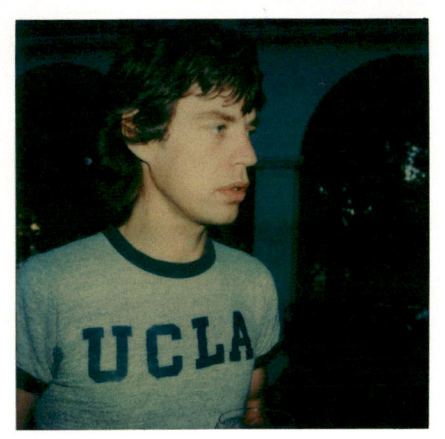
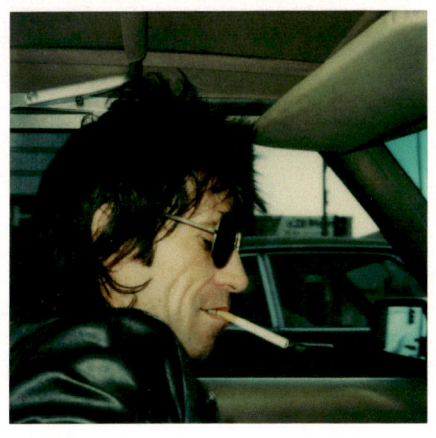

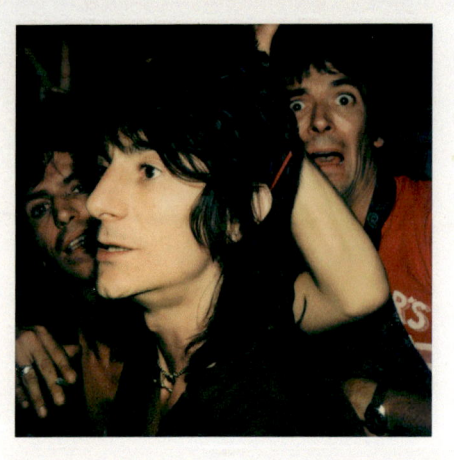
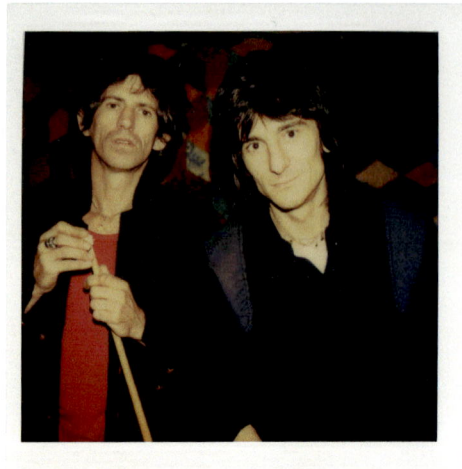
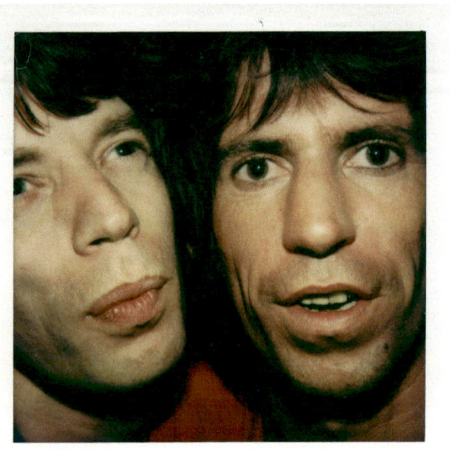
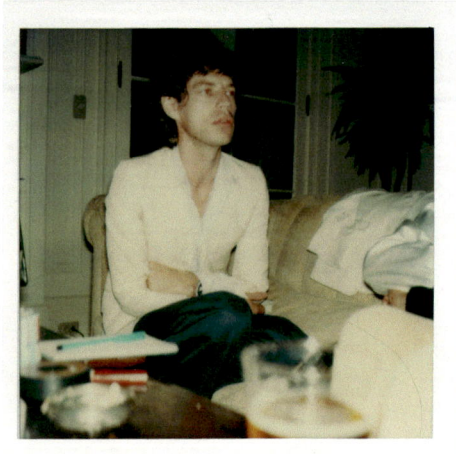
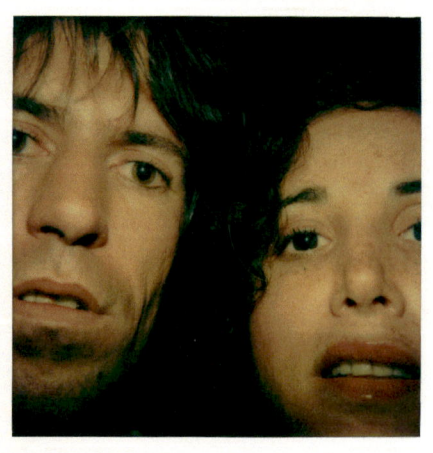
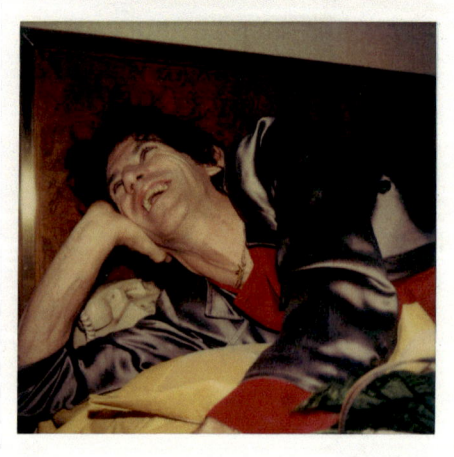

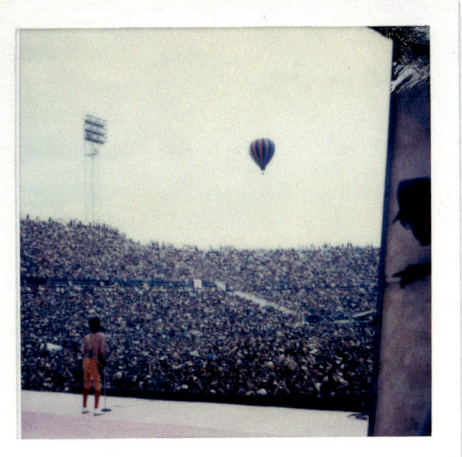 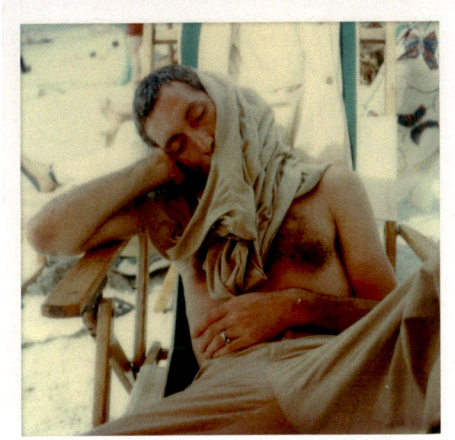

Aaron Rapoport

Cotton Bowl, Dallas, Texas, 31 October–
1 November 1981.
"The Coliseum sounded like an Ohio State–Michigan
football game in a boiler factory when mighty mite
Mick Jagger skipped on stage in a light-blue ski
jacket, white knickers with blue knee guards, white
leggings and white shoes. He jumped in the air,
twirled, danced, waved, bowed to the audience."
Jane Scott, reviewing a concert in Cleveland, Ohio,
The Plain Dealer, 17 November 1981

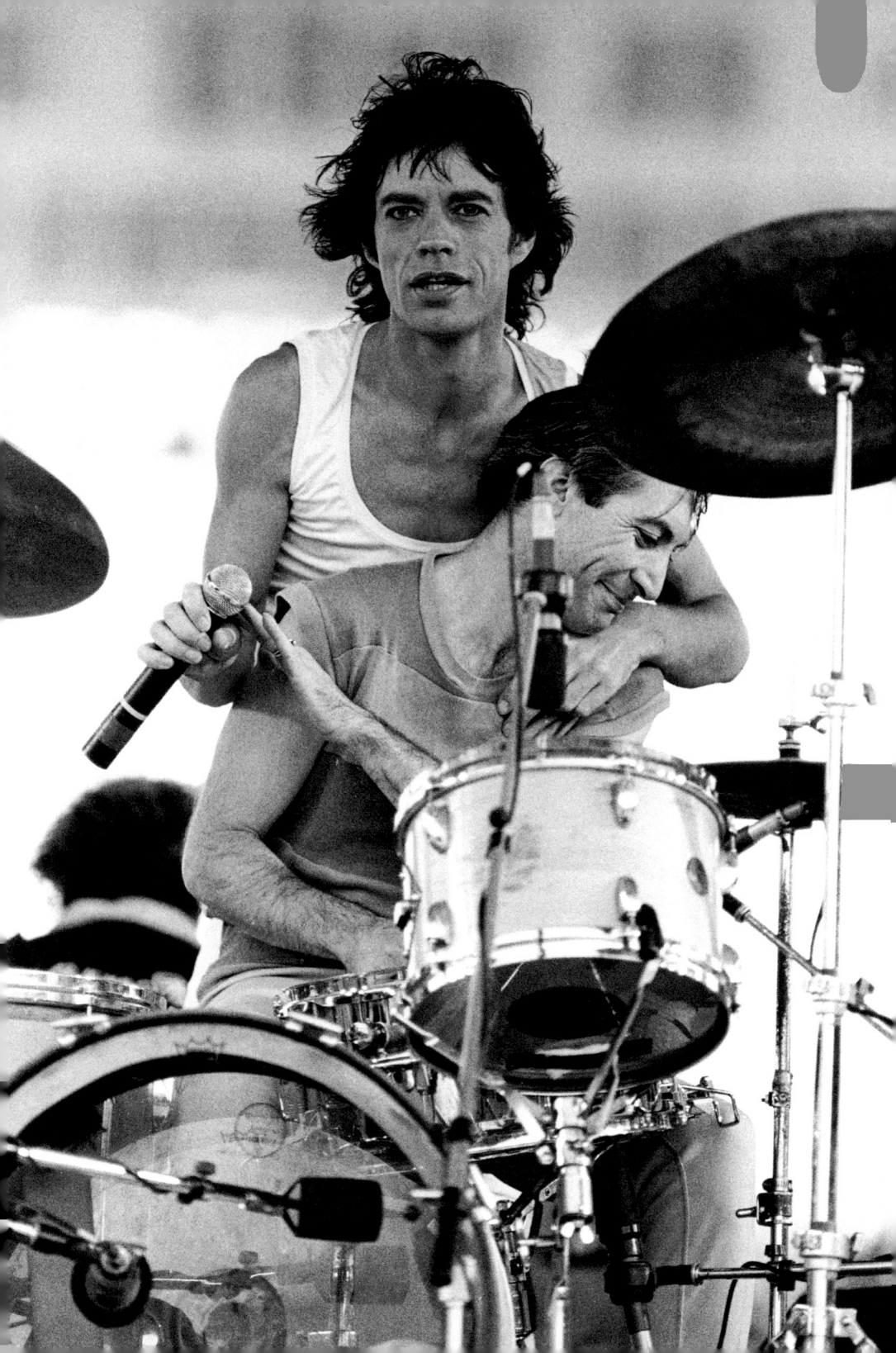

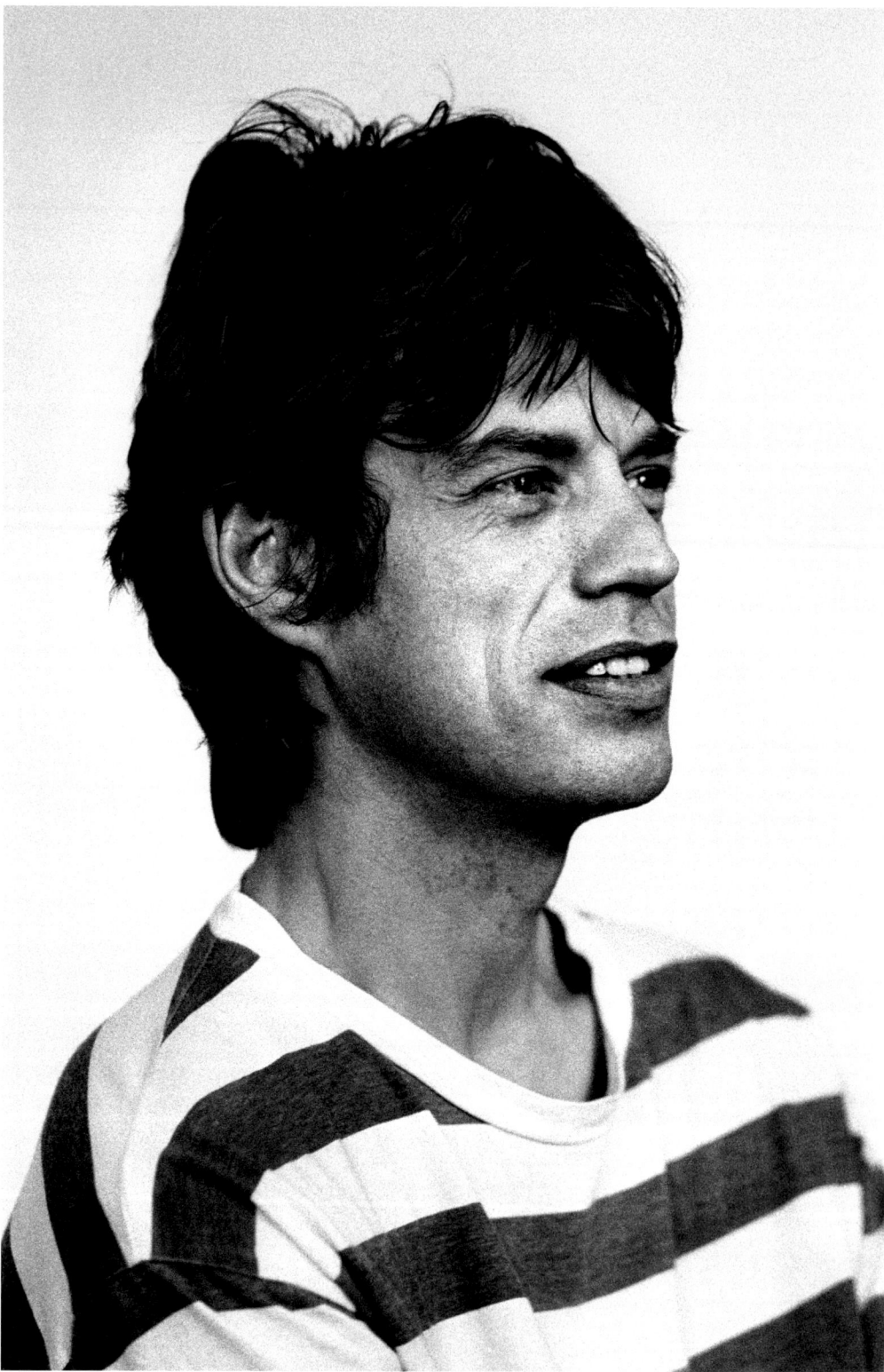

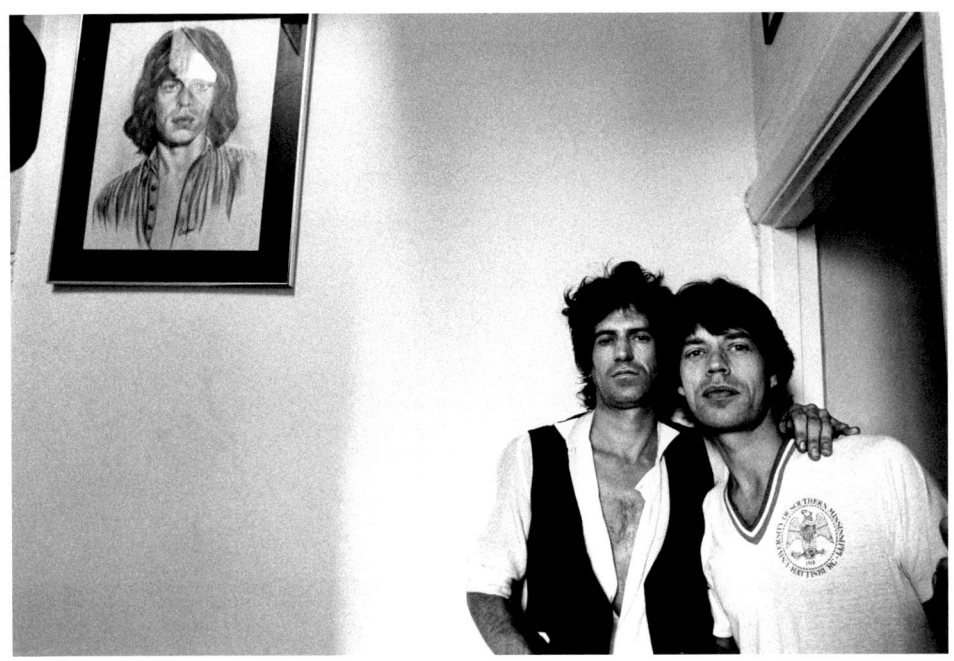

Anton Corbijn
London, 1980. Shot taken for *New Musical Express* around the release of *Emotional Rescue.* *"He is still very beautiful in my eyes, much has been said of his androgynous attraction, and I suppose my response to his physical presence confirms all that. Jagger is also such a charismatic person that he could easily make you forget his looks."* Pete Townshend, *The Times*, 25 July 1983

Anton Corbijn
London, 1980. While there were no live shows for the band in 1980, the album *Emotional Rescue* easily filled the vacuum, topping both UK and American charts on its release. Photos to augment the LP's promotion were taken in the spring of 1980, and appeared in a Mick Jagger cover feature for the 28 June edition of Britain's *New Musical Express,* under the headline "Rolling Away The Stone".

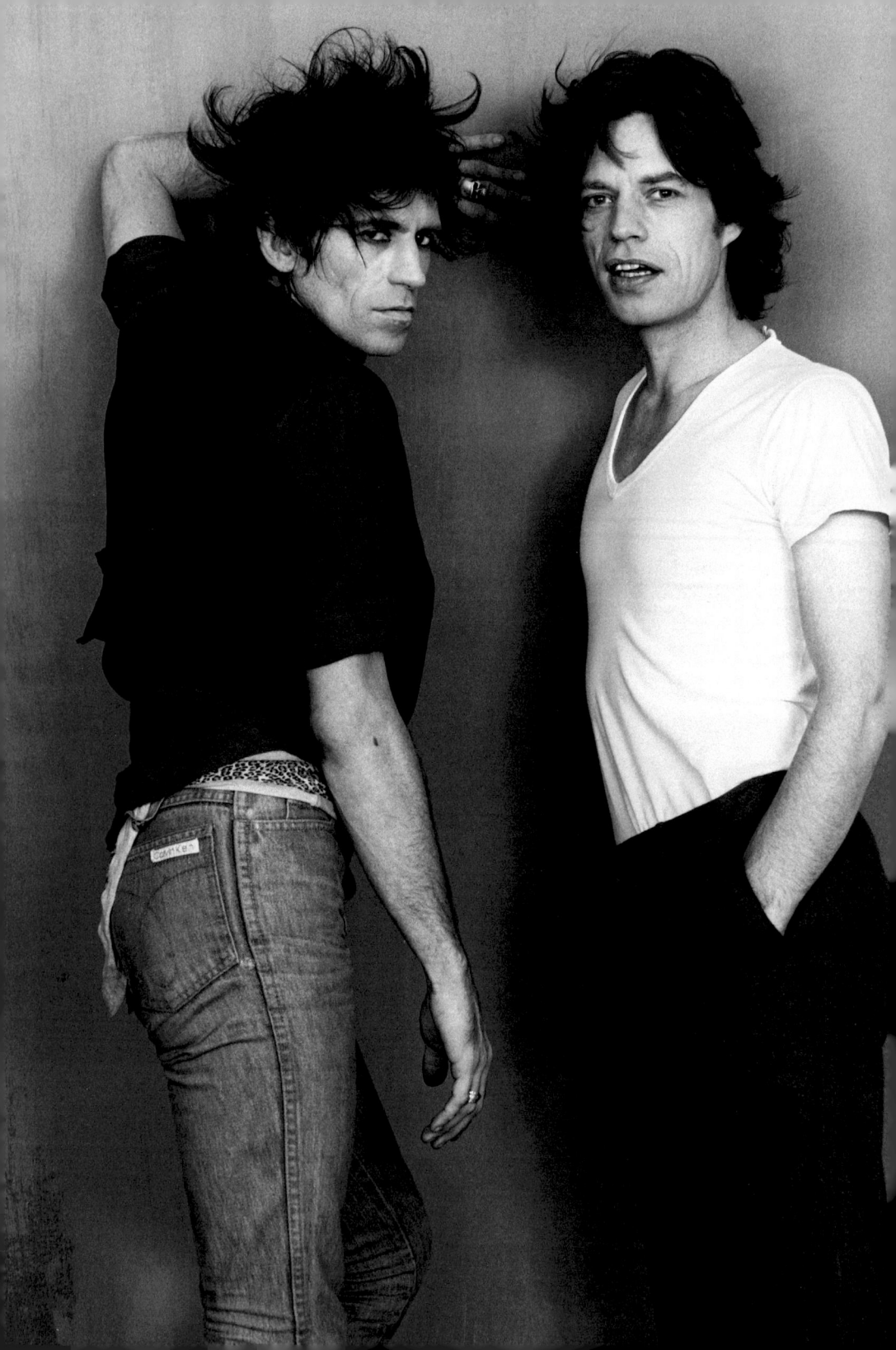

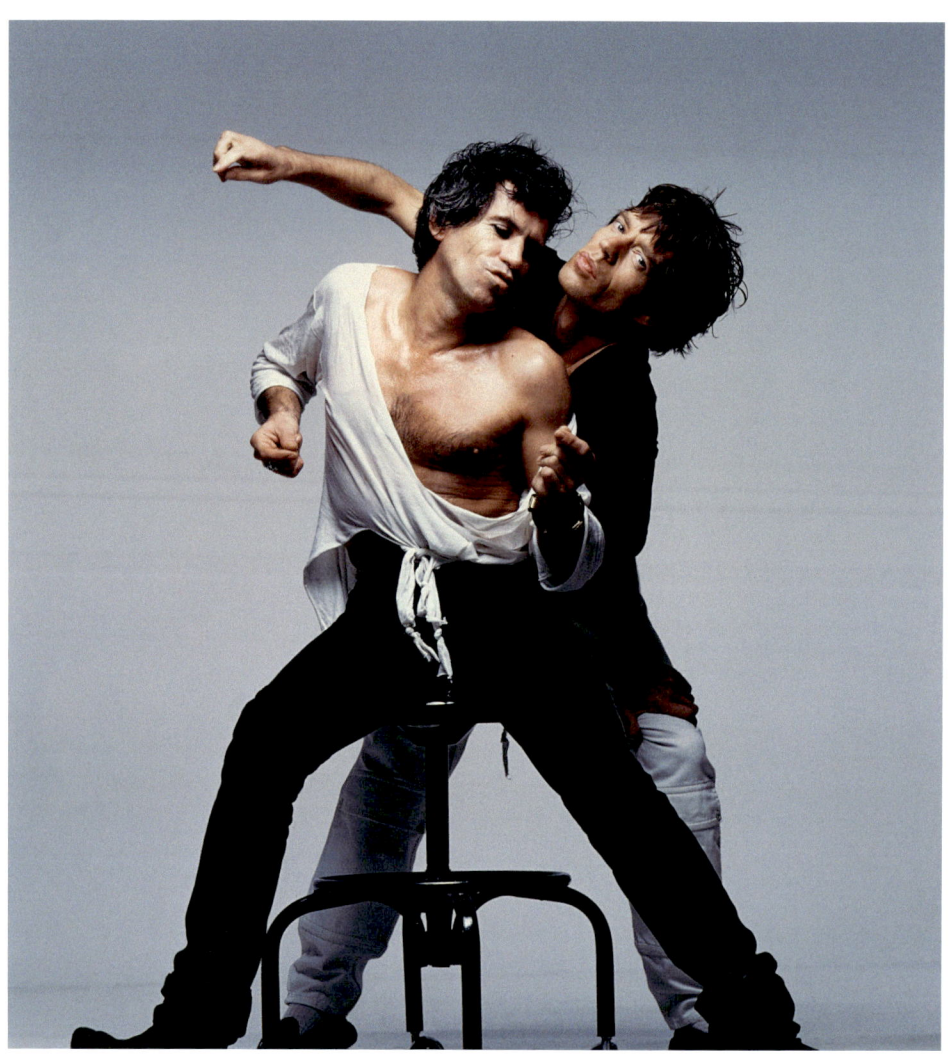

Bill King

Undercover album publicity session, New York, September 1983. *Undercover* found the band in experimental mode – both musically and lyrically. In the lead-off single, "Undercover Of The Night", Jagger's lyrics tackle the subject of political corruption in Central and South America.

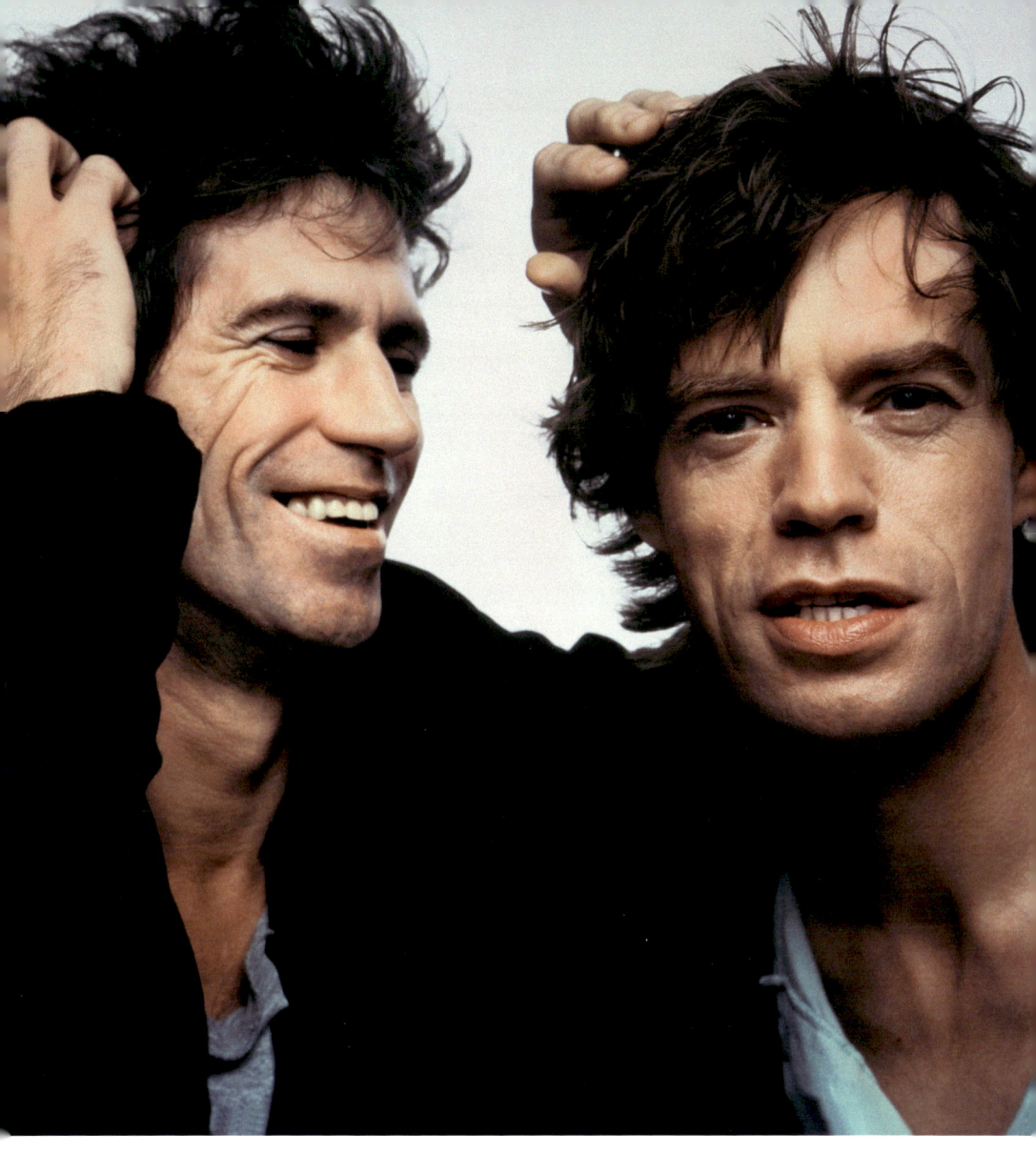

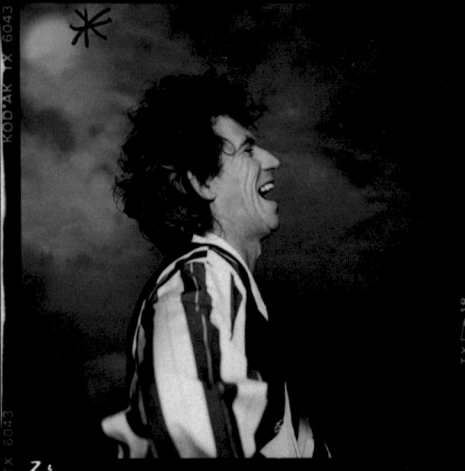

2

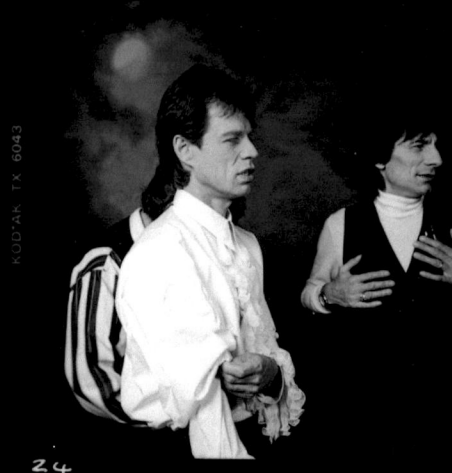

24

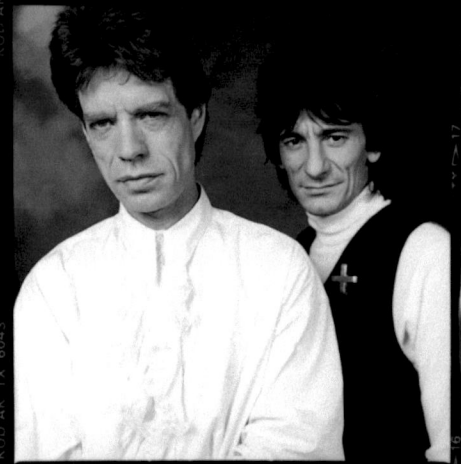

22

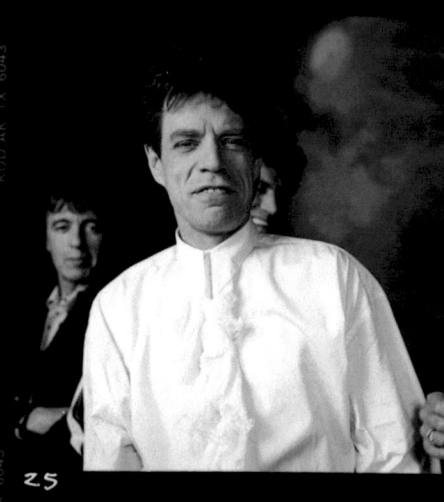

25

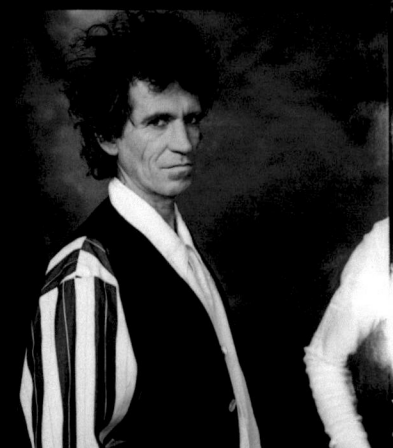

23

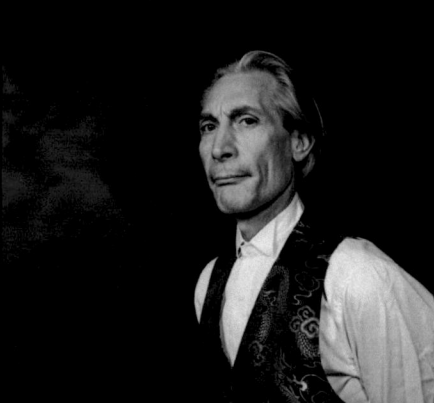

26

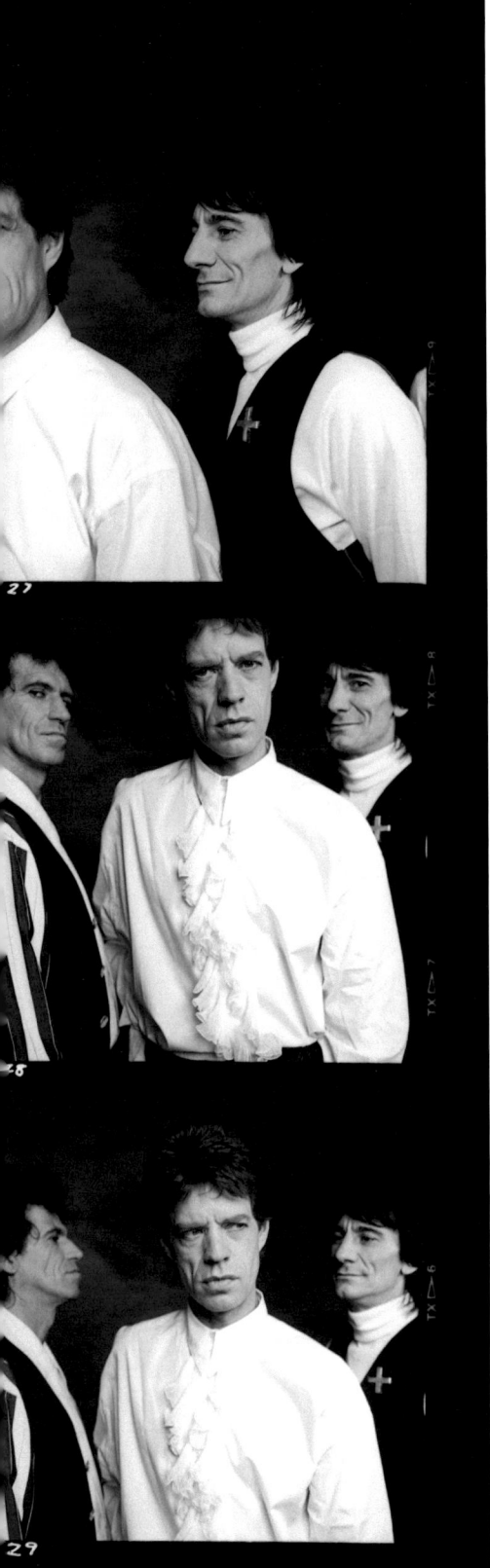

John Stoddart

London, 1989.

Preparing for the *Steel Wheels/Urban Jungle* tour of 1989–90, the most ambitious tour in rock history. The group swung through 115 shows in 18 countries, performing to an audience of over 3.25 million and in the process forging a record for the highest-grossing tour of all time.

"Just look at these guys. Giants. Golems. Geezers with a quarter-century of history together, 'a long shadow', as Keith Richards says, 'that we drag around'. Their tour starts Aug. 31 in Philadelphia; when the New York City shows were announced, some 300,000 tickets (at an average price of $28.50) were sold in a record six hours." Time magazine, 4 September 1989

Dimo Safari
New York, August 1989.
Prior to the massive *Steel Wheels/Urban Jungle* tour of 1989–90, extensive rehearsals were held in Connecticut, Long Island and finally at Veterans Stadium in Philadelphia. As was becoming customary, the group managed to slip in a warm-up show, this one at Toad's Place, a nightclub in New Haven, Connecticut, on 12 August 1989. The tour proved to be Bill's swansong with the band.
"Playing with the Stones there was always such a lot of pressure. The next album or single always had to be the best, or at least sell more. When we got together to play it was a great moment ... When I toured with the Stones it would take a month to practise all these songs we'd been playing for 30 years." Bill Wyman, *Ultimate Classic Rock* magazine, December 2012

P. 422
David LaChapelle
New York, 1992.
While originally taken to publicise Keith's 1992 solo album *Main Offender*, this iconic shot would find greater prominence on the cover of his acclaimed 2010 biography, *Life*.
"He's a good guy. He's a brilliant musician. He's had an unlikely life. If you read ten pages of this book, you won't be able to put it down. And you will understand once again, most people who really do something special, did it because of what they had inside and turns out it wasn't an accident after all." Bill Clinton, Third Annual Norman Mailer Center Gala, New York, 8 November 2011

P. 423
Herb Ritts
London, 1987.
In 1987, Mick was in the midst of pursuing a solo career – a brief interlude from the Stones that spawned several albums including *Primitive Cool*, *Wandering Spirit* and *Goddess In The Doorway*.

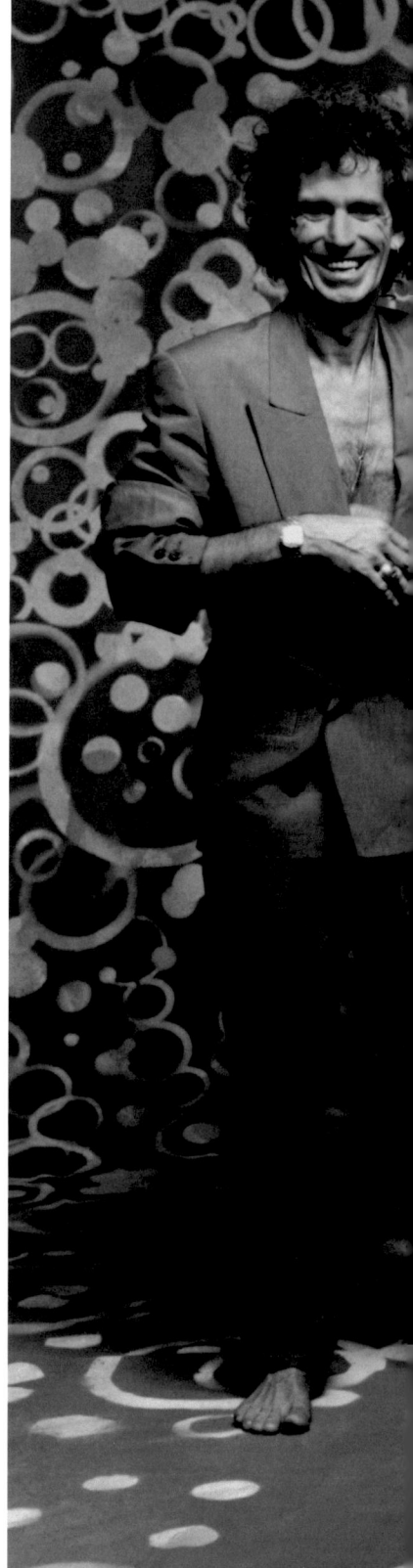

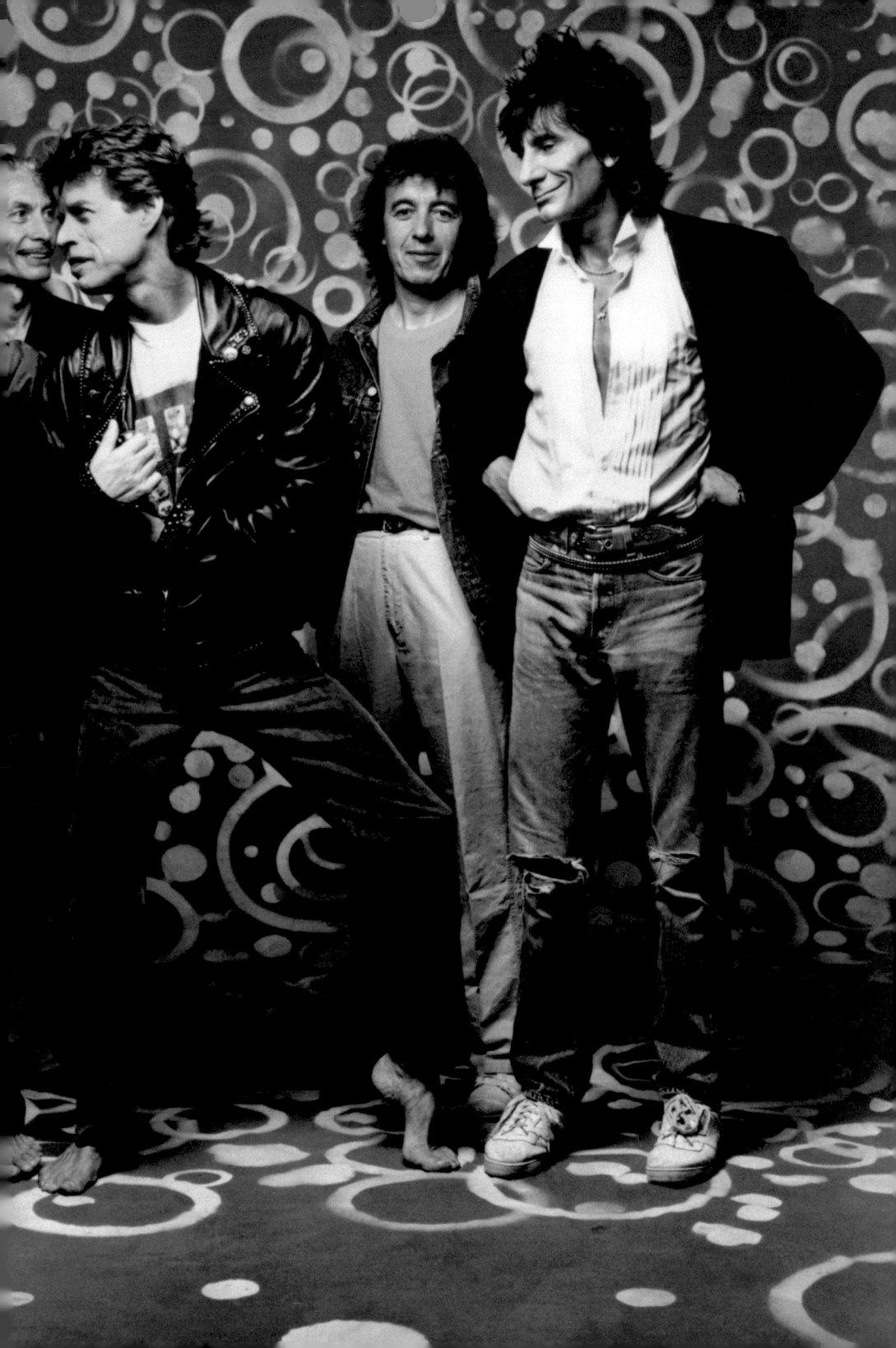

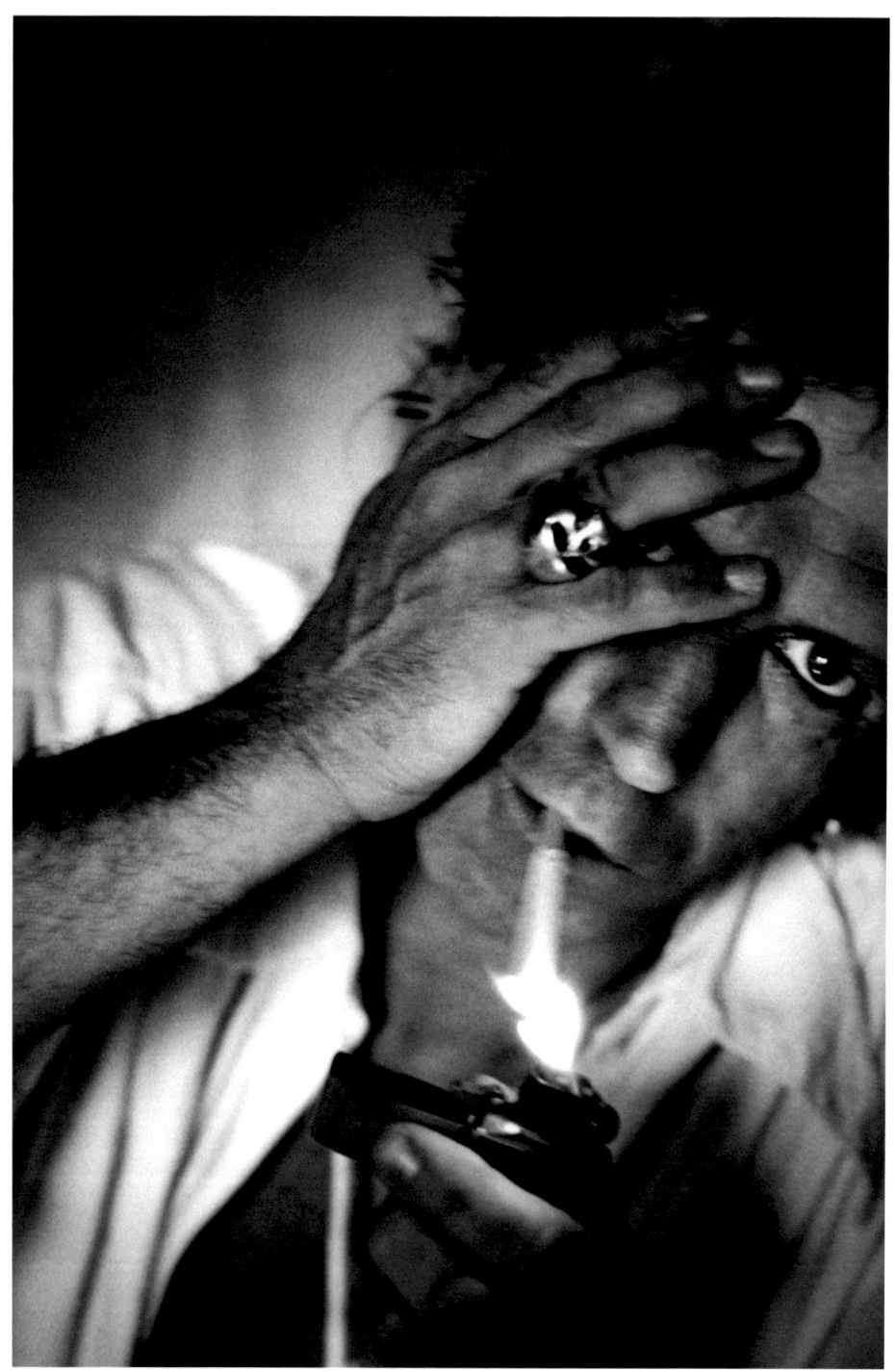

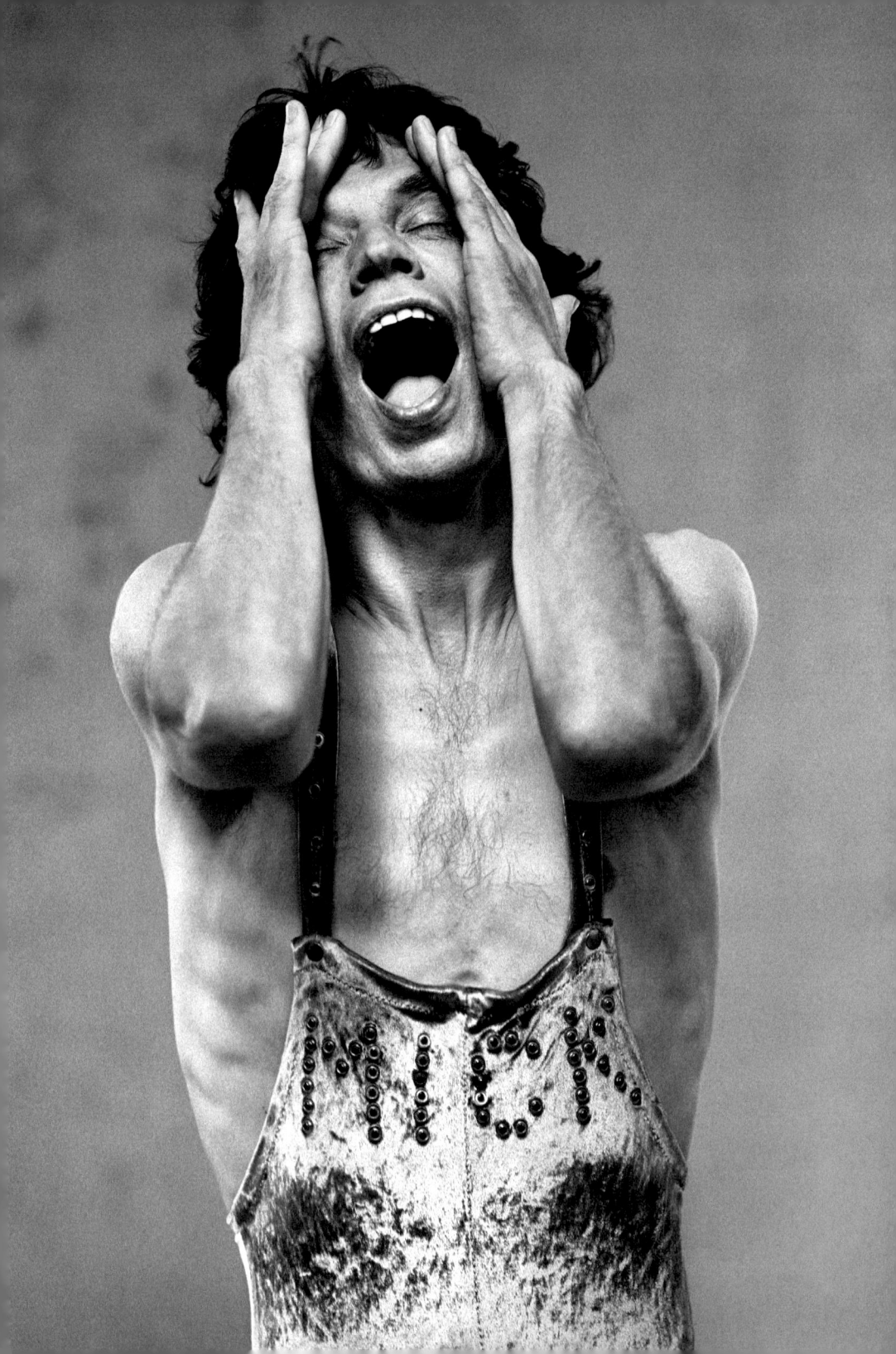

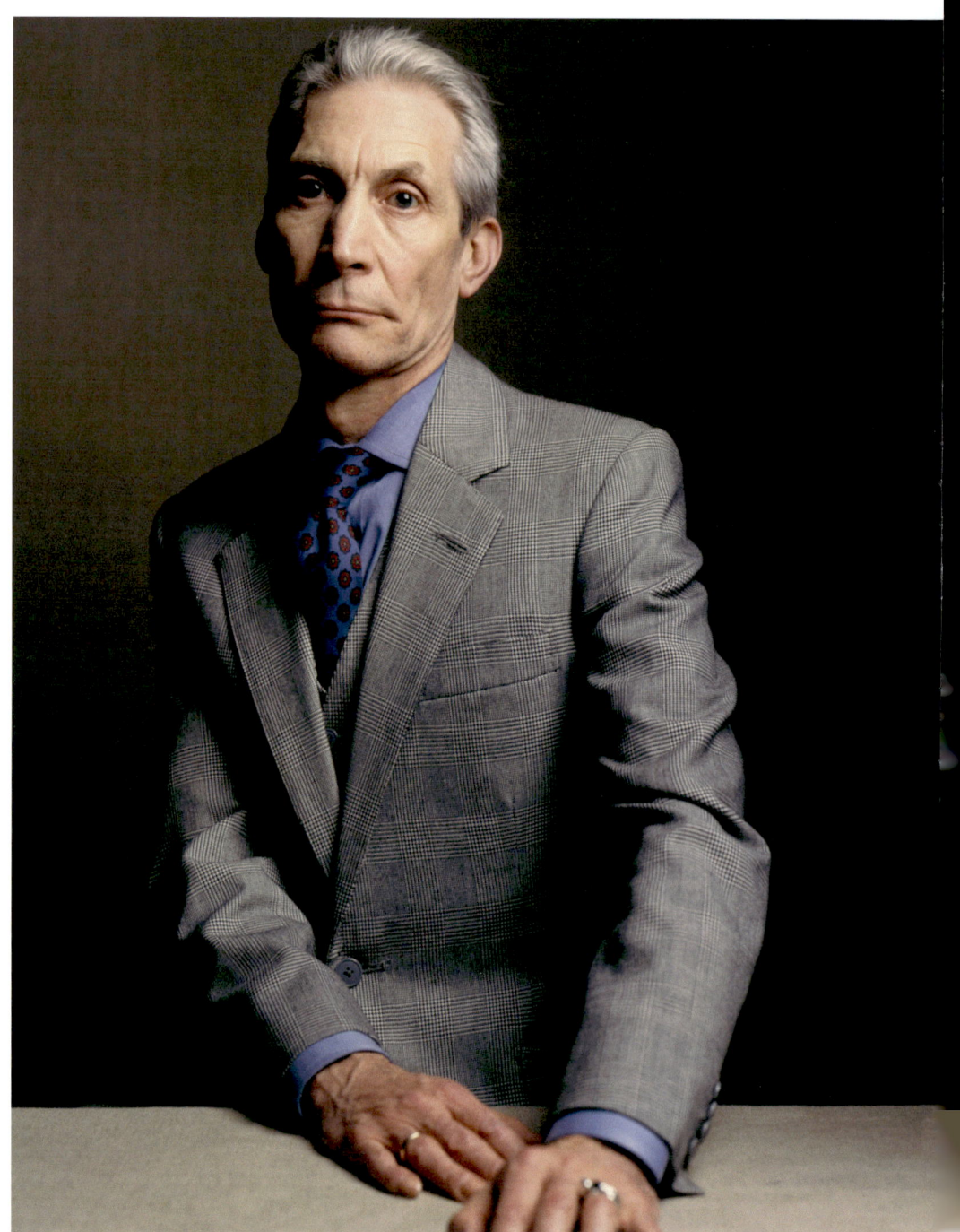

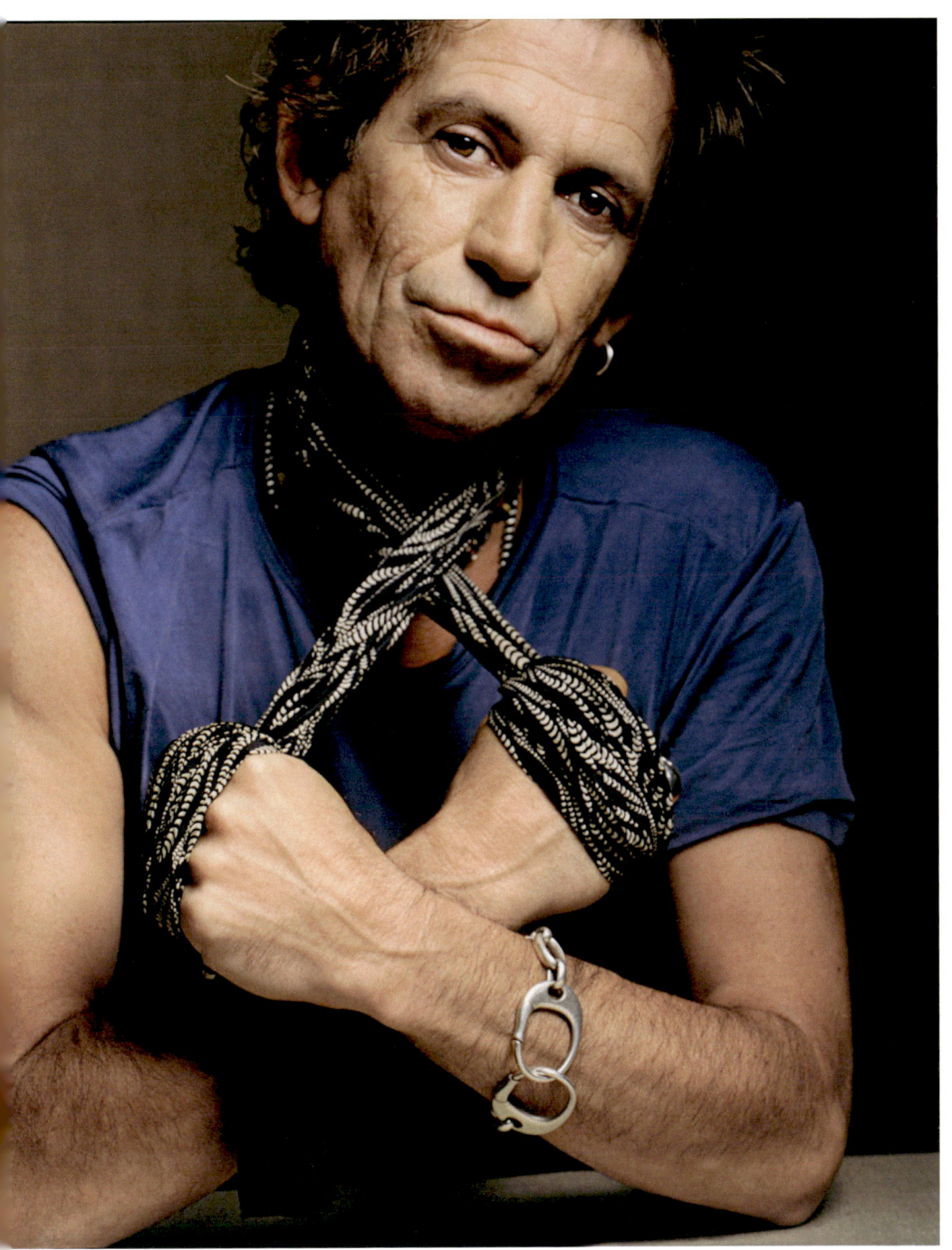

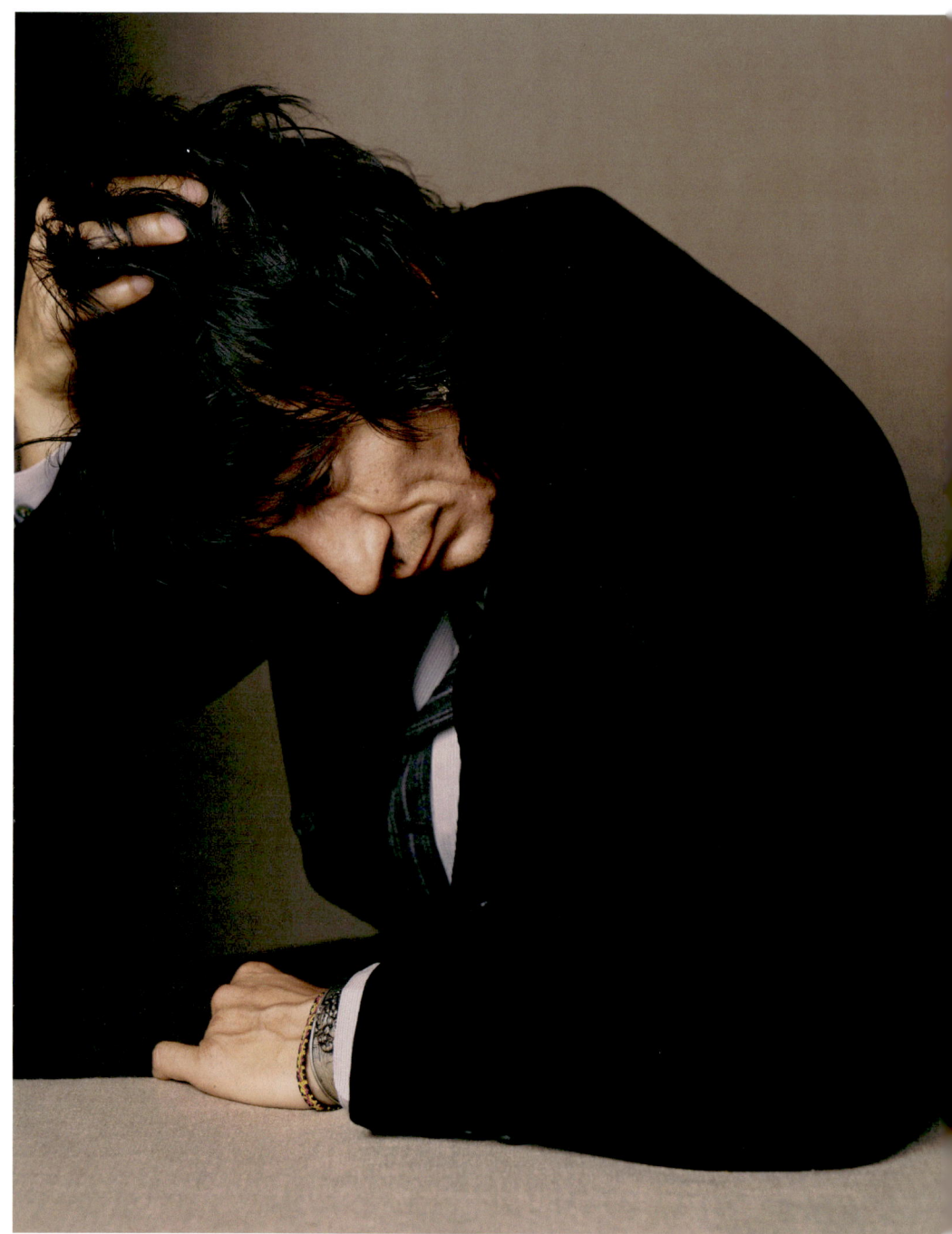

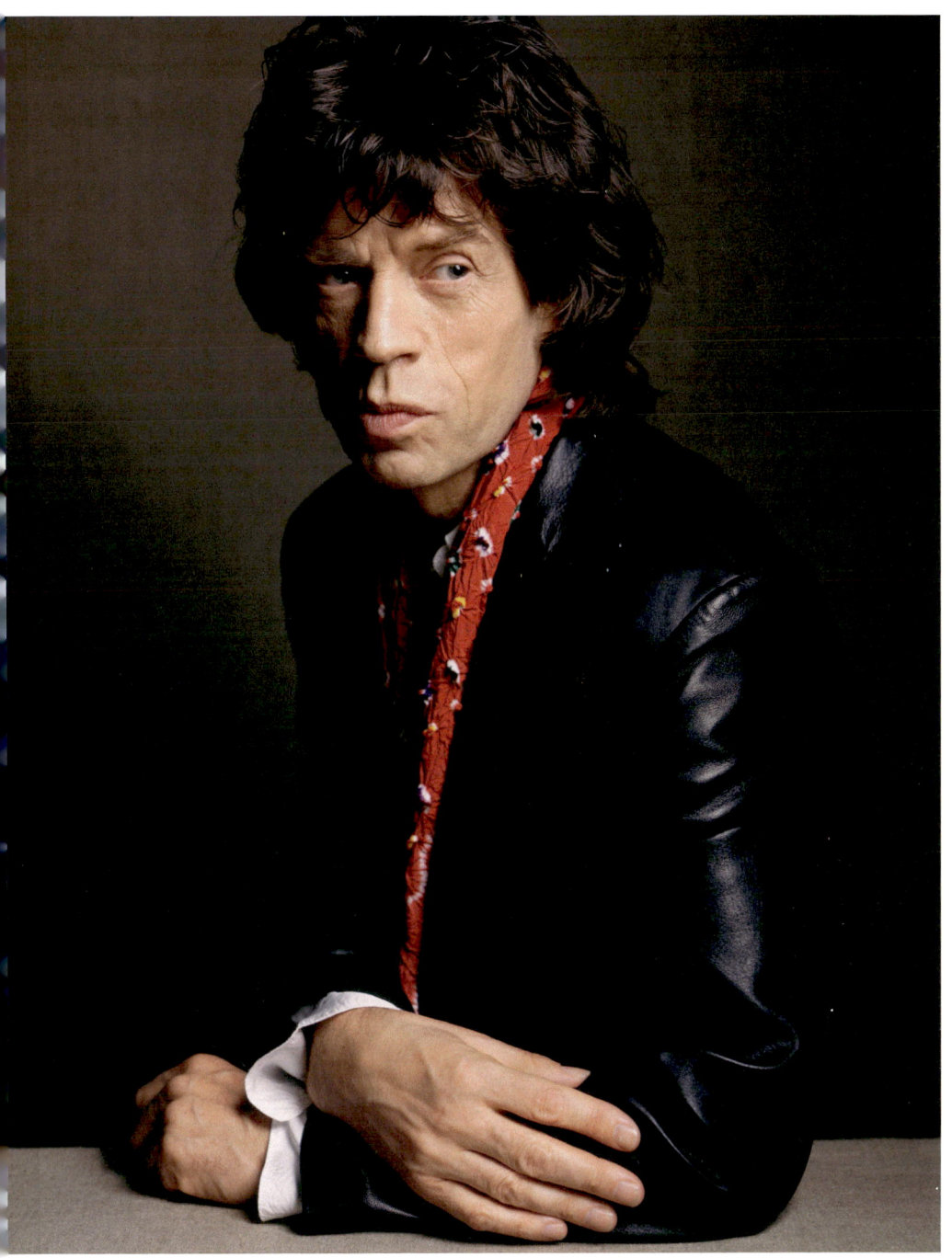

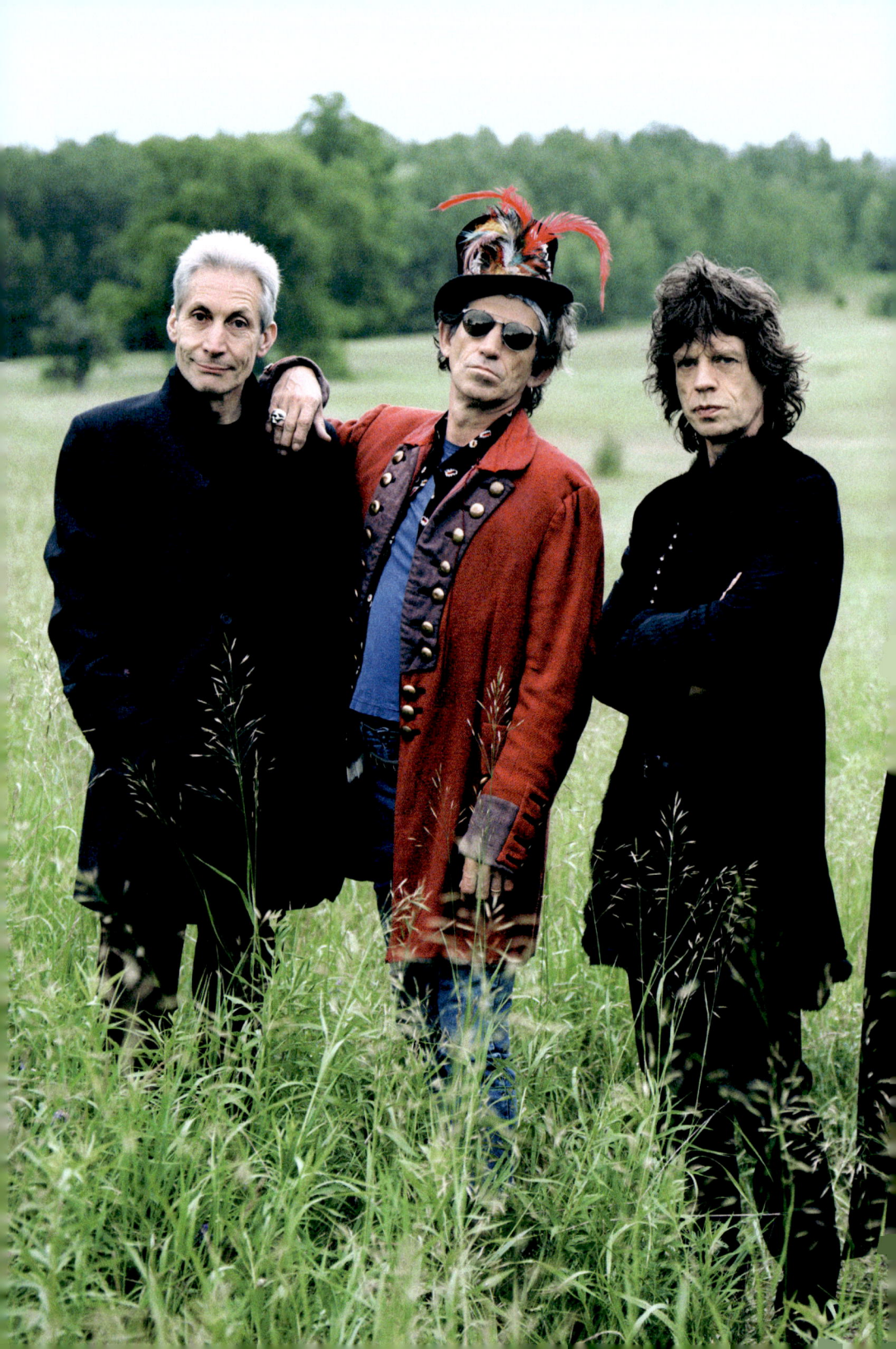

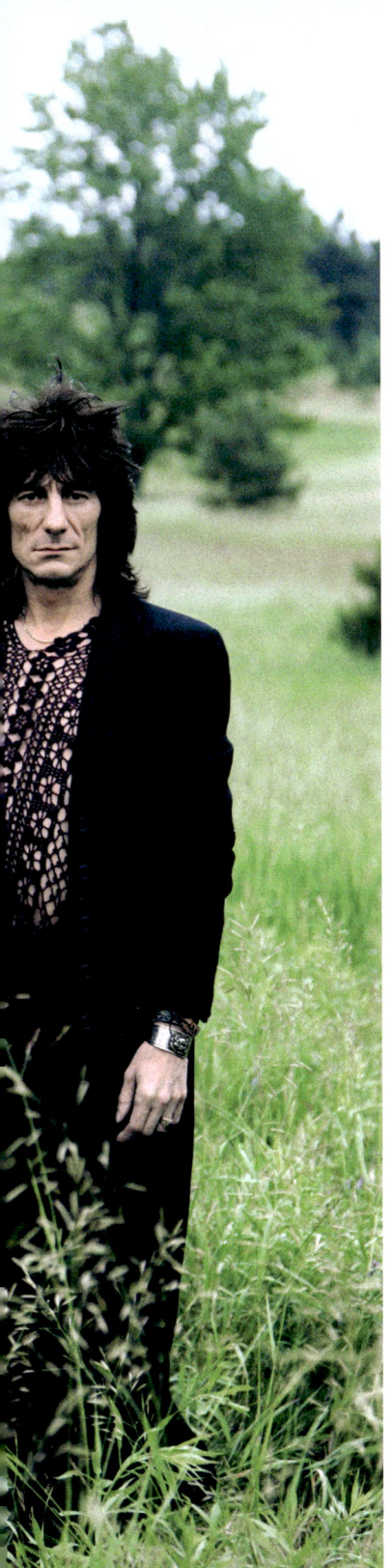

P. 424
Mark Seliger
New York, 1994.
The 1994 album *Voodoo Lounge* propelled
the Stones back to the top of the charts. Their
20th album spawned six singles and a world
tour that eclipsed all previous tours, both in size
and returns.
*"Something happens around us, and it happens
when we play. It's either magic or catastrophe
whichever way you look at it."* Charlie Watts,
interviewed in *The Rolling Stones: European
Premiere Live*, 1995

P. 425
Mark Seliger
New York, 1994.
*"Keeping a band together this long, it was bound
to hit a rocky patch somewhere. And when that
happens to most bands, that's usually it. The ship
founders on that rock forever. The strength of
the Stones is that they didn't. We went through
it all, Mick and I went through whatever we went
through, and put it all back together."* Keith
Richards, interviewed in *Voodoo Lounge Special*,
MTV Europe, 17 June 1995

P. 426
Mark Seliger
New York, 1994.
With new bass player Darryl Jones quietly filling
Bill's vacant space, the 13-month *Voodoo Lounge*
tour played 123 gigs to over 6.3 million attend-
ees, taking $ 320 million in the process.
*"It's where we operate best, on the road. Y'know
it's where we feel like normal human beings."*
Ronnie Wood, *Voodoo Lounge Special*, MTV
Europe, 17 June 1995

P. 427
Mark Seliger
New York, 1994.
*"Being interviewed is one of Mick Jagger's least
favourite pastimes, a necessity that accompanies
his career. A typical session with a journalist lasts
20 minutes. His life has been public for so long, he
sees little need to explain or justify himself and
has everything to be gained by holding on to what
privacy he has – such as the privacy of his thinking
– as well as the value of a little mystery."* Jann S.
Wenner, *Rolling Stone* magazine, 14 December 1995

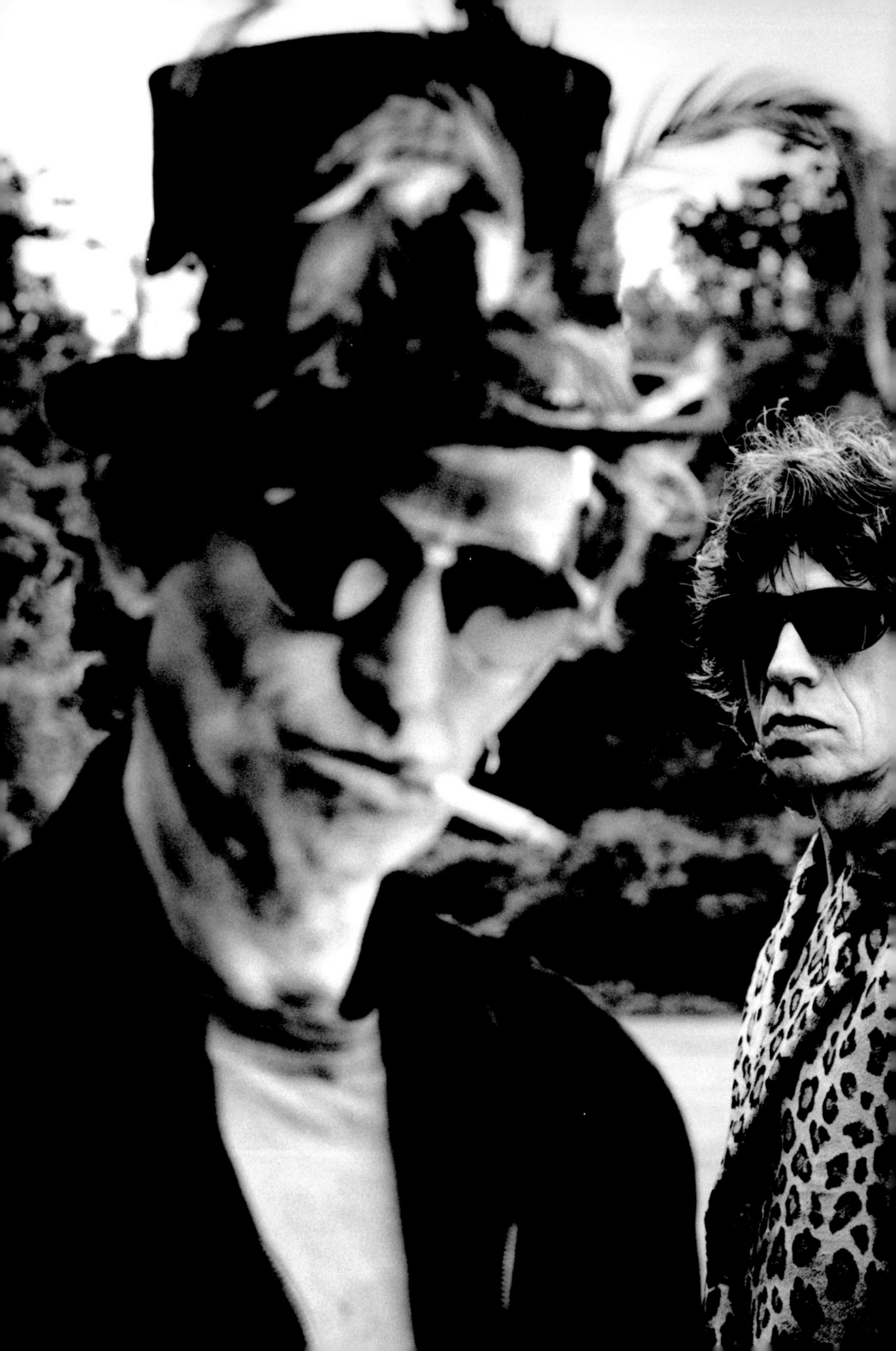

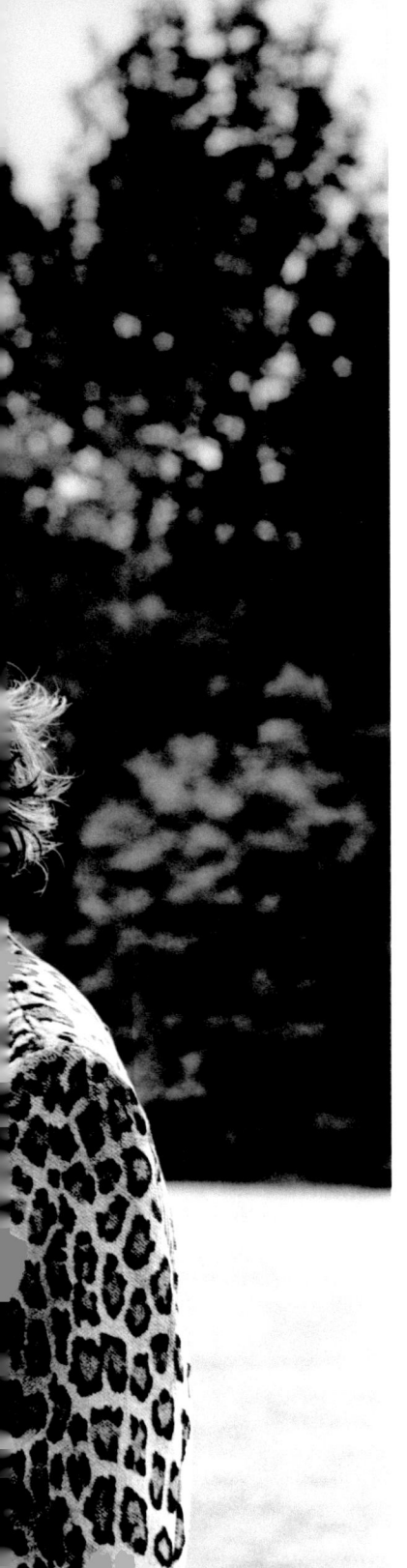

PP. 428–429
Anton Corbijn
Cover shoot for *Rolling Stone* magazine,
28 August 1995. The band spent most of June
and July 1994 preparing for the *Voodoo Lounge*
tour, rehearsing in a school gym at Toronto's
Crescent School. Keith had mixed feelings about
the city where he had been busted for drug
possession in 1977, but Toronto would become
something of a pre-tour constant for the band.
*"It's like a mutual respect. I've always felt that
about Toronto. It's been our favourite haunt
to rehearse in for some reason, a lot of it is to do
with logistics and money, I have no doubt."* Keith
Richards, *The Rolling Stones Bootleg Series*,
press kit, 2012

Anton Corbijn
Voodoo Lounge tour, CNE Stadium, Toronto,
19 or 20 August 1994.
*"Here-today, gone-tomorrow organizations
are nothing new in the concert business. But
Voodoo Lounge's sheer size and complexity sets
it apart. The stage, a futuristic monster with a
924-square-foot Sony video screen and a 92-foot-
high cobra-shaped lighting tower, requires 56
trucks to haul from city to city."* Business Week,
9 October 1994

Albert Watson
New York, 1988.
"The interesting thing about music is that it has always seemed streaks ahead of any other art form or any other form of social expression. I've said this a million times, but after air, food, water and fucking, I think music is maybe the next human necessity." Keith Richards, *Playboy*, November 1988

P.434–435
Albert Watson
Los Angeles, 1992.
In a session convened to produce a portrait for *Rolling Stone* magazine's 25th anniversary issue, Jagger was asked to share a car with a leopard. However, the creature proved to be more than just playful so a glass partition had to be built to protect the musician from any spirited advances.

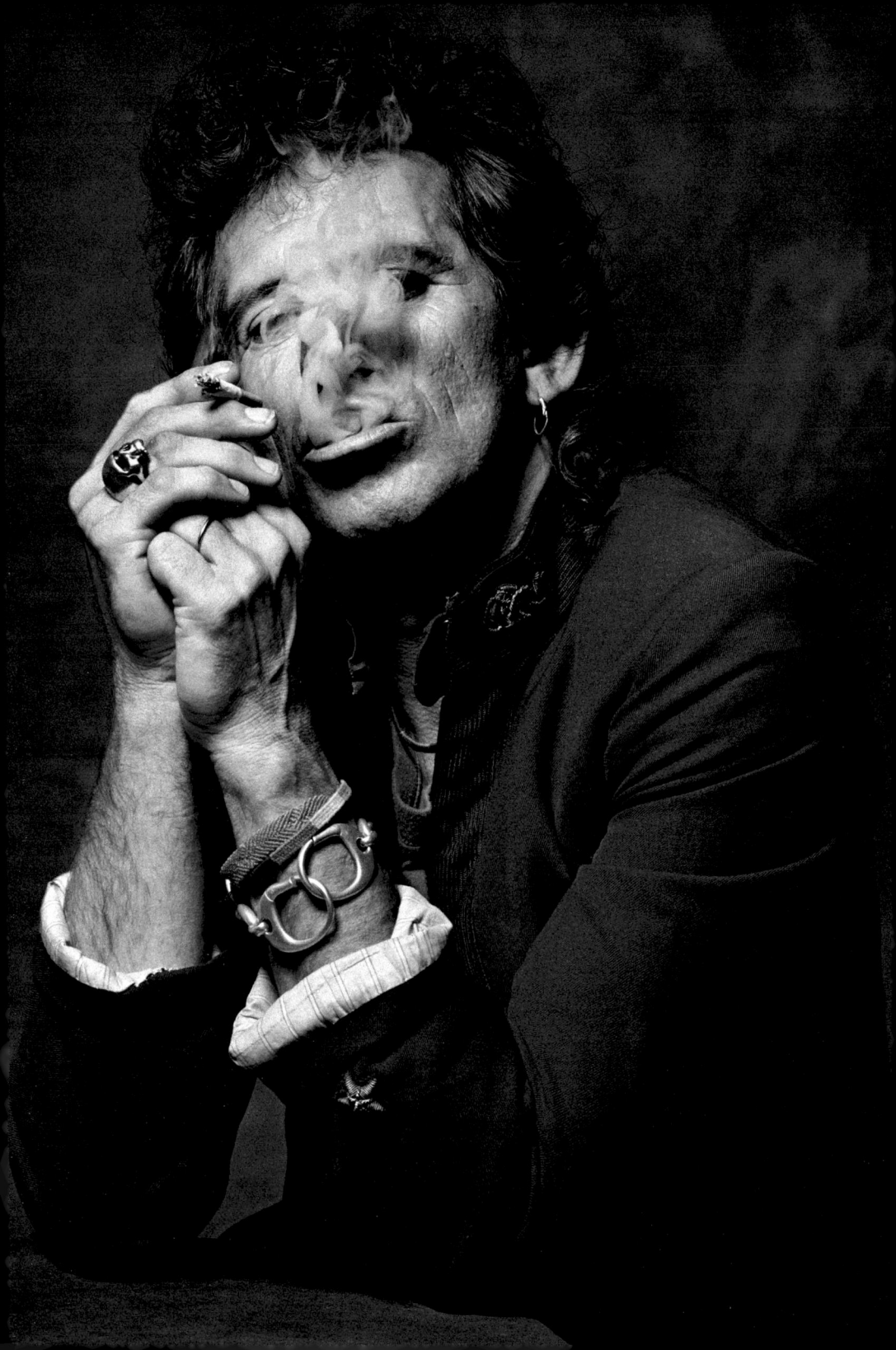

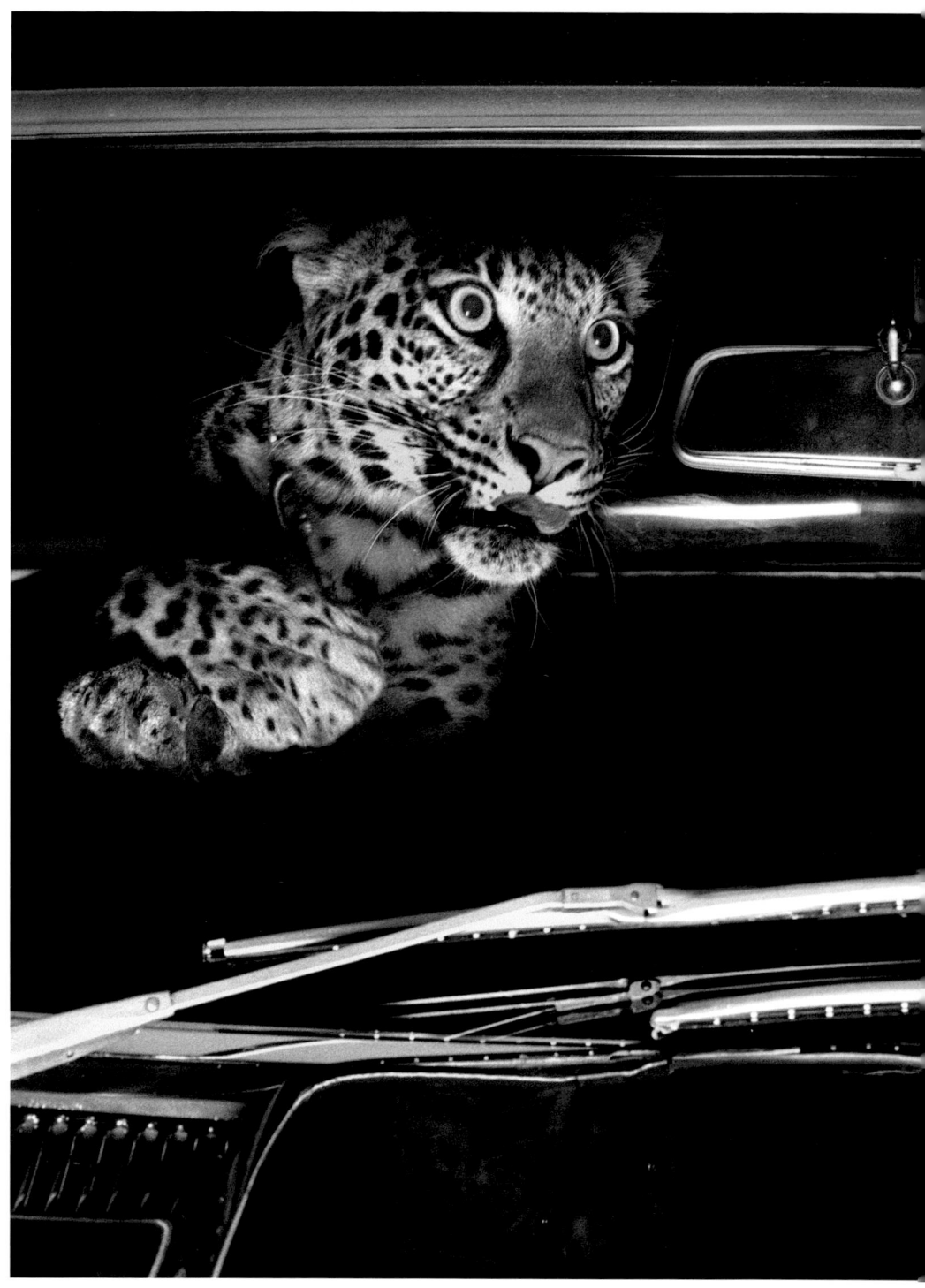

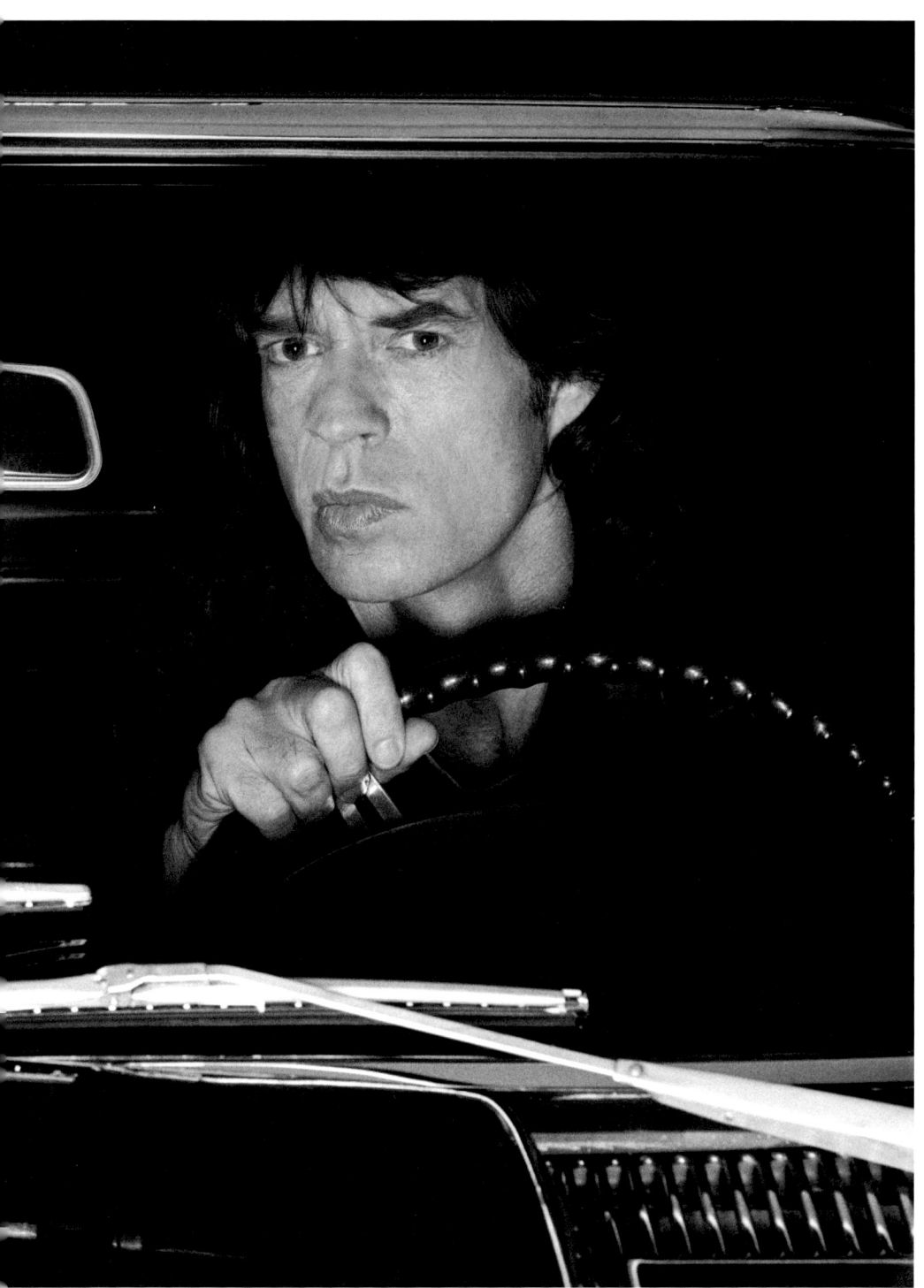

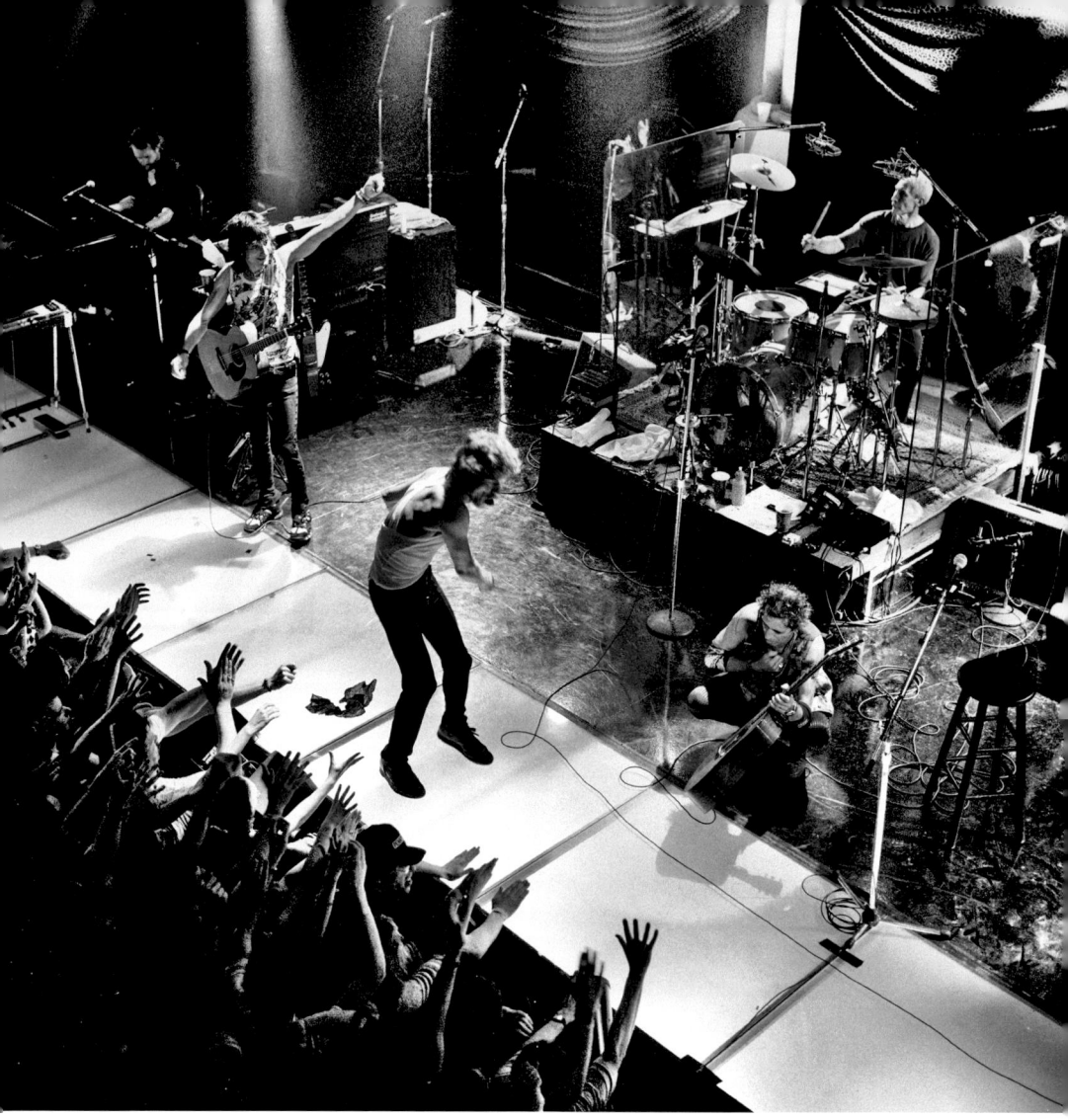

Anton Corbijn

Back to basics for two shows at Amsterdam's legendary Paradiso club on 26 and 27 May 1995. Mixing old and new material, the group put in a dynamic performance of over 20 songs that relied mainly on semi-acoustic instrumentation. Highlights were "It's All Over Now", "Shine A Light" and, for the first time, Dylan's "Like A Rolling Stone".

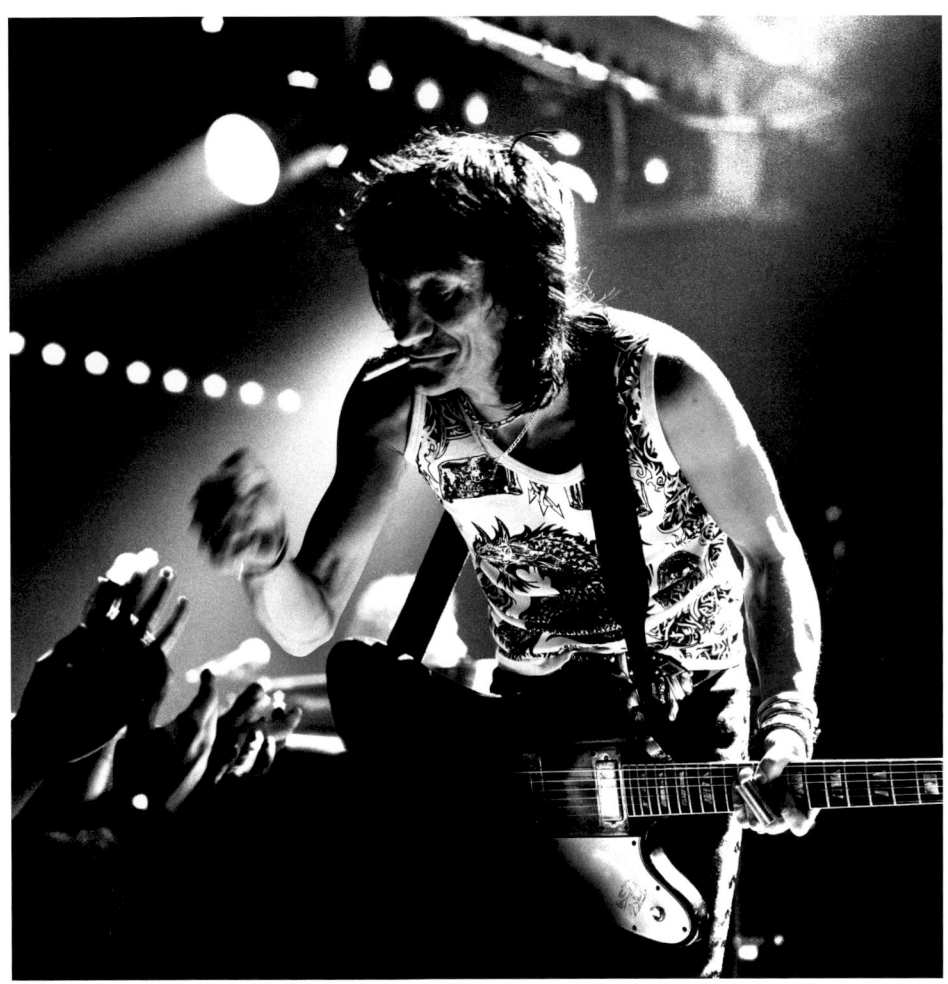

Anton Corbijn
The "club" gigs were a unique experience, and
scalpers were out in force to capitalise on the
intimacy of the Paradiso shows. With a venue
capacity of just 1,500, tickets were selling at
over $2,000 each in advance of the gig.

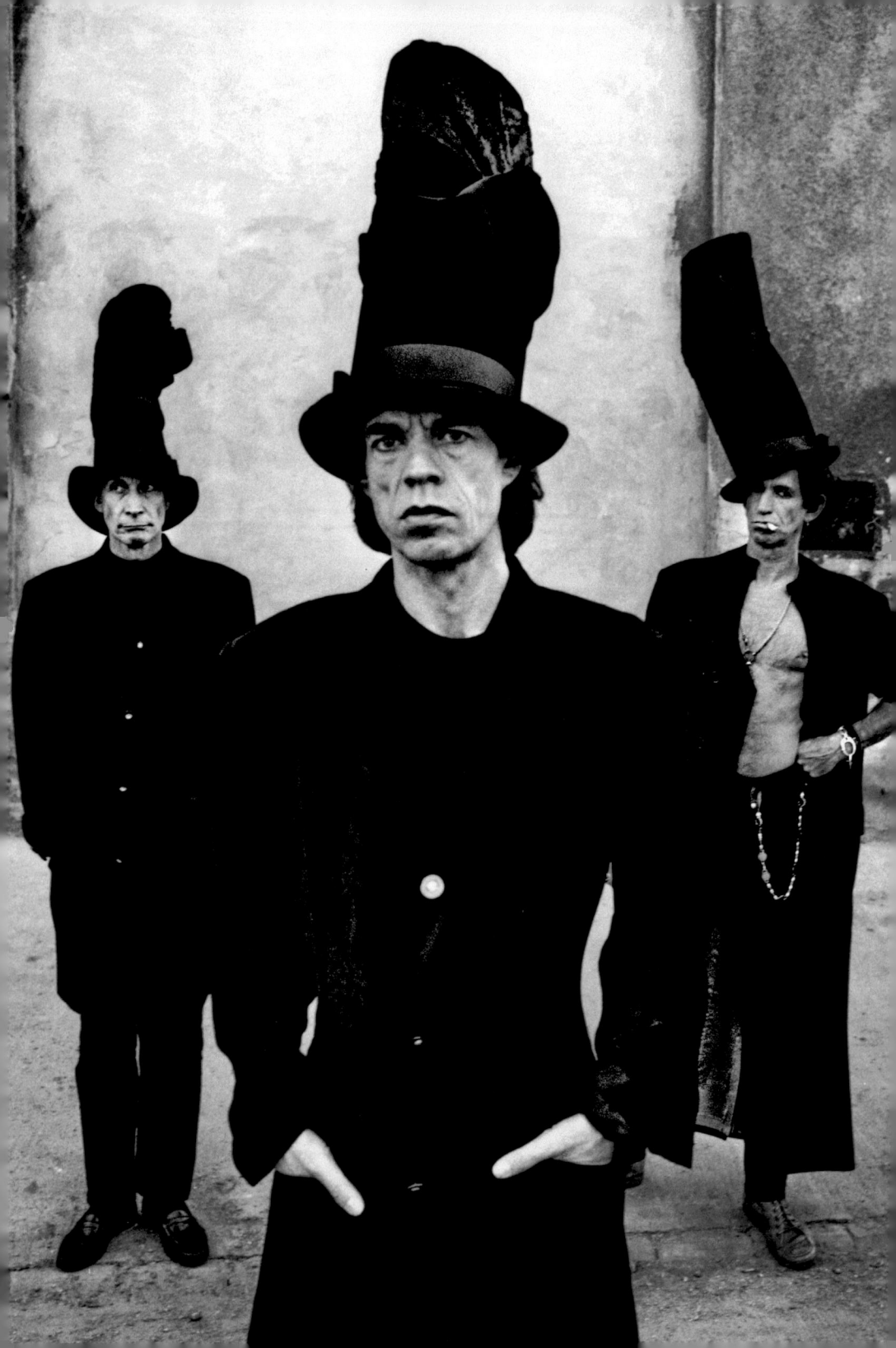

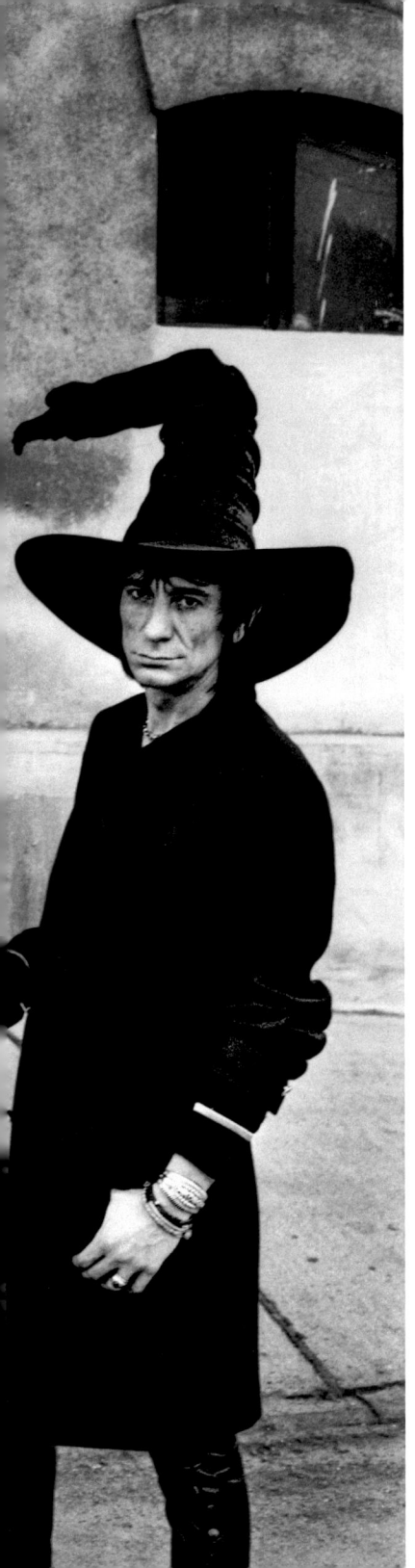

Anton Corbijn
Budapest, 8 August 1995.
Many of the 129 shows that made up the *Voodoo Lounge* tour of 1994–95 were performed in countries new to the band. Alongside the workload, there were opportunities to take a somewhat surreal approach to the traditional band portrait – such as in Budapest.

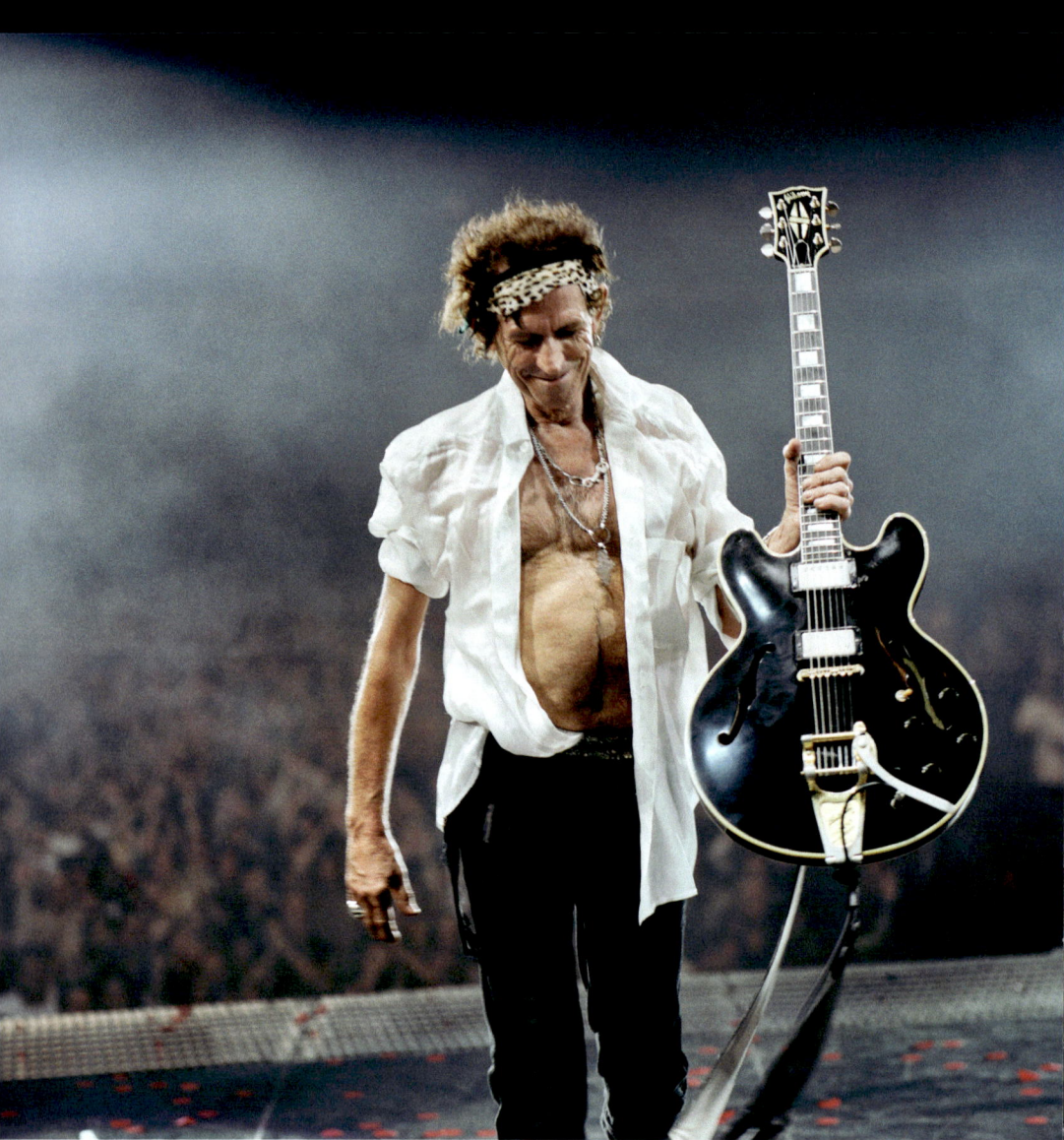

Christopher Wahl
The Air Canada Centre, Toronto, 16 October 2002.
A capacity house at Toronto's Air Canada Centre
witnessed a blistering 21-song set from the
Stones as part of the *Licks* tour.

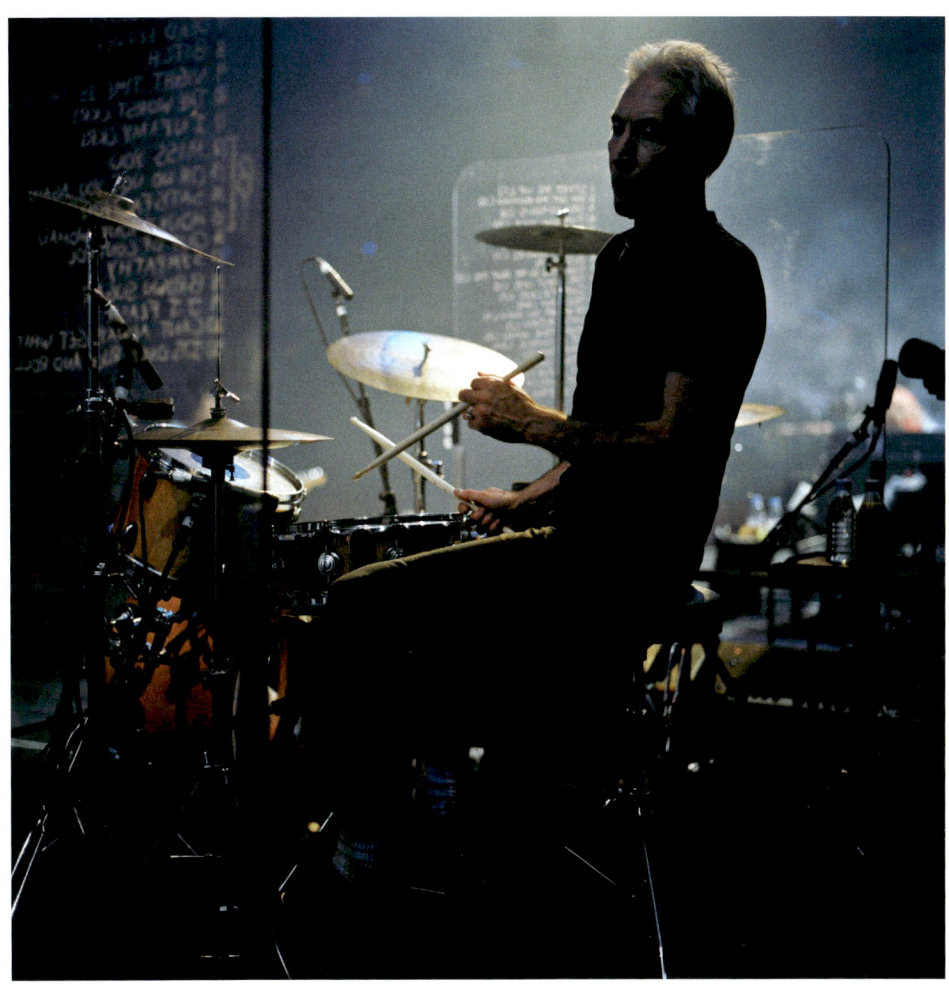

Christopher Wahl
The Air Canada Centre, Toronto, 16 October 2002.
"I can see what I'm doing now in a way. I'm more relaxed with it. And I would like to say that I wouldn't want to play with anybody else but *The Rolling Stones. I enjoy being with them and playing with them immensely. Always have done."*
Charlie Watts, *Jazziz* magazine, August 2000

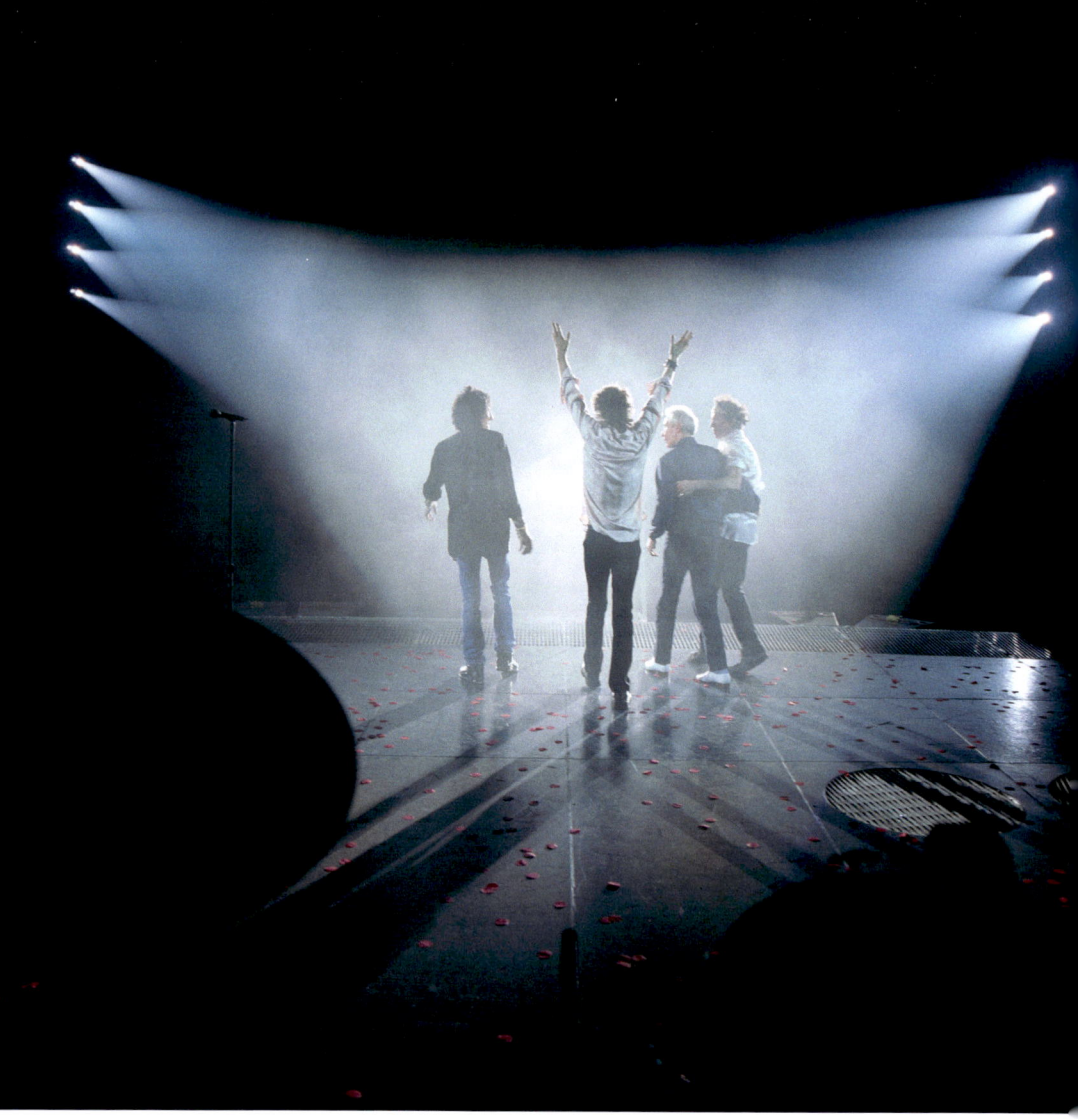

Christopher Wahl
The Air Canada Centre, Toronto, 16 October 2002.

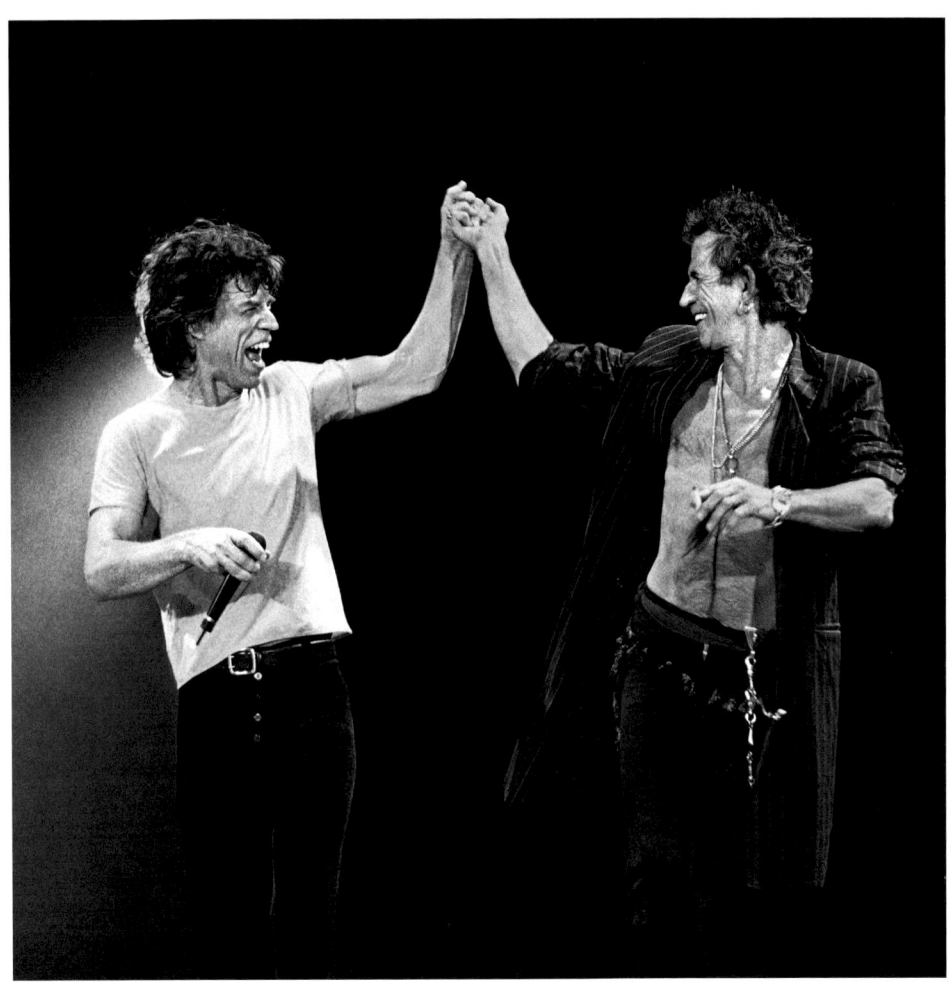

Claude Gassian

Paris, France, 25 July 1998. Thirty-four years after the band's first visit, Paris' love affair with The Rolling Stones showed no signs of abating.

The 1998 *Bridges To Babylon* European tour included a date at the massive Stade de France arena, where 80,000 fans enjoyed the 21-song set.

Anton Corbijn
Greenwood College School, Toronto,
6 August 2005.
Toronto was yet again the favoured setting
for rehearsals, and the group convened at
Greenwood College School for a month's inten-
sive preparations for the *Bigger Bang* tour.
Following full-scale dress rehearsals in an
aircraft hangar at nearby Pearson International
Airport, a two-year schedule of 147 shows
in 32 countries was ready to roll.

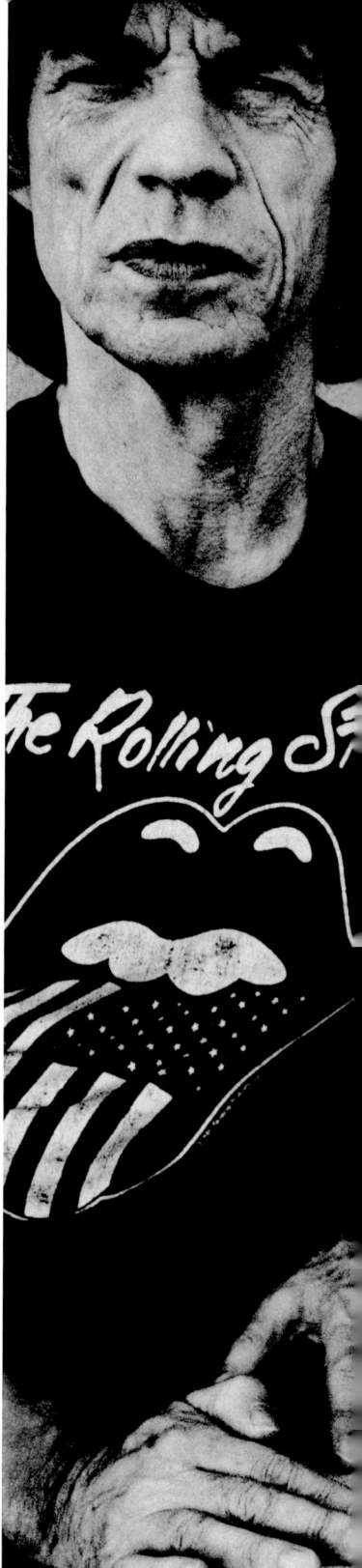

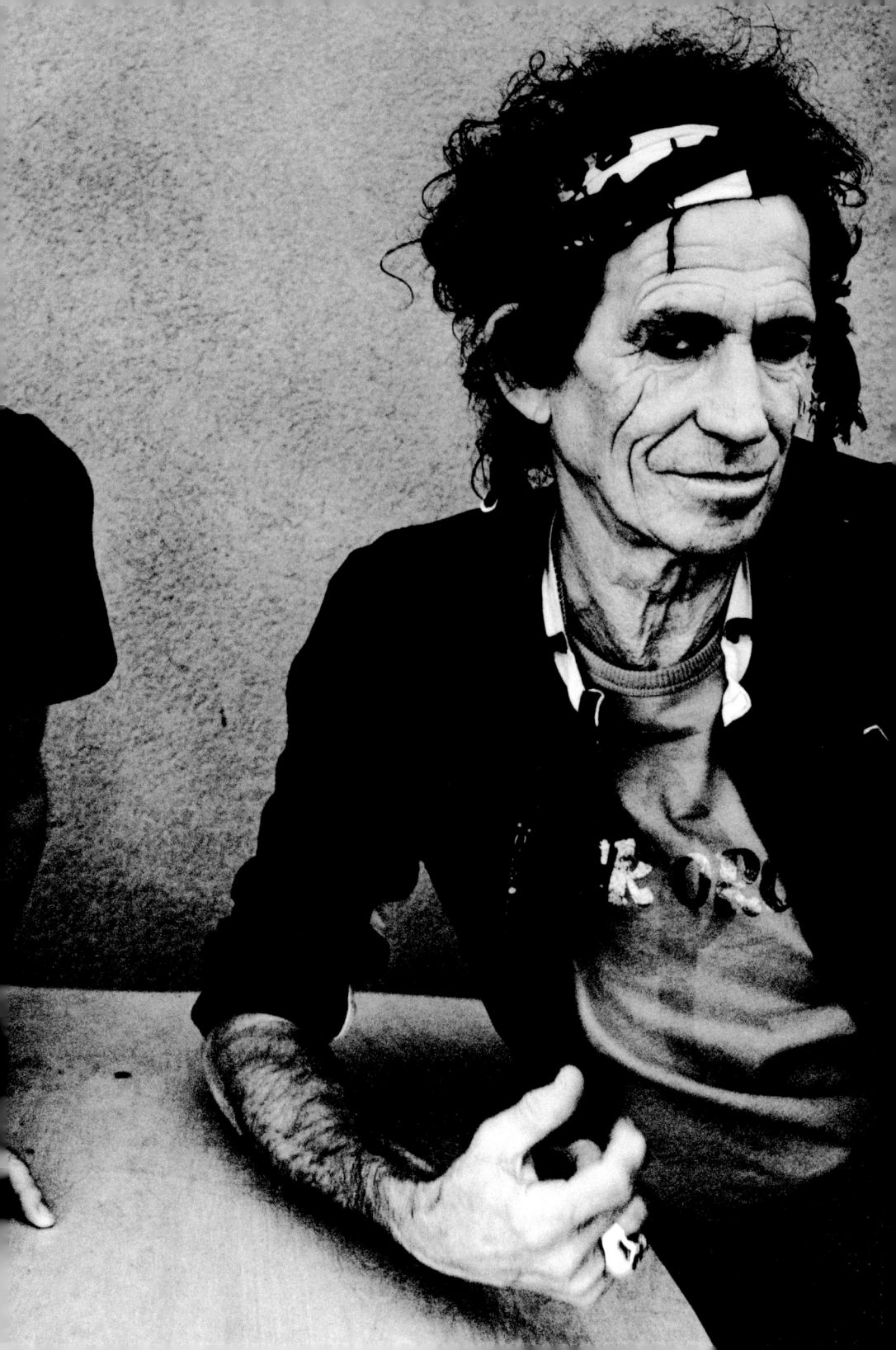

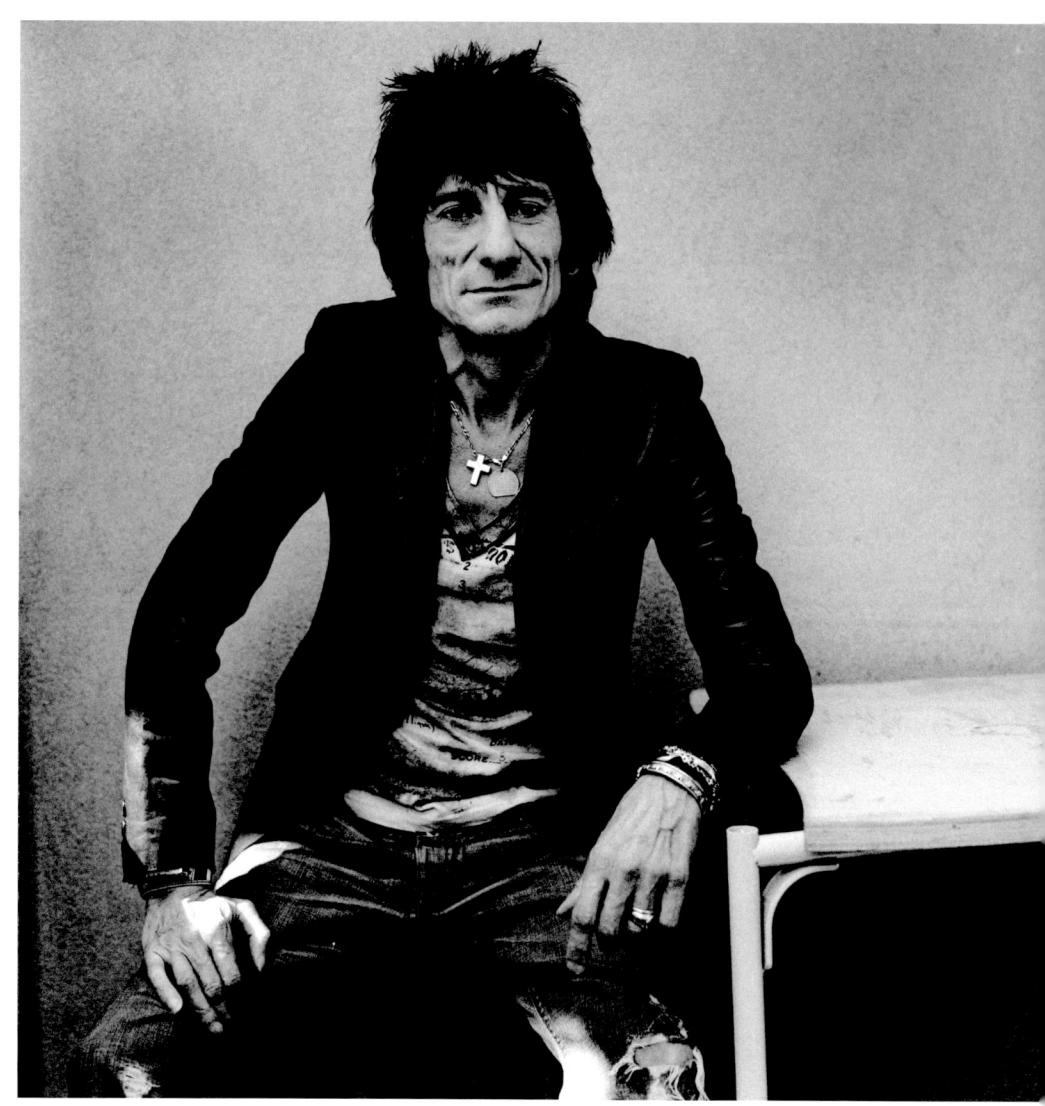

Anton Corbijn
Toronto, June 2005.
"I'm more lost when I'm not on tour. I'm in a bit of a muddle at nine o'clock – 'Where's the stage?' On tour there are people directing and supervising you. And then when you finish it's like, 'Sit down and watch TV'. Sometimes I get so bored I think 'I'll have a drink'. I don't mean any harm but I just go off the rails." Ronnie Wood, *Financial Times,* 19 July 2008

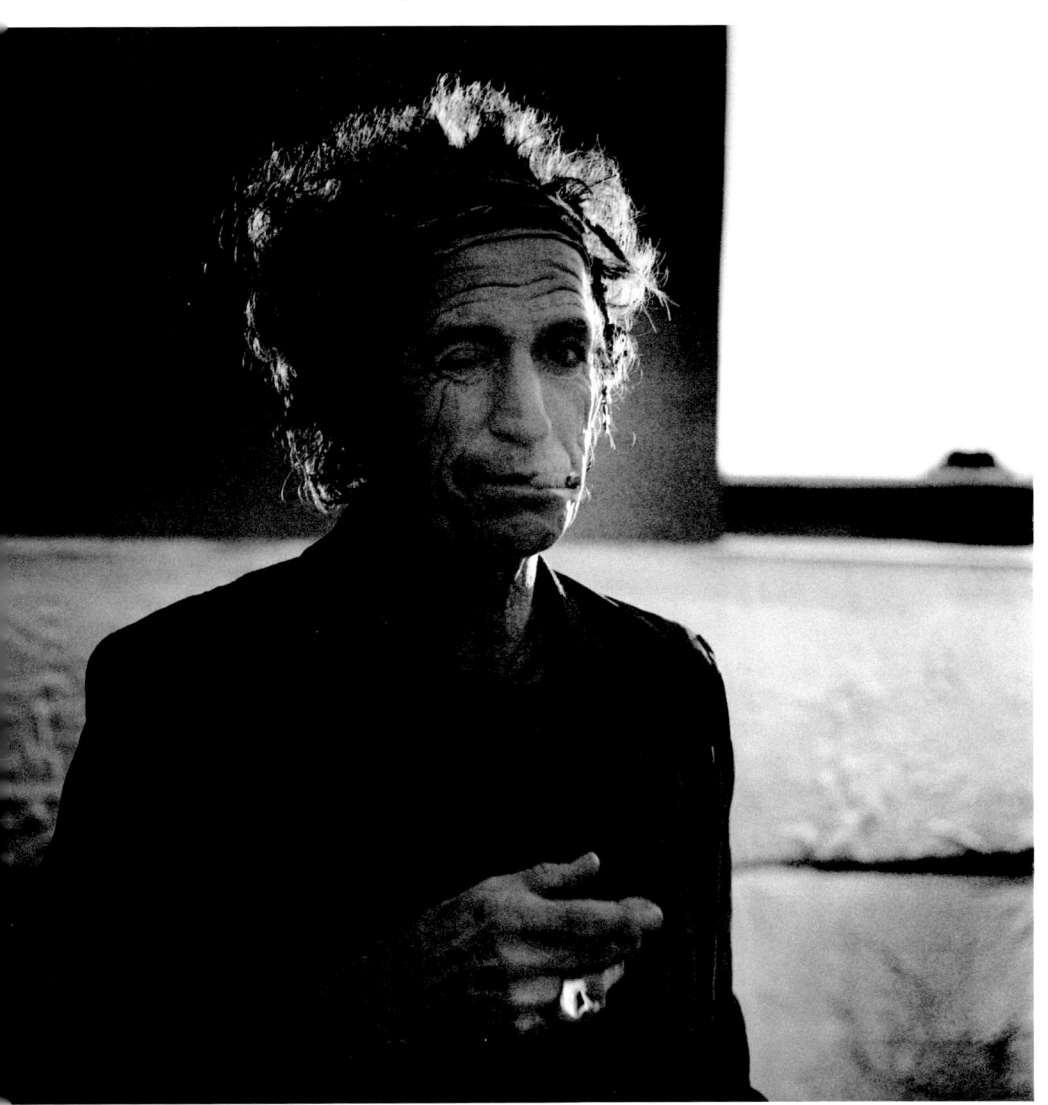

Anton Corbijn
Toronto, June 2005.
"The idea of retiring is like killing yourself. It's almost like hara-kiri. *I mean, no doubt, I intend to live to 100 and go down in history."* Keith Richards, BBC 2, *Newsnight*, 2 September 2005

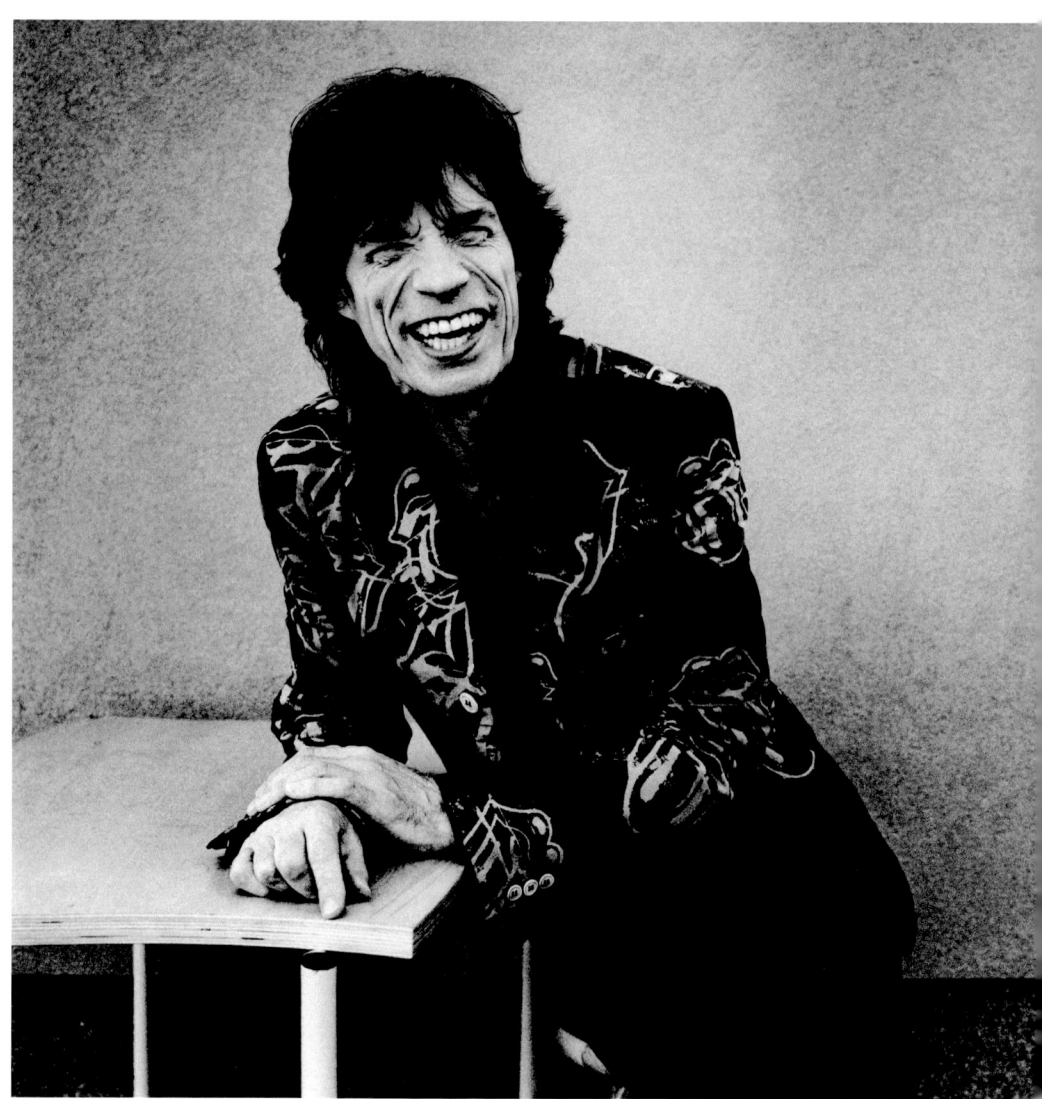

Anton Corbijn

Toronto, June 2005.

"I think it's very important to disassociate your-self from what anyone else thinks of you, because they don't really know where your mind is. So if you want, there's a mythic you, and then there's you. Or yet, in less grandiose terms, there's a stage version of you, and then there's you. And the ability to go between one and the other is the key to staying grounded." Mick Jagger, *GQ* magazine, October 2005

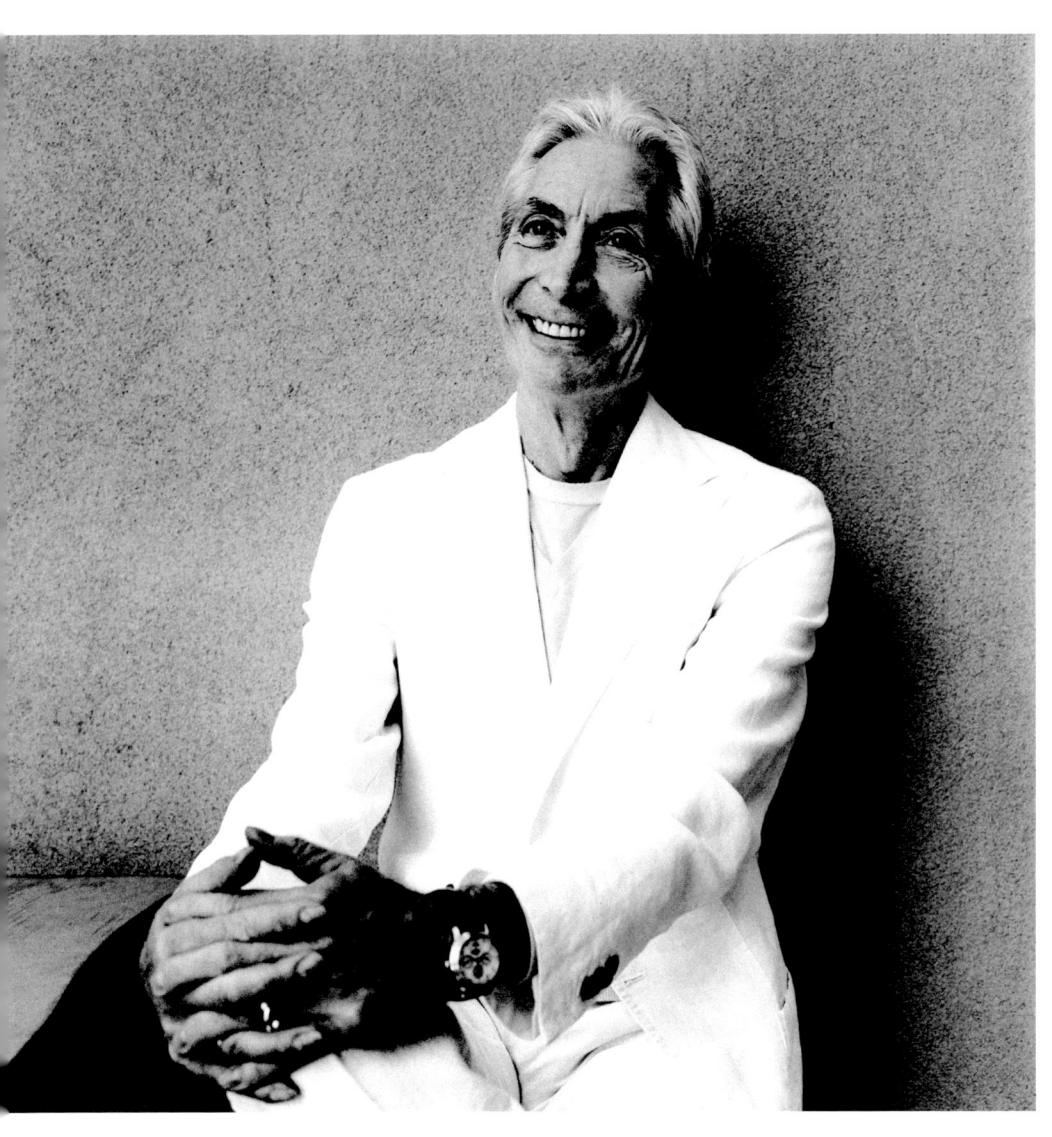

Anton Corbijn
Toronto, August 2005.

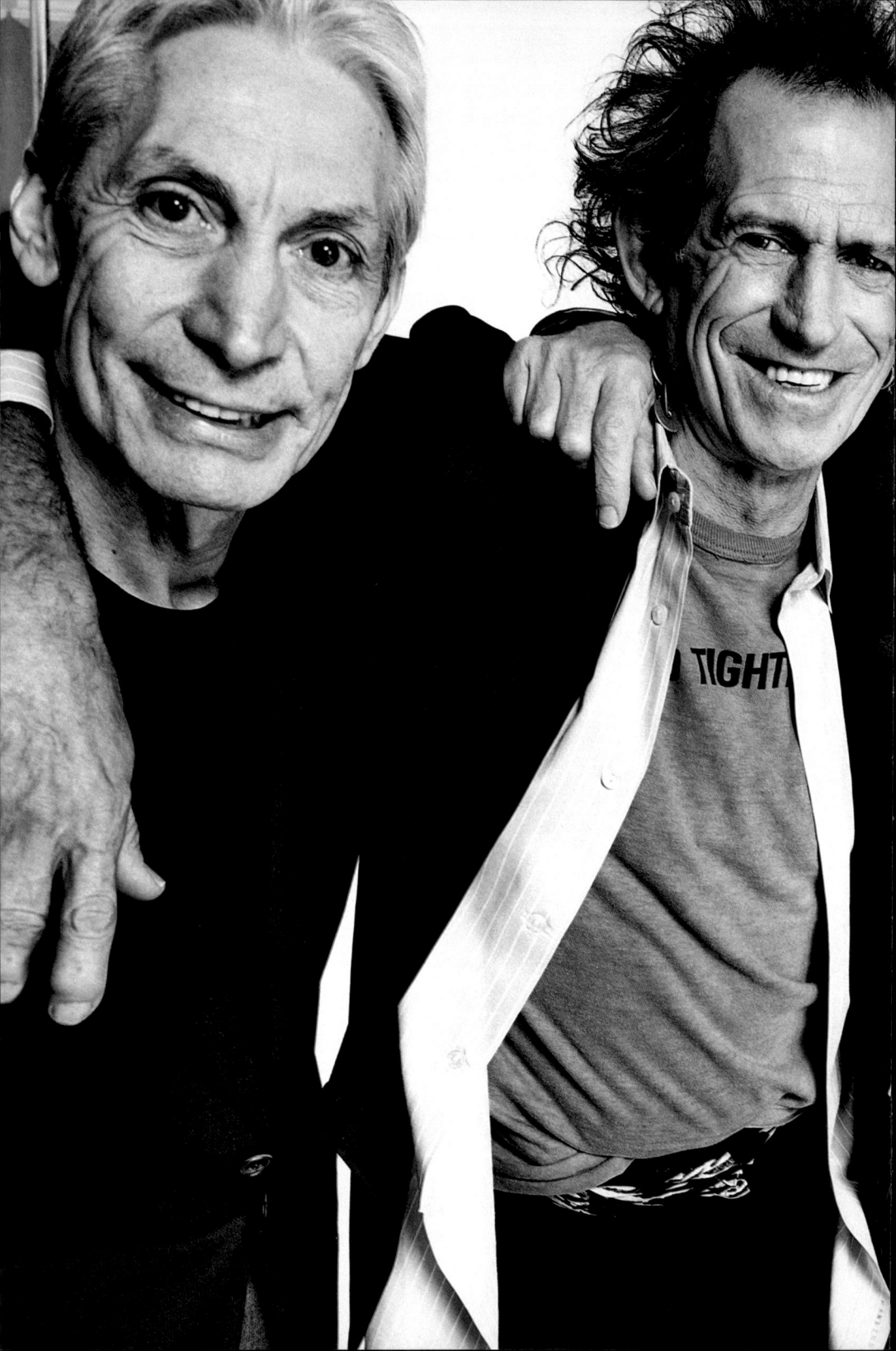

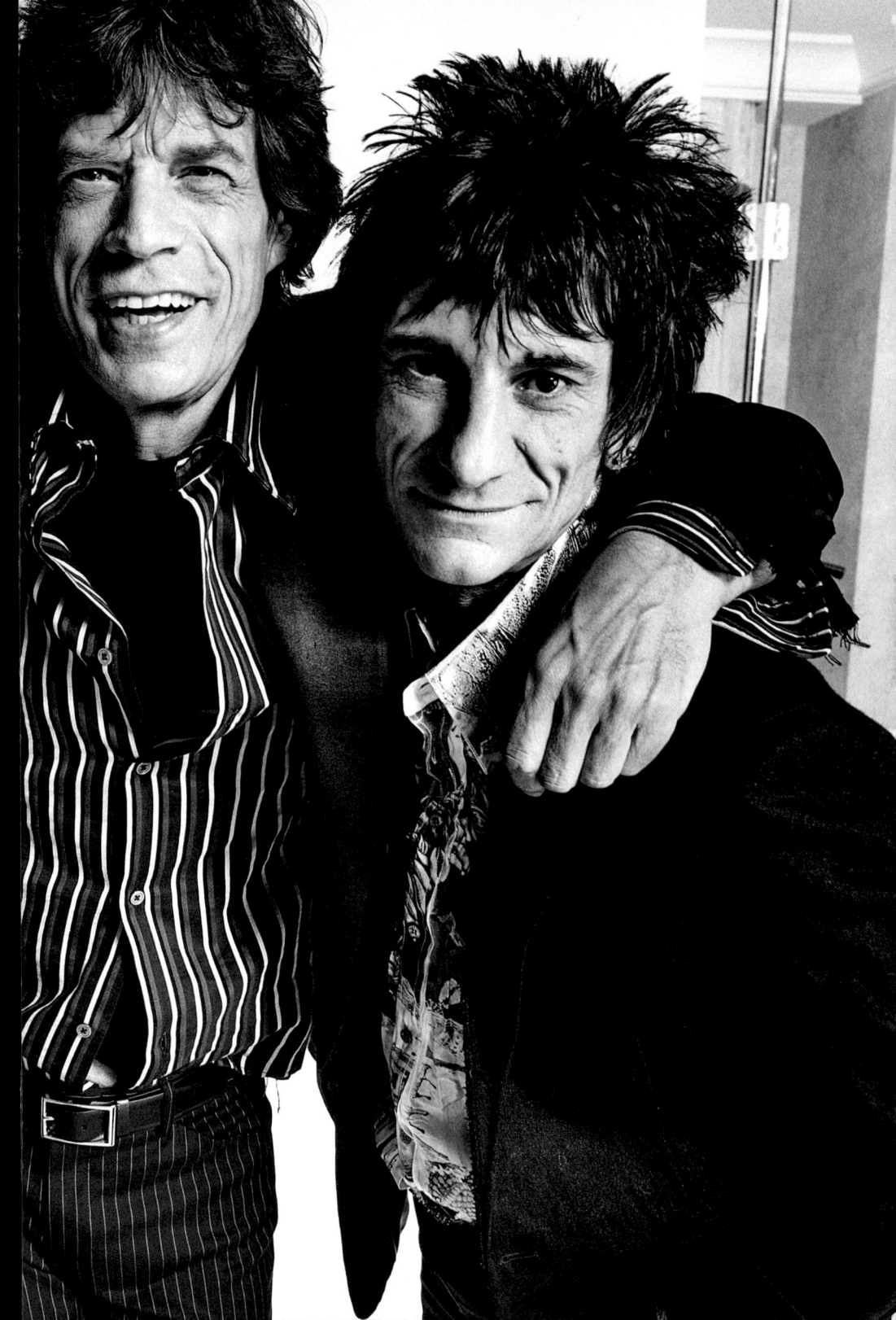

PP. 450–451

Mario Testino

Los Angeles, 2003.

"This happened at lightning speed, as I had to fly to Los Angeles from London and they only had an hour at their hotel. I would normally have turned it down but photographing the Rolling Stones was a must! I set up in the ballroom of the hotel and although the shoot was a short one, we had such a great time. The energy was so fluid and full of fun that Mick spontaneously took the camera and began directing and shooting me, just like I had been directing and shooting the band." Mario Testino, Four Seasons Hotel, Beverly Hills

Steven Klein

New York, 2005.

"Without his [Jagger's] relentless input, the group would have petered out after the recording of Let It Bleed*."* Nick Kent, *Apathy For The Devil*, 2011

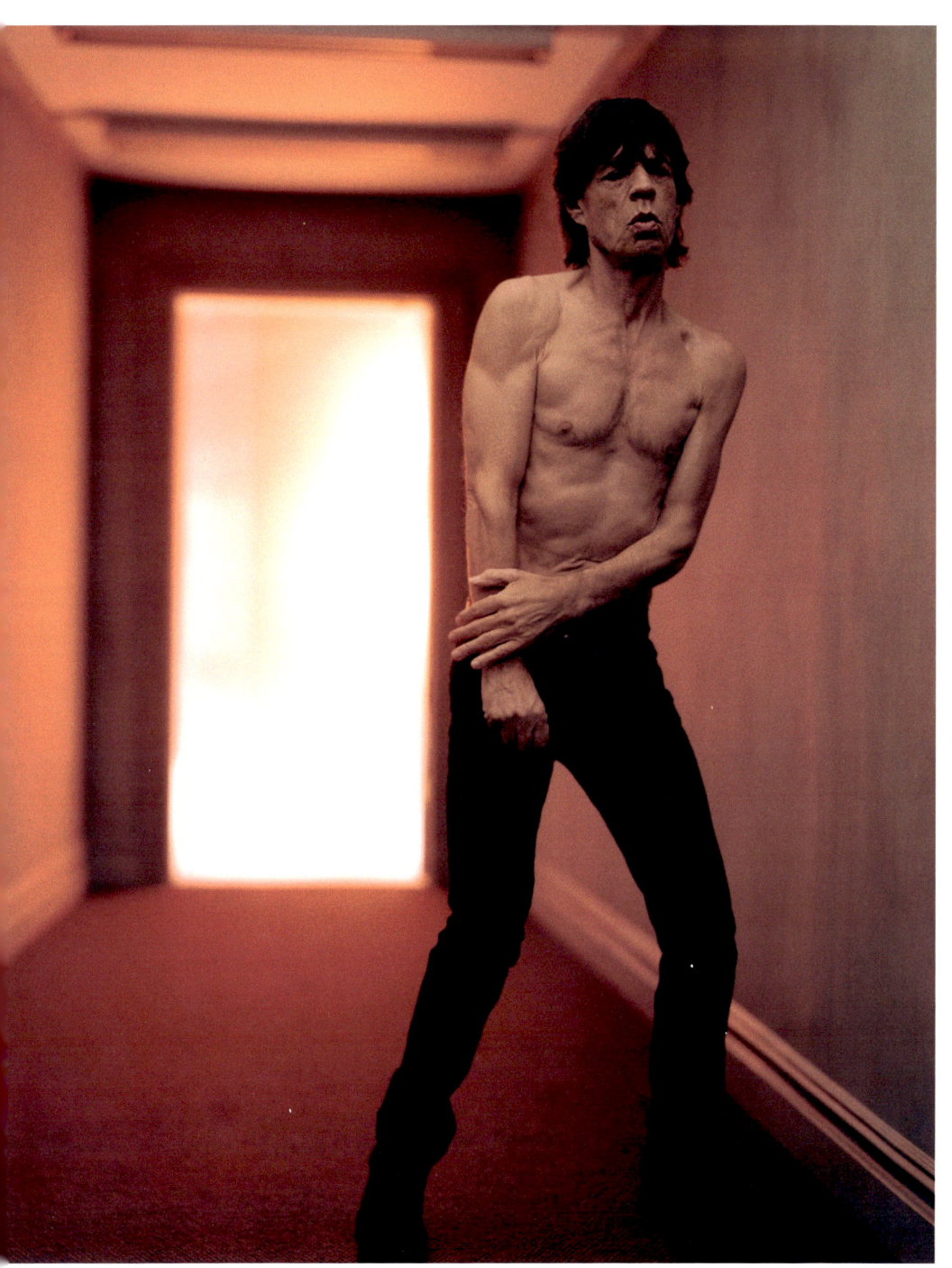

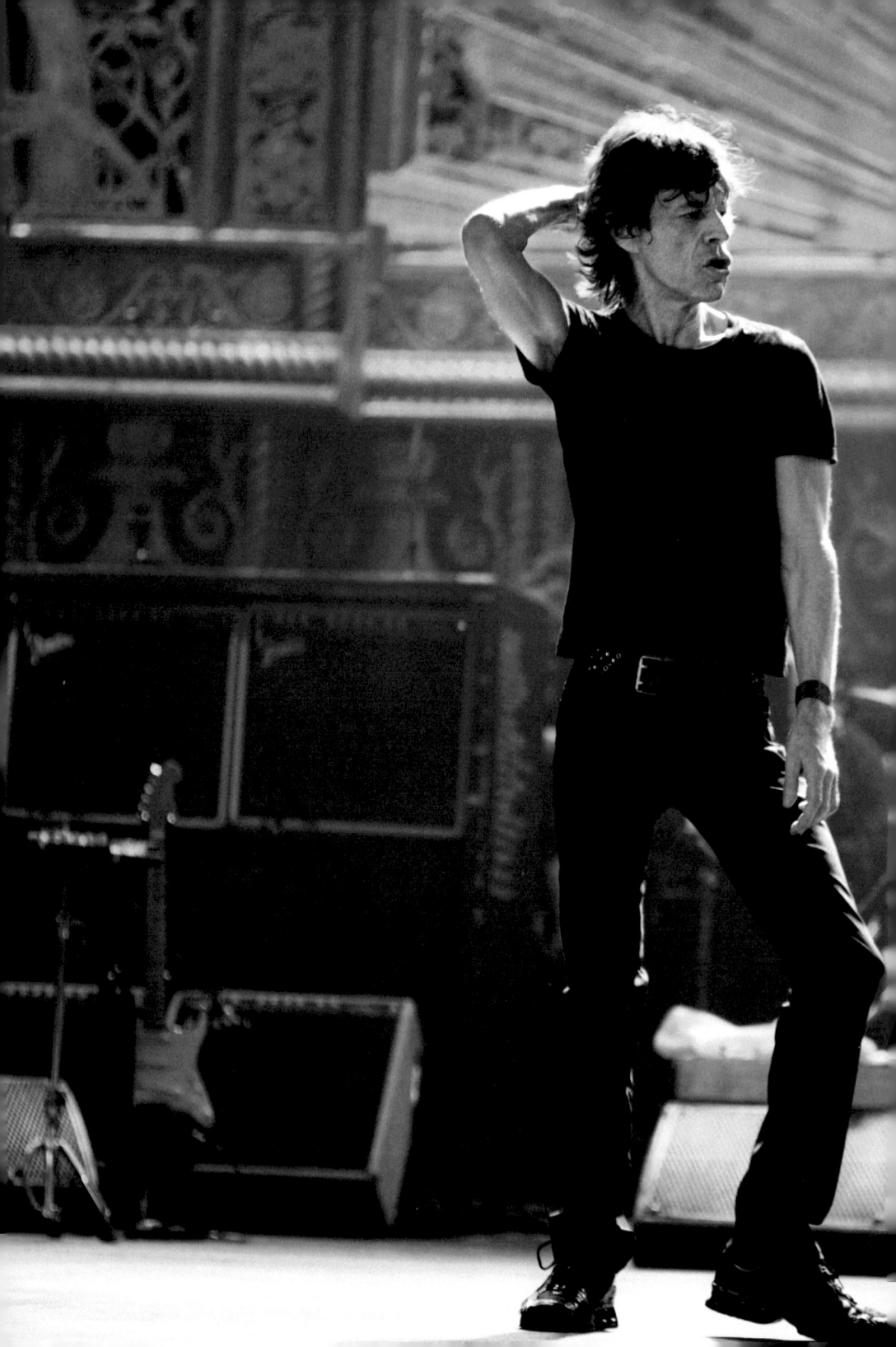

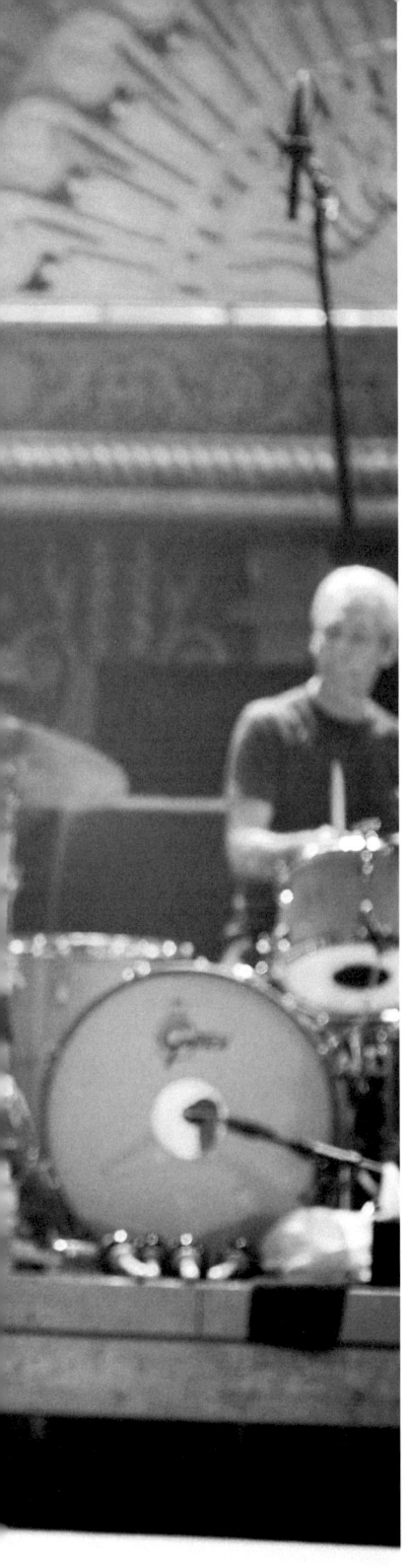

Brigitte Lacombe
New York City's Beacon Theatre hosted two intimate shows on 29 October and 1 November 2006, with just under 3,000 tickets available for each gig. Both concerts were filmed for inclusion in Martin Scorsese's 2008 concert film *Shine A Light*. *"The idea wasn't to make a documentary film, it was to capture the performance. I've always said, from when I first heard their music, 'I'm gonna get that on film some day.' It only took 40 years or so, but what can I say? And suddenly it happens."* Martin Scorsese, *Uncut* magazine, April 2006

PP. 456–457
Brigitte Lacombe
The Beacon Theatre performances benefitted the Clinton Foundation, a charity founded by President Bill Clinton.

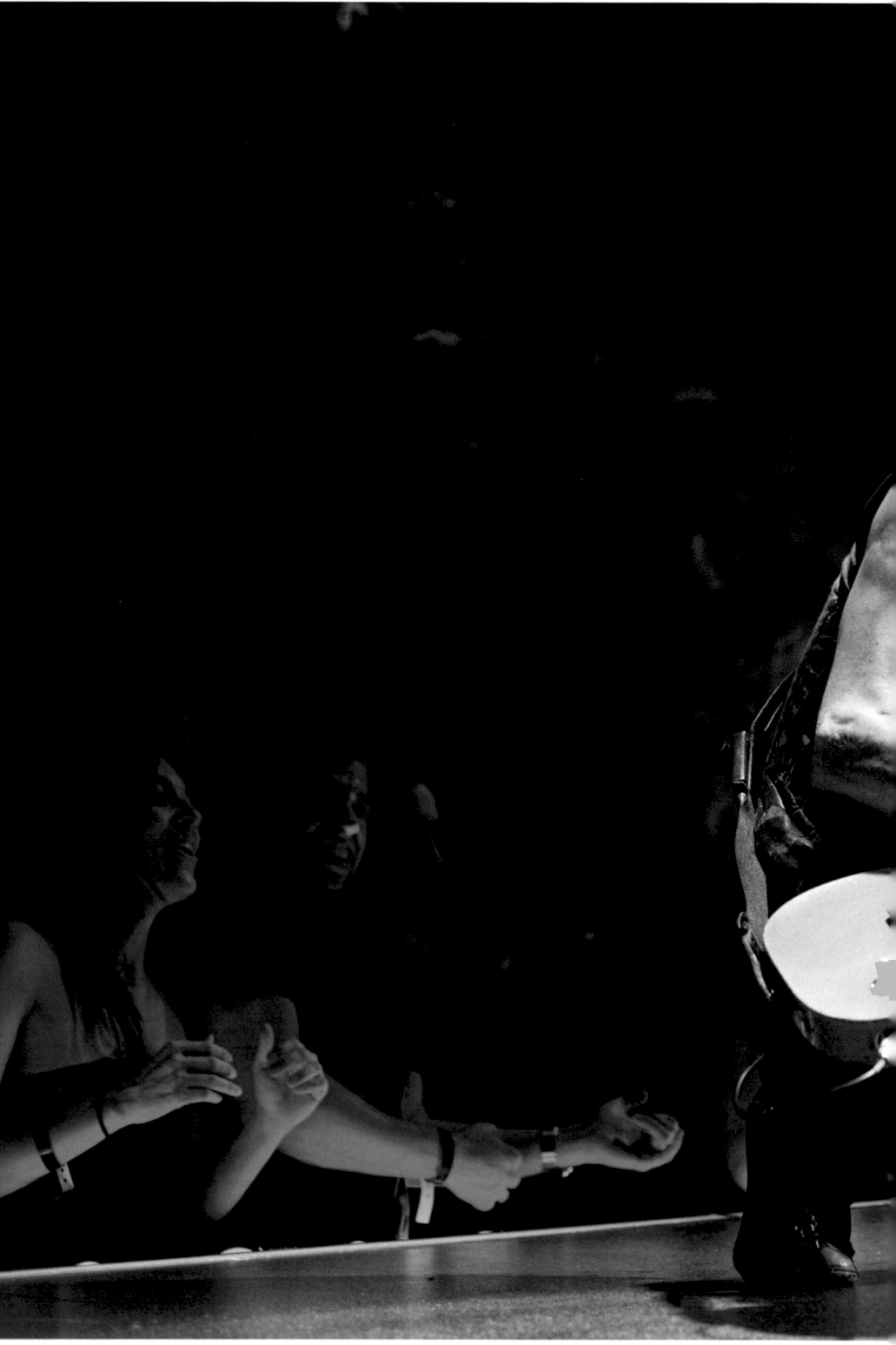

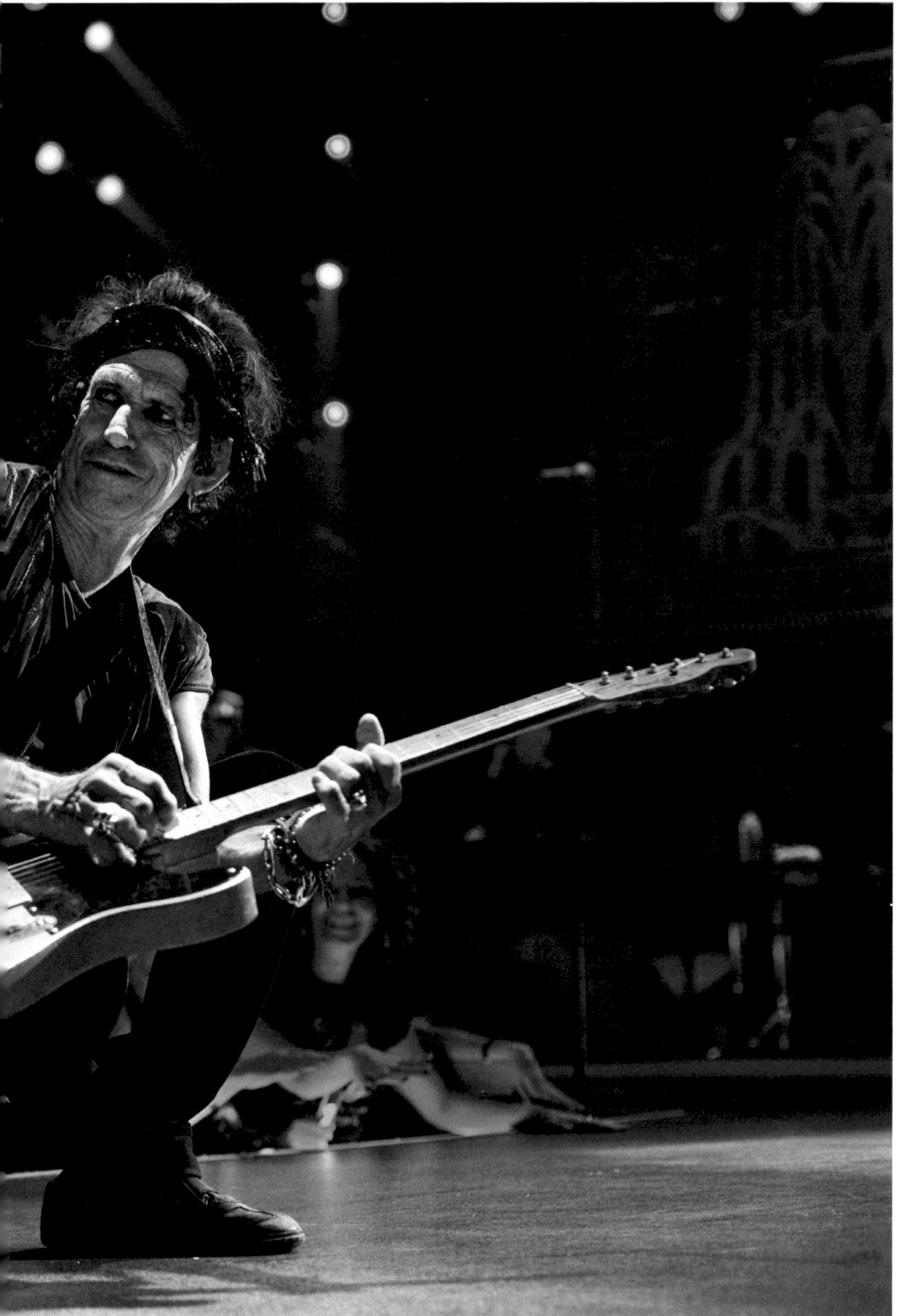

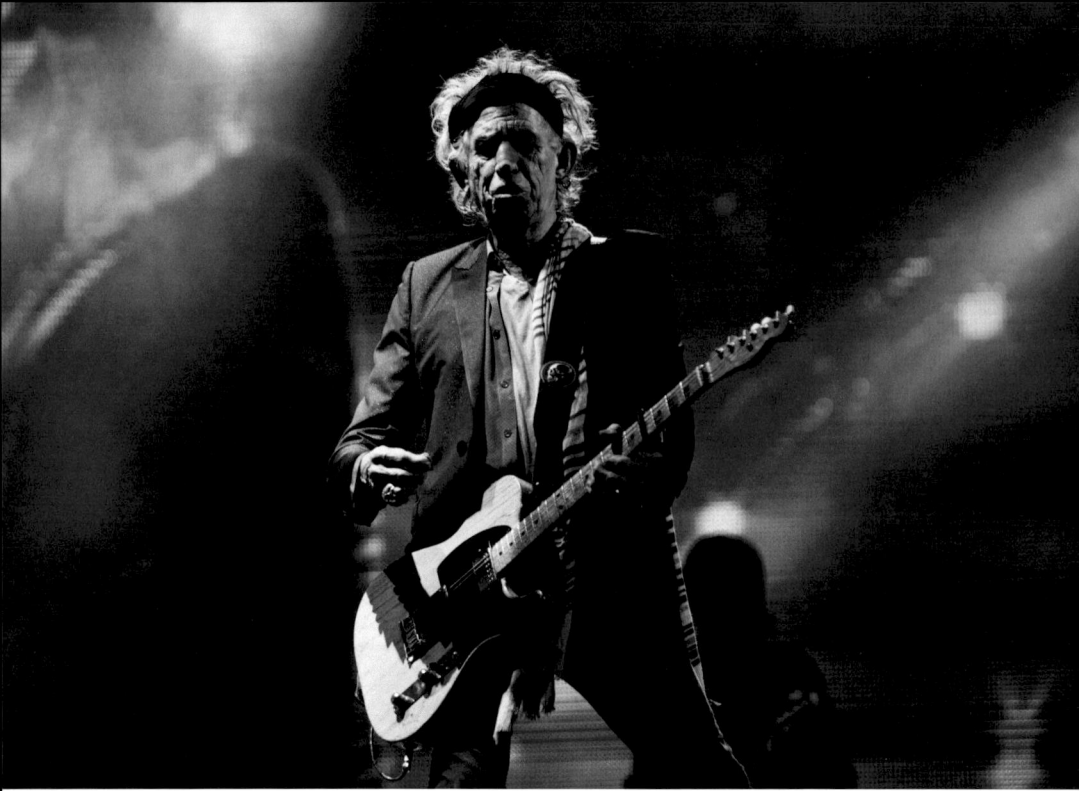

Alessio Pizzicannella
Glastonbury Festival, Somerset, 29 June 2013.
"It would be very difficult to separate myself from the Stones in any coherent form. You know, when I say 'I' I usually mean 'we'. You work with a bunch of guys that hard and that long ... And there's something to it that you don't want to – you don't want to let go, you know. I want to see how far this band will go and drop." Keith Richards in conversation with Anthony DeCurtis, New York Public Library, 29 October 2010

Alessio Pizzicannella
Glastonbury Festival, Somerset, 29 June 2013.
"It was a rip-roaring, uplifting, inspiring and quite sensational show, one that will go down in Glastonbury history." Neil McCormick, *Daily Telegraph*, 1 July 2013

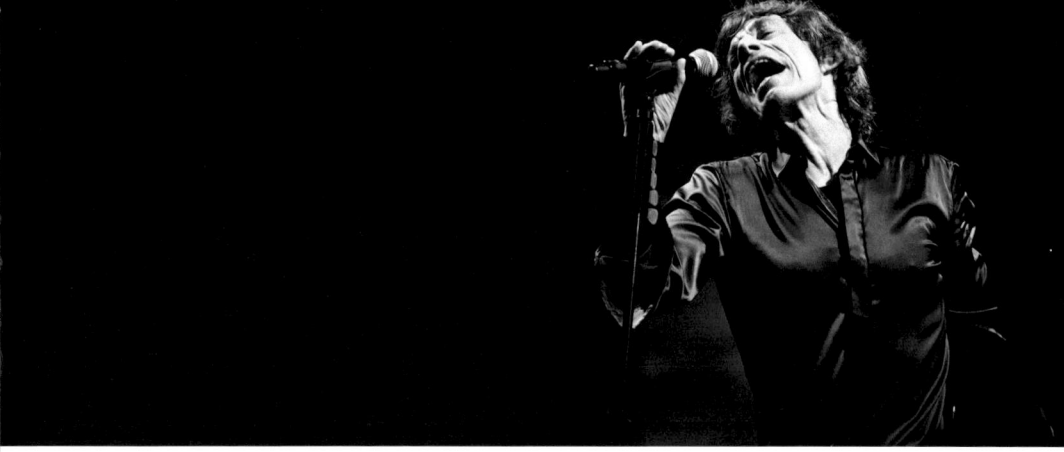

PP. 460–461
Terry Richardson
Richardson shot the cover and inside photos for the 23 May 2013 issue of *Rolling Stone* magazine. The story coincided with the *50 & Counting* tour, which started at the Staples Center in Los Angeles and ended in London's Hyde Park.

PP. 462–463
Mark Seliger
New York, April 2005.
The "Mount Rushmore" of rock assembles to promote *A Bigger Bang*. Their first studio album in eight years, *A Bigger Bang* proved an ambitious, eclectic and abrasive collection.
"They're just like every other musician, on every level. They love to play more than anything else in the world. They riff off each other. It's like a jazz group, really. There's not enough time to achieve that sort of thing twice, in your lifetime. That's why they keep going on." Don Was (producer), *Performing Songwriter*, March/April 2006

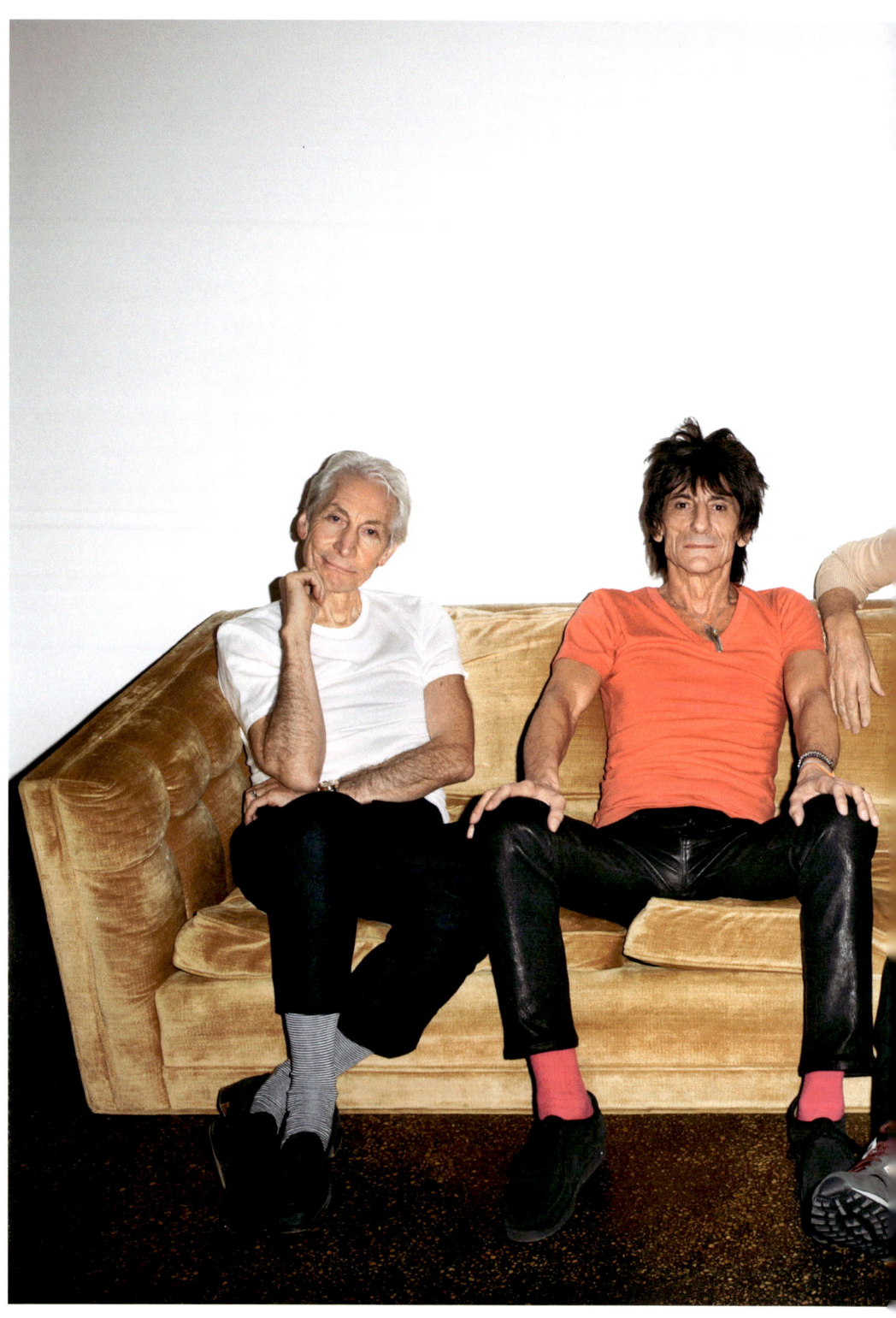

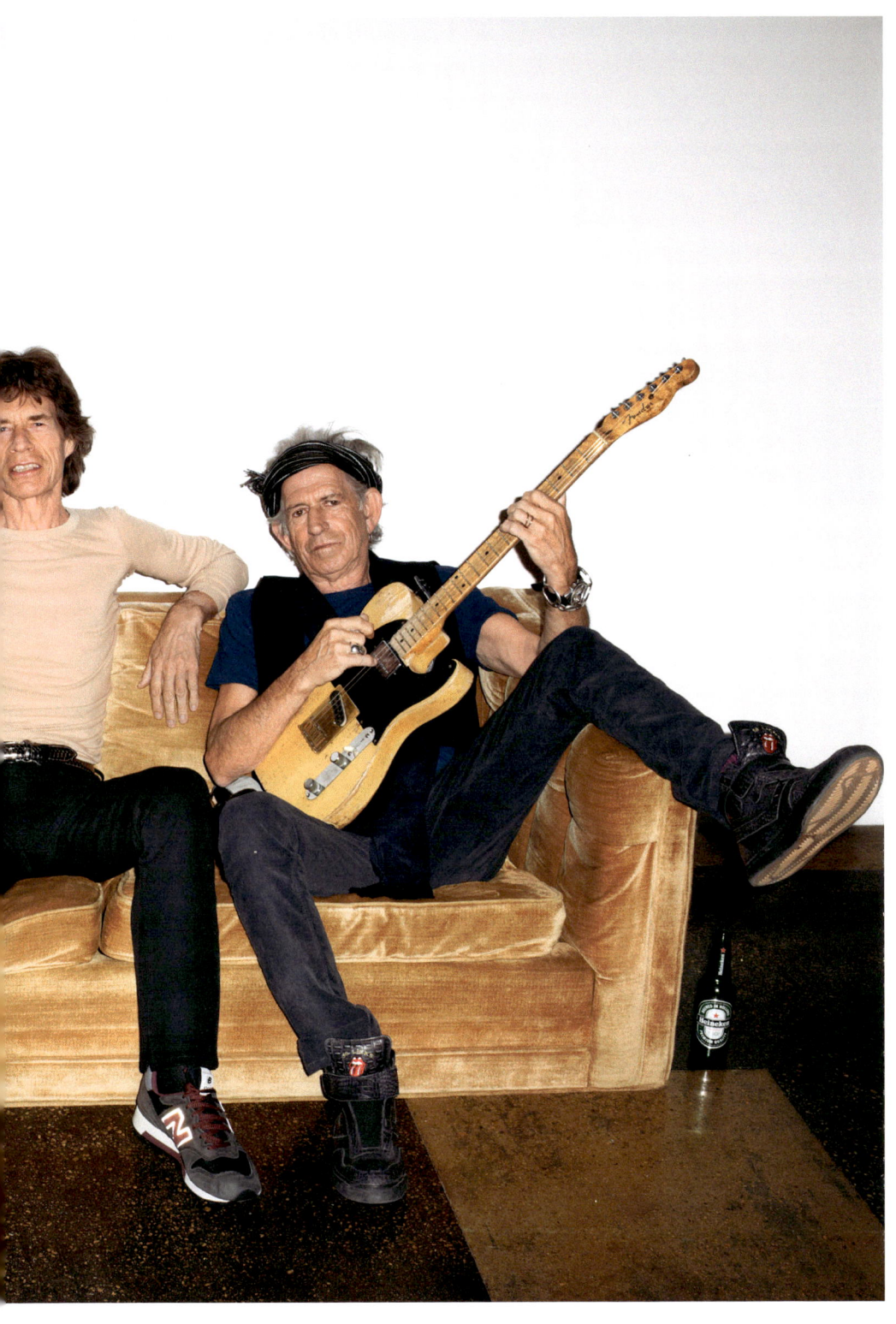

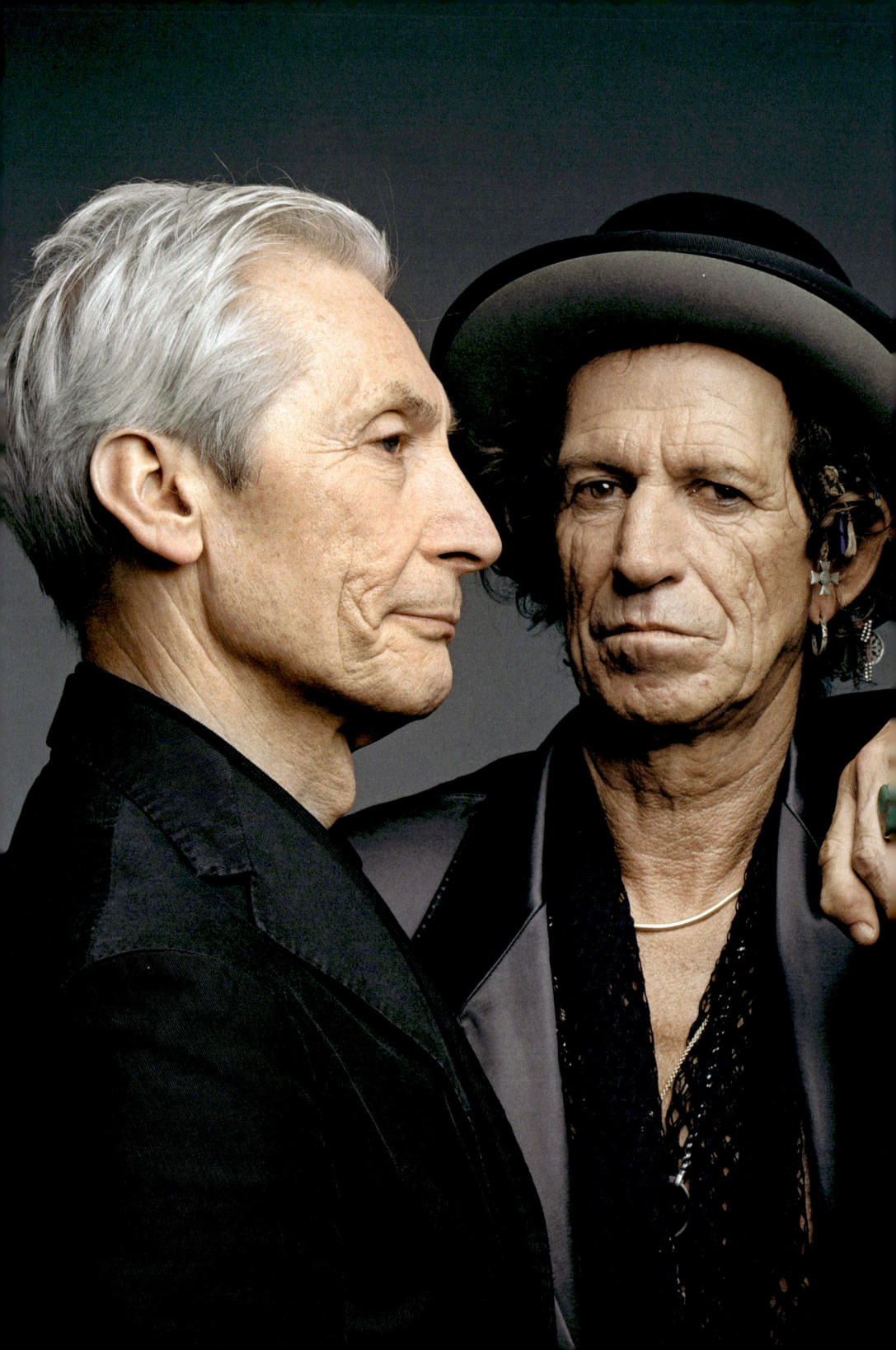

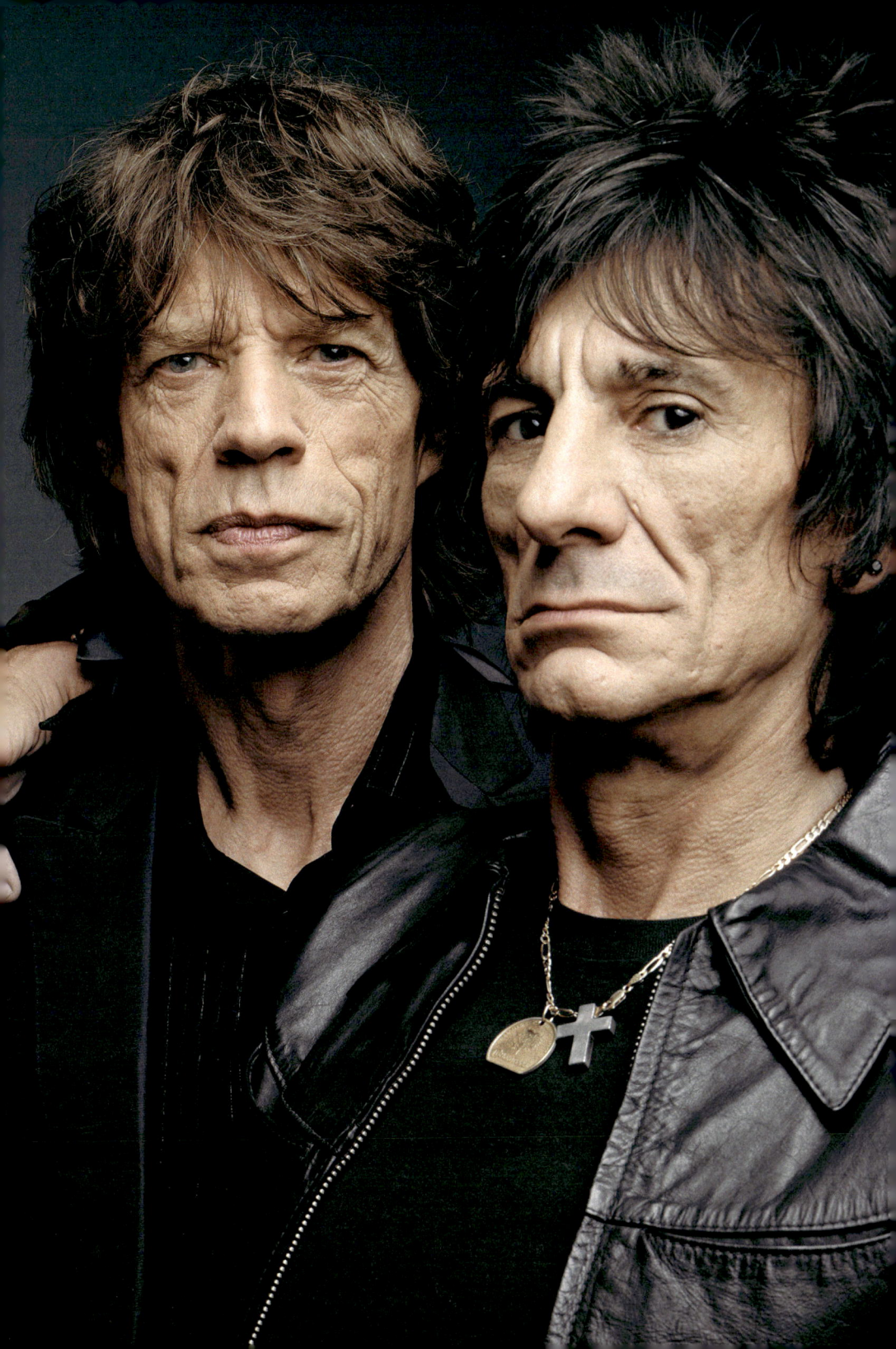

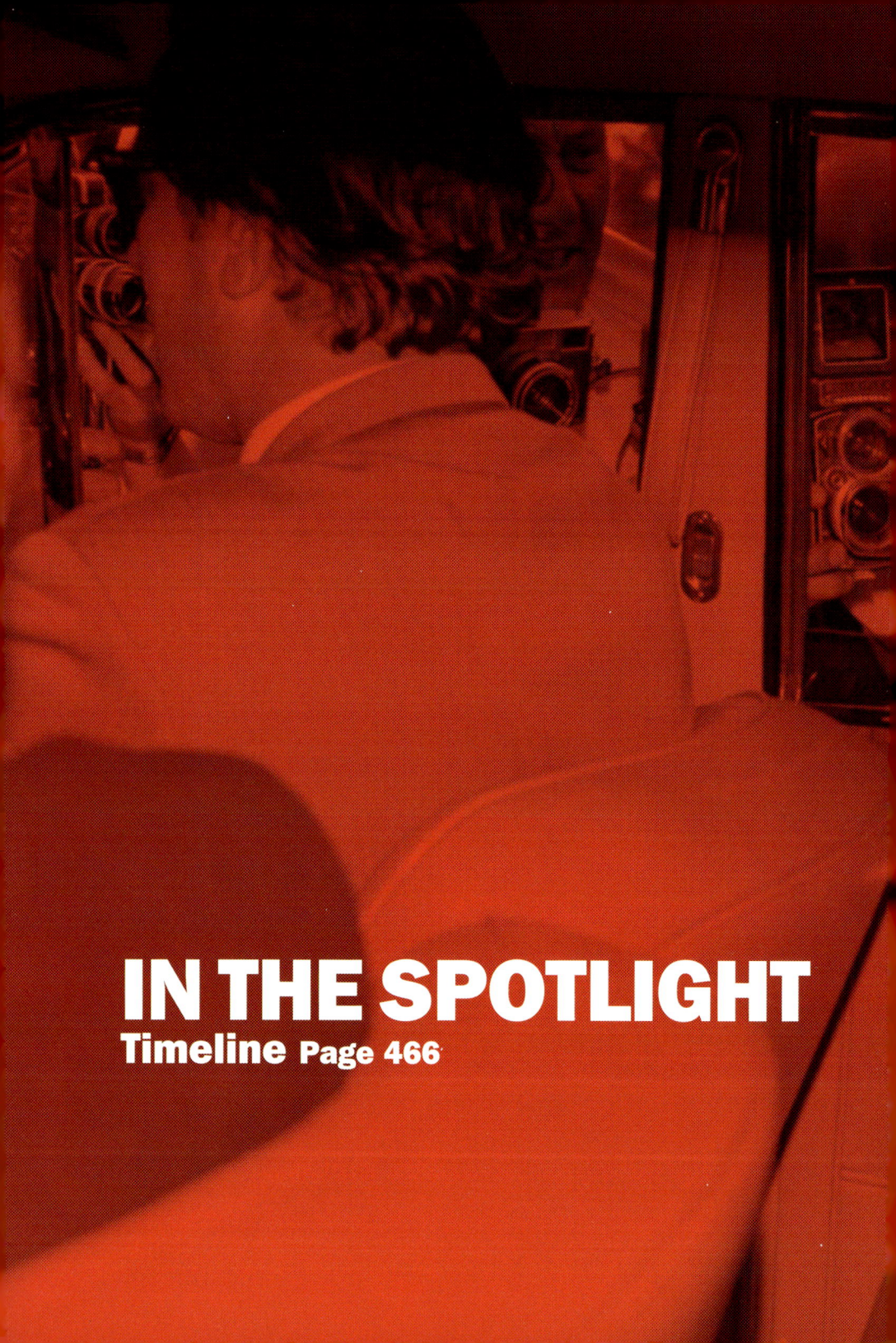

IN THE SPOTLIGHT
Timeline Page 466

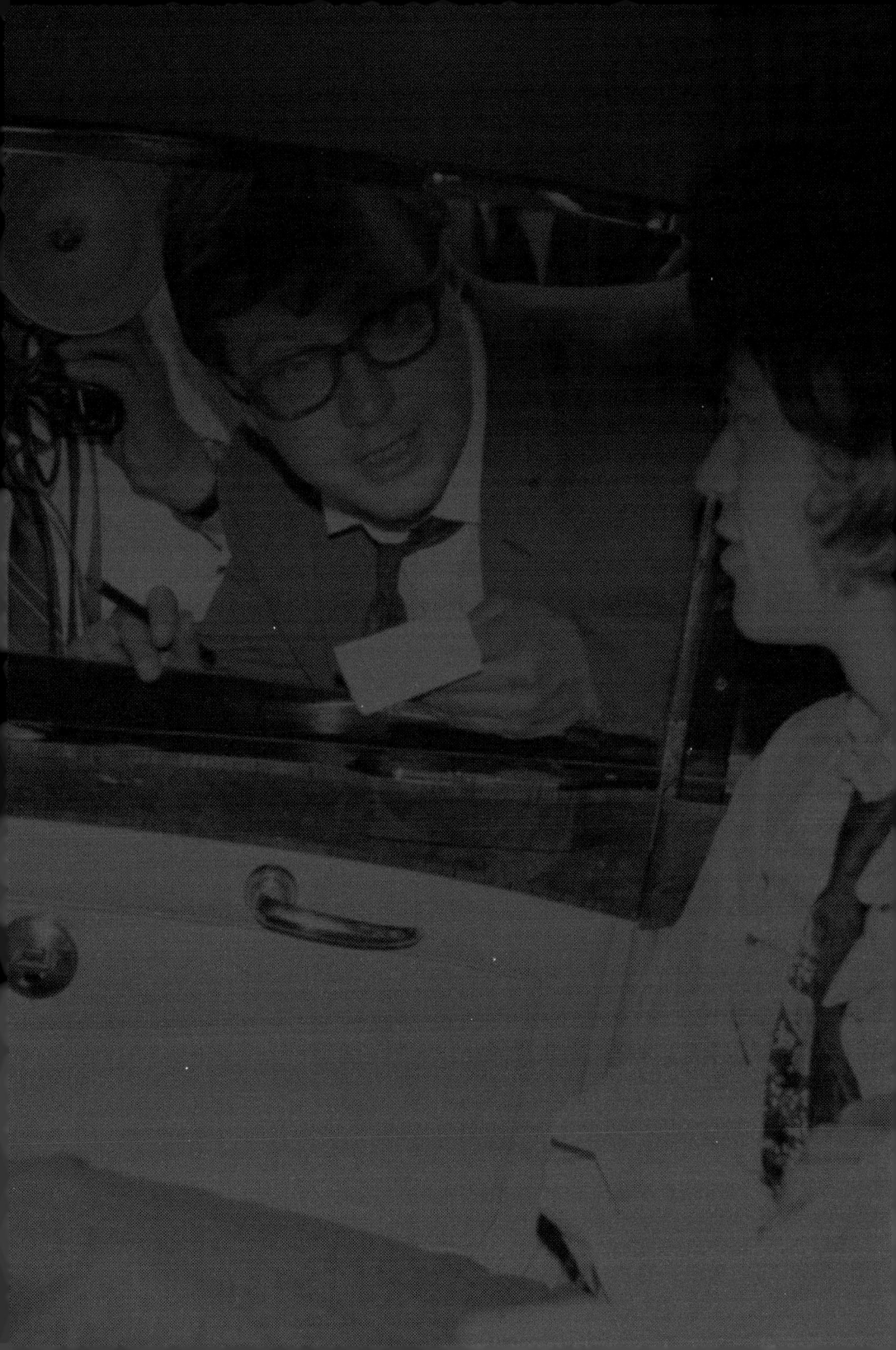

Timeline

24 October 1936
Birth of William "Bill" George Perks (Wyman) to William and Kathleen Perks of Lewisham, south London.

2 June 1941
Birth of Charles "Charlie" Robert Watts to Charles and Lillian Watts of Kingsbury, north London.

28 February 1942
Birth of Lewis Brian Hopkin Jones (Brian) to Lewis and Louisa Jones of Cheltenham, Gloucestershire.

26 July 1943
Birth of Michael "Mick" Philip Jagger to Basil "Joe" and Eva Jagger in Dartford, Kent.

18 December 1943
Birth of Keith Richards to Herbert and Doris Richards of Dartford, Kent.

1 June 1947
Birth of Ronald "Ron" David Wood to Arthur and Elizabeth Wood of Hillingdon, Middlesex.

17 January 1949
Birth of Michael "Mick" Kevin Taylor to Lionel and Marilyn Taylor of Welwyn Garden City, Hertfordshire.

1949–1952
Mick and Keith both attend Wentworth Primary School, Dartford, Kent.

17 October 1961
Keith meets Mick on Dartford Railway Station, Kent.

17 March 1962
Alexis Korner's Blues Incorporated band (featuring Charlie) debut at The Ealing Club in west London. Brian attends.

7 April 1962
Mick and Keith visit the Ealing Club to see Blues Incorporated. Later, they meet with Brian and Charlie.

May 1962
Pianist Ian Stewart responds to an ad by Brian and they start rehearsing around London. Later, Mick, Keith and bassist Dick Taylor join for rehearsals.

12 July 1962
Mick, Keith, Brian, Dick Taylor, Ian Stewart and stand-in drummer Tony Chapman perform their first gig as "The Rollin' Stones" at the Marquee Jazz Club, Oxford Street, London.

August 1962
Mick and Brian move into an apartment on Edith Grove in Chelsea, London, with Keith moving in later.

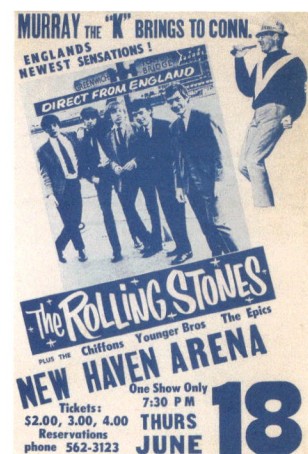

Show poster, New Haven, Connecticut, USA, 1964

December 1962
Charlie Watts leaves Blues Incorporated.

9 and 10 December 1962
Bill Wyman auditions for The Rolling Stones at The Wetherby Arms pub in Chelsea, London.

15 December 1962
Bill's first appearance with the Stones at Windsor's Ricky Tick Club.

12 January 1963
Charlie's first date with the Stones at The Ealing Jazz Club, west London.

24 February 1963
The Stones first appearance at Giorgio Gomelsky's Crawdaddy Club – hosted at Richmond's Station Hotel, Surrey.

28 April 1963
Impresario Andrew Oldham and agent Eric Easton attend a Stones gig at Richmond's Crawdaddy Club. They later meet with the band to discuss potential management duties.

1 May 1963
Andrew Oldham and Eric Easton hold a follow-up meeting with the band. Among other details, they ask for Ian Stewart to step down from the line-up. He is retained as road manager.

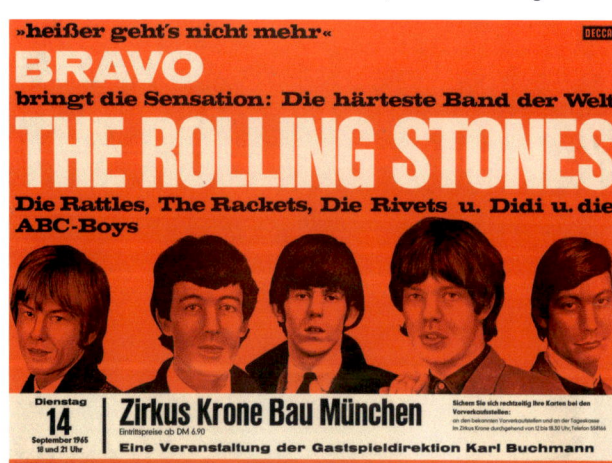

Show poster, Munich, Germany, 1965

5 May 1963
On George Harrison's recommen-
dation, Dick Rowe – Decca Records
A&R in chief – sees the Stones in
concert at the Crawdaddy Club.

6 May 1963
The Stones sign a management
contract with Andrew Oldham and
Eric Easton.

8 May 1963
Dick Rowe signs the Stones to
Decca Records.

7 June 1963
Release of first single "Come On".

7 July 1963
First national television appearance on *Thank Your Lucky Stars*.

29 September–3 November 1963
First UK tour, supporting Bo
Diddley, The Everly Brothers and
(for later shows) Little Richard.

1 November 1963
Single release, "I Wanna Be Your
Man".

6–27 January 1964
Tour of the UK.

8 February–March 7 1964
Concert tour of the United Kingdom.

21 February 1964
Single release, "Not Fade Away".

27 March 1964
At a launch party in Windsor,
Berkshire, for Andrew Loog Oldham
protégée Adrienne Posta, Mick
meets Marianne Faithfull.

16 April 1964
First UK album release, *The Rolling
Stones*.

26 April 1964
Wembley Empire Pool, London –
New Musical Express' Poll Winners
Concert.

30 May 1964
First US album release,
*The Rolling Stones – England's
Newest Hit Makers*.

1 June 1964
Arrival in New York City.

5–20 June 1964
The Stones' first United States tour.

10–11 June 1964
Recording at Chess Studios in
Chicago, Illinois.

26 June 1964
Single release, "It's All Over Now".

27 June 1964
All five Stones review the week's
record releases on a pre-recorded
edition of BBC *TV's Juke Box Jury*.

4 July 1964
Marianne Faithfull single release,
"As Tears Go By", a song written by
Mick and Keith.

5 September–11 October 1964
UK tour.

24 October–15 November 1964
Second tour of the United States.

25 October 1964
First appearance on *The Ed
Sullivan Show*.

28–29 October 1964
Santa Monica, California – Civic
Auditorium. Filming for the *Teen
Age Music International (T.A.M.I.)
Awards Show*.

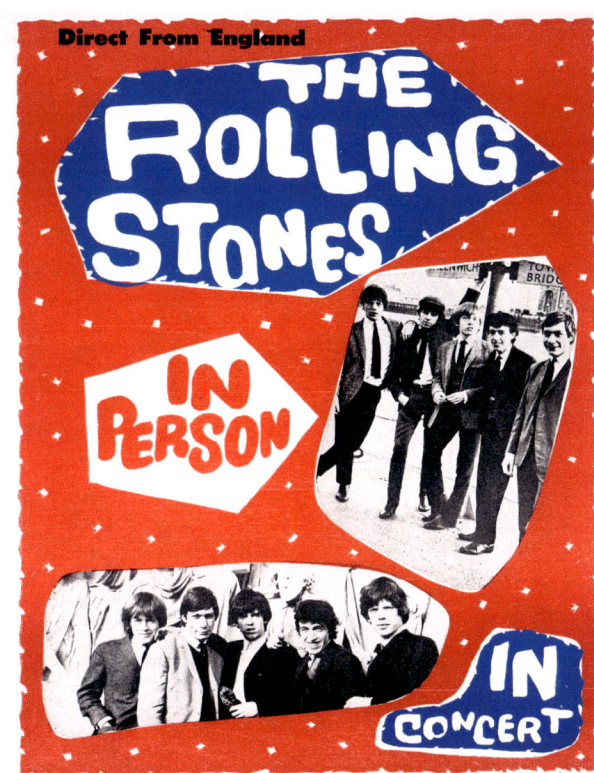

Show poster, Dayton, Ohio, USA, 1964

13 November 1964
UK single release, "Little Red Rooster".

6–8 January 1965
Tour of Northern Ireland/Republic of Ireland.

16 January 1965
Album release, *The Rolling Stones No. 2*.

22 January–16 February 1965
Tour of Australia, New Zealand and Singapore.

18 March 1965
Charges of "insulting behaviour" are levied against Bill, Brian, and Mick after being refused use of a toilet at a petrol station in London.

26 March–2 April 1965
Scandinavian tour.

11 April 1965
Wembley Empire Pool, London
New Musical Express' Poll Winners Concert.

23 April–29 May 1965
Tour of North America.

5 June 1965
Single release (US),
"(I Can't Get No) Satisfaction".

11 June 1965
EP release, *Got Live If You Want It!*

24–29 June 1965
Tour of Scandinavia.

26 July 1965
The band meets with new business manager, Allen Klein.

30 July 1965
Album release (US), *Out Of Our Heads*.

2 September 1965
Ready, Steady, Go! – a pre-recorded special edition of the show that the Stones took over with guests.

3–4 September 1965
Short tour of Northern/Republic of Ireland. Parts of the tour are filmed for later use in *Charlie Is My Darling*.

11–17 September 1965
First tour of West Germany and Austria.

14 September 1965
Backstage at Munich's Circus-Krone-Bau, Brian meets Anita Pallenberg for the first time.

15 September 1965
Gig at Berlin's Waldbühne arena is halted after 20 minutes due to rioting audience.

24 September–17 October 1965
UK tour.

25 October 1965
Single release, "Get Off Of My Cloud".

27 October–5 December 1965
North American tour.

4 February 1966
Single release, "19th Nervous Breakdown".

18 February–1 March 1966
Tour of Australia and New Zealand.

26 March–5 April 1966
Tour of Europe.

Show poster, Big Beat Show, *Australia, 1965*

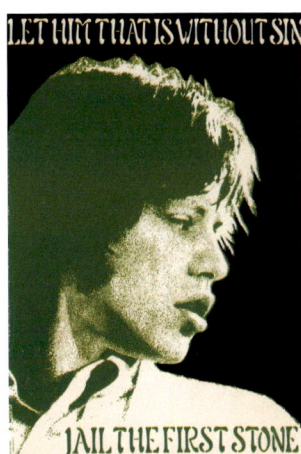

Color lithograph poster, Vroom, Netherlands, 1967

15 April 1966
Album release, *Aftermath*.

7 May 1966
Single release, "Paint It, Black".

24 June–28 July 1966
North American tour.

23 September–October 9 1966
UK tour.

December 1966
Mick's relationship with Marianne Faithfull is made public.

13 January 1967
Single release, "Let's Spend The Night Together"/"Ruby Tuesday".

15 January 1967
The Ed Sullivan Show broadcasters force Mick to change the title of "Let's Spend The Night Together" to "Let's Spend Some Time Together".

20 January 1967
Album release, *Between The Buttons*.

12 February 1967
Police raid Keith's West Wittering home in West Sussex looking for drugs.

26 February–21 March 1967
Mick, Keith and Brian plus Anita

Pallenberg, Marianne Faithfull and others embark on a holiday in Morocco. Start of Keith and Anita's relationship.

25 March–17 April 1967
European tour.

10 May 1967
Mick and Keith are charged over the 12 February Redlands drugs raid. Later that day, Brian Jones' flat in Kensington, London is raided by police.

16–18 June 1967
Brian attends the Monterey International Pop Festival in California and introduces the Jimi Hendrix Experience.

27–29 June 1967
The trial of Mick and Keith in relation to the Redlands' drugs raid takes place at Chichester Court, West Sussex. Mick is found guilty for possession of Benzedrine and is sentenced to 3 months in jail. Keith is also found guilty for allowing his property to be used for the smoking of cannabis and sentenced to 12 months' imprisonment.

30 June 1967
Mick and Keith are granted bail and released from jail on appeal.

31 July 1967
In London's High Court, Mick and Keith successfully appeal against their sentences emanating from

the Redlands trial. Following the hearing, Mick appears on Granada Television's *World In Action*.

18 August 1967
Single release, "We Love You".

20 September 1967
The Stones announce that they are no longer represented by Andrew Loog Oldham.

8 December 1967
Album release, *Their Satanic Majesties Request*.

March 1968
Mick buys a property at 48, Cheyne Walk, Chelsea, London.

17 March 1968
Mick attends a demonstration against the Vietnam War outside the American Embassy in Grosvenor Square, London.

18 March 1968
Birth of Shirley and Charlie Watts' daughter, Serafina.

24 May 1968
Single release, 'Jumpin' Jack Flash".

2 September 1968
Mick starts filming *Performance* in London.

21 November 1968
Brian purchases Cotchford Farm in East Sussex.

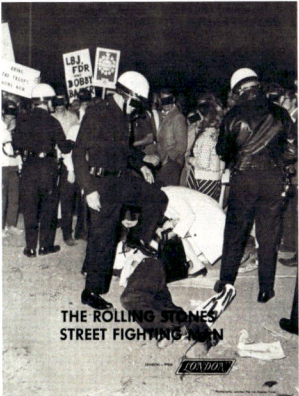
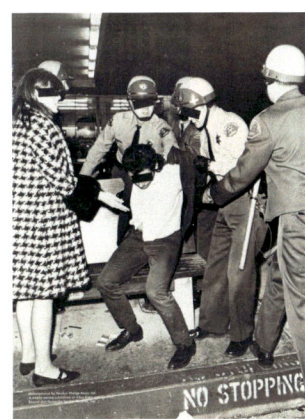

Promotion for "Street Fighting Man", UK, 1968

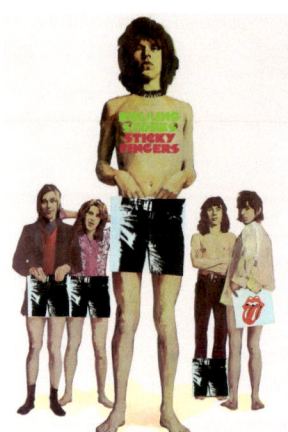

Promotional poster, **Sticky Fingers,**
1971

30 November 1968
Jean-Luc Godard's film *One Plus One (AKA Sympathy For The Devil)* featuring the Stones, receives its London premiere.

5 December 1968
Press launch for *Beggars Banquet* album release at the Gore Hotel in Kensington, London.

6 December 1968
Album release *Beggars Banquet.*

10–12 December 1968
Filming of TV special *The Rolling Stones' Rock 'n' Roll Circus* at InterTel Studios in Stonebridge Park, north London.

19 May 1969
Keith buys a house at 3, Cheyne Walk, Chelsea in London.

21 May 1969
Final Stones photo shoot with Brian present in London.

31 May 1969
Mick Taylor starts recording with The Rolling Stones.

8 June 1969
Mick, Keith and Charlie travel to Brian's Sussex home and inform him that he is no longer part of the Stones.

13 June 1969
At a press conference in London's Hyde Park the group introduce Mick Taylor and announce a free concert in the park set for 5th July 1969.

2 July 1969
While working at Olympic Sound Studios, news comes through that Brian had been found dead in his swimming pool in Hartfield, Sussex.

4 July 1969
Single release, "Honky Tonk Women".

5 July 1969
To a crowd estimated at over 250,000 the Stones headline a free concert in London's Hyde Park.

13 July–10 September 1969
Mick films *Ned Kelly* in Bungendore (near Canberra), Australia.

10 August 1969
Birth of Marlon Richards, son to Keith and Anita Pallenberg.

7–30 November 1969
North American tour.

18 November 1969
Final appearance on *The Ed Sullivan Show*.

5 December 1969
Album release, *Let It Bleed*.

6 December 1969
Free concert at Altamont Speedway, Livermore, California. 300,000-plus attendees, four births and four dead. Filmed by the Maysles Brothers as part of the film *Gimme Shelter*.

24 June 1970
Premiere of *Ned Kelly* film in London.

20 July 1970
The Stones announce they are to sever ties with Allen Klein and Decca Records, with a plan to start their own record label.

3 August 1970
Premiere of *Performance* film in New York City.

30 August–9 October 1970
European tour.

4 September 1970
Album release, *Get Yer Ya-Ya's Out!*

5 October 1970
Prince Rupert Lowenstein is appointed to coordinate the band's business affairs.

4 November 1970
Birth of Karis, daughter to Mick and Marsha Hunt.

6 December 1970
Premiere of the film *Gimme Shelter* in New York City.

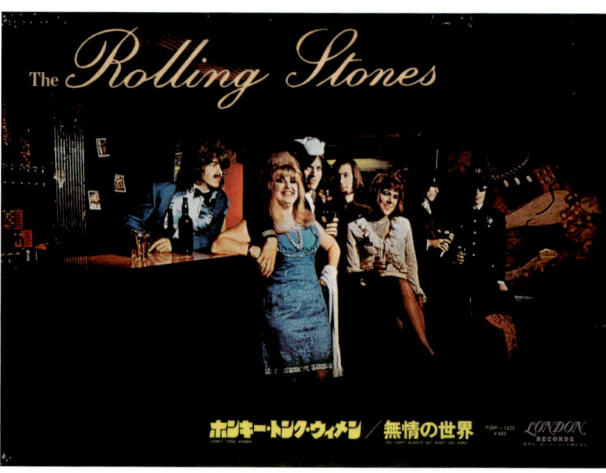

Promotional poster, Japan, 1969

4 February 1971
It is suggested that the group leave Britain to escape the country's crippling tax laws.

4–14 March 1971
UK "Farewell" tour.

26 March 1971
Private gig at London's Marquee Club in Soho – filmed ostensibly for US television.

April 1971
Keith, Charlie, Bill, Mick Taylor and their families relocate to the south of France. Mick and his partner Bianca Pérez-Mora Macías base themselves in Paris.

6 April 1971
Rolling Stones Records, the band's own label, is launched with Marshall Chess employed as president.

16 April 1971
Single release, "Brown Sugar".

23 April 1971
Album release, *Sticky Fingers*.

12 May 1971
Mick marries Bianca Pérez-Mora Macías in Saint-Tropez, France.

7 June–July 5 1971
Sessions for *Exile On Main St* begin at Keith's Villa Nellcôte residence in southern France.

21 October 1971
Birth of Jade, daughter to Mick and Bianca Jagger.

7 January 1972
Album release, *Jamming With Edward*, featuring recordings made by Mick, Charlie, Bill, Nicky Hopkins and Ry Cooder in April 1969.

14 April 1972
Single release, "Tumbling Dice".

17 April 1972
Birth of Dandelion (Angela) to Keith and Anita Pallenberg.

12 May 1972
Album release, *Exile On Main St*.

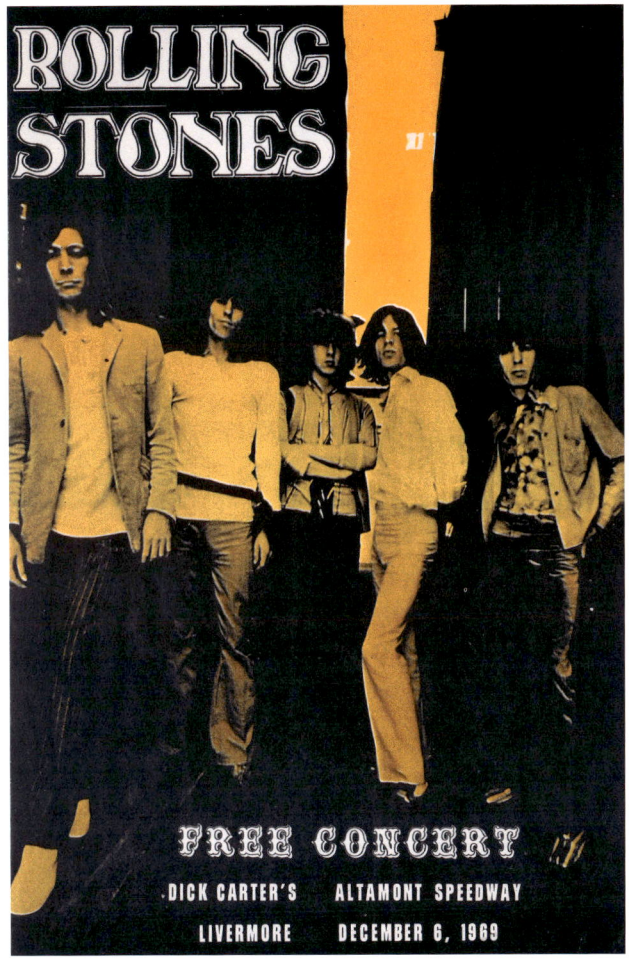

Show poster, Altamont Speedway, California, USA, 1969

3 June–26 July 1972
American tour (S.T.P.).

18 January–27 February 1973
Australasian tour.

20 August 1973
Single release, "Angie".

31 August 1973
Album release, *Goats Head Soup*.

1 September–19 October 1973
European tour.

22 October 1973
Mick Taylor's last live appearance as a member of the Stones at Berlin's Deutschlandhalle, West Germany.

14 April 1974
Premier in New York City of the 1972 American concert tour film, *Ladies And Gentlemen, The Rolling Stones*.

10 May 1974
Release of Bill's first solo album, *Monkey Grip*.

13–14 July 1974
Keith joins Ron Wood's ad hoc band for two shows at the State Gaumont Theatre in Kilburn, west London.

26 July 1974
Single release, "It's Only Rock 'n' Roll (But I Like It)".

13 September 1974
Ron's solo album release, *I've Got My Own Album To Do*.

18 October 1974
Album release, *It's Only Rock 'n' Roll*.

12 December 1974
It is announced that Mick Taylor has left The Rolling Stones.

14 April 1975
A press release announces that Ron Wood will take Mick Taylor's place in the Stones for their summer tour of the States.

1 May 1975
The Stones perform an impromptu set along 5th Avenue in New York City on a flat-bed truck. The event coincides with the announcement of the band's tour of North and South America – scheduled for later in the year.

1 June–8 August 1975
Tour of the Americas. Dates originally scheduled for Mexico, Brazil and Venezuela are cancelled.

19 December 1975
It is announced that Ron Wood is now a permanent member of The Rolling Stones.

26 March 1976
Birth of Tara, son to Keith and Anita Pallenberg.

16 April 1976
Single release, "Fool To Cry".

23 April 1976
Album release, *Black And Blue*.

28 April–23 June 1976
Tour of Europe.

4 June 1976
Keith and Anita Pallenberg's baby son, Tara, dies of respiratory failure aged just two-and-a-half months in Geneva, Switzerland.

21 August 1976
Gig at Knebworth Park (headlining Knebworth Fair), Hertfordshire, England.

30 October 1976
Birth of Jesse, son to Ron and Krissy Wood.

16 February 1977
Stones sign a four-album record deal with WEA in North America (and EMI for other territories) worth $14 million.

27 February 1977
Keith's room at Toronto's Harbour Castle Hotel is raided by Royal Canadian Mountain Police, who find quantities of heroin and other drug-related material. He is released on bail.

4–5 March 1977
Two concerts at Toronto's El Mocambo Club. Both are recorded.

23 September 1977
Album release, *Love You Live*.

19 May 1978
Single release, "Miss You".

29 May 1978
Bianca Jagger files for divorce from Mick.

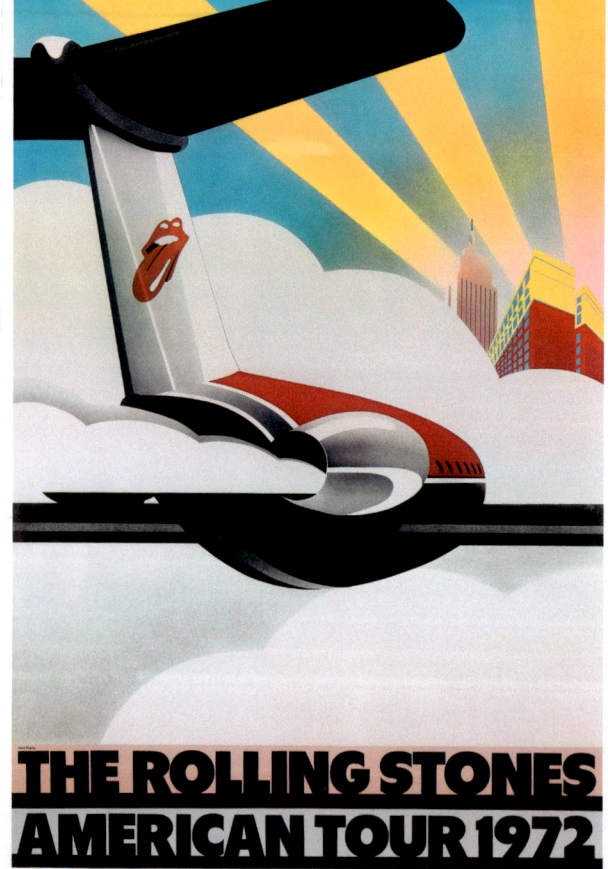

Promotional poster, The Rolling Stones American tour, 1972

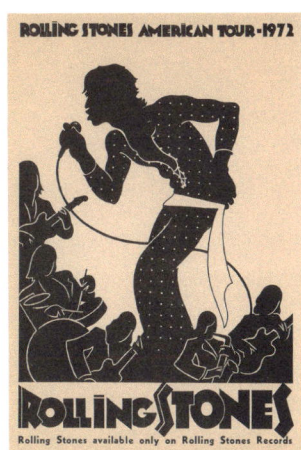

Promotional poster, The Rolling Stones American tour, 1972

9 June 1978
Album release, *Some Girls*.

10 June–26 July 1978
US tour.

15 September 1978
Single release, "Respectable".

22 October 1978
Birth of Leah, daughter to Ron and Jo Howard.

23–24 October 1978
At Toronto's New Court House, Canada, Keith is given a 12-month prohibition order in conjunction with heroin addiction treatment. In addition, he is ordered to play a benefit concert for Canada's National Institute for the Blind.

12 December 1978
Release of Keith's Christmas themed record, *Run Rudolph Run*.

22 April 1979
Two concerts at Oshawa's Civic Auditorium in Ontario, Canada, in aid of the Canadian National Institute for the Blind. Support comes from The New Barbarians.

24 April–22 May 1979
Ron and Keith, as part of The New Barbarians, begin an 18-date tour across the States.

11 August 1979
Keith and Ron appear with The New Barbarians at the Knebworth Fair festival in Hertfordshire, England.

18 December 1979
Keith meets his future wife Patti Hansen in New York City.

20 June 1980
Single release, "Emotional Rescue".

23 June 1980
Album release, *Emotional Rescue*.

July 1980
Keith and Anita Pallenberg end their relationship.

5 November 1980
Mick and Bianca's divorce is finalised in London.

January–February 1981
Mick films his contribution to Werner Herzog's *Fitzcarraldo* in Iquitos, Peru. He later pulls out after co-star Jason Robards falls ill, prolonging the filming schedule.

14 August 1981
Single release, "Start Me Up".

27 August 1981
Album release, *Tattoo You*.

25 September–19 December 1981
Tour of America.

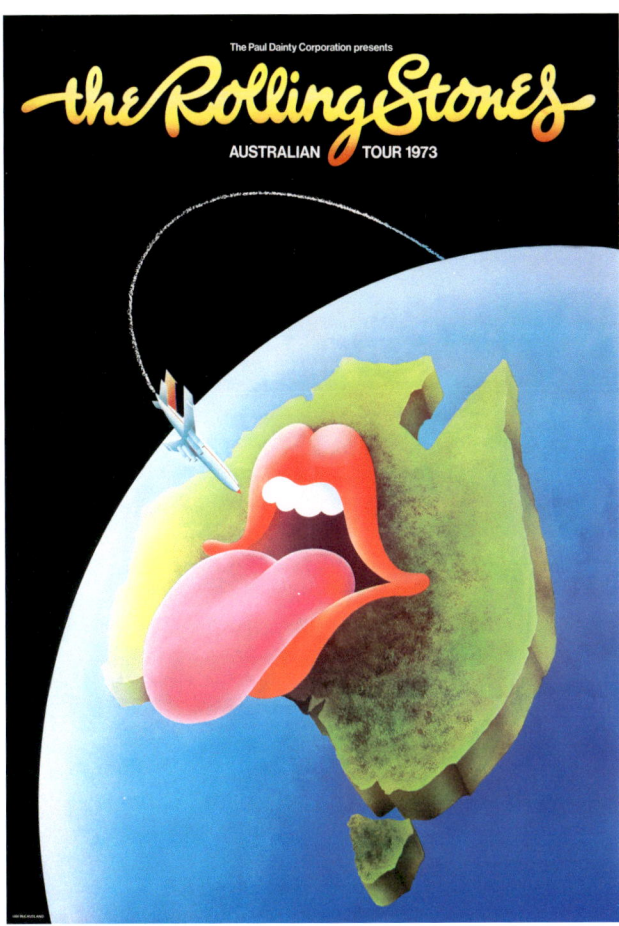

Promotional poster, The Rolling Stones Australian tour, 1973

473

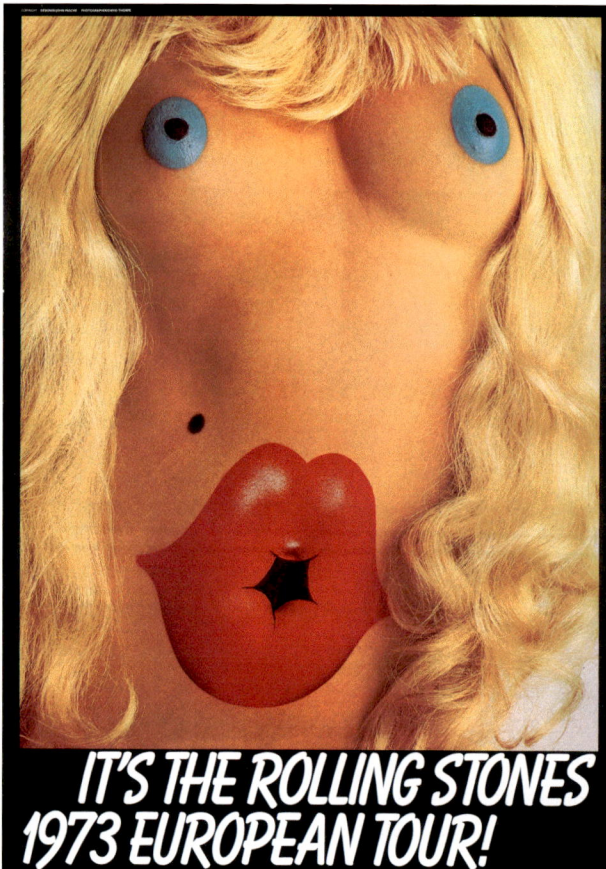

Promotional poster, European tour, 1973

14 December 1981
At Kemper Stadium in Kansas City, Mick Taylor joins the Stones for part of the concert.

26 May–25 July 1982
European tour.

26 May 1982
Keyboardist Chuck Leavell's debut with the Stones at Aberdeen's Capitol Theatre, Scotland.

30 May 1982
Surprise gig at London's 100 Club.

1 June 1982
Album release, *Still Life*.

25 July 1982
Ian Stewart's last concert working for the Stones at Leeds' Roundhay Park, Yorkshire.

18 February 1983
The band (minus Bill Wyman) attend the premiere in New York of *Let's Spend The Night Together*, the 1981 North American concert film directed by Hal Ashby.

August 1983
The Stones sign with CBS Records for a distribution deal worth $28 million. In a separate deal, Mick also signs with CBS for his solo work.

20 August 1983
Birth of Tyrone, son to Jo Howard and Ron Wood.

20–21 September 1983
Bill & Charlie and others perform at London's Royal Albert Hall in aid of Ronnie Lane's ARMS Charity that supports multiple sclerosis research.

1 November 1983
Single release, "Undercover Of The Night".

7 November 1983
Album release, *Undercover*.

28 November–9 December 1983
Charlie, Bill and Ronnie tour the States in aid of the ARMS charity.

18 December 1983
On his 40th birthday, Keith marries Patti Hansen in Mexico. Mick is best man.

2 March 1984
Birth of Elizabeth, daughter to Mick and Jerry Hall.

14 June 1984
Madison Square Garden in New York City inducts The Rolling Stones into their Hall Of Fame.

28 June 1984
Release of The Jacksons' single "State Of Shock" featuring a contribution from Mick.

2 January 1985
Marriage of Ronnie to Josephine (Jo) Howard. Keith and Charlie act as joint best men.

4 February 1985
Single release from Mick, "Just Another Night".

25 February 1985
Release of Mick's first solo album, *She's The Boss*.

18 March 1985
Birth of Theodora, daughter to Keith and Patti Richards.

25 April 1985
Release of the charity album *Willie And The Poor Boys*, featuring Bill, Charlie and others.

13 July 1985
Mick, Ronnie and Keith perform at the "Live Aid" charity concert at JFK Stadium in Philadelphia. Mick duets with Tina Turner; Keith and Ronnie appear alongside Bob Dylan.

19 August 1985
Single release, "Dancing In The Street", Mick and David Bowie's charity release for the Band Aid trust.

28 August 1985
Birth of James, son to Mick and Jerry Hall.

18 November 1985
Debut appearance of The Charlie Watts Orchestra at London's Ronnie Scott's Jazz Club. Mick and Keith attend.

12 December 1985
Death of Ian Stewart.

20 December 1985
Mick, Keith, Charlie, Ron and Bill attend Ian Stewart's funeral in Leatherhead, Surrey.

23 February 1986
At London 100 Club, the Stones perform in tribute to Ian Stewart

with guest appearances from Eric Clapton, Pete Townshend and Jeff Beck.

25 February 1986
The Stones receive a Grammy Lifetime Achievement Award from Eric Clapton at The Roof Gardens, London.

26 February 1986
Single release, "Harlem Shuffle".

24 March 1986
Album release, *Dirty Work*.

20 June 1986
Mick appears alongside David Bowie and others in aid of The Prince of Wales Trust Concert at London's Wembley Arena.

7–8 July 1986
Aretha Franklin records "Jumpin' Jack Flash" with Keith producing and playing guitar with Ron.

28 July 1986
Birth of Alexandra, daughter to Keith and Patti Richards.

15–16 October 1986
Keith appears with Chuck Berry and all-star band at St. Louis' Fox Theatre, Missouri. Both concerts are filmed for the movie *Hail! Hail! Rock 'n' Roll*.

13–24 June 1987
The Charlie Watts Orchestra US tour.

13 July 1987
Keith signs with Richard Branson's Virgin Records for solo recordings.

November 1987
Publication of Ron's art book, *The Works*.

4–25 November 1987
The band The Gunslingers, featuring Ron and Bo Diddley, tour the States.

20 January 1988
At the Waldorf Astoria in New York City, Mick inducts The Beatles into the Rock and Roll Hall of Fame.

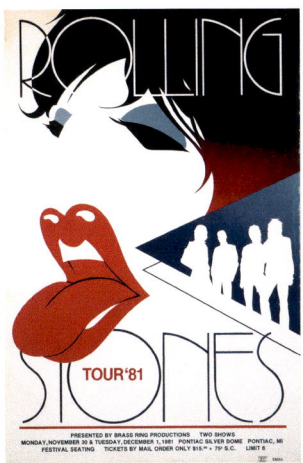

Promotional poster, Tour '81, USA, 1981

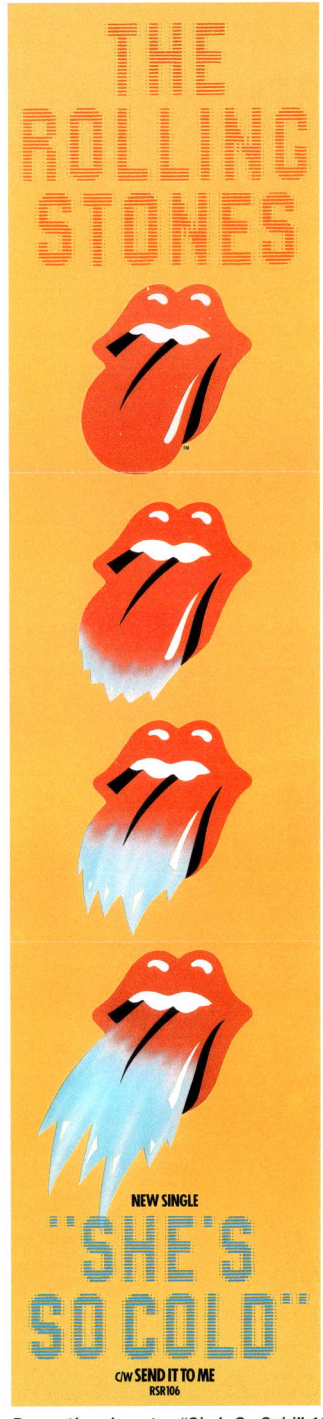

Promotional poster, "She's So Cold", 1980

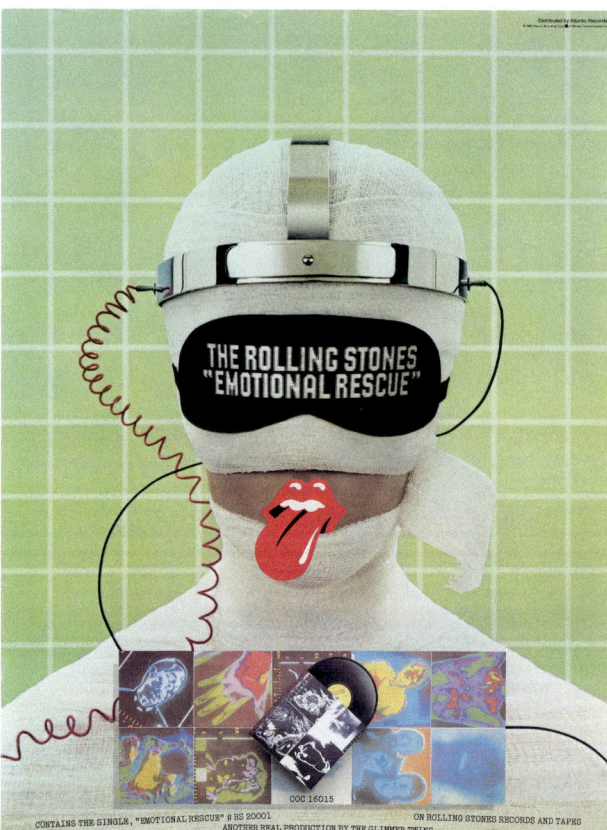

Promotional poster, Emotional Rescue, *1980*

20 February 1988
Charity concert at London's Royal Albert Hall in aid of the Great Ormond Street Hospital featuring Bill, Ron and others.

2–15 March 1988
Ron & Bo Diddley as The Gunslingers tour Japan.

15–28 March 1988
Mick's solo tour of Japan.

18–26 March 1988
Ron and Bo Diddley tour the West Coast of the United States.

22 September–5 November 1988
Mick's solo tour of Australia, New Zealand and Indonesia.

3 October 1988
Release of *Talk Is Cheap*, Keith's first solo album.

24 November–17 December 1988
Keith Richards And The X-Pensive Winos tour of America.

18 January 1989
At New York's Waldorf Astoria Hotel, the Stones are inducted into The Rock and Roll Hall of Fame by Pete Townshend. Mick, Keith, Ron and Mick Taylor are present for the acceptance and (later) perform with Little Richard, Tina Turner and others.

9 May 1989
Bill opens his restaurant/bar Sticky Fingers in Kensington, London.

31 May 1989
Keith receives the "Living Legend" Award at The International Rock Awards in New York City. He also performs with the X-Pensive Winos.

2 June 1989
Bill marries Mandy Smith in Suffolk, England.

29 August 1989
Album release, *Steel Wheels*.

31 August–20 December 1989
Steel Wheels North American tour.

27 December 1989
TV premiere of *25x5: The Continuing Adventures Of The Rolling Stones.*

14–27 February 1990
Steel Wheels tour of Japan.

18 May–25 August 1990
Urban Jungle European tour.

24 October 1990
Publication of Bill's 1960s-centred biography, *Stone Alone*.

22 November 1990
Bill divorces Mandy Smith.

18 February 1991
Mick begins filming his part in the movie *Freejack* alongside Anthony Hopkins and Emilio Estevez.

2 May 1991
The Stones receive an "Outstanding Contribution to British Music" award at the Ivor Novello song writing presentations in London. Bill and Ron collect the award.

25 October 1991
Release of *At The Max*, the concert film of the 1990 *Urban Jungle* European tour.

19 November 1991
The group sign a deal with Virgin Records worth $40 million.

10 December 1991
Release of Keith and the X-Pensive Winos album *Live At The Hollywood Palladium.*

12 January 1992
Birth of Georgia, daughter to Mick and Jerry Jagger.

19 May 1992
Charlie Watts Quintet album release, *A Tribute To Charlie Parker With Strings*.

12–23 July 1992
The Charlie Watts Quintet tour the States.

16 October 1992
Ron plays at the Bob Dylan all-star tribute concert at Madison Square Garden in New York City.

31 October–5 December 1992
Ron's *Slide On This* North American tour.

27 November–18 December 1992
Keith Richards and the X-Pensive Winos European tour.

6 January 1993
Bill announces on UK television that he has quit the Stones.

10–14 January 1993
Ron's *Slide On This* tour of Japan.

2 June 1993
Mick and Keith are inducted in The Songwriters' Hall of Fame in New York City. Keith accepts the award.

11 July 1994
Album release, *Voodoo Lounge*.

1 August–18 December 1994
The *Voodoo Lounge* North American tour with Darryl Jones on bass.

8 September 1994
At Radio City Music Hall in New York City, the Stones receive an MTV "Lifetime Achievement Award".

26 September 1994
Single release, "You Got Me Rocking".

14 January–17 April 1995
The *Voodoo Lounge* world tour (South America, South Africa, Japan, Australia and New Zealand).

26 May–30 August 1995
The *Voodoo Lounge* European tour.

13 November 1995
Album release, *Stripped*.

4–15 July 1996
The Charlie Watts Orchestra North American tour.

5 July 1996
Mick begins filming *Bent* in Glasgow, Scotland.

23 September–12 December 1997
Bridges To Babylon North American tour.

27 September 1997
Album release, *Bridges To Babylon*.

9 December 1997
Birth of Gabriel, son to Mick and Jerry Jagger.

5 January–15 February 1998
Bridges To Babylon North American tour (continued).

12 March–17 March 1998
Bridges To Babylon tour of Japan.

29 March–5 April 1998
Bridges To Babylon tour of South America.

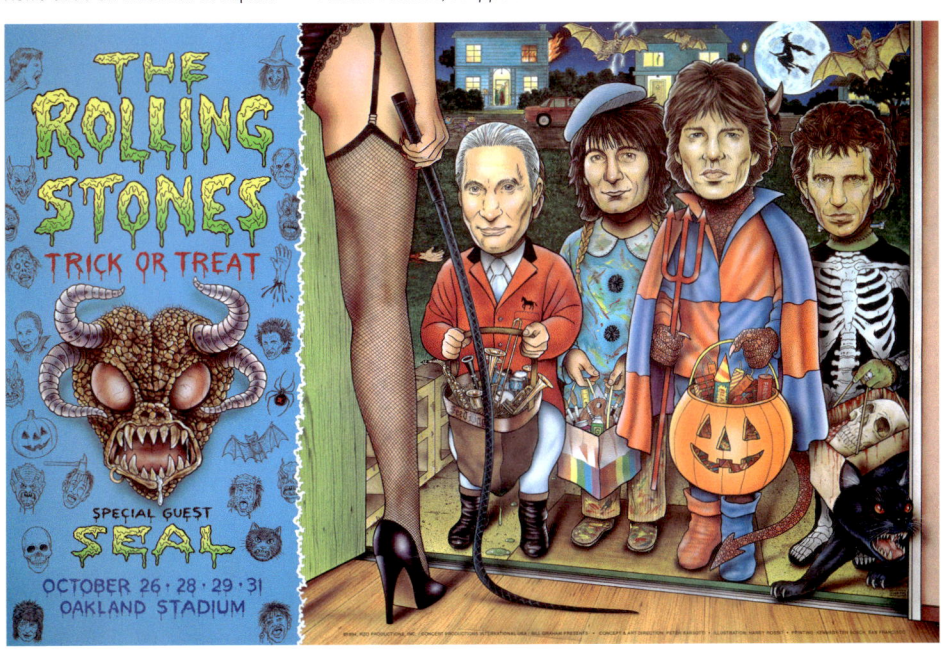

Show poster, The Rolling Stones Trick or Treat, Oakland, California, USA, 1994

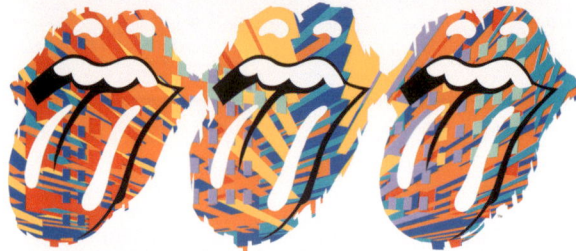

ROLLING STONES

LICKS WORLD TOUR 2002/03

Promotional poster, Licks World tour, 2002

17–26 April 1998
Bridges To Babylon North American tour (continued).

18 May 1998
Keith sustains three broken ribs after an accident in his library at home in Connecticut. As a result, the *Bridges To Babylon* European tour is postponed until June 1998.

8 June 1998
Because of new British tax laws, Rolling Stones concerts at Edinburgh (Murrayfield, 24/08/1998), Sheffield (Don Valley Stadium, 26/09/1998) and two dates in London (Wembley Stadium, 20 & 22/06/1998) are to be rescheduled for June 1999.

13 June–19 September 1998
Bridges To Babylon European tour.

11 August 1998
Historic gig in Russia at Moscow's Luzhniki Stadium.

25 January–20 April 1999
No Security North American tour.

18 May 1999
Birth of Lucas Jagger, son to Mick and Luciana Gimenez Morad.

29 May–20 June 1999
Bridges To Babylon European tour (rescheduled with additional dates).

8 June 1999
Small theatre show at Shepherd's Bush Empire in London.

3 November 1999
Keith receives a Q magazine

"Special Merit" award at London's Park Lane Hotel. The award is presented by Ron.

30 March 2000
Opening of "The Mick Jagger Centre", an arts centre housed at Dartford's Grammar School, Kent. Mick attends the opening ceremony.

18 May 2000
Mick's mother Eva dies.

26 May 2000
Funeral of Eva Jagger at Ham, Surrey with Mick, Keith, Ronnie and Charlie in attendance.

30 August 2000
Bert Richards, Keith's father, dies in Connecticut.

6 March 2001
At New York City's Beacon Theater,

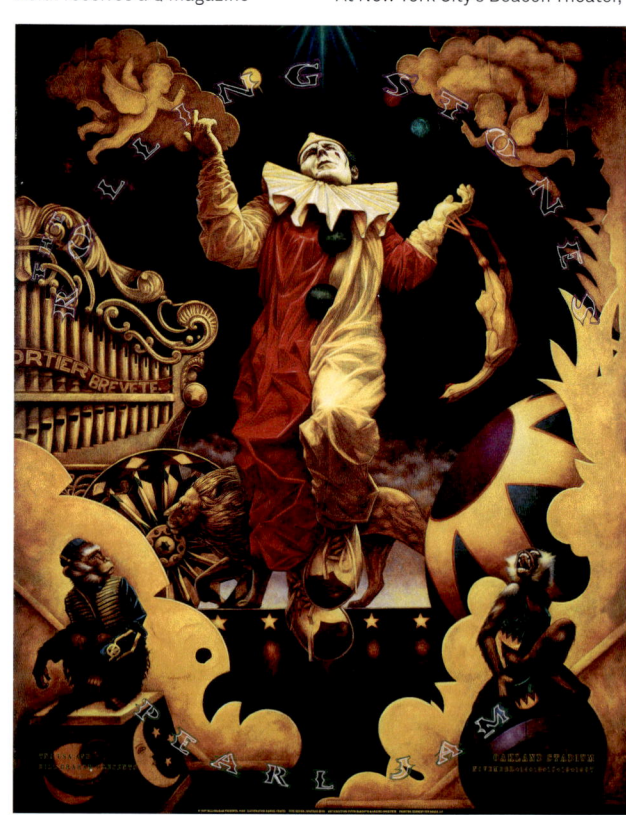

Show poster, Oakland, USA, 1997

Keith plays a set in aid of the charity The Rainforest Alliance.

23 April 2001
John Phillips (posthumous) album release *Pay, Pack and Follow* featuring Mick, Keith, Ron and Mick Taylor. (Sessions date from 1976–77.)

24 September 2001
British royal premiere in London of the film *Enigma* – co-produced by Mick.

20 October 2001
Mick and Keith appear at "The Concert for New York" at Madison Square Garden in aid of the September 11 terrorist attacks appeal.

15 November 2001
Mick performs at El Rey Club in Los Angeles, California.

22 November 2001
Television broadcast of *Being Mick*, a video diary of Jagger's filmed over a two-year period.

7 May 2002
To announce the 2002–03 *Licks* tour, the band arrives in New York City's Van Cortlandt Park by airship.

14 June 2002
It is announced in the British Queen's Birthday Honours list that Mick has been knighted for services to music.

3 September–30 November 2002
North American *Licks* tour (first leg).

21 October 2002
Publication of Bill's retrospective book *Rolling With The Stones*.

16 November 2002
Private concert at Las Vegas' The Joint, for a reported fee of $7 million.

8 January–8 February 2003
Licks tour (second leg).

6 February 2003
Performance at "Fight Global Warming" awareness concert at Los Angeles' Staples Center,

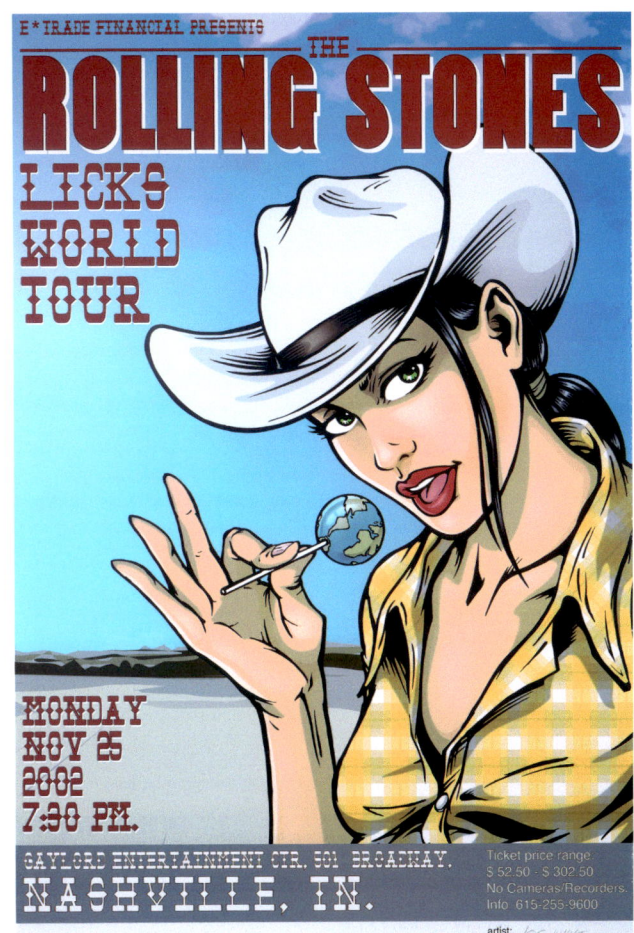

Show poster, Licks World tour, Nashville, Tennessee, USA, 2002

California. The band is introduced by President Bill Clinton.

18 February–5 March 2003
Licks Australasian tour.

7 March–10 April 2003
Licks Asian tour.

27–28 March 2003
Concerts scheduled for China (Hong Kong, Shanghai and Beijing) are cancelled due to the SARS epidemic.

4 June–2 October 2003
Licks European tour.

30 July 2003
Appearance at the "Molson Canadian Rocks for Toronto" at Downsview Park, Toronto in front of 490,000 fans.

August 2003
According to The Rolling Stones, the band's authorised autobiography is published.

7–9 November 2003
Two concerts at Hong Kong's Tamar festival site, the first time the group play the Republic of China.

12 December 2003
In the absence of Queen Elizabeth II,

Mick is knighted by Prince Charles at Buckingham Palace in London.

15 March 2004
Keith and Mick are present at the 19th Rock & Roll Hall of Fame awards in New York City, Keith inducts ZZ Top, while Mick performs similar honours for *Rolling Stone* magazine co-founder, Jann Wenner.

14 June 2004
Charlie Watts and the Tentet live album release of *Watts At Scott's*.

9–10 July 2004
Keith guests at two Gram Parsons tribute concerts in California.

18 October 2004
Soundtrack release, *Alfie*, recorded by Mick and Dave Stewart.

14 November 2004
The UK Music Hall of Fame inducts the Stones at London's Hackney Empire – Ron accepts the award.

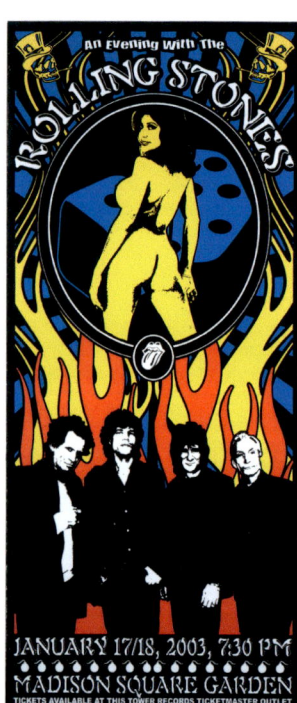

Show poster, New York City, USA, 2003

13 March 2005
At London's Theatre Royal, "Ronnie Wood and Fiends (sic)" concert. Mick guests.

21 August–3 December 2005
A Bigger Bang North American tour.

5 September 2005
Album release, *A Bigger Bang*.

10 January–8 February 2006
A Bigger Bang American tour (continued).

5 February 2006
The group perform at the traditional half-time show at the NFL Superbowl final at Ford Field, Detroit, Michigan. Broadcasters silence part of Mick's vocal during "Start Me Up".

11 February–1 March 2006
A Bigger Bang South American leg.

18 February 2006
An estimated 1.5 million people attend the Stones concert at Copacabana Beach in Rio de Janeiro, Brazil.

4 March–14 March 2006
A Bigger Bang American tour (continued).

22 March–8 April 2006
A Bigger Bang Asian tour.

8 April 2006
Performance at Shanghai's Grand Stage Theatre – their first appearance in mainland China. Three songs ("Brown Sugar", "Honky Tonk Women" and "Rough Justice") are censored by the Chinese Ministry of Culture.

11–18 April 2006
A Bigger Bang Australasian tour.

27 April 2006
Keith sustains a head injury after falling from a coconut tree while on holiday in Fiji.

11 July–3 September 2006
A Bigger Bang European tour.

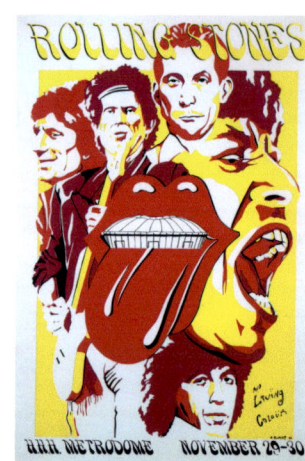

Show poster, Minneapolis, Minnesota, USA, 1989

11–15 September 2006
Keith films his part as "Captain Teague" for *Pirates Of The Caribbean: At World's End*.

20 September–25 November 2006
A Bigger Bang North American tour (continued).

29 October & 1 November 2006
Two concerts at New York City's Beacon Theatre – filmed by Martin Scorsese for the concert movie *Shine A Light*.

11 November 2006
Death of Mick Jagger's father Joe.

7 February 2007
Premiere in Berlin, Germany, of *Shine A Light* concert film.

21 April 2007
Death of Keith's mother Doris.

18 May 2007
Premiere in Anaheim, California, of *Pirates Of The Caribbean: At World's End*. Keith attends.

5 June–26 August 2007
A Bigger Bang European tour (continued).

10 June 2007
Headline performance at the Isle of Wight Festival.

25 July 2007
The band signs a new contract with Universal Music Group.

12 October 2007
Publication of Ron's autobiography, *Ronnie*.

4 April 2008
Album release, *Shine A Light*.

3 November 2009
Album and DVD release, *Get Yer Ya-Ya's Out!* (40th Anniversary Edition).

10 January 2010
Album release from The ABC & D of Boogie Woogie (featuring Charlie), *The Magic of Boogie Woogie*.

9 April 2010
The Ronnie Wood Show premieres on Absolute Radio.

11 May 2010
Premiere of the documentary *Stones In Exile* at New York City's Museum of Modern Art. Mick, Keith, and Charlie attend.

17 May 2010
Album release, *Exile On Main St* (remastered).

18 May 2010
CNN *Larry King Live*. Mick guests.

September–October 2010
Keith films his sequences for *Pirates Of The Caribbean: On Stranger Tides* at Pinewood Studios, Buckinghamshire.

16 September 2010
US theatrical re-release of the 1974 film *Ladies And Gentlemen, The Rolling Stones*.

19 October 2010
Ron Wood solo concerts at The Ambassadors Theatre in London, England (2 shows).

13 February 2011
At the 53rd Grammy Awards ceremony at Los Angeles' Staples Center, Mick sings live in tribute to the late Solomon Burke.

6 April 2011
Release of *Boogie 4 Stu*, a tribute album to Ian Stewart, featuring a new Stones song, a cover of Bob Dylan's "Watching The River Flow".

9 May 2011
At the Sony Radio Academy Awards in London, Ron is awarded Music Radio Personality of the Year.

16 September 2011
Release of the album *SuperHeavy*, featuring Mick and others.

4 October 2011
Theatrical release, *Some Girls: Live In Texas*.

8 November 2011
In New York City Keith receives The Norman Mailer Award from President Bill Clinton in honour of his autobiography, *Life*.

21 November 2011
Album release, *Some Girls* (deluxe edition).

21 February 2012
In front of President Barack Obama, Mick performs at the Red, White and Blues Concert at the White House in Washington.

26 February 2012
Keith performs at the PEN New England's Song Lyrics of Literary Excellence award for Chuck Berry, at the John F. Kennedy Library in Boston.

Show poster, América Latina Olé, Mexico City, Mexico, 2016

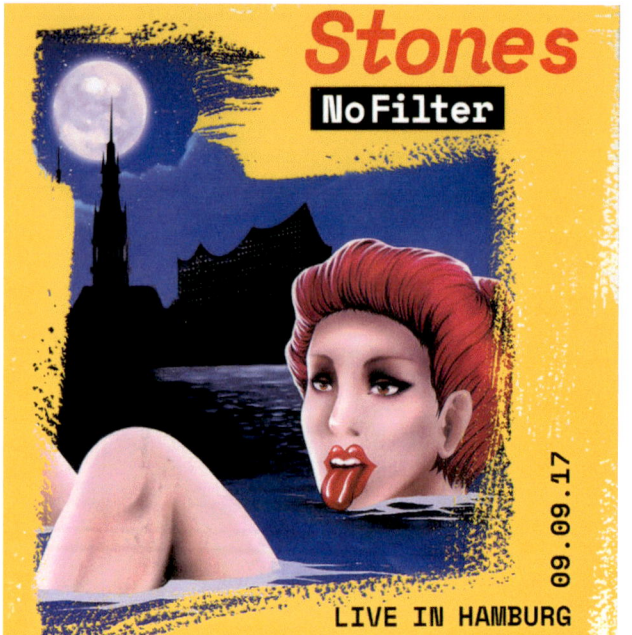

Show poster, Hamburg, Germany, 2017

17 March 2012
Charlie is present at the former Ealing Club in London at an unveiling to commemorate the club's 50th anniversary.

19 May 2012
Mick acts as co-host on NBC TV's *Saturday Night Live*. In addition to performances with Arcade Fire, Foo Fighters and Jeff Beck, Mick performs in several skits.

26 June 2012
Live album release from Charlie's band, The ABC & D of Boogie Woogie, *Live In Paris*.

10 July 2012
DVD-CD release, *Live At The Checkerboard Lounge 1981* (recordings featuring Mick, Keith, Ron and Muddy Waters in concert on 22 November 1981).

29 September 2012
The 1965 concert film *Charlie Is My Darling* is premiered in an expanded form at the New York Film Festival.

11 October 2012
Single release, "Doom And Gloom".

18 October 2012
Premiere of the documentary retrospective *Crossfire Hurricane* at The London Film Festival.

25 October 2012
In performance at Le Trabendo, Paris.

29 October 2012
In performance at Théâtre Mogador, Paris.

25 November–15 December 2012
50 & Counting tour (UK and USA).

25 November 2012
At London's O$_2$ Arena with guest appearances by Bill Wyman and Mick Taylor.

29 November 2012
Bill and Mick Taylor guest again at London's O$_2$ Arena.

11 December 2012
CBS TV's *The Late Show With David Letterman*. Mick performs in a skit

entitled "The Top Ten Things I, Mick Jagger, Have Learned After 50 Years In Rock 'n' Roll".

12 December 2012
Appearance at "121212 The Concert for Sandy Relief", benefit concert at Madison Square Garden in New York City.

15 December 2012
Performance at the Prudential Center in Newark, New Jersey. Concert broadcast as "Pay Per View" TV and online streaming service.

27 April–24 June 2013
50 & Counting tour, North American concerts.

29 June 2013
The band make their Glastonbury Festival debut in Somerset, UK.

6 and 13 of July 2013
Concerts in Hyde Park, London.

8 November 2013
Album/DVD release, *Sweet Summer Sun – Hyde Park Live*.

14 February 2014
Private concert for fans in Bondy, France, during rehearsals for the *14 On Fire* tour.

21 February–22 November 2014
14 on Fire world tour of Asia, Australia, New Zealand, and Europe.

18 March 2014
All upcoming dates on the Australasian leg of the *14 On Fire* tour are postponed following the death of Mick's partner L'Wren Scott in New York City on March 17.

20 May 2014
Prince Rupert Loewenstein, the Stones' financial advisor from 1968 to 2007, dies in London age 80.

4 June 2014
In performance at Park Hayarkon in Tel Aviv, the band's first ever appearance in Israel.

21 July 2014
Mick attends the premiere of the James Brown biopic he co-produced, *Get On Up*, at New York City's Apollo Theatre.

9 September 2014
Children's book release from Keith and daughter Theodora, *Gus & Me: The Story Of My Granddad And My First Guitar*.

25 October–22 November 2014
14 On Fire tour of Australasia, the dates rescheduled from March 2014.

30 October 2014
Album/DVD release, *From The Vault: Hampton Coliseum – Live In 1981*.

14 November 2014
Album/DVD release, *From The Vault: L.A. Forum – Live In 1975*.

2 December 2014
Long-term Stones musical associate, saxophonist Bobby Keys, dies at his Tennessee home aged 70.

12 December 2014
The Rolling Stones, an authorised definitive photographic edition is published by TASCHEN.

20 May 2015
In performance at Los Angeles' Fonda Theatre, performing the entirety of *Sticky Fingers*. The show is filmed and recorded.

24 May–15 July 2015
Zip Code tour of North America.

5 June 2015
Album release, *Sticky Fingers* (super deluxe edition).

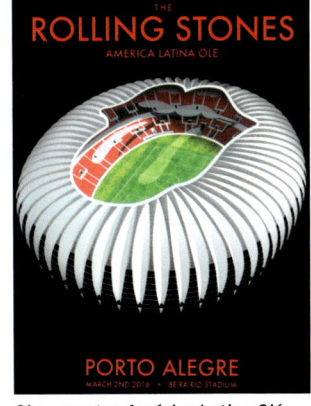

Show poster, *América Latina Olé*, Porto Alegre, Brazil, 2016

8 June 2015
Album/DVD release, *From The Vault: The Marquee Club – Live In 1971*.

17 July 2015
Download single release from Keith, "Trouble".

8 September 2015
Keith receives "Legend of the Year" award from *GQ* magazine at London's Royal Opera House. Ron is also in attendance.

8 September 2015
Release of Ron's book, *How Can It Be? A Rock & Roll Diary*.

17 September 2015
Keith attends the premiere of the Netflix documentary, *Keith Richards: Under the Influence*, at the Toronto Film Festival.

18 September 2015
Release of *Crosseyed Heart*, Keith's third solo album.

29 September 2015
Album/DVD release, *From The Vault: Sticky Fingers Live At The Fonda Theatre 2015*.

22 October 2015
Keith plays alongside Bernard Fowler, Lisa Fischer and others at a tribute for Merry Clayton at the Harlem Apollo, New York City.

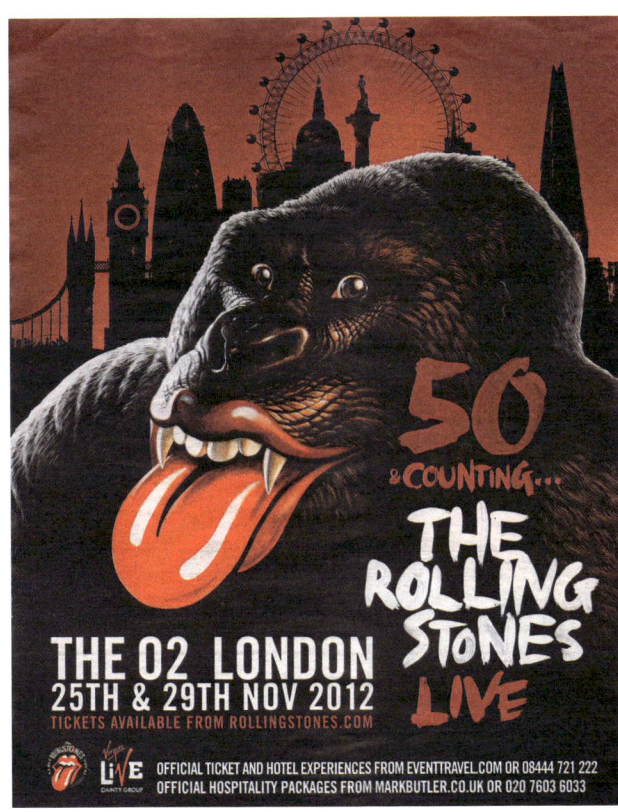

Show poster, *The Rolling Stones Live*, London, UK, 2012

25 October 2015
Keith appears on BBC Radio "Four's Desert Island Discs".

30 October 2015
Album/Blu-Ray/DVD release, *From The Vault: Live At The Tokyo Dome 1990.*

11 November 2015
Album/Blu-Ray/DVD release, *From The Vault: Live In Leeds 1982.*

3 February–25 March 2016
América Latina Olé tour of South America.

14 February 2016
Premiere on HBO TV of *Vinyl*, Mick's drama (co-created with Martin Scorsese and others) based on life in the 1970s music industry. The series will run until 17 April 2016.

25 March 2016
Free concert for an audience estimated at 500,000 at the Ciudad Deportiva de la Habana, Havana, Cuba.

4 April 2016
"Exhibitionism", a multimedia exhibition of Stones' memorabilia opens at London's Saatchi Gallery with the band in attendance. The exhibition will move to New York City and then onto other cities worldwide.

20 May 2016
Album/Blu-Ray/DVD release, *Totally Stripped* (super deluxe edition).

30 May 2016
Birth of twins Gracie Jane and Alice Rose, to Ron and Sally Wood.

23 July 2016
Keith features in a BBC TV documentary, *Keith Richards – The Origin of the Species* directed by Julien Temple.

23 September 2016
Premiere of the documentary *Havana Moon.*

3 October 2016–25 October 2016
Short North American tour,

including two dates at the Desert Trip Festival in Indio, California.

6 October 2016
Download single release, "Just Your Fool".

11 November 2016
Album/Blu-Ray/DVD release, *The Rolling Stones: Havana Moon*.

25 November 2016
Single release, "Ride 'Em On Down".

2 December 2016
Album release, *Blue & Lonesome*.

8 December 2016
Birth of Deveraux, son to Mick and Melanie Hamrick.

25 April 2017
Mick, Charlie and Ron accept "Best Blues Act" and "Album of the Year" award for *Blue & Lonesome* at the Jazz FM awards in Shoreditch, London. Charlie receives a "Gold Award" for a lifetime contribution to jazz and blues.

12 May 2017
Blu-ray/DVD release, *Olé Olé Olé: A Trip Across Latin America.*

13 June 2017
Anita Pallenberg dies in Chichester, West Sussex, age 73.

28 July 2017
Single release from Mick, "Gotta Get A Grip"/"England Lost". Charlie and Ron feature on the recording.

15 August 2017
Book release, *Ronnie Wood: Artist.*

9 September–25 October 2017
No Filter tour of Europe (first leg).

1 December 2017
Album release, *On Air* – a collection of BBC recordings.

28 January 2018
Blue & Lonesome wins "Best Traditional Blues Album" at the Grammy Awards in New York City.

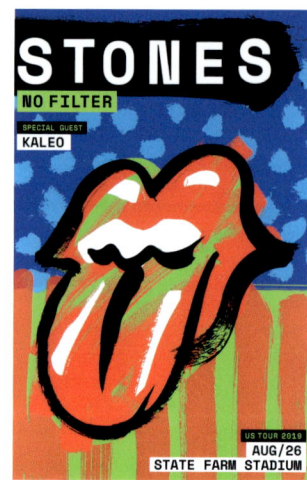

Show poster, No Filter, Phoenix, Arizona, USA, 2019

15 March 2018
Keith performs at the Love Rocks NYC benefit concert at The Beacon Theatre, New York City.

17 May–8 July 2018
No Filter tour of Europe (second leg).

13 July 2018
Album/Blu-Ray/DVD release, *From The Vault: No Security San José '99.*

13–15 November 2018
Ron performs three shows in honour of Chuck Berry at London's Ronnie Scott's Jazz Club.

16 November 2018
Album/Blu-Ray/DVD release, *Rolling Stones Voodoo Lounge Uncut.*

23 November 2018
Single release from Keith, a remix of his 1978 track "Run Rudolph Run".

4 April 2019
Mick undergoes heart surgery in New York City, necessitating the postponement of the *No Filter* North American tour for two months.

13 April 2019
Single release for "Record Store Day" 2019, "She's A Rainbow".

19 April 2019
Compilation album release, *Honk,* with expanded edition featuring live performances recorded between 2013 and 2018.

2 May 2019
The Quiet One, a documentary about Bill is premiered at the Tribeca Film Festival in New York City. It goes on release at selected US cinemas from 21 June 2019.

21 June 2019
Album/Blu-Ray/DVD release, *Bridges To Bremen*.

21 June–30 August 2019
The re-scheduled *No Filter* North American tour.

7 September 2019
Mick attends the premiere of *The Burnt Orange Heresy* at the Venice International Film Festival in which he plays a role.

12 October 2019
Premiere of documentary on Ron, *Somebody Up There Likes Me,* at the BFI London Film Festival, Shepherd's Bush. Ron attends.

8 November 2019
Album/Blu-Ray/DVD release, *Bridges To Buenos Aires.*

20 November–27 November 2019
Ron and his band tour the UK as Ronnie Wood with his Wild Five.

23 April 2020
Single, "Living in a Ghost Town", released during height of global pandemic. First original material for eight years, it is critically acclaimed and a worldwide hit.

8 May–9 July 2020
No Filter tour of North America (second leg) postponed due to Covid-19 pandemic.

22 July 2021
The rescheduled 2020 *No Filter* North American tour is announced to start in the early fall.

4 August 2021
It's made public that Charlie Watts will not be present for the tour's start, following emergency surgical procedure, and will be replaced by Steve Jordan.

24 August 2021
Charlie Watts, 80, passes away in a London hospital. His cause of death is not made public.

6 September 2021
Charlie Watts' funeral is held in Devon, UK.

26 September 2021
The postponed 2021 *No Filter* US tour kicks off at The Dome at America's Center, St. Louis, beginning with a touching montage of Charlie Watts playing.

23 October 2021
Tattoo You is re-released in a special 40th Anniversary Edition.

1 June 2022
2022 SIXTY tour of Europe starts with a concert at Wanda Metropolitano Stadium, Madrid.

3 August 2022
The *2022 SIXTY* tour concludes at the Waldbühne, Berlin.

6 September 2023
Single release, "Angry".

20 October 2023
Album release, *Hackney Diamonds*.

28 April–21 July 2024
Hackney Diamonds tour of North America.

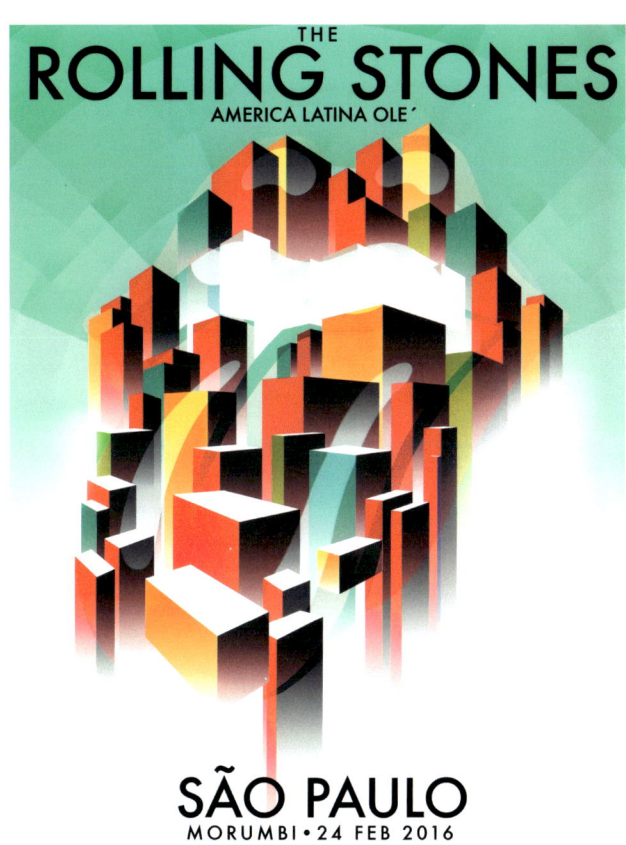

Show poster, América Latina Olé, São Paulo, Brazil, 2016

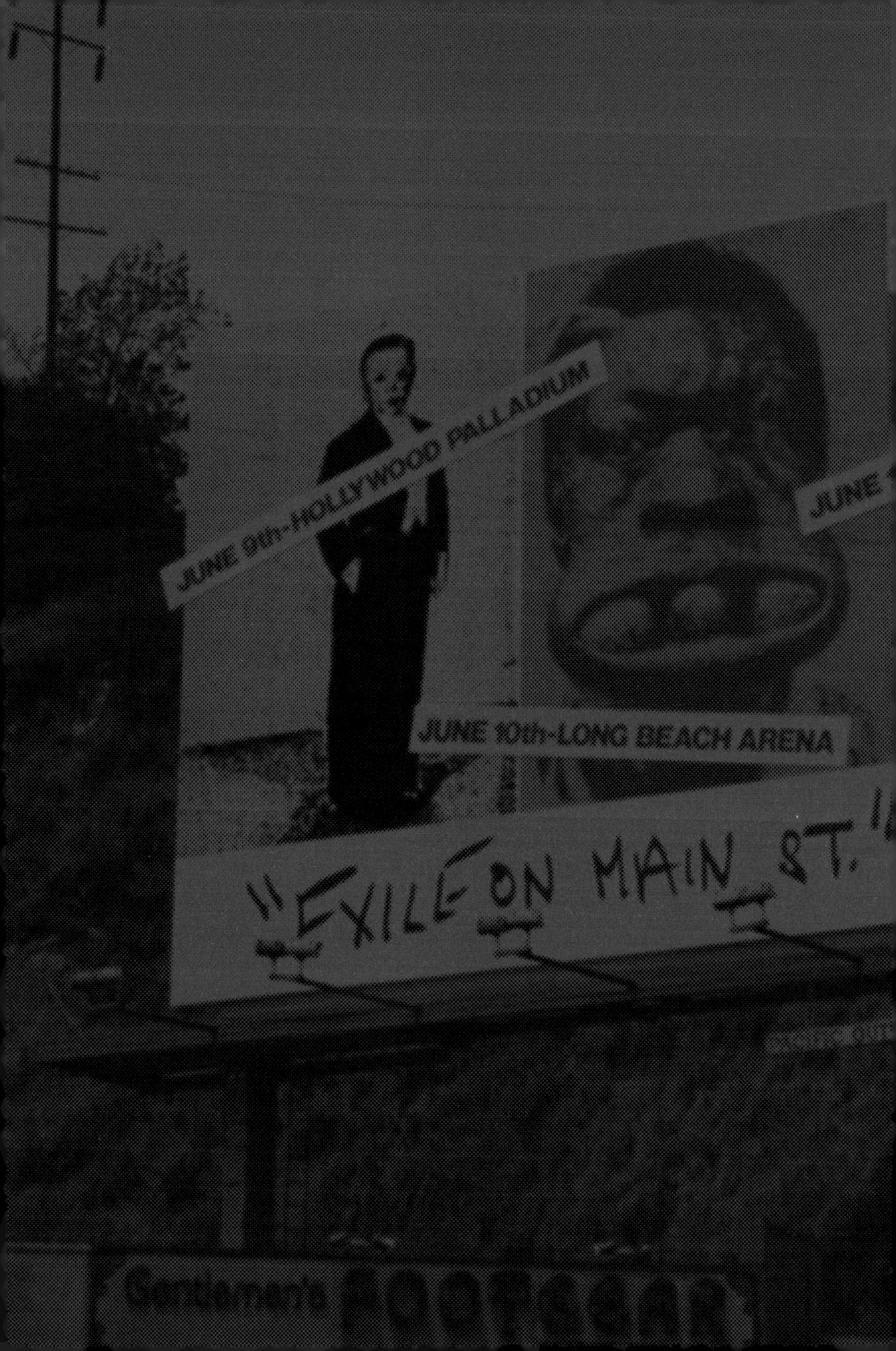
JUNE 9th-HOLLYWOOD PALLADIUM
JUNE 10th-LONG BEACH ARENA
"EXILE ON MAIN ST."
Gentlemen's

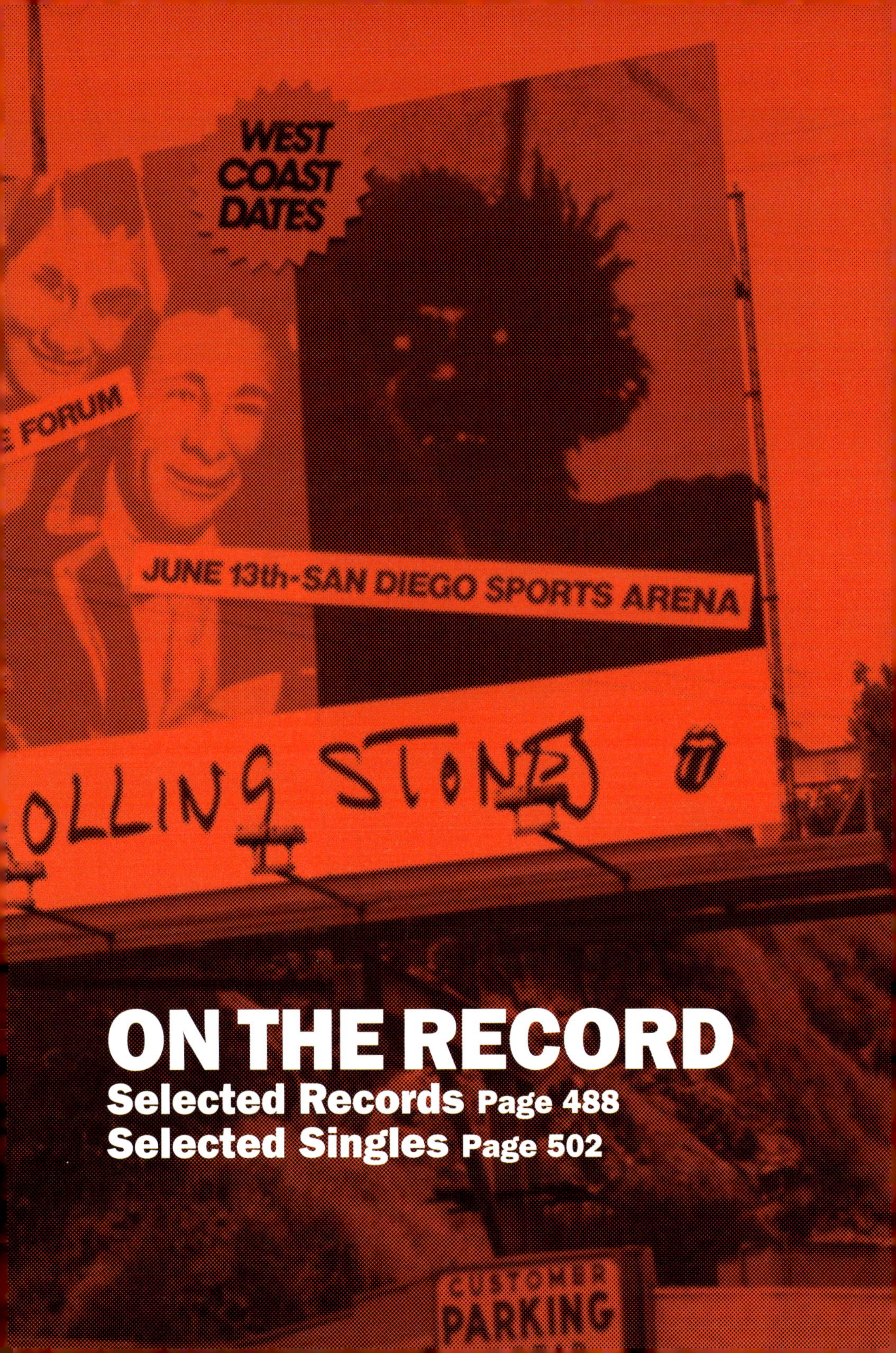

WEST
COAST
DATES

FORUM

JUNE 13th-SAN DIEGO SPORTS ARENA

OLLING STONES 77

ON THE RECORD
Selected Records Page 488
Selected Singles Page 502

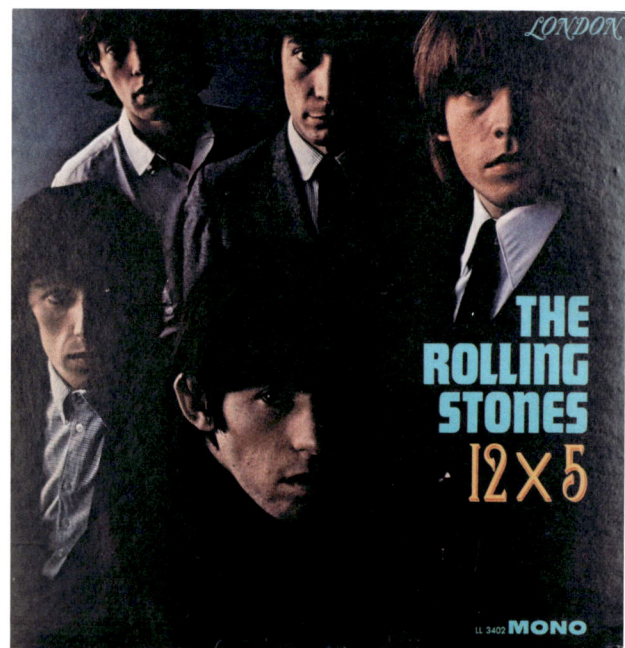

1

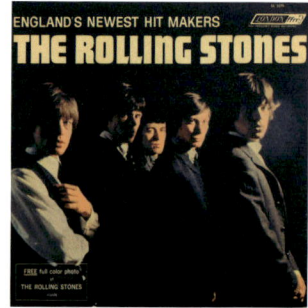

2

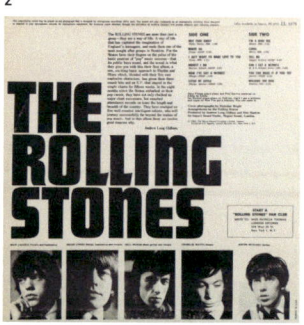

3

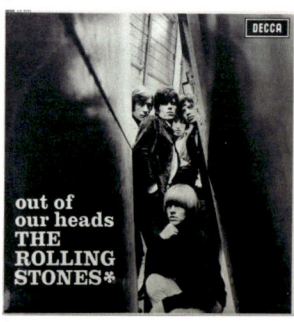

4

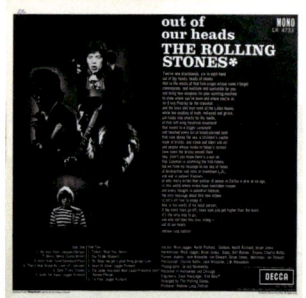

5

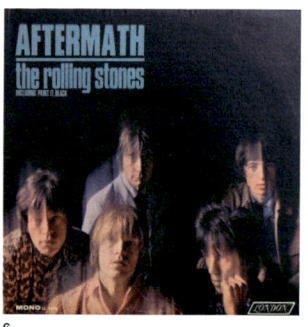

6

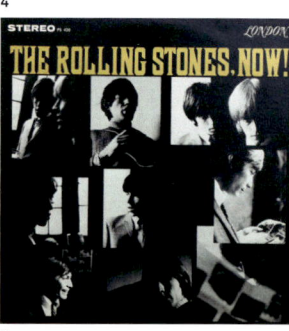

7

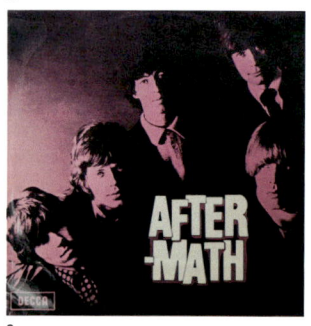

8

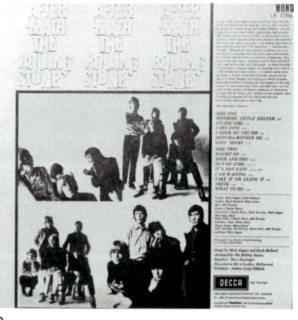

9

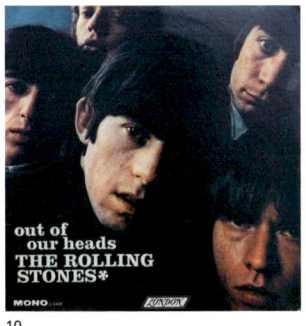

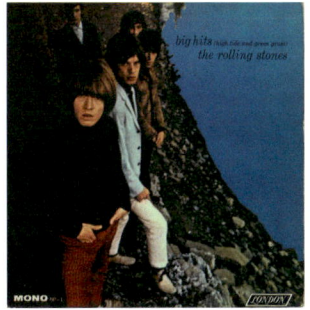

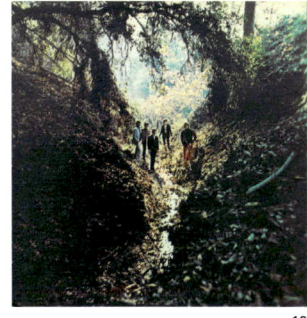

10

11

12

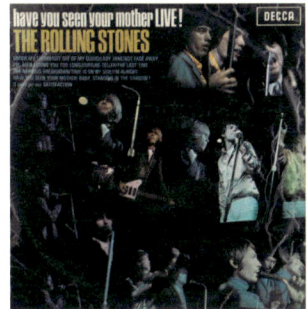

13

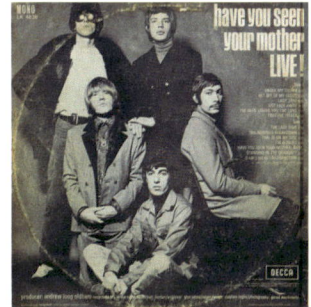

14

15

1 *12 x 5*, front cover, US release, 1964 (London/ABKCO)

2 *England's Newest Hit Makers*, front cover, US release, 1964 (London/ABKCO)

3 *England's Newest Hit Makers*, back cover, US release, 1964 (London/ABKCO)

4 *Out Of Our Heads*, front cover, UK release, 1965 (Decca/ABKCO)

5 *Out Of Our Heads*, back cover, UK Release, 1965 (Decca/ABKCO)

6 *Aftermath*, front cover, US release, 1966 (London/ABKCO)

7 *The Rolling Stones, Now!*, front cover, US release, 1965 (London/ABKCO)

8 *Aftermath*, front cover, UK release, 1966 (Decca/ABKCO)

9 *Aftermath*, back cover, UK release, 1966 (Decca/ABKCO)

10 *Out Of Our Heads*, front cover, US release, 1965 (London/ABKCO)

11 *Big Hits (High Tide And Green Grass)*, unreleased cover, 1966 (London/ABKCO)

12 *Big Hits (High Tide And Green Grass)*, back cover, US release, 1966 (London/ABKCO)

13 *Big Hits (High Tide And Green Grass)*, front cover, UK release, 1966 (Decca/ABKCO)

14 *Have You Seen Your Mother Live!*, front cover, UK for export only, 1966 (Decca/ABKCO)

15 *Have You Seen Your Mother Live!*, back cover, UK for export only, 1966 (Decca/ABKCO)

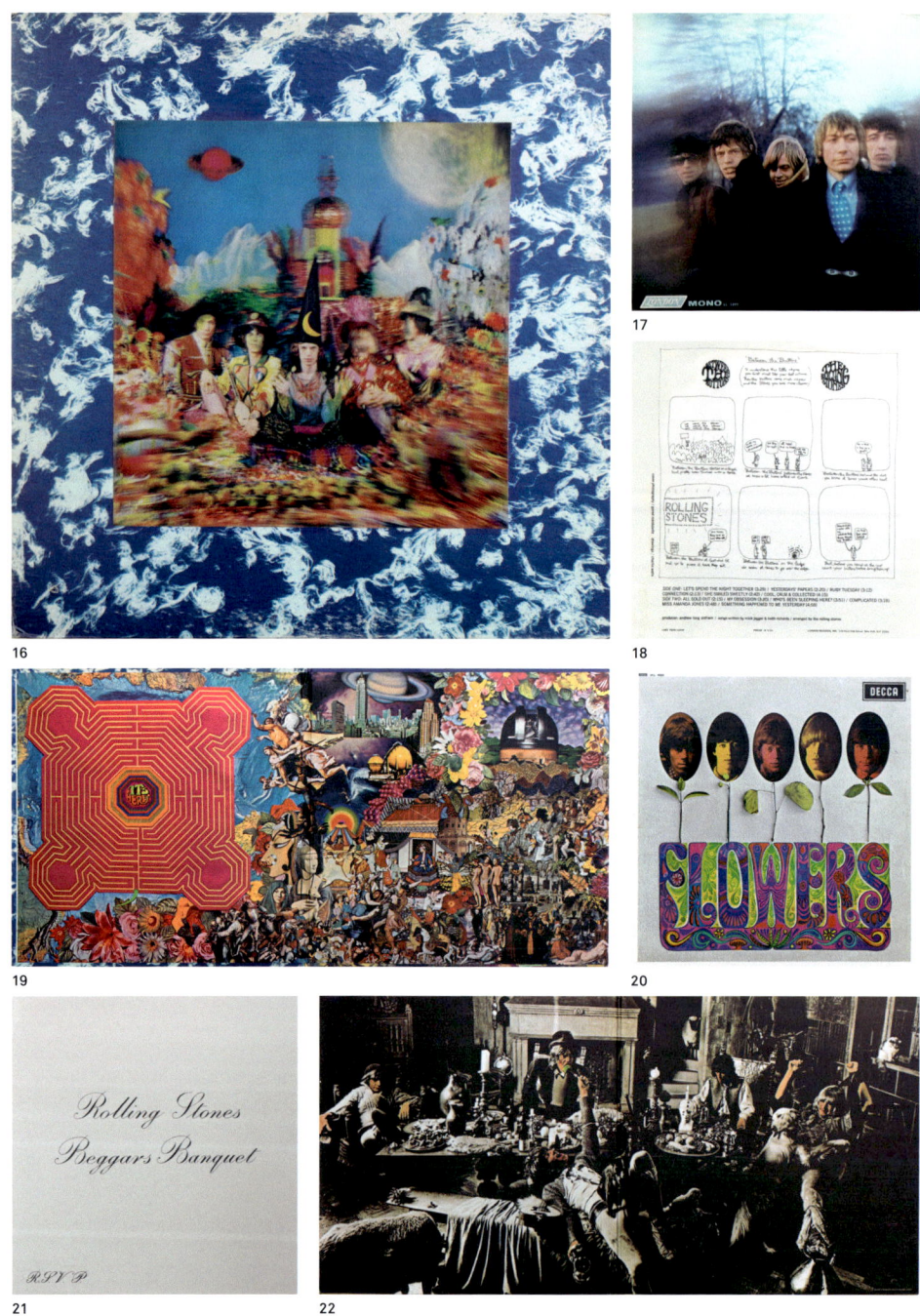

16

17

18

19

20

21

22

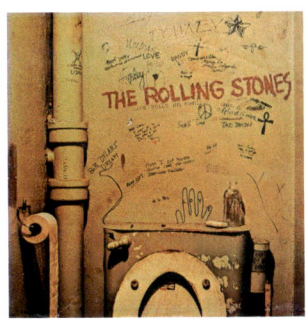

23

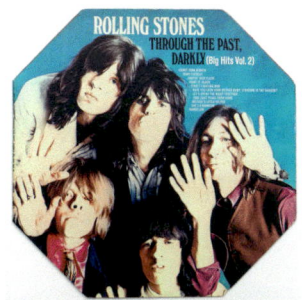

24

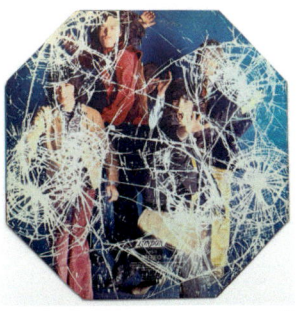

25

ROLLING STONES **LET IT BLEED** DECCA

26

27

16 *Their Satanic Majesties Request*, front cover, 1967 (Decca/London/ABKCO)

17 *Between The Buttons*, front cover, US release, 1967 (London/ABKCO)

18 *Between The Buttons*, back cover, US release, 1967 (London/ABKCO)

19 *Their Satanic Majesties Request*, inside gatefold sleeve, 1967 (Decca/London/ABKCO)

20 *Flowers*, front cover, UK export edition, 1967 (Decca/ABKCO)

21 *Beggars Banquet*, front cover, 1968 (Decca/London/ABKCO)

22 *Beggars Banquet*, inside gatefold sleeve, 1968 (Decca/London/ABKCO)

23 *Beggars Banquet*, unreleased cover, 1968 (Decca/London/ABKCO)

24 *Through The Past, Darkly*, front cover, 1969 (Decca/London/ABKCO)

25 *Through The Past, Darkly*, back cover, 1969 (Decca/London/ABKCO)

26 *Let It Bleed*, cover, 1969 (Decca/London/ABKCO)

27 *Through The Past, Darkly*, inside gatefold, 1969

28 *The Rolling Stones*, front cover (promo only), 1969 (London/ABKCO)

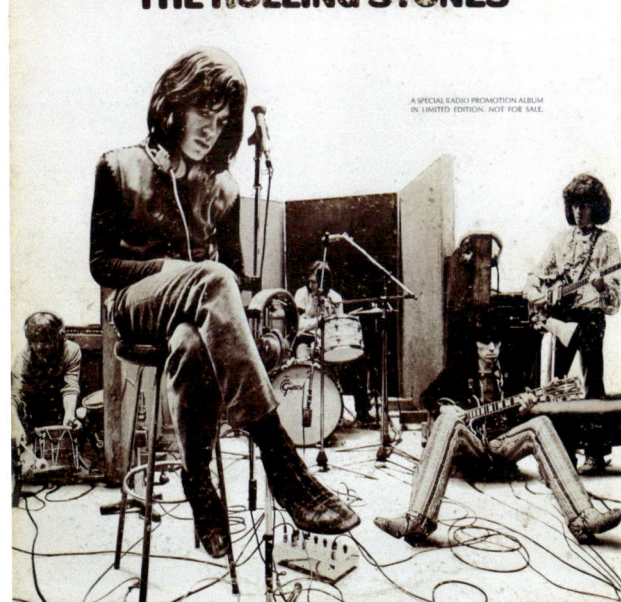

28

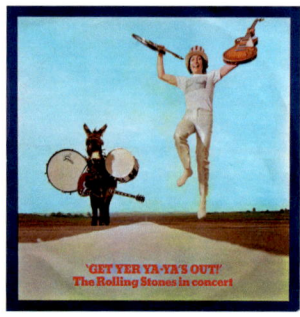

29

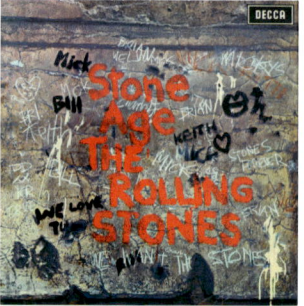

30

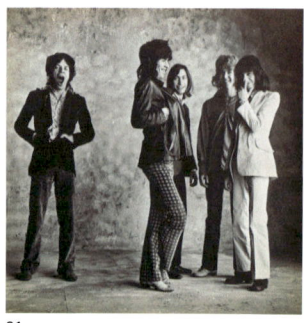

31

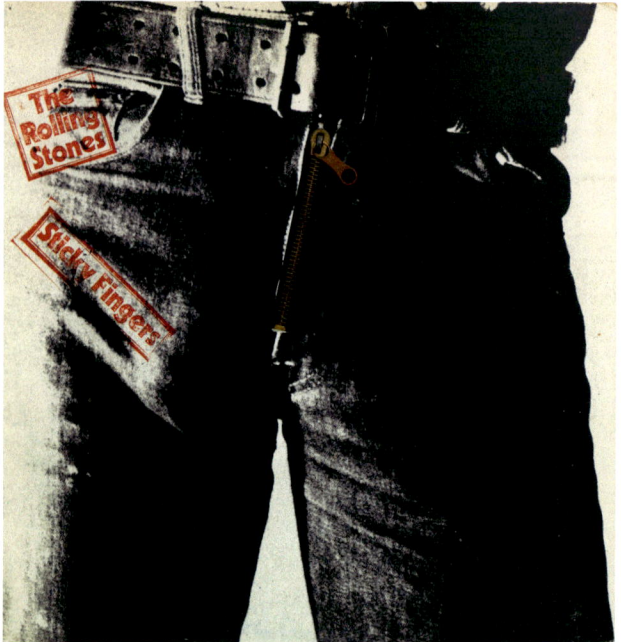

32

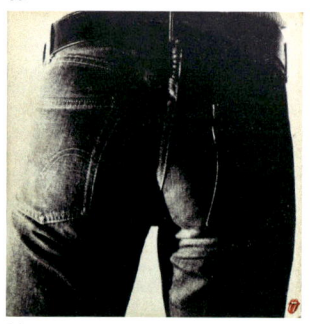

33

34

29 *Get Yer Ya-Ya's Out!*, front cover, 1970 (Decca/London/ABKCO)

30 *Stone Age*, front cover, UK release, 1971 (Decca/ABKCO)

31 *Sticky Fingers*, interior, 1971 (Rolling Stones Records)

32 *Sticky Fingers*, front cover, 1971 (Rolling Stones Records)

33 *Sticky Fingers*, interior, 1971 (Rolling Stones Records)

34 *Sticky Fingers*, back cover, 1971 (Rolling Stones Records)

35 *Sticky Fingers*, inner sleeve, 1971 (Rolling Stones Records)

36 *Gimme Shelter*, front cover, UK release, 1971 (Decca/ABKCO)

37 *Hot Rocks*, back cover, US release, 1971 (London/ABKCO)

38 *Hot Rocks*, front cover, US release, 1971 (London/ABKCO)

39 *Exile On Main St*, front cover, 1972 (Rolling Stones Records)

40 *Exile On Main St*, interior, 1972 (Rolling Stones Records)

41 *Exile On Main St*, interior, 1972 (Rolling Stones Records)

42 *Exile On Main St*, interior, 1972 (Rolling Stones Records)

43 *Exile On Main St*, interior, 1972 (Rolling Stones Records)

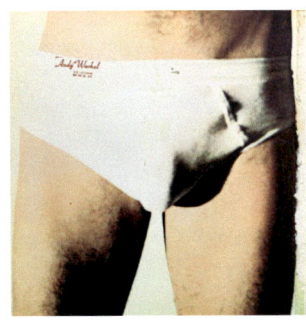

35

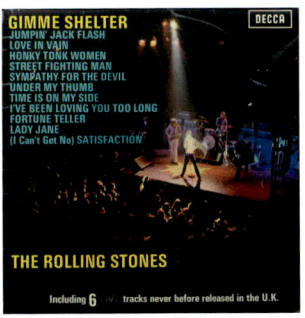

36

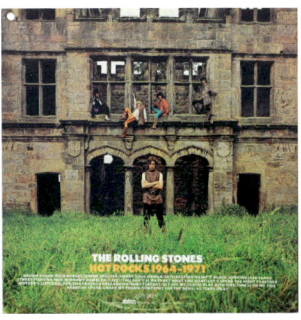

37

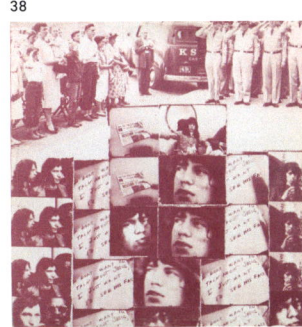

38

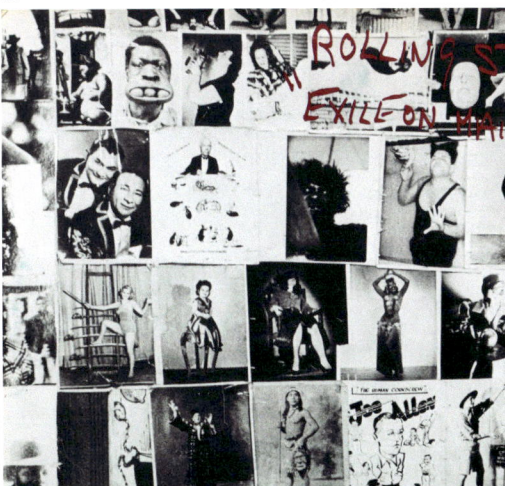

40

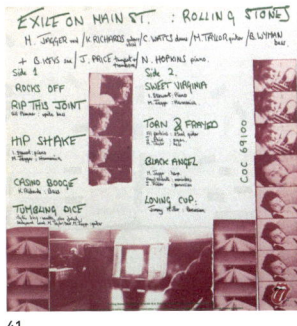

39

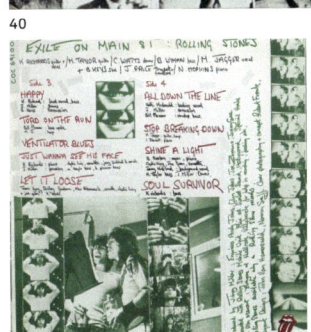

41

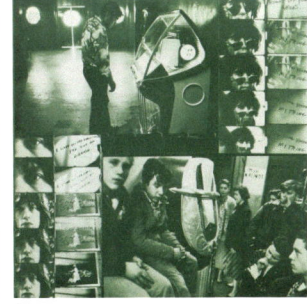

42

43

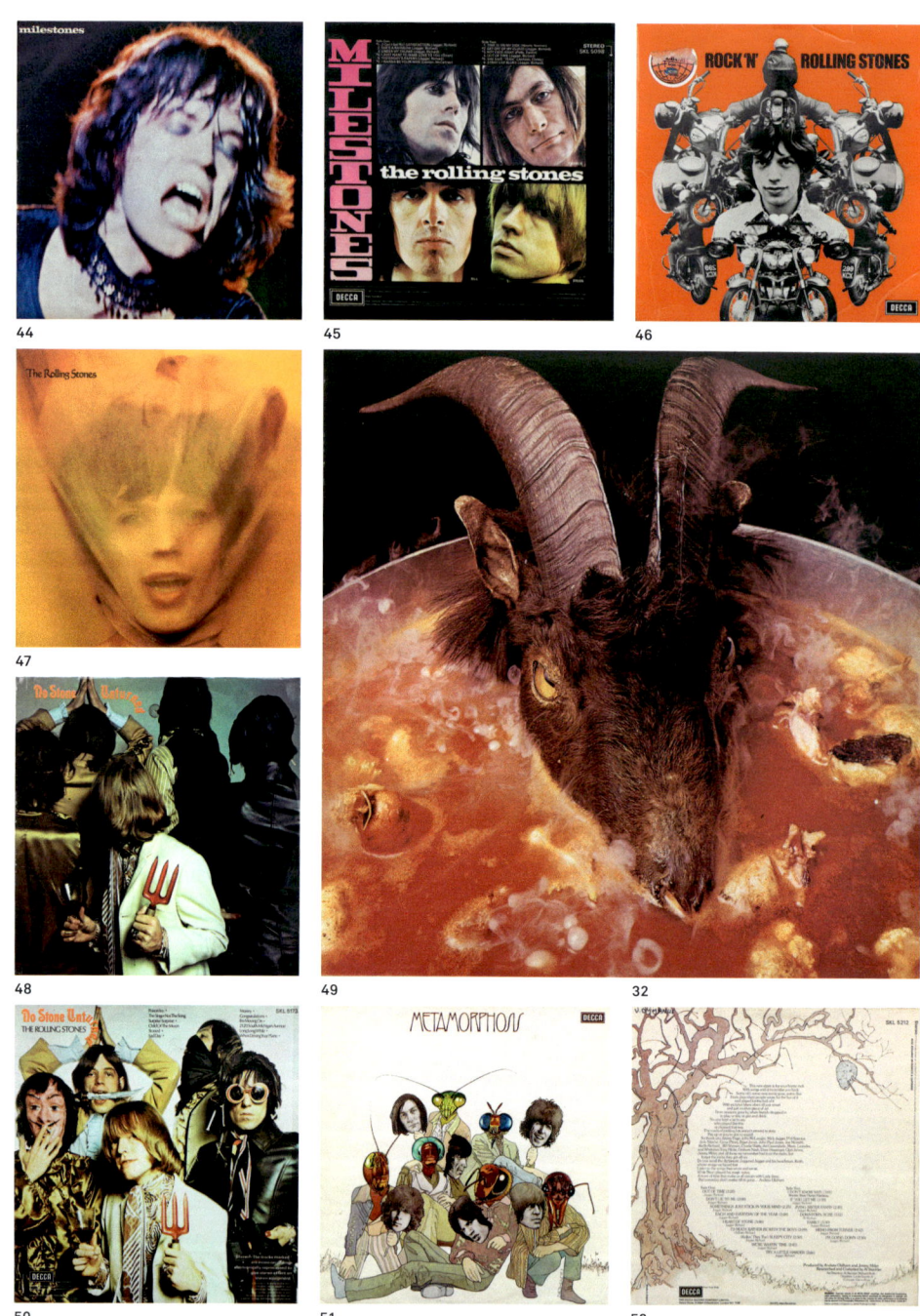

44

45

46

47

48

49

32

50

51

52

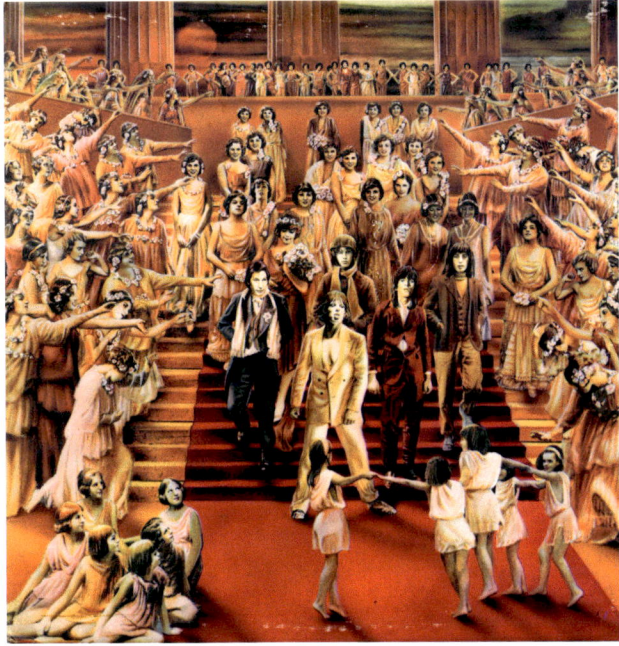

53

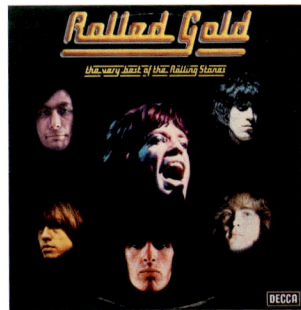

54

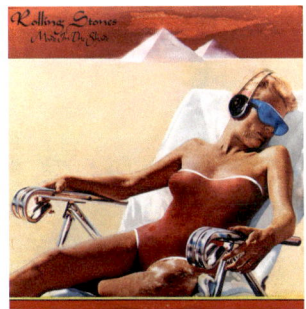

55

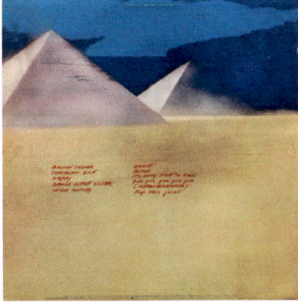

56

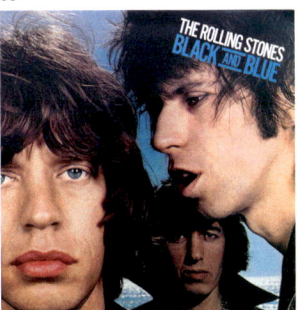

57

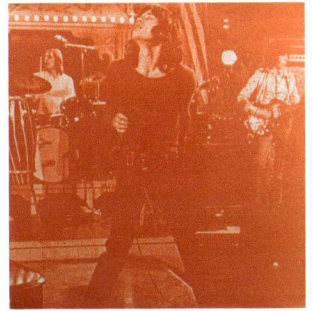

58

44 *Milestones*, front cover, UK release, 1972 (Decca/ABKCO)

45 *Milestones*, back cover, UK release, 1972 (Decca/ABKCO)

46 *Rock 'n' Rolling Stones*, front cover, UK release, 1972 (Decca/ABKCO)

47 *Goats Head Soup*, front cover, 1973 (Rolling Stones Records)

48 *No Stone Unturned*, front cover, UK release, 1973 (Decca/ABKCO)

49 *Goats Head Soup*, insert, 1973 (Rolling Stones Records)

50 *No Stone Unturned*, back cover, UK release, 1973 (Decca/ABKCO)

51 *Metamorphosis*, front cover, 1975 (Decca/ABKCO)

52 *Metamorphosis*, back cover, 1975 (Decca/ABKCO)

53 *It's Only Rock 'n' Roll*, front cover, 1974 (Rolling Stones Records)

54 *Rolled Gold*, front cover, 1975 (Decca/ABKCO)

55 *Made In The Shade*, front cover, 1975 (Rolling Stones Records)

56 *Made In The Shade*, back cover, 1975 (Rolling Stones Records)

57 *Black And Blue*, front cover, 1976 (Rolling Stones Records)

58 *Songs Of The Rolling Stones*, front cover, US promo, 1975 (ABKCO)

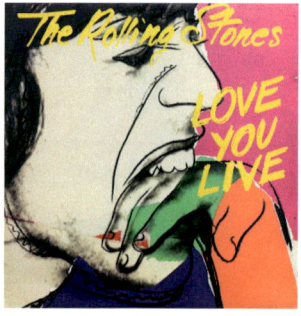
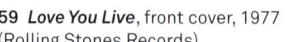
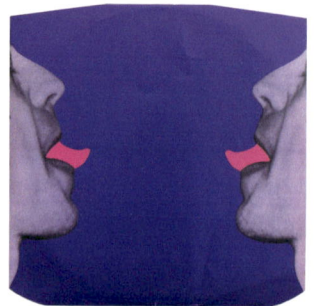
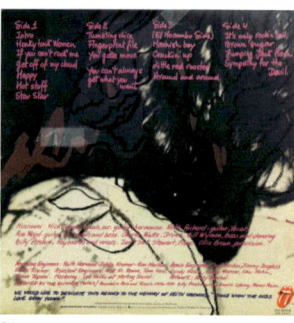

59 *Love You Live*, front cover, 1977 (Rolling Stones Records)

60 *Love You Live*, interior, 1977 (Rolling Stones Records)

61 *Love You Live*, back cover, 1977 (Rolling Stones Records)

62 *Some Girls*, front cover, 1978 (Rolling Stones Records)

63 *Some Girls*, back cover, 1978

64 *Some Girls*, interior, 1978 (Rolling Stones Records)

65 *Sucking In The Seventies*, back cover, 1981 (Rolling Stones Records)

66 *Songs Of The Rolling Stones*, front cover, US promo, 1979 (ABKCO)

67 *Emotional Rescue*, front cover, 1980 (Rolling Stones Records)

68 *Emotional Rescue*, back cover, 1980 (Rolling Stones Records)

69 *Tattoo You*, front cover, 1981 (Rolling Stones Records)

70 *Tattoo You*, interior sleeve, 1981 (Rolling Stones Records)

71 *Undercover*, front cover, 1983 (Rolling Stones Records)

72 *Still Life (American Concert 1981)*, front cover, 1982 (Rolling Stones Records)

73 *Still Life (American Concert 1981)*, interior sleeve, 1982 (Rolling Stones Records)

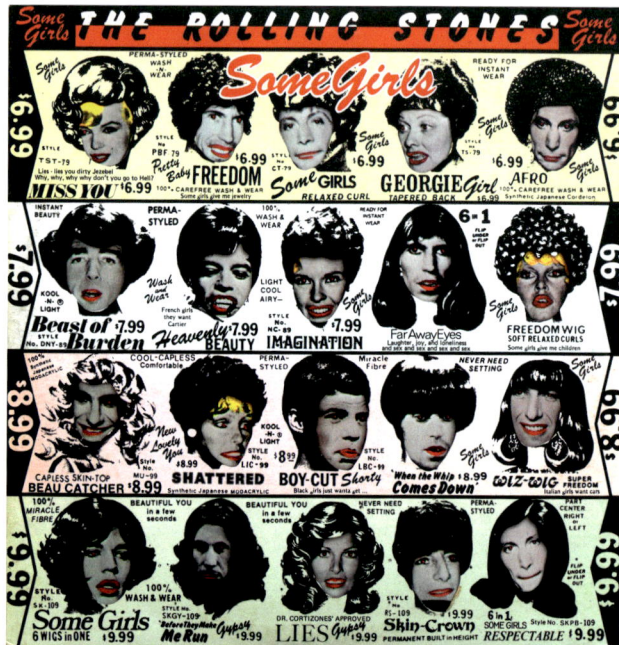

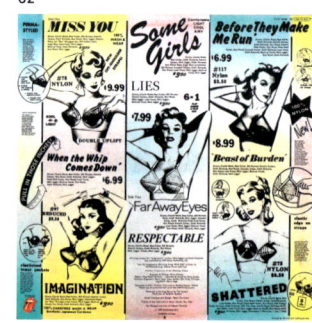

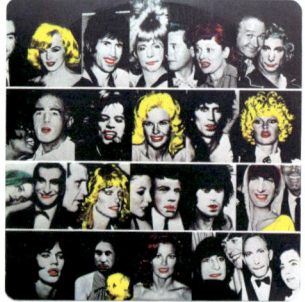

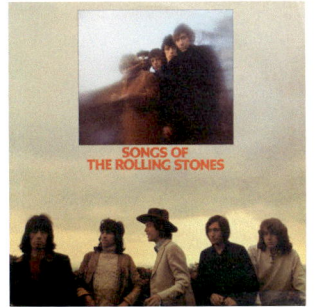

65

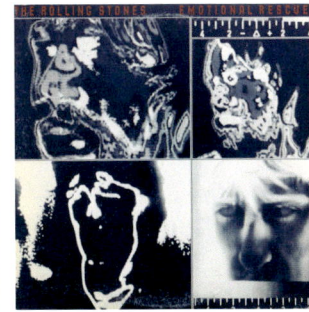

66

67

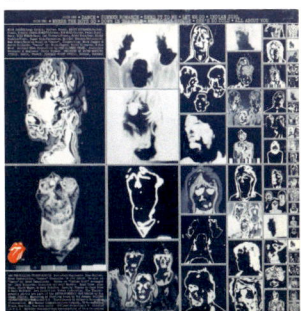

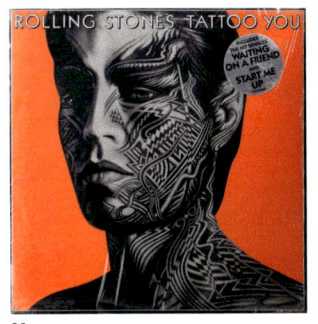

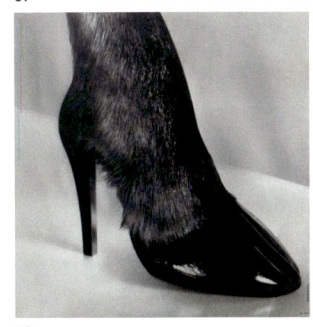

68

69

70

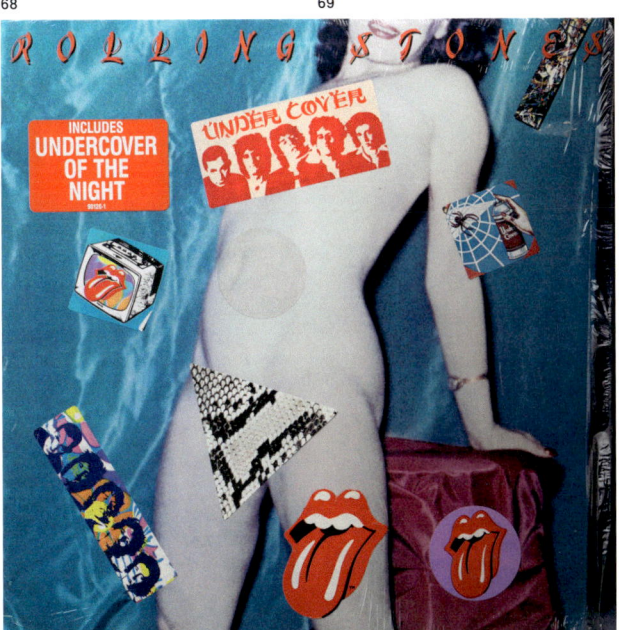

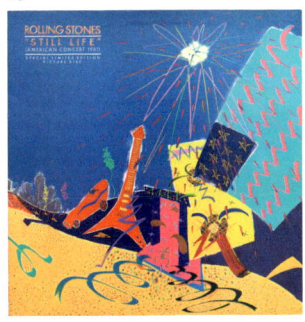

72

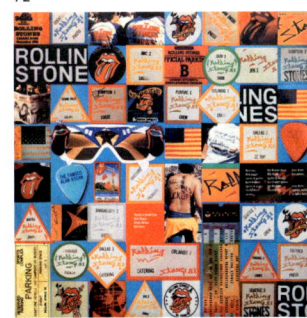

71

73

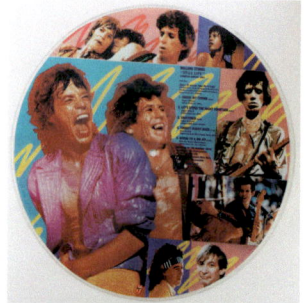

74

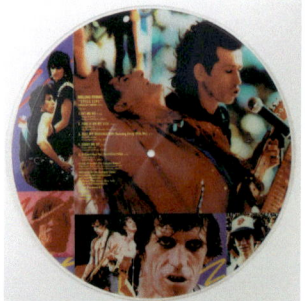

75

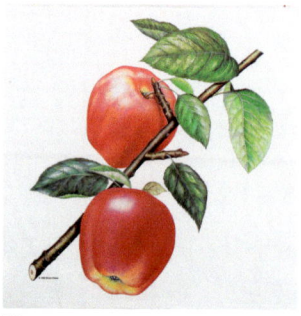

76

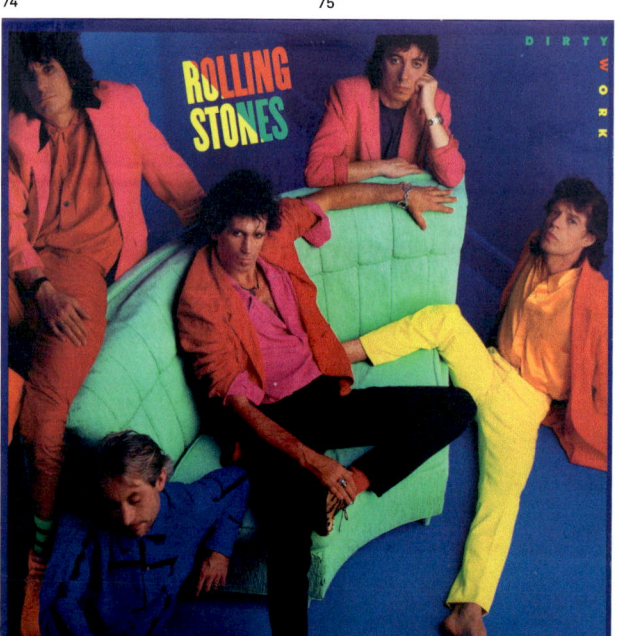

77

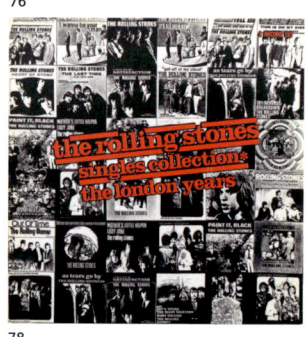

78

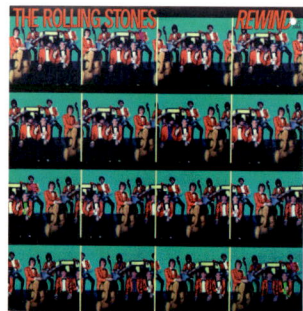

79

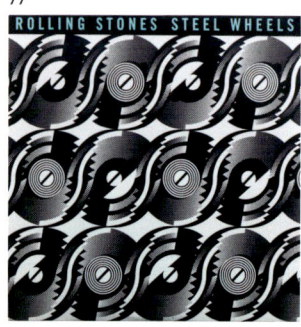

80

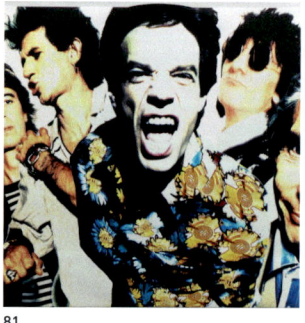

81

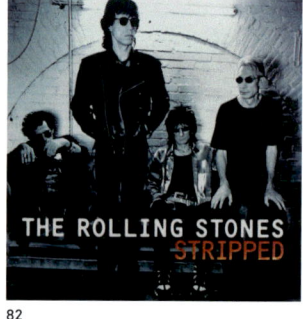

82

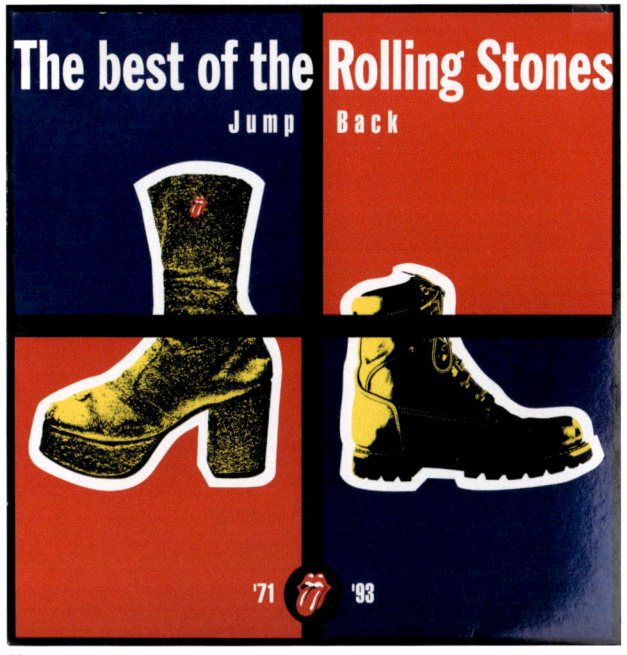

83

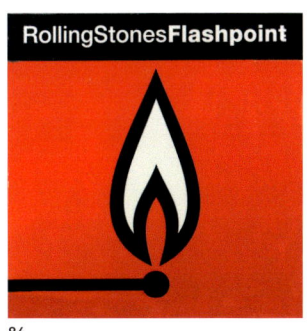

84

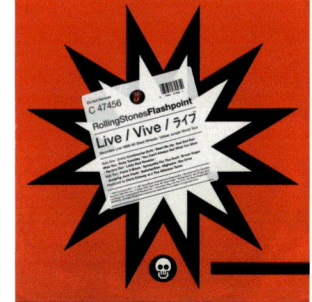

85

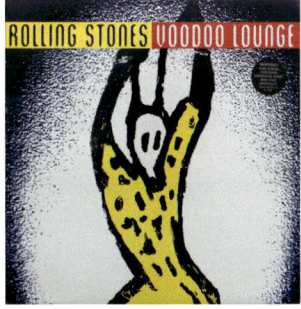

86

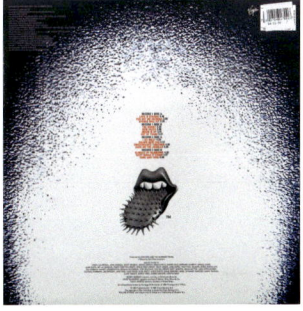

87

74 *Still Life (American Concert 1981)*, 1982 (Rolling Stones Records)

75 *Still Life (American Concert 1981)*, 1982 (Rolling Stones Records)

76 *Undercover*, interior sleeve, 1983 (Rolling Stones Records)

77 *Dirty Work*, front cover, 1986 (Rolling Stones Records)

78 *Singles Collection: The London Years*, front cover, US release, 1989 (ABKCO)

79 *Rewind (1971–1984)*, front cover, 1984 (Rolling Stones Records)

80 *Steel Wheels*, interior sleeve, 1989 (Rolling Stones Records)

81 *Steel Wheels*, interior sleeve, 1989 (Rolling Stones Records)

82 *Stripped*, front cover, 1995 (Virgin)

83 *Jump Back: The Best Of The Rolling Stones*, front cover, UK release, 1993 (Virgin)

84 *Flashpoint*, front cover, 1991 (Rolling Stones Records/Virgin)

85 *Flashpoint*, back cover, 1991 (Rolling Stones Records/Virgin)

86 *Voodoo Lounge*, front cover, 1994 (Virgin)

87 *Voodoo Lounge*, back cover, 1994 (Virgin)

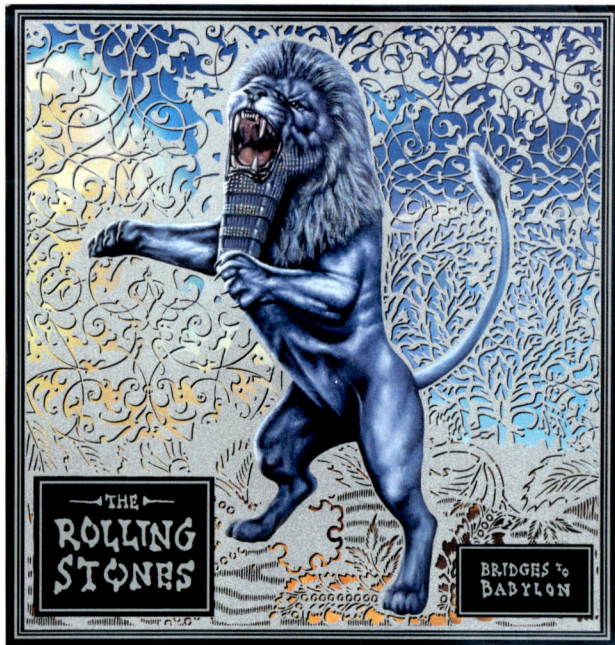

88

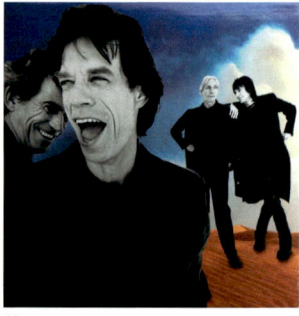

89

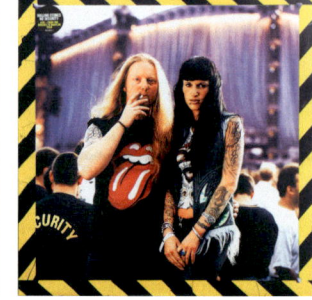

90

88 *Bridges To Babylon*, front cover, 1997 (Virgin)

89 *Bridges To Babylon*, inner sleeve, 1997 (Virgin)

90 *No Security*, back cover, 1998 (Virgin)

91 *A Bigger Bang*, front cover, 2005 (Rolling Stones Records/ Virgin)

92 *A Bigger Bang*, interior, 2005 (Rolling Stones Records/Virgin)

93 *Rarities*, front cover, UK, 2005 (Rolling Stones Records/Virgin)

94 *GRRR!*, front cover, 2012 (ABKCO/Universal Music Group)

95 *Blue & Lonesome*, front cover, 2016 (Polydor Records)

96 *Honk*, front cover, 2019 (Promotone BV/Universal Music Group)

97 *Hackney Diamonds*, front cover, 2023 (Polydor/Geffen)

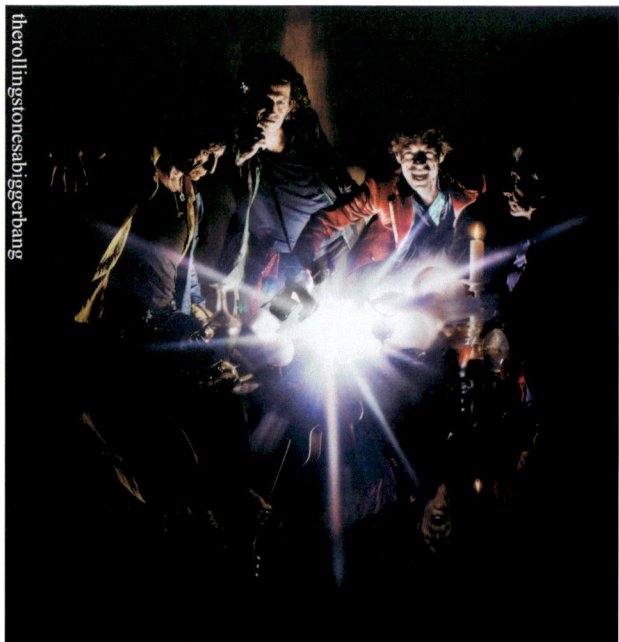

91

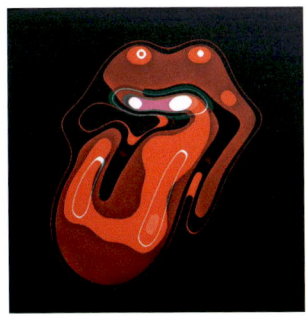

92

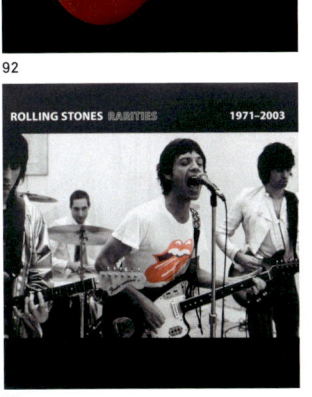

93

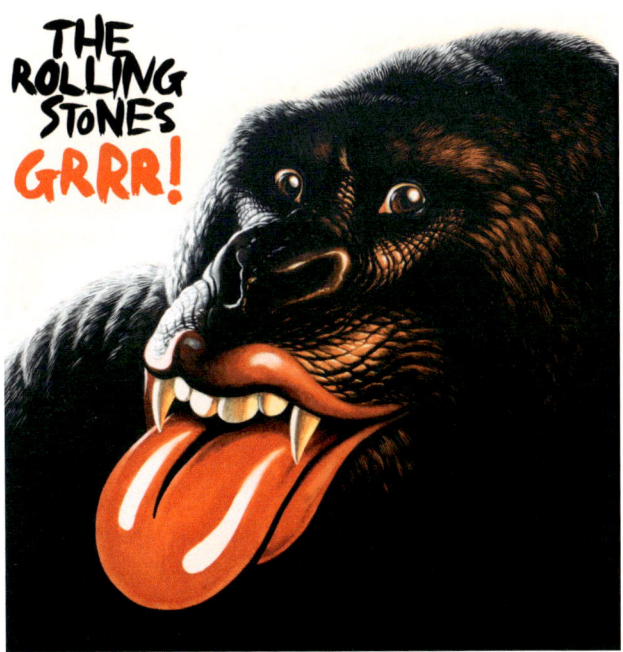

94

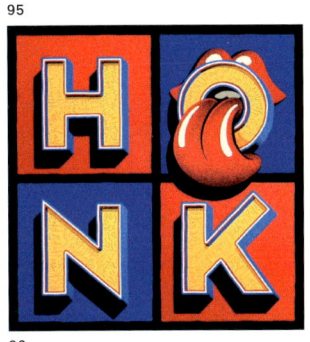

95

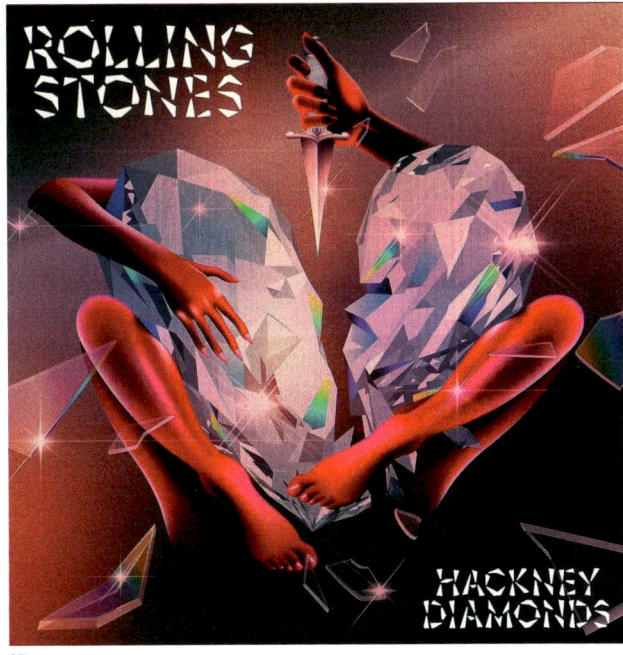

96

97

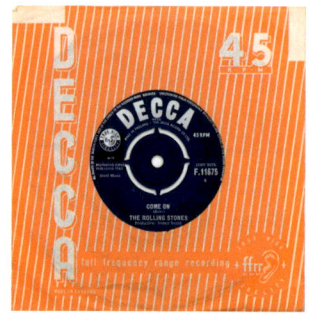

1

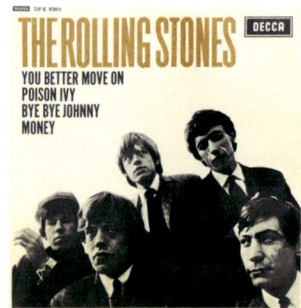

2

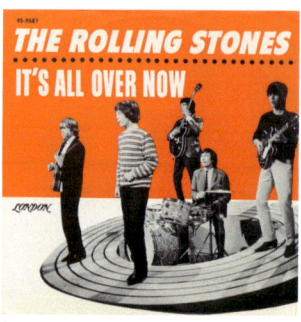

3

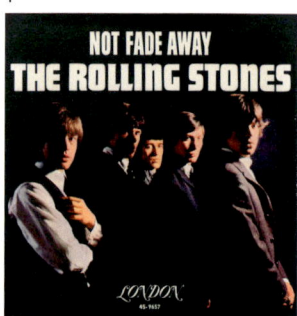

4

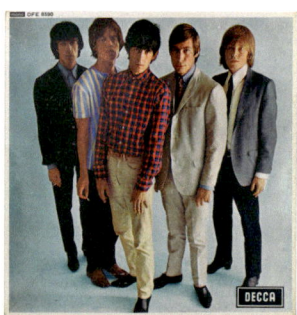

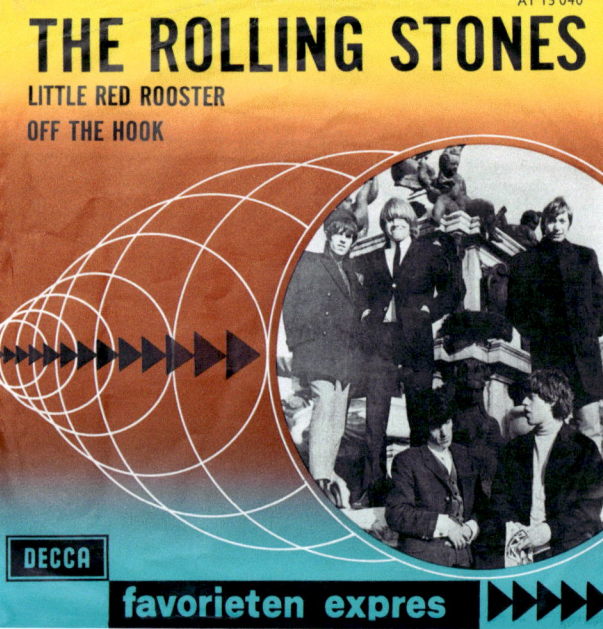

5

6

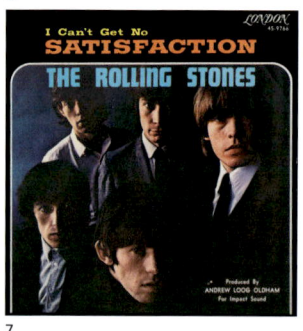

7

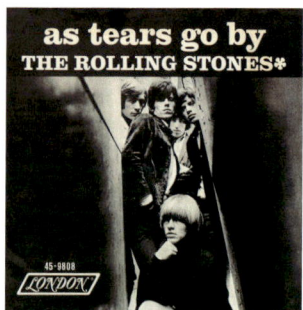

8

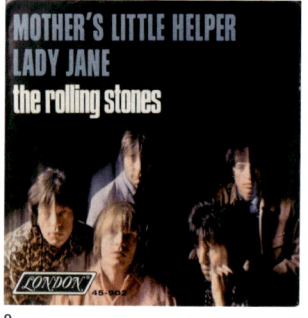

9

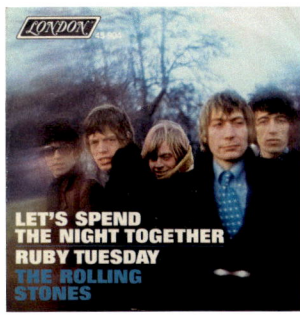

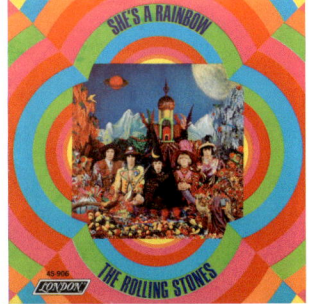

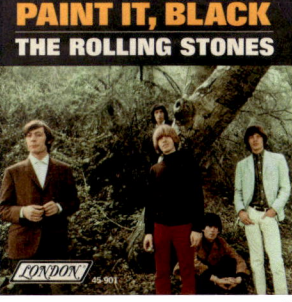

10

11

12

13

14

Jumpin' Jack Flash   The Rolling Stones

PHOTO: DAVID BAILEY   45-908   *LONDON*

15

1 "Come On", UK company sleeve, 1963 (Decca/ABKCO)

2 "You Better Move On"/"Poison Ivy"/"Bye Bye Johnny"/"Money", front cover, UK release, 1964 (Decca/ABKCO)

3 "It's All Over Now", US cover, 1964

4 "Not Fade Away", US front cover, 1964 (London/ABKCO)

5 "Five By Five", front cover, UK release, 1964 (Decca/ABKCO)

6 "Little Red Rooster"/"Off The Hook", front cover, Netherlands picture sleeve, 1964 (Decca/ABKCO)

7 "(I Can't Get No) Satisfaction", US cover, 1965 (London/ABKCO)

8 "As Tears Go By", US picture sleeve, 1965 (London/ABKCO)

9 "Mother's Little Helper"/"Lady Jane", US cover, 1966 (London/ABKCO)

10 "Let's Spend The Night Together"/"Ruby Tuesday", US front cover, 1966 (London/ABKCO)

11 "She's A Rainbow", front cover, 1967 (London/ABKCO)

12 "Paint It Black", US picture sleeve, 1966 (London/ABKCO)

13 "In Another Land", US front cover, 1967 (London/ABKCO)

14 "Street Fighting Man"/"No Expectations", front cover, 1971 (Decca/ABKCO)

15 "Jumpin' Jack Flash", US front cover, 1968 (London/ABKCO)

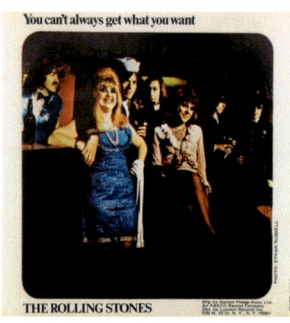

THE ROLLING STONES

16

16 "You can't Always Get What You Want", US B-side, 1969 (London/ABKCO)

17 "Brown Sugar"/"Bitch"/"Let It Rock", UK release, front cover , 1971 (Rolling Stones Records)

18 "Brown Sugar"/"Bitch"/"Let It Rock", UK release, sleeve, 1971 (Rolling Stones Records)

19 "Miss You", front cover, 1978 (Rolling Stones Records)

20 "Shattered"/"Everything's Turning to Gold", front cover, 1978 (Rolling Stones Records)

21 "She's So Cold", front cover, 1980 (Rolling Stones Records)

22 "Before They Make Me Run", front cover (promo only), US release, 1978

23 "Waiting On A Friend", A-side, UK release, 1981 (Rolling Stones Records)

24 "Going To A Go-Go", A-side, 1982 (Rolling Stones Records)

25 "Too Much Blood", front cover, 1983 (Rolling Stones Records)

26 "Time Is On My Side", front cover, UK release, 1982 (Rolling Stones Records)

27 "Undercover Of The Night", front cover, US release, 1983 (Rolling Stones Records)

28 "Undercover Of The Night", front cover, UK release, 1983 (Rolling Stones Records)

29 "She Was Hot", front cover, 1984 (Rolling Stones Records)

30 "One Hit (To The Body)", front cover, 1986 (Rolling Stones Records)

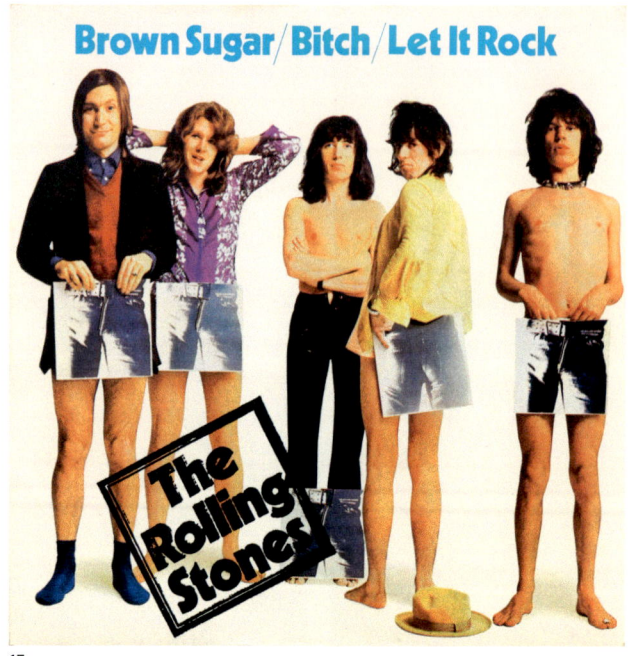

17

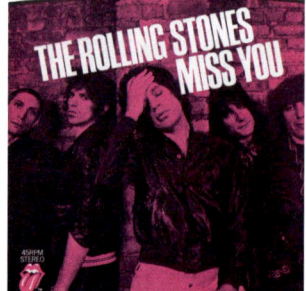

19

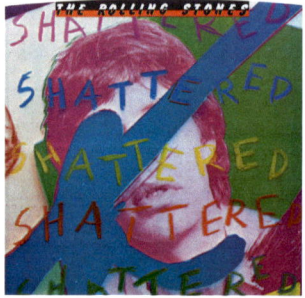

18

20

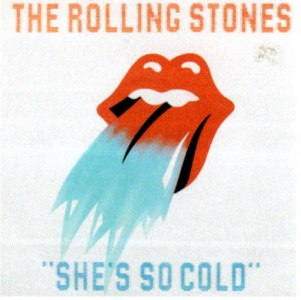

21

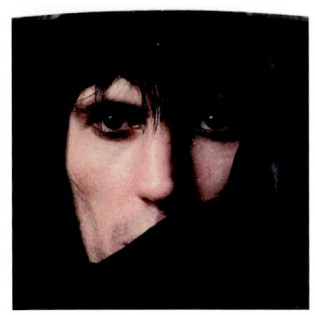

22

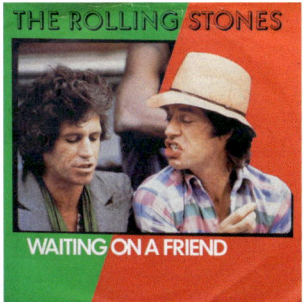

23

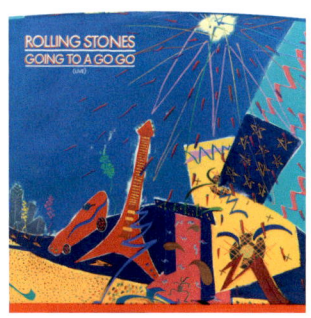

24

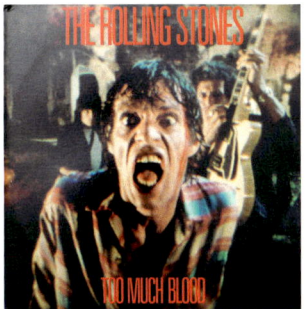
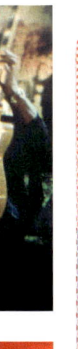
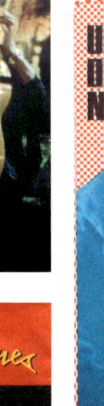

25

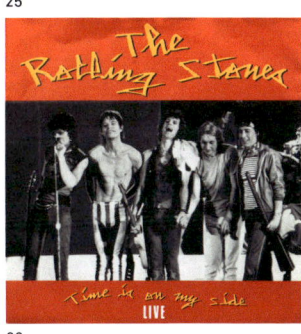

26

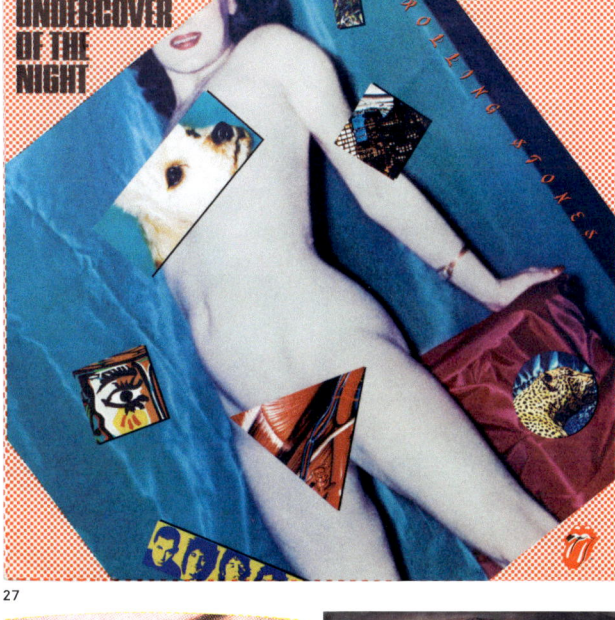

27

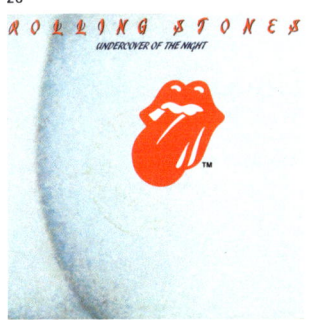

28

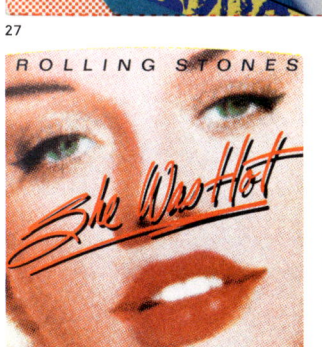

29

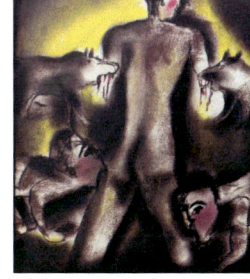

30

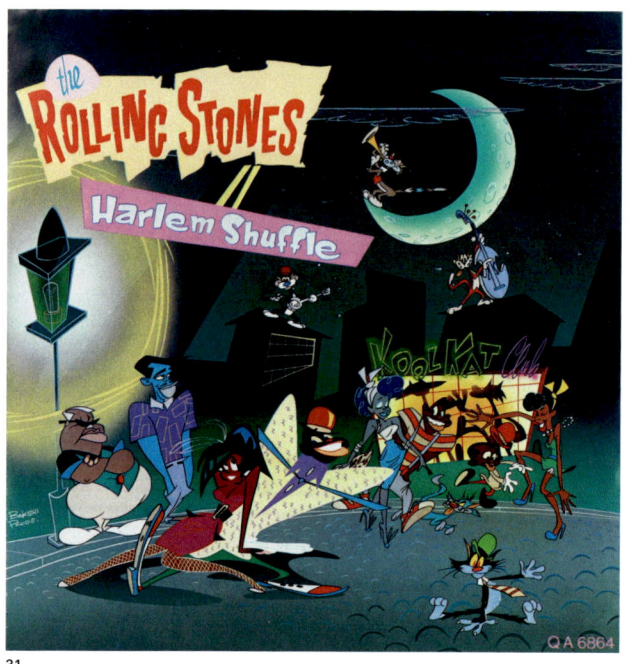

31

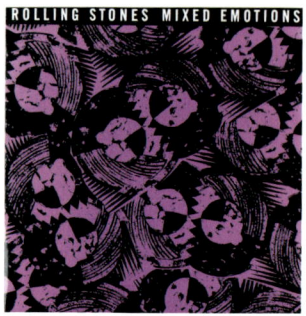

32

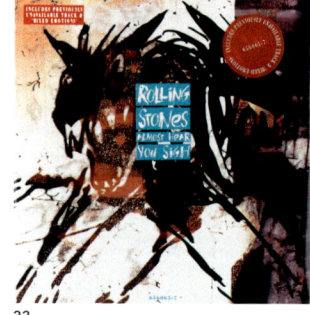

33

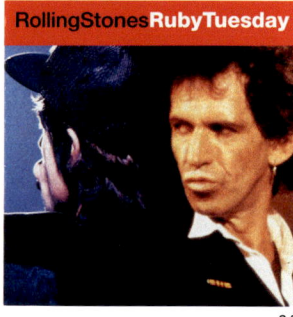

34

35

36

31 **"Harlem Shuffle"**, front cover,
1986 (Rolling Stones Records)

32 **"Mixed Emotions"**, front cover,
1989 (Rolling Stones Records)

33 **"Almost Hear You Sigh"**,
front cover, 1990 (Rolling Stones
Records)

34 **"Ruby Tuesday"**, front cover,
1991 (Rolling Stones Records)

35 **"Highwire"**, back cover, 1991
(Rolling Stones Records)

36 **"Love Is Strong"**, front cover,
1994 (Virgin)

37 **"Anybody Seen My Baby?"**,
picture disc, 1997 (Virgin)

38 **"You Got Me Rocking"**,
front cover, 1994 (Rolling Stones
Records/Virgin)

39 **"Jumpin' Jack Flash"**,
front cover, 1991 (Rolling Stones
Records/Virgin)

40 **"Rain Fall Down"**, front cover,
2005 (Virgin)

41 **"Saint Of Me"**, front cover,
1998 (Virgin)

42 **"Streets Of Love"**, front cover,
2005 (Virgin)

43 **"Doom And Gloom"**, front cover,
2012 (Universal Music)

44 **"Living In A Ghost Town"**,
front cover, 2020 (Polydor Records)

45 **"Angry"**, front cover, 2023
(Universal Music)

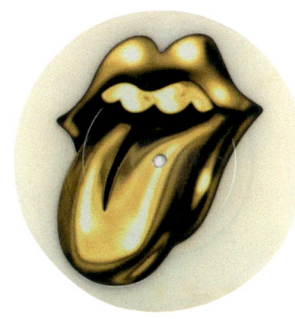

37

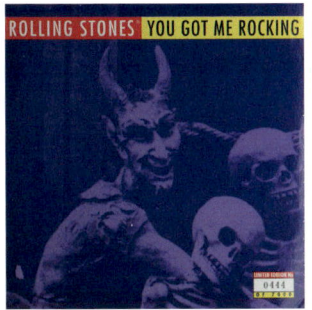

38

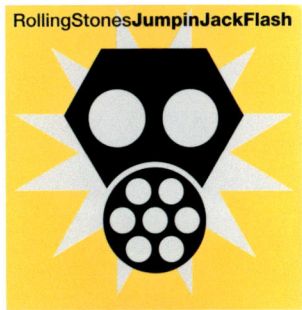

39

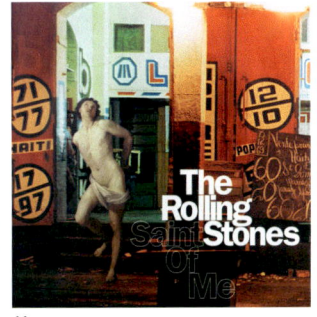

40

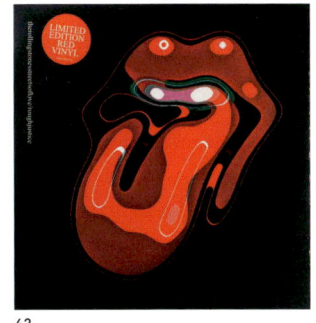

41

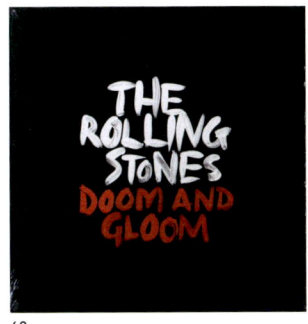

42

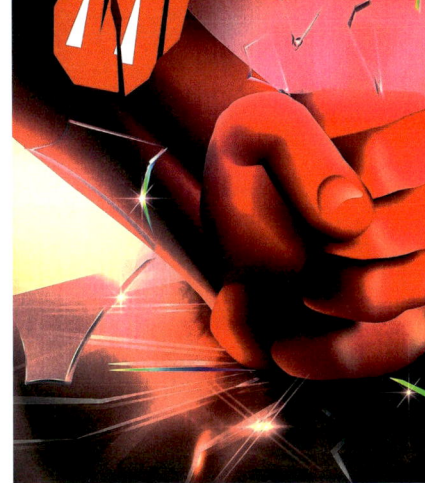

43

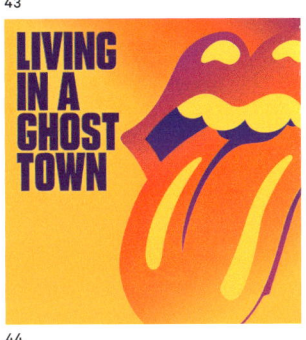

44

45

CREDITS & ACKNOWLEDGEMENTS

S.T.P.

Credits &
Bibliography

© 2025 The Andy Warhol Foundation for the Visual Arts, Inc. / Licensed by Artists Rights Society (ARS), New York 380–381
© David Bailey 38–39, 238–239, 262–263, 298–299, 348, 350–356
Photograph by David Bailey / © The Rolling Stones 298–299
Dick Barnatt / Getty Images 270–271
© Peter Beard / Art + Commerce 346–347
Collection Beyl © Thomas Beyl / Cinetext Bildarchiv 198–199, 232–233, 247, 260
Photographs by Bob Bonis © The Bob Bonis Archive 52–53, 86, 87, 88–89, 90, 91, 92, 93, 94–95, 96–97, 99
© Harm Botman 284
© Camera Press / Cecil Beaton 229, 236, 237
MichaelCooperCollection.com 214–215, 216–217, 218–219, 221, 224–228, 231, 234, 235
Photographs by Gus Coral / © The Rolling Stones 24–25, 34–35
© Anton Corbijn 2, 412–413, 428–431, 436–437, 438, 445–449, back cover
Photographs by Willie Christie 272–273
Jeremy Fletcher / Redferns / Getty Images 61
Pierre Fournier / Getty Images 168, 169
Peter Francis / Getty Images 60
Claude Gassian 396–397, 443
Photographs by Michael Geary from the Rob Weingartner Collection.

Courtesy James Karnbach 208–209
© Bubi Heilemann / rockfoto.de 275
Photographs by Hiro / © The Rolling Stones 374–378
Dezo Hoffman / Rex USA 55
Hulton Archive / Getty Images 258–259
© Michael Joseph 196–200
Photograph by Michael Joseph / © The Rolling Stones 245
Photographs by Bill King / © The Rolling Stones 416–417
© Steven Klein. From the Archive of Steven Klein, 2005 453
Eddie Kramer Archives © 2020 285
Photograph by David LaChapelle / © The Rolling Stones 422
Photograph © Brigitte Lacombe 454–457
© Annie Leibovitz 322–323, 332–333, 365, 383, 414–415
© LFI / Photoshot 68–69, 74–75, 202–203, 222–223
Lichfield / Getty Images 304–305
Photograph by David Magnus / Rex USA 207
Photographs by Gered Mankowitz © Bowstir Ltd. 2014 / mankowitz.com front cover, 76–81, 121–123, 164–165, 170–193, 200–201, 212–213
© Jim Marshall Photography LLC 294, 326, 329, 334–335, 336–337
© 1966 Paul McCartney / Photographer: Linda McCartney. All rights reserved. 166–167
© Mirrorpix 46–49, 206, 220, 248–249, 292
David Montgomery 302–303
© Andee Nathanson / All Rights Reserved 280, 281
Photographs by Helmut Newton / © The Rolling Stones 392–395
Terry O'Neill / Iconic Images 16–17, 28–33, 36–37
Denis O'Regan / Getty Images 402–403

© Norman Parkinson Ltd / courtesy Norman Parkinson Archive 42–45
© Jean-Marie Périer / Photo 12 63, 64–65, 82–83, 84–85
Pictorial Press Ltd / Alamy 22–23, 54, 57–59
Picture Alliance / AP Images 286, 287
© Jean Pigozzi 382–385
© Alessio Pizzicannella / The Hell Gate 458, 459
Popperfoto / Getty Images 26–27
Paul Popper / Popperfoto / Getty Images 50–51
Michael Putland / Getty Images 388–389, 390–391
© Aaron Rapoport 411
David Redfern / Getty Images 230
© Bent Rej 4–5, 98, 100–120, 132–133, 134, 135, 136–161, 290–291, 295, 296, 297
© Terry Richardson / Art Partner 460–461
Herb Ritts / Trunk Archive 423
© Jane Rose 404–409
Photographs by Ethan Russell. Copyright © Ethan Russell. All rights reserved. 251, 252–256, 276–279, 282, 288–289, 324–325, 330–331, 338, 341, 342–343, 344–345
Photograph by Dimo Safari / © The Rolling Stones 420–421
Jerry Schatzberg / Trunk Archive 162–163
Photographs by Norman Seeff 316, 317, 318–319, 320–321
© Mark Seliger 424–427, 462–463
© Shepard Sherbell / Getty Images 210–211
Photograph by John Stoddart / © The Rolling Stones 418–419
© Eric Swayne 40, 41, 66–67
Christopher Simon Sykes / Getty Images 358–359
Photograph by Christopher Simon Sykes / © The Rolling Stones 364, 366–367, 368–369, 370, 371, 372, 373
© Dominique Tarlé 306–307, 308–309, 310–311, 312, 313

Bibliography

Badman, Keith, Neil, Andrew,
Rawlings, Terry *Good Times,
Bad Times: The Definitive Diary of
The Rolling Stones, 1960–1969*
(London: Complete Music, 1997)

Barnard, Stephen *The Rolling
Stones: Street Fighting Years*
(London: Studio Editions, 1993)

Beaton, Cecil *Beaton in the Sixties:
The Cecil Beaton Diaries as He
Wrote Them, 1965–1969* (New York:
Alfred A. Knopf, 2004)

Bockris, Victor *Keith Richards:
The Biography* (London: Hutchinson,
1992)

Booth, Stanley *The True
Adventures of The Rolling Stones*
(London: William Heinemann Ltd,
1985)

Buck, Paul *Performance:
A Biography of the Classic Sixties
Masterpiece* (London: Omnibus,
2012)

Carr, Roy *The Rolling Stones:
An Illustrated Record* (London:
New English Library, 1976)

Charone, Barbara *Keith Richards*
(London: Futura, 1979)

Cooper, Michael, Roylance, Brian
(compiler) *Blinds & Shutters*
(Guildford: Genesis/Hedley, 1990)

Dalton, David *The Rolling Stones:
The First Twenty Years* (London:
Thames & Hudson, 1981)

Dalton, David, Farren, Mick *Rolling
Stones in Their Own Words* (London:
Omnibus Press, 1980)

Davis, Stephen *Old Gods Almost
Dead* (London: Aurum, 2002)

Jagger, Mick, Richards, Keith,
Watts, Charlie, Wood, Ronnie,
Dodd, Philip (ed.), Loewenstein,
Dora (ed.) *According to The Rolling
Stones* (London: Weidenfeld &
Nicolson, 2003)

Faithfull, Marianne (with Dalton,
David) *Faithfull* (London: Michael
Joseph, 1994)

Goodman, Pete *Our Own Story by
The Rolling Stones as We Told It to
Pete Goodman* (London: Transworld
Publishers, 1964)

Greenfield, Robert *S.T.P.: A Journey
Through America with The Rolling
Stones* (London: Aurum, 2010)

Greenfield, Robert *Exile on Main St
– a Season in Hell with The Rolling
Stones* (Philadelphia: Da Capo,
2007)

Hayward, Mark *The Rolling Stones:
On Camera, Off Guard 1963–69*
(London: Pavilion, 2009)

Hoffman, Dezo *The Rolling Stones*
(London: Vermilion, 1984)

Hewat, Tim *The Rolling Stones –
File Number 2* (London: Panther,
1967)

Kent, Nick *Apathy for the Devil:
A Seventies Memoir* (London:
Faber & Faber, 2010)

Kooper, Al *Backstage Passes:
Rock 'n' roll Life in the Sixties*
(New York: Stein and Day, 1976)

Mankowitz, Gered *Satisfaction:
The Rolling Stones Photographs
of Gered Mankowitz* (London:
Sidgewick and Jackson, 1984)

Mankowitz, Gered *The Stones
65–67* (London: Vision On, 2002)

Marshall, Jim *The Rolling Stones
1972* (London: Chronicle Books,
2012)

Marion, Larry *The Lost Rolling
Stones Photographs: The Bob
Bonis Archive, 1964–1966*
(New York: It Books/Harper Collins,
2010)

Martin, Elliot *The Rolling Stones
Complete Recording Sessions
1962–2012* (London: Cherry Red,
2012)

Nash, Will (ed.) *Stu* (London:
Out-Take, 2012)

Norman, Philip *The Stones*
(London: HarperCollins, 2012)

Oldham, Andrew Loog *2Stoned*
(London: Secker & Warburg, 2002)

Paytress, Mark *The Rolling Stones:
Off the Record* (London: Omnibus
Press, 2003)

Rawlings, Terry *Who Killed
Christopher Robin? The Truth
Behind the Murder of Brian Jones*
(London: Boxtree, 1994)

Reed, Jeremy *The Last Decadent:
A Study of Brian Jones* (London:
Creation, 1999)

Rej, Bent *The Rolling Stones:
In the Beginning* (London: Mitchell
Beazley, 2006)

Randolph, Mike *The Rolling
Stones' Rock and Roll Circus /
Photographs by Mike Randolph*
(London: Faber & Faber, 1991)

Richards, Keith (with Fox, James)
Life (London: Phoenix, 2011)

Russell, Ethan (with Van Der Leun, Gerard) *Let It Bleed: The Rolling Stones, Altamont, and the End of the Sixties* (New York: Springboard Press, 2009)

Sandford, Christopher *The Rolling Stones: Fifty Years* (London: Simon & Schuster, 2012)

Southern, Terry *The Early Stones: Legendary Photographs of a Band in the Making 1963–1973. Photographs by Michael Cooper*

(London: Secker & Warburg, 1993)

Simon Sykes, Christopher *The Rolling Stones Tour of the Americas 1975: T.O.T.A. '75 / the Diary, Photographs and Memorabilia of Christopher Simon Sykes* (Guildford: Genesis, 2005)

Tarlé, Dominique *EXILE: The Making of Exile on Main St* (Guildford: Genesis, 2001)

Vyner, Harriet *Groovy Bob: The Life and Times of Robert Fraser* (London:

Faber & Faber, 1999)

Wells, Simon *Butterfly on a Wheel: The Great Rolling Stones Drugs Bust* (London: Omnibus, 2011)

Wyman, Bill (with Coleman, Ray) *Stone Alone: The Story of a Rock 'n' Roll Band* (London: Viking, 1990)

Wyman, Bill (with Havers, Richard) *Rolling with The Stones* (London: Dorling Kindersley Publishers, 2002)

Acknowledgements

Our deepest gratitude must go first and foremost to Mick Jagger, Keith Richards, Charlie Watts, and Ronnie Wood for their commitment, creativity, and collaborative spirit at every stage of this book coming to fruition. Our thanks to Joyce Smyth and Sherry Daly for working so hard to make things happen.

A special thank you to Jane Rose for her insights, enthusiasm, and granting us access to her remarkable private archive.

This book would not have been possible without Benedikt Taschen directing and producing the entire project with his customary vision and imagination. Victoria Pearman of Jagged Films played a key role in the book's conception and execution.

From Munro Sounds/Marathon Music, Steve Daly, Barry "Spin" Mindel, Pia Squillino, Bill Bolton, and everyone at Raindrop Services. Thanks also to Bill Wyman for allowing us to publish his photographs.

Simon Wells for his enlightening captions, and to Lucy Sante, David Dalton, and Waldemar Januszczak for their eloquent and incisive essays.

The Stones collectors and experts who allowed us to tap into their knowledge and personal archives: Olaf Boehme, James Karnbach, Ira Korman, Matt Lee, Arsalan Mohammad, Andy Neil, Raj Prem and J.R. Rutherford. Additional photo research was done by Loni Efron, Julian Lass, and Rebecca Moldenhauer.

An encore of appreciation must go to The Rolling Stones for creating the soundtrack to our lives.

Reuel Golden, New York

Imprint

© 2025 TASCHEN GmbH
Hohenzollernring 53, D–50672 Köln
www.taschen.com

Original edition:
© 2014 TASCHEN GmbH

Editor: Reuel Golden, New York

Printed in Bosnia-Herzegovina
ISBN 978–3–8365–9756–2

EACH AND EVERY TASCHEN BOOK PLANTS A SEED!
Each year, we offset our annual carbon emissions with carbon credits at the Instituto Terra, a reforestation program in Minas Gerais, Brazil, founded by Lélia and Sebastião Salgado. To find out more about this ecological partnership, please check: www.taschen.com/institutoterra.
Inspiration: unlimited.
Carbon footprint: (almost) zero.

Want to see more?
Visit taschen.com to view our current publications, browse our latest magazine, and subscribe to our newsletter.

Pages 464–465
Anonymous
Freed from Brixton prison in south London on 30 June 1967, Mick's weary smile masks the trauma of three nights behind bars.

Pages 486–487
Robert Landau
Promoting both the album and the up-and-coming dates for the 1972 tour on the Sunset Strip in Los Angeles. Taken from artwork for *Exile On Main St*, each of the figures in the photographs references a band member. From left, Mick, Charlie, Bill, Mick Taylor and Keith.

Pages 508–509
Ethan Russell
Backstage passes of the 1972 *Stones Touring Party (STP)*.